Fifth Edition

PSYCHOLOGY IN TEACHING, LEARNING, AND GROWTH

Don Hamachek

MICHIGAN STATE UNIVERSITY

ALLYN AND BACON

Boston London Toronto Sydney Tokyo Singapore

This book is dedicated to the idea that an effective teacher, one who is competent and caring, wise and warm, firm but fair, will model not only what it takes to be a knowledgeable individual, but also will reflect in his or her behavior what it means to be a good person.

Editor-in-Chief, Education: Nancy Forsyth
Editorial Assistant: Christine R. Nelson
Marketing Manager: Ellen Mann
Production Administrator: Annette Joseph
Production Coordinator: Holly Crawford
Editorial-Production Service: Kelly Ricci, Spectrum Publisher Services, Inc.
Composition Buyer: Linda Cox
Manufacturing Buyer: Megan Cochran
Cover Administrator: Linda Knowles
Photo Researcher: Susan Duane

A Simon & Schuster Company
Needham Heights, Mass. 02194

A previous edition was published under the title *Behavior Dynamics in Teaching, Learning, and Growth,* copyright © 1975 by Allyn and Bacon, Inc.

Library of Congress Cataloging-in-Publication Data
Hamachek, Don.
Psychology in teaching, learning, and growth / Don Hamachek.—5th ed.
p. cm.
Includes bibliographical references and index.
ISBN 0-205-15269-4
1. Educational psychology. 2. Learning, Psychology of. 3. Child psychology. 4. Child development. I. Title.
LB1051.H2278 1994
370.15—dc20 94-6126
CIP

Printed in the United States of America

10 9 8 7 6 5 99 98

Credits are listed on page 628, which constitutes a continuation of the copyright page.

Contents

Preface

As with the previous four editions, the central thrust of this fifth edition of *Psychology in Teaching, Learning, and Growth* is on the *human* understandings, *human* meanings, and *human* experiences that are involved in teaching, learning, and growth. Within this context, I have attempted to highlight some of the central ideas, research findings, and different points of view about such matters as developmental processes involved in physical, interpersonal, and cognitive growth; about what constitutes "good" or effective teaching; about how information is processed and what we can do to ensure its retention; about what learning is, how it occurs, and what we can do to enhance achievement outcomes; and about how, as teachers, we can work toward creating the sort of positive attitude and upbeat classroom climate that encourage optimal learning and growth for students.

Educational and social science research is an ongoing process that constantly reveals fresh ways and new ideas. Because new knowledge is continually evolving, I wanted the organizational framework to be one that reflects the notion that the ideas, concepts, and theories addressed are seen primarily as starting points rather than as conclusions. There is much more to know and think about than one book can offer. Hence, the thrust of each of the five major parts is on "Toward Developing . . . ," which puts the emphasis where it properly should be, namely, on "we are moving toward" rather than on "we have arrived."

The goals I had in mind for myself as I worked on the fifth edition are those that have guided my thinking and my presentation of material from the beginning. I wanted to have the book (1) reflect a strong theoretical-philosophical overlay that is both adaptive and flexible within a developmentally eclectic framework, (2) have a solid informational base buttressed by current psychological and educational research, (3) have a fluid explanatory tone that clarifies ideas and concepts by both illustration (verbal and visual) and example, (4) have a prescriptive core that offers possible solutions to a variety of classroom problems and teacher dilemmas, and (5) include opportunities for reflective self-examination and self-discovery exercises.

I struggled with goal five because I wanted the exercises to be evident, explicit expressions of this text's emphasis on human behavior and human experience that could best be understood, or are at least more meaningfully understood, in personal terms. Thus, throughout the text, personal involvement boxes contain questions or exercises that invite you to be involved in ways that, I hope, help make your reading and learning more personally relevant.

Research has shown that learning is enhanced when we are given *advanced organizers,* which usually appear in the form of short expository paragraphs, sentences, or labels that provide a general overview or introduction to new material. I have tried to put advanced organizers into practice in four ways:

1. I have divided the book into five separate but interrelated parts, each of which deals with different ideas, issues, and concerns associated with the field of educational psychology. Each part is preceded by an overview statement designed to help you anticipate what is to come and relate each part to the others.

2. Each chapter includes a chapter outline, which consists of the major headings and subheadings within the chapter. At a glance, you have an overview of the content dealt with in any given chapter.

3. Each chapter also includes a summation of the important ideas and major concepts contained within it. I realize there may be differences about what is and what is not important; therefore, if you consider my listing of important chapter ideas as reading guidelines and study organizers rather than as conclusions, it may be easier to accept them in the spirit in which they are offered.

4. I have deliberately used many descriptive headings and subheadings in each chapter to give you a reasonably good "headline notice" of what is immediately to follow. At the end of each chapter, I have included a series of study and review questions. Each series of questions is, in a way, a test of your knowledge of the essential, "basic" content of the chapter. I am reasonably certain that if you can handle these questions, you will do quite well on any test you may take. As you go through the questions and find that there are some questions about which you are uncertain, you will find it helpful to reread the sections of the chapter where your memory is a little shaky. Chapter 6, which discusses how information is processed and remembered, contains many suggestions you may find beneficial in helping you develop study and retention strategies.

I have no illusions about this text covering all there is to know that is functional, useful information in the field of educational psychology. I have, however, attempted to include a broad sampling of the educational and psychological research findings that are related to the kinds of understandings and strategies that we can use to help us make schooling a more positive experience for both students and teachers. Thus, this text has an extensive research base because it is only through continuing research that we are able to determine what works and what does not work in upgrading and improving schooling practices.

Teaching is an enormously complex professional and personal activity. There is nothing in our subjective world of experience or in the objective arena of research that allows us to believe that there is only one particular way to be a good teacher, or for that matter, a good learner. There are many ways to be "good" at teaching and learning and each has merit depending on the teacher, student, or subject matter. It is my hope that this text will, at least in some small measure, stimulate the kind of discussion and inquiry that enables you to see that becoming a good teacher doesn't just happen. It is the result of dedication, hard work, and careful preparation. It is the cumulative outgrowth of different kinds of knowing: knowing about your subject matter, which empowers you to be a competent teacher; knowing about your students, which allows you to be an understanding teacher; and knowing about yourself, which enables you to be a self-aware teacher.

ACKNOWLEDGMENTS

The efforts of many people go into producing a book of this sort. I particularly want to thank professors Charles Bacon of Indiana University–Purdue University at Fort Wayne and Frank Stancato of Central Michigan University for their careful, critical reviews and their constructive, creative suggestions for ways that I could improve this fifth edition. It has also been my good fortune to have had the editorial expertise and support of Allyn and Bacon's Nancy Forsyth (Editor-in-Chief, Education), Christine Nelson (Editorial Assistant), and Annette Joseph (Production Administrator) during all phases of this book's production. I am especially indebted to Kristin Miller, Kelly Ricci, and Mercedes Jackson at Spectrum Publisher Services, Inc., for their very competent and meticulous attention to the countless details that are involved in converting a manuscript into a book. Finally, a big thank you to Carol DuGuay, Lisa Payne, and Joni Smith—their marvelous word processing skills transformed my scribbled drafts into a readable manuscript. As they have reminded me on numerous occasions, without them there would be no book.

I

TOWARD DEVELOPING A PSYCHOLOGICAL FRAMEWORK FOR UNDERSTANDING HUMAN BEHAVIOR AND IMPLICATIONS FOR EDUCATIONAL PROCESSES

Becoming a good teacher is a demanding and challenging undertaking. We not only have to know our subject matter but we also have to know our students, and we have to know something about ourselves. That involves a lot of knowing. We have to be academicians who know what we're talking about and psychologists and developmentalists who understand something about human nature and its various stages of maturation. Thus, in order to be good teachers, which includes both helping students learn and establishing relationships that facilitate positive teaching-learning outcomes, we need to be reasonably clear as to what our assumptions are about why people behave the way they do. Although we all have assumptions about human nature and private theories of personality, these assumptions and theories are not necessarily conscious conclusions. Hence, the purpose of Chapter 1 is to help bring you to a greater awareness of the assumptions you may have about why humans behave the way they do and to relate those assumptions to their implications for your role as a teacher and even for your behavior as a student. Chapter 1 exposes you to three major theoretical views about the psychology of human behavior, each of which has spawned assorted theoretical offshoots that have further refined and defined the original parent theories. Essentially, Chapter 1 serves as a backdrop for subsequent chapters.

Chapter 2 outlines five psychological growth models that may help you more fully understand and interpret human behavior. These models have something basic and fundamental to say about the developmental tasks that confront us at various periods in our lives, the stages we must pass through on a developmental continuum, the needs we attempt to satisfy, and the deep need we have to feel competent at something in our lives, and therefore worthwhile. Also included is the beginning of ongoing discussions of how you might convert your understanding into classroom practices that promote learning, which is, after all, what teaching is about.

Together, Chapters 1 and 2 are designed to provide you with a holistic overview of the major theoretical positions and psychological models from which we build in subsequent chapters.

What are the implications of psychoanalytic psychology for teaching and learning? How can behavioristic psychology enhance educational processes? How can we translate humanistic principles into classroom practices? What does it mean to be a self-actualized person? How is competence related to self-esteem and psychological health? What, ultimately, is a teacher's role in converting psychological theory into practical classroom use? These and many other questions are explored in Chapters 1 and 2.

1

Three Major Theoretical Positions About Human Behavior

CHAPTER OVERVIEW

IMPORTANT CHAPTER IDEAS

1. Your beliefs about yourself will significantly affect your teaching practices and your relationship to your students.
2. Psychoanalytic psychology emphasizes the idea that early childhood experiences significantly affect later adult behavior.
3. Much of our behavior is unconsciously motivated, according to psychoanalytic psychology.
4. Psychoanalytic theory has been criticized for concentrating too much on pathology and too little on normality, too much on unconscious motivations and too little on conscious processes.

5. Psychoanalytic psychology has contributed significantly to our understanding of how the behavior and self-attitudes of children can be affected, for better or worse, by how adults treat them.
6. Behavioristic psychology stresses outer experience, overt behavior, and action and reaction. It begins with the assumption that people's behaviors are shaped, molded, and maintained by forces outside themselves.
7. Consistent with this assumption, behaviorists believe that behavior can be predicted, routed, and controlled. Freedom is an illusion.
8. The use of positive, negative, and operant reinforcement strategies is associated with behavioristic approaches to teaching and learning.
9. A major criticism of behaviorism is that it overlooks the inner person by concentrating too much on the outer conditions that may be affecting that person.
10. An important lesson for education growing from behavioristic theory is that teachers are likely to be more effective when they use positive reinforcement, which encourages the learning and behaviors they desire.
11. Humanistic psychology emphasizes conscious motivation and the idea that people behave the way they do as a consequence of their perceptions of the world around them and the personal meanings they attach to those perceptions.
12. Because humanistic psychology focuses on people's perceptions and subjective experiences, the self and self-concept are important aspects of its theoretical structure.
13. A major criticism of humanistic psychology is that it is both too vague to be helpful and much too commonsensical to be scientific.
14. From a humanistic point of view, a central implication for teachers is that teaching is an interactive process involving action and reaction, moderated always by students' perceptions of what the process and the learning means to them personally.

PROLOGUE

How you behave as a teacher and how you act toward others depends largely on your implicit beliefs about why people behave the way they do. Implicit beliefs are those that are understood, although not directly stated or expressed. Our implicit beliefs may even influence the political party with which we align ourselves. It's been found, for example, that people whose beliefs tend to be more conservative than liberal and who believe that religious values are important and that abortion is wrong are likely to lean toward the politics of the Republican party. In contrast, those whose beliefs are more liberal, who believe that secular values are as important as religious ones and that abortion should be a matter of personal choice are inclined to favor the politics of the Democratic party (St. Angelo and Dyson, 1968). Whether we are Republican or Democrat (or something else), there is the implicit belief that our party will come closest to answering our deepest needs (and prejudices), and thus deserves our vote. Our implicit beliefs influence our behavior, even to the point of affecting whom we vote into office.

Just as our political views may reflect the ideologies of certain political parties, so, too, it is possible that, without knowing it, our implicit beliefs about human nature may reflect the basic tenets of certain psychological theories. What are your beliefs about human nature? Before reading further, you may find it revealing to respond to the nine-item inventory, "What Do I Believe?" (Figure 1.1). There are no right or wrong responses. Just check the "yes" or "no" space next to each statement that seems most true for you.

Each of the statements you've responded to in the inventory is related to one of the three psychological positions we discuss in the following pages. A "yes" response to at least two of the first three statements may suggest a leaning toward *psychoanalytic* thinking about human behavior. A "yes" response to two or more of statements four through six may suggest an inclination to think along the lines of *behavioristic* psychology. A "yes" response to two or more of items seven through nine may reflect a *humanistic* position related to behavior. If you found yourself answering "yes" to six or more of the statements, this does not necessarily mean that your views about behavior are inconsistent. It may mean that, for you, behavior can be viewed comfortably from various perspectives.

	Yes	*No*
1. People are essentially bad or evil by nature.	______	______
2. The first 5 years of life are probably the most important in shaping one's adult personality.	______	______
3. Unconscious forces are more dominant than conscious ones in determining behavior.	______	______
4. Most people work better and harder when the reward for their efforts is given by another person.	______	______
5. Most people's behavior can be controlled by giving them appropriate rewards when they do what you want them to do.	______	______
6. It is easier to understand people by watching their behavior than by listening to their feelings.	______	______
7. People are essentially good by nature.	______	______
8. Later life experiences are just as important as early ones in determining a course of behavior.	______	______
9. A person's conscious awareness is more dominant than unconscious forces in determining his or her behavior.	______	______

Figure 1.1. WHAT DO I BELIEVE?

These three theoretical positions—psychoanalysis, behaviorism, and humanism—represent three distinct psychological theories developed in the nineteenth and twentieth centuries, which continue to be dominant forces in psychological thought. The first theoretical wave, psychoanalysis, painted a picture of humankind as fraught with conflict and driven by destructive instincts. It was a dismal concept of human nature that emphasized unconscious, irrational forces as controlling factors in behavior. Behaviorism, the second wave, characterized human behavior as flexible, malleable, and totally controlled by external stimuli—the doomed or favored pawn of environmental fate. More recently, the third wave (frequently referred to as the "third force" movement), known as *humanistic* psychology, has emerged. Essentially, it emphasizes the goodness of human nature and stresses the idea that, if conditions are right, people will move toward realizing their potential because of internal, not external, motivations.

None of these theories is all right or all wrong. Each has something to offer to our understanding of human behavior. We humans are simply too complex to be totally understood by a single point of view. In addition, there have been, and no doubt will continue to be, too many creative approaches to solving the puzzle of the human psyche to think that one psychological theory could ever be comprehensive enough to do it all. Thomas (1992) has observed that a theory is what makes sense out of facts, an explanation of how facts fit together, which is exactly what each of the three theories does. Each theory takes the facts related to human behavior and interprets them in accordance with a particular theoretical framework, each having its strengths and weaknesses, which will be highlighted in this chapter. Remember that each of these major psychological positions is a theory of human behavior and, as such, each serves as a kind of starting place for suggestive, testable behavioral hypotheses. Each has something to teach us about the psychology of human behavior. With this in mind, we will explore the central offerings of each of these three major theories.

CLASSICAL PSYCHOANALYTIC PSYCHOLOGY: CENTRAL IDEAS

Some of the roots of contemporary personality theory go back deep into the fertile soil of traditional Freudian psychoanalytic psychology. Although nowhere near as dominant a force as it was thirty or forty years ago, it continues to send offshoots of impact into our thinking about human behavior.

The origins of this theory go back to the pioneering efforts of Sigmund Freud (1856–1939) and extend over the fifty-year period of his clinical practice and writing. Freud completed his medical degree work at the University of Vienna in 1881, where he developed an early interest in organic diseases of the nervous system. He continued his study in that area at Vienna's General Hospital until 1886. Gradually, his interests shifted from an emphasis on the purely physical aspects of the nervous system and moved in the direction of investigating possible psychological causes of nervous disorders. His ongoing involvement with patients who had various psychological problems and, significantly, his own self-analysis led Freud to believe that most psychological difficulties were unconsciously rooted in sexual conflicts.

Until Freud changed it, the psychology of human behavior was confined largely to the study of conscious states. Although Freud was not the first to realize that people are sometimes unaware of the underlying reasons for their behavior, he was the first to make a systematic study of the unconscious and to make a successful case for its existence in such everyday behaviors as slips of the tongue, dreams, missed appointments, certain "accidents," and so forth.

Personality Consists of Different Levels of Consciousness

Personality organization from a psychoanalytic point of view involves three levels of consciousness—the conscious, the preconscious, and the unconscious—that are quite different layers of awareness.

At a *conscious* level, we have all the sensory inputs and experiences of which we are aware at any given moment. Classical psychoanalytic theory suggests that only a small part of our mental life (perceptions, feelings, thoughts) is contained at a conscious level. The content of our awareness at any given time, says the theory, is largely the result of selective attention regulated by external cues. You may, for example, be aware of holding this book and reading this sentence, but there may be deeper, less conscious motivations for studying the discipline that this book represents.

There is also a *preconscious* layer of personality, which includes all the experiences that are not conscious to us at a particular moment, but which can be readily called into awareness with minimal effort. For example, until the following items are mentioned, you probably were not conscious at this moment of their existence in your mental life: your phone number, mother's maiden name, what you had for dinner last night, or the most recent movie you saw. Most of us can quickly recall items of this sort because they are preconsciously stored memories and are easily accessible. So, too, are certain emotionally important experiences we may have had, such as a memory of a car accident we were in or witnessed, the night of our high school graduation, an early romantic experience, or a time when we had to speak in front of an audience.

The real action, however, is at the *unconscious* level of the human mind. In psychoanalytic theory, the unconscious is not a hypothetical abstraction but a reality that can be demonstrated and proved. Freud, for instance, believed strongly that the really significant aspects of human behavior are shaped and molded by impulses and forces buried in the deepest corners of our psyches.

An example of the unconscious at work can be found in Shevrin's (1980) research findings, which suggest that the brain is fairly humming with unconscious thoughts and emotions. In a series of experiments with more than one hundred people, Shevrin assessed the degree of the brain's response to various kinds of subliminal (below awareness) inputs, which was done by measuring the brain's electrical response when a word or picture was flashed on a screen for a thousandth of a second. (This was accomplished by using an electroencephalograph, which records electrical activity in the brain.) After the pictures had been flashed, participants were asked to say any words that came to mind. The results were remarkably consistent. If, for example, it was a picture of a bee, most people showed a stronger brain response than if it was a picture of an abstract geometric shape (i.e., the brain was aroused more and showed an increase in electrical activity). What this suggests is that a meaningful object apparently attracts a person's attention, unconsciously, more than a meaningless one. In addition, when a picture of a bee was flashed, participants were inclined to free-associate more words related to bee—*bug, sting, honey*—than when a geometric shape was shown. The implications of this are startling and clear: a certain kind of focusing and understanding occurs at an unconscious level, even though, at a conscious level, people may not be aware of the fine distinctions they are making in their unconscious minds.

1.1 Getting to the Unconscious

If you would like to see a simple demonstration of the unconscious at work, try the following on some friends. First, ask them to quickly give the answer to the following addition problems: 4 + 4, 5 + 5, and 6 + 6. Then ask them to name their favorite color. Follow this by asking them to choose any number between 5 and 10. About 60% to 70% of the people asked to do this offer 7 as the number of their choice. When asked why they choose that number, most reply, "Well, it's the first number that came to my mind." It is indeed the first number that came to mind, but it did so because of the unconscious connection to the sequence of additions they did. Asking for their favorite color merely diverted their attention. The fact that most people don't know *why* they choose the number 7 suggests that its choice is unconsciously motivated. There are many examples of unconsciously motivated behavior in everyday life. For example, think about the colors you most like to wear. When you get beyond the idea that you "just like those colors," what do you suppose your color choice suggests about you as a person? Unconsciously, what do you suppose you communicate about yourself? It might be fun to check your introspections about this with feedback from some friends whose opinions you trust.

A helpful way to understand the organization of personality within the psychoanalytic system is to visualize a huge iceberg. Just as the major portion of an iceberg lies below the water's surface, so, too, does a major portion of the human personality lie below the level of awareness, a fact that can help us more fully appreciate that there is no doubt more to both ourselves and others than may be immediately apparent.

Ego, Superego, and Id: Personality's Major Components

Just as a person's personality can be thought of as having three levels of awareness, it can also be viewed as having structural components that cut across those levels. You can see how this looks conceptually in Figure 1.2, which helps give an idea of how the various layers of consciousness contribute to the structure of personality.

Orthodox psychoanalytic thinkers suggest that a universal set of violent urges is an instinctual part of human heritage. This pattern of primitive aggressiveness, coupled with what appeared to be an insatiable need for immediate gratification, Freud termed the *id*. Freud thought he saw two expressions of the id. On the one hand, there were urges to live, to create, and to love. Expressions of this sort he called the *life wish,* and the term *libido* was coined to symbolize that part of the life wish concerned with sexual or other affiliative relations with people. On the other hand, Freud also saw evidence of hostile, destructive impulses reflected in behavior. These, in Freud's continuing drama of personality dynamics, were called expressions of the *death wish.* You can get a feeling for Freud's (1930) ideas about the hostile and destructive side of human nature in his observation that

> Men are not gentle, friendly creatures wishing for love, who simply defend themselves if they are attacked, but . . . a powerful measure of desire for aggressiveness has to be reckoned as part of their instinctual endowment. The result is that their neighbor is to

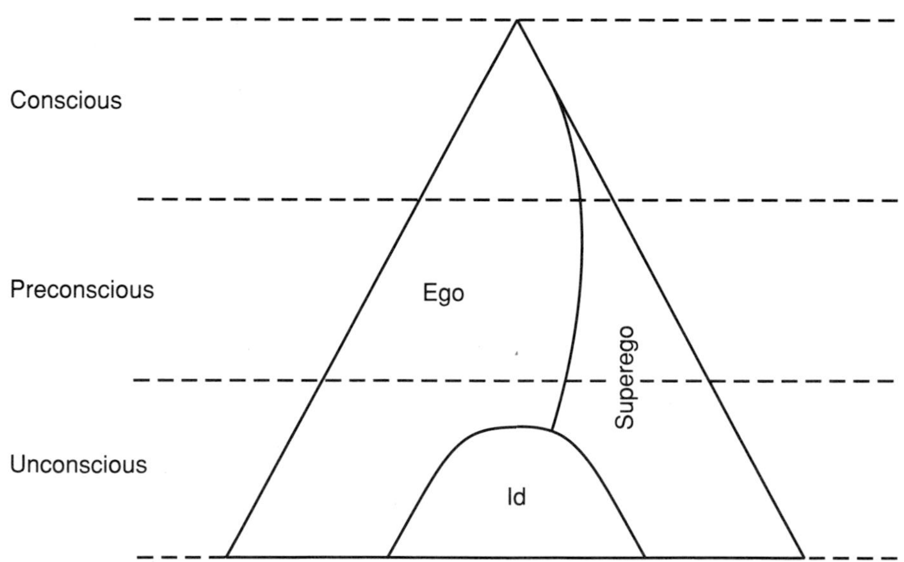

Figure 1.2. LEVELS OF AWARENESS AND RELATIONSHIP TO THE STRUCTURE OF PERSONALITY AS CONCEPTUALIZED IN PSYCHOANALYTIC PSYCHOLOGY.

them not only a possible helper or sexual object, but also a temptation to gratify their aggressiveness . . . to seize his possessions, to humiliate him, to cause him pain. (pp. 85–86)

Although the id can generate images and wishes related to immediate need gratification, it cannot begin the direct action necessary toward meeting its needs. Thus, a second key construct, the *ego,* develops to mediate between the demands of the id and the realities of the outside world. Cutting across all three layers of consciousness, it is the ego's task to keep one's overall personality in balance so as not to be overwhelmed by the id's need for immediate gratification or the superego's urgings for ongoing delays in gratification. If we should see a person constantly giving in to his or her need to have fun, seek pleasure, and avoid responsibility, we might conclude that the person has a weak ego, one not strong enough to hold his or her need for immediate gratification in check.

A third major psychoanalytic construct, namely, the *superego,* a term synonymous with conscience and concerned with the good and the bad, the right and the wrong. The superego grows and develops as children gradually incorporate the values and social standards taught by parents and other significant persons in their lives. In the psychoanalytic scheme of things, there are two divisions of the superego. One is popularly referred to as *conscience,* which discourages the expression of undesirable behavior, and the other is the *ego-ideal,* which encourages more desirable behavior. The conscience develops primarily through the influence of scorn and threats of punishment. For example, a parent may say, "You're a naughty boy for doing that," "You are bad for acting like that," or "I am ashamed of you." Thus, children eventually learn to control their behavior much as their parents would control it. Similarly, the ego-ideal develops through continued positive statements and expressions of approval, such as "Good girl" or "I like it when you behave like that," or through increased material rewards and privileges, which help children move toward the ideal of how they should behave.

The First Five Years Set the Tone

Psychoanalytic theory places a heavy emphasis on the first 5 years of life as the most critical stages of development. It is during these years, Freud maintained, that the foundations for adult personality are largely established. He believed that children pass through a predictable sequence of psychosexual stages. Individual differences in adult personality, he assumed, could be ultimately traced to the specific manner in which children experienced and handled the conflicts occurring in these stages.

What Freud did was to take observable, biological facts and give them a dynamic psychological orientation. Perhaps we can understand this better by taking a brief look at the three stages children pass through during their first 5 years, or so, of life.

Development during the first years is called the *oral stage,* and is so labeled because the focus of infants' attention and activity is centered mainly around their mouth, esophagus, and stomach. Freud concluded that babies have a great awareness of their pleasure in taking food and that they soon learn to associate the feeding process with the attitudes reflected by the adults who feed them. On a broader scale, psychoanalytic theory maintains that children psychologically incorporate much about life during this stage as they make connections between their oral needs and their experiences with food. It is speculated, for example, that infants allowed to remain too often in a state of uncertainty (tension, hunger) tend to develop into the kind of person who in later life is perpetually uncertain about whether people or circumstances can be trusted. (This idea is similar, as you will see in Chapter 2, to Erik Erikson's ideas about trust formation.) The speculation goes further to suggest that excessive tension and/or frustration of oral needs may leave a child fixated at this level of development to the extent that later adult oral activities—excessive drinking, smoking, eating, or talking—become dominant expressions of his or her life-style. What happens to children during their first year of life is seen as closely related to their later sense of security.

During the *anal stage,* encompassing the second and third years of life, the infant's attention shifts mainly to anal activity, which is particularly emphasized through parental urges for toilet training. According to Freud, the tactics employed by parents, along with their attitudes about such matters as defecation, cleanliness, and control, determine in large measure what kind of influence toilet training will have on personality and its development. Here again, there may be enduring fixations, which may result from punishment for failure to control elimination or from excessive rewards for successful control. Freud theorized that people who become fixated at this stage are inclined to show anal characteristics throughout their lives—stinginess, stubbornness, excessive neatness, compulsive perfectionism, and the like. The reasoning is that if children are made to feel unduly guilty, anxious, or unloved when they are messy or dirty, they may grow into obsessively fussy adults, forever worrying about appearances.

The *phallic* stage is theorized to occur between 3 and 5.5 years of age. It is during this stage that children grow increasingly aware of their own bodies and particularly of the pleasurable genital sensations they begin to experience. Indeed, Freud left a Victorian society flabbergasted in the wake of his assertion that childhood sexuality, with its sexual fantasy and masturbation, was a universal and normal phenomenon, a view that most people now take more or less for granted. At the phallic stage, the *Oedipus* complex (so-called after the classical Greek myth of King Oedipus who unwittingly killed his father and married his mother) occurs. This is the childhood romance we have all heard about in which a boy experiences erotic feelings toward his mother and antagonistic feelings toward his father. This same phenomenon for girls, but in reverse, is known as the *Electra* complex. Thus, according to psychoanalytic theory, the boy and the girl place themselves in the fantasied role of father and mother, respectively, out of which grow their primary identifications with the parent of the same sex.

1.2 Exploring the Deep Past

Given what you know about yourself, do you see any behaviors that come close to those aligned with either the oral or anal stage of growth that you've been reading about? The next time you have a chance, you may find it both interesting and revealing to talk to your parents or primary caretakers about what those early years were like for you. What kind of an infant were you? (Quiet? Loud? Happy? Fussy?) How did they respond to you? (On demand? On a schedule?) How were you toilet trained? Was it a relaxed process, or was it a tense struggle? Do you see any relationship between how you or any of your siblings were raised in those early years and how you behave today?

Weaknesses of the Psychoanalytic Position

Freud's ideas about human behavior are penetrating and challenging. His analysis of the human psyche has made it clear that unconscious motivations play an important part in shaping the expressions of one's behavior. Freud's theory drives home the idea that people are enormously complex creatures capable, on the one hand, of deep love and altruistic acts and, on the other hand, of deep hatred and vicious deeds. However, it was, and still remains, a controversial theory. Among the commonly cited weaknesses of this point of view are the following:

1. The theory was generated out of a preoccupation with the pathology of abnormal people. It is doubtful whether such a theory can effectively deal with the normal personality.

2. The theory was established on the basis of emotional disturbances among middle-class people in Vienna more than one-half century ago. No compelling evidence suggests that the theory is equally applicable to other kinds of people in other cultural settings.

3. Although, as suggested by the theory, humans can sometimes be characterized by their aggressive and sometimes vicious nature, studies of various cultures have shown that many people in the world are, as a group, friendly and kind. For instance, Freud's theories about instinctive destruction urges are notably absent in the behavior of African pygmies inhabiting the Ituri rain forests. They neither hurt nor kill each other even though they are highly skilled with blowguns and other deadly weapons. Violence and aggression

among people in the primitive cultures of the Maori of New Zealand and the Balinese is also notably low. In addition, there is a notable lack of violence both in the fossil record and in contemporary Kalahari tribes of South Africa, a finding that led anthropologist Richard Leakey (1981) to conclude that there is no proof in the hunter-gatherers of the Kalahari that man is an inherently violent "killer ape." So much for sweeping generalizations about humankind's instinctive destructive urges. People can be destructive to each other, but this may have as much to do with the culture in which they are raised as it does with the instincts with which they are born.

4. Some of the concepts used within psychoanalytic theory are vague and ill-defined. Freud's ideas of a death instinct would be an example of this. There are no hard empirical data for the death instinct. Drug addiction, suicide, and other self-destructive behaviors that might serve as evidence for such instincts can be explained in other ways. For example, psychoanalytic interpretations for alcoholism include such possibilities as repressed rage because of early deprivation, repression to a dependent state, or fixation at the oral stage. Contemporary explanations, however, include possible biological and perhaps even genetic bases of alcoholism and other addictions (Zucker and Gomberg, 1986). Thus, it is difficult to know what contribution death instincts might make to our understanding and explanations of addictive behavior.

5. A particular weakness of psychoanalytic theory is in its failure to pay much attention to how sociocultural factors may influence behavior. Freud, for example, attributed the distress of many of his female patients to his observation that they wanted to be more like men, a condition he referred to as *penis envy.* This rather narrow view completely overlooked the fact that women were frequently forced into subservient roles and that their frustration may have had more to do with the narrow range of life choices available to them rather than to their alleged distress over lack of a penis.

6. Another shortcoming of the psychoanalytic position is its insistence that early childhood experiences are inevitably the cause of subsequent life problems. In some cases, this may be true, but research in development across the life span suggests that one's emotional difficulties can have far more recent origins. Childhood is not the only spawning ground.

Jung and Adler: Psychoanalytic Thinkers of a Different Sort

Freud's views about the idea that human behavior is largely instinctual and that human motivation is influenced heavily by sexual considerations were viewpoints that some psychoanalysts found uncongenial. Carl Jung and Alfred Adler were both former students of Freud who broke away from his views to establish their own persuasive theories about behavior. They are both examples of neo-psychoanalytic thinkers, and each theorist has his own substantial following. (Erik Erikson, whose contributions are discussed more fully in Chapter 2, is another researcher who came from a psychoanalytic background to establish a contemporary, neo-psychoanalytic framework.)

Jung, for example, had a different view of the unconscious, which he conceptualized as having two levels: (1) the *personal unconscious,* which is similar to Freud's in the sense that it encompasses material that is repressed or forgotten and (2) the *collective unconscious,* which is that part of the human psyche filled with primordial images or archetypes consisting of primitive, tribal, and ancestral experiences garnered over the millions of years of human existence. This collective unconscious is common to all human beings and includes such universal experiences as mothers, the earth, and even the caves in which we once lived. Jung believed that these unconscious forces and images are a central part of every healthy personality.

It is also interesting to note that Jung's theory of human behavior included the idea that men and women are equal and psychologically complementary to each other. This is quite a different stance from that of Freud, who took it more or less for granted that women were inferior to men because of their stronger sexual repressions and passivity. Expressing these views in the early 1900s, Jung was far ahead of his time in recognizing that both men and women might be happier and healthier if they could be freer to experience both the masculine and feminine components of their personalities.

Alfred Adler was another early pupil of Freud, but broke with him, as did Jung, over the issue of the importance of sexuality in human behavior. Adler saw each person primarily as a social being rather than a sexual one. The essential pillar of Adlerian psychology, in terms of which the rest of it takes on meaning, is his conception of a *life plan* of the individual—the purpose, the goal, and the "end in view" that determines behavior. Adler's self is a highly personalized subjective system through which people interpret and give meaning to their experiences. Unlike Freud, who made the unconscious the center of personality, Adler stressed *consciousness* as the center of personality. He viewed people as conscious beings ordinarily aware of their reasons for behavior; more than that, they are self-conscious individuals capable of planning and guiding their actions with full awareness of what it means for their own self-realizations.

Adler saw every person as having the same goal, namely that of superiority, but he also saw countless life-styles for achieving that goal. For example, one person may try to become superior through developing his or her intellect, another may strive to be a Don Juan, and still another bends all his or her efforts toward achieving the body beautiful. The intellectual, the lady killer, the muscle builder—each has an individual life-style. The intellectual seeks knowledge; the Don Juan, women; and the muscle builder, physique. Each arranges his or her other life to achieve the end of being more or less superior to those seeking similar goals.

Other contributors to the neo-Freudian psychoanalytic movement who have given more emphasis to social and environmental factors—as opposed to purely innate or biological ones—in the development and function of personality are Karen Horney, Harry S. Sullivan, and Erich Fromm, to name a few. An excellent overview of these and other neo-Freudians can be found in volumes by Derlega, Winstead, and Jones (1991) and Peterson (1992).

Implications for Teaching and Learning

Psychoanalytic theory does not deal directly with the sort of teaching and learning that goes on in a classroom. It is a theory of behavior, not of teaching and learning. Nonetheless, it can be useful to us not only in deepening our knowledge about unconscious motivations, but also for increasing our understanding of how adults serve as models for youths to imitate and identify with.

Growing children and adolescents are malleable. They want to grow up; they want to become like the adults around them and have more power, strength, status, privileges, and freedom. What adults say to them matters. How adults behave around them makes a difference. The sensitive first-grade teacher who says, "Patrick, I really like the hard work you've done on this assignment," may be the only positive, significant adult who has ever encouraged him. Billy's warm, trusting feelings toward that teacher may be the beginning of a healthy identification with an adult who can help him grow in positive ways. However, a grouchy tenth-grade teacher who yells, "Patty, you never pronounce words right when you read," may nourish a 15-year-old girl's already existing seeds of self-doubt and self-disappointment. Consciously, Patty may decide that she will never again volunteer to read out loud or to do anything else that may risk public humiliation. Unconsciously, she may be making the sort of negative connections between learning and schooling that make her want to avoid more education rather than pursue it. Psychoanalytic psychology sensitizes us to the interplay and overlapping connections between conscious life and unconscious processes.

In summary, we can conclude the following:

1. Teachers are usually among those significant persons in a child's or adolescent's life who make a difference and who, in the context of an interpersonal relationship, can influence a youth's attitudes about him- or herself for better or worse.
2. Inasmuch as the basic framework for self-attitudes, which may last a lifetime, are established during the formative years, it is absolutely essential that teachers be positive and concentrate on what students *can* do (their strengths, possibilities, and potentials) rather than be negative and focus on what students *cannot* do (their weaknesses, shortcomings, and deficiencies).

1.3 Teachers You Have Had

Psychoanalytic psychology sensitizes us to the importance of one's early years in shaping subsequent life attitudes. Reflect a moment. Do you recall a particular teacher or teachers from your elementary school experiences that you associate with some particularly positive or negative memories? How would you say those experiences affected you, particularly when it comes to your feelings about academic matters?

BEHAVIORISTIC PSYCHOLOGY: CENTRAL IDEAS

Essentially, behavioristic psychology is a theoretical position that stresses outer experience, overt behavior, and action and reaction. It is also referred to as stimulus-response (S-R) psychology because it is an approach that seeks to understand behavior generally, and teaching and learning specifically, by studying the conditions (stimuli) *outside* a person that cause him or her to behave (respond) in certain ways. Historically, this position grew from a reaction to what was called introspectionist psychology, which, as its name suggests, was an approach to understanding behavior through close, systematic examination of a person's conscious, introspective reports. Whereas the introspectionists started by asking, "What is happening in the person's inner world?", the behavioristic approach is to ask, "What is happening in the person's outer world?"

Starting with the basic assumption that people's behavior was shaped, molded, and maintained by forces outside themselves, psychologist John B. Watson (1925) dramatically shifted the focus of psychology from inner psychic processes to outer behavior that is completely observable. Watson asserted that the proper starting point for understanding people is through the study of their *behavior*—what they do, not what they think or feel.

The early roots of stimulus-response theory were nurtured by the work of the Russian physiologist Ivan Pavlov (1906), who, in a classic experiment, conditioned a dog to salivate at the sound of a bell by the dog's associating that sound with the sight and smell of meat. Using a similar approach, Watson conditioned a child to fear a rat by substituting a loud, sudden noise for the rat. He reasoned that if he could condition a child to fear a particular kind of animal, he could presumably condition a child to fear anything else. Indeed, Watson went on to assert that if he could condition people to fear anything, he could also condition them to hate, love, or do just about anything he wanted them to do. This view was probably best expressed by Watson (1919) when he flamboyantly asserted, "Give me a dozen healthy infants, well formed, to bring them up in any way I choose and I'll guarantee you to take any one at random and train him to become any type of specialist I might select—doctor, lawyer, artist, merchant-chief, and, yes, even beggar-man and thief, regardless of his talents, penchants, tendencies, abilities, vocations and race of his ancestors" (p. 10).

Behavior Is Lawful: Freedom Is a Myth

Although few contemporary behaviorists would agree that Watson could do what he promised in the preceding statement, those subscribing to behaviorism would substantially agree that behavior can be dramatically altered, shaped, controlled, and manipulated through the use of reinforcements.

The late B. F. Skinner (1971), a former Harvard psychologist and one of the leading proponents of behaviorism, triggered a national stir with his book, *Beyond Freedom and Dignity,* in which he asserted that the idea of human freedom is really a myth. Skinner's thinking runs counter to the traditional views of humankind as made up of autonomous individuals possessing a measure of freedom and personal dignity. According to Skinner, we attribute freedom and dignity to humans only because we retain the myth of the inner person who is somehow independent of the controlling influences of his or her environment. Skinner insisted that no such creature exists. For example, Skinner repeatedly asserted that *all behavior is lawful,* which, from a behavioristic perspective, means that an individual's behavior is entirely a product of, and can be understood purely in terms of, the objective world. We witness one individual commit a serious crime and another perform a great service for humanity. *It is important to understand that to be a behaviorist both expressions of behavior result from an interplay of identifiable variables that completely determine behavior.*

Is such a world of behavioral manipulation really possible? Skinner and those who subscribe to what has been called his *radical behaviorism* believe it is. The way to manipulate behavior, Skinner proposed, is through *behavioral technology,* a developing science of control that aims to change the environment rather than people, seeks to alter actions rather than feelings, and shifts the customary psychological emphasis from the world inside people to the world outside them. Central to the behavioristic approach is a method of conditioning, based on reinforcement, that has been used with uniform success on laboratory animals—giving rewards to mold the subject to behave in predictable ways. According to Skinner and his followers, the same technique can be made to work equally well with humans. How would this work? Let us take a look at some of the basic principles involved.

1.4 Is Anyone Really Free?

How do you respond to the idea that freedom is a myth, which is basically a view that says people are the products of their conditioning. More specifically, it says that, since who we are at this moment is the outgrowth of a particular history of reinforcements, we only *think* we are free. Skinner implied that the process of living itself subjects people to a variety of experiences that condition them to behave in predictable ways, thus making the idea of freedom largely an illusion, a myth. What are your thoughts about this?

Reinforcement and Conditioning: Basic Behavioristic Principles

A central principle in behavioristic theory is the idea that behavior that has a satisfying effect—satisfaction of a desire, escape from punishment, relief from fear—will be learned, but behavior that has an unpleasant effect or consequence—lack of reward, frustration of a desire, fear—will not be learned.

Basically, we are more apt to repeat those behaviors for which we have been rewarded. If you study hard for an exam and receive what you consider a high grade, you will be likely to study hard for your next exam also. In other words, when a pleasant reward follows a specific behavior, then this behavior is likely to be repeated at some future time under similar conditions. Animal trainers, for example, have honed this very basic principle into an exact science. Whether it is a dog, dolphin, monkey, or killer whale, each is rewarded with kindness and/or food when in the process of learning a new trick and doing it correctly.

The consequences of reinforcement can be nicely seen in an informal experiment conducted by a group of psychology students who planned that on alternate days they would: (1) laugh at anything even remotely funny in the instructor's lecture, and (2) not even crack a smile no matter what the professor said or did (Verplanck, 1956). These experimenters (conspirators, actually) reported that until the instructor caught on to the game there was vast day-to-day variation in the amount of humor or attempted humor in lectures. For instance, on days his humor was reinforced, the instructor seemed to double his efforts to be funny. However, on days when his best jokes met with stony silence, lectures became grimly serious. Of course, similar effects of reinforcement on verbal behavior have been produced less dramatically, but more quantifiably, in laboratory investigations.

Conditioning is the other important concept associated with the behavioristic position. Basically, there are two conditioning processes—*classical* (or Pavlovian) and *operant* (or instrumental).

Classical conditioning is probably the simplest of all forms of learning. It is what we see in the eyes of a child who was burned when he or she sees fire. What this means is that a *conditioned stimulus* (the sight of fire) takes on the potential to evoke the *response* (fear) formerly reserved for the *unconditioned stimulus* (actual heat of the fire). Most people will automatically respond to anything that actually burns them, but to react before being burned—to respond to the sight of fire—is learned behavior based on experience. It is a *conditioned response,* much the same as Pavlov's dog salivating at the sound of a bell.

An example closer to home would be that of a youngster who has been conditioned to fear school. For example, I know a high school student who is so fearful of school that even the thought of going makes him anxious. What this means is that a *conditioned stimulus* (the thought of school and what happens there) has the potential to evoke the response (fear, anxiety) formerly reserved for the *unconditioned stimulus* (actual experiences with failure and humiliation). Most students will automatically respond to school-failure experiences. But to respond before a failure (in other words, to the anticipation of a failure) is a learned behavior based on experience. This is what you call a conditioned response. The boy had literally been conditioned to fear school because of his frequent experiences with failure. In contrast, a teenage neighbor of mine is conditioned the other way. She loves school because she associates it with success and positive feelings about herself.

While classical conditioning involves a change in the stimulus that causes a response, operant conditioning involves a selection, from many responses, of the one that habitually will be given in a stimulus situation. In the classical conditioning process just discussed, the person in question receives his or her reinforcement regardless of what each does in the learning situation. By contrast, what people do in an operant conditioning situation has everything to do with this being reinforced. That is, their behavior is *instrumental* for the reward to occur. They must in some way *operate* within their environment to get rewarded. Therefore, the actions rather than the scheduling determine the frequency and rate of reward.

A teacher-friend of mine has nicely implemented the basic principles of operant conditioning in a technique to involve his more quiet students in class discussions. What he does is direct his comments or questions to shy, bashful students whenever it appears that their hands are even close to being raised. For example, one of his quieter students had merely raised his hand to scratch his ear, and the teacher wondered what his *opinion* was (not what he *knew*—that's a different order of question) about some of the ideas being expressed regarding the topic at hand. The student was a bit flustered at first, but he did express some opinions. Without making a big deal of it, the teacher praised the boy for contributing and the class went on. By responding to a partially raised hand and publicly praising a quiet, shy boy, a wise teacher had planted the seeds of a healthy connection in this boy's mind between raising his hand, contributing, and feeling good about the classroom situation. The boy's quiet behavior did not change overnight, but through techniques like this, my friend slowly helped encourage this shy youngster to increase the amount of times he volunteered in class. Others, as well, became involved in class discussions.

1.5 Is Manipulation Wrong?

Issue is sometimes taken with the idea that a teacher might do something that is designed to manipulate students' behavior. As one student put it, "I think it's highly unethical to deliberately manipulate students through the use of rewards or what is called 'operant conditioning' techniques. I don't care what the end result is. Students become mere objects and no longer in control of their own behavior."

How do *you* feel about this issue? Would you do anything such as my teacher-friend did?

Positive and Negative Reinforcement: How Each Works

Positive and negative reinforcement are key concepts in behavioristic psychology, but they are easily misunderstood. The basic principle is this: *Both types increase the probability of response* (Klein, 1987). *Positive reinforcement* is the net result of something *being added* (a positive reinforcer) to a situation when a response is made. For instance, a response may be positively reinforced if it involves, say, winning an award, getting praised, or earning more money. Athletes who win trophies, ribbons, and other signs of recognition are encouraged to continue their competitive efforts; students who hear favorable comments from teachers are inclined to try harder in class; and salespersons who win money bonuses for top sales may redouble their efforts.

Negative reinforcement, in contrast, is what happens *when something is removed* (a negative reinforcer) from a situation when a response is made. For example, a response may be negatively reinforced if the removal of extreme heat or cold or a threatening situation is the consequence. A colleague of mine taught in a small rural high school in the southern United States that, because of lack of air conditioning, would get particularly warm during certain months of the year. He noted that during these months more students than usual misbehaved in class and were sent to the principal's office, which consisted of a cluster of three rooms, *each air conditioned.* Without realizing it, my colleague and other faculty members were unwittingly removing students from a hot, aversive learning situation (a negative reinforcer) and sending them to a place where they could, quite literally, cool off. (By the way, once the staff realized what might be happening, misbehavers were sent to another non-air conditioned room. Misbehaving did not stop, but it did drop significantly.)

Sometimes, unfortunately, the entire school experience becomes a negative reinforcer and, as a consequence, thousands of students drop out. Dropping out removes the threat of more failure and, as research has shown, a significant number of dropouts' self-esteem gets *higher* once they leave school (Rumberger, 1987). A way, then, to remove the negative reinforcement (school) is to drop out of it. The fact that many dropouts end up with higher self-esteem (positive reinforcement) may help explain, at least in part, why so few go back.

A too-casual interpretation of behaviorist principles can be very misleading. It would be erroneous to assume, for instance, that randomly applied positive reinforcers will be effective or that the same positive reinforcers will work for all individuals. For example, teachers sometimes fail to understand why their students behave so poorly or are not performing better in class. A teacher may say something like this: "Here I've given my students the best instruction possible, I've given them stars, attention, praise—why are they misbehaving? Why aren't they achieving better?" The hidden assumption here seems to be one that suggests that, with all these positive reinforcers, the students should be doing much better. Indeed, a vague knowledge of reinforcement principles may lead this teacher to conclude that behaviorism is an impractical theory and that positive reinforcement does not work. The teacher needs a more complete understanding of the reinforcement principles. Perhaps the stars, attention, and praise are not made contingent on desirable behaviors; that is, maybe the teacher indiscriminately provides his or her reinforcements without being certain that the reinforcers are the specific consequences of particular behaviors.

Another possibility may be that at least some of what the teacher does is not serving as reinforcement; perhaps giving stars, attention, or praise is more reinforcing for the teacher than for the students. A teacher, for example, may praise his or her students because he or she feels insecure and uses praise more as a means to manipulate students' good will rather than as a method for sincerely acknowledging students' efforts. Over time, students come to sense this, and praise loses its effectiveness. In another instance, a teacher may praise so indiscriminately that it no longer has special meaning. Further, the students' misbehavior and low achievement may be more positively reinforced by peer input than by teacher feedback.

Advocates of behavioristic approaches are in high agreement that conditions are *most desirable when our actions gain us something* (positive reinforcement) and *least desirable when we must behave in a certain way in order to escape from something* (negative reinforcement). Certain school situations are loaded with negative reinforcers. In some classrooms, for example, the activities are so dull and boring that any behavior that results in the students' not having to do the work is highly negatively reinforced. If cutting classes, being expelled from the room, or creating havoc in the classroom succeeds in certain students being removed from an aversive learning environment (a negative reinforcer), then these behaviors can be expected to increase. In fact, some students may be conditioned to repeat those same behaviors regularly.

1.6 Positive Versus Negative Reinforcement

Can you think of examples of things you did (or do) in your own life—not necessarily school-related—that were/are done primarily because of the benefits of negative reinforcement (i.e., things you have done or do that make it possible to avoid an unpleasant experience)? What are some things you have done or do that seem more related to the pleasant outcomes of positive reinforcement (i.e., things you do or have done with the idea in mind of *getting* something rather than *avoiding* it)? How would you describe the differences in your feeling state when your behavior is motivated by the anticipation of positive as opposed to negative motivation?

Although we could certainly enlarge our picture of the behavioristic position with such related concepts as extinction, partial reinforcement, contingency reinforcement, conditioning, stimulus generalization, schedules of reinforcement, and so on, it is sufficient for our purposes to know that what we have discussed represents some of the basic principles of behavioristic theory.

Actually, there is no single behavioristic position; there is, rather, a cluster of overlapping positions more or less resembling each other but at the same time each possessing distinctive characteristics. For example, one position emphasizes the contiguity of stimulus and response (the simultaneous occurrence of the two is regarded as a sufficient condition for a connection to be established). Psychologists associated with this position are W. K. Estes and E. R. Guthrie. Still another position, very much related to the contiguity view, stresses the importance of reinforcement in order to stamp in the desired response. Psychologists frequently associated with this position include E. L. Thorndike, J. Dollard, N. Miller, C. Hull, and K. Spence.

Still another behavioristic position asserts that there are at least two fundamental kinds of learning, and, therefore, theory must encompass both of them. Briefly, this position suggests that learning can be divided into two processes, conditioning or *sign learning,* with fear as a basic component, and *solution learning,* with habit formation as the key feature. This position is probably best known as Mowrer's revised two-factor theory. (Gredler [1992] and Klein [1987] contain excellent overviews of behavioristic theories and theorists.)

Some Criticisms of Behavioristic Theory

Behaviorism has been mostly criticized for allegedly depersonalizing or dehumanizing our basic nature because of its emphasis on *quantifying* and *objectifying* human behavior too rigidly.

Indeed, it is precisely because of its emphasis on quantifying behavior and objectifying humankind that behaviorism meets it stiffest resistance. The very idea of supporting an objective psychology that develops a technology for controlling and manipulating human behavior through the systematic, deliberate use of reinforcement is frightening to some, and appalling to many.

Some of the major questions and criticisms regarding the control issue were raised by Carl Rogers (1956).

> They can be stated very briefly: Who will be controlled? Who will exercise control? What types of control will be exercised? Most important of all, toward what end or what purpose, or in pursuit of what value, will control be exercised? . . . If we choose some particular goal or series of goals for human beings and then set out on a large scale to control human behavior to the end of achieving these goals, we are locked in the rigidity of our initial choice, because scientific endeavor can never transcend itself to select new goals. Only subjective human persons can do that. . . . If, however, a part of our scheme is to set free some "planners" who do not have to be happy, who are not controlled, and who are therefore free to choose other values, this has several meanings. . . . It means that if it is necessary to set up an elite group which is free, then this shows all too clearly that the great majority are only slaves—no matter by what high-sounding name we call them—of those who select the goals. (p. 1063)

Criticism aimed at the behavioristic position always seems to revolve around two major issues: Is there really no such thing as a subjective, inner person capable of making free choices? and can people—and, if possible—*should* people be controlled through an advanced behavioral technology that controls the environment? The critics say "yes," there is an inner person, and "no," we should not control behavior. Albert Bandura (1977) has made the case that human beings are capable of choosing how they will respond because many types of human behavior are under what he calls *anticipatory control.* That is, we are able to observe the effects of our behaviors and anticipate the consequences—not always and not perfectly, but to an extent. As a result, we are capable of significantly controlling our behavior by choosing between alternatives and thereby *producing* predetermined consequences. Even among those identified with behaviorism, opinions differ about how much free choice people have and the extent to which human behavior can be controlled. These are touchy issues, both inside and outside the confines of behavioristic theory.

1.7 What Would You Do?

Consider this for a moment. If you had your choice between being able to make it possible for all youths to experience academic success by systematically controlling the school environment with the techniques discussed in this section, or allowing all youths the freedom to learn as determined by their own free will, which would you choose? Why? In which system would you prefer to be a student? Why?

Implications for Teaching and Learning

One of the most powerful implications of behavioristic theory for teaching and learning deals with the use of reinforcement, particularly positive reinforcement. Remember that positive reinforcement happens when something is added to a situation as a response is made, causing a pleasing result *to the receiver.* We use this type of reinforcement all the time, but are likely to call it praise, a compliment, a flattering remark, or a gift. When we are the receivers of positive reinforcement, we usually feel good (although not always, if we feel it is overdone or that we do not deserve it). If we feel good we are more likely to repeat the behavior that elicited the reinforcement in the first place.

In various books devoted partly or entirely to the application of behavioristic principles (e.g., Bigge, 1982; Gredler, 1992; Hill, 1982), it is possible to find highly detailed descriptions of how reinforcement can be used according to various schedules of reinforcement. For example, schedules can be *continuous* (a reward is provided for every correct response) or *intermittent* (only some of the correct answers are rewarded). If reinforcements are intermittent, then teachers, or whoever is doling them out, can choose to reinforce a proportion of the correct answers (a *ratio* schedule), or they may dole out the reinforcements on a time basis (an *interval* schedule). In a ratio schedule, the teacher might, for example, decide to reinforce one out of every three correct responses, while in an interval schedule he or she might reinforce one correct response every 30 seconds. Within these two options are still two more choices. The reinforcer might choose to reinforce correct responses in a predetermined fashion (*fixed* schedule) or in a more haphazard manner (*variable* schedule). Or, to really confuse matters, the reinforcer might combine a number of these schedules and triumphantly claim that he or she is using a mixed or *combined* schedule. Figure 1.3 may help you see what these schedules look like in relation to one another. It is not likely that we will find many teachers who set out to reinforce their students' efforts on a variable ratio schedule, fixed interval schedule, or any other kind of schedule. Rather, we are more likely to find teachers moving with, and responding to, the flow of classroom life without regard for a particular schedule of responses. Wise teachers know that positive reinforcement, discriminately dispensed and genuinely given, can serve as a powerful motivator, an outcome consistently found in research related to learning and motivation (Bates, 1979; Boggiano and Main, 1986).

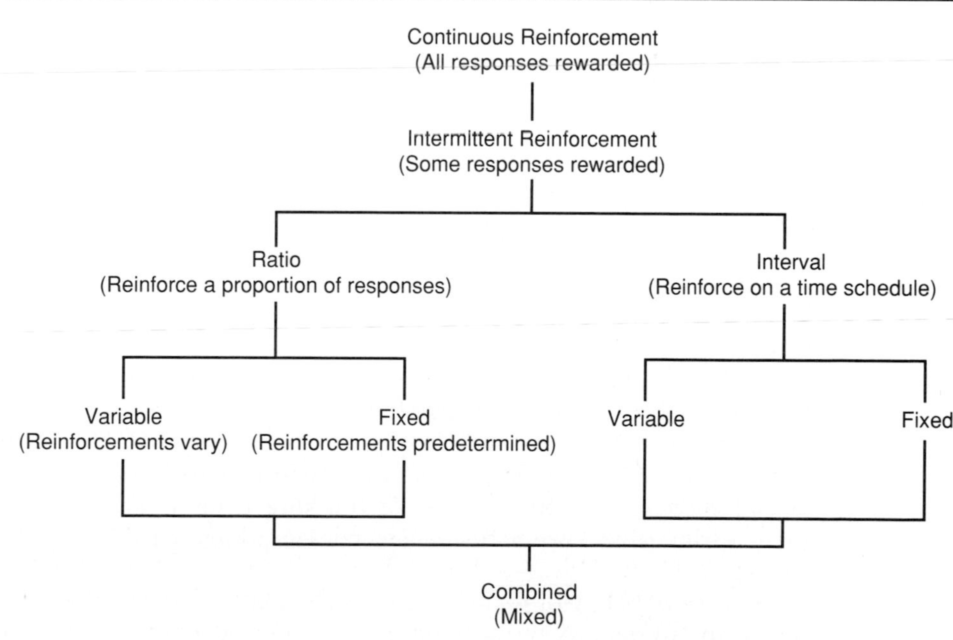

Figure 1.3. OVERVIEW OF VARIOUS TYPES OF REINFORCEMENT SCHEDULES.

Positive reinforcement does not necessarily have to be in the form of tangible tokens of approval such as stars, prizes, medals, money, or a place on the honor roll, although tangible rewards of this sort can be, and are, effective. Sometimes, the most effective rewards are embedded in satisfying relationships between students and teachers.

1.8 How Did You Feel?

> Think about the last time an instructor gave you some attention or showed some interest in your work. How did you feel? Generally, how would you describe your attitude toward the instructor and the class? What happens to you when you receive no attention or, worse, negative attention? How do those feelings—good or bad—affect your behavior inside and outside the class?

Overall, the net effect of positive reinforcement is that it helps students have the feeling that they have been *added to* and, as a consequence, they may feel more encouraged to come back to school to get more of the same. The net effect of negative reinforcement is that students may learn to avoid school experiences (cause trouble, drift off in fantasy, drop out) as a way of evading negative experiences that are humiliating and ego deflating.

Perhaps one of the most important implications of the behavioristic position for teaching and learning is the inherent stimulus potential of the teacher. A teacher's presentation, tone of voice, manner of dress, personality, and so on, all have stimulus potential in the sense that each characteristic will cause students to respond in different ways and for various reasons. In other words, stimulus potential helps us to understand what it is about ourselves that may be causing students to respond favorably or unfavorably.

Let us turn now to still another view of human behavior—one that considers the inner person, which is an entity rejected by behavioristic theory.

HUMANISTIC PSYCHOLOGY: CENTRAL IDEAS

The idea of a *humanistic psychology* was the project of a group of psychologists who, under the leadership of Abraham Maslow in the early 1960s, worked to establish a viable theoretical alternative to psychoanalytic theory and behaviorism, the two influential psychological currents at that time. Unlike the others, humanistic psychology is not a single organized theory or system but is a collection of convergent lines of thinking from Western philosophical sources (primarily, existentialism) and contemporary psychological thought (Hamachek, 1987).

The view of behavior that grows out of humanistic theory focuses on how humans are influenced and guided by the personal meanings they attach to their experiences. It stresses not so much people's biological drives as their goals; not so much their past experiences as their current circumstances; and not so much environmental forces as perceptions of those forces. Hence, the emphasis is on the subjective qualities of human experience and the personal meaning of experiences to a person, rather than on his or her objective, observable, measurable responses.

This humanistic view of behavior represents what is sometimes called the third force in psychology in that it distinguishes itself from the psychoanalytic and behavioristic positions by focusing on the positive aspects of people, their inner-directed, conscious motivations and self-directed goals. Whereas psychoanalytic theory, by stressing the power of instinctual drives and unconscious motivations, and behavioristic theory, by focusing on the controlling power of external conditions, deemphasize the idea of freedom of choice, humanistic psychology underscores the importance of human choice in everyday behavior. Along these lines, Maslow (1968a) has noted:

> Life is a continual series of choices for the individual in which a main determinant of choice is the person he already is. . . . We can no longer think of the person as "fully determined" where this phrase implies "determined only by forces external to the person." The person, insofar as he *is* a real person, is his own main determinant. Every person, is, in part, "His own project" and makes himself. (p. 193)

The idea of personal freedom is an important issue in the humanistic-perceptual framework. We may not use the freedom we have or we may misuse it, but in this framework it is there for the taking.

1.9 Do You Have a Choice?

> Suppose a couple of people aligned with the psychoanalytic and/or behavioristic positions were observing you read this book and they asked you the following question: "Since you have to read that book to pass the test and eventually the course, aren't you in a position of being unfree to choose *not* to read that volume?" Do they have a point? Or not? How would you respond to the implied charge that you are not free to choose to read this book?

The Nature of Human Behavior: A Humanistic Perspective

James Bugental (1965), the first president of the American Association for Humanistic Psychology, has suggested five basic postulates for the humanistic-perceptual view that may help give additional perspective to this frame of reference for understanding human behavior.

1. *Humans, as humans, supersede the sum of their parts.* We are more than the accumulation of our various part-functions. This is something like saying that Marvin Hamlisch's score for *A Chorus Line* is more than the summation of the number of individual musical notes that went into composing it.

2. *Humans have their being in a human context.* Our unique human nature is expressed through our relationship to our fellows and, in that sense, humanistic psychology is always concerned with a person's interpersonal potential.

3. *Humans are aware.* Whatever our degree of consciousness, we are aware of ourselves and our existence. We do not move from one experience to the next as if they were discrete, independent, and unrelated episodes. The way we behave in the present is related to what happened in our past and connected to our hopes for the future.

4. *Humans have choice.* Phenomenologically, choice is a given of experience. When aware, we can choose and thereby become a participant in experience, not a bystander.

5. *Humans are intentional.* Whenever people make choices, they demonstrate their intent. People intend through having purpose, through valuing, and through seeking meaning in their lives. Our intentionality, or conscious deliberateness as you might call it, is the basis on which we build our identity and distinguish ourselves from other species.

In humanistic psychology, terms such as *self-actualization, self-fulfillment,* and *self-realization* carry important meanings. Each conveys the idea of who one is. What one can become depends on one's choices and self-perceptions. Indeed, the whole idea of self is an important one, an idea we turn to next.

The Self: A Key Construct

With so much emphasis on how people perceive themselves—on personal meanings, values, choices, subjective experiences, and perceptions—it seems only natural that the idea of self or self-concept, should be the centerpiece of humanistic theory.

The self is the private picture each of us has regarding who we think we are, what we think we can do, and who we think we can be. It is that part of our personality of which we are conscious.

Over time, the idea of self-concept has emerged as a kind of unifying principle of personality for psychologists and educators with a humanistic bent. It offers a way for taking into account the subjective experience of each individual and for understanding the meaning of that experience from his or her point of view.

Why is the self important within the humanistic frame of reference? Social psychologist M. Brewster Smith's (1976) observations help put that question in perspective.

We are partly creatures of our own images. . . . It makes a difference to me how I think about myself. Am I free or not free? Do I control my life? Do I have a core worth searching for? There is a growing body of evidence in psychology that the answers people give to such questions make a tremendous difference in happiness, the decisions they make, the way they treat people—how they live, how they die. (p. 74)

The self occupies a central seat of importance in psychology because it underscores the idea that it is how people perceive themselves and the world in which they live that determines their intrapsychic feelings and interpersonal behaviors. A self-concept point of view allows for the opportunity to consider self-perceptions as the intervening variable between the stimulus and the response. Rather than its being an S-R world, one that some feel negates the person, it becomes an S-P-R (Stimulus-*Person*-Response) world, one that others feel elevates the person, at the same time establishing a frame of reference for explaining why behaviors may vary from one person to another even though stimulus conditions are the same. The conditions may be the same, but the way they are perceived may differ.

All in all, the self is central in the humanistic perceptual view of humankind. It emphasizes the individual as each person sees him- or herself and, even more, it underscores the role of consciousness in human behavior. The self-concept idea has grown in popularity and scientific respectability in recent years, and it continues to grow both in stature and empirical substance.

Criticisms Aimed at Humanistic Theory

When humanistic psychology is discussed by its critics, three major criticisms tend to stand out. They are as follows:

1. In the first place, humanistic psychology has been criticized because it is too vague in the sense that some of its main tenets are ambiguous and subject to individual interpretation (Child, 1973). *Authenticity,* a favorite concept among humanistically inclined educators and psychologists, is a good example. Critics wonder how it is possible to recognize an "authentic" person or an "authentic" act. A person described as a "fully functioning" individual or a student engaged in a "real and meaningful learning experience" would be examples of other vague concepts.

A bothersome aspect of authenticity is that it is difficult to verify conceptual conclusions in the usual ways. How, ask the critics, can we verify or confirm the existence of an authentic person, a fully functioning individual, or a real and meaningful learning experience? How can we go beyond the subjectivity involved in deciding what, for example, is "authentic"? This, of course, leads to problems in accumulating objectively verified knowledge. The critics wonder, How can we objectify "real" learning when what is "real" is so subjectively determined? That is, what is real for one student may be unreal to another. How do we know whom to believe?

2. A second major criticism of humanistic psychology is that it seems too much like common sense and too little like science. The idea behind this seems to be the notion that humanistic approaches are sometimes viewed as derivatives of a naive type of phenomenology, which, translated, means that there is more to understanding human behavior than a study of conscious processes may allow us to observe. In the early days of humanistic psychology's emergence, Smith (1950), for example, noted that:

> such a psychology of consciousness has an element of commonsense appeal. . . . It does make sense to the layman; it accords with what he is ready and able to recognize in himself . . . because it overstates his claims, however, it may tend to promote the state of affairs away from which we have been striving—every man his own psychologist. (p. 517)

I suppose we might quarrel about whether it is a bad idea to work in the direction of helping persons to be their own psychologists—I see that as a gain, not a loss—but the fact remains that it is a criticism worth considering for its moderating effect.

3. Still a third criticism leveled at the humanistic position is what Child (1973) calls a "trend toward sentimentality." From the critics' point of view, this means that there is more to understanding human behavior than that which is embodied in simple religious optimism, in emphasizing the power of positive thinking, or in stressing the infinite capacity of the human will to achieve good.

All in all, critics of humanistic psychology view it as being too "soft," not rigorous enough to encourage the sort of tough, objective scientific investigations necessary to render it more than a "commonsense" psychology.

Implications for Teaching and Learning

From a humanistic point of view, a major purpose of education is to help develop each student's individuality, to assist him or her in realizing the uniqueness and potential that already exists within. These are broad goals and probably no more or less than any teacher would want regardless of his or her view of human behavior. The difference lies not in the goals, but in the means for achieving them. I think Maslow (1968b) stated the difference most clearly when he wrote:

> We are now being confronted with a choice between two extremely different, almost mutually exclusive conceptions of learning. One is what I want to call for the sake of contrast and confrontation, *extrinsic learning*, i.e., learning of the outside, learning of the

impersonal, of arbitrary associations, of arbitrary conditions, that is, of arbitrary meanings and responses. In this kind of learning, most often it is not the person himself who decides, but rather a teacher or an experimenter who says, "I will use a buzzer," "I will use a bell," "I will use a red light," and most important, "I will reinforce this or that." In this sense, learning is extrinsic to the learner, extrinsic to the personality, and is extrinsic also in the sense of collecting associations, conditionings, habits, or modes of action. It is as if these were possessions which the learner accumulates in the same way that he accumulates keys or coins and puts them in his pocket. They have little or nothing to do with the actualization or growth of the peculiar, idiosyncratic kind of person he is. (p. 691)

This does not mean that extrinsic learning and the conditions that promote it are unimportant. It means, rather, that the emphasis is on intrinsic learning and those conditions that foster it.

A major implication for educational processes growing from this point of view is the emphasis on helping each student decide for him- or herself who he or she is and what he or she wants to be. Students can think for themselves, they have conscious minds that enable them to make choices, and through their capacity to make choices they will develop the sense of self necessary for productive, actualizing lives. In other words, part of a teacher's job is to assist students in finding out *what is already in them* that can be refined and developed further.

Another major implication growing from this point of view is the idea that in order to effectively teach students we must try to understand them from their point of view. This is consistent with a little truism growing out of perceptual psychology: we tend to behave in terms of what we *believe* to be true—not what *is* true, but what we believe to be true about reality as we *perceive* it (Combs, Richards, and Richards, 1976). If we are to be effective teachers, then we should attempt to see the world as the student sees it, accept it as the student's truth, and not attempt to force him or her into changing. This does not mean that a teacher should not challenge what a student believes or avoid presenting him or her with alternatives. It only suggests that to be effective *a teacher would be well-advised to start where the student's perceptions are, and not where his or her own perceptions happen to be at the moment.*

This view values individuality, personal choice, and, indeed, values themselves. It starts with the idea that students are individuals, and it strives to help students become more like themselves and less like one another. The teacher assists, helps, and ministers to growing, living, dynamic human beings already in the process of becoming. A significant implication emerging from this point of view is that good teaching is best done through a process of helping students explore and understand the personal meanings that are inherent in all of their experiences.

Humanistically inclined teachers tend to be as concerned with understanding the inner student as they are with manipulating the external environment; they are as interested in their students' current lives as they are in their early histories; they are as involved with the discovery of subjective, personal meanings to explore further as they are with looking for objective, observable behaviors to reinforce; they tend to be as concerned with the question of what is a good relationship as they are with what is a good reward.

It would not be correct to conclude that all one has to do to be classified as a humanistic teacher is create an unconditionally accepting climate that allows students to choose their own learning. Teachers who approach teaching with this attitude may not be rigid and authoritarian, but they are no less dogmatic than those who believe that the traffic flow of learning should always be determined by the teacher. As will be discussed in Part III, many students function better and learn best when they are given considerable direction and guidance. It is altogether possible for a teacher to provide both specific structure and explicit expectations and still be a humanistic teacher. Basically, a humanistic approach to education is one that affirms the idea that teaching and learning are interactive processes, interested in helping students reach their potential for optimum growth.

1.10 Which View Do You Prefer?

> You have been exposed to three major points of view about how to think about human behavior, particularly as it relates to teaching and learning. Each has a certain emphasis, a certain slant. How would you rank those viewpoints in terms of your identification with, and preference for, the point of view associated with each? Which one(s) best reflect(s) your own feelings regarding how to think about human behavior? Can you explain why you feel as you do?

EPILOGUE

Each of the theoretical positions discussed in this chapter has something important to say about behavior and the nature of humankind. Psychoanalytic psychology helps us better understand and appreciate the power of unconscious motivations and the contribution of past experiences to current behavior. Behavioristic psychology provides us insight into the basic processes of conditioning and how outside stimuli can influence behavior. Humanistic psychology provides us a way of understanding behavior from the point of view of the person doing the behaving, and of appreciating the idea that how people behave or how students learn is a function of *their* perceptions of the world, not our own.

It would not be accurate to say that one theoretical position is better or more effective than another, but it is possible that you may find yourself attracted to one particular viewpoint more than to others. However, leaning one way or another does not mean that we cannot gain from the lessons, the evidence, or the experience of points of view different from that to which we are inclined.

If, for instance, we believe that our students are simply products of past experiences or victims of social conditioning, then we are in a poor position to consider the motivation potential in the further goals students may set for themselves or in the personal aspirations they are striving to meet. However, if we believe that there is no such thing as intrinsic motivation, then we may expend needless energy devising ways to keep students extrinsically awake, interested, and alert. We could be so caught up in the idea that students should be free to do their own thing, make their own choices, arrive at their own decisions, and so on, that we may overlook those students who may need some direction, guidance, and structure in order to perform at their best.

As you will learn in the pages ahead, the lesson from research and experience is clear: students learn in various ways and are motivated for various reasons. This suggests that, as teachers, we have to be as flexible in our view of human behavior as possible.

It is natural to project those qualities we value in ourselves onto other people and to believe that most other persons learn, live, and behave as we do. However natural it is, our projections are not always accurate. Although we have many overlapping behaviors, values, and styles of living, each of us is unique. What fits one person does not necessarily fit another. In order to be effective teachers, we first have to be flexible and open enough to use the best of what various points of view regarding human behavior and human learning have to offer. Each of the theoretical positions we have examined has something to teach about understanding the behavioral dynamics that go on inside and outside the classroom, and their presence will be felt as undercurrents throughout this text.

STUDY AND REVIEW QUESTIONS

1. If someone asked you how psychoanalytic psychology changed our approach to understanding behavior, how would you reply?
2. Can you briefly describe the first five stages of growth as described by a psychoanalytic theory?
3. What are some of the basic criticisms of psychoanalytic theory?
4. As examples of neo-psychoanalytic theorists, how do Jung and Adler differ from Freud regarding views of human behavior?
5. How would you describe the implications for teaching and learning that can be derived from psychoanalytic thinking?
6. In what basic way does behavioristic psychology differ from psychoanalytic psychology?
7. Can you explain why some behaviorists would say that human freedom is largely a myth?
8. How would you explain the terms *reinforcement* and *conditioning?* How do they work in conjunction with each other?

9. How do positive and negative reinforcement work? Can you give an example of how each might be used in a classroom?
10. What are some of the basic criticisms of behavioristic theory?
11. What are the major implications for teaching and learning derived from behavioristic theory?
12. How does humanistic psychology differ from psychoanalytic and behavioristic psychology?
13. If you were asked to explain the humanistic approach to understanding behavior, what would you say?
14. Why is the role of the self important in humanistic thinking?
15. When humanistic psychology is criticized, what points are usually made?
16. What major implications for teaching and learning can be derived from humanistic psychology?

REFERENCES

Bandura, A. *Social Learning Theory.* Englewood Cliffs, NJ: Prentice Hall, 1977.

Bates, J. A. "Extrinsic Reward and Intrinsic Motivation: A Review with Implications for the Classroom." *Review of Educational Research,* 1979, *49,* pp. 557–576.

Bigge, M. L. *Learning Theories for Teachers,* 4th ed. New York: Harper & Row, 1982.

Boggiano, A. K., and Main, D. S. "Enhancing Children's Interest in Activities Used as Rewards: The Bonus Effect." *Journal of Personality and Social Psychology,* 1986, *51,* pp. 1116–1126.

Bugental, J. *The Search for Authenticity.* New York: Holt, Rinehart and Winston, 1965.

Child, I. L. *Humanistic Psychology & the Research Tradition: Their Several Virtues.* New York: Wiley, 1973.

Combs, A. W., Richards, A. C., and Richards, F. *Perceptual Psychology: A Humanistic Approach to the Study of Persons.* New York: Harper & Row, 1976.

Derlega, V. T., Winstead, B. A., and Jones, W. H., eds. *Personality: Contemporary Theory and Research.* Chicago: Nelson-Hall, 1991.

Freud, S. *Civilization and Its Discontents.* London: Horgarth, 1930.

Gredler, M. E. *Learning and Instruction: Theory into Practice.* New York: Macmillan, 1992.

Hamachek, D. "Humanistic Psychology: Theory, Postulates, and Implications for Educational Processes." In J. A. Glover and R. R. Ronning (Eds.), *Historical Foundations of Educational Psychology* (pp. 159–182). New York: Plenum, 1987.

Hill, W. F. *Principles of Learning: A Handbook of Applications.* Palo Alto, CA: Mayfield, 1982.

Klein, S. B. *Learning: Principles and Applications.* New York: McGraw-Hill, 1987.

Leakey, R. E. *The Making of Mankind.* New York: Dutton, 1981.

Maslow, A. H. *Toward a Psychology of Being,* 2nd ed. Princeton, NJ: VanNostrand, 1968a.

Maslow, A. H. "Some Educational Implications of Humanistic Psychologies." *Harvard Educational Review,* 1968b, *38,* pp. 685–696.

Pavlov, I. P. "The Scientific Investigation of the Psychical Faculties or Processes in the Higher Animals." *Science,* 1906, *24,* pp. 613–619.

Peterson, C. *Personality,* 2nd ed. Fort Worth: Harcourt Brace Jovanovich, 1992.

Rogers, C. "Some Issues Concerning the Control of Human Behavior." *Science,* 1956, *30,* pp. 1057–1066.

Rumberger, R. W. "High School Dropouts: A Review of Issues and Evidence." *Review of Educational Research,* 1987, *57,* pp. 101–121.

St. Angelo, D., and Dyson, J. W. "Personality and Political Orientation." *Midwest Journal of Political Science,* 1968, *12,* pp. 202–223.

Shevrin, H. "Glimpses of the Unconscious." *Psychology Today,* 1980, April, p. 128.

Skinner, B. F. *Beyond Freedom and Dignity.* New York: Knopf, 1971.

Smith, M. B. "The Phenomenological Approach to Personality Theory: Some Critical Remarks." *The Journal of Abnormal and Social Psychology,* 1950, *45,* pp. 516–522.

Smith, M. B. "Our Many Versions of the Self." *Psychology Today,* 1976, February, pp. 72–75.

Thomas, F. M. *Comparing Theories of Child Development,* 5th ed. Belmont, CA: Wadsworth, 1992.

Verplanck, W. S. "The Operant Conditioning of Human Motor Behavior." *Psychological Bulletin,* 1956, *53,* pp. 70–83.

Watson, J. B. *Psychology from the Standpoint of a Behaviorist.* Philadelphia: J. B. Lippincott, 1919.

Watson, J. B. *Behaviorism.* New York: Norton, 1925.

Zucker, R. A., and Gomberg, E. S. L. "Etiology of Alcoholism Reconsidered." *American Psychologist,* 1986, *41,* pp. 783–793.

SELECTED READINGS OF RELATED INTEREST

Baldwin, J. D., and Baldwin, I. J. *Behavioral Principles in Everyday Life,* 2nd ed. Englewood Cliffs, NJ: Prentice Hall, 1986. An excellent source for exploring how behavioral principles can be applied both inside and outside the classroom.

Derlega, V. J., Winstead, B. A., and Jones, W. H., eds. *Personality: Contemporary Theory and Research.* Chicago: Nelson-Hall, 1991. Explores the many dimensions of personality and includes discussions of how personality theories help us to understand behavior.

Hamachek, D. "Humanistic Psychology: Theory, Postulates, and Implications for Educational Processes." In J. A. Glover and R. R. Ronning (Eds.), *Historical Foundations of Educational Psychology* (pp. 159–182). New York: Plenum, 1987. A basic overview of humanistic psychology beginning with its early roots in humanism. Discusses contemporary implications for teaching and learning.

McAdams, D. P. *The Person: An Introduction to Personality Psychology.* Fort Worth: Harcourt Brace Jovanovich, 1990. Contains particularly good discussions about psychoanalytic and humanistic psychology and theorists associated with each.

Peterson, C. *Personality,* 2nd ed. Fort Worth: Harcourt Brace Jovanovich, 1992. Presents a fine overview and analysis of the major theories of personality and research supporting each position.

2

Psychological Models for Understanding Behavioral Dynamics

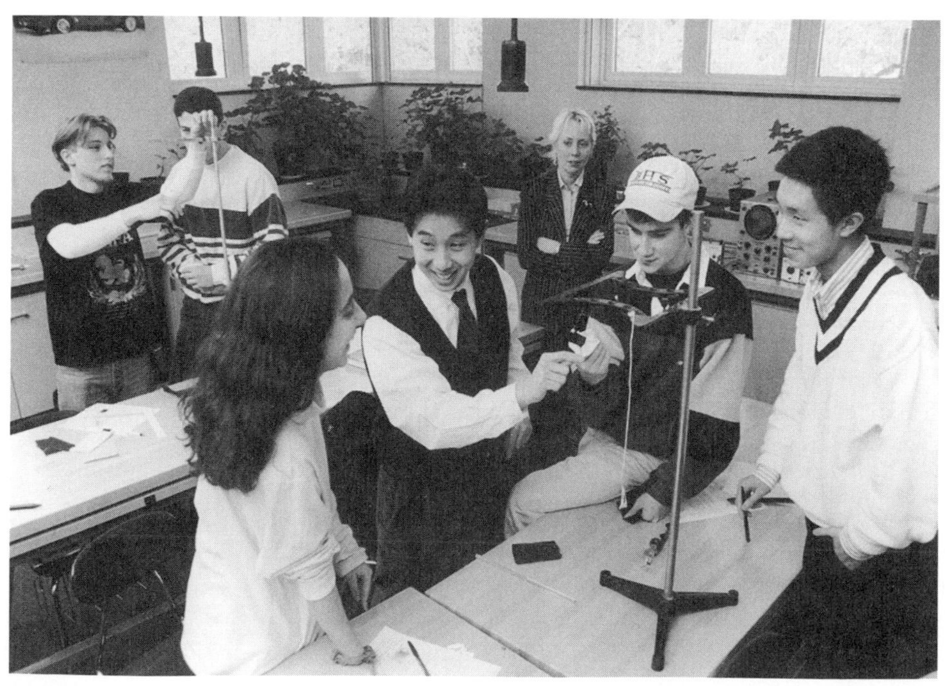

CHAPTER OVERVIEW

IMPORTANT CHAPTER IDEAS

1. According to Havighurst, developmental tasks consist of certain skills, attitudes, and understandings that a person is confronted with at various growth stages.
2. Each growth stage is associated with specific developmental tasks that must be accomplished before moving to subsequent growth stages.
3. According to White, one's sense of competence is roughly proportional to the number of successes one has in doing things that are personally important.
4. As viewed by White, the drive or motivation to be competent is an inherent desire to have an effect on one's environment.
5. High self-esteem and feelings of competence are positively related.
6. Feelings of competence (or incompetence), according to White, begin in the early school years.
7. According to Maslow, moving in the direction of being a self-actualized person is synonymous with reaching the potential that is within the self.
8. Self-actualization theory is basically an optimistic view of human nature, which sees humankind as essentially and innately good and stresses the importance of knowing more about such human conditions as joy, love, and well-being.
9. A person's lower, and more basic, needs in Maslow's hierarchy must be satisfied in order for movement in the direction of self-actualization to occur.
10. According to Rogers, a fully functioning individual has a more internal than external locus of evaluation.
11. In Rogers' theory, most perceptions adopted by the individual are those that are consistent with his or her concept of self.
12. According to Erikson, one's social-emotional development progresses through eight psychosocial stages beginning at birth and ending in the retirement years.
13. Each stage represents a "psychosocial crisis," or turning point, when one's potential and vulnerability are greatly increased, a time when things may go either well or badly depending on one's life circumstances.
14. We are likely to find in every person a certain ratio between the positive and negative qualities associated with each stage, which, when the ratio is more positive, will help him or her to cope more successfully with subsequent stages.
15. Some measure of psychological health and a sense of personal competence are goals within reach of every school-age youth and every adult.

PROLOGUE

The primary purpose of this chapter is to present the broad outline of five time-tested psychological models that can help us understand and interpret human behavior. The models that we examine in this chapter are reflections and refinements of the three theoretical positions discussed in Chapter 1. For example, Robert Havighurst's developmental task model, which stresses the importance of certain tasks being completed at certain ages, underscores a basic behavioristic principle, namely, when behavior is appropriate or successful it tends to be repeated, thus enhancing the possibility of further learning. Both Robert White's concept-of-competence model and Erik Erikson's psychosocial stages model emphasize—as does psychoanalytic theory—that the early years have a deep impact on one's subsequent growth and development. Abraham Maslow's self-actualization model and Carl Rogers' fully functioning person model reflect a more humanistic slant, each emphasizing the inner person, conscious processes, and the importance of self-perceptions.

The five models discussed in this chapter are offered as a kind of framework for thinking about why humans behave as they do, and for understanding some of the deeper needs and motivations that may trigger certain behaviors. Just as it is important for a doctor to have working knowledge of human physiology in order to treat specific patients, so too is it important for a teacher to have fundamental knowledge of human psychology in order to teach specific students.

Why is it important to accomplish certain developmental tasks at certain stages of growth? How does progression through psychosocial stages influence development? How are competence and self-esteem related? What does it mean to be a fully functioning or self-actualized person? What can teachers do to encourage a healthy self-concept in all students? By the end of this chapter you should have some ideas about how to respond to questions of this sort.

THE DEVELOPMENTAL TASKS MODEL (ROBERT HAVIGHURST)

As growth proceeds along a developmental continuum, each new stage of development, according to Havighurst (1972, 1980) ushers in new tasks—skills, attitudes, understandings, accomplishments—that must be met before a person can move to a higher level of development. These are referred to as *developmental tasks,* which Havighurst (1972) says occur

> At or about a certain period in the life of the individual, successful achievement of which leads to happiness and to success with later tasks, while failure leads to unhappiness in the individual, disapproval by society, and difficulty with later tasks. (p. 2)

Havighurst has divided the life span into six periods. Each period is associated with specific tasks that must be met and accomplished before moving to

Infancy and early childhood (birth to 6 years)	*Middle childhood (6–12 years)*	*Preadolescence and adolescence (12–18 years)*
Learning to walk. Learning to take solid foods. Learning to talk. Learning to control the elimination of body wastes. Learning sex differences and sexual modesty. Achieving physiological stability. Forming simple concepts of social and physical reality. Learning to relate oneself emotionally to parents, siblings, and other people. Learning to distinguish right and wrong and developing a conscience.	Learning physical skills necessary to ordinary games. Building wholesome attitudes toward oneself as growing organism. Learning to get along with agemates. Learning an appropriate masculine or feminine social role. Developing fundamental skills in reading, writing, and calculating. Developing concepts necessary for everyday living. Developing conscience, morality, and a scale of values. Achieving personal independence. Developing attitudes toward social groups and institutions.	Achieving new and more mature relations with agemates of both sexes. Achieving a masculine or feminine social rolc. Accepting one's physique and using the body effectively. Achieving emotional independence of parents and other adults. Achieving assurance of economic independence. Selecting and preparing for an occupation. Preparing for marriage and family life. Developing intellectual skills and concepts necessary for civic competence. Desiring and achieving socially responsible behavior. Acquiring a set of values and an ethical system as a guide to behavior.

Early adulthood (18–35 years)	*Middle age (35–60 years)*	*Later life (60–)*
Selecting a mate. Learning to live with a marriage partner. Starting a family. Rearing children. Managing a home. Getting started in an occupation. Taking on civic responsibility. Finding a congenial social group.	Achieving adult, civic, and social responsibility. Establishing and maintaining an economic standard of living. Assisting teenage children to become responsible and happy adults. Developing adult leisure-time activities. Relating oneself to one's spouse as a person. Learning to accept and adjust to the physiological changes of middle age. Adjusting to aging parents.	Adjusting to decreasing physical strength. Adjusting to retirement and reduced income. Adjusting to death of spouse. Establishing an explicit affiliation with one's age group. Meeting social and civic obligations. Establishing satisfactory living arrangements.

Figure 2.1. DEVELOPMENTAI TASKS FROM INFANCY THROUGH LATER LIFE.

subsequent growth stages. Figure 2.1 itemizes the specific tasks associated with each major growth stage. Each series of developmental tasks is a complex organization of problems that all individuals encounter in one form or another at certain stages in their lives. Unless a person meets the demands of these problems and resolves them adequately as they occur, it is likely that he or she will encounter developmental problems in subsequent stages. For example, unless a person meets the developmental task of achieving new and more mature relations with the opposite sex during the preadolescent and adolescent years (ages 12–18), then it may be difficult to move to the next developmental task of selecting a mate, existing happily in a marriage, and starting a family. Many youthful marriages run into trouble because one developmental task (getting married) was taken on before a prior developmental task (learning how to relate to members of the opposite sex) was completed.

The developmental task idea is a useful framework insofar as it reminds us that different skills and attitudes are acquired at different times along the developmental continuum. Further, it helps us to see that there is a certain hierarchy of personal and interpersonal skills that have to be learned at particular times in one's life in order to progress to the next higher level of personal and social development. The developmental task model also helps to remind us that one of the major goals of an educational enterprise is the creation of experiences and opportunities to assist youth to accomplish the tasks before them.

2.1 Assessing Your Progress

As you look at the developmental tasks outline in Figure 2.1, how would you assess your growth and development through the stages you have gone through so far? Are there particular tasks that you perhaps did not learn as well as others and had to go back and learn? For youth 6 to 18 years, which tasks would you say that schools should have particular responsibility for teaching?

THE CONCEPT-OF-COMPETENCE MODEL (ROBERT W. WHITE)

One way of looking at competence is to think of it as an outgrowth of what one feels after the successful completion of a task or course of study. This may indeed be one way of acquiring it. However, Robert W. White (1959, 1960), in two provocative and still timely papers, proposed a quite different view of competence. Quite simply, White proposed the existence of a new drive or motivation, inherent in the child, which is called *effectance.* Effectance is the inherent desire to have an effect on one's environment. It is what you might call a built-in motivation to be competent. Indeed, White regards the innate human drives, such as hunger, thirst, and sex, as relatively unimportant compared to the drive for effectance. He reasons that the effectance drive is as innate as other primary drives. Our most important motivated behaviors are not derivatives of sexual or erotic interests, as a more Freudian view would suggest, but have independent status.

Competence and Self-Esteem Go Hand In Hand

To some extent self-esteem (self-prizing, self-valuing) develops from doing new things and doing them successfully. A child's initial acts of reaching, grasping, pulling, crawling, standing, and eventually walking without help are done intentionally and, to the degree that they are successful, they can leave a child with a happy sense of efficacy, of being good at something. You can check this out yourself. The next time you have an opportunity to observe a young boy (or girl) take his first tottering steps alone, do not watch his feet; watch his face, because that is where you can see his feelings of efficacy and success. As he tries to walk a few feet from one support to another, he knows whether he succeeds or fails. An appreciative adult audience may encourage him, but he does not require approval to know that he has succeeded. Mind and muscle have been pitted against an invisible force trying to force him to the floor, and they have proved equal to the task (competent).

Although it is true that we can enhance our own feelings of self-esteem by seeing ourselves as good at something it would be erroneous to conclude that the dividends of self-esteem were minted entirely from within. There has to be a balance. Research has consistently shown that self-esteem has two sources: an inner source, the degree of effectiveness of one's own activity; and an external source, the opinions of others about oneself (Frey and Carlock, 1989; Hamachek, 1992). Both are necessary and important, but the former is steadier and more dependable.

Fortunately, owning a healthy sense of self-esteem does not depend on being competent in all things one does. For example, 10-year-old Mary may be particularly good in math and social studies, but not as good in drawing, writing, and other fine-motor skills. In spite of these shortcomings, she still has fairly high self-esteem because of her successes in math and social studies. Her self-esteem might be even higher if doing well in writing or drawing is not particularly important to her. One's sense of personal competence is heavily dependent on doing well in those areas and on those tasks that one *wants* to do well, which means that there is something to lose (i.e., self-esteem) if one does poorly.

It is also true that when people—young or old—feel deeply incompetent to the point of having an inferiority complex, we usually find them forever making unfavorable comparisons between themselves and others. For example, John hears one of his peers make an intelligent response in class, which causes him to lament what he considers to be his inferior intellectual status. His friends get him to join in a pinochle game, and he has a chance to deplore his mediocrity at cards. A buddy happens by with a pretty date, and this causes him to squirm because, secretly, he would like to ask a pretty girl out, but does not for fear of being turned down. In other words, a single day may provide John with opportunities to feel inferior in a dozen ways. But it is not those dozen inferiorities that bother him. Rather, it is the more pervasive fact that he does not have a sufficient sense of competence about anything to help him form a nucleus of self-esteem necessary to feel worthy. Not feeling particularly competent in anything, he feels somewhat incompetent in everything. In the absence of one or two things about his accomplishments that he could feel good about, he behaves as if he were incompetent in practically everything within his potential to do.

2.2 Looking at Your Own Competence and Self-Esteem

You might be able to understand the relationship between competence and self-esteem in a more personal way by looking at how being really good at something has affected your own self-regard. Think of some times in your life when you've been quite successful at something you've done. How did that experience impact your self-esteem? Can you think of some times in your life when you have done poorly or at least less than you had expected? How did those experiences affect your self-esteem?

The Early Years: Their Effect on Competence

The influence of success and failure on one's feelings of competence is particularly critical during the early elementary years. For example, William Glasser (1969), writing out of his many years of psychiatric experience with children, has observed:

> The critical years are between five and ten. Failure, which should be prevented throughout school, is most easily prevented at this time. When failure does occur, it can usually be corrected during those five years within the elementary school classrooms by teaching and educational procedures that lead to fulfillment of the child's basic needs. The age beyond which failure is difficult to reverse may be higher or lower than ten for any one child, depending upon the community he comes from, the strength of his family, and his own genetic resources; regardless of those variations, however, it is amazing to me how constant this age seems to be. Before age ten, a good school experience can help him succeed. After age ten, it takes more than a good school experience and unfortunately, shortly after age ten he is thrust into junior and senior high situations where he has much less chance for a corrective educational experience. Therefore, although children can be helped at any school level, the major effort should be made in the elementary school. (pp. 27–28)

Early family experiences also contribute significantly to a child's sense of competence and self-esteem. For example, Coopersmith (1967) noted from his research that children with high self-esteem are more likely to have parents who provide direct experiences of success, the means of achieving success, and handling adversity in a realistic yet nondestructive manner. For example, not long ago I heard a father say to his 5.5-year-old son, "Chris, you're just not *good* enough to ride a two-wheeled bike yet." A more appropriate and less ego-damaging response to his son's pleas for a new bike might have been something along the lines of, "Chris, you're not quite *big* enough yet. In another six months or so we'll see how much you've grown and then we'll test you out." To say that Chris is not good enough, which is, in fact, an assessment of his competence, does nothing to encourage him to think positively about his potential to *become* good. However, to say that Chris is not *big* enough is to realistically appraise the problem for what it is—a problem of size, not skill. This way Chris can see the problem for what it is and also retain good feelings about himself. The experiences children have during their early years play an incredibly important role in the development of feelings of competence.

2.3 Observe the Classes You Are In

For the next week or so, you may find it interesting and insightful to pay particular attention to interactions that go on between students and instructors in the various classes you are taking. What do you hear being said that helps to build competence and confidence in students? In yourself? How would you describe those classrooms where it seems to be easier to develop a healthy sense of competence? How about those classrooms where it seems to be more difficult?

Psychological Health as Related to Competence

White's (1959) competence model suggests that there is more to the human motivational system than the urge to satisfy basic physical needs. It is a view that allows us to tender the possibility that the really ubiquitous and important motives in life are the drives to be active, to explore, to manipulate, to control one's destiny, to produce, and to accomplish. Implicit in this notion is the idea that many forms of cognitive and social behavior, which were originally thought to be derived from other, more instinctual motivations, may themselves have an innate or inborn basis in the structure of the nervous system. Thus, we may struggle to read a difficult book or complete a project not merely because the tasks are instrumental to the gratification of a primary drive, but in part, because certain activities are intrinsically pleasurable. We are not only tension *reducers,* but also tension *producers.*

Competence leads to positive self-esteem, and positive self-esteem leads to psychologically healthier people (Hamachek, 1982, 1992; Jourard and Landsman, 1980). As youths come to know their strengths, it becomes increasingly possible for them to actualize their potentials to become what they can, an idea to which we now turn as another example of a psychological model for understanding behavior.

THE SELF-ACTUALIZATION MODEL (ABRAHAM MASLOW)

Abraham Maslow's (1987) view of personality development has a distinctly humanistic flavor in the sense that it focuses primarily on human interests and values as well as on human meanings and experiences. It also stresses the idea that the cosmos is one and interrelated, that any society is one and interrelated, and that all persons are individuals but interrelated.

Basically, the idea of self-actualization refers to a person's constant striving to realize the potential within and to develop inherent talents and capabilities. Self-actualizing behavior is what we see when people strive to be the best they can be.

Above all, self-actualization theory is an optimistic, hopeful view of human nature, viewing humankind as essentially and innately good. Maslow admonished psychology for its pessimistic, negative, and limited conception of human behavior. It was his view that psychology has examined humankind's frailties but has overlooked its strengths. Where is the psychology, he asked, that takes into account such human emotions and conditions as joy, love, understanding, and well-being to the same extent that it deals with depression, hate, ill-will, and sickness? Why is it that we have a very rich vocabulary for psychopathology but a very meager one for health or transcendence? If humankind is bad, it is because the environment is bad and not because of any inherent rottenness. Destructiveness and violence, for example, are not innate to humans; rather, humans become destructive when their inner nature is twisted, denied, or frustrated. Although Maslow admits that the thin thread of our potential for self-actualization may be overcome by a poor culture, bad parenting, or faulty habits, it never completely disappears.

Striving, reaching beyond oneself, looking ahead, and transcending the usual, mundane ways of living are important dimensions of the self-actualization model. Maslow's self-actualization theory and White's concept-of-competence model share interesting similarities. White, you remember, established a substantial case for an inherent motivation called effectance. Humans have a need to do more than simply satisfy basic needs. Maslow (1987), in a similar vein, has noted that

> The gratification of basic needs does not in itself automatically bring about a system of values in which to believe and to which one may commit himself. Rather, we have learned that one of the possible consequences of basic need gratifications may be boredom, aimlessness, anomie and the like. Apparently we function best when we are striving for something that we lack, when we wish for something that we do not have, and when we organize our powers in the service of striving toward the gratification of that wish. The state of gratification turns out to be not necessarily a state of guaranteed happiness or contentment. It is a moot state, one that raises problems as well as solving problems. (pp. xxi–xxii)

As you can see, whether the motivation is the desire to have an effect or striving for something we lack, both suggest what most of us know from experience: most people have a need to grow further, to move beyond where they are at the moment.

2.4 Does Striving Make a Difference?

What do you think about Maslow's observation that "we function best when we are striving for something that we lack, when we wish for something that we do not have?" Do you find yourself, for example, functioning better when striving for something? What examples of this can you think of? What implications do you see in Maslow's observations for teaching and learning?

Self-actualizing behavior, then, is aimed not at simply restoring one's equilibrium or status quo but at some sort of improvement. Attainment of one goal usually unlocks new confidence and creates new incentives for further growth. However, it is important to realize that before people of any age can mobilize themselves to aim for a goal as lofty or as noble as anything we might fit under the heading "self-improvement," they first must have their more basic needs satisfied. Let us turn our attention to this idea.

Maslow's Basic Needs Hierarchy

First, it is important to realize that self-actualization theory distinguishes between basic or deficiency needs and growth or actualization needs. Deficiency needs are what Maslow has called lower-order basic needs, in the sense that a deficiency in any one or more of these needs prevents one from going on to the higher-level growth needs. Altogether, there are eight levels of needs in Maslow's hierarchy, beginning with the most basic physiological needs and moving progressively higher to the growth needs. Figure 2.2 gives you an overview of each of the levels within the needs hierarchy. The first four levels are labeled deficiency needs as a way of underscoring the idea that a deficiency in any one level makes it difficult to be terribly concerned about moving to the higher-level growth needs. For example, when our physiological needs are threatened, chances are very good that we will not be too concerned about whether we are loved and appreciated. Or, moving up the scale, if our esteem needs are not met, chances are rather good that we will not be terribly concerned about actualizing ourselves.

According to the theory, within every person there is a hierarchy of need priorities. Each represents a level of personal functioning that one must successfully achieve or satisfy before there can be movement to the higher levels. There are eight levels of need priority arranged along a hierarchy of prepotency, as Maslow defined it. Even though the first four needs are lower-level needs, they are as important as those higher up on the ladder.

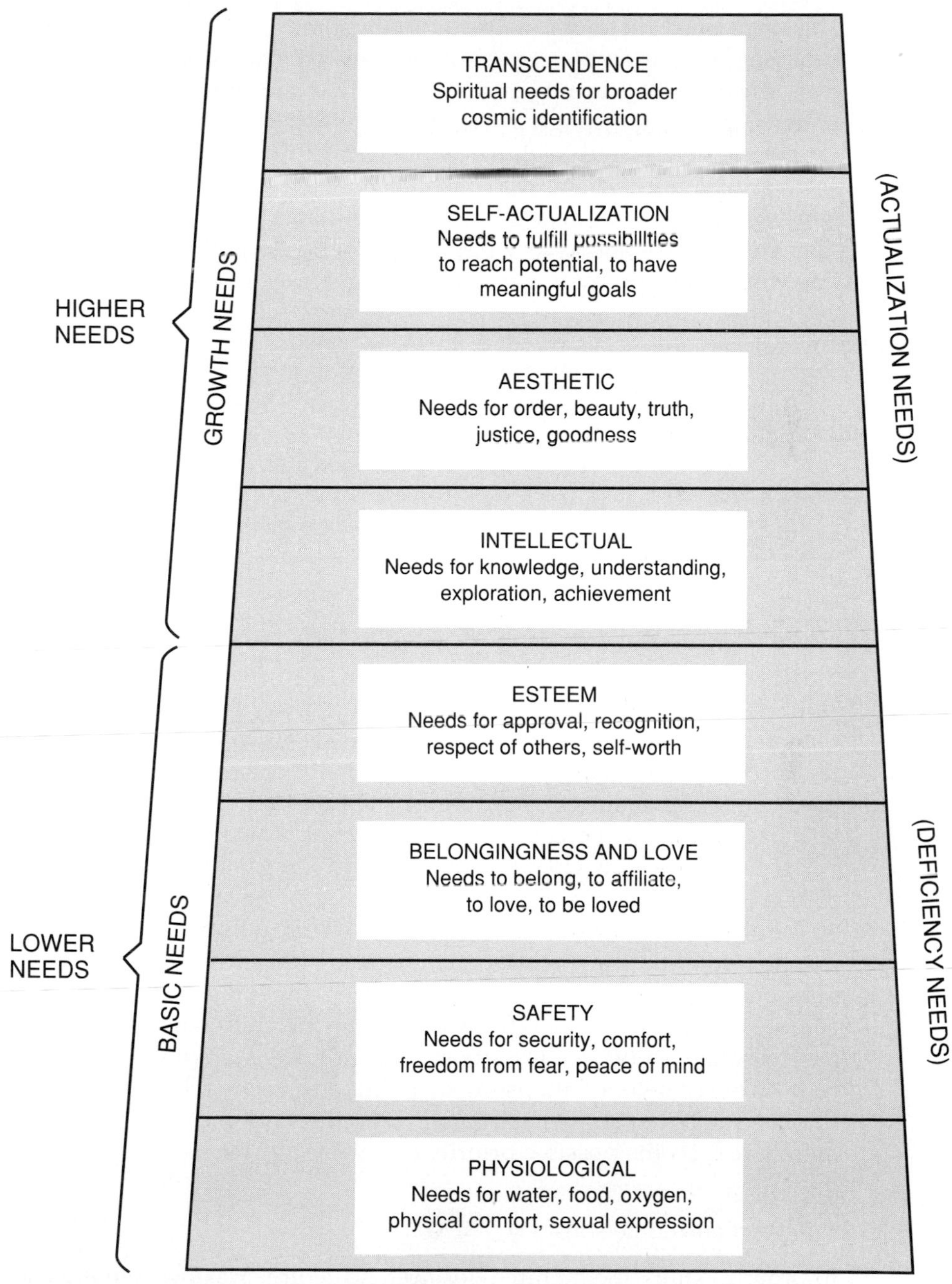

Figure 2.2. MASLOW'S HIERARCHY OF NEEDS (LOWER-LEVEL NEEDS MUST BE SATISFIED IN ORDER FOR HIGHER-LEVEL NEEDS TO BE REACHED).

How Basic Needs Influence Behavior

Maslow's need hierarchy helps us understand many expressions of human behavior. If, for example, 6-year-old Johnny goes to school hungry, he may not care much about learning how to read that morning. If 12-year-old Joan's parents are going through a wrenching divorce, which threatens Joan's need for belongingness and love, we can understand why she seems unmotivated to do school work. If you have just received a low grade on a paper or exam, which threatens your need for achievement and learning, it is not difficult to see why you may not be very responsive to the aesthetic world around you—a fine work of art, pretty flowers, a dazzling sunset, and so forth.

2.5 How Has Your Behavior Been Influenced?

Can you think of any examples from your own experiences that illustrate how being stuck at a lower-level need has interfered with doing something at a higher level? For instance, how is your work and study affected after, say, an argument with a loved one or after receiving an emotionally distressing letter from home? How would you explain this in terms of Maslow's need hierarchy?

Degrees of Satisfaction in the Basic Needs Hierarchy

Maslow's hierarchy of basic needs is not fixed in some kind of permanent staircase relationship. It would not be correct to say that if one need is satisfied, then another automatically emerges. What seems to happen is that most normal people are partially satisfied and partially unsatisfied in all of their basic needs at the same time. A more realistic appraisal of the hierarchy would be in terms of decreasing percentages of satisfaction as we move up the need scale. According to Maslow (1987), "It is as if the average citizen is satisfied perhaps 85% in his physiological needs, 70% in his safety needs, 50% in his love needs, 40% in his esteem needs, and 10% in his self-actualization needs" (p. 28). As for the idea of the emergence of a new need after satisfaction of a lower need. This emergence is not a sudden, abrupt happening, but rather a gradual emergence by slow degrees from nothingness. A child who gradually comes to feel reasonably safe in a classroom does not, for example, suddenly feel that now he or she belongs and is cared about and esteemed by all. This takes time. If a need does not show itself clearly, that does not mean it does not exist—it merely reflects the possible priority of lower-level needs.

Examples of Self-Actualized Persons

In order to study the hierarchy of need structure, Maslow initially conducted a unique type of research. What he set out to do was to find a group of healthy, balanced, integrated, successful, actualizing people. *Successful* here meant the full use and exploitation of talents, capacities, and potentialities. Within this framework, he came up with forty-nine persons from public and private life; some were well-known personalities, other historical figures. Examples of those included for study are Abraham Lincoln, Thomas Jefferson, Walt Whitman, Henry David Thoreau, Eleanor Roosevelt, Jane Addams, Albert Einstein, Albert Schweitzer, Aldous Huxley, and Adlai Stevenson. Historical figures were studied by way of biographical and autobiographical sources, while living persons were investigated through personal interviews and contact with their friends and relatives.

After studying those healthy, self-actualizing individuals, Maslow was able to sort out fifteen basic personality characteristics that distinguished them from "ordinary" people. This is not to suggest that each person he studied exhibited all fifteen self-actualizing characteristics; each did, however, exhibit a greater number of these characteristics in more varied ways than might be expected in a less self-actualized individual.

Behavioral Characteristics of Self-Actualizing Persons

The personality characteristics that most frequently distinguish self-actualizing people (Maslow, 1987) are as follows:

1. They are realistically oriented.
2. They accept themselves, other people, and the natural world for who and what they are.
3. They are spontaneous in thinking, emotions, and behavior.
4. They are problem-centered rather than self-centered in the sense of being able to devote their attention to a task, duty, or mission that seems particularly cut out for them.
5. They have a need for privacy and even seek it out on occasion, needing it for periods of intense concentration on subjects of interest.
6. They are autonomous, independent, and able to remain true to themselves in the face of rejection and unpopularity.
7. They have a continuous freshness of appreciation for, and a capacity to stand in awe again and again of, the basic goods of life.
8. They have frequent "mystic" or "oceanic" experiences, although not necessarily religious in character.
9. They feel a sense of identification with humankind as a whole in the sense of being concerned not only with their own immediate families, but with the welfare of the world as a whole.
10. Their intimate relationships with a few specifically loved people tend to be profound and deeply emotional rather than superficial.
11. They have democratic character structures in the sense of judging people and being friendly not on the basis of race, status, or religion, but rather on the basis of who other people are as individuals.

12. They have a highly developed sense of ethics and are inclined to choose their behavior with reference to ethical implications.
13. They have an unhostile sense of humor, which is expressed in their capacity to make common human foibles, pretensions, and foolishness—rather than smut, sadism, or hatred of authority—the subject of laughter.
14. They have a great capacity for creativeness.
15. They resist total conformity to society.

2.6 Are You a Self-Actualizer?

A person does not have to be Eleanor Roosevelt or Thomas Jefferson to approach some level of actualization. As you look through the behaviors associated with self-actualized people, which ones seem to fit you best? Whom have you known in your life who was (or is) a self-actualized person? What kind of an effect has that person had on you?

Psychological Health and Self-Actualization

At first glance it may seem that the idea of self-actualization is too far removed from the grasp of the average youth or adult to be a realistic goal. Not true: Psychological health does not necessarily mean possessing all the self-actualizing characteristics previously listed to the same degree or, for that matter, at the same time. Self-actualization is not a destination at which one arrives but is, rather, a goal toward which one is constantly moving. It is, in its broadest sense, a life-style, a manner of relating to oneself and others.

At first glance, it may appear that one has to be practically perfect in order to approach some level of actualization. Maslow (1987) put that idea to rest when he observed self-actualized people in his study:

> These people are *not* free of guilt, anxiety, sadness, self-castigation, internal strife, and conflict. . . . What this has taught me I think all of us had better learn. *There are no perfect human beings*. . . . To avoid our disillusionment with human nature, we must first give up our illusions about it. (pp. 145–147)

This seems an important insight, particularly for perfectionistic people who are forever disappointed in themselves and others.

There is one final point to be made, and that has to do with the difference between pseudo and authentic self-actualization. Healthy self-actualization does not mean that people go about doing what they want without regard for social customs or others' feelings. Pseudo self-actualization is very likely to be the undisciplined release of impulses of one who behaves something like a spoiled brat—who, in effect, self-actualizes at other people's expense. Pseudo-actualizing behavior says, in so many words, "I'm doing this for my sake, because it *feels* right, no matter what the consequences." Authentic self-actualizing behavior says, "I've considered my feelings and yours, and as long as I do not hurt other people, I will go through with my plan." (If you would like to explore self-actualization further, *Self-Actualization: An Annotated Bibliography of Theory and Research* by Welch, George, and Medieros (1987) would be a helpful source.)

Being aware of the dynamics of self-actualizing behavior can assist us in developing in our students those attitudes, values, and behaviors most conducive to healthy living. When students are encouraged to actualize their potentials, in whatever area they might be—science, English, metalworking—they at the same time move in the direction of becoming what Carl Rogers has called "fully functioning" individuals. Let's briefly examine what this means.

THE FULLY FUNCTIONING PERSON MODEL (CARL ROGERS)

"Fully functioning" is a concept that has evolved from many years of psychotherapeutic educational practice and research by Carl Rogers. In many ways it is similar to the idea of self-actualization in the sense that it refers to the behavior of people who have grown in the direction of psychological health.

Whereas Maslow studied healthy people in his effort to construct a model for healthy personality development and expression, Rogers' ideas about the healthy personality have come primarily from his work with clients in psychotherapy and his work as an educator. Rogers' views of what constitutes a fully functioning person do not have their origins in his observation of people at their lowest ebbs of despair, but rather in the processes they go through and the characteristics they reflect as they move in the direction of developing a self that is uniquely their own.

According to Rogers (1961) people en route to becoming fully functioning usually exhibit characteristics such as the following:

1. They tend to move away from facades. That is, they move away from a self that they are not and toward a self that they really are.
2. They tend to move away from "oughts"; they gradually reflex their compulsion to be what they "ought" to be or "ought" to become.
3. They tend to move away from meeting others' expectations and move toward meeting their own expectations.
4. They tend to move away from pleasing others and begin to be more self-directed.
5. They tend to be more accepting of themselves and are able to view themselves as people in the process of becoming. They are not easily upset by the fact that they do not always hold the same feelings toward a given experience or person or that they are not always consistent. The striving for conclusions or end states seems to decrease.

6. They tend to move toward being more open to their experiences in the sense of not having always to blot out the thoughts, feelings, perceptions, and memories that might be unpleasant.
7. They tend to move in the direction of greater acceptance of others. They seem more able to accept the experience of others even though it may differ from their own.

As you can see, the thrust of Rogers' fully functioning model is always in the direction of living in closer harmony with one's inner self. Rogers (1962) says it nicely:

> They accept the realization that the meanings implicit in their experiencing of a situation constitute the wisest and most satisfying indication of appropriate behavior. I think of one client who, toward the close of therapy, when puzzled about an issue, would put his head in his hands and say, "Now what is it I'm feeling? I want to get next to it. I want to learn what it is." Then he would wait, quietly and patiently, until he could discern the exact flavor of the feelings occurring in him. Often I sense that the client is trying to listen to himself, is trying to hear the messages and meanings which are being communicated by his own physiological reactions. No longer is he fearful of what he may find. He comes to realize that his own inner reactions and experiences, the messages of his sense and his viscera, are friendly. (p. 28)

Ideas Central to the Model

The self, which is a basic concept in Rogers' theory, has numerous features, the most important of which are as follows:

1. The self strives for consistency.
2. A person behaves in ways that are consistent with the self.
3. Experiences that are not consistent with the self are perceived as threats and are either distorted or denied.
4. The self may change as a result of maturation and learning.

The behavioral dynamics behind how a person's self is expressed in behavior are discussed in a series of nineteen propositions formulated by Rogers (1951). These are related to his ideas about how a healthy person strives to function. Seven of the most basic propositions are as follows:

1. Every individual exists in a continually changing world of experience, of which he or she is the center. In this sense, each person is the best source of information about him- or herself.
2. Each individual reacts to his or her perceptual field as it is experienced and perceived. Consequently, knowledge of the stimulus is not sufficient for

predicting behavior; one must know how the person is perceiving the stimulus and what it *means* to that person.

3. Each individual has a basic tendency to strive, actualize, maintain, and enhance the experiencing organism.
4. As a result of interaction with the environment, and others, a person's self-picture is formed: an organized, fluid, but consistent conceptual pattern of perceptions of characteristics and relationships of the "I" or the "me."
5. Perception is selective, and the primary criterion for selection is whether the experience is consistent with how a person views him- or herself at the moment.
6. Most ways of perceiving adopted by the individual are those consistent with his or her concept of self.
7. When a person perceives and accepts into one integrated system all of his or her sensory and visceral experiences, then he or she is in a position to be more accepting and understanding of others as separate and *different* individuals.

For example, students who feel insecure about what they perceive as their own lack of intellectual skill may tend to criticize or move away from those people they consider to be brighter than they are. However, if they can accept their own intellectual skills as they are, then they may be less inclined to berate the intellectual skills of others.

Psychological Health and the Fully Functioning Person

A central concept stressed time and again in Rogers' writings is that of trust, particularly trust in oneself. One of the reasons persons are fully functioning is that they have learned to trust themselves enough to take more risks; they are able to put their best hunches on the line and do what feels right or appropriate to them. Perhaps we can understand this "trust in self" idea if we look at some of the everyday choices that many of us face from time to time: "Do I want to go out with him if he calls again?" "Shall I have just one more drink?" "Would it be better to take twelve credits this term or fifteen?" "What would be the best choice for me, to accept company A's offer or company B's?"

As most of us probably know from experience, sometimes we make our most ill-considered judgments and our greatest blunders when we remain closed to our inner feelings, to our best hunches, or to the quiet but persistent voice of experience advising us to either go ahead or slow down. Thus, an individual may persist in the idea that "I can handle just one more," when openness to the results of his or her past experience with liquor would indicate that this was hardly correct. A love-struck young woman may see only the glorious qualities of her boyfriend, whereas a more open (and honest) attitude toward her experience with him would indicate that he is not so perfect after all.

Fully functioning people tend to trust their own choices. In Rogers' (1961) words:

> Less and less do they look to others for approval or disapproval; for standards to live by; for decisions and choices. They recognize that it rests within themselves to choose; that the only question that matters is "Am I living in a way which is deeply satisfying to me, and which truly expresses me?" (p. 119)

2.7 How Fully Functioning Are You?

Consider yourself for a moment. Where is your locus of evaluation? Out there? Inside yourself? How important is it to you what others think—about how you look, about your choice to be a teacher, about what you say in class, about what you eat? Whose evaluation is *really* most important to you? Yours? The other person's? How fully functioning do you see yourself, as described by Rogers?

Basically, growing in the direction of being a fully functioning person involves living in closer harmony with one's own potential and listening to the wisdom of one's own experiences. It means developing a locus of control that is less situated outside of oneself and more embedded in the inner person.

Some people develop an internal locus of control while others seem to have one that is more externally located. Erikson's psychosocial stages model can help us understand better how this happens.

THE PSYCHOSOCIAL STAGES MODEL (ERIK ERIKSON)

Erik Erikson is a psychoanalyst who has developed a new and different way of looking at the developmental phases involved in psychological growth. Although Erikson was influenced by Freudian analytic theory, his own psychosocial growth model is more expansive and humanizing. Freud, for example, viewed personal dynamics in relation to the classic matrix of the child–mother–father triangle. Erikson, however, considers individuals in relation to their parents in the context of a family and in relation to the broader social-cultural heritage in which families live.

You saw in Chapter 1 that the Freudian view of humans is somewhat dismal, warning of the social doom we may face if left to our own strivings. Erikson does not see it that way. In fact, the main thrust of his psychosocial model is to point out the developmental opportunities that each of us has to triumph over the psychological hazards of living. While Freud gave his energies to the study of pathological development, Erikson has focused on the successful and healthy solution of the developmental crises that are associated with each of his psychosocial stages.

According to Erikson (1980, 1982), each individual passes through a succession of eight psychosocial stages, beginning at birth and ending in the retirement years. Five of those stages are experienced during the first 20 years of life and the remaining three during adulthood. The eight psychosocial stages and the approximate time span usually associated with each are as follows:

1. Trust versus mistrust (birth to 18 months)
2. Autonomy versus shame and doubt (18 months to 3 years)
3. Initiative versus guilt (3 to 6 years)
4. Industry versus inferiority (6 to 12 years)
5. Identity versus identity confusion (12 to 18 years)
6. Intimacy versus isolation (18 to 35 years)
7. Generativity versus self-absorption (35 years to retirement)
8. Integrity versus despair (retirement years)

Erikson has observed that each stage represents a "psychosocial crisis," or turning point, when both potential and vulnerability are greatly increased—a time when things may either go well or badly depending on one's life experiences. In every person, we are likely to find a certain ratio between the positive and negative qualities associated with each stage, which, if the ratio is on the side of being more positive, will help him or her to cope more successfully with later crises.

The idea of acquiring a healthy ratio between positive and negative ego qualities is an important one, but one that sometimes gets left by the wayside when the focus is almost wholly on only the positive outcomes of each psychosocial stage. As Erikson (Evans, 1981) expressed it:

> When these stages are quoted, people often take away mistrust and doubt and shame and all of those not so nice, "negative" things and try to make an Eriksonian achievement scale out of it all, according to which in the first stage trust is "achieved." Actually, a certain ratio of trust and mistrust in our basic social attitude is the critical factor. When we enter a situation, we must be able to differentiate how much we can trust and how much we must mistrust, and I use mistrust in the sense of a readiness for danger and an anticipation of discomfort. (p. 15)

Although we would hope for greater weight on the side of positive ego qualities, if that is all we considered when assessing the overall health of the self's development, we could easily overlook the possible value to be found in the negative ego qualities associated with each stage. The following are a few examples: a certain amount of mistrust helps people to be less gullible and more cautious; a certain readiness to feel shame and doubt helps people behave appropriately and pursue assertively goals that are important to them; the capacity to feel guilt helps people make correct moral judgments and behave responsibly toward others; being in touch with what it is like to feel inferior helps people stay motivated to do their best; and a certain degree of identity confusion helps people sharpen their self-perceptions and make new adjustments in light of new experiences and changing life circumstances.

Each stage builds upon the psychological outcomes of the previous stage(s), although not according to a rigid timetable. For example, when development proceeds normally, with no outstanding traumatic events to derail its progress, the attitude of basic trust that develops during Stage 1 helps children feel safe enough to expand the range and diversity of their experiences and in the process develop an attitude of autonomy in Stage 2. Trusting their environment and feeling the necessary autonomy to move freely in it, children reinforce the attitude of initiative associated with Stage 3. This encourages the industry of Stage 4, an attitude that emerges as children learn to control their lively imaginations and apply themselves to formal education. With the fundamental groundwork laid—basic trust, autonomy, initiative, and industry—youth are ready for the monumental challenge of Stage 5, establishing an identity, a sense of who they are as individuals. Out of all this emerges an overall personality, which, when things go well, houses an essentially positive self-concept.

Of course, there may be a breakdown during any of the five psychosocial stages that would predispose an individual to a greater likelihood of acquiring a higher ratio of any of one or more negative ago qualities, such as mistrust, shame and doubt, guilt, and inferiority, which then increases the probability of a greater degree of identity confusion and subsequent life adjustment problems.

The first five stages are stressed in this discussion ahead, primarily because these first five psychosocial periods are so fundamental to all that happens subsequently in one's life.

Stage 1: Trust Versus Mistrust (Birth to 18 Months)

The first task of an infant is to develop what Erikson (1980) has called "the cornerstone of a healthy personality," a basic sense of trust in him- or herself and the surrounding environment. The first year of children's lives is a time when they are completely and utterly dependent on the outside world to tend to their basic needs. If their assorted needs—for example, for a bottle when hungry, dry diapers when wet, warm blankets when cold, or a protecting adult when frightened—are not met with reasonably predictable consistency, they may gradually develop a sense of mistrust for the world around them.

As conceived by Erikson, the capacity to depend on other persons has its roots in the first year or so of life. This does not mean that if infants are raised in an emotionally unpredictable environment they are irreversibly fated to grow into nontrusting adults. It does mean that if a basic sense of trust is not laid during the first year, it becomes increasingly difficult to establish in later years.

2.8 Are You a Trusting Person?

Do you allow yourself to get close to others? Can others get close to you? Do you tend to wonder about others' ulterior motives? Do you worry about being used? Do you find it hard to share your possessions, the "things" of your life? People who have trouble trusting usually answer "yes" to questions like these. What experiences in your life do you believe have had the most impact, positively or negatively, on your capacity to trust others? If someone asked you whether the ability to trust was an important quality for teachers to have, how would you respond? *Why* would you respond that way?

Stage 2: Autonomy Versus Shame and Doubt (18 Months to 3 Years)

This second phase of growth is a time when children discover that their behavior is their own. They begin to assert their newly discovered sense of autonomy in ways with which we are all familiar: "No, let me do it." "Don't help me." "Let me do it by myself." Erikson reasons that children experience conflicting pulls: one to assert themselves and the other to deny themselves the right and capacity to make this assertion. To live in a healthy way during this stage means to expand one's limits assertively, to act on one's own terms, and to insist on one's own boundaries.

Adults can encourage a healthy sense of autonomy during this phase through a wise balance of firmness and permissiveness. Letting young children do whatever they please is not a healthy way to help them find their strengths because they have nothing against which to measure themselves. The responsibility for establishing reasonable limits rests with parents and teachers. Children are pliable; if they know and fully understand the range of their limits, what they can do and what they cannot do, their growth has a greater chance of being healthy.

However, limits that are too restrictive or are too punitive, and/or adults who are too protecting can interfere with growing children's natural inclination to want to test their wings and to try themselves out in different ways. People of any age who have not tested themselves are invariably plagued with self-doubts because they are uncertain about what they can or cannot do. Shame is the other part of this feeling, which, as Erikson (1963) puts it, is an emotion that "supposes that one is completely exposed and conscious of being looked at: in a word, self-conscious" (p. 253).

Children who grow up in a shame-based environment are self-conscious for a reason: they are fearful of doing something wrong (again) and being belittled or embarrassed. Shame is what is felt when there is a fear of condemnation from the outside. Children (and adults) who have trouble doing certain things in public, for example, speaking in front of groups, dancing when others may be watching, playing a musical instrument when someone is listening, often come from backgrounds in which they were emotionally reduced and publicly humiliated for being less than perfect (Kaufman, 1989).

Feelings of shame can be stoppers. When experienced too often and too long at an early age, children grow fearful of exploring new avenues of adventure and learning. As a consequence, feelings of autonomy and independence that grow naturally from being successful adventurers into new territories fail to develop. At this critical stage, if children do not have sufficient opportunities to develop a sense of autonomy, the sense of initiative associated with Stage 3 is more difficult to attain.

Stage 3: Initiative Versus Guilt (3 to 6 Years)

At no time in children's development are they ready to learn more quickly and avidly than during this stage of their growth. It is a time when children begin slowly but surely to expand the geography of their social boundaries. Having acquired some measure of conscious control over themselves and their environment, children can now move rapidly forward to new challenges in ever-widening social and spatial spheres. Erikson reasons that the very act of moving more assertively into the social world is the beginning of a process that helps children see that they do have a certain amount of power (in terms of being able to make things happen), and that life has a purpose for them. This is a time when they can express their autonomy in behavior, which we call *initiative.*

It is also during this stage that children begin to develop a conscience, or a sense of right and wrong. However, if the capacity to feel guilt is overtaxed by moralistic and/or punitive parents and teachers, children can easily develop a feeling of badness that can seriously inhibit healthy urges to test themselves in an expanding social world.

Children are particularly vulnerable to adult input during this growth period. Children's natural sense of initiative is easily blocked when they are ridiculed for failing or made to feel guilty for being less than perfect. Like shame, guilt can be a stopper. It is a potential block to children's development when the adults in their lives express too much disapproval, causing them to feel they have done something wrong and thereby inhibiting their willingness to try again. Thus, guilt surfaces and initiative fades.

When it comes to autonomy versus shame and doubt, and initiative versus guilt, how do you see yourself? Do you easily feel self-conscious in front of groups? Or do you feel you can assertively voice your view regardless of the number who may be listening? Do you have initiative, the capacity to get things started? Or do you procrastinate until the last moment? Do you get easily embarrassed and feel shame quickly? Some people are quick to feel guilty, even about the smallest things. How about you? What part would you say that shame and guilt play in your life? If those emotions seem to be a fairly prominent part of your life, can you explain how your early life experiences may have contributed to their development?

Stage 4: Industry Versus Inferiority (6 to 12 Years)

The major theme of this stage is reflected in children's determination to master and succeed at whatever they are doing. It is a time when children become ready to apply themselves to given skills and tasks that go far beyond the mere expression of using their bodies in play. They develop industry (i.e., they adjust themselves to real-world demands to be more industrious). Play activities remain an important part of children's growth during this phase because it is through play that they begin to master some of the basic social and physical skills necessary for mature adult living.

In sum, during this phase of growth children can learn to have a healthy view of themselves through their increased competence in doing things. In learning to accept instruction and to win recognition and approval by producing "things," they open the way to the capacity for work enjoyment in later years. The danger in this period is the development of a sense of inadequacy and inferiority in children who do not receive recognition for their efforts.

Stage 5: Identity Versus Identity Confusion (12 to 18 Years)

As the potency of sexual maturity is ushered in, the innocence of childhood fades into the background. Young boys and girls pear into mirrors and are startled to see new faces developing and new bodies forming. As the comfortable dependency of childhood draws to a close, latent growth processes suddenly begin to speed up, and critical questions step center stage: Who am I? Who do I *want* to be? What will I do with my life? Caught somewhere between the children they once were and the adults they will become, adolescents face a real crisis in identity. Erikson (1950) quotes an aphorism posted in a Western bar that captures the flavor of this growth stage: "I ain't what I ought to be, I ain't what I'm going to be, but I ain't what I was" (p. 139).

Achieving a sense of identity as well as overcoming a sense of identity confusion are the polarities of this developmental stage. Changes in adolescents' biology trigger changes in adolescents' psychology. As their body image changes, so, too, does their self-image. Adolescents in this period are conscious of who they are and how they might be coming across to others, and the self-consciousness that began in Stage 2 grows more intense. It is this self-consciousness that motivates adolescents to try themselves out in new ways, to experiment with various identities to see which one fits best.

The identity issues of Stage 5 are self-concept issues. They are more likely to be resolved favorably if the previous four stages have been resolved on the side of positive ego resolutions—more trust than distrust, more autonomy than shame and doubt, and so on. If, however, there have been too many negative ego resolutions during the four preceding stages, this, as Erikson (1980) has observed, may result in identity confusion. Identity confusion is more than not knowing who one is (identity), it is not knowing for sure what one can do (initiative, industry), not knowing whether one can do what needs to be done (autonomy) and, in some instances, not even knowing whether anyone can be counted on to help (trust). Like logs floating down a river, identity confusion problems form a log jam when the normal flow of one's developmental current carries with it too many negative ego resolutions that come together at the same time.

2.10 How About Your Own Identity?

As you think about your own growth between 12 and 18 years of age, what stands out for you? What major changes have occurred in your self-image since you were an adolescent? What sort of identity confusions did you feel in adolescence? What did you feel most confused about? How did your experience in school help or hinder your own struggle to develop an identity?

As mentioned earlier, more is being said about Erikson's first five stages then there will be about the last three stages because what happens in the initial 18 years or so of life is so critical in shaping everything that happens from that time on. As a way of consolidating our discussion to this point, Figure 2.3 provides an overview of the sort of behaviors that are likely to be associated with each of the first five psychosocial stages (Hamachek, 1985). For example, people who, as young children, had essentially positive experiences with emotionally dependable adults may tend to show more signs of trust than mistrust in their behaviors. As suggested in Figure 2.3, they will tend to invest in relationships, reflect an open, unsuspicious attitude, and be more likely than not to share both themselves and their possessions. However, people who, as young children, had essentially negative experiences with emotionally unde-

Outward signs of healthy growth	*Outward signs of less healthy growth*
I. *Expressions of trust*	I. *Expressions of mistrust*
1. Invests in relationships	1. Avoids relationships
2. Open, unsuspicious attitude	2. Suspicious, closed, guarded
3. Lets go of mother	3. Unwilling to let go of mother
4. Welcomes touching	4. Loner and unhappy
5. Good eye contact	5. Poor eye contact
6. Shares self and possessions	6. Does not share self or possessions
II. *Expressions of autonomy*	II. *Expressions of shame and doubt*
1. Independent	1. Procrastinates frequently
2. Not easily led	2. Has trouble working alone
3. Resists being dominated	3. Needs structure and directions
4. Able to stand on own two feet	4. Has trouble making decisions
5. Works well alone or with others	5. Is easily influenced
6. Assertive when necessary	6. Embarrassed when complimented
III. *Expressions of initiative*	III. *Expressions of guilt*
1. Is a self-starter	1. Is easily depressed
2. Accepts challenges	2. Puts down self
3. Assumes leadership roles	3. Slumped posture
4. Sets goals—goes after them	4. Poor eye contact
5. Moves easily, freely with body	5. Has low energy level
IV. *Expressions of industry*	IV. *Expressions of inferiority*
1. Wonders how things work	1. Timid, somewhat withdrawn
2. Finishes what is started	2. Overly obedient
3. Likes "projects"	3. Procrastinates often
4. Enjoys learning	4. An observer, not a producer
5. Likes to experiment	5. Questions own ability
V. *Expressions of identity*	V. *Expressions of identity confusion*
1. Certain about sex-role identity	1. Doubts about sex-role
2. Not so susceptible to peer pressure	2. Lacks confidence
3. Plans for future	3. Overly hostile to authority
4. Challenges adult authority	4. Overly obedient
5. Tends to be self-accepting	5. Tends to be self-rejecting

Figure 2.3. BEHAVIORS ASSOCIATED WITH HEALTHY AND LESS HEALTHY DEVELOPMENT DURING ERIKSON'S FIRST FIVE PSYCHOSOCIAL STAGES.

(Reprinted from Hamachek, D. E., "The Self's Development and Ego Growth: Conceptual Analysis and Implications for Counselors." *Journal of Counseling and Development, 64,* 1985, pp. 136–142. Copyright © ACA. Reprinted with permission. No further reproduction authorized without written permission of the American Counseling Association.)

pendable adults may tend to show more signs of distrust than trust in their behaviors. They may be inclined to avoid relationships, to be somewhat suspicious of others, and have trouble sharing themselves or their possessions. We all do this from time to time—avoid relationships, become suspicious of others, and so forth—however, whether or not it is truly unhealthy depends on the extent to which it is done. The individual who avoids a relationship with a *particular* person who may have done something hurtful one time is one thing. The individual who avoids relationships with practically everyone, even those who are friendly, is another thing. Also, it is important to remember that it is the ratio of healthy to less healthy growth signs at either end of the continuum, rather than the absolute number of behaviors.

Stage 6: Intimacy Versus Isolation (18 to 35 Years)

Childhood and youth are at an end. This is a time, if all has gone well, when each of us begins our participation as adult members of Western society. According to Erikson (1980), all of the growth experiences to this point have prepared the youth to participate in a close, trusting relationship with a member of the opposite sex. Whereas graduation from adolescence requires a sense of identity, graduation from the first stage of adulthood requires a sense of shared identity, which some find in marriage and others in various living-together arrangements.

Stage 7: Generativity Versus Self-Absorption (35 Years to Retirement)

This is that period in persons' lives when they literally generate or produce whatever it is that gives them a sense of personal creativity. *Generativity* does not refer to procreation, but rather involves an individual's total efforts to be useful as a parent, worker, husband, wife, participant in the community, and so on. The danger in this period is that some individuals are unable to release themselves from the web of their own self-doubt.

Stage 8: Integrity Versus Despair (Retirement Years)

Finally, as adults witness the development of a new generation, they gain a fuller perspective of their own cycle and are in a position to reach the fullest sense of trust that Erikson (1963) views as the "assured reliance on another's integrity" (p. 267). The first developmental theme (a sense of trust) evolves into the final one. Thus, this final phase is an outgrowth of the seven phases preceding it. It involves a sense of wisdom, a philosophy of life, and an inner peace, all of which have roots in early trust, youthful independence, vigorous initiative, established identity, and a sense of generativity (Hamachek, 1988, 1990).

This completes our brief overview of five psychological growth models. You can see that growth along a developmental continuum means that there are certain social-emotional tasks to accomplish, certain competencies to acquire, certain lower-level needs to satisfy, and certain ego conflicts to resolve in route to becoming an emotionally healthy and contributing member of society. Let us turn our attention now to some things that teachers can do to encourage these outcomes.

WAYS TO PROMOTE HEALTHY SELF-ATTITUDES IN STUDENTS

A sense of competence, a self-actualizing spirit, and a fully functioning approach to life are acquired and learned through experience. What people acquire and learn, they can be taught. An adequate, healthy self-concept is not a gift reserved for a chosen few, but a possibility available to every student who goes through school.

One way of achieving this goal is to view it as a self-sustaining circular process. Consider Figure 2.4 as an example. A healthy, positive school experi-

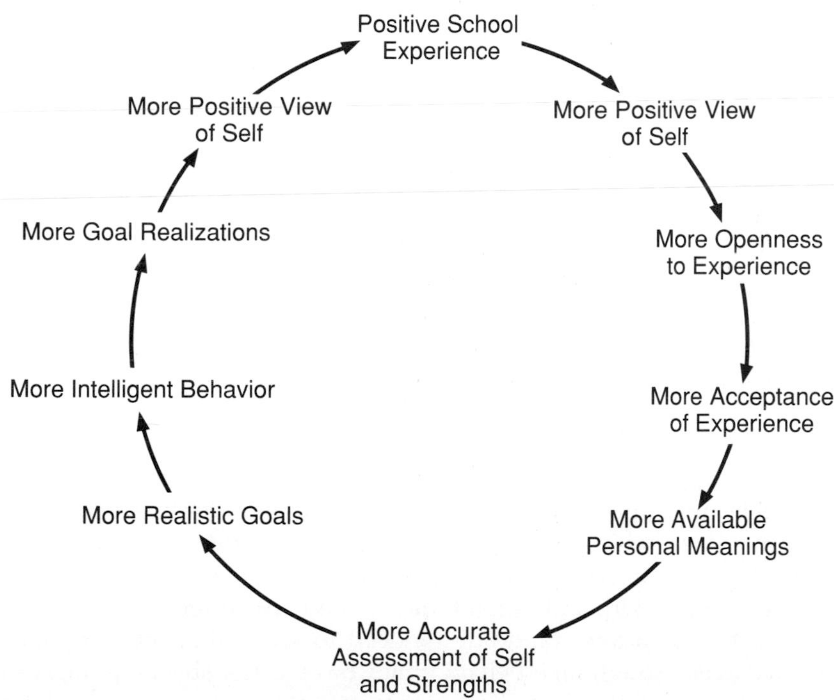

Figure 2.4. THE CYCLE OF POSITIVE GROWTH.

ence is both the product and producer of adequate, competent teachers and students. Undoubtedly, you can recall from your own memories how certain school experiences are not available to all students. Rather than learning about their possibilities and capabilities, some students learn about their limitations and shortcomings. Consider some examples of what a few students remember their teachers saying to them or about them (Purkey and Novak, 1984):

> On the first day of school, the teacher came in and said he wasn't supposed to teach this basic class, but that he was stuck with us.
>
> The teacher said, "That's crazy! What's the matter with you?" His negative attitude stood out like a bump on your nose.
>
> My teacher told me I was the worst kid she ever taught.
>
> The teacher said to me in front of the whole class: 'I really don't think you're that stupid.' (p. 14)

2.11 What Memories Do You Have?

Think back to your elementary and high school days. What memories do you have of things that were said to you or about you by teachers that put a damper on your school experience? How were you affected? On the other side, what sorts of things were said to you or about you by teachers that enhanced your school performance? How do you suppose these experiences will affect your behavior as a teacher?

Helping youths develop their confidence and competence is a process we can help facilitate. Let us look at some specific ways for doing this.

Develop an Accepting Attitude

This demands no elaborate machinery or organization. If you intend to be a teacher, an important requirement is that you like the age group you plan to teach. It means accepting a growing person not only for what he or she is, but for where he or she is. Does this mean we have to accept the youngster who kicks us in the shins or disrupts the class? Sure it does! Rejecting the person and rejecting the act are different things. We may not like a specific behavior, but that does not mean we have to reject the person as a whole. It is better to say, "John, I will not tolerate any more of that behavior," than to say, "John, you're a rotten kid, and I won't tolerate you any longer!"

Youth of all ages (and adults) need to know that they are liked and accepted even though their behavior may be objectionable at times. A simple "Hi there, Joan," a friendly smile, an encouraging note on a returned test, or just calling students by their first names can work wonders in establishing a positive classroom climate.

Give Students a Chance to Express Their Feelings

School should be a place where youth can test and expand the range of their emotional and intellectual potentials. It should be a place where they can express their deepest thoughts and feelings. Psychologists have long known that persons who are most alienated from themselves are those who have been taught to *think* feelings without *having* feelings. Students are frequently asked questions like, "What do you know about this?" or "What does the book say about that?" But they may be less frequently asked questions such as "How do you *feel* about that?" or "What is your *attitude* toward this?" Consider an example of what is meant here:

Ten-year-old Laurie no sooner walked in the door after school one day than she began to cry. Her mother asked her what was wrong and in sobbing tones Laurie explained that the teacher chose another girl over her to play on the kickball team, and she (Laurie) felt terrible because she didn't know if the teacher just didn't like her or if she was too poor a kickball player. Laurie had held her sad, confused feelings all day for fear of someone seeing them. It is too bad that Laurie had to hold back sad feelings for six hours before being in a setting safe enough to express them. School can be the best place in the world for youngsters to understand themselves and the world in which they live. In order to make this more possible, we must first provide the necessary conditions for helping students to be open to not just what they know, but to what they feel.

Create Opportunities for Classroom Interaction

Sometimes we take students' opportunities for classroom participation more or less for granted, forgetting that not all young people have equal opportunity or, for that matter, equal assertiveness necessary to get involved. Research shows that many students do their best work when interaction opportunities are the greatest (Schmuck and Schmuck, 1992). Interaction can be improved by more democratic classroom organization, by encouraging more possibilities for free interchange of opinion in discussion, by small-group activities, and by activities that call for sharing and joint participation. Interaction activities not only offer students opportunities to be heard, but chances to be successful. Of course, there is always the chance that one *will not* be successful; hence, the risk involved. That risk can be minimized by at least lauding the effort when the product comes up short.

Establish Firm, Fair, and Explicit Rules

Sometimes youth misbehave not because they are given too much freedom (although that could be a reason), but because they do not know the rules of what is appropriate behavior and what is not. Fairness, along with firmness and clearly defined limits, are a very good way of making it clear to students that we *expect* them to live up to certain standards. Indeed, setting firm rules that are consistently enforced can communicate two kinds of messages. One is that we care enough about our students to set rules for them in the first place, and the other is that we can be counted on to be fair when enforcing those rules. (This concept is discussed further in Chapter 14.)

Having explicit rules and regulations does not inhibit freedom; in fact, students can feel even freer once they know what does and what does not count, where the boundaries are, and how far they can go.

Make Sure Each Student Experiences Some Success

Almost without exception, the research done on the effects of failure on school achievement points to the conclusion that success tends to encourage students to raise their level of aspiration, whereas failure generally causes students to lower it (Clifford, 1979, 1984). Success, for most people, is an affirming, positive happening that feeds egos and fuels motivation. It helps students (and practically anyone else) in two ways: (1) they can feel good about themselves (internal reward) because they have done well in something, and (2) it provides an opportunity for others to respond favorably and positively (external reward) to the person behind the accomplishment.

It seems generally true that if people are to have a chance to succeed in life, they must first experience success in one important domain of their lives. For most children and adolescents, this important domain is school.

EPILOGUE

The main objective of this chapter has been to stress the positive aspects of living and to underscore the processes that serve as available routes to a mentally healthy life from the point of view of five psychological models.

The developmental task idea, described by Havighurst, is a framework for looking at the specific problems, undertakings, or tasks that occur at various stages of growth, which are necessary to master before moving to higher levels of development. Each life stage has its own demands and expectations, and if we are to be wise teachers and sensitive parents, we need to be aware of these.

From Erikson we learn that a person's self goes through different phases as one progresses through the eight stages of psychosocial development. His is a developmental framework to help us understand that even though growth is a continuous process certain critical times or crises occur at various points in the life cycle, each of which must be successfully resolved before one can effectively meet the subsequent psychosocial stage.

The need to be effective or good at something is a need we all share, and it is around this need that Robert White has built a strong case for competence as a primary stimulus for human motivation. Success, as they saying goes, breeds success, but a student's striving for success or mastery can be quickly stifled or at least seriously inhibited if he or she experiences too much failure at an early age. A sense of competence is a primary prerequisite to healthy development.

Maslow's self-actualization model is a direct outgrowth of investigations of healthy people. This point of view focuses on human possibilities rather than on human deficiencies. It is a theory of human motivation that underscores the hierarchical nature of needs behind human behavior.

Rogers' fully functioning person model is similar to Maslow's in the sense that it, too, is a way of underscoring the possible and positive in human behavior. Both indicate not only the signs but also the possible routes to healthy development.

All in all, research and clinical evidence strongly suggest that psychological health and a sense of competence are goals within reach of every school-age youth and every adult. Perfection is not our goal, improvement is, and this is a goal toward which each of us can aim ourselves and the students we teach.

You have been introduced to three theoretical positions and five psychological models to help you better understand and interpret human behavior, and to see some of the major implications these positions and models have for classroom practices.

Now that we have looked at some psychological models for growth, we will make our objective in Part II a more detailed understanding of the actual developmental processes involved from birth through adolescence.

STUDY AND REVIEW QUESTIONS

1. What is a developmental task? Why is it important that the particular developmental tasks associated with particular growth stages be accomplished before moving to subsequent stages?
2. How do Havighurst's developmental tasks differ from Erikson's psychosocial stages?
3. Can you explain why negative ego resolutions, particularly in any of the first four of the eight psychosocial stages, interfere with positive ego resolutions in subsequent stages?
4. Why is it that children who grow up in shame-based environments are so self-conscious and cautious?
5. Robert White has theorized that each person is born with an inherent drive or motivation for *effectance.* What does this mean? How is this ideal related to the development of self-esteem?
6. Failure is always hazardous to one's psychological health, but why is it even more so during a child's early school years?
7. What are the essential ingredients in Maslow's theory of self-actualization? How is his basic needs hierarchy related to the idea of self-actualization?

Explain why lower (basic) needs control whether higher (growth) needs are met.

8. What similarities do you see between Maslow's self-actualized person and Rogers' fully functioning person? What differences do you see?
9. What can teachers do to help their students develop positive attitudes about themselves and hopeful outlooks about their possibilities?

REFERENCES

Clifford, M. M. "Effects of Failure: Alternative Explanations and Possible Implications." *Educational Psychologist*, 1979, *14*, pp. 44–52.

Clifford, M. M. "Thoughts on a Theory of Constructive Failure." *Educational Psychologist*, 1984, *19*, pp. 108–120.

Coopersmith, S. *The Antecedents of Self-Esteem*. San Francisco: Freeman, 1967.

Erikson, E. H. "Growth and Crises of the Healthy Personality." In M. J. E. Senn (Ed.), *Symposium on the Healthy Personality* (pp. 91–146). New York: John Macy, Jr., Foundation, 1950.

Erikson, E. H. *Childhood and Society*, 2nd ed. New York: W. W. Norton, 1963.

Erikson, E. H. *Identity and the Life Cycle*. New York: W. W. Norton, 1980.

Erikson, E. H. *The Life Cycle Completed: A Review*. New York: W. W. Norton, 1982.

Evans, R. I. *Dialogue With Erik Erikson*. New York: Praeger, 1981.

Frey, D., and Carlock, C. J. *Enhancing Self-Esteem*, 2nd ed. Muncie, IN: Accelerated Development, 1989.

Glasser, W. *Schools Without Failure*. New York: Harper & Row, 1969.

Hamachek, D. *Encounters with Others: Interpersonal Relationships and You*. New York: Holt, Rinehart and Winston, 1982.

Hamachek, D. "The Self's Development and Ego Growth: Conceptual Analysis and Implications for Counselors." *Journal of Counseling and Development*, 1985, *64*, pp. 136–142.

Hamachek, D. "Evaluating Self-Concept and Ego Development Within Erikson's Psychosocial Framework." *Journal of Counseling and Development*, 1988, *66* pp. 254–360.

Hamachek, D. "Evaluating Self-Concept and Ego Development in Erikson's Last Three Psychosocial Stages." *Journal of Counseling and Development*, 1990, *68*, pp. 677–683.

Hamachek, D. *Encounters with the Self*, 4th ed. Fort Worth: Harcourt Brace Jovanovich, 1992.

Havighurst, R. S. *Developmental Tasks and Education*, 3rd ed. New York: David McKay, 1972.

Havighurst, R. S. "More Thoughts on Developmental Tasks." *Personnel and Guidance Journal*, 1980, *58*, pp. 330–335.

Jourard, S. M., and Landsman, T. *Healthy Personality*, 4th ed. New York: Macmillan, 1980.

Kaufman, G. *The Psychology of Shame*. New York: Springer, 1989.

Maslow, A. H. *Motivation and Personality*, 3rd ed. (Revised by R. Frager, J. Fadiman, C. McReynolds, and R. Cox, Eds.) New York: Harper & Row, 1987.

Purkey, W. W., and Novak, J. M. *Inviting School Success: A Self-Concept Approach to Teaching and Learning*, 2nd ed. Belmont, CA: Wadsworth, 1984.

Rogers, C. R. *Client-Centered Therapy*. Boston: Houghton Mifflin, 1951.

Rogers, C. R. *On Becoming a Person.* Boston: Houghton Mifflin, 1961.

Rogers, C. R. "Toward Becoming a Fully-Functioning Person." In *Perceiving, Behaving, and Becoming.* Yearbook of the Association for Supervision and Curriculum Development. Washington, DC; National Education Association, 1962.

Schmuck, R. A., and Schmuck, P. A. *Group Processes in the Classroom,* 6th ed. Dubuque, IA: Brown, 1992.

Welch, I. D., George, A., and Medieros, D. *Self-Actualization: An Annotated Bibliography of Theory and Research.* New York: Garland, 1987.

White, R. W. "Motivation Reconsidered: The Concept of Competence." *Psychological Review,* 1959, *66,* pp. 297–333.

White, R. W. "Competence and the Psychosocial Stages of Development." In M. R. Jones (Ed.), *Nebraska Symposium on Motivation.* Lincoln: University of Nebraska Press, 1960.

SELECTED READINGS OF RELATED INTEREST

Evans, R. I. *Dialogue with Erik Erikson.* New York: Praeger, 1981. Evans explores Erikson's thinking about the ideas that motivated the development of his psychosocial theory. A very readable and revealing little book.

Hall, C. S., Lindzey, G., Lochlin, J. C., and Manosevitz, M. *Introduction to Theories of Personality.* New York: Wiley, 1985. An excellent source for those who want to know more about the major psychological theorists who have shaped much of the thinking of twentieth-century psychologists. Basic tenets and postulates of sixteen major theoretical views are examined.

Peterson, C. *Personality,* 2nd ed. Fort Worth: Harcourt Brace Jovanovich, 1992. Provides detailed, comprehensive discussions about many of the theorists studied in this chapter. A very readable, engaging volume.

Waters, P. L., and Cheek, J. M. "Personality Development." In V. J. Derlega, B. A. Winstead, and W. H. Jones (Eds.), *Personality: Contemporary Theory and Research* (pp. 113–148). Chicago: Nelson-Hall, 1991. A succinct overview of Rogers' position and research associated with his work, along with other personality theorists.

Welch, I. D., George, A., and Madieros, D. *Self-Actualization: An Annotated Bibliography of Theory and Research.* New York: Garland, 1987. A particularly helpful volume for those who wish to survey the vast amount of thinking and research spawned by self-actualization theory.

TOWARD UNDERSTANDING GROWTH DYNAMICS INVOLVED IN PHYSICAL, PSYCHOLOGICAL, COGNITIVE, AND MORAL DEVELOPMENT

Part I introduced you to some major psychological theories and conceptual frameworks that have expanded our understanding of and thinking about human behavior. The major objectives of Part II are to examine the growth dynamics and behavioral outcomes associated with school-age youngsters as they progress through their elementary and high school years. With this in mind, our task in the following chapters is to explore what developmental psychologists have discovered as being major age-level characteristics associated with each of these growth periods. Before we can become successful teachers, it is important to be knowledgeable about the developmental dynamics of the group with which we are working. Thus, the three chapters included in this part of the text are designed to acquaint you with interesting information and facts associated with development during two major growth periods: between the ages of 6 and 12 and 13 and 18. Each growth stage has its own unique characteristics and each leaves an indelible imprint on youngsters as they progress through it.

In Chapters 3 and 4, we look at the physical, social, emotional, and intellectual changes associated with middle childhood and adolescence. In addition, some major implications that these changes have for teaching practices and teacher behavior are discussed.

Because intellectual ability and moral development are so intimately connected to success in school and healthy personal and interpersonal growth, we turn our attention exclusively to these matters in Chapter 5, where we explore how both intelligence and moral development change in form and expression as students move through middle childhood and adolescence.

These chapters are introductory overviews aimed at helping you keep in mind the students you will one day be teaching. In addition, they serve as an important backdrop for later chapters that explore learning, teaching, and classroom management.

3

The Elementary Years

Behavioral Dynamics and Age-Level Characteristics

CHAPTER OVERVIEW

IMPORTANT CHAPTER IDEAS

1. Between the ages of 6 and 12, basic values are shaped, a sense of industry or inferiority is learned, self-concept is molded, and feelings of positive or negative self-esteem develop.
2. Physical development during the elementary years is primarily a change in becoming more balanced proportionately, rather than an increase in sheer size.
3. Body build and size influence children's personality development to the extent that these facets of growth affect how others respond to them. Overweight children are especially at risk for negative feedback.
4. Elementary-age children more readily believe what is said about both their person and performance than they ever will again. Their self-concepts are

incompletely formed, which makes them very susceptible to feedback from adults and peers.

5. About two-thirds of all childhood accidents occur before age 9, and boys have the majority of these.
6. The development of many same-sex friends and less time spent at home are natural, expected social behaviors.
7. Children in this age group are naturally critical of one another.
8. This is a restless and active age. Activity-oriented relationships and games demanding large-muscle involvement are preferred over verbally oriented relationships and quieter, more passive games.
9. Elementary-age children are emotionally vulnerable. They tend to absorb, uncritically and spongelike, much of what happens around them—for better or worse.
10. If not monitored, children tend to eat a lot of high-calorie junk food, which, in sufficient quantities, can have an adverse effect on behavior.
11. Vocabulary, particularly language recognition, grows dramatically.
12. The ability to conceptualize grows rapidly during middle childhood; concepts come to have more validity, status, and accessibility.
13. A child's brain grows in size and complexity, corresponding to an increased capacity for inductive and deductive reasoning.
14. There is research indicating differences in the organization of the brains of boys and girls for verbal and spatial skills, which may account for some of the sex differences in learning.
15. The developmental goal of middle childhood is disorganization, not improvement, so that a higher level of social, emotional, and intellectual integration can be achieved.

PROLOGUE

Some remarkable changes occur between the ages of 6 and 12. Like a caterpillar going through metamorphosis, the undifferentiated self we saw during the early years begins to expand and unfold into a more differentiated, identifiable pattern of behavior that we gradually associate with a child's personality. These are the years in a child's development when he or she becomes increasingly more aware of and responsive to an ever-widening array of influences, ranging from their parents to playmates, television, and comic books. It is a time when boys do not particularly care for girls, when girls are indifferent to boys (but not so much so), and when both sexes find their greatest satisfaction and pleasure in being with other kids, preferably of the same age and gender. It is a time for large-muscle development and small-muscle refinements, and for an energy supply that can leave the adults in their world breathless. Depending on where they live, elementary-age youngsters graduate from a tricycle to a two-wheeler (with many variations in riding, such as with no hands, sideways, and standing up); they learn to swim and dive (belly flops are more like it); they learn to dribble a basketball and play soccer, baseball, and football; and they learn to master simple small-muscle acrobatics such as ear wiggling, finger snapping, and bubblegum blowing. It is a time when, in a wider social context, they continue to develop and expand the personality characteristics that began to emerge during the preschool years. It is also a time when cognitive processes continue to evolve slowly from the purely concrete, black-and-white thinking that emerges during the later middle years and adolescence.

Unless there are dramatic shifts in life circumstances, children in these middle years will continue to grow in the direction they started. Overall development will be slower and less dramatic than it was during the first five or so years of life, but it will be steady and on course.

Psychologically, a great deal happens to children between the ages of 6 and 12. Basic values are shaped and formed, a sense of industry or feelings of inferiority are learned, self-concept is molded, feelings of negative or positive self-worth develop, and primary attitudes about life itself are planted as emotional seedlings in each child's mind to be nurtured or neglected, depending on life experiences in the years ahead.

PHYSICAL DEVELOPMENT: BASIC CHARACTERISTICS

When children enter middle childhood their physical shape and appearance change markedly. The round, cherubic appearance of babyhood stretches out, giving most children a more slender appearance. This occurs because of a growth spurt and because of increased participation in diverse physical activities that affect muscle growth and body build.

Actually, physical development during the elementary years is primarily a move toward greater balance of proportion rather than an increase in sheer size. Children grow more slowly during their elementary years than they did earlier or than they will in adolescence. For example, by 8 years of age, the arms and legs are nearly 50% longer than they were at age 2, yet overall height has increased by only 25% (Shonkoff, 1984).

As you can see in Table 3.1, boys and girls are about the same average height until age 9, although boys tend to be slightly heavier in the early years. For the next four years or so, girls spurt ahead of boys, and by age 11, the average girl is about 57 inches tall. The average boy the same age is about 56.5 inches tall. By the time the average boy reaches 12 years of age, he will have reached about 84% of his mature adult height, while girls reach approximately 92.6% of their mature adult height at the same age. It is not until 13.5 to 14 years of age that boys overtake girls in height, and not until 14.5 to 15 years of age that they overtake girls in weight (Tanner, 1990). It is important to keep in mind that the growth figures in Table 3.1 are expressions of what is average for

Table 3.1. AVERAGE HEIGHT AND WEIGHT OF BOYS AND GIRLS BETWEEN AGES 6 AND 12

	Height		*Weight*	
Age	*Inches*	*Centimeters*	*Pounds*	*Kilograms*
Girls				
6	45.5	115.0	43.0	19.0
7	47.0	120.5	49.0	21.5
8	49.5	126.5	55.0	25.0
9	52.0	132.0	63.0	28.5
10	55.0	138.5	72.0	32.0
11	57.0	144.5	81.5	37.0
12	59.5	151.0	92.0	41.5
Boys				
6	45.5	116.0	46.0	21.0
7	48.0	121.5	51.0	23.0
8	50.0	127.0	56.0	25.5
9	52.0	132.0	62.0	28.0
10	54.5	137.5	69.5	31.5
11	56.5	143.5	78.0	35.5
12	59.0	149.5	88.0	39.5

Source: U.S. Department of Health, Education, and Welfare, Health Resources Administration, National Center for Health Statistics, and Center for Disease Control, 1977.

any given age. Many healthy, robust children are smaller or larger than the average for their age group. The range of normal growth is so great that if 8-year-olds who were among the tallest and heaviest 10% of their classmates were to stop growing for a year while their classmates continued to grow normally, the 8-year-olds would still be taller than one-half of their peers and heavier than three-quarters of them (National Center for Health Statistics, 1976).

There are also some striking changes in the general cast of a child's facial features during the middle childhood years. The fat pads that fill out the preschooler's cheeks gradually dwindle away, leaving a formerly rounded face with a far leaner appearance. The oversized forehead housing a rapidly growing brain gets progressively smaller as the rest of the child's face catches up with cranial development. Then, of course, there are those years between ages 6 and 8, depending on the child, when the baby teeth are lost (or does the tooth fairy take them?), and what was once a cute smile becomes a silly, toothless grin. When permanent teeth arrive to fill the gaps, they frequently appear disproportionately large in relation to the jaw available to them. The baby teeth drop out approximately in the order in which they came in, beginning with the lower front teeth and moving systematically back. Later losses of baby teeth are not as noticeable because they occur farther back in the mouth, but the shedding of old teeth and the eruption of permanent ones goes on until age 10 or 12. Actually, it is not until adolescence, when the nose cartilage expands and the jaw develops further, that the face catches up to the teeth in size, and children begin to look like the adults they are slowly becoming.

3.1 What Did Your Changes Look Like?

You may find it an eye-opening experience to dig out some of your old pictures and line them up in chronological order from the time you began elementary school to when you completed high school. You can see for yourself the remarkable changes that occurred. Notice in particular how your facial characteristics have changed.

As with height, weight increases are also slow and fairly uniform at this age. At the end of the middle years, the average 12-year-old girl weighs approximately 92 pounds and the average boy of the same age weighs 88 pounds. Girls tend to be slightly heavier than boys during the second half of these middle years, and this difference is exaggerated even more when girls begin their puberty spurt (earlier than boys) during the closing years of childhood. How much a child weighs depends to some extent on his or her particular body build, which can range from extreme ectomorphy (thin) to extreme endomorphy (fat). Figure 3.1 presents the three basic body builds associated with mesomorphic, endomorphic, and ectomorphic types.

Body Types Influence Others' Perceptions

Children as young as 6 to 10 years of age have been found to be in reasonably close agreement when it comes to assigning certain personality traits to particular body types. Staffieri (1967), for example, found that boys in this age group had a strong tendency to stereotype certain body builds in predictable ways. He noted, for instance, a remarkable similar tendency for boys with endomorphic builds (obese, heavy) to be perceived as socially offensive and delinquent, while ectomorphic boys (tall, thin) were viewed as retiring, nervous, shy, and introverted. Mesomorphs (athletic, muscular) and ectomorphs were chosen as the most popular by their peers, whereas endomorphs were less popular, knew that they were unpopular, and were less accepting of their own body image. Similar results have been found for elementary-age girls (Casky and Felker, 1971; Staffieri, 1972). It is interesting and instructive to note that these stereotypes began as early as the preschool years (Walker, 1962, 1963).

Because body image greatly influences overall self-image, being overweight can cause special problems (LeBow, 1984). This is especially likely to happen for those whose weight is 20% to 30% more than the usual weight for their height and bone size. One is considered obese when one's weight is 30%

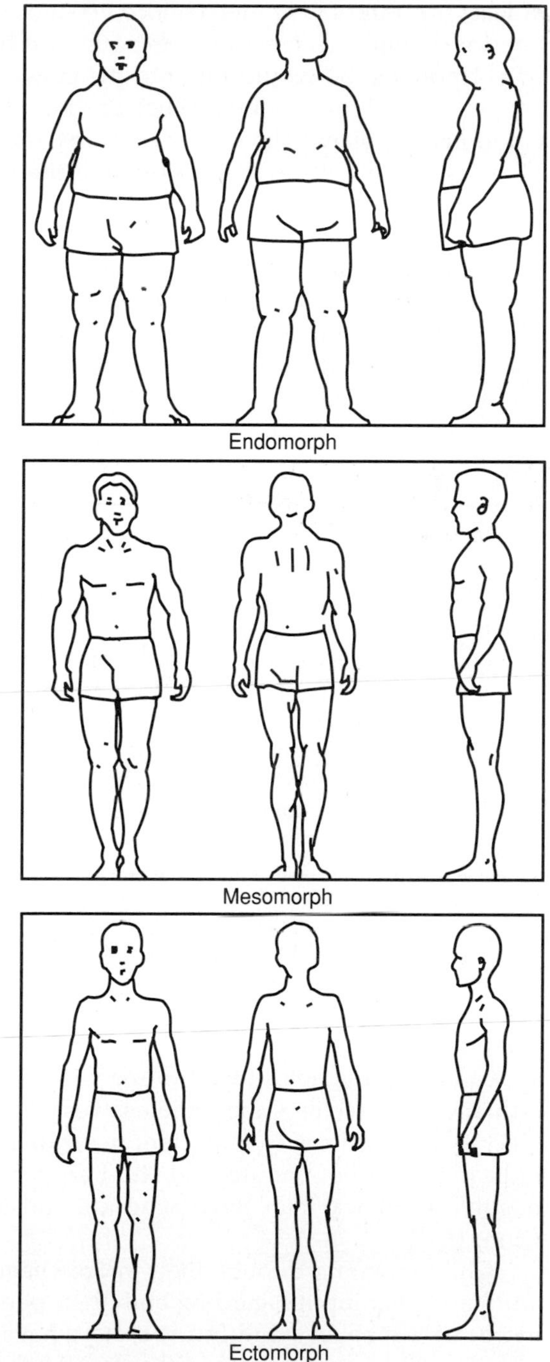

Figure 3.1. THREE BASIC BODY BUILDS SEEN IN BOTH SEXES AT ALL AGES.

or more above the normal range for one's size and build, something that befalls at least one out of every ten children (Winock, 1975). The average 12-year-old boy, for example, weighs about 88 pounds. If his weight is in the neighborhood of 114 pounds, he would fall into the obese range. Children who are excessively overweight (endomorphic) are not only likely to have more social-emotional problems, they also run more risk of a variety of minor and major illnesses (LeBow, 1986). Perhaps one of the reasons that overweight children are viewed as less popular and have more social problems is that they are not able to run and move as freely and agilely in play as their peers. Because they are not able to keep up as easily, they may be excluded more frequently. This leads to feelings of rejection, which foster a negative self-concept, often leading directly to unhealthy substitutes, such as candy bars, soft drinks, ice cream, and other high-calorie foods that make a bad problem worse. Unless broken, it is a vicious cycle.

3.2 Too Much TV Is Bad for One's Health and Waist

Research in recent years has pointed to a not-so-surprising finding: the more television that overweight children and adolescents watch, the less likely they are to lose weight. Also, the more overweight they are, the more likely it is that they will show early signs of cardiovascular disease (Jelinek, 1990). Up to age 17, most children watch television three to four hours per day. While they watch, they are not only bombarded with messages about high-calorie foods, they are usually sampling some. It has been estimated that the prevalence of obesity in children increases about 2% for each additional hour of television beyond three hours watched daily (*University of California, Berkeley, Wellness Letter,* 1987). If a parent asked you how to stop children from watching so much television, what suggestions would you offer?

We cannot say that a child's personality is a result of a certain body type, but we can say that body type plays an important part in determining the feedback he or she gets from others. Indeed, considering the feedback that any person—young or old—both gives and receives purely on the basis of physical appearances, it is not difficult to see how children's physical proportions can influence their feelings about themselves simply by affecting how other people react to them. This is an important realization, particularly in light of research indicating that both adults and children perceived as attractive receive more positive feedback than those who are considered less attractive (Dion and Dion, 1987).

Children going through their middle years are *extremely* receptive to both adult and peer input regarding both their person and their performance. They more readily believe and incorporate what is said about them during these middle years than they ever will again. It behooves all of us who work with or teach growing children to remind ourselves that what we may consider to be harmless perceptions ("Billy, you are so clumsy," or "Betty, you are always so sloppy-looking.") may, if a child hears them often enough, be converted in the child's mind to *self-conceptions.* Over time, Billy may conclude, "I'm pretty clumsy," and then, precisely because of his self-consciousness, fulfill that conception by tripping over his own feet. Betty may conclude, "I'm not very pretty," and unwittingly choose clothes that make her look unattractive.

Physical Growth and Its Implications for Teachers

1. *Children have their greatest number of accidents in their first nine years of life.* About two-thirds of all childhood accidents occur before age 9, with boys of all ages more likely to have accidents than girls. In fact, the leading cause of death (and third leading cause of injury) in children is accidents (Thomas, Groër, and Droppleman, 1993). Inasmuch as middle-grade children are using their bodies in new and frequently daring ways for the first time, it is not surprising that there are more injuries during this growth phase. Teachers can help children in this age group by giving them honest feedback and appropriate cautions about the limits of their physical skills and abilities; for example, "That may be a bit heavy for you to carry, Johnny," or "Try this instead, Jenny, it's not so high."

2. *Gross-motor (large-muscle) skills far outstrip fine-motor (small-muscle) coordination, particularly among children during grades one through three.* This is one of the reasons there are so many tumbles and falls; the large muscles for running are there, but the coordination for all that machinery is still developing. Large-muscle activities—running, skipping, hopping, climbing, wrestling, and so forth—are not only desired, but necessary expressions of restless new muscles begging to be used. Try not to schedule too many quiet activities at one time. It is helpful to allow for break time, even if only to stand up and stretch or to walk around the room for a few minutes.

3. *Early elementary-age children's enthusiasm for life is frequently greater than their available energy (relatively small lungs can transport only so much oxygen), and they need rest periods to recoup.* Scheduling quiet activities, such as reading or art, after recess or gym is a good way to allow them to recoup.

4. *Children in the upper elementary grades gradually exhibit greater smoothness and command of small-muscle expression, which is reflected in better coordination in activities ranging from handwriting to skateboarding to batting a ball.* You can expect better detail work and longer periods of concentration from most children in grades four through six. However, energy levels remain high, making it difficult for children to sit still for extended periods. Allow a certain amount of time for moving about and talking.

5. *Bone and ligament growth is not yet complete and, as a consequence, they are not able to withstand extremely heavy pressure or continuous stress.* It is for a good reason that elementary-age boys and girls should not run or throw for extended periods. Wise coaches know the wisdom of frequent substitutions during physically demanding games. Children at this age are not particularly good at reading their own body signs and, if left to their choices, will more often than not push their bodies and endurance beyond safe limits. They may not want adult intervention ("Okay gang, we've had enough for now."), but they do need it.

6. *Visual maturity is usually reached somewhere between 6 and 8 years of age.* Peripheral vision at these ages is fully developed and elementary-age children are able to discriminate very fine differences in color. There are, however, wide individual differences in visual acuity: some children are far-sighted (see best at a distance) and others near-sighted (see best at close range). Unfortunately, sometimes neither parents nor teachers are aware of such problems, because of either a lack of testing or a lack of feedback from the child. Children with sight problems are not apt to say anything. From their point of view, nothing is wrong because this is the way it has always been. Be sensitive to the child who squints a lot or who complains of headaches after reading.

7. *The immunological system becomes functionally mature during the early school years.* The body becomes increasingly efficient in fighting the three or so significant infections per year that the average child catches. Colds, gastrointestinal system infections, and allergic disorders account for about 71% of school absenteeism (Schuster and Ashburn, 1980). Because cold viruses are transmitted primarily by hand-to-hand contact, with the infested hand eventually carrying thousands of germs to the main portals of entry (the nose and eyes), teachers and students can reduce the number of colds and other infectious diseases they get by simply washing their hands more often.

8. *On the average, girls reach puberty somewhere between 12 and 13 years of age, yet can begin as early as 9. As noted earlier, boys mature a bit later, reaching puberty on the average by age 14, with the age range between 11 and 18 years.* Concern and curiosity about sex are practically universal phenomena, particularly as children near puberty. There are many questions, and both boys and girls profit most from accurate answers given directly and honestly within the framework of common sense and each school's existing guidelines for sex education.

9. *The middle years of childhood are a time of good health, slower growth, large-muscle development and small-muscle refinement, and increased skill development.* It is a time when a child sheds his or her baby physical self and gradually assumes the body proportions and facial dimensions of his or her adult physi-

cal self. Physical growth is one aspect of middle childhood; social growth is still another, a topic to which we now turn.

3.3 What Was Your Own Early Growth Like?

Think back over your own middle-school years and the physical development you experienced at that time. Were you small for your age? Large? About right? How did your physical development affect the way you related to others? The feedback you got? How did it influence the way you felt about yourself? How did the adults in your life affect your feelings about your physical self at that time? In your life today, do you see any residue, for better or worse, of those early influences?

SOCIAL DEVELOPMENT: BASIC CHARACTERISTICS

Between ages 6 and 12, children take giant strides toward becoming competent social members of their culture. They are away from their families for increasingly longer periods of time, they invest themselves in a broader range of peer relationships, and they spend considerable energy mastering critical developmental and culturally imposed tasks. By the end of this growth period they are on the threshold of adolescence, with varying degrees of readiness to assume new, expanded responsibilities and relationships.

In the classical Freudian view of emotional development, the middle years represent the so-called "latency period," which is characterized by the repression of sexual drives. From Erik Erikson's psychosocial point of view, children develop either a sense of industry or feelings of inferiority, depending on how successful they are in meeting new demands, solving problems, and "making it" interpersonally.

Overview of Social Development Outcomes and Their Implications for Teachers

1. *Children become increasingly social during this stage of development.* They begin to develop more individual friendships, which are almost exclusively same-sex friendships. Friendship bonds are important, offering opportunities for youngsters to find out about themselves and others in the more objective world of peer relationships. Indeed, research indicates that children with few or no friends run increased risks of interpersonal problems and emotional disturbances as they get older, probably because they feel increasingly alone in a society of peers that becomes more and more social (Shaffer, 1993).

There are at least three implications here for teachers: (1) build on children's natural affinity for social involvement by planning a certain number of activities that enable them to work in pairs or in small groups; (2) keep an eye open for lonely, isolated children (sociograms can be useful tools here) so that you can give them some confidence-building attention and help involve them with others; and (3) recognize that children this age not only *want* to interact with others but *need* to as part of their development.

2. *Quarrels and squabbles are frequent and natural at this level.* Elementary-age children do not yet have well-developed social skills and resort quickly to more primitive, aggressive methods of resolving conflict. *Aggression* has been defined as simply "an act that injures or irritates another person" (Eron, 1987). Hartup (1974) has pointed out that whereas we are more apt to see expressions of instrumental aggression (object-oriented) among preschoolers, we are more likely to see expressions of hostile aggression (person-centered) among elementary-age youths. Basically, this means that interpersonal conflicts shift from fights involving objects (toys, personal possessions) to fights involving egos (self-esteem, personal pride). Thankfully, physical aggression decreases from about age 7, only to be replaced by an increase in verbal aggression (Patterson, 1984).

Boys and girls deal differently with conflict. Maccoby's (1980) review indicates that boys (males generally) tend to predominate as both the agents and victims of aggression, being more aggressive both physically and verbally than females.

As a teacher, it will be helpful to both the children and your mental health to realize that children's occasional squabbles and fighting are normal by-products of this stage. Children, particularly those in grades one through three, are still quite egocentric, a characteristic that carries with it a tendency to see things only from their own point of view, which is one of the reasons they may have more interpersonal conflicts. The frequency of interpersonal conflicts is reduced as children move into the upper elementary years and become more capable of what Selman (1980) has called *perspective taking,* the ability to see things from the other person's point of view. Teachers can help this process along by encouraging students to see how their words and deeds affect others ("Chris, look at John—see how badly he feels about what you did?").

Unless children are actually hurting one another, a rule of thumb is to let them work out their own problems. It is part of the business of growing up.

3. *Children during this age span are naturally critical of one another; they tend to have favorite scapegoats.* Diplomacy and tact are noticeably absent during middle childhood. Youngsters this age are inclined to say what they feel and express it with gusto and feeling, particularly in the lower elementary grades. Their inclination to editorialize freely about others' shortcomings and to exaggerate existing flaws can probably be explained in at least two ways: (1) in the process of growing up most children are frequently admonished, corrected, and criticized by their parents, and they freely pass it on; and (2) children, at this point, simply have not grown up enough to move beyond the self-

centeredness that blocks their view of the effect they have on others. How many adults do you know who are *still* that way?

Teachers play an important role in helping youngsters see that helping others and being sensitive to others' needs and feelings are valued behaviors. Sometimes children simply need to be calmly given feedback about how they can hurt others by what they say and do. This helps them take the other person's perspective. It is best for children to see those who teach them model the sort of sensitivity and tact that promotes positive solutions to interpersonal conflict.

4. *Social relationships tend to be activity-oriented at this stage.* This is a restless age. Children enjoy doing active things with others or playing catchy, entertaining games that involve chance and that conclude quickly. At one moment, playing soccer or kick-the-can is the thing. At another moment, playing simple card games will do. Children like being involved in activities with one another. Unlike adolescents, who can sit and talk for hours, elementary-age children relate better when there is something specific and concrete to do, giving them an outlet for their enormous energy reserves along with a focus for their social interactions.

When you teach, you will find this age of youngsters quite responsive to opportunities for interacting with one another in gamelike activities. Spelling bees or arithmetic contests that involve, say, one group of children working cooperatively together against another group, usually provoke considerable interest and motivation, while at the same time being good learning activities.

3.4 What Kind of Social Child Were You?

You can begin to grasp the nature of children's social development by reflecting back over your own growth in this area. What memories do you have about how you related to other kids your age? Did you have lots of friends and mix freely with others, or were you more on the fringe of social groups? Do you see any resemblances between the way you behaved as a social youngster and the way you function as a social person in adulthood? How does an awareness of your own social development help you understand other children's social development?

EMOTIONAL DEVELOPMENT: BASIC CHARACTERISTICS

Children between the ages of 6 and 12 are emotionally vulnerable. Their self-concepts are still in the process of forming, which means that they are particularly susceptible to the feedback they get from adults and peers. If feedback is essentially positive and ego-enhancing, children will be more apt to develop an exploring sense of industry, which is the foundation to the sort of healthy risk-taking behavior associated with positive self-concept development. If feedback is essentially negative and ego-deflating, then children will be more likely to develop low self-esteem and feelings of inferiority.

Child development literature is replete with examples of how and why children's experiences can have such powerful effects, for better or worse, on both their self-concept development and academic learning (Elkind, 1988; Hamachek, 1992; Marshall, 1989; Missildine, 1963). The reason that children are so easily influenced and molded during these years is that they are not well defended psychologically. For example, if a second grader fails a spelling test, he or she is more likely to believe that mark (i.e., incorporate it, internalize it) than is a twelfth-grade boy with a positive view of himself and a history of doing well in school who fails a geometry test. The twelfth grader can blame his performance on a fluke, deny its importance, rationalize his lack of study, or blame it on his teacher. So long as his performance is inconsistent with his concept of self, he can defend himself against the loss of self-esteem. The second grader, however, does not yet have a well-defined self with which he or she can, or has to be, consistent. Hence, whether it is a failed or successful experience, the elementary-age child can offer far less resistance to its impact and will be a much less critical recipient of its place in his or her evolving sense of self. Elementary-age children do not yet have a consolidated self-system to serve as the framework within which they can evaluate other people's evaluations of them. Thus, children this age are more apt to accept as true the feedback, positive or negative, that they hear.

Overview of Emotional Development Outcomes and Their Implications for Teachers

1. *The first four years of school (approximately, ages 6 to 10) are a critical period in development in that behavioral tendencies crystallized at this time persist into adulthood.* Longitudinal research (studies of the same people over long periods of time) points clearly to the idea that the kind of adults we are today is very much related to those particular personality characteristics that were consolidated during the early primary years (Moss and Susman, 1980). Particular emotional-social characteristics such as aggressiveness in males and passivity in females are especially predictable outcomes in the adult behavior of children observed with these tendencies. Both the content and direction of a child's emotional growth are influenced more than we may realize during the elementary school years. What teachers say can dramatically affect, positively or negatively, a child's emotional stability and self-concept development.

2. *During this stage of growth, children are typically eager to please a teacher. Most children want to be liked, and they want to know they are liked in return.* They are quite responsive to praise and recognition. Wise teachers can use this in posi-

tive ways by giving them reinforcing feedback ("What a good idea, Jane," or "That's an excellent drawing, John."), which encourages children to stay motivated, and helps them like you, themselves, and school.

3. *Children grow increasingly in their need for emotional independence and in their ability to express their feelings.* Compared to preschoolers, whose range of emotional expression is limited, school-age children's repertoire of emotions becomes more specific, diverse, and sophisticated. Teachers can be helpful in at least two ways as children develop emotionally: (1) they can respect children's needs to do more for themselves (they want to be big and prove it); and (2) they can help children express their emotions in healthy, constructive ways. ("Susie, I know you're angry, but calling Jerry a cross-eyed donkey only makes it worse. Just tell him that when he behaves like that you really feel angry. You don't have to call people names to let them know how you feel.")

4. *If not monitored, children tend to eat a lot of junk food, which can have an adverse effect on their emotions due to alterations in body chemistry and brain metabolism.* Some children may be hyperactive, aggressive, depressed, or show mood swings because they are suffering from what has been called the "overconsumption syndrome" (Bland, 1982). Basically, this is a disorder caused by an excessive diet of empty-calorie foods, those containing a lot of sweets, but little in the way of essential vitamins and minerals. When the body is shortchanged of these important micronutrients, brain functions and behavior can be disturbed because brain cells are not receiving the right proportion of vitamins and minerals to convert glucose received from the blood into energy. Research has shown that when the brain receives too little energy to operate normally, aggression, depression, and other symptoms can result (Barton, 1990). Children do not know this. They know only that candy and soft drinks taste good, and they want more. Teachers can help both children and parents be more aware of the relationship between food consumption and behavior. Have you ever noticed from your own experience that too great a consumption of sweets can leave you somewhat lethargic and depressed?

3.5 Watch Children's Emotional Expressions

There are many opportunities to watch and listen to young children (in streets, on playgrounds, in your own family), and as you do, pay attention to how they express their emotions. Some children seem quiet, shy, even frightened, and tend to keep their feelings in check. Other children are emotionally open and outgoing. Pay particular attention to the interactions you see going on between children and the significant adults in their lives. What kinds of interactions tend to close down children emotionally? What kinds of interactions seem to encourage more emotional openness and spontaneity?

COGNITIVE DEVELOPMENT: BASIC CHARACTERISTICS

Children this age are gluttonous learners. They learn everywhere and from everyone. Everything is so new to them that practically everything they do is a learning experience.

Sometime during the beginning of the school years, for some children around age 4 and for others as late as age 7 or 8, a major change in cognitive functioning takes place and is reflected in various general and specific learning readiness—general school readiness, number readiness, and so forth. Each child, on his or her own timeframe, enters what might be called a state of general intellectual readiness and cognitive preparedness to do school-related work. This is partly a function of having more experience with life itself and partly a function of increased brain growth.

Although middle-grade children are eager learners, intellectual development slows during this period. From Bloom's (1976) studies, for example, it has been estimated that about 50% of mature intelligence is developed by age 4, another 30% by age 8, and the remaining 20% during the remainder of the middle childhood years. Let's be sure we understand this. To say, for instance, that about 80% of children's intelligence is developed by age 8 does not mean that they know 80% of all that they can learn about. It *does* mean, however, that by age 8 most children have developed about 80% of their *innate ability* for learning. How that innate ability is developed, of course, depends very much on the environment (e.g., homes, schools, parents, opportunities, and so on) to which children are exposed.

Vocabulary development, which is a reflection of cognitive growth, increases dramatically during the middle years. By the time they reach about 6 years of age, children have acquired a recognition vocabulary of between 8000 and 14,000 words (Berger, 1986). This is a very impressive performance, especially in light of evidence from the 1930s suggesting that children's recognition vocabularies did not develop to that extent until they were about 12 years of age (Seashore and Eckerson, 1940). Improved teaching methods, along with enlightened ideas about what young children are really able to learn, have contributed to a steady increase in children's vocabularies in the past fifty years. Studies continue to confirm that children from well-educated families tend to increase their vocabularies more than do those from families in which parents have less education and that girls, on the whole, continue to develop larger vocabularies than boys (Seward and Seward, 1980).

Although most of our everyday grammatical constructions are mastered by about age 6, actual knowledge of syntax continues to develop throughout elementary school, perhaps because children become more competent in using grammar to understand connections between words. By the time children are about 8 years old, they are not easily fooled by word order to apparent meaning. For example, Chomsky (1969) found in her research that only children younger than 8 would be likely not to understand the idea that the subject of a sentence is usually the noun preceding the verb (e.g., would read "John promised Mary to shovel the driveway" and conclude that Mary would do the shoveling). Research by deVilliers and deVilliers (1978) indicates that children younger than age 6 or 7 have difficulty understanding the passive voice, but by middle childhood most children understand that "the truck was bumped by the car" does not mean that the truck did the bumping.

Words are stepping-stones to more sophisticated cognitive development. Reciprocally, cognitive development enhances both word recognition and word usage. All in all, research indicates that it takes about the first seven or eight years of life to master the basic rules of syntax and grammar (Rice, 1989). This is true even in languages where grammatical structure is relatively simple. For example, as pointed out by deVilliers and deVilliers (1978), the subjunctive is much less complicated in Russian than in English, but Russian children do not master the subjunctive earlier than English-speaking children because the concept must first be understood before the form can be mastered. In order for this concept to be grasped, a certain amount of maturation, learning, and brain development must take place.

Intellectual Functioning and Brain Development

The human brain is an awesome tangle of neuronal complexity. At birth, a baby's brain is about 25% of its adult weight; by age 5 it has reached 90% of its adult weight (Tanner, 1990). In terms of the brain's early development, perhaps the most significant is that occurring during the second, third, and fourth years, when the growth of cross-modal zones connect one area of the brain with others (Groves and Reboc, 1988). This is important because these connections enable children to expand their cognitive powers as they learn to think in terms of associations. For example, they can associate or connect the sound of a horn with the sight of a car, or the sight of an orange with its taste, and eventually the sound of the spoken word "horn" with sound and sight and "orange" with sight and taste. It is the beginning of what Piaget (1973) referred to as the concrete-operational stage of intellectual development, a time when a child thinks more like an adult. Basically, this involves the capacity for deductive reasoning (from the general to the particular). Thus, children begin to think and reason abstractly, although there are wide individual differences among them.

As highly related as brain maturation is to learning, there is no exact correspondence between brain growth and cognitive development. Some children, for example, began reading at age 4, or even at age 3, when their brains are immature. In addition, the fact that brain maturation and cognitive development occur at the same time does not prove that brain maturation causes cognitive development. Children's intellectual development may cause brain maturation or at least move it along at a more rapid rate. As an example of this possibility, there is interesting evidence showing that rats raised in an enriched psychological environment, with objects to manipulate, various paths to explore, and problems to solve, not only develop thicker and heavier cerebral cortexes than those that live out their lives in an impoverished environment, but also have more complicated patterns of interconnecting dendrite branching among neurons than do disadvantaged rats (Greenough, Black, and Wallace, 1987; Rosenzweig, 1984).

It is tantalizing evidence, suggesting that if you enhance the intellectual environment the brain grows larger—at least among some rats. However, it is not as simple as it seems. We all know about particular persons who have come out of impoverished backgrounds and who have done remarkably well in school and/or life. We no doubt can think of others who, in spite of their richly endowed backgrounds, have been miserable failures. Cognitive development, brain growth, and environment interact in ways that are only beginning to be understood. It is certain that each influences the other. Further, it is worth noting that a rich, varied environment has never been shown to stand in the way of learning and cognitive development.

Conceptual Ability Develops Rapidly

The capacity to conceptualize or see things in appropriate categories or groupings develops rapidly in middle childhood. By definition, a concept is a mental grouping of events or objects that are, on the surface, distinct, yet alike in a more general way. There are, for example, about 7.5 *million* distinguishable differences in colors. By categorizing these colors into a dozen or more color groupings, we manage to deal with these vast differences quite well. Thus, we can talk about the concept "red" and not let the 100,000 or so different shades of red stand in the way of our communication. In a similar way, a concept like "fruit" allows us to group a great number of objects, such as apples, oranges, grapes, bananas, and so on, under a similar heading. Thus, it is possible to tell 8-year-old Jimmy that fruit is good for him without having to list individually all the food objects that are fruit.

Favell (1970) has documented this dramatic progression in conceptual ability by detailing how concepts change markedly in terms of *validity, status,* and *accessibility* during middle childhood.

You may have noted how a 2-year-old's concept of the word "toy" or "father" is often personalized and reference-specific to *his* toys and *his* father. He does not understand yet that toy and father are concepts that have reference to many types of play objects and adult males that, once they meet particular criteria, can be generally classified under the labels "toy" and "father." Most 7-year-olds, however, have no problem with this. They know that toy or father can refer either to something of theirs or someone else's. In that sense, these concepts become more *valid* for them insofar as their meaning is more similar for all people.

Concepts assume greater *status* during the middle years as a child is able to more clearly articulate his or her meaning. For instance, a 3-year-old's concept of "weather" is fuzzy at best, whereas a 9-year-old's understanding of this concept is more exact, clear, and stable over time, enabling him or her to talk about various kinds of weather, given differing conditions and seasons of the year. A 3-year-old says, "Weather is all over outside." A 9-year-old says, "It can be cold or hot outside, but it depends on if the sun is out." In this sense, concept development during middle childhood gains more status, or power, which helps children to see the differences among both objects and events.

Concepts become more *accessible* to this age group. If you ask a 4-year-old about the concept "size," he very likely will say that he does not know, although his behavior must very well suggest that he does have some comprehension of these concepts. For instance, two 4-year-old boys were building different sized forts of wet sand on a beach. One said to the other, "Your fort is bigger than mine." The other answered, "Yes, mine's the biggest in the whole world." A few moments later I asked the first boy how he would compare the size of those two forts. He answered, "Well, they're just big forts, that's all." His friend was equally puzzled by the idea of comparing size, although each had made obvious references to size in their earlier spontaneous comments. An 8-year-old would have little difficulty talking about the concept of size and using it in his reasoning to conclude something such as, "My fort is twice as big as John's."

Children develop a great number of concepts during their elementary school years, a number that varies widely from child to child when factors such as basic intelligence, opportunity for learning, and socioeconomic background are taken into account. We need to remember that the ability for conceptual learning is not something that happens all at one time, but is a gradual process that evolves during the elementary years—slower for some children and faster for others.

Formal and Informal Conceptual Rules Emerge

Whereas concepts are symbols that represent a set of common attributes of persons, places, objects, events, or experiences, rules are ways of categorizing relations among concepts. Understanding rules is also a major intellectual skill and cognitive activity that commences with vigor during middle childhood.

Both formal and informal rules play important parts in children's cognitive functioning. Most of children's beliefs are based on informal rules, and their major purpose is to help children bring some order and predictability to what they experience in an increasingly complex life. Once children leave the refuge of their parents' wings, life does get more complicated, and in the absence of adults who interpret life for them, children must work harder to understand it better themselves. Hence, the evolvement of many informal rules. "Crosswalks are dangerous," "Matches can burn," and "Ice is cold," are examples of the many informal rules that help children cope more effectively.

Formal rules, however, state relationships between aspects that are always true and specifiable. For instance, the formal mathematical rule $3 \times 10 = 30$ implies a fixed relationship between the concepts 3 and 10 when subjected to the process of multiplication. The formal spelling rule of "*i* before *e* except after *c*" implies a fixed relationship between two vowels when juxtaposed with the letter *c*.

Overview of Cognitive Development Outcomes and Their Implications for Teachers

1. *Elementary school students are eager, enthusiastic learners. They are naturally curious, which is why, at least in the beginning, they are natural learners.* There is a certain amount of energy and zest associated with children's natural curiosity. They want to know why, how, and where, and they tend to be both impatient and undisciplined when it comes to exploring their world. Be careful not to plan for long periods of time to be spent on a single topic. Insofar as is possible, give students opportunities to pursue their own particular interests within a given unit of study. Doing something of their choice gives students a chance to exploit and expand their curiosities, which may be a helpful way to channel their enthusiasm along constructive routes. For example, you might offer choices of special projects such as reading a particular book, making a special report, or being a peer helper to a classmate who needs some assistance.

2. *Students in the middle school years learn best when they can participate in concrete, hands-on experiences.* Jean Piaget's investigations of children's intellectual development leaves little doubt that elementary-age youth learn best by doing (Bybee and Sund, 1982). We can use this knowledge by giving pupils as many opportunities as possible for doing, trying, testing, and trial-and-error experimenting so that they can see for themselves how things work. For example, students' learning about the concept of money will be enhanced by actually giving and receiving change for a specified amount. They will more readily grasp the idea of rectangles, circles, or triangles by handling examples of each, rotating them, cutting them into two pieces, refitting them, and so on. Increasingly, children grow skilled in operations involving mathematical reasoning (with wide individual differences here) and become better able to work problems in their heads as well as on paper. All in all, the middle-grade child moves steadily in the direction of becoming a more logical person.

3. *Sex differences in specific abilities and general academic performance begin to emerge.* It is important to notice the word "emerge" here. These differences are not nearly as clear during the elementary years as they are during adolescence and beyond. Evidence shows that, on the average, girls tend to be superior in

spelling, reading, word fluency, and mathematical computation than boys. However, boys tend to do better in mathematical reasoning, in tasks involving understanding spatial relationships, and in solving insight problems (Jacklin, 1989).

Why do these emerging differences exist? The answer to this is somewhat equivocal at this time. On one hand, research suggests that boy/girl differences in verbal and mathematical ability might be more a matter of maturation than of sex per se (Waber, 1976). For example, boys and girls who matured early were found to do better in verbal skills and poorer in spatial skills. The reverse was true for boys and girls who matured late. Because girls mature earlier than boys, this could account for their superior verbal skills. Conversely, because boys mature later, this could account for their superior abilities on spatial tasks. On the other hand, evidence suggests that sex differences in learning are not so much a product of different rates of overall physical maturation as they are a product of specific differences in rate of brain development. Neurophysiological research findings are showing that females' left brain hemispheres—the hemisphere primarily responsible for linguistic, mathematical, and analytical skills—activate more readily than do males' (Goleman, 1978; Shucard, 1982). This left-hemisphere brain difference is observable as early as 3 months of age and may be yet another way females develop their verbal and language skills more rapidly than boys. Not only do girls become more adept at the specialties of this favored half of the brain, but also there is evidence to suggest that they enhance the development of this side by increasing stimulation of it (Huttenlocher et al., 1991: Hyde, Fennema, and Lamon, 1990).

We have to interpret this research cautiously. First, when we look at specific individuals, generalized conclusions begin to break down. Second, there is an ongoing interplay between one's environment and heredity and between one's hormonal physiology and personal psychology. Things are never as simple as they seem when it comes to understanding human behavior.

You will no doubt enhance your effectiveness as a teacher by keeping in mind that there really are some general differences in the learning processes of boys and girls. For example, because the brains of boys and girls seem to be organized differently for verbal and spatial skills, reading may draw on different parts of the brain in the sexes. Learning to read is not purely a linguistic skill; learning to recognize letters, for instance, is a spatial process. Teaching reading by the phonics methods stresses sound recognition, mainly a left-hemisphere function, while the look-say method calls for recognizing words on sight, an approach that involves both hemispheres. Because girls are more likely to have spatial abilities on both sides of the brain (something that occurs later for boys), they are more likely to learn about as well either way. Perhaps a teaching approach that combines both phonics and look-say methods would be best in order to accommodate these natural sex differences.

There are sex differences in learning. They are not very noticeable during the elementary years, but they become progressively more observable as middle childhood nears its conclusion. Our sensitivity to these differences can help us develop a deeper appreciation for the idea that both psychology and biology play a part in learning and school achievement.

UNDERSTANDING MIDDLE CHILDHOOD

This is a time when previously established patterns of a child's personality are broken up or loosened, so that emerging adolescent changes can be incorporated. The outcome of this developmental phase is not *improvement* but *disorganization* (not permanent disorganization, of course, but disorganization for future growth). Indeed, disorganization must occur, or a higher level of organization and integration cannot be achieved. Children do not become adults by simply growing bigger and better. If all the children did was improve their personalities, then they very likely would end up as oversized children or infantile adults. Among other things, growing into an adult means leaving behind and/or drastically modifying some of what the child has been, thereby becoming something else in more mature and complex ways.

The middle years are primarily "disassembly" years and are designed to prepare a child for the physical and psychological changes that occur during adolescence. Existing personality patterns are loosened so that change can take place.

EPILOGUE

Middle childhood is indeed a remarkable age. The changes that occur are so slow and subtle that a youngster can go from childhood to adolescence almost before we are aware of it. Indeed, more than one parent has wondered, "What ever happened to my little boy/girl?" Middle childhood goes so quickly, but as it is happening it seems to be moving hardly at all. There is a good reason for this, and it has to do with the fact that physical growth is more steady in middle childhood, which makes month-to-month changes less apparent than years of change. By age 12, the average boy has attained about 84% of his full height, and a girl about 92% of hers.

Children's sense of self expands and develops in many ways during these years. They not only grow bigger and stronger, but smarter and more knowing. It has been estimated that a child reaches about 80% of his or her innate ability for learning by about 8 years of age. That may be true, but they also reach about 150% of their curiosity when they are 6 years of age and continue their insatiable hunger for knowing through their middle childhood years. Not all children, of course, have the same kind of hunger. One child, for example, might enjoy doing things that are more physical in nature and that allow him or her to use his or her body. Another child might appreciate activities that are more intellectual in nature and that encourage him or her to use his or her mind. Most growing children, if given half a chance, will try out both their minds and their bodies during middle childhood and, somewhere along the way, discover those talents, interests, and personal strengths that will eventually help them uncover their own individual identities.

Middle childhood has been called the latent period in a child's growth because it is a time of relatively little in the way of sexual development. It would probably be more accurate to say that this is a time of relatively little in the way of sexual interests. Boys and girls continue in their development as sexual persons, but, for the moment, have neither the interest nor the hormones to be much more than aware of each other's differences and platonic in their close relationships.

Intellectually—from their own angle of judgment—most elementary-age children operate on the naive assumption that the world is as it seems to be. Hence, most children during these years are not very skilled at verbal logic. Their thinking is more concrete, more black-and-white. In addition, their verbal thought lags behind their verbal logic. For instance, they deal with the problems of right and left, of degree and order, and of social relations *in practice,* long before they can handle the same issues in words and in thought separate from action. It is not until the end of the elementary years that children begin to show signs of *verbal* facility in reasoning. Although they might begin to be curious about mechanical causes and effects somewhere between 7 and 10 years of age, they probably will have little success with causal thinking until 11 or 12 years of age. The implication for teachers is clear: the more opportunities there are for elementary-age youngsters to actually *do* things, such as manipulate, experiment, touch, feel, examine, and so forth (as opposed to simply thinking about things abstractly), the more likely it is that learning will occur.

Children's allegiance to their peers, whether they happen to be some kids from down the street or the neighborhood "gang," is a perfectly normal outgrowth of a self that is expanding its social boundaries and interpersonal contacts. It is behavior that says, "I am growing up; I can take care of myself; I need to talk to others kids with parent problems; I want to see how strong I am and what my chances for survival are with those who will judge me impartially." It is all part of the process of maturing and becoming independent, processes that cannot happen unless children have as many opportunities as possible for relating to their own kind and holding their own under a variety of conditions and circumstances.

Middle childhood is another stage in a continuous cycle of growth. It is a time when most children begin to consolidate a self-image and integrate a personality that, for better or worse, will serve as the foundation on which a more complex personality will be built.

STUDY AND REVIEW QUESTIONS

1. What does it mean when we say that physical development during the elementary years is primarily one of proportion rather than size?
2. Although a child's personality is not determined by this or that body type, it is influenced by it. Can you explain what this means?
3. Why is it not a good idea to expect elementary school children to sit still for extended periods?
4. Why is middle childhood sometimes referred to as the "latency period?"
5. It is said that the squabbles and fighting of middle childhood are normal by-products of that age. Can you explain why this is so?
6. Can you explain why elementary-age children spend so much time in activity-oriented play?
7. Children between the ages of 6 and 12 are emotionally vulnerable. Explain *why* this is so.
8. Why are the first four years of school so critical to a child's emotional development?
9. If you were asked to explain the basics of a child's cognitive development during the middle years, what would you say?
10. What does research suggest about the effect of environment on brain growth?
11. What part do formal and informal conceptual rules play in children's cognitive development?
12. Explain why hands-on experiences are so important to successful learning among elementary children.
13. What does it mean when we say that the main outcome of middle childhood is disorganization rather than improvement?

REFERENCES

Barton, L. "Food, Mood, and Behavior." *USAir Magazine,* 1990, July, pp. 82, 84–85.

Berger, K. S. *The Developing Person Through Childhood and Adolescence,* 2nd ed. New York: Worth, 1986.

Bland, J. "The Junk-Food Syndrome." *Psychology Today,* 1982, January, p. 92.

Bloom, B. J. *Human Characteristics and School Learning.* New York: McGraw-Hill, 1976.

Bybee, R. W., and Sund, R. B. *Piaget for Educators,* 2nd ed. Columbus: Merrill, 1982.

Casky, S. R., and Felker, D. W. "Social Stereotyping of Female Body Image by Elementary Age Girls." *Research Quarterly,* 1971, *42,* pp. 251–255.

Chomsky, C. *The Acquisition of Syntax in Children from Five to Ten.* Cambridge, MA: MIT Press, 1969.

deVilliers, J. G., and deVilliers, P. A. *Language Acquisition.* Cambridge, MA: Harvard University Press, 1978.

Dion, K. L., and Dion, K. K. "Belief in a Just World and Physical Attractiveness Stereotyping." *Journal of Personality and Social Psychology,* 1987, *52,* pp. 775–780.

Elkind, D. *The Hurried Child,* rev. Reading, MA: Addison-Wesley, 1988.

Eron, L. D. "The Development of Aggressive Behavior from the Perspective of a Developing Behaviorism." *American Psychologist,* 1987, *42,* pp. 435–442.

Flavell, J. H. "Concept Development." In P. H. Mussen (Ed.), *Carmichael's Manual of Child Psychology,* 3rd ed. Vol. I. New York: Wiley, 1970.

Goleman, D. "Special Abilities of the Sexes: Do They Begin in the Brain?" *Psychology Today,* 1978, November, pp. 48–59, 120.

Greenough, W. T., Black, J. E., and Wallace, C. S. "Experience and Brain Development." *Child Development,* 1987, *54,* pp. 1286–1296.

Groves, P. M. and Rebec, G. V. *Introduction to Biological Psychology.* Dubuque, IA: Brown, 1988.

Hamachek, D. *Encounters with the Self,* 4th ed. Fort Worth, TX: Harcourt Brace Jovanovich, 1992.

Hartup, W. W. "Aggression in Childhood: Developmental Perspective." *American Psychologist,* 1974, *29,* pp. 336–341.

Huttenlocher, J., Haight, W., Bryk, A., Seltzer, M., and Lyons, T. "Early Vocabulary Growth: Relation to Language Input and Gender." *Developmental Psychology,* 1991, *27,* pp. 236–248.

Hyde, J. S., Fennema, E., and Lamon, S. J. "Gender Differences in Mathematics Performance: A Meta-analysis." *Psychological Bulletin,* 1990, *107,* pp. 139–155.

Jacklin, C. N. "Female and Male: Issues of Gender." *American Psychologist,* 1989, *44,* pp. 127–133.

Jelinek, P. "Studies Find Health, TV, Weight Linked in Kids." *Detroit Free Press,* September 5, 1990.

LeBow, M. *Childhood Obesity.* New York: Springer, 1984.

LeBow, M. "Child Obesity: Dangers." *Canadian Psychology,* 1986, *27,* pp. 275–285.

Maccoby, E. E. *Social Development.* San Diego: Harcourt Brace Jovanovich, 1980.

Marshall, H. H. "The Development of Self-Concept." *Young Children,* 1989, *44,* pp. 44–51.

Missildine, W. H. *Young Inner Child of the Past.* New York: Simon & Schuster, 1963.

Moss, H. A., and Susman, E. J. "Longitudinal Study of Personality Development." In O. G. Brim, Jr., and J. Kagen (Eds.), *Constancy and Change in Human Development* (pp. 530–597). Cambridge, MA: Harvard University Press, 1980.

National Center for Health Statistics (NCHS). *Vital Statistics.* NCHS Growth Charts, 1976, 253 (Suppl.), U.S. Department of Health, Education, and Welfare.

Patterson, C. J. "Aggression, Altruism, and Self-Regulation." In M. H. Bornstein and M. E. Lamb (Eds.), *Developmental Psychology: An Advanced Textbook.* Hillsdale, NJ: Lawrence Erlbaum, 1984.

Piaget, J. *The Child and Reality.* New York: Grossman, 1973.

Rice, M. L. "Children's Language Acquisition." *American Psychologist,* 1989, *44,* 149–156.

Rosenzweig, M. R. "Experience, Memory, and the Brain." *American Psychologist,* 1984, 365–376.

Schuster, C. W., and Ashburn, S. S. *The Process of Human Development: A Holistic Approach.* Boston: Little, Brown, 1980.

Seashore, R. H., and Eckerson, L. D. "The Measurement of Individual Differences in General English Vocabularies." *Journal of Educational Psychology,* 1940, *31,* pp. 14–38.

Selman, R. *The Growth of Interpersonal Understanding.* New York: Academic Press, 1980.

Seward, J. P., and Seward, G. H. *Sex Differences: Mental and Temperamental.* Lexington, MA: Lexington Books, 1980.

Shaffer, D. R. *Developmental Psychology,* 3rd ed. Pacific Grove, CA: Brooks/Cole, 1993.

Shonkoff, J. P. "The Biological Substrate and Physical Health in Middle Childhood." In W. A. Collins (Ed.), *Development During Middle Childhood: The Years from Six to Twelve* (pp. 24–69). Washington, DC: National Academy Press, 1984.

Shucard, D. "Linking Sex with Learning." *Science Digest,* 1982, March, p. 99.

Staffieri, J. "A Study of Social Stereotype of Body Image In Children." *Journal of Personality and Social Psychology."* 1967, *7,* pp. 101–104.

Staffieri, J. "Body Build and Behavioral Experiences in Young Females." *Developmental Psychology,* 1972, *6,* pp. 125–127.

Tanner, J. M. *Fetus into Man: Physical Growth from Conception into Maturity,* 2nd ed. Cambridge, MA: Harvard University Press, 1990.

Thomas, S. P., Groër, M., and Droppleman, P. "Physical Health of Today's School Children." *Educational Psychology Review,* 1993, *5,* pp. 5–33.

University of California, Berkeley, Wellness Letter, 1987, June, p. 2.

Waber, D. P. "Sex Differences in Cognition: A Function of Maturation Rate?" *Science,* 1976, *192,* pp. 572–573.

Walker, R. N. "Body Build of Behaviors in Young Children: I. Body Build & Nursery School Teachers' Ratings." *Monographs of the Society for Research in Child Development,* 1962, *27*(3).

Walker, R. N. "Body Build & Behavior in Young Children: II. Body Build & Parents' Ratings." *Child Development,* 1963, *34,* pp. 1–23.

Winock, M., ed. *Childhood Obesity.* New York: Wiley, 1975.

SELECTED READINGS OF RELATED INTEREST

Bee, H. *The Developing Child,* 6th ed. New York: Harper Collins, 1992. This fine text treats in greater detail many of the ideas about physical, social, and cognitive development only touched on in this chapter. A very readable book.

Mussen, P. H., Conger, J. J., Kagan, J., and Huston, A. C. *Child Development and Personality,* 7th ed. New York: Harper Collins, 1990. Written by acknowledged experts in child development, this volume has been around for many years. Parts three and four are particularly relevant to our discussion related to social and cognitive development in this chapter.

Segal, J., and Yahraes, M. *A Child's Journey: Forces that Shape the Lives of Our Young.* New York: McGraw-Hill, 1978. If I were to recommend a single book to give a person interested in knowing more about why and how children grow and develop the way they do, this would be it. Written to be read and understood.

Webb, P. A. *The Emerging Child: Development Through Age Twelve.* New York: Macmillan, 1989. One of the better books available that focuses on the early years of growth. Excellent section on personality and self-concept development.

4

The Adolescent Years

Behavioral Dynamics and Age-Level Characteristics

CHAPTER OVERVIEW

IMPORTANT CHAPTER IDEAS

1. Adolescence is not a universal happening; it is, in fact, a relatively recent phenomenon in Western societies.
2. Change is the outstanding characteristic of the adolescent years, which includes changes in physical features, emotionality, social functioning, and cognitive skills.
3. One can be psychologically adolescent long after physical adolescence has ceased.

4. Pace and rate of growth vary widely *between* the two sexes and *within* each sex.
5. Early-maturing boys enjoy certain personal and interpersonal advantages that are related to their accelerated growth. Slower-growing boys might experience somewhat more difficult times during their teenage years, but they are as likely to be successful in adulthood as anyone else.
6. Early-maturing girls tend to be taller and stockier than other girls in their age group, which makes many of them feel self-conscious and out of place.
7. Whereas the faster-growing boy may be a recipient of admiration for his advanced maturity, the faster-growing girl may be a recipient of concern because of her advanced sexuality.
8. Drug consumption, particularly alcohol, is a major problem among adolescents. More teenagers are killed in alcohol-related automobile crashes than all other accidents combined.
9. Each year about one million unmarried American girls between ages 15 and 19 become pregnant, which is almost 1 out of 10, a rate more than double that of the next highest countries.
10. A great many adolescent activities are done in groups and in same-sex or opposite-sex pairs. This is a normal outgrowth of increased involvement in peer group activities.
11. Whereas peer group values influence short-range plans, parental values are more likely to influence long-range goals.
12. The emotional life of the typical adolescent is a series of fluctuating ups and downs, which is quite normal for this state of development.
13. The search for a self-concept that fits is a major task of adolescents.
14. Adolescents are probably no more likely than any other age group to experience the problems and stresses of everyday living, but they *are* facing many of these problems for the first time, which might make their problems seem worse to them than they really are.
15. Intellectual abilities expand from thinking primarily in concrete here-and-now terms to the capacity to reason conceptually and hypothetically.
16. Although adolescents are better able to understand another person's point of view, they still have trouble understanding how that other point of view could be different from their own—an advanced state of egocentrism.

PROLOGUE

Change is the overriding feature of adolescence. Everything about the adolescent is altered, including physical characteristics, emotional functioning, social interactions, and cognitive ability. For example, between ages 11 and 15, depending on whether one is a boy or a girl, an adolescent may grow as much as 6 inches and gain as many as 30 pounds. Hair begins growing where it has never grown before, acne often erupts on various parts of the upper body and face, boys experience wet dreams, and girls begin menstruation. Socially, there are a greater number of group activities. Cliques are formed within these groups when friendships grow deeper and become more important. As new hormones surge through developing bodies, boy/girl relationships grow simultaneously more confusing, tempting, and exciting because of the complex chemistry and emotions of awakening sexuality. Cognitively, the typical adolescent shifts from thinking primarily in concrete here-and-now terms to thinking abstractly and hypothetically. All in all, adolescence is a time for adjusting to an influx of interactive biochemical and psychological changes, all of which are necessary to move from the safety of childhood dependency toward the challenge of adult maturity. It is a time for facing important questions: Who am I? Who do I want to be? How am I coming across to others? What do I want from my life? It is a time for making the transition from dependence to independence and, in the process, formulating an identity that incorporates the child into the adult that is emerging. There are innumerable starts and stops, and stumbles and falls in the process. It is all part of growing up and growing away.

We begin our journey through adolescence by turning first to an important question.

WHAT IS ADOLESCENCE?

This question is not as self-evident as it may seem. There has always been, and continues to be, some confusion about the meaning of adolescence. There is a reason for this.

Adolescence is neither a universal happening nor does it have lengthy historical credentials. The *Oxford English Dictionary,* for example, traces the term only to the fifteenth century. Prior to that, the idea of childhood hardly existed, let alone childhood beyond puberty, as the term adolescence suggests. The early Greeks and Romans, for instance, did not view what we call adolescence as a separate growth stage, except for the relatively brief one- to two-year period it took to develop from sexual immaturity to sexual maturity. Although the Roman emperor Claudius was regarded by his Claudian and Julian relatives to be somewhat dull and slow in developing, he nonetheless married at age 12 and became emperor at age 13. Shakespeare's tragic heroine Juliet was only 14 at the time of the fateful events in her abbreviated life.

The leap from childhood straight into adulthood with no adolescent apprenticeship was typical not only of classical culture but also of the Middle Ages and Renaissance as well. Early cultures were not age graded. For both those who went to school and those who did not, the age of adulthood in most of early Western culture was 7 years old. Even today, adolescence as a separate growth stage is often a nonexistent concept in some cultures. Within some hunting cultures, childhood is considered to be over by age 8, and within some agrarian cultures, it ceases anywhere between ages 10 and 12 (Dusek, 1991).

The prolonged postponement to full adult status after puberty is a relatively recent phenomenon in Western societies. Until several hundred years ago in Western society, and persisting even today in many tribal cultures, the physical changes accompanying puberty, usually celebrated by some type of ceremonial observance, automatically opened the doors to adulthood. However, as Western societies grow more complex, industrialized, and technological, the period of childhood apprenticeship has been extended so that adolescence is now a bona fide and important developmental period. It has been lengthened because, as the number of adult roles and responsibilities has multiplied, an increasingly longer period of learning in preparation for adult status has become necessary.

Although our culture contains numerous "micro-rites" of passage to signal an adolescent's entrance into adulthood, there is no universal indicator of adulthood. Indeed, those micro-rites that do exist may even conflict with one another. For example, although it is now possible under the Twenty-Sixth Amendment for all 18-year-olds to vote in all elections, the age at which a young person can buy alcoholic beverages may be set anywhere from age 18 to 21, depending on his or her state of residence. In some states the minimum age required in order to obtain a driver's license is 16, while in others it is 18. And, of course, one needs to be only 18 to become a member of the armed services.

All in all, there is a good bit of confusion about what adolescence means and when it ends. Adult ambiguity about adolescence reinforces adolescents' ambiguity about themselves. For instance, if you are to address a group of adolescents, how would you express the salutation? Do you call them "teenagers?" "Boys and girls?" "Ladies and gentlemen?" It's difficult to know what is appropriate.

It may be helpful to think of adolescence in terms of its two major components: psychological adolescence and physical adolescence.

Psychological Adolescence

In a purely *psychological* sense, the meaning of adolescence refers more to a life-style, an attitude, a way of looking at the world that begins with puberty and ends when one is relatively independent of parental control. As you know from your own observations, the cessation of psychological adolescence can vary from individual to individual. Most youths are eager to grow up and to become economically independent and emotionally responsible adults. As this occurs, psychological adolescence is left behind, and young adulthood begins. Some youths, however, do not easily make this transition and persist as psychological adolescents into their twenties and, sadly, sometimes even into their thirties.

Adolescence, then, begins with signs of sexual maturity in both physical and social development and ends when young people become self-supporting, responsible, and are accepted in most ways by the reference-group peers toward whom they look for some measure of approval, recognition, and advice. I want to emphasize the importance of shifting one's needs for approval, recognition, and advice to the peer group because the major symptom of persisting psychological adolescence is the continued dependence on parents as a major source of approval, recognition, and guidance. Jourard (1968), for example, found that many undergraduate college students who used the counseling center had more trouble talking to their peers than to their parents, which would suggest that older adolescents who have not weaned themselves away from parents are more apt to have social-emotional problems than those who are more independent and peer related. One does not have to give up completely the idea of needing anything from one's parents, whether it be their counsel or their love, in order to be a mature adult. Concern centers on the *degree* to which an individual remains dependent on his parents and needs them for emotional and social support when physical adolescence is completed. A 27-year-old man who continues to live at home when he could be supporting himself or a 23-year-old woman who gives up her vocational plans because her parents disapprove could very well be psychologically adolescent in their dependency ties and ability to think for themselves.

Psychological adolescence, then, has reference to the idea that a person is basically dependent on parents for economic support and/or at a level of psychological development similar to what we might expect of adolescents of a particular age.

Physical Adolescence

In a strictly *physical* sense, adolescence is a universal phenomenon. What varies are the meanings and expectations that various cultures and subcultures place on youth as they move through this growth stage. Physically, adolescence commences with the prepubertal growth spurt and ends with the attainment of full physical maturity. Although physical maturity is difficult to define with precision, it usually refers to reaching the upper limits of one's genetic potential for endocrine development, skeletal growth, and total height.

4.1 When Is an Adolescent No Longer Adolescent?

What is it about the adolescent growth stage that makes it so difficult to determine when it starts and when it ends? Why do you suppose it is that, as a culture, we are so ambiguous about adolescence, particularly in terms of the time span it should occupy? To think about this in a more personal way, how will you (or did you) know your own adolescence was over?

PHYSICAL DEVELOPMENT: BASIC CHARACTERISTICS

Adolescence includes several distinct periods of developmental change. Pubescence (sometimes called preadolescence) refers to the two years preceding puberty and to the physical changes occurring during that time. Puberty follows pubescence and is marked by specific indicators of sexual maturity. For girls, puberty is the onset of menstruation, and for boys, the most valid indicator is probably the presence of live spermatozoa, or male reproductive cells, in the urine. This may or may not coincide with the emergence of pigmented pubic hair, which is the most observable outer sign of sexual maturity in boys (Tanner, 1990).

An adolescent's body changes markedly in form and function during this stage of development. Boys develop wider shoulders, and girls, wider hips. Strength and stamina increase, and correspondingly, so does the capacity for work and play. Girls buy their first bras, and boys shave their first whiskers.

Arm and leg growth reach their peak during early adolescence, which accounts for the long, gangly look that some youngsters have at this time. In addition, evidence suggests a general "going-togetherness" of growth (Garrison, 1976). For example, there is a close correspondence between the onset of menstruation and the age when the bones of the fingers become fused. Appearance of pubic hair in boys is closely associated with skeletal development of the hand. Similar relationships are apparent in other aspects of skeletal and muscle growth, as well as primary and secondary sexual development. When growth is occurring in one part of the body, it is going on in other parts as well.

Growth Occurs at a Rapid but Variable Rate

Development progresses at a rapid rate with the onset of puberty. There is a dramatic increase in body size, corresponding changes in body composition, and a rapid development of reproductive organs.

Research has consistently shown that in every age group some youngsters will be ahead of their peers in terms of physical, mental, social, and emotional development, while others will lag behind (Schuster, 1980). For example, the growth spurt may begin as early as 9.5 years or as late as 13.5 in boys. Most boys, however, begin their growth acceleration at about 12 years, reach a growth peak between 13.5 and 14 years, and decline sharply to pre–growth-spurt rates by about 15.5. Growth goes on at a slower pace for several years thereafter. On the average, boys grow eight inches between the ages of 11 and 15.

For girls, the adolescent growth spurt may be as early as 8.5 years (seldom) or as late as 11.5 years. The average girl, however, begins her stint of rapid acceleration at about age 10, reaches a peak between 11.5 and 12 years, and then decreases to pre–growth-spurt rates by about age 13. Boys' growth continues, but at a slower pace, for the next several years. On the average, girls grow about four inches between the ages of 11 and 14. Figure 4.1 may help give you a visual idea of the variations in growth rate between boys and girls in the same age groupings. During this period of rapid growth in height, boys increase their weight by an average of twelve pounds and girls by about ten pounds. Part of this weight gain can be attributed to an increase in fatty tissue around the hips and thighs for girls and a broadening of the shoulders and increased lean-muscle tissue for boys (Garbarino, 1985).

Along with the increase in height and weight during this period, some less dramatic changes also occur. For example, the low forehead becomes higher and wider, the mouth widens and the lips fill out, and the slightly receding childhood chin begins to assert itself. The nose grows larger and loses much of its pudginess. In addition, the large head, characteristic of the childhood years, continues to become smaller in proportion to total body length. (Actually, it does not really grow smaller, but appears to because the trunk and extremities are growing so rapidly.) Because of these critical changes, most youngsters between the ages of 11 and 13 look increasingly like the adults they are becoming, at least so far as facial features are concerned.

Hormonal Activity Increases

Many of the most noteworthy physical changes that occur during adolescence are those stemming from altered endocrine functioning due to an increased output of hormones from the pituitary gland (Dreyer, 1982). This gland, located in the brain, is primarily responsible for growth and serves to monitor the hormone balance of the body. The gonadotropic hormone secreted by the pituitary stimulates the activity of the gonads or sex glands, which in turn produce the sex hormones and the growth of mature sperm in males and ova in females.

In the female, hormones from the ovaries (estrogen) stimulate development of the breasts, uterus, fallopian tubes, and vagina. In addition, estrogen produces the secondary sex characteristics, including the growth of pubic and axillary hair, increased activity of the sweat glands, and a broadening of the hips.

In the male, hormones from the testes (testosterone) stimulate growth of the prostate gland, seminal vesicles, penis, and such secondary characteristics as broadened shoulders, a deeper voice, and, as in the female, growth of pubic and axillary hair and increased sweat gland activity. In addition, male hormonal activity stimulates muscle development so that males grow both stronger and larger. In many cases, the plumpness of late childhood is replaced by a firmer, more angular build, although there are many individual differences.

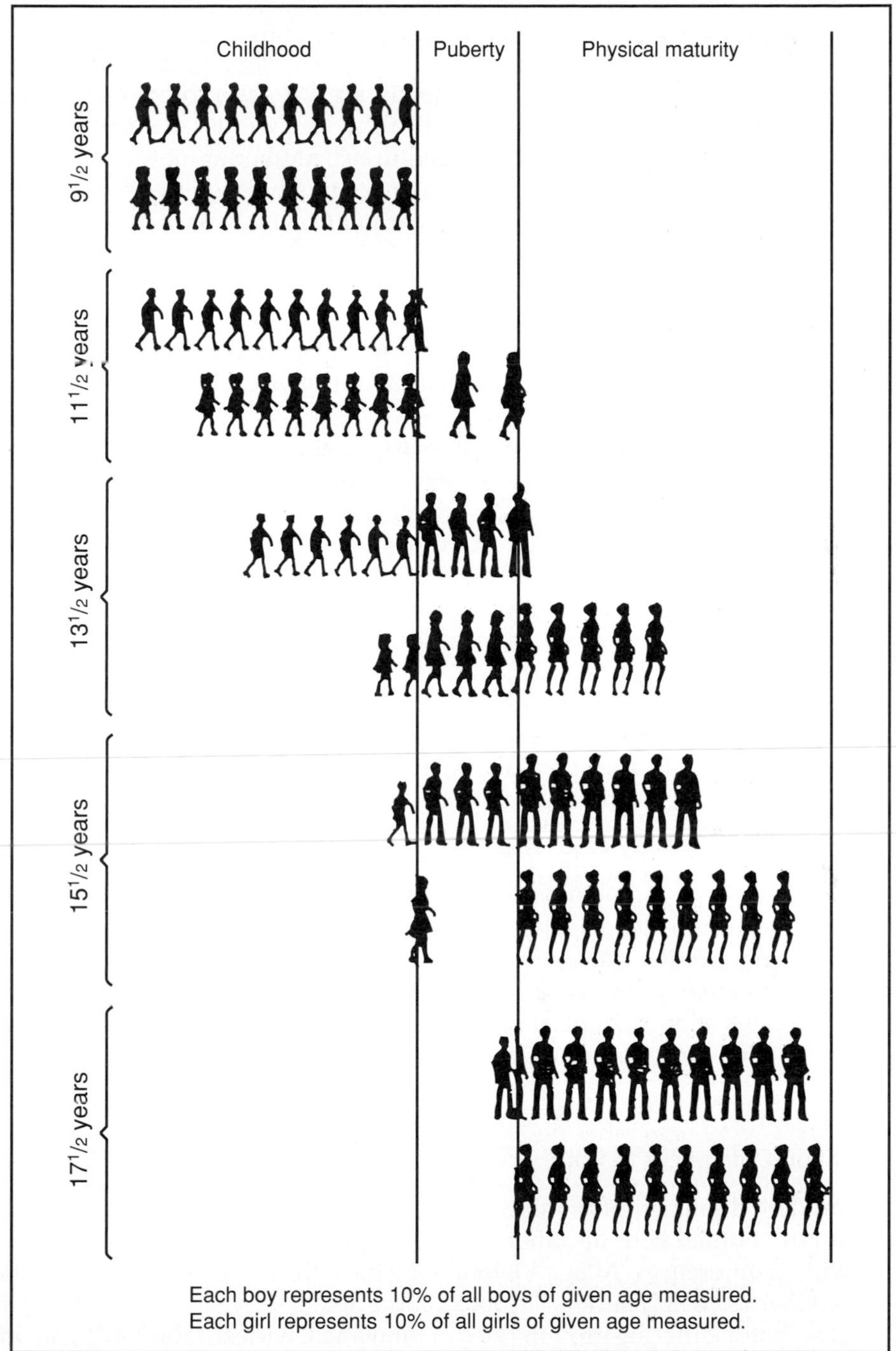

Figure 4.1. RELATIVE AGES AT WHICH BOYS AND GIRLS MATURE.

Adolescents Grow Bigger and Faster

If bigger is better, then the youths of today are a great improvement indeed. Compared to his father at maturity, a healthy boy will be one to two inches taller and ten pounds heavier; compared to her mother at maturity, a healthy girl will be about one inch taller and two pounds heavier. (Remember, these are averages, so we can expect to find many individual variations.) One hundred years ago, males did not reach their full adult height until age 25; today, most boys accomplish that by age 18 or 19 (Chumlea, 1982). It is interesting to note, by the way, that 17- to 19-year-old girls average about three pounds *lighter* than their counterparts fifty years ago, a fact that undoubtedly reflects changes in both dietary habits and ideas about physical attractiveness (Dion, 1986).

Further, girls are reaching sexual maturity at an earlier age. For example, over the past 150 years or so, the average age of menarche in Western societies has dropped from 14 or 15 to 12, which may be due in part to improved nutrition and sanitation. In support of this view, Tanner (1981) has noted that in technologically simple societies in New Guinea, for instance, the average age of menarche is still 15 to 18 years. This is also true among adolescent girls in rural Mexican villages, where nutrition and sanitation may be poor. However, in the more developed parts of Mexico, girls begin menstruation at about the same age as girls in the United States and Western Europe.

Are we destined to become a species of giants, forever growing bigger and faster? We can only speculate about this, but the evidence available so far suggests that the growth spurt may be leveling out. Dreyer (1982) cites, for example, that the age at which boys attain full growth and girls reach menarche in industrial nations began to stabilize in the 1950s. The well-fed segments of these populations seem to be reaching their maximum potential. One physical anthropologist has estimated that under optimal conditions, the average height of the human male will be about six feet (Krogman, 1970). In order to have that as an average, remember that some men will have to be as short as five feet and as tall as seven feet. Basketball players and jockeys will still be in abundance for future generations.

Effects of Maturation Differences in Boys

It would no doubt simplify matters if all boys the same age grew at about the same rate, but, as with all other aspects of growth, there is a wide range of individual differences. At age 13, John may have the body of a 17-year-old boy, while Charles, who really is 17, looks more like a 13-year-old. What are the effects of these differing growth rates in John and Charles? (You can get an idea of what a fast-maturing and a slow-maturing boy of the same age look like in Figure 4.2.) Because adolescents tend to be enormously preoccupied with their

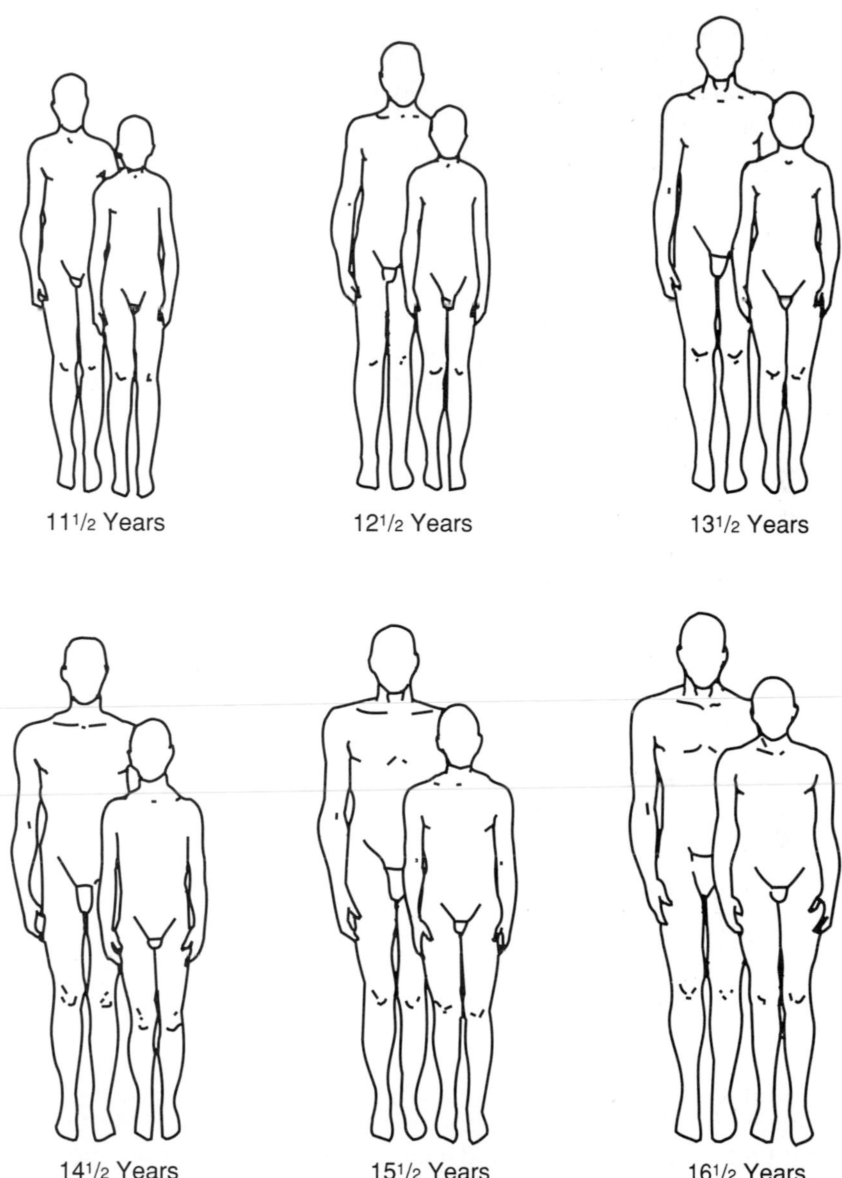

Figure 4.2. DIFFERENTIAL GROWTH OF AN EARLY-MATURING AND A LATE-MATURING BOY.

(From Shuttleworth, F. K. "The Adolescent Period: A Pictorial Atlas." *Monographs of the Society for Research in Child Development* [Ser. no. 59]. 14 [1949]. Copyright © The Society for Research in Child Development, Inc.)

appearance and body changes, rate of growth has both short-term and long-term effects. On the whole, research has consistently found that, for boys in particular, maturing slightly ahead of one's peers is accompanied by distinct social advantages (Gross and Duke, 1980; Lerner and Foch, 1987; Mussen and Jones, 1957; Petersen, 1987). Faster-growing boys such as John, for example, tend to have more positive self-concepts. They are inclined to be more independent, self-confident, and self-reliant than their slower-growing peers. In addition, they report higher levels of personal satisfaction and more positive feelings about themselves. Perhaps a reason for this is that they tend to be more widely accepted and liked by both peers and adults. All of these findings may help explain why early-maturing boys tend to be more matter-of-fact about themselves, and why they have less need to strive for status and recognition. This general air of confidence may be one of the reasons why they are frequently chosen for leadership positions in high school. Research suggests that boys who mature early are poised, relaxed, good-natured, and relatively stable. It is worth noting that boys who mature at an average age have about as many relative advantages as those who mature early (Clausen, 1975).

Slower-maturing boys such as Charles, however, tend to have a somewhat more difficult time of it (Lerner and Foch, 1987; Mussen and Jones, 1957; Petersen, 1987; Weatherly, 1964). Boys who mature late tend to be anxious, tense, and dependent. In addition, they are more likely to behave in childish, affected, and attention-seeking ways, which might explain why they are apt to be less accepted by their peers, more dominated by their parents, and chosen for so few leadership positions. During adolescence, at least, late maturers suffer as many disadvantages as early-maturing boys enjoy advantages.

Although life for slower-maturing boys is somewhat dismal to begin with, the picture brightens as they catch up and move into young adulthood. Findings from ongoing longitudinal and in-depth studies indicate that early maturers perhaps pay a price for their moment of glory in adolescence, and that late maturers are compensated for their early agonies (Peskin, 1973; Siegel, 1982). As adults, early maturers tend to be anxious about not doing well or not being liked, concerned about appearances, and somewhat rigid about how they live their lives.

However, these same insecure, anxious, late-maturing boys tend to be more expressive, curious, and flexible as adults. Surprisingly, they are apt to have better senses of humor and handle ambiguous situations more easily than their faster-growing cohorts, a behavior that reflects their flexibility. Having to work a bit harder to survive in a tough world may be one of the reasons they have learned to be flexible and develop a sense of humor. It is a little easier with these qualities. In addition, late-maturing boys simply have more time to prepare for their status as an adult.

To summarize: early-maturing boys do seem to enjoy certain personal and interpersonal advantages in adolescence primarily because others' perceptions and expectations of them are positive. This obviously helps them feel good about themselves. On the positive side, this frequently lends itself to competitive advantages (e.g., notice the size of football and basketball team members). On the negative side, it sometimes means that the adolescent boy responds to expectations sometimes determined more by size and appearance than by other aspects of maturing. Later-maturing boys appear, and sometimes behave, younger than they are, which only makes it more difficult for them to survive in the fickle social world of their peers. Available evidence suggests that they are, as young adults, as much on the path to making it as anyone else, and perhaps, in some cases, even more so because of the adaptive strategies they had to learn when younger.

4.2 As a Male, What Was Your Physical Growth Like?

This may be a good time for a little reflection. Think back over your own adolescence. What do you remember about the growth status of boys at your school who were popular, well-liked, athletic, and leaders in various ways? How about those who may not have enjoyed those advantages? What similarities or differences in behavior do you see between what research has found between faster- and slower-growing boys and what you remember from your own experiences? If you are male, how does this discussion fit your own experience in adolescence?

Effects of Maturation Differences in Girls

The outcome of early or late maturation for girls is somewhat more complex than it is for boys. (Figure 4.3 will give you an idea of the growth differences between the typical early-maturing and late-maturing girls.) Whereas a faster-maturing boy tends to be heavier and taller than his peers, a rapidly growing girl may only be stockier and heavier, but not necessarily taller than her peers. This can cause self-image problems, since a heavier, stockier body runs counter to the tall, slim ideal, at least in North America (Dion, 1986). Early-maturing girls encounter another problem. Because girls begin to mature sooner than boys, something that faster growers do on an even earlier schedule, rapidly developing girls look especially conspicuous in the sixth and seventh grades. (A quick look at the faster-growing girls between ages 11.5 and 12.5 in Figure 4.3 will help you see why.) This can trigger two problems. First, since faster-growing girls in those grades look very much unlike their female counterparts, they feel self-conscious and different. As expressed by an early-maturing young lady while discussing personal feelings about her own growth experience, "I didn't like what was happening to me at all. I felt like I was a woman before I was through being a girl and I was only in the sixth grade." Second, particularly for girls who develop rapidly in the sixth, seventh, and eighth

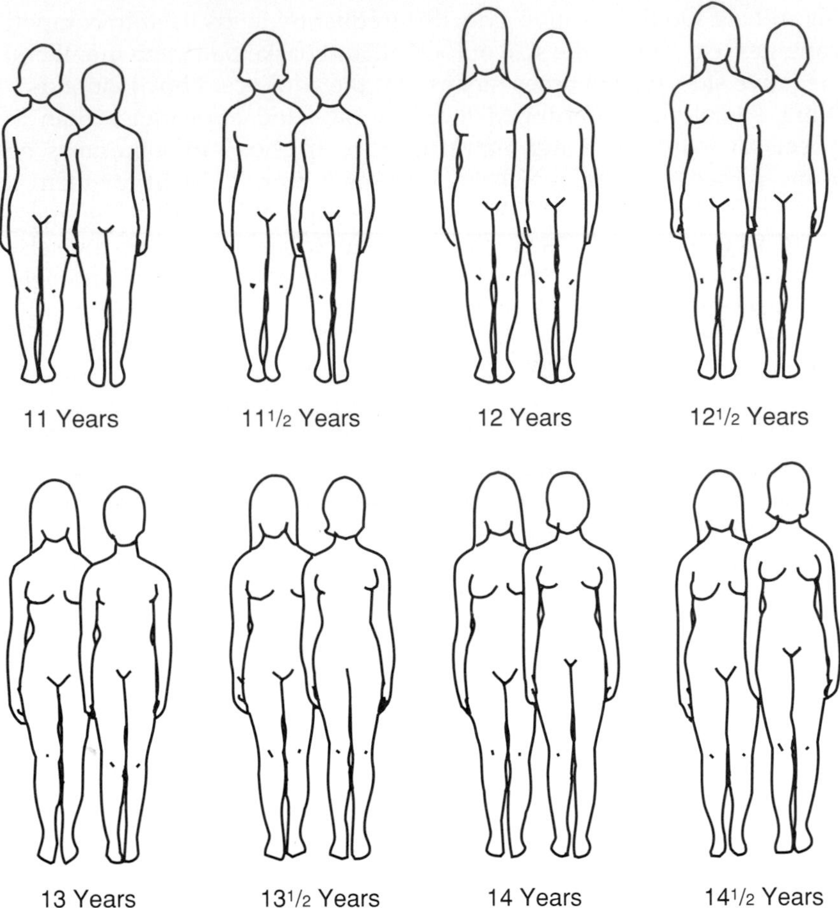

Figure 4.3. DIFFERENTIAL GROWTH OF AN EARLY-MATURING AND A LATE-MATURING GIRL.

(From Shuttleworth, F. K. "The Adolescent Period: A Pictorial Atlas." *Monographs of the Society for Research in Child Development* [Ser. no. 59]. 14 [1949]. Copyright © The Society for Research in Child Development, Inc.)

grades, is the difficulty that these girls have interacting with boys in their own age group. Although they have reached puberty and are ready to socialize with boys, most boys have not yet made that transition. It should not surprise us when we find an early-developing seventh-grade girl look favorably and hopefully at a tenth-grade boy.

The early-maturing boy is welcomed into the ready-made roles of school leader and athlete. Both parents and peers (and coaches) admire him. The welcome mat to maturity is much smaller for early-maturing girls. Rather than see her blossoming physique as simply a sign of early maturity, it is more likely to be viewed as a source of potential sexual trouble. Parents might brag about a son's manly size; they are not as likely to crow about a young daughter's curvaceous figure.

Overall, research shows that, for girls, as opposed to boys, the rate of physical maturation is a much less influential variable mediating personality development (Brooks-Gun and Petersen, 1983; Hamachek, 1980). Why should this be? One possible reason might be related to the fact that the cultural sex-role prescription for males in our society is relatively clear, and places a high value on attributes associated with physical strength, coordination, and athletic deftness, especially in the adolescent and young adulthood years. For girls, the feminine sex-role prescription is still somewhat ambiguous and is therefore not as likely to be connected to any specific pattern of physical attributes.

Slow but steady progress is being made in destereotyping how young girls and women are supposed to be. Indeed, one of the healthy outgrowths of the women's movement seems to be a gradual shift in social expectations away from traditional, stereotyped views about what constitutes masculine and feminine behavior to a more realistic stance that recognizes that a girl can be strong and assertive without being masculine and that a boy can be warm and sensitive without being effeminate. As social expectations change, adolescent boys and girls might feel freer to experience and develop more aspects of their total selves, rather than just the culturally accepted aspects.

4.3 As a Female, What Was Your Physical Growth Like?

Given what you have just read about the effects of differential growth rates in girls, how does the knowledge we have about this square with your own observations and experience? If female, how do the research findings fit with your experience as an early- or late-maturer? Given your particular growth rate at that time, what was most difficult for you? What kinds of adjustment problems did you have? What did teachers do that made it harder or easier for you as you went through your own physical development?

Overview of Physical Development Outcomes and Their Implications for Teachers

1. *Growth accelerates rapidly, especially for boys, some of whom add as much as six inches and twenty-five pounds in a single year.* This period of rapid growth can begin as early as the sixth grade and involves almost all junior high students. There are great variations among individual students of the same sex and, particularly, there are dramatic physical development differences between boys and girls. For example, looking back at Figures 4.2 and 4.3, you can see

that 12.5-year-old girls are already as advanced developmentally as 14.5-year-old boys.

As teachers, we can be aware that these dramatic changes in growth during adolescence have both physical and psychological consequences. How adolescents react to such changes, including their perceived attractiveness or unattractiveness and their treatment of others, greatly affects how they evaluate themselves. This is why physical and psychological development are highly interrelated (Petersen, 1981). As a teacher, you can help your students accept themselves as changing persons by using your awareness of those changes in understanding ways. As an example of what I mean here, I remember that as a ninth-grader in high school, I desperately wanted to go out for the football team, but I felt "I'm just not big enough," a concern that I expressed to Mr. Kranz, our physical education teacher. He patiently explained to me some of the very growth facts we have been considering in this chapter, especially the idea that it was not uncommon for some boys to grow more slowly than others. He suggested that, since both of my parents were a bit above average height, I would probably grow more in the next couple of years. He outlined a simple weight-lifting program that would help me add some bulk and advised me not to worry about it, that I would grow more in good time. I was an enormously relieved 14-year-old boy, and I have never forgotten those 15 minutes with Mr. Kranz. I did, by the way, take his advice about lifting some weights, and between the weight-lifting and adding a couple inches of stature, this happy 15-year-old made the team the next year. I have often wondered how it may have turned out if Mr. Kranz had not shared with me his time, knowledge, and understanding.

2. *The adolescent years are the healthiest years of life when compared to later years and judged in terms of mortality rates and causes of death.* When adolescents do meet death, it is more likely to be from some form of violence rather than from disease. Car crashes, homicide, and suicide, in that order, account for almost 80% of deaths among adolescents and young adults between 15 and 24 years of age (Seifert and Hoffnung, 1987). Up to 50% of all fatal automobile crashes are alcohol related, which translates into approximately 25,000 deaths annually (Jaccard and Turrisi, 1987). Of this number, it has been estimated that about 14,000 of those deaths are adolescents and young adults, which is more than all other accidents combined (Seifert and Hoffnung, 1987).

Drug consumption, including alcohol, is a serious problem, one involving huge numbers. Spickard and Thompson (1985) estimated that as many as 3.3 million teenagers alternate between using alcohol and illegal drugs. Among the 18 to 25 year age group, 72% report that they are current users of alcohol (U.S. Census Bureau, 1988). Although there are signs of a reduction in the use of marijuana and other drugs, it is worth noting that alcohol and other drug use after high school is predictable from senior-year drug use (Johnson, O'Malley, and Bachman, 1985).

Adolescence is a time for testing and experimentation, which is why reckless things are sometimes done, such as drinking too much, driving too fast, and in other ways going beyond the limits of reason and safety. As teachers, we face the challenge of both modeling and teaching responsible ways of living without falling into the trap of being preachy and moralistic.

3. *Many adolescents have confused ideas about their sexual feelings and relationships.* It is a small wonder that there is confusion. Parents, churches, and society in general say no, do not do it. Peers, erotic movies, stimulating reading material, suggestive dress, and raging hormones say yes, go ahead.

Many do go ahead, and some become very young mothers and fathers. Each year, about one million unmarried girls between the ages of 15 and 19 become pregnant, which, startlingly, is almost 1 out of 10 (DeRidder, 1993). This rate is more than double those in the next highest countries, England and Wales. In an effort to find out why so many more American girls are getting pregnant than girls in countries similar to the United States in economic background and development, Brozan's (1985) analysis of studies related to this problem revealed some interesting facts. American teenagers are no more sexually active than their foreign peers. Nor is the difference due to higher abortion rates abroad—they are much higher here. For example, 60 out of every 1000 American women have had an abortion by age 18. In contrast, the rates are 30 per 1000 in Sweden, the next highest country in abortion use, and 7 per 1000 in the Netherlands, which ranks lowest. Maternity and welfare benefits do not appear to promote teenage pregnancy either, because other countries provide more generous support.

Why, then, do so many more American teenagers get pregnant? The answer seems to lie in the peculiarly American combination of a liberal sexual climate and a reluctance to help teenagers avoid pregnancy. Teenage sex is an intensely emotional issue in America, and one that taps into deep religious convictions. Whereas the goal of many U.S. lawmakers and religious groups is to promote abstinence as well as responsible sex among the young, the goal of public policy in most European and other countries is aimed at preventing teenage pregnancy. It is interesting and instructive to note that the countries with the lowest rates have easily accessible and free contraceptives for young people, with no required parental notification. These countries also have comprehensive sex education programs throughout their school systems.

As teachers, there is probably not much we can do directly to help adolescents with sexual problems and conflicts (this is a volatile political-religious issue in most schools), but what we can do is answer questions honestly, and realistically accept adolescent sexuality as a necessary part of growing up. It is easy to moralize to young people about how they "should" behave, but nothing is likely to turn off an adolescent boy or girl more quickly. With the AIDS scourge becoming a worldwide concern, there is an even greater urgency for sane and rational responses to the problem of teenage sexuality.

4.4 A Pregnancy Question

> Let us say you have been selected to be on a committee of adults and teenagers who have been charged with the responsibility of developing a policy statement that will influence: 1) whether sex education classes are taught in your school, and 2) if they are taught, what the content of those classes should be. What recommendations would you argue for?

SOCIAL DEVELOPMENT: BASIC CHARACTERISTICS

Adolescence is an intensely social period in the developmental continuum. Although most adolescents were also fairly social and interactive during their middle childhood years, the social experiences they have as teens are accompanied by a large psychological difference, namely enormous self-consciousness. Preoccupied as they are with their changing bodies and newly felt social status as semi-adults, younger adolescents tend to constantly monitor their appearance and actions. It is as if they are on stage playing before what Elkind (1980) has called an "imaginary audience." Thus, much of their behavior is shaped to impress that audience, especially its critics, or to conceal aspects of themselves they want to keep hidden. If you can imagine what it would feel like to walk across the front of a large room filled with people, all of them looking in your direction (or so you think), you may have an idea (or a memory) of what it is like to be a self-conscious adolescent.

A great many adolescent activities are done in groups, in subgroups or cliques with the groups, and in same-sex or opposite-sex pairs. The participants' primary motivation is not necessarily to know others (although that is part of it), but to know themselves through feedback from others.

Overview of Social Development Outcomes and Their Implications for Teachers

1. *Peer group relationships become increasingly important during the junior high and high school years.* Peer group influence hits its peak during the high school years, and then, after high school, begins to decline as young people go their separate ways. However, during the junior high and high school years, adolescents have a "youth culture" of their own, overlapping with, yet separate from, the larger society in which they live.

The peer group has an enormous impact on an adolescent's social development and sense of self. Why is the adolescent peer culture so successful in shaping the behavior and self-attitudes of young people? In a timeless response to this question, Medinnus and Johnson (1969) answer as follows:

> It succeeds because it is dangerous and exciting and requires real skills . . . because it is *not* based on such things as class distinctions, which are contrary to our expressed adult values system but not to our actual behavior; because it is based on the idea that the individual should be judged in terms of personal attributes and accomplishments; because it is in many ways more humane and accepting of individual differences than adult cultural values; because it is concerned with expanding self-awareness at a time when people have few means of discovering themselves; because it is against sham; and because it fulfills the needs of young people better than does the adult culture. (p. 709)

At least six important functions have been identified that are most directly associated with peer group involvement (Hamachek, 1980). They are as follows:

a. To some extent, *the peer group takes the place of the family;* a youngster can feel a particular status, or lack of it, independent of his or her family. This is invaluable preparation for adulthood because it gives one a chance for more objective feedback than parents can usually provide.

b. *Peer group membership is a useful stabilizer* during a period of rapid transition. In light of the incredible hormonal, developmental, and social changes that occur during the brief period of adolescence, it is comforting to know that others are going through the same thing. As one 16-year-old boy put it, "I hate these dumb pimples, but I'd hate them more if I was the only one who had them."

c. *The peer group can be an important source of self-esteem* in the sense of being important to someone outside the primary family unit. Of course, it can work the other way, too, particularly for the adolescent who is isolated or scapegoated.

d. *The peer group insulates and protects* adolescents to some extent from the coercions that adults are likely to impose on young people. When adolescents say something on the order of "Everyone else is going (or doing it, or wearing it, or whatever), why can't I?" they are raising what has become an almost universal wail of defensive protest designed to persuade restricting adults to change their minds. As you can imagine (or remember from your own adolescent years), there is safety in lodging this protest while holding membership within the security of one's peer group. There is both safety and strength in numbers, and membership in the peer culture provides a little of each.

e. *The peer group provides an opportunity to practice by doing.* Dating, participation in extracurricular activities, and bull sessions about life, sex, future goals, and the world in general are important rehearsals for eventual adulthood.

f. *The peer group offers an important source of feedback.* Although adolescents might have that "imaginary audience" to whom they act out their parts and play their various roles, they also have that real audience—their peers. Teens are constantly commenting on one another's "performance." It is feedback that, because of its objectivity and honesty, helps them fine-tune how they present themselves to others and how they feel about themselves. Girls are better at giving and receiving feedback because they spend more time talking and disclosing to each other, an affinity that persists into adulthood. Boys, however, might give and get less feedback, at least from one another, because the things they do together are, when compared with girls' activities, more activity oriented (Berndt, 1982; Tesch, 1983).

Please do not conclude that boys seldom talk to each other in disclosing, personal ways. They do interact at that level, but not as *much* as girls do. It is a matter of degree. Females are inclined to engage in more face-to-face interactions (men do more side-by-side activities) and are more skilled than men in doing so, which may explain why males, from adolescence onward, tend to prefer to talk to females about personal matters (Brehm, 1985).

2. *Peer group values and outlooks are likely to influence short-range plans, but parents are more likely to influence long-range goals.* Although teenagers as a group move initially in the direction of the more liberal peer group, when it comes to life-shaping choices such as occupational preference, moral-ethical development, and political behavior, they are more inclined to lean in the direction of the primary family values (Conger, 1991; Crites, 1980; Gallatin, 1980).

It appears that when an adolescent has to decide what to wear, what kind of haircut to get, or what to do on the weekend—decisions that have to do with social or identity needs—what his or her friends are wearing or doing will make the greatest difference. However, when adolescence is wrapped up in the album of high school memories, the young adults looking back on them will be reflecting the values and outlooks that look suspiciously like the parental values they once questioned.

There are exceptions to this. For example, where parental warmth and a sense of equal rights within the home are minimal, as is sometimes the case, the peer group might provide both the security and the models that youngsters need. The greater the wall between the adolescent and his or her family, the more important the values of the peer culture are likely to become. When this happens, family input diminishes and peer input increases as a reference source for both short- and long-range thinking and planning.

As a teacher, it is helpful to remember that in the eyes of adolescents you are a member of the adult world whose values they are questioning. It is a necessary part of growing up. If you can keep that in mind, it might help you to both understand and accept the idea that your impact on them might not be felt so much in the short run, when they are immersed in their own adolescent defensiveness, as it will be remembered in the long run when they become adults themselves. Your influence on them in terms of what they learn is right around the corner; in terms of what they become, that is further down the road.

4.5 How About Your Own Peer Experiences?

When you reflect back to your teen years, how did peer relationships influence your development at that time? As you look at it more objectively now, what are some specific examples of how peer pressure influenced your behavior? How was the peer group important to your social-emotional development? Consider this: would you choose to allow your own children to associate with the same sort of gang or clique that you once did, and do some of the same things you did? Will that be a good thing for them? Why or why not? Can you think of anything else to add to the list of peer group functions just discussed?

EMOTIONAL DEVELOPMENT: BASIC CHARACTERISTICS

The emotional life of the typical adolescent is a series of fluctuating ups and downs, with the ups being very up and the downs being very down. Nothing, for example, is more exhilarating than being in love for the first time, and nothing is more despairing than falling out of love for the first time. Lacking an experiential base against which to measure their highs and lows, life for adolescents usually seems much better or a lot worse than it really is. Adolescence is a time for shedding the comfortable dependency of childhood and preparing for the independence of adulthood. Emotionally, adolescents tend to be less stable because a great deal is happening in this metamorphosis between childhood and adulthood.

Overview of Emotional Development Outcomes and Their Implications for Teachers

1. *Adolescence is not so much a period of "storm and stress" as it is a time of change and redefinition.* Overall, the usual pattern of development in adolescence is essentially positive. For example, Petersen (1987) found in her study of 335 adolescents that more than 50% seemed to be almost trouble-free, while approximately 30% of the total group had only intermittent problems. Only about 15% had ongoing problems of a more serious sort.

2. *Although adolescents are no more likely than any other age group to experience the problems and stresses of day-to-day living, it is helpful to remember that they are experiencing these problems for the first time and might have somewhat more difficulty coping with them.* In addition, there are enormous pressures to achieve, to get good grades, and to prepare oneself for work in a society that is growing increasingly more specialized and technological.

Adolescents have to make many emotional adjustments. The adolescent might have to adjust to any or all of the following:

a. From going to the same school, attending classes in the same room, with the same classmates and the same teacher, to attending various classes, each with a new set of classmates and a different teacher.

b. From being among the largest, oldest, and most experienced students in elementary school to being among the smallest, youngest, and least sophisticated in high school.

c. From having to think ahead only as far as tomorrow to increased pressure to think ahead to the future.

d. From depending almost entirely on parents to take care of all the basic needs to assuming increased responsibility for taking care of one's own needs.

e. From thinking essentially and simplistically in terms of "What can I do?"—with allowance, time, friends, and so on—to thinking more abstractly along the lines of "Who am I, and what do I want to be?"

As teachers, we need to remember that each adjustment is a necessary prerequisite to eventual adult responsibility. These adjustments are not always easy to make and adolescents need as much support and guidance as we can muster in helping them through these times. Among other reasons, this is why counseling and guidance programs and personnel are so important in junior and senior high school.

3. *Depression is the most common emotional experience among adolescents.* Some depressions are more severe than others, but for the most part practically every teenager experiences depression to some degree. It is part of the moodiness we frequently associate with teenage behavior. So many things happen simultaneously—psychologically, physically, and socially—that one simply feels overpowered from time to time. Depression can be a consequence of such feelings and frequently is a natural, normal response to circumstances that seem larger than life and to feelings that leave one with a sense of helplessness and lowered self-confidence. Depression is a kind of time-out period, an opportunity for regrouping one's thinking and recharging the emotional battery (Mayo Clinic, 1989).

Be careful not to overrespond to adolescent depression. Remember that things usually seem a bit worse than they really are to the typical teenager. A supportive, nonjudgmental response from you as a teacher can work wonders. (Say, "I know how it feels to be down, Chris; hope you feel better soon," rather than, "Oh, come on, Chris, it's silly to feel that way. Nothing is that bad.")

The seriousness of a depressed, or any other, emotional state is usually measured in terms of its duration and intensity. If it lasts a long time (beyond two days is a long time) and seems deep and profound, you have clues to a problem possibly serious enough to refer to the counseling office. Studies have shown that girls might be more likely than boys to experience depression (Clarizio, 1993). In part, this might be because girls tend to be raised to be somewhat more sensitive to interpersonal issues than boys, and therefore are more subject to hurt and despondency. It could also be, as one theory suggests, that girls are socialized in a way that makes them believe they have less control over their lives than do boys. As a result, they might be more prone to the development of what Seligman (1975) has termed *learned helplessness,* an emotional state that degenerates easily to depression. There is a great deal we can do as teachers to help adolescent girls see that they are capable of controlling their lives and shaping their own destinies. We can make the effort to continue to encourage them to focus on a broader range of occupational and academic goals in order to help them see beyond the traditional sex-role stereotypes of men and women.

Depression can be a prelude to suicide, a tragic outcome that has been increasing among teenagers. As can be seen in Figure 4.4, there has been a dramatic increase in the number of suicides among both white and black adolescents since 1960 (U.S. Bureau of the Census, 1983–1989). The rates for blacks and females are slightly lower, with black females rating lowest. Overall, the suicide rate among older adolescents has tripled since 1950, although it has decreased slightly in recent years (*Report of the Secretary's Task Force on Youth Suicide,* 1989). It is interesting (and distressing) to note that, among both sexes, firearms and explosives account for the greatest number of *completed* suicides, whereas drugs or poisons account for the greatest number

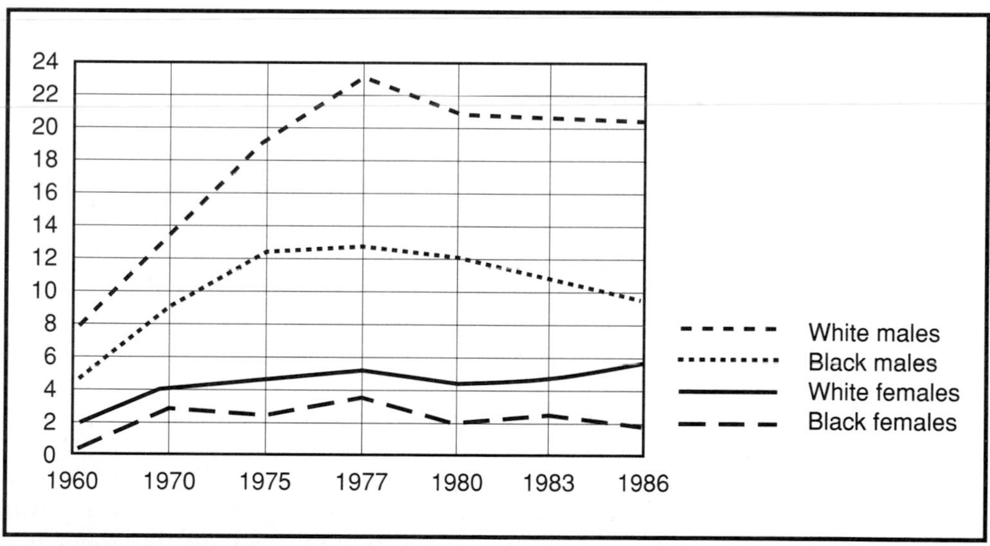

Figure 4.4. DEATH RATES (PER 100,000) FROM SUICIDE AMONG 15- TO 24-YEAR-OLDS, 1960–1983.

(From U.S. Bureau of the Census, *Statistical Abstract of the United States, 1983–1989.* Washington, DC: U.S. Government Printing Office, 1983–1989.)

of *attempted* suicides. Although both adolescent and adult females outnumber the males in the number of attempted suicides, completed suicides are more common among males (Curran, 1987, *Report of the Secretary's Task Force on Youth Suicide,* 1989). It is worth noting that the depression that usually precedes suicide is usually accompanied by a loss of interest in the surrounding world, a change for the worse in school grades, and talk about feeling helpless or hopeless.

Whether we hear about a suicide possibility directly or indirectly, it is something to be taken seriously. Most people who feel as though they want to kill themselves are deeply confused about whether they really want to die. Talking about suicide or the actual attempt are frequently cries for help. It is worth noting that most persons who attempt suicide let someone know about it before they attempt it (Clarizio, 1993).

4. *The search for a self-concept that "fits" is a major psychological thrust during adolescence.* Remember, adolescence is primarily a "breakup" period—a time for breaking up the familiar behaviors of childhood and preparing new behaviors for adulthood. It is not always an easy task, which is why Erik Erikson referred to this fifth step in his psychosocial ladder of development (see Chapter 2) as the "identity versus identity confusion" stage. Expect to see a fair amount of emotional shifting in adolescent behavior. They are leaving a very dependent stage and getting ready for a different stage—one that demands and reinforces independence. The transition period of adolescence is a time for getting ready for new expectations. As Marcia (1980) has pointed out, there is a delicate balance between a positive identity and identity confusion, which could lead to a negative identity.

As teachers, we can help adolescents move in the direction of positive identity development by avoiding rigid, dogmatic expectations for how they should behave, think, and dress. They need to experiment with themselves and with themselves in relation to others. We can also work on deeply appreciating and accepting a basic trademark of adolescence: the need to be different—to have one's own language, dress, values, justice, and outlooks. The need to be different is as much an effort to be unlike the children they recently were as it is to be different from the adults that surround them. In order to find out what you can do and who you are, you first have to find out what you can do on your own.

Necessarily, adolescents are a reactionary group. They are reacting to the little children they recently were and to adults who continually admonish them to grow up on one hand, while simultaneously treating them as though they were not grown up on the other. When working with adolescents, it will be helpful to see their reactionary behavior for what it usually is, namely, a developmental phenomenon designed to help them test their limits, not a personal attack on your value system. Be patient, and try not to be reactionary yourself.

4.6 Where Would You Send Your Kids?

There is by no means universal agreement on the suggestion that teachers can help adolescents move in the direction of positive identity development by avoiding rigid, dogmatic expectations for how they should behave, think, and dress. Some say that if adults, generally, and school, specifically, had more clear-cut expectations for how teenagers should behave, think, and dress, there would be fewer problems. Supposedly, this helps adolescents discipline their behavior and intellectual processing at a time when they need it most. Private and parochial schools are sometimes referred to as successful examples of how explicit, tougher expectations can bring about positive results. If you were one of those students who went to a private or parochial school with tough expectations, how did it work for you? If you had a chance to send children of your own to that kind of school, would you? What arguments would you offer for your choice?

COGNITIVE DEVELOPMENT: BASIC CHARACTERISTICS

Important changes in children's cognitive skills begin to occur around 11 or 12 years of age. They shift away from the concrete, specific, black-and-white thinking of the preadolescent years into the more mature, abstract reasoning skills associated with adult problem solving. It is the beginning of what is called a "period of formal operations" (Inhelder and Piaget, 1958). The term *formal* is a reflection of the development of *form,* or structure of thinking. It is a way of highlighting the growing ability to *form* hypotheses.

Probably the most important general feature of formal-operational thought is the new relationship between the real and the possible. For example, when confronted with a problem, elementary school children work with the facts at hand. They use their intellectual abilities to examine the parameters of the problem, to make comparisons with what is known in the world around them, and to do some trial-and-error problem solving, if possible. They do not speculate on unknown alternatives or what might be. If you were to ask 9-year-old Jimmy what the earth would be like if there were no sun, he might simply say that the earth *has* a sun, or he might say that it would be dark all the time. He keeps his feet planted firmly on the ground of facts, standing clear of the ambiguous arena of hypothetical possibilities. The real world is what matters to him.

Youngsters who have grown into the formal-operational mode of thinking, however, approach problems the other way around (Flavell, 1985). Hypothetical possibilities come first, and reality second. Fourteen-year-old Cindy would have more to say about the consequences of no sun than 9-year-old Jimmy because she is able to think not only about actual events, but about hypothetical situations. Cindy, for example, would probably realize that a sunless earth could never exist, but she can still reason about it. She might speculate that millions would die, heat would come only from volcanoes, survivors might live underground, and so forth. She can think not only about what is possible but also what is impossible.

Bybee and Sund's (1982) review of Piaget's research indicates that the evolution of formal thinking processes reaches its completion during adolescence. Somewhere between the ages of 11 and 15, youngsters develop and refine their capacity to think in terms of symbols. That is, real or concrete entities can be symbolically represented so that spatial, temporal limitations can be transcended. In this way, symbols enable them to think at a level detached from concrete reality. Whereas an elementary-age child in the concrete thinking stage might ask, "What is it that makes me live?" a 15-year-old tenth grader might ask, "What is the meaning of life?"

In order to test Piaget's assumptions and findings about the development of formal thinking, Case and Collinson (1961/1962) presented a group of boys and girls from ages 7 to 18 with written materials in history, geography, and literature. Each child was asked questions about the material and then scored as giving an *intuitive* answer (lowest level of thinking), a *concrete* answer (next highest level), or a *formal* answer (highest level).

For instance, after reading a passage about an English church reformer, Dunstan, the child was asked, "Was Dunstan a good man? Why?" If a child either failed to reply or said something such as, "He was a good man and did as he was told, so that made him good," the child was said to be giving an intuitive answer. If, however, the child answered, "Yes, he was a good man because he made the church better," the response was scored as being a concrete answer. A child was scored at the formal-operational level for responses such as, "He was good in some ways but not in others, because he was trying to make the church powerful, although I don't think he was right in being cruel to those who disagreed with him." Here the child is able to appropriately use words such as "powerful," "cruel," and "disagreed," which are really conceptual labels that represent complex behaviors. This sort of reasoning enables a child to see that Dunstan was neither all good nor all bad and that, although it may be a legitimate aim to make the church powerful (a hypothesis), it does not necessarily follow that it is desirable to cruelly suppress disagreement (a deduction).

The results were clear. Age 11 was the earliest age at which children gave formal or concrete, rather than intuitive, responses. Between 11 and 13 years of age, the children were giving more formal answers than intuitive or concrete answers. However, it was also noted that the combined number of intuitive or concrete answers was greater than, or equal to, the number of formal answers given between ages 11 and 13. It was no contest between the ages of 14 and 18. Here, formal answers outweighed intuitive and concrete responses by about eleven to one.

The results generally support Piaget's theory of intellectual development and the relation between particular ages and stages of thinking. However, we should note that the findings of Case and Collinson (1961/1962) also suggested that many children are at times able to engage in formal verbal reasoning *before* age 11. What seems to happen is that from ages 7 to 15 there is a steady increase in the tendency to think formally; there is no sudden appearance of this higher-level thinking. Eleven years may be roughly the age when it becomes a *favored* way of thinking, and not when it *first* begins to develop or to be used.

Depending on the circumstances, young adolescents can, therefore, think intuitively, concretely, or formally. The older they are, the more likely they are to think formally. How soon formal thinking makes its appearance and becomes dominant will vary from person to person because, like all other behavioral expressions, it is a function of not only innate intelligence, but also of experience, social class, ethnic background, and previous learning.

The change in adolescents' abilities to think in more abstract ways is not just a function of experience, although that is very important, but it is also a function of corresponding changes in brain growth and structure (Thatcher, Walker, and Guidice, 1987).

Overview of Cognitive Development Outcomes and Their Implications for Teachers

1. *The ability to conceive "what might be" is an essential characteristic of the formal operational thought processes that emerge in adolescence.* Whereas younger children deal only with concrete reality (concrete-operational thinking), formal-operational adolescents are more capable of thinking about both the reality they can see and the reality they can imagine if circumstances were altered. This frequently leads to a fair amount of idealistic thinking, so characteristic of adolescents. We should not be too alarmed by this. As adulthood approaches, ideas and behavior are tempered by experience and living, and most individuals learn for themselves that complex problems cannot be easily solved with idealistic and simplistic approaches.

This ability to think and reason symbolically is neither something that happens all at once nor is it a capacity that occurs at the same time for all individuals. Just as there are individual differences in intelligence, there are similar differences in conceptual skills. As teachers, we need to keep these differences in mind as we think about instructional strategies to take advantage of students' expanding intellectual abilities. Adolescents like to think about things, to imagine beyond the moment. Their cognitive capacities are budding with new possibilities, which is, perhaps, one of reasons why they find rote memorization and factual regurgitations so boring.

2. *Although adolescents are better able to understand another's point of view, they are still likely to assume that the other person's perception is the same as their own.* Elkind (1980) has identified this phenomenon as a new expression of egocen-

trism, which is the tendency to assume that others think and feel the way you do—hence, the egocentric quality characteristic of adolescent thinking. Adolescents tend to reflect this type of thinking in the thoughts they have about themselves and in their more abstract thinking about the world in general. For example, the adolescent who is self-conscious about his or her weight or appearance is certain that others are noticing the very thing he or she is concerned about. The adolescent who believes the solution to world hunger is simply to give our excess grain and wheat to needy persons and nations might have trouble understanding why there are those who disagree.

In a more abstract way, adolescent egocentrism sometimes takes the form of zealous idealism. In their thinking about the world and a perfect society, adolescents often arrive at what they see as ultimate solutions to inequality and social injustice. They are frequently frustrated when they find that not everyone shares their view of a perfect reality.

Intellectual growth, like all other aspects of growth, takes time. It takes a certain amount of experience with life and living to fully appreciate the idea that people have differing ideas and ways—that there can be different, but equally good, solutions to the same problem. Adolescents are in the process of gaining this experience. It is part of growing up—in this case, intellectually. As teachers, we are more apt to be successful with adolescents if we remember that a certain amount of idealistic, egocentric thinking is a normal outcome of blossoming intellectual skills that, for most, will be honed and moderated by more exposure to reality.

4.7 Think About How You Thought

You have just read about how the structure and content of intellectual processes changes in early adolescence—it becomes more complex, abstract, idealistic, and so forth. As you think about your own adolescent years, particularly the early ones, can you think of some examples of how your own way of thinking about life, school, and yourself changed as you moved into that stage known as "formal operations?" For instance, can you recall some examples of when your thinking about how to solve personal problems or even global problems may have been more idealistic than realistic?

EPILOGUE

Adolescence represents a very special time in the chronology of a young person's developmental history. As youngsters move from junior high to high school, they not only grow as physical persons, but also develop as psychological and cognitive persons. Middle childhood is a time when they begin to develop a more definitive self-image. Adolescence is a stage when youngsters work on refining that self-image and begin to develop, at a deeper level, those special feelings of being unique individuals.

A great many changes occur in adolescents' lives between 11 and 18 years of age. They grow bigger, taller, and heavier; glandular eruptions convert them from persons indifferent to sex to persons whose awakening sexuality adds an entirely new dimension to how they see themselves; parental authority (and practically everything else associated with parents) is questioned with increasing frequency and intensity; what one's friends think, do, and wear becomes a reference for both thought and action; and intellectual processes move from thoughts about everyday, concrete, here-and-now happenings to complex social issues and the meaning of life itself.

Although the adolescent self seldom reaches full maturity during adolescence, it nonetheless makes significant strides in that direction. In order to mature completely and to assume the responsibilities of adult life, adolescents have to outgrow the child life they once had. Adolescence is a tenuous, fragile moment on the developmental continuum, marked by continual shifts in emphasis, direction, and expression. When we talk about the adolescent self, what we refer to is a type of experimental personality style that may change, chameleonlike, at a moment's notice, depending on the strength of current social fads. Probably the most important consideration to keep in mind regarding the adolescent self is that it is incompletely formed and that many of its expressions are simply temporary mimicries of the youth culture in which it is nurtured. Persons who work with, or who are the parents of, adolescents would do well to keep in mind that teenagers must experience a great deal of changing and growing. Sometimes we forget this and act as if the normal stresses of growing up are symptoms of personality malfunction and disorder.

Growing up means growing away, and that is not easy. One part of the adolescent boy or girl wants to feel safe and protected by parents who love them and tell them what to do, while another part wants to reach out to new experiences and take on new challenges. In a sense, it is a personal civil war. The conflict would not be half as troublesome if it were just a simple struggle between children and parents. Its complexity grows from the revolt of the maturing self against the baby self. Frequently, parents, teachers, and other authority figures are dragged into the strife because they are all mixed up in a young person's mind with the baby self. It may be helpful to remember this so we can understand that some of the rebellious behavior of adolescents. This behavior is not so much a rebellion against their parents or against their love for their parents as it is against their dependency on them and other authority figures. Falling out of love with one's parents is the first step an adolescent boy or girl must take toward falling in love with another person.

Adolescents are not so much in revolt as they are in search of workable guidelines for their lives, for their work, and for their relationships—goals not unreasonable for any stage of development.

STUDY AND REVIEW QUESTIONS

1. What are some of the reasons for the confusion about what adolescence means and when it ends?
2. How would you explain the difference between psychological adolescence and physical adolescence?
3. Can you explain the effects of early versus late maturation in boys?
4. Can you explain the effects of early versus late maturation in girls?
5. What does research say about the long-term effects of early and late maturation in boys and girls?
6. If you were asked why so many American adolescents have confused ideas about sexual expression, how would you respond?
7. What important functions does peer group involvement play in an adolescent's social development?
8. Ordinarily, family values are more likely than peer group values to influence an adolescent's long-term goals. Sometimes, however, family relationships are such that peer group values have a significant impact on long-term goals. Can you explain why this sometimes happens?
9. What common emotional adjustments must be made by adolescents when they shift from elementary school to secondary school?
10. What does it mean when adolescence is referred to as a time for finding a self-concept that "fits?" What part can teachers play in this process?
11. Can you explain what it means when adolescents' cognitive growth is discussed as a time for the development of formal-operational thought? What implications does this have for teachers in terms of how teaching is done?
12. Why is it that so much idealistic thinking goes on in adolescence?
13. What does it mean to say that egocentrism is characteristic of adolescent thinking?
14. How can teachers use what they know about adolescent cognitive growth and function to improve their teaching?

REFERENCES

Berndt, T. J. "The Features and Effects of Friendship in Early Adolescence." *Child Development*, 1982, *53*, pp. 1447–1460.

Brehm, S. *Intimate Relationships.* New York: Random House, 1985.

Brooks-Gun, J., and Petersen, A. C., eds. *Girls at Puberty: Biological and Psychosocial Perspectives.* New York: Plenum, 1983.

Brozan, N. "U.S. Leads Industrialized Nations in Teen-Age Births and Abortions." *New York Times,* March 13, 1985, p. 1.

Bybee, R. W., and Sund, R. B. *Piaget for Educators,* 2nd ed. Columbus, OH: Merrill, 1982.

Case, D., and Collinson, J. W. "The Development of Formal Thinking in Verbal Comprehension." *British Journal of Educational Psychology,* 1961/1962, *31–32,* pp. 103–111.

Chumlea, W. C. "Physical Growth in Adolescence." In B. B. Wolman (Ed.), *Handbook of Developmental Psychology.* Englewood Cliffs, NJ: Prentice Hall, 1982.

Clarizio, H. *Assessment and Treatment of Depression in Children and Adolescents,* 2nd ed. Brandon, VT: Clinical Psychology Publishers, 1993.

Clausen, J. "The Social Meaning of Differential Physical and Sexual Maturation." In S. Dragastin and G. H. Elder, Jr. (Eds.), *Adolescence in the Life Cycle.* New York: Wiley, 1975.

Conger, J. J. *Adolescence and Youth,* 4th ed. New York: Harper Collins, 1991.

Crites, J. O. "Career Development." In J. F. Adams (Ed.), *Understanding Adolescence: Current Developments in Adolescent Psychology,* 4th ed. Boston: Allyn & Bacon, 1980.

Curran, D. K. *Adolescent Suicidal Behavior.* Washington, DC: Hemisphere Publishing Corporation, 1987.

DeRidder, L. M. "Teenage Pregnancy: Etiology and Educational Implications." *Educational Psychology Review,* 1993, *5,* pp. 87–107.

Dion, K. K. "Stereotyping Based on Physical Attractiveness: Issues and Conceptual Perspectives." In C. P. Herman, M. P. Zanna, and E. T. Higgens (Eds.), *Physical Appearance, Stigma, and Social Behavior.* Hillsdale, NJ: Lawrence Erlbaum, 1986.

Dreyer, P. H. "Sexuality During Adolescence." In B. B. Wolman (Ed.), *Handbook of Developmental Psychology.* Englewood Cliffs, NJ: Prentice Hall, 1982.

Dusek, J. B. *Adolescent Development and Behavior,* 2nd ed. Englewood Cliffs, NJ: Prentice Hall, 1991.

Elkind, D. "Strategic Interactions in Early Adolescence." In J. Adelson (Ed.), *Handbook of Adolescent Psychology.* New York: Wiley, 1980.

Flavell, J. H. *Cognitive Development,* 2nd ed. Englewood Cliffs, NJ: Prentice Hall, 1985.

Gallatin, J. "Political Thinking in Adolescence." In J. Adelson (Ed.), *Handbook of Adolescent Psychology.* New York: Wiley, 1980.

Garbarino, J. *Adolescent Development: An Ecological Perspective.* Columbus, OH: Merrill, 1985.

Garrison, K. C. "Physiological Development." In J. F. Adams (Ed.), *Understanding Adolescence,* 3rd ed. Boston: Allyn & Bacon, 1976.

Gross, R. T., and Duke, P. M. "The Effect of Early vs. Late Maturation on Adolescent Behavior." *Pediatric Clinics of North America,* 1980, *27,* pp. 71–77.

Hamachek, D. "Psychology and Development of the Adolescent Self." In J. F. Adams (Ed.), *Understanding Adolescence: Current Developments in Adolescent Psychology,* 4th ed. Boston: Allyn & Bacon, 1980.

Inhelder, B., and Piaget, J. *The Growth of Logical Thinking from Childhood to Adolescence.* New York: Basic Books, 1958.

Jaccard, J., and Turrisi, R. "Cognitive Processes and Individual Differences in Judgments Related to Drunk Driving." *Journal of Personality and Social Psychology,* 1987, *53,* pp. 135–145.

Johnson, L. D., O'Malley, P. M., and Bachman, J. G. *Use of Licit and Illicit Drugs by America's High School Students, 1975–1984.* Rockville, MD: National Institute on Drug Abuse, 1985.

Jourard, S. M. "Healthy Personality and Self-Disclosure." In W. G. Bennis, E. H. Schein, F. I. Steele, and D. E. Berlow (Eds.), *Interpersonal Dynamics,* rev. Homewood, IL: Dorsey Press, 1968.

Krogman, W. M. "Growth of Head, Face, Trunk and Limbs in Philadelphia White and Negro Children of Elementary and High School Age." *Monographs of the Society for Research on Child Development,* 1970, *35*(3), Serial No. 136.

Lerner, R. M., and Foch, T. T., eds. *Biological-Psychological Interactions in Early Adolescence: A Life-Span Perspective.* Hillsdale, NJ: Lawrence Erlbaum, 1987.

Marcia, J. E. "Identity in Adolescence." In J. Adelson (Ed.), *Handbook of Adolescent Psychology.* New York: Wiley, 1980.

Mayo Clinic Health Letter, Depression. 1989, February.

Medinnus, G. R., and R. C. Johnson. *Child and Adolescent Psychology.* New York: Wiley, 1969.

Mussen, P. H., and Jones, M. C. "Self-Conceptions, Motivations & Interpersonal Attitudes of Late- and Early-Maturing Boys." *Child Development,* 1957, *28,* pp. 243–256.

Peskin, H. "Influence of the Development Schedule of Puberty on Learning and Ego Functioning." *Journal of Youth and Adolescence,* 1973, *2,* pp. 273–290.

Petersen, A. C. "The Development of Self-Concept in Adolescence." In M. D. Lynch, A. A. Norem-Hebeisen, and K. Gergen (Eds.), *Self-Concept: Advances in Theory and Practice.* Cambridge, MA: Ballinger, 1981.

Petersen, A. C. "Those Gangly Years." *Psychology Today,* 1987, September, pp. 28–34.

Report of the Secretary's Task Force on Youth Suicide, Vol. 1. *Overview and Recommendations.* Washington, DC: U.S. Government Printing Office, 1989.

Schuster, C. S. "Biosocial Development of the Adolescent." in C. S. Schuster and S. S. Ashburn (Eds.), *The Process of Human Development: A Holistic Approach.* Boston: Little, Brown, 1980.

Seifert, K. L., and Hoffnung, R. J. *Child and Adolescent Development.* Boston: Houghton Mifflin, 1987.

Seligman, M. E. P. *Helplessness: On Depression, Development, and Death.* San Francisco: Freeman, 1975.

Siegel, O. "Personality Development in Adolescence." in B. B. Wolman (Ed.), *Handbook of Developmental Psychology.* Englewood Cliffs, NJ: Prentice Hall, 1982.

Spickard, A., and Thompson, B. R. *Dying for a Drink.* Waco, TX: World Books, 1985.

Tanner, J. M. "Growth and Maturation During Adolescence." *Nutrition Review,* 1981, *39,* pp. 43–55.

Tanner, J. M. *Fetus into Man: Physical Growth from Conception to Maturity,* 2nd ed. Cambridge, MA: Harvard University Press, 1990.

Tesch, S. "A Review of Friendship Development Across the Lifespan." *Human Development,* 1983, *26,* pp. 266–276.

Thatcher, R. W., Walker, R. A., and Guidice, S. "Human Cerebral Hemispheres Develop at Different Rates and Ages." *Science,* 1987, May, pp. 1110–1113.

U.S. Bureau of the Census. *Statistical Abstract of the United States, 1983–1989.* Washington, DC: U.S. Government Printing Office, 1983–1989.

U.S. Bureau of the Census. *Statistical Abstract of the United States.* Washington, DC: U.S. Government Printing Office, 1988.

Weatherly, D. "Self-Perceived Rate of Physical Motivation and Personality in Late Adolescence." *Child Development,* 1964, *35,* p. 1209.

SELECTED READINGS OF RELATED INTEREST

Atwater, E. *Adolescence,* 3rd ed. Englewood Cliffs, NJ: Prentice Hall, 1992. This text presents a nicely balanced view of adolescence. It is written within a framework that promotes the idea of mediated effects, which suggests that the primary developmental changes of adolescence are influenced by the surroundings in which they occur, reflecting the combined effects of nature and nurture.

Chilman, C. S., ed. *Adolescent Sexuality in a Changing American Society.* New York: Wiley, 1983. Explores a wide range of issues and concerns related to adolescent sexuality, with Chapter 1 written by experts in this area. Comprehensive overview, easy-to-read, and one of the few texts of its kind.

Damon, W., and Hart, D. *Self-Understanding in Childhood and Adolescence.* Cambridge, MA: Cambridge University Press, 1988. A somewhat more technical book than you will find a general adolescence text to be, but the only book of which I am aware that provides a comprehensive look of how children and adolescents come to understand themselves during the first two decades of life.

Leigh, G. K., and Peterson, G. W., eds. *Adolescents in Families.* Cincinnati: Southwestern, 1986. Excellent discussions related to drug use, adolescent sexuality, effects of divorce, minority issues, self-concept development, and much more, all in the context of how this relates to adolescents' family experiences.

Lipka, R. P., and Brinthaupt, T. M., eds. *Self-Perspectives Across the Life-Span.* New York: State University of New York Press, 1992. Contains two excellent chapters devoted to the issues of self-concept and self-esteem during adolescence. A fine overview of current theoretical views and research related to self-concept stability and change during adolescence.

Rice, F. R. *The Adolescent,* 7th ed. Boston: Allyn & Bacon, 1992. A comprehensive overview of adolescence covering social, emotional, physical, and intellectual aspects of development. Very readable.

Shaffer, D. R. *Developmental Psychology: Childhood and Adolescence,* 3rd ed. Belmont, CA: Brooks/Cole, 1993. A research-oriented text that discusses how research findings and theory can be used in applied settings. I like it because it is written in clear, uncluttered language that is easy to understand. It is also a particularly attractive book visually.

5

Developmental Processes Involved in Intellectual Growth and Moral Reasoning

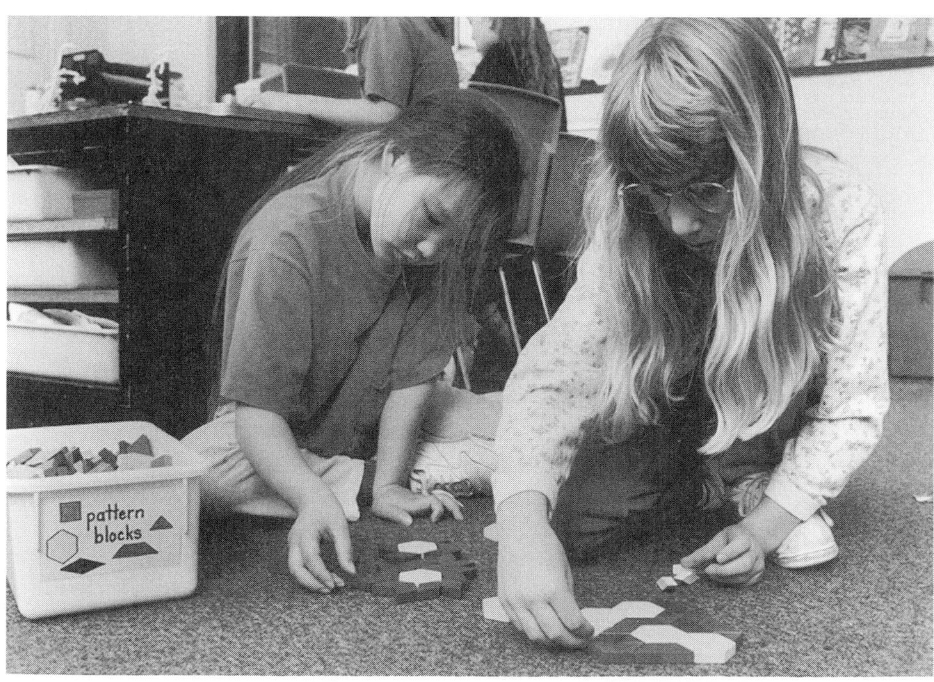

CHAPTER OVERVIEW

IMPORTANT CHAPTER IDEAS

1. What we call intelligence is a combination of many distinct abilities, which may vary widely from person to person.
2. Intelligence as conceptualized by six psychologists:
   a. Intellectual functioning consists of one general (*g*) factor and several specific (*s*) factors (Spearman).
   b. One's level of intelligence is determined by the number of neural connections in the brain (Thorndike).
   c. Intelligence consists of seven components or families of abilities, which, although related, function relatively independent of one another (Thurstone).
   d. Intelligence is a complex, three-dimensional structure, whose components interact to produce 120 abilities (Guilford).
   e. Intelligence is of seven types, enabling people to be intelligent in different ways (Gardner).
   f. There are three components to intelligence that enable some people to be strong analytically, others to be skilled creatively, and still others to have well-developed practical intelligence (Sternberg).
3. Intelligence is not only the capacity for abstract thinking, but also the ability to learn from experience (develop common sense), the capacity to know oneself and relate to others, the faculty for logical thinking, the skill involved in language usage, the aptitude for creative output, and the capacity for concrete thinking. It is now recognized that there are many ways to be intelligent, and not all of them are directly related to the ability to do schoolwork.
4. Intelligence begins as a series of simple reflex actions and then grows increasingly more organized and adaptive through a process of assimilating new information and accommodating old information to fit new interpretations of reality.
5. According to Piaget, intelligence develops in four sequential stages, each marked by characteristic and identifiable ways of thinking.
6. Research on brain development indicates that there are four major spurts in brain growth that correspond closely to Piaget's stages, suggesting a biological basis for intellectual development.

7. Although there is debate whether intellectual development grows in stages or in a more continuous, unbroken line, evidence suggests that specific mental abilities can only be learned at particular times along that growth continuum.
8. Specific teaching strategies are associated with each stage of intellectual growth, starting with concrete, hands-on experiences in the early phases, to increasingly more complex experiences demanding higher-level reasoning and hypothetical thinking.
9. Vygotsky's social cognitive theory is characterized by three underlying themes, which include: (1) the importance of culture, (2) the role of language, and (3) the idea of one's zone of proximal growth.
10. Vygotsky has speculated that students have what he referred to as "zones of proximal development," which are middle points or areas where they may not be able to solve problems alone but are capable of doing so with some outside help.
11. A major implication of Vygotsky's influence is that the school's educational environment be structured in such a way as to encourage students to function at a level slightly in advance of their current developmental level, thus stretching them into their zones of proximal development.
12. Both heredity and environment contribute to the extent and degree of intellectual growth; research continues into the relative impact of each element.
13. Intellectual development grows faster during the first twelve or so years of life, and then gradually decreases.
14. Intellectual development as measured by IQ tests is positively related to achievement in school, although there are many exceptions at the level of individual performance (higher IQ students may not do well, and lower IQ students may do quite well).
15. Because of the possibility of test bias, considerable caution needs to be exercised when considering IQ scores as assessments of intellectual development and ability.
16. Teachers cannot change their students' intellectual heredity, but they can have considerable influence in creating a favorable environment.
17. Piaget has theorized that children go through three stages of moral development, which range from not being concerned at all about rules when they are preschoolers to developing and understanding that not only are there rules, but that there are degrees of wrongdoing, and punishment relative to those rules.
18. Kohlberg extends Piaget's ideas by proposing three broad levels of moral development subdivided into six stages, with each stage building on the moral aspects of the previous stage.
19. In Kohlberg's view, those in the lower stages of moral development behave morally either to avoid punishment or to get rewards, while those in the highest stages are more apt to behave morally because of agreement with the rules rather than blind obedience to them.

20. Moral development goes along with intellectual development insofar as becoming more intelligent means, among other things, becoming more aware of the world in which one lives, and of becoming more sensitive to how one's choices to be hurtful or helpful to oneself or others can influence the course and quality of life.

PROLOGUE

Is there anything more frightening about the human animal than its intelligence? Human accomplishments are at the same time majestic and frightening. As for majesty, humans are able to build a spaceship that takes men and women to the moon and back. As for frightening possibilities, humans are able to build a single bomb capable of leveling an entire city and killing thousands. Intelligence assembled the press that printed this book, invented the light that illuminates this page, and is responsible for the assorted technology that may surround you at this very moment.

What is intelligence? How should it be defined? Is it genetically determined, or is it influenced more by environment? Can we get smarter? Can one's IQ be raised? Is there just one general type of intelligence of which each of us has more or less, or are there different types or expressions of intelligence that are distributed differentially among people? What kind of relationships are there between cognitive functioning, brain growth, and brain size?

For more than ninety years questions of this sort have been, and continue to be, carefully scrutinized in research into the growth, nature, and expression of intelligence. To this day, there are ongoing debates, some with political-social overtones, about how to define intelligence and how best to encourage its development. Probably no other component of one's development can influence self-concept so powerfully for better or worse, whether it comes from one's own private evaluation of intellectual ability or from an outside assessment. Is there any more powerful compliment than to be regarded as smart? Is there any more devastating insult than to be viewed as dumb?

Then there is the question of moral development. How do children acquire a sense of right and wrong? Indeed, how do people of any age decide what is right and wrong, and what is good and bad behavior? Are there stages of moral development? Is moral development related to intellectual ability? Are there ways to encourage higher levels of intellectual ability and moral behavior?

Our task in this chapter is to better understand the nature and expression of intelligence, which we do by examining six distinct, yet overlapping, views on this subject. Then we look at how intellectual growth occurs over time as described by Jean Piaget. We also consider the contributions of Lev Vygotsky, a psychologist in the former Soviet Union, whose theorizing about the nature of children's thinking and language development has stimulated new ideas about intellectual growth. In addition, we look at the effects of environment and heredity on intelligence, and conclude with an explanation of moral development, particularly as this process has been described by Jean Piaget and Lawrence Kohlberg.

Let us begin with an important question.

WHAT CONSTITUTES INTELLIGENCE?

The word *intelligence* is derived from a translation of "dia-noesis," a term Aristotle used to describe the abstract qualities involved in all intellectual processes, including perception, sensation, imagination, memory, and reasoning. Aristotle was not far off, since most definitions of intelligence do involve the processes he mentioned, along with some others.

Actually, there is no one definition of intelligence; there are many. Some of the more common definitions include such considerations as the ability to do the following:

1. Profit from experience.
2. Solve problems.
3. Adjust and relate to one's environment.
4. Think abstractly.
5. Perceive relationships.
6. Behave competently and effectively.
7. Learn.

None of these definitions is mutually exclusive of the others, and, in fact, the better we are able to do any one of the seven definitions mentioned, the better we are able to do the others. If we can perceive the relationships between events or ideas, we very likely can learn. If we can learn, we can profit from experience. If we can profit from experience, we can behave more competently and effectively, and so on. There might be semantic distinctions among the seven definitions, but in terms of what we think of as constituting intelligence, they are more on the order of overlapping components of cognitive ability rather than separate and unrelated divisions of it.

Intelligence, then, is not just one kind of ability or talent, but is, rather, a combination of many abilities or components that compile the package we label "intelligence." Although two people might have similar intelligence scores as derived from an IQ test, they might have quite different intellectual abilities.

One thing seems certain: wherever learning is, intelligence is, too. We could not put it the other way and say that wherever intelligence is, learning is sure to follow because, unfortunately, it does not always work that way. We probably all know persons—young and old—who by most standards are intelligent enough, but who, for one reason or another, simply refuse to learn from either their own experience or from someone else's. Intelligent people do not always use their capacity for learning (they are frequently labeled "underachievers" in school), but whenever learning does occur, there has to be some measurable degree of intelligence present.

In order to understand what intelligence is, let us turn our attention to six distinct, but overlapping, viewpoints on the nature of intellectual functioning.

Intelligence Consists of Both General and Specific Components (Spearman)

In the pioneering days of research into the nature of intelligence, Charles Spearman (1927) theorized that intellectual functioning does not consist of many abilities, but of one general (*g*) factor and several specific (*s*) factors. He defined the *g* factor as a mental energy that people draw on for everything they do. Essentially, the *g* factor is one's ability to perceive relationships. *S* factors, however, are specific to given tasks. For example, one particular *s* factor might be involved in arithmetic and another involved in spelling or reading, but a minimal amount of *g* factor is necessary for dealing with and understanding all three subjects. Within this framework, it is possible for a person to have a high level of general intelligence and still be less capable in a particular area than someone with a high *s* factor in that same area. Usually, however, the more *g* factor a person has, the more *s* factors are at his or her command. This is consistent with research that suggests that persons with above-average (or below-average, as the case may be) aggregate intelligence scores tend to be somewhat above average (or below average) in most things they attempt (Resnick, 1976).

Quantity of Neural Connections Determines Intelligence (Thorndike)

Edward L. Thorndike (1927) offered a quite different view of the nature of intelligence from those that preceded. Essentially, his thinking revolved around the idea that the quality of intellectual functioning is due to the number and kind of neural connections. A bright person, for example, simply has more neural connections of an adequate nature than a dull person, a view that, in light of recent brain research, might have more merit than even Thorndike thought possible (Groves and Rebec, 1988; Restak, 1984). Although Thorndike perceived every mental act as different from every other one, some acts were seen as having enough elements in common to justify three general groupings or components of intelligence: (1) concrete thinking—the ability to deal with black and white situations and circumstances, (2) social thinking—the ability to deal with people, and (3) abstract thinking—the ability to deal with ideas. As we go along, you will see how these categories are similar to the constructs other theoreticians have formed for their thoughts about intelligence.

Intelligence Consists of Seven Primary Abilities (Thurstone)

Intelligence is conceptualized as a collection of related mental abilities rather than as a single generalized capacity for thinking. Louis L. Thurstone's (1938) theory of primary mental abilities, for example, conceptualized intelligence as consisting of seven components or families of closely related abilities. Not all psychologists have agreed with these categories, but the categories have weathered the tests of time and scientific scrutiny long enough to qualify them as more generally accepted components of intelligence. They are qualities of intellectual functioning easily recognized, in that they are so much a part of everyday living. They are as follows:

1. *Space factor.* This refers to the ability to visualize objects in space; for example, it is the ability a good quarterback uses to complete long passes, or the ability to judge whether we have time and room to pass a car when another car is approaching in the other lane. Although most intelligent people seem reasonably well supplied with the space factor, some are lacking in this primary ability. Some intelligent people, for example, have trouble parking a car.

2. *Number factor.* Those who rate high in this function are usually good at manipulating numbers, as in balancing a checkbook or making change. We would expect that accountants and cashiers, for example, would be high in this ability.

3. *Verbal comprehension.* People high in this ability typically read faster, have large vocabularies, and, naturally enough, seem to understand more of what they read. They would be more likely to quickly interpret a proverb, such as "All that glitters is not gold," than a person whose verbal comprehension was not as high.

4. *Word fluency.* People high in this ability seem to be adept at using words. A simple test for word fluency is to ask someone to write as many girls' or boys' names (beginning with the letters *Ch-* or *Fr-*) as he or she can in a few minutes. Some can produce a string of names, while others have a terrible time.

5. *Ability to memorize.* Oddly enough, the ability to memorize is not necessarily related to other mental abilities. That is, those with good memories may or may not be blessed with other primary abilities. More than that, there seem to be several types of memory abilities. For example, there appears to be a

difference between the ability to memorize intentionally—for instance—and the ability to recall past experiences.

6. *Inductive reasoning.* This is the ability to discover the underlying rule or principle in the material with which one is working. It is the ability to arrive at useful generalizations from limited information. We would suspect, for example, that successful football coaches or police detectives would be high in this ability.

7. *Perceptual speed.* This is the ability to identify objects quickly. For example, those high in this function can understand more easily than most others entire sentences without having to examine each word carefully and are more able to comprehend entire paragraphs without looking microscopically at each sentence. It is the ability a good quarterback uses when scanning the entire field of potential receivers to find an open player, without spending undue time looking at each receiver.

5.1 Where Are Your Intellectual Strengths?

How would you rate yourself on Thurstone's seven factors? Where are your strengths? Do you see any relationship between what you see as your strengths and weaknesses and your success in particular courses you have taken or the career you have chosen? Do strengths/weaknesses in any of these factors seem to run in your family? Which ones?

Intelligence Consists of Three Dimensions (Guilford)

J. P. Guilford's (1967) "structure-of-intellect" model is by far the most complex and comprehensive model of intelligence. Basically, Guilford theorized that intelligence consists of three basic dimensions: (1) *mental operations*—processes of thinking, (2) *contents*—what we think about, and (3) *products*—the results of our thinking. Figure 5.1 shows how these three dimensions interact with each other. Note that mental operations are divided into five subcategories, including (1) *cognition*—integration of old and new information, (2) *convergent thinking*—focuses on one answer or solution, (3) *divergent thinking*—explores new possibilities, (4) *evaluation*—judgments about how good or suitable something is, and (5) *memory.* The content component refers to the particular cognitive mode a person may be in at a given moment: *symbolic, figural* (graphic), *semantic,* or *behavioral* (motor). The product that can grow from this might be units, classes, relations, systems, transformations, or implications. (If you think that this is unbelievably complicated, you have a lot of company.)

On the positive side, Guilford's model alerts us to the enormous complexity of human intelligence. It also helps us see that in relatively complex forms of learning, such as problem solving, several combinations of abilities might be required, depending on the nature of the problem. It also highlights differences between convergent and divergent thinking, which has helped us to better understand some of the basic cognitive differences between somewhat average and very bright students.

On the negative side, the model has proven to be too complex to be much help as a guide for predicting cognitive outcomes or planning instructional activities. In addition, the 120 mental abilities that are theoretically possible in the 5 × 4 × 6, three-dimensional model in Figure 5.1 are not as separate as Guilford believed. Research has consistently found many significant, positive correlations among them, suggesting that they are overlapping abilities, not separate entities (Kail and Pellegrino, 1985).

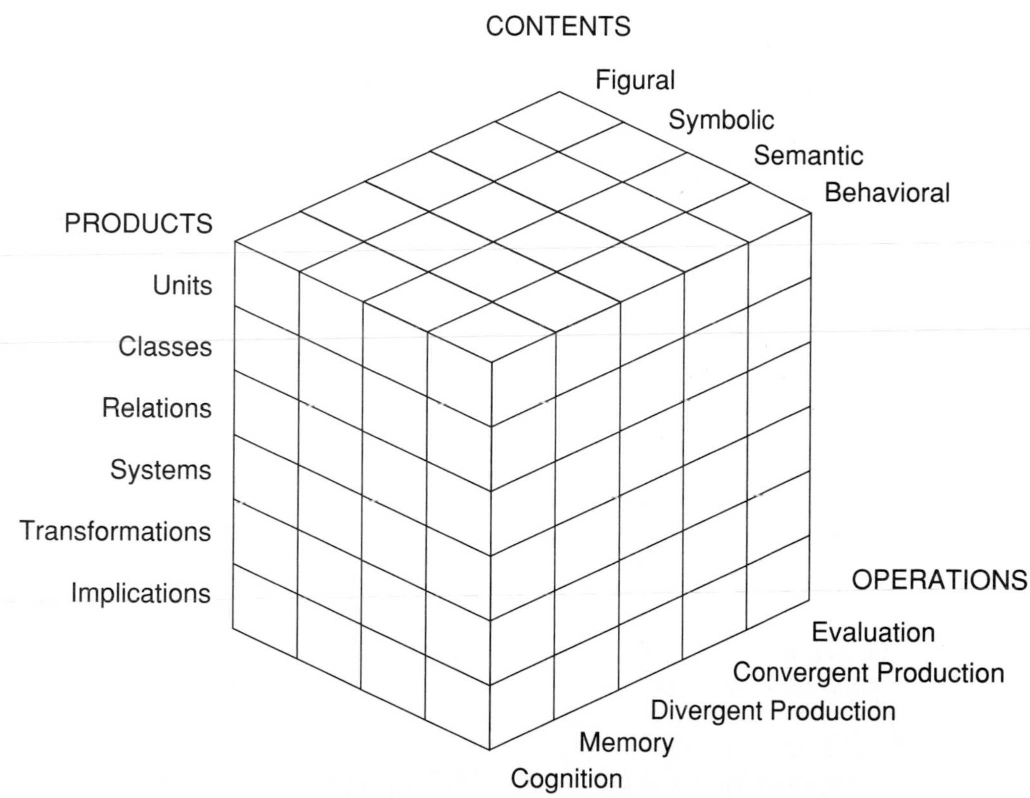

Figure 5.1. GUILFORD'S THREE-DIMENSIONAL STRUCTURE-OF-INTELLECT MODEL.

(From J. P. Guilford. *The Nature of Human Intelligence.* New York: McGraw-Hill. Copyright 1967 by McGraw-Hill, Inc. Reproduced with permission.)

Intelligence Composed of Multiple Intelligences (Gardner)

Howard Gardner (1983) is one of a growing number of psychologists who believes that intelligence, far from being a unitary power of the mind, consists of a set of mental abilities or "intelligences," as he calls them, that not only manifest themselves independently, but probably also spring from distinct areas of the brain. While working at a Veterans' Administration (VA) hospital, Gardner was struck by the cruel and exquisite selectivity with which disease and injury can damage the mind. He noted, for example, that patients with a right-hemisphere brain lesion might read flawlessly but be unable to interpret what they read. Left-hemisphere–damaged patients might lose the ability to speak but be able to sing lyrics to songs because the musical right-hemisphere was still intact.

Gardner hypothesizes that there are at least seven broad categories of intelligence. The first three are fairly conventional, fitting as they do with other ideas about mental ability, but the remaining four are more controversial because they are more unconventional in terms of what is usually called intelligence. They are as follows:

1. *Linguistic or verbal intelligence*—the ability to understand and use words.
2. *Logical/mathematical intelligence*—the ability to reason abstractly and conceptually using deductive or inductive modes of thought.
3. *Spatial intelligence*—the ability to perceive the world of objects accurately, imagine transformation and modifications of what one sees, and re-create visual experiences from memory.
4. *Musical intelligence*—the ability to recognize variations of tone and pitch, and a capacity to combine tones to create new sounds.
5. *Bodily/kinesthetic intelligence*—the ability to use one's body and muscle structure in a coordinated, planned way.
6. *Interpersonal intelligence*—the ability to deal effectively with others.
7. *Intrapersonal intelligence*—the ability to know one's own feelings and to understand one's own behavior.

In defense of the label "intelligence," Gardner has argued that each of the seven abilities can be destroyed by particular brain damage, each is shown in highlighted form in the talents of gifted persons or savants (otherwise below-average intelligence persons who are capable of a specific and spectacular mental feat, such as doing long, complicated math problems in their heads or memorizing entire pages of a book after one reading), and each involves specific mental skills.

Gardner (1984) maintains that when people are evaluated on only one measure, they are cheated of recognition for other skills they may be good at. In this view,

> There is no single "horizontal" capacity such as memory, perception, problem solving, learning, or originality that cuts across diverse contents. Rather, individuals can have a

> good or bad memory, can be rapid or slow learners, can exhibit novel or stereotypical thinking in any one of these intelligences. . . . In this view, there is no general "brightness" or "smartness." People can be "smart" or "dumb" in one area, but this tells us nothing about their intelligence in other domains. (p. 700)

Gardner admits that the mental abilities most valued in the Western world are linguistic and logical/mathematical intelligences. He notes, however, that the importance of the seven intelligences has shifted over time and varies from culture to culture. In a hunting society, for example, it is more important to have extremely good control of your body (bodily/kinesthetic intelligence) and know your way around (spatial intelligence) than to add and subtract quickly. In Japanese society, the ability to work cooperatively in groups and to arrive at joint decisions (interpersonal intelligence) is highly valued. Whereas schools in the first fifty years or so of this century focused on linguistic and interpersonal skills, contemporary schools focus more on linguistic and logical/mathematical abilities. Gardner (1983) speculates that linguistic abilities will become even less important in schools in the near future as logical/mathematical abilities become more important for computer programming.

The point is that, although both logical/mathematical and linguistic intelligences are important today, it will not always be that way. Hence, Gardner's argument is that we need to be sensitive to the fact that what is valued as far as intelligence is concerned is changeable, something we need to keep in mind as we plan curricula and teach students.

5.2 Are There Advantages to a Broader View of Intelligence?

Most psychologists have no trouble with Gardner's first three intelligences; they tend to fit traditional thinking about intelligence. It is the last four that are most questioned. If you were asked to defend the idea of broadening the definition of intelligence to include skills such as musical ability, bodily/kinesthetic abilities, and interpersonal and intrapersonal talents, what would you say? What advantages (or disadvantages) can you see in considering these seven intelligences when working with young people?

Intelligence Consists of Three Major Components (Sternberg)

Robert Sternberg (1985) has offered a view of mental abilities that questions the common assumption that "smart is fast." This assumption underlies the overwhelming majority of IQ and aptitude tests, but is one that overlooks the evidence suggesting that smartness is not always associated with quickness.

First, it is well documented that a *reflective* rather than an *impulsive* style of problem solving tends to be associated with higher ability to solve problems (Baron, 1982). Jumping to conclusions without adequate reflection can lead to false starts or erroneous thinking. How often, for example, do our snap judgments turn out to be poor ones, if not wrong ones? Yet the vast majority of intelligence tests are timed, which forces the taker into an impulsive mode.

Second, research suggests that persons who are highly intelligent tend to spend relatively more time than less intelligent persons on global, higher-order planning, and less time on local, problem-specific planning (Mulholland, Pellegrino, and Glaser, 1980; Sternberg, 1981). Brighter people tend to be more reflective in their efforts to understand the terms and parameters of a problem than are less bright ones, something that takes more, not less, time.

Finally, in a study in which individuals were free to spend as long as they liked solving insight problems, a quite high correlation, 0.75 (1.00 is a perfect correlation), was found between time spent on the problems and measured IQ (Sternberg and Davidson, 1982). These findings suggest that more able individuals do not easily give up when confronted with problems, and that persistence and involvement are highly related not only to successful outcomes, but also to higher IQs.

For Sternberg, the critical aspect of what constitutes intelligence is not necessarily the speed with which one arrives at a solution, but the process one uses to get there. Thus, Sternberg (1985) has suggested a "triarchic theory of intelligence," a point of view that says there are different ways to be smart and that processing information quickly does not mean it was done accurately or correctly. Sternberg theorized that there are three aspects of intelligence: componential, experiential, and contextual.

Componential intelligence is that facet of people's mental ability that enables them to reason logically, to think analytically, to identify connections among ideas, and to see various aspects or components of a problem. It is the type of intelligence typically associated with people who do well on achievement and IQ tests. People with high componential intelligence might do quite well on multiple-choice or true-false tests and might be especially skilled at critiquing and analyzing arguments. Tests such as the *Scholastic Aptitude Test* (SAT) and the *Graduate Record Exam* (GRE) (which determine the futures of thousands of students) are primarily geared to assess componential thinking. This is one kind of intelligence, but not the only one. As observed by Sternberg, "A lot of people are very good analytically, but they just don't have good ideas of their own" (Trotter, 1986, p. 58).

This is where *experiential intelligence* comes in, a facet of mental ability associated with a person's capacity to combine disparate experiences in insightful ways. People high in this type of intelligence may not have the best test scores, but they are able to come up with creative and ingenious ways to see new combinations and possibilities in the world around them. Sternberg and Davidson (1982) concluded from their research that experiential intelligence consists of three types of insight: *selective encoding, selective combination,* and *selective comparison.*

Selective encoding is the ability to focus on critical information. Einstein, for example, developed the startling concept that if a person were to fall from the roof of a house and, in the process of falling, release an object, the object would remain, relative to him or her, in a state of rest. He concluded from this mental picture that a person falling from the roof of a house was both in motion and at rest *at the same time,* which proved to be a critical step in his efforts to reconcile his general theory of relativity with Newton's theory of gravity. (It is interesting to note that Einstein was a somewhat mediocre math student in high school. One might wonder how Einstein the high school math student would have done on the math section of our contemporary SAT tests.)

Sternberg and Davidson's second type of insight is termed *selective combination,* which involves putting facts together to get the big picture. For example, the wind had been blowing dust around for millions of years, but it was not until 1901 that H. C. Booth thought of using wind in reverse, creating the first vacuum cleaner. Similarly, other people had the same facts as Charles Darwin, but he saw how to combine these facts in a new way, and thus was born his theory of evolution.

Sternberg and Davidson's third type of insight, *selective comparison,* is the ability to see an old thing in a new way, or a new thing in a new way. Some examples are Elias Howe, who perfected his sewing machine by designing a needle with a hole at the bottom rather than at the top, and Benjamin Franklin, who, to avoid changing from one pair of spectacles to another, cut the lenses of each pair in half and stuck the unlike halves together to make the world's first bifocals. Experiential intelligence, then, is the capacity to not only make sense of our experiences, but also to reorder, recombine, and reinterpret our experiences in new and possibly creative ways.

5.3 Can You Think of Some Examples?

As you have seen, selective encoding, selective combination, and selective comparison are three ways that one's experiential intelligence can be expressed. What kinds of examples can you think of that would further illustrate the three ways of reflecting experiential intelligence? Are there things you have done in your own life that are examples of one or more of these three modes?

Contextual intelligence is the third type of mental ability. Basically, it is the type of intelligence people use in the context of their external world. It is one's practical intelligence, or common sense, which might loosely be defined as all of the important things they never teach you in school. In Sternberg's view, there are a lot of people who do not do particularly well on tests, but who are extremely intelligent in a practical sense. Although this kind of intelligence does not fit into the academic world, it is intelligence, and, as such, Sternberg believes it should be considered along with all other expressions of human mental abilities.

The task facing Sternberg and others who wish to expand the current view of intelligence is to find ways to measure these new dimensions of mental skill, an area that is currently being studied (Sternberg, 1985, 1984). For example, one possibility is to devise intelligence tests that can measure what one has learned from particular school courses. Such a test could be devised through the use of problems that require little in the way of prior knowledge, but do require some insight. Consider two questions that involve this type of insight (see footnote * for answers).

1. If you have both black and brown socks in your drawer, mixed in the ratio of 4 to 5, how many socks will you have to take out to make sure you have a pair of the same color?
2. Water lilies double in area every 24 hours. At the beginning of the summer there is one water lily on the lake. It takes 60 days for the lake to become covered with water lilies. On what day was the lake one-half covered?

5.4 Is "Common Sense" Really Intelligence?

> Most psychologists have no trouble with Sternberg's componential and experiential components of intelligence, but some wonder about the necessity (or importance) of the third type, contextual or practical intelligence, referred to by some as "common sense." If you were to take a position related to whether this kind of intelligence should be considered in any formal definition of intellectual ability, which side would you take and why?

WHAT CAN WE CONCLUDE ABOUT THE NATURE OF INTELLIGENCE?

Intelligence is a complex blend of many types of mental abilities, a fact that is apparent in the overview provided by Figure 5.2. Although there are different theories about what it is exactly that goes into the tapestry of intelligence, the six views we have just examined share descriptive strands. For example, each view recognizes that a capacity for abstract thinking is related to intelligence, although this capacity has various names, such as inductive reasoning, cognition, logical/mathematical, or componential. Three of the six views recognize a type of social intelligence that Thorndike called social thinking, Gardner

---

*Answers to word puzzles: 1. 3 socks. 2. Day 59.

termed interpersonal intelligence, and Sternberg labeled contextual intelligence. Four of the six positions—experiential intelligence, divergent thinking, inductive reasoning, and abstract thinking—share the idea that intelligence also consists of the ability to see possibilities where, at first glance, none are apparent. As you can see in Figure 5.2, aspects of the capacity to think concretely are also included in the consideration of what constitutes intelligent behavior. This is reflected in Spearman's *s* factor, Thorndike's concrete thinking, Guilford's convergent thinking, and Sternberg's contextual intelligence, and is implicit in Thurstone's space, number, and memory factors and in Gardner's spatial and bodily/kinesthetic intelligences. Of course, none of these mental abilities are discrete components. They are all related in overlapping ways, some more so than others.

New research and fresh thinking about the nature of cognitive ability are allowing us to see that intelligence has many facets. The implications of this are vast and enormously hopeful, particularly for classroom teachers who face an immense sea of intellectually varied students on a daily basis. It is now valid to consider a broader view of intelligence: it is not only the capacity for abstract thinking, but also the ability to learn from experience (to develop common sense); the capacity to know oneself and to relate to others; the faculty

Spearman (1904)	*Thorndike (1927)*	*Thurstone (1938)*
2 Basic Factors *g*-eneral *s*-pecific	*3 Types of Thinking* Concrete Social Abstract	*7 Primary Abilities* Space factor Number factor Verbal comprehension Word fluency Memory ability Inductive reasoning Perceptual speed
Guilford (1967)	***Gardner (1983)***	***Sternberg (1985)***
5 Mental Operations Cognition Convergent thinking Divergent thinking Evaluation Memory	*7 "Intelligences"* Logical/mathematical Linguistic Spatial Musical Bodily/kinesthetic Interpersonal Intrapersonal	*3 Components* Componential intelligence Experiential intelligence Contextual intelligence

Figure 5.2. SIX MAJOR THEORETICAL VIEWS ON THE COMPONENTS OF INTELLIGENCE.

for logical thinking; the skill involved in language usage; the aptitude for creative output; and the capacity for concrete thinking. Some students might not be good at math, but they might be skilled in reading, writing, or even in athletics where they can use their physical intelligence. Other students might do rather poorly in activities involving physical abilities (bodily/kinesthetic intelligence), but well in math or subjects that require verbal fluency.

There are, it appears, many different ways to be intelligent. Some students express their intellectual strengths in the classroom, some reflect it in their social and interpersonal skills, while still others show their greatest intelligence in their abilities to work with their hands, to play musical instruments, or perhaps to compete in athletics. However, there are many students (and adults) who do not have a single outstanding ability, but who are moderately endowed in many different areas.

There are many expressions of intelligent behavior. Because students are slow in math or reading does not necessarily mean that they are unintelligent. It could mean that they have not had as many opportunities for learning in those areas or that they really do have aptitude deficits in math and/or reading and, as a consequence, have developed other outlets for their intellectual potential. Intelligence is far more than the ability to pass a test. The ultimate test of intelligence is one's ability to succeed in life, and we need only look around us to see that there are many ways to accomplish that type of success.

5.5 What Is Your View of Intelligence?

Imagine the following scenario: John is a high school senior who has lettered in three varsity sports and will graduate with a 2.2 grade point average. He has been offered athletic scholarships to several small colleges. In contrast, William has never been coordinated enough to go out for any sport, much less letter in any of them, but will graduate with a 3.8 average and attend a large university on an academic scholarship. If you were asked to make a case for which student was more "intelligent," how would you respond?

INTELLECTUAL DEVELOPMENT AS DESCRIBED BY PIAGET

The late Swiss biologist-psychologist Jean Piaget has probably done more to advance our knowledge of intellectual development and stimulate research in this area than any other person. His theoretical observations (1983, 1976, 1970) have been formulated from a vast base of information gathered through years of observing, interviewing, and testing children of all ages.

Early in his career, Piaget made an important discovery. While administering intelligence tests to children, he observed that the same wrong answers were frequently given by children in the same age range. He also noted that children of various ages were giving wrong answers common to their respective age groups. This led him to hypothesize that, rather than older children simply knowing more than younger ones (a quantitative difference), the thought processes of the two groups are qualitatively different.

Central to Piaget's thesis is the idea that a child's intelligence develops in sequential stages, each marked by characteristic and identifiable ways of thinking. The development of each stage is influenced partly by nature and partly by nurture. The child is somehow programmed to master logical thought in predictable developmental stages, with this development dependent on vigorous interaction with the child's environment. Thus, intelligence is not innate to a child; it is something a child helps to create through his or her own activity. For example, until age 5 or 6, most children think that ten pennies that are stacked are quantitatively fewer than when they are spread out in a row. By age 7 or 8, most children understand that the number of pennies does not change, no matter how they are arranged. Children might have the innate ability to grasp a mental picture, but they learn it only though interaction and experience with their environment.

In Piagetian theory, all children construct and constantly revise their own models of reality by going through four sequential stages of intellectual growth. Intelligence begins as a series of simple reflex actions (the infant turns and moves its head in search of a nipple, and sucks when it is found). From this point on, the *mental schema* and *cognitive functions* grow increasingly more organized and adaptive through a process of assimilating new information so that it fits with what is known, and through accommodating old information so that it coincides with new interpretations of reality. Figure 5.3 offers an overview of these basic processes, which are ongoing and occur at increasingly higher levels of complexity from childhood through adulthood. Let's turn our attention to the four sequential stages of intellectual development that are central to Piaget's theory.

The Sensorimotor Stage (Birth to 2 Years)

During this stage of intellectual growth, learning is almost totally dependent on immediate sensory experiences and assorted motor activities. The child's interactions with the environment are governed by overt actions, either physical (e.g., grasping, reaching, sucking, and so forth) or sensory (e.g., seeing and hearing). Initially, a baby does not "think" in the sense of planning or intending, but rather explores and discovers more or less by chance. It is not long, however, before a baby mouths and handles objects intentionally in various ways, depending on what the object is—nipple, toy, thumb, and so on. Within the first month of life, babies begin to follow moving objects with their eyes, suggesting an increased attentiveness to their environment. Within the first several months of life, you can see them reach for objects (suggesting intention-

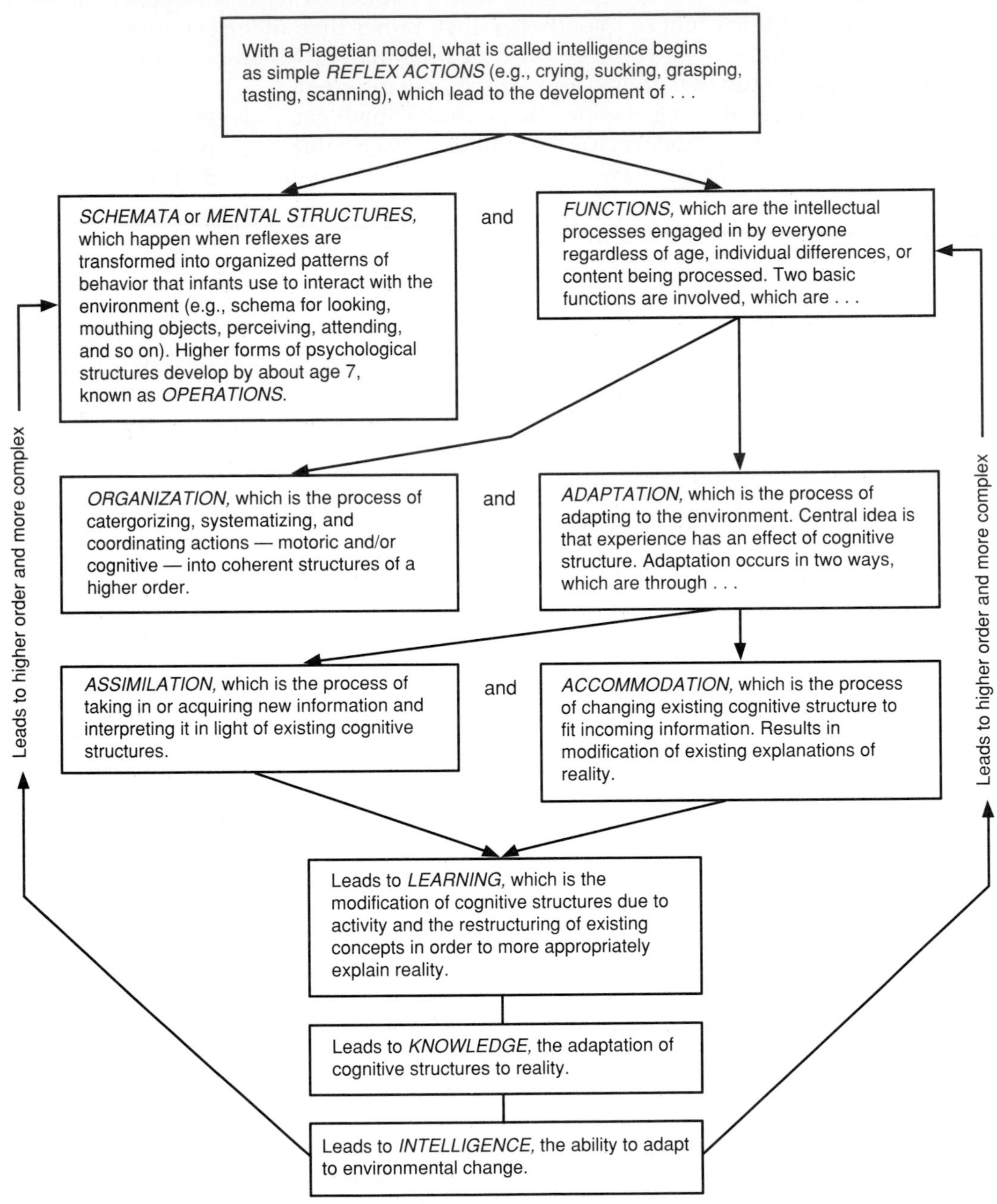

Figure 5.3. BASIC PROCESSES IN PIAGET'S THEORY OF INTELLECTUAL DEVELOPMENT.

ality). At about the fourth or fifth month, we can see a baby both looking *and* reaching for moving objects (suggesting the beginning of perceptual-motor coordination). Cognitive structures quickly grow more refined and highly organized in the first year of life.

The pace of intellectual development is very much influenced by the opportunities a child has for sensory stimulation. Ross (1974), for example, found that 12-month-old babies not only played with and handled novel toys more than familiar toys, but they also remained in rooms with novel toys longer than they did with familiar toys. In other words, novelty and variety tend to capture babies' attention and encourage longer periods of sensorimotor involvement.

The kind of adult–child interaction that occurs also has a great influence on intellectual development at this time. Bradley and Caldwell (1976) found in a thirty-month longitudinal study of twenty-seven black and white, male and female babies that there were significant increases in IQ scores among those children whose mothers were actively involved with them and who provided appropriate and varied playthings. They found significant decreases in IQ among children who came from homes where the environment was poorly organized and less stimulating.

Intellectual Characteristics of the Sensorimotor Stage

Through ongoing sensory and motor explorations, children develop a primitive idea of *object permanence,* the realization that objects continue to exist even when they are out of sight. It is an initial but unconscious insight into the nature of reality. The infant can crawl or totter away from a toy or blanket and return to find it still there. Through sensory and motor explorations, children slowly develop an overall idea of *time, space,* and *causality.* They learn that there is a time to go to bed, to get up, and to eat, and that there is a yesterday, today, and tomorrow. They learn about space as they have opportunities to crawl under, inside, or behind things. They learn about causality when they cry and are fed, and when they knock something over and are admonished. These are the foundational experiences on which subsequent experiences are built. Adequate opportunities for learning about object permanence, time, space, and casualty are very important in the early years.

Egocentrism, the inclination to see things only from one's own point of view, is both characteristic and normal at this age. It takes some time and experience for very young children to learn that the world is not structured according to their point of view alone.

Experimentation, the intentional manipulation of objects, ideas, or events, is another characteristic of the sensorimotor stage. It is a vitally important one, particularly because it reflects not just exploratory behavior, but an exploratory *attitude.* This attitude and behavior can be encouraged, even at a very young age. Rheingold, Stanley, and Cooley (1962) reported that 3-month-old babies, who touched a ball in their crib designed to turn on a short film with musical background, showed more ball-touching behavior than babies who were not rewarded for touching the ball. Exploratory behavior was enhanced when paired with visual and auditory rewards. In another study, White (1965) found that babies who received extra handling as well as large doses of visual stimulation engaged in more visual exploratory activity than babies who were given only normal caretaking.

Circularity, the repetition of behaviors such as sucking, throwing, squeezing, crying, or some combination of these acts, is a characteristic of this age that possibly encourages a primitive sense of mastery or competence. Have you ever watched a 15-month-old child throw a spoon, ball, or both many times with a glow of triumph after each fling?

Imitation, copying another person's behavior, is another feature of this stage. Piaget believed that this was an expression of a baby's effort to understand and become part of his or her reality. It is an incredibly powerful force in early learning. For better or worse, young children absorb the basic ingredients of the environment in which they find themselves by imitating the sights and sounds around them. It is both a conscious and an unconscious process.

Facilitating Cognitive Development in the Sensorimotor Stage

1. Provide young children with a wide range of sensory experiences involving touching, feeling, grasping, sucking, moving, looking, and listening.
2. Give young children a lot of variety. Have a selection of toys and objects of various sizes, colors, and textures available so that you can interchange them. Advise parents with infants that mobiles hung above the crib are an excellent way of providing children with simple but rich visual experiences. Those that combine sights and sounds are particularly interesting to young children.
3. Demonstrate various ways for playing with toys, stacking blocks, or making simple block construction designs.
4. Encourage imitation by repeating sounds, gestures, or body movements that you want the child to learn.
5. Reward young children with smiles, hugs, and verbal feedback that reflect your pleasure when they try something new.
6. Contrive experiences that encourage a degree of repetitive behavior. For example, young children are often enamored of air-filled clowns that are weighted at the bottom and bounce back when knocked over.
7. Avoid overloading the child with too much stimulation and variety. Moderation is the wisest course. Young children need a certain amount of repetition and familiarity in order for the assimilation and accommodation processes to function properly. Too much at one time can overwhelm them.

5.6 What Captures a Young Child's Attention?

Whenever you have a chance, watch for things that capture the attention of children under the age of 2. If you have friends or relatives with children in this age group, it would be quite educational to observe the children whenever you can. You may even find it instructive to ask your parents, if they are available to you, what they remember of your behavior during your first couple of years. What things captured your attention?

The Preoperational Stage (2 to 7 Years)

Up to this stage, children's intellectual skills rest primarily in the ability to use their senses and to interact with the world through movement. During the preoperational stage, something new is added—language. Piaget (1967) observed that language is essential to cognitive development in three basic ways:

1. Language allows us to communicate ideas and thoughts, thus beginning the process of socialization.
2. Language assists thinking and memory, both of which are the internal processing of events and experiences.
3. Language allows a person to construct mental pictures and images, which allows one to conduct mental experiments.

This is called the *preoperational* stage because children's thinking at this time is guided more by intuition (i.e., knowledge without rational thought or inference) than by logic. As Piaget used the term, a *mental operation* refers to truly logical acts or thoughts. Two- to 7-year-old children are not there yet, although we may begin to see the inception of logical processes in some 7-year-olds and a few 6-year-olds.

Intellectual Characteristics of the Preoperational Stage

Although children in this stage use very little logic, they do engage in more abstract thinking than they were capable of in the sensorimotor stage. For example, they are able to use *nonverbal symbolism*, which is the use of objects in ways other than those for which they are designed (a big box turned upside down becomes a dark cave; a broom becomes a speedy horse). With this capacity, preoperational children can play house, school, store, and cops and robbers by using only a few props and imagining the rest. When my daughter, Debbie, was in this stage, she was fond of inviting me into her "kitchen"—a corner of the rec room—for a "dinner" that she had cooked on her play stove. Blocks of wood were bread, bowls of water were our favorite soups, and shredded paper was a special pudding. My daughter, like many 6-year-olds, was very convincing in her imaginary play. On more than one occasion, when through "eating," I had the strange sense that I really *had* eaten something!

Children in this stage are also able to use *verbal symbolism,* which allows language to represent objects, situations, experiences, and events. A child, for example, might ask why the sun goes down behind the trees or might tell you that a particular cloud formation looks like a "doggy." In both instances, language is being used to get information or to communicate a perception.

During this second stage of cognitive development, children's language behaviors, similar to the manipulative activities of the sensorimotor stage, are generally characterized by *egocentrism, repetitiveness, experimentation,* and *imitation.*

Language behavior is largely *egocentric* because, as Piaget (1973) noted, a child in this stage

> talks either for himself or for the pleasure of associating anyone who happens to be there with the activity of the moment. This talk is egocentric, partly because the child speaks only about himself, but chiefly because he does not attempt to place himself at the point of view of his hearer. (p. 32)

Children's egocentric language grows somewhat more encompassing between 3.5 and 5 years of age. For example, Mueller (1972) observed that when two children in this age group were playing and one child said something, the other child answered or said something appropriate more than 60% of the time. Another 23% of the time the child at least paid attention to his or her partner, which suggests both an inclination and a capacity to grow beyond a consuming self-centeredness.

The *repetitiveness* so characteristic of children's behavior in the sensorimotor stage is now reflected in their language usage. Nothing delights 2- and 3-year olds more than repeating newly learned words and phrases, listening repeatedly to their favorite stories, or repetitiously pointing out the words and pictures they know in their storybooks. It is self-reinforcing to be able to remember increasingly more words and pictures from recognition alone. It is the stuff of which a sense of mastery and competence is built.

Language experimentation is a big part of the preoperational stage. Children like using new words and talking in new ways, such as speaking in a fast or slow manner, using nonsense words, or playing with tongue twisters (e.g., "Sally sold seashells by the seashore."). At your present level of intellectual development, you probably take your language usage more or less for granted, but have you ever found yourself deliberately looking for ways and excuses to use an interesting new word you learned? Reinforcement and satisfaction are associated with using that new word, and so it is with young children.

Research is clear in pointing out that environmental circumstances have a great deal to do with the breadth and degree of a child's verbal experimentation (Grimm, Goff, and Ashburn, 1980). Opportunities for practicing language are critical to verbal development. For example, Lovitt and Smith (1972) have shown that simply asking children with poor speech to explain and to invent stories about pictures can greatly improve children's verbal performance.

Language imitation is the fourth major intellectual characteristic of the preoperational child and is closely related to experimentation. Imitative speech is a largely conscious process of copying the language sounds that children hear in the world around them. You can see them doing this when they use a toy telephone or when they get involved in the various roles associated with playing house or school. Imitative speech is the primary vehicle that children use to expand their awareness of the world. Parents and teachers can greatly influence verbal learning, for better or worse. Along this line, Piagetian psychologist Ruth Beard (1969) has observed:

> All evidence suggests that in addition to the provision of a stimulating environment, attention from adults and older children, especially in answering questions and in conversation, is immensely important to developing in this stage. It is in these respects that many children from poor environments suffer. (p. 55)

By the end of the preoperational period, most children begin to show signs of outgrowing their egocentrism. They come to understand that a given situation can be viewed in various ways. They do, however, tend to retain a sort of egocentrism in their feelings; that is, they might find it difficult to understand that someone else feels differently about a situation than they do. This aspect of egocentrism does not change much until adolescence, and it might never be lost completely. As adults, many of us are still unable to understand another person's emotional perspective. How many times have we heard someone say, "I can't understand how he or she could feel that way"?

Between the ages of 5 and 7, children begin to think in terms of classes, to handle concepts, and to see simple relationships. Thinking at this time is largely intuitive because even though they may be able to grasp particular concepts (e.g., knowing that oatmeal and cornflakes are both cereals), they do not really understand how or why. Children also begin to develop a gradual awareness of conservation of mass, weight, and volume; that is, they begin to see that an amount remains the same even if transferred to a different-sized container.

Facilitating Cognitive Development in the Preoperational Stage

1. Be prepared to do a lot of listening. Preoperational children do a great deal of talking, frequently repeating their favorite stories and experiences. For them, new language skills are like new toys. Let them play with these emerging skills without always correcting them and giving crash courses in basic English.

2. Practice correct language skills yourself. Talk to children, respond, ask questions, do whatever you can to encourage language use. Be a good model.
3. Encourage children to describe, to look at, and to draw things from various perspectives. This helps them learn that there is more than one way to see the world. Ask questions such as, "How would that look from a mountain top?" or "How might that seem to a person who could not see?"
4. Be patient and tolerant when children have trouble explaining something. A young child's reply to "Why did you do that?" is frequently "Because," or "I don't know." Remember that preoperational children have difficulty reflecting on their own thoughts and acts.
5. Concentrate on facilitating intellectual development rather than on trying to accelerate it. Provide preoperational children with opportunities to explore their environment and to experiment with what they find in it. They love to construct, to tear down, and to start all over again.

The Concrete-Operational Stage (7 to 11 Years)

This is the time in intellectual development when children begin to acquire the ability to perform what Piaget refers to as *operations*—cognitive maneuvers based more on logical reasoning than on intuitive functioning. Children show increasing concern about *why* things are happening. In addition, there is a shift from egocentrism to *relativism,* the ability to think from different perspectives and to think simultaneously about two or more aspects of a problem.

Intellectual Characteristics of the Concrete-Operational Stage

During this stage, children grow increasingly more capable of performing specific actions (operations) that have an impact on objects or events as long as they are concretely present. Hence, it is called the concrete-operational stage. (Keep in mind that the term *operations* is a Piagetian term for what are usually called "intellectual skills.")

A basic operation we see in this stage is that of *conservation,* the law that states that liquids and solids can be changed in shape without altering their volume or mass. For example, in the preoperational stage, children are able to form and to talk about simple concepts, such as the quantity of liquid, but they are easily confused once the apparent quantity is changed. However, an 11-year-old who watches water being poured from a tall, narrow glass into a short, broad glass knows that the amount of water is the same, regardless of the glass in which it is held.

Decentration, another characteristic of this stage, refers to the ability of a child to consider more than one characteristic of an object at the same time. Whereas a 4-year-old tends to concentrate only on the height of a glass and concludes that more water is in it, an 11-year-old is able to consider both height *and* volume. In doing this, the older child uses *reversibility,* an operation that allows him or her to imagine what conditions were like before they were altered. As adults, we do this often without even thinking about it. For example, you transfer some money from your savings account to your checking account. Does this mean you have less money? Assuming you do not spend it right away, you will not because you recognize that transferring money from one account to the other still leaves you with the same amount. This would hold true no matter how you transferred the money. This is the basic idea behind reversibility.

When children acquire these operations, they become increasingly able to use elementary deductive reasoning. However, they still depend a great deal on actual contact with concrete reality. They are not able to handle hypothetical problems or abstract issues. Most 11-year-olds could probably understand a problem such as the following:

> Sally is shorter than Debbie.
> Barbara is taller than Debbie.
> Who is taller, Sally or Barbara?

"Shorter" and "taller" are familiar words. The 11-year-old has a concrete idea of what taller is in relation to shorter. Yet, he or she would have considerable trouble with a question such as the following: if you assume that there are ten hours in a day and thirty minutes in an hour, how many minutes would there be in a week? In order to answer this question, a child would have to imagine an unreal and nonexistent time structure along with using hypothetical considerations to solve the problem. The question is abstract and hypothetical; thus, it is beyond the intellectual capacities of most children at this stage of intellectual development.

5.7 Some Research You Can Do on Conservation

If you can arrange access to some children who are age 7 and younger and others who are age 8 and older, you can see the principle of conservation in action. All you need is a tall, narrow glass and a short, broad glass. How do 4-year-olds respond to water being poured from one to the other? Will they suddenly "see more" if the water is poured from the short glass to the tall one? What are their responses? What do they give as reasons? Compare these with those of the older children. What are the differences?

Facilitating Cognitive Development in the Concrete-Operational Stage

1. Be as concrete and specific as possible when teaching children between the ages of 7 and 11. Use as many visual examples as possible, such as

hands-on objects, maps, charts, pictures, anything you can think of to make word abstractions concrete.

2. Remember that there are wide individual differences in the ability of children to perform the concrete operations of this stage (conservation, decentration, reversibility, and classification). Make it a practice to know your students well. Get a feel for what each one is able to do.
3. Provide as many opportunities as possible for interacting with the environment in tangible, tactile ways. For example, if teaching about shapes, arrange to have props available that represent different possibilities (i.e., square, rectangular, triangular, or circular) that the children are able to see, touch, and look at from various perspectives.
4. Encourage children to think in terms of cause-and-effect relationships by offering them opportunities to speculate on the outcomes of events or experiences and to give reasons for their speculations. For example, a fifth-grade teacher I know uses this principle in teaching her students that ordinary tap water contains valuable minerals and nutrients necessary for growth by feeding one plant tap water for two weeks and a similar plant distilled water. The students speculated about what might happen, and then kept an eye on the actual consequences of the two feedings. They learned first by talking and then by observing. It was a good learning experience.
5. Help students to be less egocentric by giving them opportunities to both listen to and express the ideas and views of others. For example, a sixth-grade teacher I know successfully teaches about the facts and feelings associated with the ignominious days of slavery in America by having her students role-play a little drama she concocted involving buyers, sellers, and slaves in a marketplace. Then the students talked about the experience. Her students learned a great deal, both at an objective, factual level and at a subjective, affective level.

The Formal-Operational Stage (11 Years and Older)

Somewhere between the ages of 11 and 15, children's intellectual capacities develop to the level at which they are able to do more hypothetical thinking and trial-and-error reasoning. A 15-year-old is able to imagine the earth rotating in its orbit around the sun and relate the idea of rotation and orbit to sunrises and sunsets. A preoperational child, however, would probably need an actual model of the sun and the earth in order to understand these relationships. This is a basic characteristic of children in this stage—they are able to see more in their heads, abstractly and hypothetically. The term *formal* refers to the development of a *form* or structure of thinking. You could even think of it as the growing capacity to *form* hypotheses.

Intellectual Characteristics of the Formal-Operational Stage

A significant change in intellectual ability can be seen in a youngster's ability to concentrate more on possibilities than on realities. For example, a pre-operational child who sees a picture of a car wrecked in an accident might simply conclude that it hit a tree and went into a ditch. An adolescent at the formal-operations stage might suggest a variety of causes, ranging from a slippery road, to poor brakes, or to a sleepy driver. The adolescent's ability to conceptualize and hypothesize beyond the concrete data leads to all sorts of possibilities.

As noted by Ginsburg and Opper (1979), the expanding intellectual skills of adolescence is not without its problems:

> Having just discovered capabilities for abstract thought, [the adolescent] then proceeds to exercise them without restraint. Indeed, in the process of exploring his new abilities the adolescent sometimes loses touch with reality, and feels that he can now accomplish everything by thought alone . . . whereas earlier he could love his mother or hate a peer, now he can love freedom or hate exploitation . . . the possible and the ideal captivate both mind and feeling. (pp. 204–205)

It is the exercise of these intellectual powers without restraint and the loss of touch with reality that sometimes results in adolescents and adults locking horns. Adolescents are inclined to be impatient with parents or other adults who fail to find quick solutions to complex problems. They frequently see many alternatives to the way things are presently done and, in the absence of a sufficient experiential base for making wise decisions, their proposed solutions to economic and social ills tend to be more idealistic than ideal. It is not until later in the adolescent years, when they begin to see the complexities of interpersonal relationships and of economic and social problems, that adolescents develop a more tempered understanding of the world in which they live. They begin to see that complex problems are not solved by simple solutions.

The Capacity for Formal Thinking Varies Widely

The ability to engage in formal-operational thinking is not an automatic occurrence. In fact, Piaget (1974) himself observed that most adults were probably capable of using formal-operational thought in only a few areas, those being where they had the greatest interest or experience. In their research with college students representing three different majors (physics, political science, and English), DeLisi and Staudt (1980) came up with data that supported Piaget's observation. They found, for example, that although most students were able to use formal-operational thinking when confronted with problems similar to those found in their own majors, only about one-half of them were able to use formal-thinking processes when they were asked to find solutions to problems outside their own majors. Not only are there large numbers of adolescents and adults who do not use formal-operational thinking, but there also is a wide age range among those who do. For example, Higgens-Trenk and Gaite (1971) have shown that only about one-half of the 17-year-olds they studied reached the apex of that stage. In contrast, Brainerd (1975) and Ennis (1975) found that some children as young as age 8 or 9 could perform the operations associated with adolescent thinking.

Some of the criticisms of Piaget's work have been aimed at his description of formal-operational thinking. Basically, the critics have said that Piaget's portrait of formal operations is too idealistic and his standards for thinking are too high (Flavell, 1985). Most adults are neither capable of, nor interested in, that sort of logical, scientific reasoning Piaget associated with this stage. The truth is, most adults are not scientists. This does not mean that they are incapable of scientific thinking, but it does suggest that they do not apply formal operations automatically or consistently.

Remember that, in this stage of formal operations, as in the other three stages, there is a considerable range of individual differences in students' readiness and their abilities.

Facilitating Cognitive Development in the Formal-Operational Stage

1. It is particularly important to remember that a fair number of students between ages 11 and 14 will still be in the preoperational stage and, thus, not as quick in picking up on activities or discussions that are too abstract.
2. With this in mind, it is a good idea to have a good stock of concrete learning aids on hand. These aids will be helpful to youth who overlap the preoperational stage, and they will be helpful to more advanced students in testing their reasoning and in checking their answers visually. For example, not all students can "see" where a certain country is in their minds; a globe can help.
3. Be wary of the tendency to blame students for not working hard enough if their work is below average. Not working hard enough is sometimes the cause, but even the most determined students can not do more than their level of cognitive development will allow.
4. Remember that some students at this stage are more concerned with possibilities than realities. When class discussions become unrealistically abstract and hypothetical, point out to your students the facts of the matter and ask for practical solutions.
5. Be tolerant of and patient with a certain amount of idealistic thinking. More experience with life will moderate this. Students who are embarrassed or made fun of for their ideas might not cease their idealistic ways, but they might stop talking about them.

Can you think of some examples of when your own thinking processes began to evolve from concrete-operational to formal-operational processes? How was this kind of thinking reflected in your behavior in terms of how you processed information about yourself and the world around you?

Weaknesses and Limitations of Piaget's Theory

One of the major questions raised about Piaget's theory is whether cognition develops through four successive stages, as he proposed (Gelman and Baillargeon, 1983). Piaget's critics have argued that if there are separate stages and if children's reasoning at each stage is based on a particular set of mental operations, then once children have mastered these operations they should be fairly consistent in solving all problems requiring those operations.

This view grows directly from a major premise of Piaget's theory, which is that at each stage of cognitive growth children possess an underlying structure of logic. If this is true, we could expect that children at any given stage would use similar logic in dealing with a variety of problems. We should, in other words, expect to see similar mental processes.

However, the research findings of Keating and Clark (1980), Klausmeirer and Sipple (1982), Martorano (1977), and Roberge and Flexer (1979) suggest that this kind of consistency does not always exist across different tasks. Achenbach and Weisz (1975), for example, found that 4- and 5-year-olds might succeed in correctly arranging colored objects from light to dark, but fail to put a group of blocks in order correctly from longest to shortest. If the ability to put objects in correct serial order is a basic concept, why is it that children are able to apply it to some tasks, but not others?

Piaget's response to this question was that, although there is an overall structure to each stage, all the skills constituting that structure do not emerge at precisely the same time. The results of a three-year longitudinal study by Tomlinson-Keasey and her colleagues (1979), who tested the same group of children from the first grade through the third grade, tended to confirm Piaget's observation. They found that there were differences among children in the same grade in their abilities to deal with the conservation of mass, weight, and volume (the idea that even though the shape of a ball of clay can be changed, its mass is conserved). They also found that a child's position on these conservation tasks stayed approximately the same throughout the three years of testing. A 6-year-old who was able to understand conservation of mass continued to be ahead of the other children later on. A later-developing child went through the same sequence about two years later.

This and other research shows that while all concrete operations tasks are not mastered at the same time by all children, there is a sequence involved.

John Flavell (1985), a major interpreter of Piaget, has argued that these differences in the emergence of various intellectual skills show that cognitive development occurs as a continuous, gradual process rather than in four major stages, as Piaget's theory suggests.

The problem with any stage theory of development is that there will always be individual differences among children of similar ages in physical, social, or intellectual growth and along a particular stage continuum. Nonetheless, the weight of the evidence suggests that by the end of any given stage of cognitive development, most normally developing children are able to do most of the intellectual tasks associated with that stage. Hence, we would expect to find the greatest variability in intellectual ability at the beginning of a new stage rather than at the end. Intellectual development is continuous to the extent that it is an ongoing process, but it grows in stages to the extent that certain mental operations need to be learned at four different times, or stages, along that continuum.

Another weakness of Piaget's theory is that it tends to promote the underestimation of the intellectual abilities of younger children. For example, research by Gelman, Meck, and Merkin (1986) and Miller and Gelman (1983) points to the strong possibility that preschool children understand more about the concept of number than Piaget thought. Newer research shows that as long as preschoolers work with only three or four objects at a time, they are able to tell that the number remains the same, even though the objects are spread apart or grouped close together. To Piaget, the children may have appeared to be confused or unable to do this because the problems he gave them were too difficult and the directions too confusing.

The bottom line is that younger children may be more intellectually competent for their age than Piaget imagined. For example, rather than learning that objects are permanent, they may have simply learned how to look for them, which may suggest that we are born with more innate cognitive tools than Piaget gave credit for.

No theory is ever perfect. Piaget's is no exception. Although new research has pointed to some weaknesses in his conceptual offerings about the nature of cognitive growth and functioning, the general tenets of Piaget's theoretical framework continue to serve as valid guidelines on how to enhance children's learning at all levels. Thomas (1992) who has done a comparative analysis of various theories of development, comments on Piaget:

> I am convinced that the greater part of Piaget's writings is valuable and accurate. After studying his works, I feel that we can understand the development of children's thinking processes far better than before. . . . I feel that the theory rates a high mark. (p. 318)

Let us turn our attention to yet another viewpoint on children's intellectual development.

VYGOTSKY'S SOCIAL-COGNITIVE THEORY

Lev Semenovich Vygotsky was a Russian psychologist who made major contributions to the field of psychology in the 1920s. However, because of disputes within the Soviet Union's psychological community, his work was suppressed (like so many other things in the former Soviet Union), and it was not until 1962 that his work began to appear in English translations. While Piaget's conception of a child was that of a "little scientist" who alone constructs an understanding of the world, Vygotsky (1978, 1986) believed that a child's cognitive development depends much more on language and social support.

Vygotsky's social-cognitive theory is characterized by three underlying themes, which include: (1) the importance of culture, (2) the role of language, and (3) the idea of a zone of proximal growth. The theory has a strong social emphasis and places a high value on interactive opportunities and experiences in order to promote cognitive development.

Culture plays an important part in Vygotsky's theory because it is viewed as the social medium in which children interact with the more competent members of their social environment, including more capable peers and adults. These people serve as intellectual guides, providing the information and stimulation necessary for cognitive development. This kind of intellectual assistance is referred to as *scaffolding*, a term used to suggest the idea that children use this kind of social support to help them construct the intellectual foundation that will eventually enable them to solve more problems on their own.

A major theme in Vygotsky's theory is the idea that children begin to use language, not only as a means to communicate with others, but also to plan and guide their own activities. One of the ways they use language is through the involvement of *inner speech*, which is, basically, the process of using language to talk one's way through the steps needed to accomplish a certain task. How many times, for example, have you heard yourself say, "now, let's see, the first thing I have to do is . . . and then I'll . . . "? Inner speech is used to help us solve problems by clarifying what needs to be done and verbally outlining the steps needed to follow through. Palincsar and Brown (1989) have found a positive relationship between children's inner speech and task performance, which suggests that inner speech does indeed help young students solve problems.

Another of Vygotsky's main themes revolves around his idea that every child has a sphere or zone of current capabilities, which he referred to as a child's *zone of proximal growth*. What this zone refers to is the idea that at any given point in children's intellectual growth there are certain problems that they are close to being able to handle. At such times, children need to be encouraged, perhaps by clues, reminders, gentle prodding, more instruction, or whatever it takes to bring them to the edge of new knowledge. Some problems, of course, can be solved without help. Other problems are clearly beyond some children's capacities to understand, no matter how clear and detailed the explanation. Wertsch (1985) has indicated that a child's zone of proximal development is a kind of middle point—the point at which a child cannot solve a problem alone but is capable of doing so with some adult guidance or the help of a more advanced classmate. In Vygotsky's view, instruction and learning can occur at this point because this is when students have a real readiness for new knowledge.

5.9 An Example of Guiding Students within Their Zone of Proximal Development

Although his class was very interested, a seventh-grade science teacher was having trouble getting some of his students to see how an airplane's wings enabled it to fly by creating a low pressure area over the top of the wings and a high pressure area underneath them. Diagrams on the board did not quite do it. So, to illustrate the point, he brought a large fan to class, turned it on high, and had his students take turns holding their hands in the shape of an airplane's wings in front of the fan. Experiencing the natural lifting sensation in their hands drove the point home. His students now understood how an air pressure differential was created to enable airplanes to fly. A creative teacher found a novel way to teach an abstract idea, thus helping his students acquire new knowledge within what Vygotsky referred to as their zone of proximal development.

Implications of Vygotsky's Views

Three educational implications can be extracted from this brief overview of Vygotsky's social-cognitive theory. First, the theory underscores the importance of language in the development of intellectual functioning. The theory stresses the idea that language is a social and cultural phenomenon that is centrally involved in the development of higher mental processes. Thus, the importance of language development is seen as a critical and urgent part of every school curriculum, especially when children are beginning to develop language skills.

Second, Vygotsky's theory highlights the idea that cognitive development is strongly affected by students' cultural and social environments. Specifically, the theory suggests that children's educational environment be structured in such a way as to encourage them to function at a level slightly in advance of their current developmental level. The idea is that students should be put in situations in which they have to stretch their minds to understand, but in which support and assistance from the teacher or peer helpers are always available.

The third implication is critical. Because teachers are advised to present materials that are slightly ahead of their students' developmental level, it is imperative that teachers know their students as well as possible in order to stay within, but at the upper levels of, their zones of proximal development.

5.10 A Way to Keep Interest

Have you ever noticed how a problem, puzzle, or project that is somewhat difficult, but not unsolvable, will keep your attention and hold your interest longer than one that is too easy? Essentially, this is the idea behind presenting students with material slightly ahead of their current developmental level. It keeps them interested.

INTELLECTUAL FUNCTIONING AND BRAIN DEVELOPMENT

Sitting at the top of your spine, floating in a shock-absorbing fluid, and protected by about one-half of an inch of bone, is nature's greatest invention, the human brain. If you are a woman, your brain weight is just under three pounds; if you are a man, it is slightly over. This weight difference is not surprising because women are, on average, smaller than men. When that fact is taken into account, the brain proportions are much the same for both sexes. In any case, brain size in the human animal is not very important. The largest human brain known weighed six pounds; it belonged to a mentally defective person. What is inside the brain, not its size, is what matters.

We might better understand and appreciate intelligence and intellectual development if we first have an understanding of the development of this remarkable organ.

Overview of the Brain's Development

Research in recent years has taught us a great deal about the brain's growth and functioning (Groves and Rebec, 1988; Kolb, 1989; Maranto, 1984). The brain begins to develop about three weeks after conception. Thousands of new brain cells develop each minute, with growth being especially rapid between the second and third months. By birth, the brain's weight is close to one pound, about one-third of its eventual weight. Those parts of the brain that regulate basic processes, such as breathing, circulation, and consciousness, are fully developed at birth, as they must be for the child to survive. Brain functions less critical to immediate survival, such as those controlling language use and mobility, mature after birth.

The brain adds its second pound during the first year of life, with much of this growth occurring in the cerebellum, located under the bump on the base of the head. Functioning much like the brain's automatic pilot, the cerebellum coordinates the responses of muscle groups involved in some of the complicated, unconscious movements we engage in, such as walking, playing tennis, or typing. As the cerebellum develops, a child begins to crawl, then walks, and eventually runs.

The third, and final, pound develops between ages 2 and 16, a period of movement from the initial helpless, wordless state of the infant to the independent, communicative state of the mature adult.

The brain is composed of a communications network of at least ten billion neurons, approximately the number of hairs on the heads of 100,000 persons. It would take about 100,000 neurons to fill a space the size of a pinhead. Each neuron is linked synaptically to thousands of other neurons (Figure 5.4). In fact, the web of connections between neurons in the top layer of the brain—called the neocortex—is so dense that it would measure an incredible 10,000 miles per cubic inch if strung out (Jastrow, 1981). The final pound of the adult three-pound brain involves the growth of more remote axon/dendrite extensions throughout the neural network, along with an insulating layer of myelin around the axons. Not only has this final sixteen ounces of growth been found to have an enormous impact on the brain's capability, but its growth also corresponds roughly to Piaget's stages of intellectual development.

Brain Growth and Relationships to Piaget's Stages

Continuing research in brain development is pointing to the possibility that brain growth between the ages of 2 and 16 does not occur continuously, but develops in four, four-year cycles: 3 to 10 months, 2 to 4 years, 6 to 8 years, 10 to 12 (plus) years, and 14 to 16 (plus) years (Epstein, 1979a, 1980, 1990; Hudspeth and Pribram, 1990). (Ten months to 4 years is one cycle, 4 years to 8 years a second cycle, and so on.) It has been noted that there is a period of rapid growth at the beginning of each cycle, followed by a period of relative dormancy as the new growth is integrated into the existing cognitive system. (We see this same pattern in nature. A tree branch, for example, grows very rapidly during the spring and then is relatively dormant until growth begins anew the following spring.) You can see in Table 5.1 that brain growth roughly overlaps the stages of intellectual development identified by Piaget.

Table 5.1. CYCLES OF BRAIN GROWTH AND COGNITIVE CORRELATES

Growth period	*Integration period*	*Cognitive correlates (Piaget)*
3–10 mos.	3–10 mos.	Sensorimotor stage movement
2–4 yrs.	4–6 yrs.	Preoperational stage Language development Fusion of thought and language
6–8 yrs.	8–10 yrs.	Concrete operational stage Reading/writing
10–12+ yrs. (female brain grows faster than male brain)	12–14 yrs.	Formal operational stage Abstract thought and problem solving
14–16+ yrs. (male brain grows faster than female brain)	16 yrs. and throughout adult life	Self-awareness and problem finding

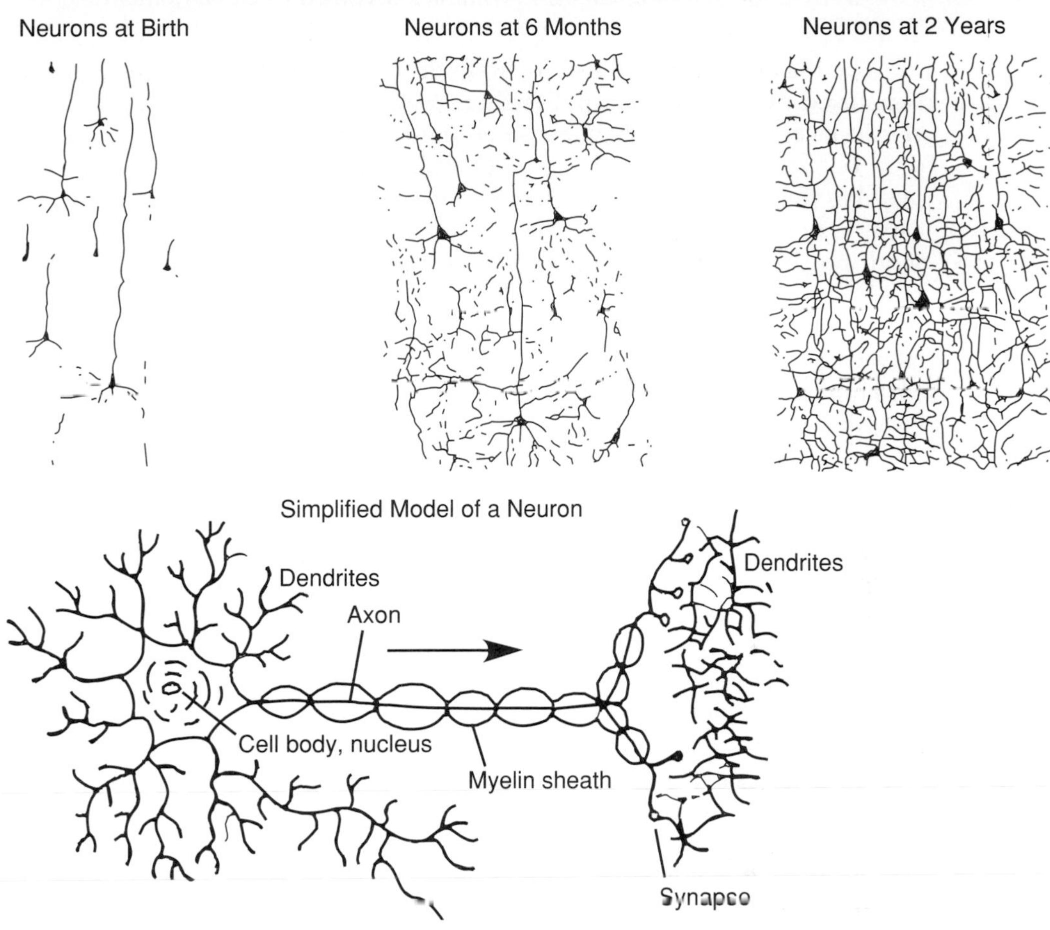

Figure 5.4. A SHORT LESSON IN NEURONAL GROWTH AND BIOCHEMISTRY. Neurons form the brain's communication network. Highly interconnected, they regulate consciousness, perception, thought, and action. Information is processed in neurons in a three-step sequence. First, a large number of short, tubular projections on the cell body, called *dendrites,* receive chemical information from other junctures called *synapses.* The information comes in the form of coded molecules, called *neurotransmitters,* that are released at the synapse and electrically relayed to other neurons through a long projection known as an *axon.* When this information reaches the end of the axon, it releases stored neurotransmitters that are synaptically connected with the dendrites of surrounding neurons. At maturity, a single neuron may be in direct contact with over 1000 nearby and distant neurons through axon/dendrite connections. Since axons transmit chemical information electrically, they are wrapped in what is called a *myelin sheath* to ensure that messages will not be lost because of a loss of power. (Multiple sclerosis, for example, involves a breakdown of the myelin sheath, resulting in many short-circuits along transmitting lines.) As the brain gains its final pound of weight between the ages of 2 and 16, its billions of axons and dendrites are developing synapses and extending out to other neurons throughout the neural network. It is this kind of microcellular growth that permits the brain to develop increasingly more extensive, complex, and reliable interneural connections. The end product is the gradual development of a potentially broader and more efficiently functioning mind.

The idea for a linkage among brain growth and Piaget's stages is further supported by the research of Thatcher, Walker, and Guidice (1987). Using an electroencephalograph, they measured brain wave activity of 577 normal children between 2 months of age and adulthood. (Measures such as this are possible because the brain is something of a self-contained electrical plant capable of generating about twenty-five watts of power, thus enabling it to send information through its trillions of connections at about 250 miles per hour.) Thatcher, Walker, and Guidice (1987) found five major increases in the rate of brain growth, inferred from changes in brain wave activity, that occurred from birth to about 3 years of age, from 4 to 7, from 8 to 10, from 11 to 14, and from 15 years of age to adulthood. You can see how closely these growth periods correspond to Piaget's stages.

Implications for Teaching Practices

Epstein's analysis of brain development research concluded with the observation that about 85% of all children's brain growth falls into the five major growth cycles described previously. This growth pattern has been observed in normal children from a range of countries and cultures. Although this is a very high percentage, we need to keep in mind that brain growth for about 15% of children is either slower or more rapid than the rest. In addition, it is important to remember that although most children of the same age are experiencing somewhat similar rates of brain growth, many individual differences in intellectual performance still exist. Similar brain size does not mean similar abilities and aptitudes. Heredity and environment are also involved.

Brain growth research indicates that major periods of brain development are likely to occur in six of the K to 12 years (grades 1, 2, 5, 7, 9, and 10), and it occurs throughout the year in a normal classroom group. This suggests that a good number of students will experience their growth during the summer, which might help explain why some might not have done very well in the previous school year; their neuronal development just was not ready. Simply being aware of this as a possibility might temper your judgment of students' academic performances. Some students fail to perform well because they simply do not try. Other students fall short because, neurologically, they are not ready to comprehend particular material. The growth of the entire child must be taken into account.

Research also indicated that normative sex differences exist in brain growth patterns. Epstein's (1979b) findings indicate that brain growth in girls tends to occur earlier than in boys with each of the major growth periods. Elementary teachers, who have said for years that boys should not begin school until they are 6 or 7 years old, might have had a point. Girls are generally ahead of boys in all phases of growth, including brain development, during the first twelve or so years of life. Boys' brain growth does not match girls' until they are between the ages of 14 and 16, which is when their physical development also catches up.

We cannot easily change these biological facts, but we can allow them to sensitize us to the idea that the rate and timing of brain development might have something to do with why some students understand the material at hand, while others do not.

Although there is a significant database suggesting a general relationship between brain growth and Piaget's stages of intellectual development, another brain researcher, Robert McCall (1990), has urged that we be cautious about making educational decisions based on relatively new information. Thus, brain research continues. With more knowledge about its functions, we will undoubtedly be better able to develop curriculum and teaching methods to take advantage of the brain's unfolding readiness to learn.

THE EFFECTS OF NATURE AND NURTURE ON INTELLIGENCE

There are two facts about the relative effects of nature and nurture on intelligence that have withstood the rigors of research and the test of time, and about which most psychologists would agree. The first is that environment does indeed have a strong impact on a person's development, generally, and intellectual growth, specifically. It does not take sophisticated studies to demonstrate that children raised in impoverished homes or by neglectful, abusive families will generally not turn out as well as children raised in stimulating, warm, and supportive homes. Environment can, and does, make a difference. If the environment is changed, the behavior of a child also changes, a process called *malleability.* Improvements in the environment enhance the child's behavior. For example, Scarr and Weinberg (1983) have shown that when children from deprived backgrounds are adopted into intellectually enriched homes, their IQ scores and school achievement improve significantly.

Another important point to consider is that genes do not fix behavior; rather, they establish a range of possible reactions to a range of possible experiences to which one may be exposed. Many believe the myth that if a characteristic is genetic, it cannot be changed. This is not necessarily true. We know, for example, that there is a very high correlation (approximately 0.90, which is not far from a perfect 1.00 correlation) between height and heredity. In spite of the high correlation between these two factors, the average height of people in the United States and Japan has increased several inches in the past seventy years. Better nutrition and sounder health practices have contributed to this increase in height. In other words, by improving specific environmental conditions, genetic potential has been changed. Tuberculosis (TB) was once highly hereditary, but now the bacillus that carries the disease is so rare that contracting TB depends less on one's genetic susceptibility and more on one's likelihood of exposure. The heredity of TB is now low. Therefore, those who argue that one's IQ or intelligence is subject largely to hereditary influences, and thus not subject to change, fail to give credit to our ability to influence performance in the future.

Environment and genes are in constant interaction. At the level of the individual it is not possible to specify how much either one is contributing; however, at the level of statistical generalization involving large numbers of persons, the results from large-scale studies involving twins (both fraternal and identical) suggest that nature and nurture each contribute an average of 50% to children's development (Tellegin et al., 1988; Segal, 1990). Twin studies are a rich source of information on the relative effects of heredity and environment because if there are dramatic differences between identical twins reared apart (remember, they share the *same* genes), those differences can be attributed to the environment. Thus, twin studies are a natural way to control for the effects of heredity on behavior.

We cannot alter one's genes, but we can have a significant influence on the environment in which one's genetic potential is expressed. Along these lines, an observation by Bloom (1969) is worth considering:

> Psychologists and geneticists may wish to speculate about how to improve the genetic pool—educators cannot and should not. Educators must be environmentalists—bridled or unbridled. It is through the environment that they must fashion the educational process. Learning goes on by providing the appropriate environment. If heredity imposes limits—so be it. Educators must work with what is left, whether it be 20 percent of the variance or 50 percent. (p. 50)

SCHOOL PERFORMANCE AS RELATED TO INTELLIGENCE

People frequently wonder whether students' measured intelligence is related to how well, or how poorly, they do in school. The fact is, intelligence tests tend to predict school achievement rather well, at least for large groups. Research indicates that general intelligence tests typically have a positive correlation with achievement, between 0.50 and 0.60; this holds true for a great variety of courses and subjects (Bloom, 1976; Sattler, 1988). Again, a perfect correlation being 1.00, 0.50 and 0.60 are considered moderately high. Some students with high IQs do not do that well in school, and some lower IQ students do quite well. On the whole, however, students with higher IQ scores are more likely to be among the high achievers in school than those students with lower scores.

It is not surprising to find a positive correlation between IQ and achievement, because there is a 90% to 95% overlap between material included in intelligence tests and material found in both standardized and classroom achievement tests. A telling characteristic of the correlation between intelligence test scores and achievement is that scores tend to be highest for subjects heavily dependent on verbal and reasoning ability, perhaps reflecting the fact that the tests sample these abilities more than others.

Another question frequently asked is whether those who score higher on IQ tests also achieve more in life. The answer to this is much less clear. What is clear is that people with higher IQs usually complete more years of school. However, when years of education are consistent, intelligence scores and school achievement are not highly related with either income or success in later life. Factors that cannot be measured by an IQ test, such as desire, willingness to work hard, motivation, social skills, or just plain luck, make a big difference in a person's success. It has been consistently noted, however, that the average IQ scores of members of different occupational groups vary considerably. Those with the highest average scores tend to be top civil servants, research scientists, and professors, while those with the lowest average scores tend to be found in unskilled occupations. Within every group, however, there are those with higher and lower scores (Sattler, 1988).

A word of caution: when considering relationships between achievement in school and IQ, we cannot say that IQ causes high or low achievement. We can say for certain that high or low IQ scores and high or low school performance tend to go together. There are, however, many individual exceptions.

5.11 How Important Is Intelligence?

When you think about persons you have known who have succeeded in life (or are succeeding) and those who have not, what personal qualities about them tend to stand out? In your experience, how important is intelligence in determining one's success? Where would you rank it on your list of important personal qualities?

There Are Limitations to What an IQ Test Can Predict

In no case is there a perfect correlation between measured ability and achievement. Too many variables other than sheer intelligence enter into how a person performs. At best, an intelligence test can indicate the possible range of a person's potential, but it is practically useless for predicting whether he or she will reach that potential. For example, Wallach's (1976) research with college students shows that scores on the SAT, which correlate highly with IQ scores, do not predict either quality or number of accomplishments in music, art, or science, even though they do predict college grades. Wallach also found that the IQs of outstanding mathematicians and chemists were not much higher than those who were not doing outstanding professional work. It would appear that among above-average IQ adolescents and adults, differences in IQ (say between 110 and 140) are not correlated with creative accomplishments or productivity in one's profession. IQ is only one factor in the total makeup of an individual. Other factors such as interest, perseverance, motivation, opportunity, and self-concept greatly influence how intellectual ability is developed and used. Strong determination and hard work can make up for many deficiencies. Intelligence tests cannot measure such qualities.

A Note of Caution About IQ and Minority Groups

We need to be particularly careful when considering possible relationships between IQ scores and school achievement among minority students, whether they happen to be nonwhites or poor whites. There is always the possibility of test bias, which is a very real problem when measuring the intellectual aptitude of minority students. Scheuneman (1981), for example, found evidence of test bias against minority groups in 58% of the SAT results in his review of the literature. Not all persons would agree that intelligence tests are biased; rather, as suggested by Lissitz (1982), they are simply unfair. However, there are some psychologists and educators who side with Jensen (1980), who has asserted that intelligence tests are generally unbiased for minorities.

Are they really unbiased? The evidence is mixed. For example, Green and Farquhar (1965) did not find a relationship between academic aptitude test scores and grades for black male high school students. They did, however, find positive correlations for white and black female students. Tests of achievement *motivation* were positively correlated with grades for black and white students of both sexes. This means that high or low motivation tends to go with high or low achievement. The significance of this is that a student's *motivation* to achieve was a better predictor of school success than intelligence tests, particularly for black males. Again, we are back to the idea that intelligence tests might unfairly assess minority students whose lack of opportunity for learning puts them at a disadvantage when it comes to taking standardized mental tests.

The caution, simply put, is to use IQ test data and standardized achievement test scores carefully and wisely. No test score is an absolute. It is only one more piece of information about a student. High scores do not automatically lead to school success, and low scores do not inevitably point to school failure. Environmental factors, as well as genetic ones, do influence test results. Remember, however, that school can be a very powerful environmental factor that might help move test results and school performance in a positive direction.

Be cautious not to begin with low expectations. *Labeling* a student as "disadvantaged," "slow," "dumb," and so on could be the beginning of a self-fulfilling prophecy, which can cause both teacher and student to behave in ways that make the labels come true.

MORAL REASONING: ITS DEVELOPMENT AND EXPRESSION

Children's moral reasoning is very much affected by their cognitive and intellectual development. Basically, moral development refers to one's sense of ethics or to one's knowledge of right or wrong. Issues related to morality develop whenever one child is in a position to help or hurt another. Because children have a lot of contact with one another, issues related to helping or hurting arise rather often; for example, deciding whether to "borrow" a friend's bike without asking, for example, or deciding whether to share a candy bar with a friend.

As suggested by these illustrations, morality has several components and, to varying degrees, each requires at least three cognitive skills. First, children must learn to identify how the choices they make can affect other children's welfare. For example, what would be the consequences of taking Billy's favorite toy to school without permission? Second, children have to learn how to use good moral judgment—how to behave in ways that truly help others. If Jane does not want one-half of the candy bar, John must learn that forcing it on her does not really constitute a good deed. Third, children must learn the appropriate skills for implementing moral judgments and behaviors. When Jean's friend falls down and begins crying, Jean may sympathize deeply, yet not know how to respond. Should she say something, and if so, what? Should she run to get help or just offer a handkerchief?

These complexities help explain why children's moral behavior lacks consistency. For example, at one time or another, almost every child cheats at schoolwork and tattles or betrays a friendship. These lapses may be the consequence of difficulties with any one of the three cognitive skills involved in moral behavior, ranging from lack of sensitivity to others' welfare, to poor judgment about how to behave appropriately, and to lack of savvy about how to implement good intentions.

In an effort to make sense of such complexities, cognitive development theorists such as Jean Piaget and Lawrence Kohlberg have tried to explain how children form their beliefs about right and wrong and how they make moral judgments. Two major stage theories of moral development have grown out of their efforts: a relatively simple one by Piaget and another more complex one by Kohlberg, who was one of Piaget's followers. Let us turn our attention first to Piaget's theory.

Piaget's Theory of Moral Development

Piaget's groundbreaking book, *The Moral Judgment of the Child* (1964), laid the foundation for our current understanding of moral reasoning in childhood. Interested in how rules develop among children, Piaget attempted to find out what children mean by "lies" or "telling the truth" and how they developed their ideas about authority or legitimacy. His conclusions were based on research with Swiss children ages 6 to 12 from a variety of social backgrounds.

Basically, Piaget used two methods for gathering his data. One was to watch children playing, join their game (his favorite was marbles), and then question them about the rules of the game—what the rules were, who made them up, whether they could be changed, and so on. A second approach was to present children with pairs of stories of childlike transgressions, after which he asked them which of the two were "naughtier." For example, in one story, a boy named John is called to dinner. As John opens the dining room door, it hits a tray holding fifteen cups, all of which break upon hitting the floor. In another story, a boy named Henry tries to get some jam from a cupboard while his mother is out of the house. Balanced precariously on a chair, he reaches for the jam and knocks over a cup, breaking it. The outcomes are discussed in the paragraphs that follow.

Piaget's observations of children's marble games and their responses to the stories led him to conclude that there are three stages of moral development. Until they reach age 4 or 5, children are essentially *premoral,* which, loosely translated, means that they are not particularly concerned about rules. For example, when a couple of 3- or 4-year-olds play marbles, each is likely to have his or her own idiosyncratic rules. Who cares if one's hand is in the marble ring? What does it matter if you move a couple of marbles out of the way to have a clear shot with your own shooter? The point is to have fun. Most parents and other adults understand that preschoolers really do not know the rules that govern everyday living and so are more tolerant when small children break rules. A 3-year-old might carry on a lively conversation during a church service; most 6-year-olds would know better.

From about age 5 to age 10, children enter the second stage of moral development, which Piaget called *moral realism.* It is during this time that children develop what Piaget termed a *morality of constraint.* Children during this stage take rules very seriously; they tend to view behavior as either right or wrong, and they assume that everyone views behaviors in the same way. The morality of constraint is based largely on admiration and fear of adults, who are seen as all powerful and all knowing.

Children in this second stage of moral development tend to judge behavior in terms of its consequences, with little regard for a person's intentions. For example, they see the boy in the story who broke fifteen cups as naughtier than the boy who broke one cup simply because the first boy broke more cups. The fact that it was accidental is not important. At this age, they are not able to distinguish between accidents and misdemeanors.

At about 10 years of age, children begin to move into Piaget's third stage, namely, *moral relativism,* a time when children show signs of developing what Piaget terms a *morality of cooperation.* Their perspective of punishment broadens as they come to understand that different degrees of wrongdoing demand different degrees of punishment. Thus, when they hear about a boy who breaks his little sister's toy, children in this stage are likely to suggest that the boy give his sister one of his toys (reciprocity) or arrange to have the broken toy fixed (restitution). Peer interaction is critical to the shift in moral reasoning during this stage. Playing and working with peers on an equal basis offers children more freedom from adult authority and, thus, more opportunities for negotiating their own points of view, cooperating to reach mutual goals, and participating in joint decisions. Rules are no longer followed simply because they are rules; they can be changed if there is a majority. Others are not evaluated solely on the objective consequences of their behaviors. By age 11 or 12, children consider a person's intentions before making a moral judgment.

Thus, a child moves from the preschooler's mentality of anything goes, there are no wrongs or rights, to an elementary school child's absolute reliance on adult authority, to a preteen's increased readiness and ability to see that moral behavior is something derived from within and through dialogue with others.

Kohlberg's Cognitive Theory of Moral Development

Kohlberg (1969, 1981, 1985) has extended Piaget's theory by proposing three broad levels of moral development subdivided into six stages rather than just two, and by proposing that these span almost the first half of life. Kohlberg's theoretical model is based on his analysis of interviews of 10- to 16-year-old boys in a twelve-year longitudinal study. These boys responded to a series of ten moral dilemmas in which they had to choose between acts of obedience to rules and authority and the needs and welfare of others that conflicted with the regulations.

5.12 What Would You Do?

In Europe, a woman was near death from cancer. There was one drug that might save her, a form of radium that a druggist in the same town had recently discovered. The druggist was charging $2000, ten times what the drug had cost him to make. The sick woman's husband, Heinz, went to everyone he knew to borrow the money, but he could only borrow about half of what it would cost. He told the druggist that his wife was dying and asked him to sell the drug cheaper or let him pay later, but the druggist refused. The husband became desperate and broke into the druggist's store to steal the drug for his wife. Should the husband have done that? Why or why not? (Kohlberg, 1969). This is one of the moral dilemmas used by Kohlberg in his research? How would you respond? Which of the stages of moral development in Figure 5.5 would your behavior reflect?

Kohlberg was interested not in whether his subjects thought the husband was right or wrong, but in how they explained their judgments. He believed that changes in the structure of their moral reasoning would be revealed in the explanations they offered; Kohlberg was correct. There were many reasons offered by the subjects for why they chose an obedient or a need-served behavior. Kohlberg's analysis of those reasons led him to his six-stage theory of moral development. Figure 5.5 provides you with an overview of the three levels and six stages that constitute Kohlberg's framework for moral development. A central point in Kohlberg's theory is that moral development occurs in stages. Although the order of the stages is fixed, the stages do not occur at the same age for all people. Many people never reach the higher stages of moral development, and some adults are forever stuck in stage one or two, where the concern is primarily one of avoiding punishment and gaining rewards.

Similar to Piaget, Kohlberg believes that stages of moral reasoning are determined by the cognitive capabilities of individuals. Both Piaget and Kohlberg theorized that each stage of moral development builds on the moral

---

LEVEL 1. Preconventional Morality. Typical of children up to age 9. Referred to as *preconventional* because children are relative naive about the conventions or rules of society.

Stage 1: Obedience and Punishment Orientation. Children at this stage behave in order to avoid punishment. The goodness or badness of one's behavior is determined by the physical consequences. Those in authority have the power and should be obeyed.

Stage 2: Naive Hedonistic and Instrumental Orientation. Children in this stage behave (conform to do as they are told) to gain rewards. Children judge their behavior as good if it is instrumental in satisfying their own needs and/or brings them some benefit in return—e.g., "I'll pick up my room if I can stay up a half hour longer tonight."

LEVEL 2. Conventional Morality. Typical of 9- to 20-year olds. Termed conventional morality because most 9- to 20-year olds conform to the conventions of society because they are the rules of society.'

Stage 3. Good Boy/Nice Girl Orientation. In this stage, people evaluate their behavior as good or bad in terms of its conformity to existing rules and regulations. Obeying and respecting authority is seen as essential.

LEVEL 3. Postconventional Morality. Usually reached only after age then, and by only a small proportion of adults. Labeled *postconventional* because the moral principles that underlie the conventions are understood but not blindly accepted.

Stage 5: Social Contract and Individual Rights Orientation. Here there is a flexibility of moral beliefs that was lacking in earlier stages. Whether a behavior is good or bad, right or wrong, is determined more by mutual agreement than by blind obedience to authority.

Stage 6: Morality of Self-Chosen Universal Principles. In this stage, moral behavior is determined by one's ability to live up to, and behave consistently with, one's own self-chosen ethical ideals, rather than the imposed standards of others.

Figure 5.5. KOHLBERG'S STAGES OF MORAL DEVELOPMENT.

---

concepts of previous stages. If you examine Figure 5.5, you can see that the six stages form a progression in two ways: first, earlier stages reflect more egocentric thinking than do later stages; and second, earlier stages require more specific or concrete thinking than is seen in later stages. For example, in Stage 1 (obedience and punishment orientation), children do not distinguish between what they think is right and what the world tells them is right; they simply accept the authorities' judgment. By Stage 4 (law and order orientation), they begin to realize that there can be different points of view about right and wrong, but they still take for granted the existing conventions for society as a whole. They cannot yet fully appreciate the possibility of purposely modifying society's existing rules and conventions. It is not until Stages 5 and 6, which have to do with orientations related to individual rights and self-chosen universal principles, that the individuals begin to see the possibility of changing a society's existing rules and conventions. This does not mean that individuals are compelled to do this, only that at this level of moral development they see choices where none previously existed.

In his early descriptions of moral development, Kohlberg suggested that only about 20% of the population reaches Stages 5 and 6 of moral reasoning. Because so few persons were ever found who truly reflected Stage 6 reasoning, its status as a legitimate stage of moral development was reduced to that of a theoretical ideal; it seemed a remote possibility for most people (Colby and Kohlberg, 1984). Apparently, there are few Mahatma Gandhis, Mother Teresas, or Martin Luther King, Juniors, among us. In addition, Kohlberg has found that Stage 5 reasoning is not universal, but depends in part on advanced education.

Critical Evaluations of the Theories

Because most of the attention has focused on Kohlberg's more complex and comprehensive model, evaluation of Piaget's theory has been somewhat limited. It did, however, serve as a kind of building block for Kohlberg's more extensive ideas. In fact, a central criticism of Piaget's theory is that it is too simplistic to account for the complexities of moral reasoning (Rest, 1983).

Kohlberg's theory has received mixed reviews. On one hand, there is evidence to show that it has endured rather well, having been tested over a twenty-year period on a wide variety of children, adolescents, and adults (Colby et al., 1983; Snarey, 1985). On the other hand, Hoffman's (1980) review of research led him to conclude that morality may not necessarily progress in stages, although he did say that Kohlberg's stages "nevertheless provide a valid description of the changes in moral development that occur in society" (p. 301).

One of the major weaknesses of Kohlberg's original theory was pointed out by Carol Gilligan (1982), who questioned Kohlberg's system for scoring levels of moral development because it did not account for sex differences.

This was a legitimate criticism because Kohlberg's original research involved only males. Gilligan's main point was that females tend to be concerned with relationships and responsibilities, whereas males typically center their responses more dispassionately on rights and rules. Because Kohlberg's stages of moral reasoning are structured primarily on the basis of rules, the tests of moral development involving females often made it appear as though their moral development was less mature than males'. It is criticism well taken, and it prompted Kohlberg (1985) to make revisions in his scoring scheme to correct this possible bias.

Probably the most frequently voiced criticism of Kohlberg's theory is that it deals with moral reasoning, or what we *say* should be done, rather than with actual behavior, or what we really *do*. Remember that Kohlberg's conclusions about moral development are based on what his subjects said they *would* do when confronted with assorted ethical dilemmas, which taps their reasoning and may or may not be the same as how they might actually behave in similar circumstances. There is some question, too, about whether ability to reason at a particular stage has much to do with actual reasoning in real-life situations or with actual behavior (Reimer, Paolitto, and Hersch, 1983).

It should be noted, however, that even the harshest critics have not altogether disregarded the theories proposed by Piaget and Kohlberg. Rather, they have pointed to weaknesses, to areas that need further research, and to conclusions that should be questioned, not necessarily discarded.

Implications for Teaching Practices

Moral development and intellectual development go hand in hand. Becoming more intelligent means, among other things, becoming more aware of the world in which one lives and becoming more sensitive to how one's choices to be helpful or hurtful to oneself or others can influence the course and quality of life. It is these choices and their consequences that determine the depth and quality of one's conscience development, one's sense of right and wrong. Children who are raised in environments where basic physical and/or emotional survival is at stake might be less well developed when it comes to morality because they are so concerned with themselves that they fail to see how their behavior affects others. Some children are so spoiled that they have the idea that their needs and desires are the only ones that count.

However, children raised in environments in which they are loved and know it, and in which they are taught that their behavior can have positive or negative consequences, depending on their choices, are in a far better position to develop a healthy conscience.

There are certain things teachers can do to help facilitate healthy conscience development and moral reasoning. Some suggestions are as follows:

1. Help children at all ages understand the idea that they always have more than one choice as to how to behave and that they are responsible for the

consequences of their behavior. For example, Billy's fourth-grade teacher reminded him of the class rule: when a person is disruptive during lesson time, that person stays in during recess. "The choice is yours," the teacher told Billy. Billy continued misbehaving; therefore, Billy stayed in during recess. As a result, Billy learned about choices and consequences.

2. Be aware that what children really learn in a lasting way is what they see in your behavior. For example, Mr. Johns, a sixth-grade teacher, broke up a fight in the hall between two boys in his class. Before deciding what to do about it, he set them both down and heard each boy's side. They had had an argument over an unopened candy bar each claimed to have found. Mr. John's solution: they would share the bounty—one boy would cut the bar in half and the other boy got to choose the half he wanted. Would you say the boys learned something about fairness?

3. Set time aside for periodic classroom discussions related to important interpersonal issues that involve moral choices and decisions. For elementary school students, discussions that focused on sibling rivalry, teasing, prejudice, and obeying parents would probably stimulate discussion. For high school students, discussions about cheating, drinking, drugs, conformity, and unpopularity would undoubtedly spark interest. In order to ensure that such discussions are as helpful and constructive as possible, Eismen (1981) has suggested the following guidelines for teachers:

a. Encourage students to see others' perspectives, perhaps by switching to the other person's point of view.
b. Help students connect values and actions and spot inconsistencies when they occur.
c. Make sure students are listening to one another by having them acknowledge and perhaps restate what others are saying.

4. Create a classroom climate that allows for differences, while at the same time allowing ample time for discussion about those differences (e.g., opinions, ideas, preferences, choices, and so on). Discussion helps people to see that even though there are differences, there can still be acceptance.

5. Remember that teaching children and adolescents to reason morally and ethically is an effort to help them conduct their lives in such a way so as to live harmoniously with others and, in the process, behave with the kind of decency and fairness that allows them to enhance life for both themselves and their fellow humans.

EPILOGUE

Intelligence is, indeed, a complex phenomenon. Not only are there different levels of intelligence, but there are also different kinds of intelligence, such as the ability to think abstractly, the ability to behave competently in social situations, and the ability to learn from a book or from experience. Intelligence is not just one thing, but a combination of many abilities or components that, as a total package, we label intelligence. Each person possesses a package of that sort, but the contents vary from one individual to the next.

This chapter explores six major theoretical positions that explain intellectual functioning. First, Spearman believes that intelligence consists of one general (*g*) factor and several specific (*s*) factors. The *g* factor refers to one's overall mental power, while the *s* factor is related to the ability to do certain specific tasks. Second, Thorndike's position suggests that intelligence is determined by the number of neural connections in the brain—the richer the neural network, the higher the intelligence. Third, Thurstone believes that intelligence consists of seven components or families of abilities, which, although related, function relatively independently, so that a person proficient in one is not necessarily so in another. Fourth, Guilford believes that intelligence is a complex, three-dimensional structure consisting of *operations, contents,* and *products,* which interact to produce 120 distinct abilities. Guilford's model helps us to see how information can be acquired, stored, and used to generate new information. Fifth, Gardner theorizes that there are seven types of "intelligences" that enable persons to be intelligent in different ways, which range all the way from logical-mathematical intelligence to intrapersonal intelligence. In this view, there is no general "brightness" or "dumbness." People can be "smart" or "dumb" in one area, but this tells us nothing about their intelligence in other domains. Sixth, Sternberg's "triarchic" theory consists of the following types of intelligence: (1) *componential*—the ability to think logically and analytically; (2) *experiential*—the ability to not only make sense of our experiences, but to reorder, recombine, and reinterpret them in new ways; and (3) *contextual*—the kind of intelligence people use in the context of their everyday worlds, which we know better as practical intelligence or common sense.

Jean Piaget has helped us to see that intellectual growth is a developmental process that goes through sequential stages, each characterized by identifiable ways of thinking. In the first two years of life (*sensorimotor stage*), infants are primarily concerned with learning about physical objects and their immediate sensory world. In the next four to five years (*preoperational stage*), children are preoccupied with language development; that is, thinking is guided more by intuition (knowledge without rational thought) than by logic. Repetitive use of words and phrases is quite characteristic of the preoperational child. From age 6 or 7 to about age 11 (*concrete-operational stage*), children acquire the ability to perform operations, cognitive maneuvers based more on logical reasoning than intuitive functioning. At this time, they show increasing skills in *decentering*—the ability to consider more than one characteristic of an object at the same time; *conservation*—the ability to see that certain properties of objects (e.g., volume or mass) remain the same despite transformations in their appearance; *reversibility*—the capacity to imagine what things were like before they were altered; and *classification*—the process of grouping objects or events in terms of their common properties. From 11 to 15 years of age through adulthood (*formal-operational stage*), children and adolescents show an increasing ability to "see" more in their heads, hypothetically and abstractly. For the first time, they are able to understand double messages—irony, double entendre, and the resonance of aphorisms.

Whereas Piaget's conception of a child was that of a "little scientist" who alone constructed an understanding of the world, Vygotsky proposed a model of children's cognitive development that depends more on language and social support. An essential feature of Vygotsky's theory is the idea that each child has what he terms a *zone of proximal development,* which represents a kind of middle point, the point at which a child cannot solve a problem alone but is capable of doing so with some guidance. In Vygotsky's view, this is where instruction and learning can best occur because it is when students have a real readiness for new knowledge.

Recent findings in brain growth research suggest that between the ages of 2 and 16 the brain develops in four, four-year cycles. The growth cycles closely overlap with Piaget's four stages of intellectual development, suggesting a biological basis for cognitive growth.

There is convincing evidence that both heredity and environment significantly contribute to intellectual growth. It is difficult to measure with precision just how much each contributes; however, that is a more academic issue than a practical one. As teachers, heredity is an uncontrollable factor, but there is a great deal we can do about the students' environment.

There is a positive correlation between school performance and intelligence as measured by IQ tests. The correlation is particularly positive between IQ scores and school subjects heavily dependent on verbal reasoning ability, perhaps because tests sample these abilities more.

Caution is in order when using intelligence tests as predictors of academic ability for minority groups. The evidence for test bias against minorities—nonwhites and poor whites—is mixed, which suggests that we need to interpret such data cautiously and carefully so as not to begin with self-fulfilling low expectations.

Jean Piaget was the first psychologist to offer a framework for understanding the moral development of children. His is a relatively simple three-stage framework. Basically, it is a theory that says children under age 5 are rarely concerned about rules (*premoral*); those between 5 and 10 years of age begin to take rules very seriously and see behavior as either right or wrong (*moral realism*); and at about age 10 they begin to broaden their perspective to recognize that there are degrees of wrongdoing and degrees of punishment (*moral relativism*).

Lawrence Kohlberg extended Piaget's three-stage theory into six stages, proposing that these stages span almost the first half of one's life. Similar to Piaget, Kohlberg theorizes that stages of moral reasoning are determined by the cognitive capabilities of individuals and that each stage of moral development builds on the moral concepts of previous stages. In Kohlberg's view, children in the first stages (younger than age 9) behave as they should either to avoid punishment (Stage 1) or get rewards (Stage 2). Youths in the next two stages (ages 9 to 20) behave properly either because they are more concerned about others' approval or disapproval than about their physical power (Stage 3), or because they have a strong desire to obey and respect authority (Stage 4). Those in the last two stages (ages 20 and over) obey the rules and conventions that have been determined more by mutual agreement than by blind obedience (Stage 5), or because what is obeyed or judged as right or wrong is determined by one's own self-chosen ethical principles (Stage 6). There are very few who fit these last two stages, and so few in Stage 6 that it is now regarded only as a theoretical ideal.

In spite of the many criticisms leveled at Piaget's and Kohlberg's theories of moral development (especially Kohlberg's, because it is more complex), they have withstood the scrutiny and retained enough credibility to remain among our best guides at this point for understanding the human reasoning involved in moral choices.

STUDY AND REVIEW QUESTIONS

1. If you were asked to define intelligence, how would you respond?
2. How does Spearman differentiate between *general* intelligence and *specific* intelligence?
3. Can you identify and briefly explain the seven primary abilities that Thurstone associated with intelligence?
4. When Gardner says that there is no general "brightness" or "smartness" among people, what does he mean? How would you interpret this to someone who did not understand his view?
5. Can you explain the essentials of Sternberg's triarchic theory of intelligence?
6. What is the difference between divergent and convergent thinking?
7. If you were asked to explain intelligence, what would your answer be? (Remember, you are not asked to *define* it, but to explain what it is.)
8. Can you identify the four stages of intellectual development described by Piaget?
9. What are the basic characteristics of each of Piaget's stages in terms of one's intellectual ability?
10. If you were to consult with a group of teachers about how to encourage cognitive development during the preoperational, concrete-operational, and formal-operational stages of intellectual growth, what advice would you give them?

11. If someone were to ask you if intellectual development occurs in stages of growth or if it is continuous, how would you reply?
12. What are the basic differences between Piaget's and Vygotsky's theories of cognitive development?
13. How would you explain Vygotsky's zone of proximal development to teachers so they could take advantage of its educational implications?
14. What does research on brain development suggest about the relationship between Piaget's stages of intellectual growth and brain growth?
15. Consider the following statement: if a particular characteristic is genetic, it cannot be changed. Is this true or false? Can you support your answer?
16. Piaget has identified three stages of moral development: premoral, moral realism, and moral relativism. Can you explain the major differences among these three when it comes to the sort of moral reasoning associated with each?
17. Can you identify and briefly describe Kohlberg's six stages of moral development?
18. In what ways are Piaget's and Kohlberg's theories of moral development similar? How are they different?
19. What criticisms are leveled most frequently at Piaget's and Kohlberg's theories of moral development?
20. If you were to advise teachers as to how they could help facilitate healthy moral development, what would you say?

REFERENCES

Achenbach, T. M., and Weisz, J. R. "A Longitudinal Study of Developmental Synchrony Between Conceptual Identity, Seriation, and Transitivity of Color, Number, and Length." *Child Development,* 1975, *46,* pp. 840–848.

Baron, J. "Personality and Intelligence." In R. S. Sternberg (Ed.), *Handbook of Human Intelligence.* New York: Cambridge University Press, 1982.

Beard, R. M. *An Outline of Piaget's Developmental Psychology for Students and Teachers.* New York: Basic Books, 1969.

Bloom, B. S. "Replies to Dr. Jensen's Article." *ERIC Clearinghouse on Early Childhood Education,* 1969, *3.*

Bloom, B. S. *Human Characteristics and School Learning.* New York: McGraw-Hill, 1976.

Bradley, R. H., and Caldwell, B. M. "Early Home Environment and Changes in Mental Test Performance in Children from Six to Thirty-Six Months." *Developmental Psychology,* 1976, *12,* pp. 93–97.

Brainerd, C. J. "On the Validity of Propositional Logic as a Model for Adolescent Intelligence." Paper presented at the *Society for Research in Child Development,* Denver, April, 1975.

Colby, A., and Kohlberg, L. "Invariant Sequence and Internal Consistency in Moral Development Stages." In W. M. Kurtines and J. L. Gewirtz (Eds.), *Morality, Moral Behavior and Moral Development.* New York: Wiley, 1984.

Colby, A., Kohlberg, L., Gibbs, J., and Lieberman, M. "A Longitudinal Study of Moral Development." *Monographs of the Society on Child Development*, 1983, *48*, (Serial No. 200).

DeLisi, R., and Staudt, J. "Individual Differences in College Students' Performance on Formal Operations Tasks." *Journal of Applied Developmental Psychology*, 1980, *1*, pp. 201–208.

Eisman, J. W. "What Criteria Should Public School Moral Education Programs Meet?" *The Review of Education*, 1981, *7*, pp. 213–230.

Ennis, R. H. "Children's Ability to Handle Piaget's Propositional Logic: A Conceptual Critique." *Review of Educational Research*, 1975, *45*, pp. 1–41.

Epstein, H. T. "Correlated Brain and Intelligence Development in Humans." In M. Hahn (Ed.), *Development and Evolution of Brain Size: Behavioral Implications*. New York: Academic Press, 1979a.

Epstein, H. T. "Growth Spurts During Brain Development: Implications for Educational Policy." In J. Chall (Ed.), *Education and the Brain*. National Society for the Study of Education Yearbook. Chicago: University of Chicago Press, 1979b.

Epstein, H. T. "Some Biological Bases of Cognitive Development." *Bulletin of the Orton Society*, 1980, *30*, pp. 46–62.

Epstein, H. T. "Stages in Mental Growth." *Journal of Educational Psychology*, 1990, *82*, pp. 876–880.

Flavell, J. H. *Cognitive Development*, 2nd ed. Englewood Cliffs, NJ: Prentice Hall, 1985.

Gardner, H. *Frames of Mind: The Theory of Multiple Intelligences*. New York: Basic Books, 1983.

Gardner, H. "Assessing Intelligence: A Comment on 'Testing Intelligence Without IQ Tests.' " *Phi Delta Kappan*, 1984, June, pp. 699–700.

Gelman, R., and Baillargeon, R. "A Review of Some Piagetian Concepts." In P. Mussen (Ed.), *Carmichael's Manual of Child Psychology. Vol. 3: Cognitive Development* (E. Markman and J. Flavell, Vol. Eds.) New York: Wiley, 1983.

Gelman, R., Meck, E., and Merkin, S. "Young Children's Numerical Competence." *Cognitive Development*, 1986, *1*, pp. 1–29.

Gilligan, C. *In a Different Voice*. Cambridge, MA: Harvard University Press, 1982.

Ginsberg, and Opper. *Piaget's Theory of Intellectual Development: An Introduction*, 2nd ed. Englewood Cliffs, NJ: Prentice Hall, 1979.

Green, R. L., and W. W. Farquhar. "Negroe Achievement Motivation and Scholastic Achievement." *Journal of Educational Psychology*, 1965, *56*, pp. 241–243.

Grimm, W. A., Goff, S. M., and Ashburn, S. S. "Language Development During Childhood." in C. S. Schuster and S. S. Ashburn (Eds.), *The Process of Human Development: A Holistic Approach*. Boston: Little, Brown, 1980.

Groves, P. M., and Rebec, G. V. *Introduction to Biological Psychology*, 3rd ed. Dubuque, IA: Brown, 1988.

Guilford, J. P. *The Nature of Human Intelligence*. New York: McGraw-Hill, 1967.

Higgins-Trenk, A., and Gaite, A. J. H. "Elusiveness of Formal Operational Thought in Adolescents." *Proceedings of the 79th Annual Convention of the American Psychological Association*, 1971.

Hoffman, M. L. "Moral Development in Adolescence." In J. Adelson (Ed.), *Handbook of Adolescent Psychology*. New York: Wiley, 1980.

Hudspeth, W. J., and Pribram, K. H. "Stages of Brain and Cognitive Maturation." *Journal of Educational Psychology*, 1990, *82*, pp. 881–884.

Jastrow, R. *The Enchanted Loom: Mind in the Universe.* New York: Simon & Schuster, 1981.

Jensen, A. R. *Bias in Mental Testing.* New York: The Free Press, 1980.

Kail, R., and Pellegrino, J. W. *Human Intelligence: Perspectives and Prospects.* New York: Freeman, 1985.

Keating, D. P., and Clark, L. V. "Development of Physical and Social Reasoning in Adolescence." *Developmental Psychology,* 1980, *16,* pp. 23–30.

Kohlberg, L. *Stages in the Development of Moral Thought and Action.* San Francisco: Harper & Row, 1969.

Kohlberg, L. *Philosophy of Moral Development.* San Francisco: Harper & Row, 1981.

Kohlberg, L. *The Psychology of Moral Development.* San Francisco: Harper & Row, 1985.

Klausmeirer, H., and Sipple, T. S. "Factor Structure of the Piagetian Stage of Concrete Operations." *Contemporary Educational Psychology,* 1982, *7,* pp. 161–180.

Kolb, B. "Brain Development, Plasticity, and Behavior." *American Psychologist,* 1989, *44,* pp. 1203–1212.

Lissitz, R. W. "Review of 'Bias in Mental Testing' by A. A. Jensen." *Educational Researcher,* 1982, *11,* pp. 25–27.

Lovitt, T. C., and Smith, J. O. "Effects of Instruction on an Individual's Verbal Behavior." *Exception Children,* 1972, *38,* pp. 685–693.

Maranto, G. "The Mind within the Brain." *Discover,* 1984, May, pp. 34–43.

Martorano, S. C. "A Development Analysis of Performance on Piaget's Formal Operations Task." *Developmental Psychology,* 1977, *13,* pp. 666–672.

McCall, R. B. "The Neuroscience of Education: More Research is Needed Before Application." *Journal of Educational Psychology,* 1990, *82,* pp. 885–888.

Miller, K., and Gelman, R. "The Child's Representation of Number: A Multidimensional Scaling Analysis." *Child Development,* 1983, *54,* pp. 1470–1479.

Mueller, E. "The Maintenance of Verbal Exchanges Between Young Children." *Child Development,* 1972, *43,* pp. 930–938.

Mulholland, T. M., Pellegrino, J. W., and Glaser, R. "Components of Geometric Analogy Solution." *Cognitive Psychology,* 1980, *12,* pp. 252–284.

Palincsar, A., and Brown, A. "Classroom Dialogues to Promote Self-Regulated Comprehension." In J. Brophy (Ed.), *Advances in Research in Teaching,* Vol. 1. Greenwich, CT: JAI Press, 1989.

Piaget, J, *The Moral Judgment of the Child.* Translated by M. Gabain. New York: The Free Press, 1964.

Piaget, J. *Six Psychological Studies.* New York: Vintage Books, 1967.

Piaget, J. *Science of Education and the Psychology of the Child.* New York: Grossman, 1970.

Piaget, J. *The Language and Thought of the Child.* New York: World Publishing Co., 1973.

Piaget, J. *Understanding Causality.* Translated by D. Miles and M. Miles. New York: Norton, 1974.

Piaget, J. *The Psychology of Intelligence.* Totowa, NJ: Littlefield, Adams, 1976.

Piaget, J. "Piaget's Theory." In P. H. Mussen (Ed.), *Carmichael's Manual of Child Psychology,* Vol. 1. New York: Wiley, 1983.

Reimer, R. H., Paolitto, D. P., and Hersh, R. H. *Promoting Moral Growth: From Piaget to Kohlberg,* 2nd ed. New York: Longman, 1983.

Resnick, L. B. (Ed.). *The Nature of Intelligence.* Hillsdale, NJ: Lawrence Erlbaum Associates, 1976.

Rest, J. "Morality." In P. Mussen (Ed.), *Handbook of Child Psychology,* Vol. 4. New York: Wiley, 1983.

Restak, R. *The Brain.* New York: Bantam Books, 1984.

Rheingold, H. L., Stanley, W. C., and Cooley, J. A. "A Method for Studying Exploratory Behavior in Infants." *Science,* 1962, *136,* pp. 1054–1055.

Roberge, J. J., and Flexer, B. K. "Further Examination of Formal Reasoning Abilities." *Child Development,* 1979, *50,* pp. 478–484.

Ross, H. S. "The Influence of Novelty and Complexity on Exploratory Behavior in Twelve-Month Old Infants." *Journal of Experimental Child Psychology,* 1974, *17,* pp. 436–451.

Sattler, J. *Assessment of Children,* 3rd ed. Philadelphia: Saunders, 1988.

Scarr, S., and Weinberg, R. A. "The Minnesota Adoption Studies: Malleability and Genetic Differences." *Child Development,* 1983, *34,* pp. 260–267.

Scheuneman, J. D. "A New Look at Bias in Aptitude Tests." In P. Merrifield (Ed.), *Measuring Human Abilities (New Directions in Testing and Measurement* (no. 12). San Francisco: Jossey-Bass, 1981.

Segal, N. L. "The Importance of Twin Studies for Individual Differences Research." *Journal of Counseling and Development,* 1990, *68,* pp. 612–622.

Snarey, J. R. "Cross-Cultural Universality of Socio-Moral Development: A Critical Review of Kohlbergian Research." *Psychological Bulletin,* 1985, *97,* pp. 202–232.

Spearman, C. *The Abilities of Man.* New York: Macmillan, 1927.

Sternberg, R. J. "Intelligence and Nonentrenchment." *Journal of Educational Psychology,* 1981, *73,* pp. 1–16.

Sternberg, R. J. "Testing Intelligence Without I. Q. Tests." *Phi Delta Kappan,* 1984, June, pp. 694–698.

Sternberg, R. J. *Beyond IQ: A Triarchic Theory of Intelligence.* New York: Cambridge University Press, 1985.

Sternberg, R. J., and Davidson, J. E. "The Mind of a Puzzler." *Psychology Today,* 1982, June, pp. 37–44.

Tellegen, A., Lykken, D. T., Bouchard, T. J., Wilcox, K. J., Segal, N. L., and Rich, S. "Personality Similarity in Twins Reared Apart and Together." *Journal of Personality and Social Psychology,* 1988, *54,* pp. 1031–1039.

Thatcher, R. W., Walker, R. A., and Guidice, S. "Human Cerebral Hemispheres Develop at Different Rates and Ages." *Science,* 1987, *236,* pp. 1110–1113.

Thomas, R. M. *Comparing Theories of Child Development,* 3rd ed. Belmont, CA: Wadsworth, 1992.

Thorndike, E. L. *The Measurement of Intelligence.* New York: Columbia University Press, Teachers College, 1927.

Thurstone, L. L. "Primary Mental Abilities." *Psychological Monographs,* 1938, *1.*

Tomlinson-Keasey, C., Eisert, C. B., Kahle, L. R., Hardy-Brown, K., and Keasey, B. "The Structure of Concrete Operational Thought." *Child Development,* 1979, *50,* pp. 1153–1163.

Trotter, R. J. "Profile–Robert Sternberg: Three Heads Are Better Than One." *Psychology Today,* 1986, August, pp. 56–62.

Vygotsky, L. S. *Mind in Society: The Development of Higher Mental Processes.* Cambridge, MA: Harvard University Press, 1978.

Vygotsky, L. S. *Thought and Language.* Cambridge, MA: MIT Press, 1986.

Wallach, M. A. "Tests Tell Us Little About Talent." *American Scientist,* 1976, *64,* pp. 57–63.

Wertsch, J. V. "Adult–Child Interaction as a Source of Self-Regulation in Children." In S. Yussen (Ed.), *The Growth of Reflection in Children.* Orlando, FL: Academic Press, 1985.

White, S. H. "Evidence for a Hierarchial Arrangement of Learning Processes." In L. P. Lipsitt and C. C. Spiker (Eds.), *Advances in Child Development and Behavior,* Vol. II. New York: Academic Press, 1965.

SELECTED READINGS OF RELATED INTEREST

Eysenck, H. J., and Kamin, L. *The Intelligence Controversy.* New York: Wiley, 1981. This small book is actually a debate by two internationally known psychologists who have opposing views about the nature and shaping of intelligence. Eysenck seeks to persuade the reader that genetic factors determine intelligence, while Kamin argues on the side of environment. It raises many questions worth thinking about.

Gardner, H. *Frames of Mind: The Theory of Multiple Intelligences.* New York: Basic Books, 1983. Gardner discusses his basic ideas and outlines the theory on which his idea of multiple intelligences is based. Provides many insights into how each of his seven "intelligences" functions.

Kohlberg, L. *The Philosophy of Moral Development.* New York: Harper & Row, 1981. Kohlberg details the basic tenets of his theory of moral development. This basic book serves as a starting place for Kohlberg's own views on his somewhat controversial work.

Mayer, R. E. *Thinking, Problem Solving, and Cognition,* 2nd ed. New York: Freeman, 1992. An excellent source for readers who want to dig deeper into the nature and expression of cognitive functioning. Contains a particularly good chapter on Piaget and his tests of intellectual growth.

Rosser, R. A. *Cognitive Development: Psychological and Biological Perspectives.* Needham Heights, MA: Allyn & Bacon, 1994. This book shows how what we learn about children's thinking applies to all of us and our understanding of the origins of mind. Emphasizes the biology of cognition and attempts to bridge the gaps between child study, animal research, and neuroscience.

Vygotsky, L. S. *Thought and Language.* Cambridge, MA: MIT Press, 1986. An overview of Vygotsky's main ideas related to the development of language and intellectual ability within a constructivist framework.

TOWARD UNDERSTANDING LEARNING

INFORMATION PROCESSING, STRATEGIES FOR ENHANCING LEARNING AND MOTIVATION, ROLE OF SELF-CONCEPT AND EXPECTATIONS, AND MEASUREMENT OF LEARNING OUTCOMES

The missions of an educational system are to promote learning, to facilitate the acquisition of knowledge, and to enlarge the minds of its students so that each is better able to find his or her own path. In the best of worlds, we hope that students learn more than the mere memorization of facts. The necessary intellectual skills that enable them to think critically, the basic interpersonal skills that allow them to develop meaningful relationships, and a foundation for their understanding of their own interpersonal possibilities so that they can make wise decisions about their futures are desired as well. For these things to occur, we must know something about the dynamics of learning, a topic explored in various ways in this part of the book. We examine learning, discuss some methods of encouragement, analyze various learning styles, and provide some suggestions for retaining knowledge. We look at how one's self-concept influences learning, how motivational strategies enhance it, and how measurement techniques assess the outcomes.

In order for learning to occur, the massive amounts of information to which we are exposed on a daily basis must be processed and stored in our memories for future use. Chapter 6 explores a point of view called "information processing" that helps you understand how information is processed and what you can do to help yourself and your students store specific information so that it is not easily forgotten.

Chapter 7 introduces you to two major theoretical views on how learning occurs, examines the strengths and weaknesses of each system, and explores their implications for teaching practices. We will also examine various styles of learning and how to recognize them in the students we teach.

Chapter 8 examines the processes, dynamics, and importance of motivation in human learning. We will consider some important ways motivation can be affected—for better or for worse—by praise and criticism, by success and failure, and by cooperative and competitive classroom situations. We will also look at the idea of less-structured instructional approaches to see what research says about their motivational effects.

Chapter 9 exposes you to a systematic exploration of the ways in which self-concept variables can influence learning and school achievement. We will try to understand why early school experiences are so crucial in determining the course of subsequent school achievement. In addition, we will explore why, and how, a student's self-concept of ability to do schoolwork is related to actual learning. Teacher expectations play a part in this, and we will take a careful look at the "psychology of expectations" and why they work the way they do.

Chapter 10 explores the matters of measurement and evaluation of learning, some ways for doing this, and some specific suggestions for constructing reliable and fair examinations.

On the whole, Part III focuses on the larger issues of learning, learning processes, and learning differences, and gives many considerations and suggestions for facilitating learning as a positive experience for students.

6

Information Processing

A Model of How Learning and Memory Occur

CHAPTER OVERVIEW

IMPORTANT CHAPTER IDEAS

1. Information-processing theory borrows generously from computer models to explain how information is taken in (encoded), processed, stored, and retrieved.
2. Most of the information around us at any one time is not actually processed in our conscious minds.
3. Attention and perception determine what is entered into our awareness. Attention allows information to enter into our awareness, and our perceptions give it meaning.

4. Although it is said that "seeing is believing," it would be more accurate to say that "believing is seeing," because what we see is shaped by prior knowledge.
5. Much of what goes into the first stage of our information-processing system (sensory register) is forgotten and permanently lost.
6. Short-term memory is very limited in both the time and the amount of information it can handle.
7. Unless new information in short-term memory is rehearsed and used, it is generally lost in about twenty seconds.
8. Long-term memory is where our knowledge, conscious and unconscious, is stored.
9. Information in long-term memory can be stored in unlimited amounts and is retained indefinitely.
10. Episodic, semantic, and procedural memories are components of long-term memory, each with its own particular memory emphasis.
11. The more completely that new information is processed and integrated with other information, the more likely it is that we will remember it.
12. Metacognition is a process that involves "knowing about knowing."
13. Research has shown that there are particular strategies that can be used to enhance learning and long-term memory.
14. The retrieval of information stored in long-term memory is a key component to successful information-processing.
15. Information is lost or forgotten because it decays through lack of use, is blocked by other learning, or is repressed for psychological reasons.
16. Information-processing research is helping us to understand why we forget and how we can enhance memory processes.

PROLOGUE

There is hardly a moment in our lives when we are not surrounded by a jungle of sensory information. At this moment, there may be someone talking in the room next door, music may be playing in the background, or an open window may give you access to outside sights and sounds. Even the chair on which you are sitting is a tactile reminder that periodically causes you to shift your posture to a more comfortable position. No matter where we turn, there are sights, sounds, smells, tastes, and tactile sensations. How do we make our way through this endless array of sensory input? How do we process all the information to which we are exposed? Why do we forget so much of what we process? What can we do to enhance our retention of information?

The purpose of this chapter is to examine these and related questions. It is not possible to fully grasp the dynamics of learning without first understanding how information is processed so that it *can* be learned. Thus, we turn our attention to what cognitive psychologists have called an "information-processing model," which helps us to understand how learning occurs and how to enhance the memory of that learning.

At this moment, you are processing the information on this page. What does this mean? How does it occur? By the end of this chapter, you will be better able to answer questions of this sort and will have some idea of how to *remember* the answers.

Let us begin with a basic question.

WHAT IS MEANT BY INFORMATION PROCESSING?

Basically, the information-processing point of view is a theoretical model that attempts to explain how we acquire information, how we sort and organize it, and how we retrieve that information when needed. Because computers are so much a part of our lives, it is no coincidence that our ideas about information processing are loosely modeled on the way computers process information; for example, before a computer can function, it must be fed data that is *encoded* (represented) in a form that can be processed and stored in a manner that allows it to be *retrieved* later. Similar to the computer, the human brain takes in information, transforms the information to give it meaning, stores and locates it, and generates the necessary responses. In this way, information processing involves gathering and representing information meaningfully, or *encoding;* storing information, or *retention;* and recovering information when needed, or *retrieval.* Thus, the human brain with its neurons and synapses and their networks of interconnections might be compared to the transistors, resistors, capacitors, chips, and relay systems of computers. Similarly, the process involved in receiving, organizing, storing, and retrieving information in the brain might be compared to the programmed functions of the computer.

The computer analogy is offered to help you get a general idea of what information processing is about. There are important differences; for example, whereas both the computer and the brain store information in memory (the computer on microchips, the brain in its neurons), what the computer stores does not change with time (unless damaged). There is considerable debate as to whether what goes into our memories is as unchangeable (Kent, 1981). In addition, it is far easier to retrieve information from a computer (touch the right key) than from the human brain. Even relatively recent knowledge can be difficult to retrieve; for example, three days ago you knew what clothes you were wearing and what you had for dinner that night. Are you able to retrieve that information now? If that data had been entered into a computer, it would still be there. For the human brain, however, it is not as easy. The brain tends to be more selective about what it retains in memory, and what is retained is not always easily retrieved.

Basic Assumptions About How Information Is Processed

The behavioral basis for information-processing rests on three major assumptions (Miller, 1983), each of which is based on a substantial body of research conducted by cognitive psychologists interested in finding out how human learning occurs. The first assumption is that information is processed in steps or stages. Ordinarily, these steps include: (1) attending to a sensory input, (2) transforming the input into some kind of mental image, (3) comparing the mental image with information already stored in memory, (4) assigning meaning to the image, and (5) acting on the image in some way.

A second assumption is that there are limits to how much information can be processed at each stage. Although the absolute amount of knowledge humans can acquire is theoretically infinite, it is clear that new information must be acquired slowly and gradually if it is to be retained.

The third assumption has to do with the idea that the human information-processing system is interactive. That is, what we already know (what is stored in memory) influences and is influenced by what we perceive and attend to in the world around us. Thus, from an information-processing perspective, learning occurs, or is likely to occur, when there is an interaction between an environmental input (the *information* that is to be learned) and a learner who *processes,* or transforms, the information. For example, a psychologist interested in conducting research related to information processing would try to find ways to study what goes on in students' minds as a teacher explains how to calculate the number of cubic feet in a box or while students search for the correct answers on an objective test. The psychologist would be less interested in what the students learned and remembered, and more interested in *how* they learned and *how* they remembered what they had learned.

The information-processing model is helpful in understanding the *how* of learning, something that should become even clearer after we cover the components that constitute its working machinery.

COMPONENTS OF THE INFORMATION-PROCESSING MODEL

Figure 6.1 is a schematic overview of the basic components and inner workings of a typical information-processing model, derived from the work of several cognitive psychologists (Atkinson and Shiffrin, 1968; Gagné, 1985). Other models may include variations of this model's features, but each contains the same basic components you see in Figure 6.1, and each resembles the flowcharts customarily used to portray computer programs. The three boxes inside the dotted-line box represent cognitive components in which information may be held, transformed, and stored. The arrows depict the flow of internal processing. The long rectangle at the top of the figure represents the human dynamics that control the flow of information throughout the system.

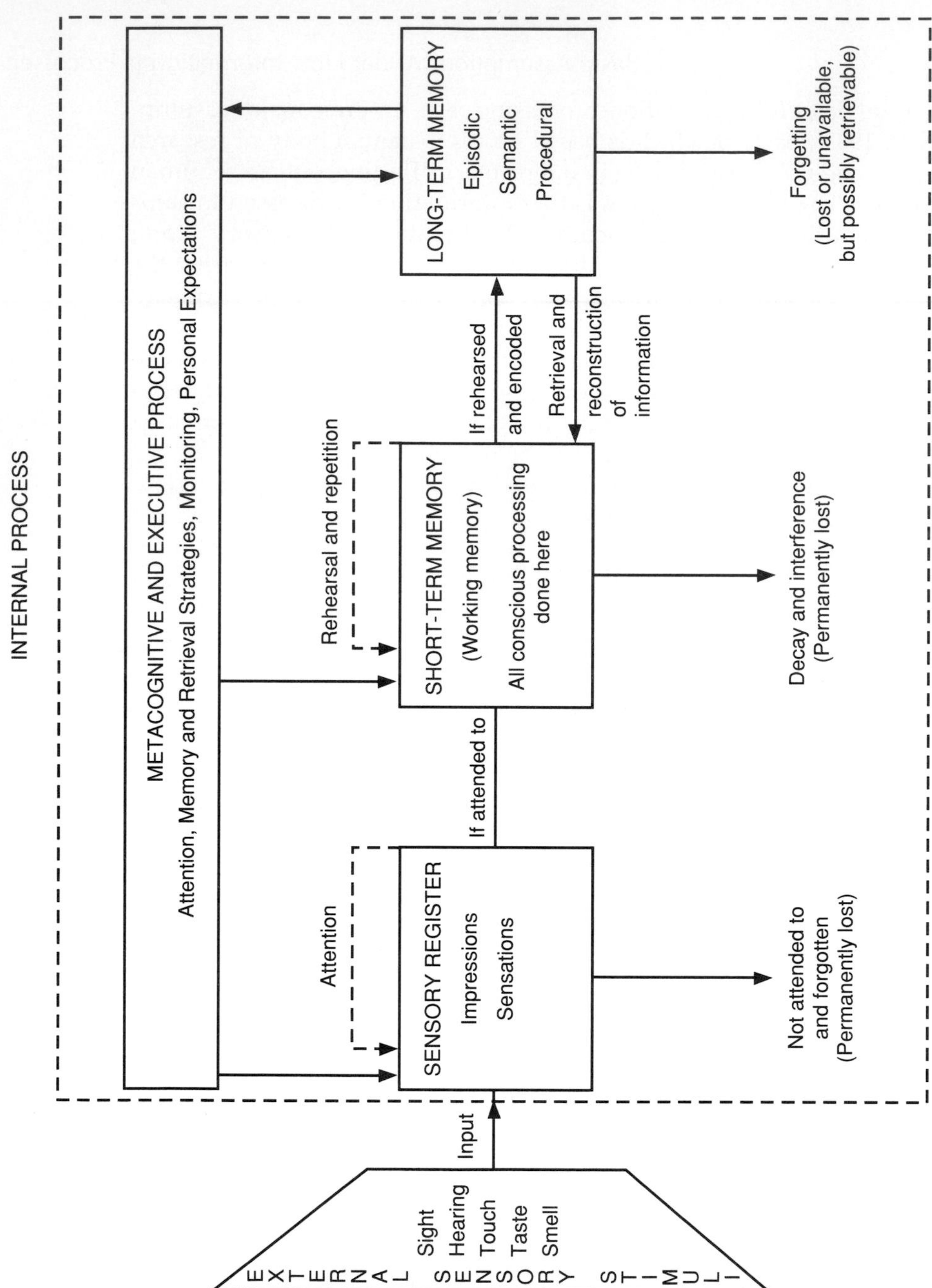

Figure 6.1. INFORMATION-PROCESSING MODEL OF LEARNING AND MEMORY.

(Adapted from Gagné and Driscoll [1988], and Mayer [1981].)

We now turn our attention to a more careful examination of each component of this model. Keep in mind, however, that what we are discussing is a *model*—a metaphoric illustration of what happens in the human mind. It is not meant to be a literal description of the way things actually are in our brains.

Sensory Register

On the left side of Figure 6.1, you see that any number of external sensory stimuli can serve as inputs to the sensory register, including sight, hearing, touch, taste, and smell. Given the rich input possibilities associated with each of these senses, it is not surprising that our sensory receptors are constantly bombarded with stimuli from our immediate environment. Consider carefully the questions in Box 6.1.

6.1 Our Bombarded Sensory System

You may find it a rich and revealing experience to stop your reading for a moment and allow assorted sensory inputs into your consciousness. Are there sounds around you that you were not aware of before you tuned into them? Is there an odor in the air that you were not aware of? Now that you consciously think of it, is there a taste in your mouth that you had not noticed? Are there tactile sensations you can be aware of from the position in which you find your body at this moment? If you were to count the nonvisual sensory stimuli that surround you, what do you come up with? It is amazing how many different sensory stimuli were affecting you and how little of it was part of your consciousness.

Although we are surrounded by a virtual ocean of sensory stimuli, we are aware of only a small portion of it. Music can be in the background, but not actually heard. Contact between body and chair is real, but not consciously felt. Clearly, the bulk of the stimulation around us at any given moment is never actually processed, which is to say it does not become part of our *cognitive structure.* The label given this unprocessed sensory stimulation is *sensory register.* When input from an environment affects a sensory receptor, it produces a stirring of neural activity lasting for only a brief time (one to two seconds), during which it is held in sensory memory, or what is called the "sensory register." Basically, the sensory register is sometimes viewed as a sensory buffer, a one-way station, located between the external environment and internal memory (Rosenzweig and Leiman, 1982).

Because the sensory register holds all input briefly, we have a chance to make sense of it, but only if we pay attention long enough to organize and give meaning to the input so that it can be passed to short-term memory. We cannot possibly perceive everything, so we selectively attend to certain inputs in the sensory register and look for recognizable patterns (Lindsay and Norman, 1977). Attention and perception are critical during the sensory register stage.

Role of Attention

Attention is critical in two ways. For example, by *not* attending to every variation in sound, movement, color, smell, and tactile sensation, we protect ourselves from being overwhelmed by information overload. By *selectively* attending to sensory stimuli, we increase the possibility of processing information that seems relevant enough to be transferred to short-term memory, and perhaps later, to long-term memory.

The capacity for attention is limited. Unless we are very skilled at doing two demanding tasks, we probably cannot do them both at the same time. For example, when you were first learning how to drive, play the piano, or knit, you had to concentrate. Now, these tasks can be done automatically, while your attention is given to another task.

6.2 What Happens When Attention Is Diverted?

Here is something you can try that might heighten your awareness of the importance of attention in assimilating new material or in learning a new task. As you read the short paragraph that follows, silently count from fifty backwards.

Recognizing words quickly and accurately is one of the cornerstones of skilled reading. Phonics improves the ability of children to identify words and sound out new ones. Sounding out the letters in a word is similar to the first tentative steps of a toddler: it helps children gain a secure verbal footing and expands their vocabularies beyond the limits of basic reading.

See how difficult it is to concentrate on two tasks at the same time? When attention is diverted, learning and memory suffer.

The point is, in order for new sensory input to register and move along the continuum from short- to long-term memory, we must first pay attention to it. When input received through our various sensory receptors is not given our attention, it is lost and permanently forgotten. We can get an idea of how this works by reflecting for a moment on what usually happens at parties: people are moving in and out of conversations, music may be playing in the background, and everyone seems to be talking at the same time. You may find yourself halfheartedly participating in a four-way conversation (and only half attending to it), when suddenly, in a nearby group, you hear your name mentioned and your attention is aroused. Perhaps a topic is brought up in which you have a keen interest; suddenly you find yourself paying closer attention to another conversation rather than to the original one.

The implications for teachers are far-reaching. In order to promote learning, teachers must first master the art of getting students' attention. Eye-catching displays, novel approaches, surprise events, variations in pacing, changes in voice level, and unexpected beginnings are ways of focusing attention and keeping students alert and on-task.

6.3 Attention Grabbers

I had a tenth-grade chemistry teacher who was especially creative at designing ways to capture our attention. For example, he might start class by announcing that those of us who were wearing shades of blue-green would be chosen to respond to questions. Of course, this was sufficiently ambiguous to keep us guessing and alert because we were never quite sure whether he would find these tones somewhere on our apparel. At other times, he would invite each of us to submit two true–false questions concerning the material covered in that session. He would choose the best of these questions to include on the weekly quiz. Quiz points quickly added up, so we jumped at the possibility of having questions we knew for sure would be on the test. It was a fun class taught by an interesting teacher who had a knack for the unexpected, which was great for grabbing and *keeping* attention. What examples can you think of that illustrate things teachers have done to focus students' attention?

Influence of Perception

As soon as stimuli from the outside world are received by sensory receptors, the mind immediately begins to work on them. This is where perception enters the picture. The sensory images of which we are conscious are not necessarily the same as the ones that we saw, heard, or felt. Perception of stimuli is not the same as reception of stimuli. Rather, perception is influenced by who we are as individuals and our particular way of viewing the world. A popular maxim is "seeing is believing." However, it would probably be more accurate to say that "believing is seeing," for what we see is shaped and limited by our previous learning and prior experiences.

Thus, perception refers to the meaning we attach to the information received through our sensory receptors. The meaning we give our perceptions is a mixture of objective reality and the way we organize our information. Smith (1975) states the following:

> It is important to grasp that the eyes merely look and the brain sees. And what the brain sees may be determined as much by cognitive structure as by the information from the world outside. We perceive what the brain decides is in front of our eyes.

You can get an idea of what is meant here by looking at the marks below:

If I asked you what the word is, you would undoubtedly say "zoo." If, however, I were to ask you what the number is, you would say "200." Although the marks are the same, your perception of them changes to match your expectation of them, representing either a word or a number.

Whatever we perceive in the world around us, we tend to view in terms of *figure* and *ground* components. For example, when looking at a picture of a group of people, we might focus on a particular individual and note the details of that person. The rest of the picture becomes less important and drifts into the background. The person we are looking at is the *figure* that stands out, while the rest of the picture is the *ground,* ambiguous and undifferentiated.

You can find examples of figure–ground relationships in Figure 6.2. In each example, what do you see at first glance? When you look at the woman, you see either an old witchlike face (what most people see the first time) or a pretty young woman wearing a boa. In the next picture, you see either a vase or the silhouettes of two faces peering at each other. When one part of either of these images becomes figure, the rest fades into ground. We cannot perceive both components at the same time. At the level of teacher–student relationships, we can find many examples of the figure–ground phenomenon in perceptions. For example, Teacher A might have heard that Michael had been a big troublemaker the year before. As a result, even Michael's most minor misdeeds are perceived by Teacher A as evidence of his persistent troublemaking tendencies, even though in actuality he is no more of a behavior problem than other students, perhaps even better behaved than most. His misdeeds are figure in Teacher A's perceptions, while his positive qualities are ground, and therefore less likely to be seen. (We examine these dynamics more fully in Chapter 9, where we discuss how teacher expectations can become self-fulfilling prophecies.)

Perception, then, is an important part of the sensory register phase of information-processing because it determines the kind of meaning that is assigned to various sensory stimuli. The way we perceive the world around us can dramatically influence what we pay attention to and how we behave, an idea nicely illustrated in the following example cited by Combs, Richards, and Richards (1988):

> Several years ago a friend of mine was driving in a car at dusk along a Western road. A globular mass, about two feet in diameter, suddenly appeared directly in the path of the car. A passenger screamed and grasped the wheel attempting to steer the car around the object. The driver, however, tightened his grip on the wheel and drove directly into

Figure 6.2. EXAMPLES OF SHIFTING FIGURE–GROUND RELATIONSHIPS.

the object. The behavior of both the driver and the passenger was determined by his own *perceptions.* The passenger, an Easterner, saw the object in the highway as a boulder and fought desperately to steer the car around it. The driver, a native Westerner, saw it as a tumbleweed and devoted his efforts to keeping his passenger from overturning the car. (p. 17)

From one point of view, the object perceived was a boulder and thus something to veer around, while from another point of view, the object perceived was a harmless weed. One person's perception triggered a panicky reaction, while the other person's perception led to a calm response.

6.4 It Depends on Your Perceptions

Gloria Cooper (1980) put together a compilation of newspaper headlines that have appeared in various U.S. newspapers. Each headline has two different meanings, depending on their interpretation. Although the headline writers undoubtedly had a perfectly innocent meaning in mind, it is clear that what is seen depends on one's perception:

DRUNK GETS NINE MONTHS IN VIOLIN CASE
LEGALIZED OUTHOUSES AIRED BY LEGISLATURE
ROBBER HOLDS UP ALBERT'S HOSIERY
NEW MISSOURI U. CHANCELLOR EXPECTS LITTLE SEX
STUD TIRES OUT
STATE DINNER FEATURED CAT, AMERICAN FOOD

Implications for Teachers

Information can be processed only if it registers in our sensory system. Whether a particular stimulus is registered depends on our *attention* to it, and *how* it is registered depends on our *perceptions* of it. The implications of these concepts are simple, but at the same time, enormous. Four important implications to remember are as follows:

1. If we want our students to learn, then we must first find ways to keep their attention.
2. Attention is most easily captured and kept by events, experiences, and occurrences that are unique, novel, and periodically different.
3. Perceptions determine how students interpret their sensory world and perceptions may vary among students. Recognizing this truth can help those of us who teach remember that different students will be interested (or bored) by different subject matter and teaching approaches. There is no one way of learning or teaching that will benefit all students in the same manner.
4. Competent preparation, novelty, variety, interesting presentations, and a sense of humor will help keep most students attentive, receptive, and perceptive to new information.

Short-Term Memory

The first of the two main storage systems for information processed through the sensory register is called "short-term memory" and is represented by the middle box in Figure 6.1. It consists of what is in our consciousness at any given time, and has been referred to as a kind of "scratch pad" for thinking (Mayer, 1981). Short-term memory contains all that is in our immediate awareness, thus constituting the raw material needed for thinking. For this reason, short-term memory is frequently referred to as "working memory," a level that draws attention to the function of this level of cognition rather than simply to its duration (Klatzky, 1980).

New information that is put into short-term memory is retained only briefly, probably for about twenty seconds or so. Information can be held for a longer period to mentally rehearse the information until it is no longer needed; for example, you might remember the names of several people, a phone number, or the directions you were just given to a person's house by repeating the information in your mind.

Short-term memory is limited not only in the length of time it can hold new information, but also in capacity. In early experimental research on this matter, Miller (1956) concluded that only about five to nine new items of information can be held in short-term memory at one time. That is, our immediate conscious awareness is limited to this number, and as new items come in, they tend to force out what is already there. You can get an idea of how this works by doing the exercise in Box 6.5.

6.5 How Good Is Your Short-Term Memory?

Consider the following list of seven phone numbers. Look at the first two phone numbers and try to remember them. Then look at the next two and try to remember them along with the first two numbers. Then add the last three numbers to your memory. How many telephone numbers can you remember?

355-6684	251-6240	487-3743
337-4592	482-1020	339-1121
	795-3484	

It is important to keep in mind (in other words, remember in short-term memory) that what we are discussing is the retention and recall of *new* information. Although you are probably experiencing difficulty remembering the telephone numbers in Box 6.5, which are new to you, you are undoubtedly able to recall five or more previously learned, older phone numbers that you frequently use. These numbers, along with thousands of other bits of information, are retrievable because they are in long-term memory. When you need that information, you retrieve and work with it in short-term memory, where it stays as long as you are consciously using it.

The idea of "consciously using it" is a key concept. Remember that we hold the information we are thinking about at any given moment in short-term memory for approximately twenty seconds. (As an example of this, do you now remember any of the telephone numbers in Box 6.5?) After twenty seconds or so, a time limit that varies slightly from person to person, the information is either permanently lost or stored in long-term memory.

At first glance, it may seem that a memory system with a twenty-second time limit is not very useful. However, without at least this amount of time you would have already forgotten what was read in the previous five or six sentences, making what you are reading at this moment difficult to understand. Conversely, it would be to our disadvantage to remember forever every sentence we ever read. Retrieving particular items of information from an endless list of sentences would be impossible. Thus, it is helpful to have a component such as short-term memory that provides temporary storage.

Actually, the apparent limitations of short-term memory are not as serious as they might seem. Although we cannot easily attend to more than five to nine individual items, a process called "chunking" dramatically improves our capacity for short-term memory. Because it is the *number* of bits of information, not the *size* of each bit, that causes problems for short-term memory, separate bits of *related* information can be chunked or grouped together in some meaningful way. For example, rather than trying to remember the first two phone numbers in Box 6.5 by their seven separate numbers, it is easier to remember them in groups. Thus, 355-6684 might be chunked as 355/66/84, and 377-4592 as 377/45/92. Now, rather than there being fourteen digits to recall, there are six groups of digits, a far easier task. Chunking is frequently used by radio and television advertisers, particularly when they want us to call in our orders. Rather than presenting us with an eleven-digit telephone number to dial in order to subscribe to a year of the magazine *Running and Health,* we are advised to dial 1-800-RUN-FAST. Which do you think you would remember more easily, 1-800-786-3278 or 1-800-RUN-FAST?

In summary, short-term memory is that part of our information-processing system in which we deal with a limited number of items, or chunks, of information in conscious awareness. Without continued rehearsal and use, this information is generally lost from memory in about twenty seconds. The major value of short-term memory is that it enables us to store information long enough to make sense of the words and data with which we are dealing at the moment. When we have rehearsed and transformed input into meaningful information, it then has a chance of being encoded in long-term memory, a system we turn to next.

Long-Term Memory

Long-term memory is where we store all the information we possess about the world—all that we *know,* but which is not in our immediate consciousness. Some of the important differences between short-term and long-term memory are juxtaposed in Figure 6.3. Whereas short-term memory is an active, dynamic, conscious process, long-term memory is a more passive, unconscious process. Although information enters quickly into short-term memory and is easily accessible, it is handled only in limited amounts, held for only about twenty seconds, and easily disrupted. Information in long-term memory, however, enters more slowly, is not as easily accessible, can be stored in unlimited amounts, is retained indefinitely, and is not easily disrupted. Cognitive psychologists subdivide long-term memory into at least three components: *episodic memory, semantic memory,* and *procedural memory* (Tulving, 1985, 1972).

Episodic memory is associated with our recall of particular times and places, and thus is a storage place for many of our personal experiences. Recalling

Short-term memory	*Long-term memory*
Information—	Information—
1. enters quickly.	1. enters slowly.
2. is immediately accessible.	2. is not easily accessible.
3. is retained briefly (20 sec.).	3. is retained indefinitely.
4. is easily disrupted.	4. is not easily disrupted.
5. Capacity is limited (5-9 items).	5. Capacity is unlimited.

Figure 6.3. DIFFERENCES BETWEEN SHORT-TERM AND LONG-TERM MEMORY.

what we ate for breakfast this morning, our first day in kindergarten, or details of our high school graduation day are examples of episodic memory. Episodic memory tends to have a strong visual aspect to it; for example, we can sometimes recall the information on a particular page by remembering where it was located on that page. We are more likely to have strong visual memories about episodes in our lives that elicited high levels of emotional arousal. Emotional arousal intensifies attention, which is one reason many of our early episodic memories are of fear, shame, physical pain, death, and the birth of siblings. An example of this is the detail with which most of us can recall where we were and what we were doing at the exact moment we heard about the tragic explosion of the *Challenger* spacecraft on January 28, 1986.

Semantic memory involves knowledge of general facts, principles, and concepts that are not connected to particular times and places. Semantic memory is mentally organized in networks of connected ideas or relationships referred to as schemata (Anderson, 1985; Chang, 1986). A *schema* (the singular form) thus becomes a mental pattern, or guide, for organizing our understanding and interpretation of the world around us. A schema is similar to an outline, with various ideas or concepts grouped under larger, more generic categories. If, for example, you were interested in learning more about the various kinds and classifications of minerals, you could enhance your efficiency by developing a schema that allowed you to organize separate chunks of information into a few manageable clumps. You see an example of this kind of schema in Figure 6.4. Notice how each part of the clump can be associated with other parts, thus helping us to remember the various components of our mineral schema. The efficacy of this approach has been demonstrated in clever experiments by Bower and his associates (1969), who found that students who used this clump approach remembered significantly more information than students who did not. The concept of schema is also illustrated in Figure 6.4, which

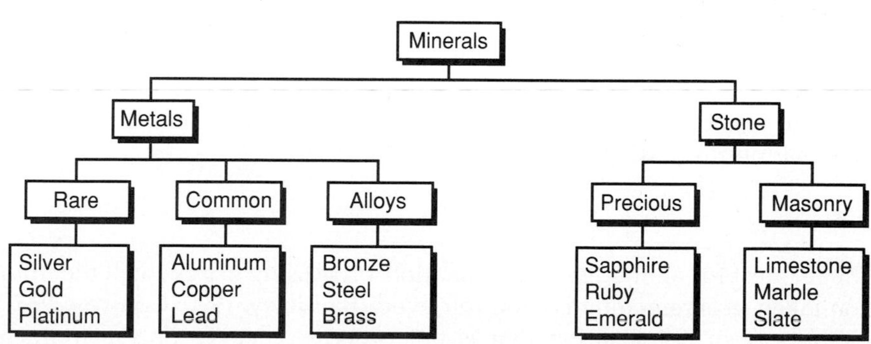

Figure 6.4. AN EXAMPLE OF A SCHEMA FOR ORGANIZING INFORMATION INTO RELATED CLUMPS.

provides a framework for deciding which details are important, what information to look for, and what to remember about the internal process associated with information-processing.

6.6 Tapping into Your Semantic Memory

What ideas or images come to mind when you see each of the following words? How would you describe the persons associated with each word?

Scientist	Lawyer	Feminist
Republican	Democrat	TV Evangelist

Although you may not be aware of it, each of these names, or labels, serves as a schema in the sense that each brings to mind particular descriptive images that help you organize your understanding of each label. Although we do not organize our schemata as neatly and deliberately as suggested in Figure 6.4, in a less conscious way we do tend to organize our knowledge of the world we live in around certain general facts, ideas, and preconceptions that constitute the schemata of our semantic memories.

Procedural memory refers to "knowing how" as opposed to "knowing that" (Anderson, 1983). The ability to ride a bike, to drive a car, to play a piano, or to type are examples of skills retained in procedural memory. This type of memory is apparently stored in a series of stimulus-response pairings. For example, a person may not have ridden a bike for years and then do perfectly well once he or she rides one again. Specific stimuli have awakened particular responses. If the bike leans one way (a stimulus), the rider leans the other (a response), thus maintaining both balance and physical well-being.

As noted earlier, we transfer information from sensory register to short-term memory through the process of attention, and we maintain it in short-term memory largely through rehearsal (repetition, practice). However, the transfer of information from short-term to long-term memory involves more than simple rehearsal and repetition. It involves *encoding,* a process of transforming and representing information in such a way that it can be organized and stored for retrieval. This can occur at different levels of abstraction and organization, which brings us to an important idea associated with information-processing.

Memory and Retrieval

The real test for all models of information-processing is how well the information taken in is remembered and retrieved (Baddeley, 1990; Conway, 1991). As we have seen, information that is not processed leaves only a momentary sensory impression (sensory register), information that is merely rehearsed fades in a matter of seconds (short-term memory), and information that is processed to a greater degree is more likely to end up in long-term memory.

Craik and Lockhart (1972) and Craik (1979) take this a step further in their levels-of-processing model by proposing that the determination of how long information is remembered is not *where* it is stored, but how completely new data is analyzed and integrated with other information.

For example, you might see a dog, but pay little attention to it. This represents the lower level of processing, and you are not likely to remember the dog. It was but a fleeting impression in your sensory register. You might have given a name to the dog, such as "Tawny" or "German shepherd." Once named, the dog is more likely to be remembered. The highest level of processing, however, would involve giving additional meaning to your perception of the dog. For example, you might remember having had a dog that looked similar to this one, or you might think to yourself that having a German shepherd would give you a feeling of great security, because you have heard that they are great watchdogs. According to the levels-of-processing theory, the more completely new information is analyzed and integrated with other information, the more likely it is that we will remember it.

This idea is illustrated in a study by Bower and Karlin (1974), who had two groups of students from one university look at the yearbook pictures of students from another university. One group of students was asked to classify the pictures as "male" or "female," while the other group was asked to classify the pictures as "very honest" or "less honest." The group classifying the pictures in terms of honesty remembered them far better than the group who simply categorized the pictures in terms of gender. Presumably, classifying pictures on an honesty continuum involved a higher level of information-processing than was required of simple gender classification.

A related levels-of-processing model is Pavio's (1971) dual-code theory of memory. The basic hypothesis is that information is retained in long-term memory in two ways: visually and verbally, which correspond to episodic memory and semantic memory, respectively. This theory states that information processed both visually *and* verbally is retained better than information processed only one way. It has been demonstrated that we are more likely to remember a face when we associate it with a name, and a name when we connect it to some personal characteristic of its owner. For example, some years ago I knew a man whose first name was Cole, a name I always had trouble remembering. One day it occurred to me that his negative attitude about everything made me think of black coal. With that association, "coal" for "Cole," I never again forgot his name. (Five years have passed since I saw him last and it is *still* fresh in my mind.) Association is the trick of the trade for many stage performers who must memorize a great deal of material.

Metacognitive and Executive Processes

The final components of the information-processing model we want to examine are the metacognitive and executive processes that monitor and divert the system's cognitive activities (Garner and Alexander, 1989). The two processes appear in the long narrow box at the top of Figure 6.1. Basically, these are the processes involved in assessing a learning problem, determining learning strategies with which to approach the problem, evaluating the effectiveness of the chosen strategy, and making modifications where necessary. Executive processes monitor the internal processes of the overall information-processing system.

The functioning of the executive processes is based on *metacognition,* a term referring to the idea of "knowing about knowing" (Flavell, 1985). Essentially, metacognition involves the study of how we think about our own thinking in order to develop strategies for learning. The skills of metacognition provide us with ways of estimating the effects of our efforts, and they enable us to anticipate how well the material will be remembered later. Metacognitive knowledge helps us to organize material to facilitate learning and retention, and it enables us to see that certain rehearsal and review strategies are more effective than others for specific types of material.

6.7 Finding Ways to Know About Knowing

Assume you are faced with taking an objective test in a history course in which there is a particular emphasis on remembering dates, historical figures, and significant historical events, and assume you know you are going to take an essay test in your educational psychology course covering material related to major theoretical views about human behavior. What factors should you take into consideration in developing a study plan? How do you then prepare for each of these exams? Your consideration of questions like these are an example of metacognition. You are finding ways to know about knowing.

Sternberg (1983) identified nine groups of executive skills (metacognitive strategies), which include: (1) identifying a problem; (2) selecting a problem-solving process; (3) selecting a strategy; (4) selecting a mode of representation, such as outlines, diagrams, charts, tables, and so on; (5) allocating resources; (6) monitoring progress; (7) sensitivity to feedback; (8) incorporating feedback into ongoing cognitive processes; and (9) implementing selected strategies.

You can see that the nine categories of executive skills are broadly defined; they represent general decisions about possible approaches one can use as cognitive strategies for processing information. The nine executive skills, or metacognitive strategies, previously identified are indications of *what* needs to be done as a first step. The next step is to find out *how;* in other words, what skills and strategies are actually used in the process of acquiring, organizing, and remembering information. However, before we look at strategies that can be used to enhance memory, let's first examine an important question.

WHY DO WE FORGET?

Although we have every good intention to set the alarm, to buy a loaf of bread on the way home, or to remember the formulas we know will be on an exam, we manage to forget. Why? What keeps us from remembering even the things we *want* to remember? With the information-processing model as our framework, let's look at some possible explanations that have been proposed by some cognitive theorists (Sherry and Schacter, 1987).

Short-Term Memory and Forgetting

Decay and interference appear to be the primary means by which information is lost in short-term memory. To say that information has been lost through decay is an abbreviated way of saying that it has disappeared due to lack of use. Because short-term memory lasts only a brief time, it does not take long for unused information to fade away. Whether discussing muscle power or brain power, there is considerable truth in the old adage that says "use it or lose it."

Forgetting due to interference is fairly straightforward. It basically refers to the idea that learning new information interferes with remembering old information. Because the limited capacity of short-term memory is quickly filled, previous information is the first to go. If, for example, I asked you to remember the names Jenny, Carol, George, and Richard, you would probably handle that easily enough. However, if ten seconds later I asked you to remember the names Jean, Debbie, Allen, and Dan, you might have trouble remembering the first four names. In fact, without looking back, what *were* the first four names? You can see how interference works. It doesn't take much.

Long-Term Memory and Forgetting

When we lose information from short-term memory, it is lost forever; for example, you probably put the names cited in the previous paragraph into short-term memory. Can you recall the last two names in each of the two sets of four names? Most people would have trouble doing this because there was no need to remember them, and thus the names flitted in and out of short-term memory. Information that is stored in long-term memory, however, is never completely lost, although it may be difficult to retrieve (Baddeley, 1990; Roitblat, 1987). There are several reasons for this difficulty, one of which may be that we sometimes intentionally desire to repress particular memories, an idea that goes back to Freud. There may be some truth to this, but this theory fails to explain why we remember certain painful experiences vividly, while some of the more pleasant experiences in our lives are forgotten.

Another reason has to do with the idea that interference causes forgetting in long-term as well as short-term memory. That is, newer information and experiences can interfere with, or cloud, older memories (Houston, 1986). One type of interference is *proactive inhibition,* which can occur when previous knowledge makes it difficult to remember new knowledge. For example, you learn A, and later, you learn B, only to discover that knowing B gets in the way of recalling A.

Another kind of interference is *retroactive inhibition,* which is what can happen when the assimilation of new information gets in the way of remembering already stored information. This can occur, for example, when the learning of new material (B) works backward and hampers your recall of older information (A) (Houston, 1986).

We can see the interference phenomenon in the lives of teachers, particularly those who have been teaching for a while and have been exposed to many students with similar names. It becomes increasingly easy to confuse new names with old names that had similar faces. This is an illustration of proactive inhibition. Conversely, once teachers learn the names of their present group of students, they sometimes have trouble remembering the students they once had. This is an example of retroactive inhibition.

The idea of forgetting due to interference does not contradict the view that nothing is really forgotten once it is stored in long-term memory. The reason for this is that the interference is not necessarily occurring in long-term memory itself, but in the mechanism for trying to recall information from long-term memory and bring it back to short-term memory (Norman, 1982). Thus, the problem very likely resides in the retrieval process, which leads us to consider . . .

STRATEGIES FOR IMPROVING LONG-TERM MEMORY

In an effort to find ways to enhance memory, Weinstein and Mayer (1985) identified five specific learning strategies, which they defined as "behaviors and thoughts that a learner engages in during learning and that are intended to influence the learner's encoding . . . in a way that facilitates the way in which the learner . . . selects, acquires, organizes, or integrates new knowledge" (p. 315). These are called *rehearsal strategies, elaboration strategies, organizational strategies, comprehension-monitoring strategies,* and *affective strategies.* Each works primarily to enhance long-term memory, which, whether looked at from the point of view of teachers or students, is the most important component of the information-processing model. Each strategy is a way of facilitating the encoding of information, which, as mentioned earlier, is a process of representing information meaningfully so that it can be retained (stored) and retrieved when needed. Let's briefly consider how each works:

1. *Rehearsal strategies.* Rehearsal means to repeat material by either speaking aloud or writing. When focusing on brief rote-learning tasks (e.g., a list of dates, names, formulas), rehearsal might involve simply repeating the material several times to aid in memorizing it. When learning more complex tasks (e.g., dividing by fractions, remembering parts of speech), rehearsal might involve copying material, taking selective notes, underlining important parts, outlining key ideas, and then rereading the material.

2. *Elaboration strategies.* Basically, this idea involves making connections between new information and more familiar material. Material elaborated on when first learned is easier to recall later. The more one item of information is associated with others, the more routes there are to the original information. For rote-learning tasks, elaboration strategies might include generating sentences that relate to the material to be learned, forming mental images that are associated with the material, or using various mnemonic devices. A simple mnemonic that one could use to remember the five learning/thinking strategies discussed would be to take the first letter of each strategy and associate a new word with it so that the five new words form a new sentence. For example, the five strategies—rehearsal, elaboration, organizational, comprehension-monitoring, and affective—might be represented by a mnemonic such as the following:

R -ambo
E -ats
O -atmeal
C -ookies
A -loud

By remembering one sentence (Rambo Eats Oatmeal Cookies Aloud) rather than trying to remember five terms, you have a better chance of retrieving the individual terms. This also illustrates chunking, discussed earlier in the chapter. Don't worry if the mnemonic you come up with doesn't make much sense. In fact, the sillier and the more ridiculous a mnemonic sounds, the more likely that you will remember it because of its novelty and uniqueness.

For more complex learning that goes beyond simple rote memorization, strategies that include paraphrasing (putting ideas into your own words), summarizing, looking for analogies, answering questions, and describing how new information relates to existing knowledge are effective ways to elaborate on what is immediately known.

3. *Organizational strategies.* This refers to the strategy of structuring material in such a way as to highlight its hierarchical nature of the similarities and differences among the components being learned. For tasks that involve simple rote learning, organizational strategies might be as simple as placing new

information in lists or clusters. Organizational strategies for more complex, meaningful learning might take the form of outlining a chapter, creating a hierarchical network of concepts, or making diagrams showing relationships, similarities, or differences among concepts. Figures 6.1 and 6.4 are examples of this approach.

4. *Comprehension-monitoring strategies.* Basically, the strategies in this category include the things we do to check our own learning, such as noting and taking action on material we fail to understand, self-questioning to check understanding, establishing subgoals and assessing progress in achieving them, and modifying our approaches to learning when necessary.

5. *Affective strategies.* Research shows that the way we feel—our mood, or *affect*—can have a powerful impact on memory and learning (Bower, 1981). Affective strategies include those things we do to deal with emotional states that might impede learning, such as establishing and maintaining motivation, focusing attention, dealing with anxiety, and managing time effectively. Regular exercise, relaxation techniques, and setting up a regular schedule and sticking to it, along with striking a balance between work and play, are helpful, healthy ways to maintain positive affect.

Processing information and retaining what we learn do not simply happen by themselves. Although a good deal of what we think about is processed automatically and without any particular awareness on our part, research (Flavell, 1985; Garner and Alexander, 1989; Klatzky, 1984; Manning, 1991) points clearly to the conclusion that long-term memory results when we adopt the types of metacognitive strategies previously stated.

A Time-Tested System for Learning Enhancement

One of the most practical and widely used approaches to learning enhancement is F. P. Robinson's (1970) SQ3R system, so named as an acronym for what the system is about: *survey, question, read, recite,* and *review.* The fact that SQ3R was introduced by a book in its fourth edition after twenty-five years is, in itself, testimony to the value of the system. A slight variation made on that system by E. L. Thomas and H. A. Robinson (1972), called PQ4R, tacked on an additional R for *reflection.* The P stands for *preview,* which means, basically, the same thing as the S in Robinson's first step, *survey.*

Let's say, for example, you have a textbook that is organized into chapters, similar to this one. You not only have to read them, but also to remember as much as possible for examination purposes. Using the PQ4R system, you would proceed with the six steps outlined next:

1. *Preview.* Begin by skimming through the assigned chapter, with particular note taken of chapter subheadings. Read the chapter summary, if there is one.

Your objective is to get a general overview, a "feeling" for the chapter. Look for three to six core ideas.

2. *Question.* Generate several major questions; for example, "what is the point of this chapter?", "what is its major theme?", and so on. Turn the first subheading into a question; this is a way of searching for the answer to that question. You could, for example, convert the subheading for this section into a question such as, "what are the SQ3R and PQ4R systems?". Write the question in your notebook.

3. *Read.* Read to answer that question. Actively search for it. When you find the answer or answers, jot down the page numbers next to the question. (You will refer to that later.)

4. *Reflect.* Try to make the materials you are reading meaningful. Relate them to your own life, making connections between what you are reading and what you already know.

5. *Recite.* After reading the section under the first subheading, look away and attempt to answer your question. Use your own words, and cite an example. If you are unable to do this, look over the materials again. There is no rule stipulating that you must absorb all the material you read the first time through—few can do this. Sometimes it takes two or three attempts. Jot down key phrases or words in the margins of your notebook. Repeat steps two, three, and four with each new subheading. When you are finished reading the chapter, you will have a series of questions with the page noted on which each answer is found, as well as key phrases in one margin of your notebook so that you can cover them up. What you have amounts to your own exam of the chapter, which is more comprehensive than your instructor can give you because your exam covers *all* the material in the chapter. Test yourself. When you do not know the answer, check your key phrases or words to see if they trigger the correct response. Go back to the pages from which you have taken your questions for details you have forgotten. (I can report from personal experience that this particular "exam" system helped me prepare for more tests than I care to remember in my college days.)

6. *Review.* When you have finished going through your own exam, go back over your questions and notes in order to get an overview of the key points. Check your memory by answering the particularly difficult questions. Try not to get discouraged when the answers do not come. Understanding new material and committing it to memory takes time. Research testing the effectiveness of this system has been quite favorable. In one study (Adams, Carnine, and Gersten, 1982), elementary-level students who used the PQ4R system recalled more information on both immediate and delayed tests than other students. Other research (Meyer, Brandt, and Bluth, 1980) has shown that students who

follow a book's structure to organize their own memory of the material are able to recall more than students who do not. Still other research (Hamilton, 1985) shows that students who generate their own questions and use the questions in the text remember more of what they read than students who do not. Simply stated, helping readers to be more aware of what they are reading enables them to more easily remember it. Generating one's own questions as well as using those in a text is another way of keeping attention focused and on-task, which is crucial in both the theory and practice of information processing. Most often we forget because our attention to a topic (information, question, a name, a face, etc.) is too short. The first step to encoding and storing new information is having a person's complete attention.

6.8 Important Steps in Remembering New Information

To briefly encapsulate what information-processing theory and research teach us about the things we need to do to put new information into long-term memory, consider the following:

1. Pay *attention* to the material. To be sure you are doing this:
   a. Repeat the material as soon as possible.
   b. Highlight important points.
2. *Rehearse* the material in different ways. You might:
   a. Form mental images or associations, such as *M*onkeys *V*ery *E*arly *M*ade *J*umping *S*eem *U*tterly *N*atural *P*ractice. (The first letter in each word stands for a planet in the solar system.)
   b. Paraphrase new material; give it personal meaning.
   c. Organize material so that it makes sense to you.
   d. Identify main ideas; develop summary schemes such as this one.
3. *Monitor* your progress by asking:
   a. Have I covered all the material?
   b. Do I understand the main points?
   c. Can I explain the main points?

Additional Specific Strategies for Memory Enhancement

When learning new material it is sometimes necessary to remember lists of names, formulas, labels, or other such factual data. What follows are some suggestions for being more successful in this kind of learning. As a package, they represent ways to make learning more efficient and manageable, as well as suggestions for coming up with creative associations and for keeping one's own psychology and physiology ready for maximum performance.

1. *Use part learning.* Break the material to be learned into manageable sections; learn each section, or part, and then practice linking the parts together

after each section is mastered. This is particularly helpful for memorizing long lists. Be sure to change the order of the list to be memorized; a person's tendency is to learn the beginning and the end of a list more thoroughly than the middle. If you always study the list in the same order, you might overlearn the beginning and the end and shortchange your memory of the middle section.

2. *Use mnemonic devices.* One mnemonic device is the successive-comparison system, based on the idea that if two ideas are blended vividly in the mind, recalling one of them will automatically lead to the recall of the other. Suppose, for instance, that you have a series of words to learn beginning with the words *lion, milk,* and *rowboat.* You commit *lion* to memory as your starting point and then associate *lion* and *milk* in an exaggerated image of a lion swimming in a tub full of milk, at which point you add a *rowboat* bobbing along next to the lion. In this way you continue down your list of words, making an effort to come up with exaggerated, even silly, associations. You are building more and more neural connections among items on the list, which makes them increasingly difficult to forget.

Mnemonics can also be rhymes or jingles that help you to link otherwise unrelated words or concepts. How often have we heard "thirty days hath September, April, June . . ." as a way of remembering the number of days in a given month; "spring forward, fall back" as an aid to setting clocks for daylight saving time; "every good boy does fine" as a way of remembering the lines of the treble clef (E-G-B-D-F); or the grammatical rule, "*I* before *e,* except after *c,* or when sounding like 'Ay,' as in neighbor or weigh."

Another kind of mnemonic that is helpful in creating associations is the pegword method, which is a way of learning new lists of items by associating them with numbers connected to an image. Lindsay and Norman (1977) have suggested ten simple words that incorporate rhymes to make a list easier to learn.

One is bun.	Six is sticks.
Two is shoe.	Seven is heaven.
Three is tree.	Eight is gate.
Four is door.	Nine is time.
Five is hive.	Ten is hen.

When you know these particular pegwords, new lists of items to be learned can be connected to these words through imagery. Suppose, for instance, that on your way home you have to pick up a book at the library, go to the cleaners, visit the grocery store, and stop by the post office for some stamps. Using the number-imagery system, you might imagine your book sandwiched between two buns' that have dripped ketchup on your shoes, which means they have to be cleaned at the cleaners. Next, you could see an empty ketchup bottle hanging from a tree inside a grocery store. Finally, you might imagine a huge door stamped into the side of a wall. Remember, your associations can be totally nonsensical. They only have to make sense to you. The number one reminds you of a bun, which triggers the image of a book sandwiched between two buns; the number two reminds you of shoes that now have ketchup on them, which reminds you of the cleaners; and so on. The more associations, the richer and more varied the neural connections, and the more of those, the better the memory. (Without looking back, can you remember what is associated with tree and door?)

3. *Overlearn the material.* Retention of new material can be enhanced if practice or review continues beyond the first errorless reproduction of the new information. Driving a car after months of not driving, typing after years of not typing, playing the piano after months of not playing, or reciting the multiplication table that we learned in fourth grade are examples of things we have overlearned.

As a technique for increasing the capacity for retention and enhancing learning, overlearning new material is most advisable in two particular situations: (1) when learning specific, concrete material, such as grammar rules, multiplication tables, names, dates, the periodic table, or football plays; and (2) when there has been a long interval between the learning of material and its recall. Encouraging students to overlearn abstract principles or concepts that they do not understand is *not* wise, however, because it invites them to simply memorize new material without knowing what it means. We are not likely to remember what we do not understand.

4. *Distribute study and practice.* New material, similar to medicine, can be taken in large or small doses. Study might be concentrated into relatively long, unbroken periods of work, or spread over several shorter sessions. Almost without exception, research shows that spacing new learning over a longer time span, with frequent study sessions, is a more effective means of maximizing retention than trying to "cram" during an all-night marathon. Even if an examination is to be given the next day, shorter study periods interspersed with study of other material is a wiser tactic than trying to learn a large amount of material in a single session. There is good reason for this. Brain research indicates that, at a biochemical level, a short-term memory process begins immediately after something new is learned. This quickly fades, however, unless there is an opportunity for it to be consolidated in long-term memory, a process involving the production of ribonucleic acids and the stimulation of higher enzymatic activities in brain cells (Groves and Rebec, 1988). This process is too complex to discuss; it is enough to know that it takes time and is facilitated by repetition. Hence, what we study in a hurry, with no chance to review, is soon forgotten.

5. *Sleep after studying, not before.* Sleep, according to Hoddes (1977), helps memory if it *follows* study. If sleep precedes study, it can be more detrimental

to memory than no sleep. The procrastinator approach—sleep before you learn—is not helpful. In fact, a short sleep just prior to new learning can seriously reduce retention; this is called the "prior-sleep" effect. An example of this could be awakening in the middle of the night, talking briefly, and then going back to sleep and remembering little, if anything, of what was said. Hoddes' research suggests that sleep increases the release of a hormone called "somatotropin," which, until one is fully awake and the hormone has returned to normal levels, tends to disrupt memory functions.

If you do not plan to relearn the material you study, the best advice is to sleep four or more hours, if possible, between the time you study and the time you have to recall the information. Do not sleep before you study unless you allow yourself plenty of time in which to fully awaken before seriously studying.

6.9 Take Your Knowledge to Bed with You

This should be easy. The next time you have to take a test, review the material the night before the exam, and let that be the last thing you do before going to sleep. Go over the major points and the key ideas, and take those thoughts to sleep with you. Find out for yourself if this tactic helps memory. Remember to give the material your full attention. One of the reasons you are more apt to remember is that there is nothing to interfere with what you've learned, which reduces what we have already discussed about retroactive inhibition. Try this system. I think you will be pleased with the results.

TEACHING STRATEGIES THAT CAN ENHANCE RETENTION AND LEARNING

To conclude this chapter, let us look at a checklist of ideas that teachers could use as a general guideline in applying basic information-processing principles in classroom settings. These are meant to be general guidelines only; specific translations from theory and research to practice depend on many variables, such as teachers, students, age group, and subject matter. The guidelines are as follows:

1. *Make sure you have the students' attention and look for ways to keep it.*
   a. Create a signal that lets students know class is beginning. Stand behind a desk or lectern, flick the lights, or raise your hand. For example, I know a high school teacher who whistles and an elementary school teacher who rings a small bell. Do what works for you.
   b. Be a moving target; vary your pitch and tone of voice. Let your hands and body be part of a total communications system.
   c. Let students know the objectives of each class session. This focuses their attention.
   d. Use students' names when talking to them; ask challenging but answerable questions. Do not always ask factual questions; occasionally, ask for

opinions, something that everyone has. This takes the pressure off having to provide the "right" answer. Placing too much pressure on having the correct answer may create excessive anxiety, an emotional state that can narrow attention.

e. Let humor and laughter be a natural part of each class; these help students to be relaxed and receptive, feelings that can enhance learning, rather than making them feel tense and defensive, which can interfere with learning.

2. *Help students separate important information.* This helps them focus their attention.
   a. Provide either a written or an oral overview (or both) of the material to be covered.
   b. As class goes on, relate the material to the objectives of the lesson.
   c. When making an important point, *say* it is important, and give students time to make notes about it. Encourage them to do so in their own words.
   d. Rephrase important points and ask questions about them, encouraging discussion when appropriate.

3. *Help students see relationships between information they have learned and new information.*
   a. Diagrams, outlines, and flowcharts are helpful in linking items of information so that relationships can be seen.
   b. Review what students already know so that they can be more aware of possible connections between previous knowledge and new input. An elementary teacher, for example, had students review their knowledge of addition before getting into a lesson on multiplication. A junior high school science teacher had his students talk about how a kite manages to stay in the air, and then moved the discussion of the aerodynamics of flight.
   c. Give assignments that encourage students to use new information along with information already known. For example, a high school science teacher asked some students to study only prior to going to bed the night before a quiz, and others taking the same quiz to study only immediately after waking in the morning. He wanted his students to see for themselves how study and sleep interact. (The quiz was not graded.) The students who studied before going to sleep did better overall than the students who studied immediately following sleep. It was quite an unscientific study, but the results were consistent with more scientific ones.

4. *Give students opportunities for repetitive study and for review.*
   a. Begin class with a quick review of material previously covered.
   b. Short, frequent quizzes encourage students to go over material.

   c. Allow time for questions about previously covered material.
   d. Give students plenty of feedback to ensure that what they are repeating and reviewing is correct.

5. *Reduce memorization to a minimum; keep meaning and comprehension at a maximum.*
   a. Help students to understand *why* and *how* X relates to Y, and not just that it does. For example, a sixth-grade teacher, wanting her students to understand the relationship between the size of an object and its mass, brought a tennis ball and a lead ball of a similar size to school. By weighing each object separately on a scale, she was able to teach her students how to distinguish between mass and weight, thus demonstrating how gravity acts on an object in relation to its mass.
   b. A fourth-grade teacher asked his students to figure out how many times the number 5 would have to be subtracted from 20 to reach a zero sum. They performed this simple operation (e.g., 20 – 5 – 5 – 5 – 5 = 0) and found that 5 could be subtracted four times. Then the teacher had students divide those same numbers (e.g., 20 ÷ 5 = 4) to help them understand that division is, in the case of specific number combinations, a short form of subtraction.

Getting students' attention and giving them opportunities to use, rehearse, and work with new information in meaningful ways while it is in short-term memory are necessary prerequisites for properly encoding new information in long-term memory.

EPILOGUE

Information-processing theory is a way of conceptually thinking about how information is taken in from the outside world, how it is stored in memory, and how it is retrieved when needed. Processing, basically, proceeds in three stages. Initially, select stimuli (e.g., sights, sounds, odors, etc.) are taken in through one of five channels and recorded in our sensory register (sometimes called sensory memory), which holds, for a matter of seconds, only raw, unprocessed data. The key to sensory-register function is *attention.* If we do not attend to the vast array of sensory information around us, it is quickly and permanently lost. If, however, any aspect of this sensory input is attended to, it passes into short-term memory.

Short-term memory is the second phase of information processing and consists of what is in our immediate consciousness at any given time. It is also called *working memory,* in that this is where we consciously work with new or retrieved information. Our short-term memory holds information for about twenty seconds or so, after which the information is either permanently lost or stored in long-term memory. The key to short-term memory function is *re-*

hearsal, which refers to data that is processed and then transformed into meaningful information so that it can be encoded in long-term memory.

Long-term memory is where we store everything we know—information of which we are not immediately conscious. Whereas short-term memory can handle only limited amounts of information for brief periods of time, long-term memory can handle unlimited amounts of information and retain it indefinitely. Long-term memory is thought to have at least three components: (1) episodic memory (times and places); (2) semantic memory (facts, principles, and concepts); and (3) procedural memory (specific physical skills and abilities). Long-term memory is similar to a storage tank: what we are not using is stored there until retrieved. Once retrieved, the actual processing of information goes on in short-term memory.

Metacognition is a term for the process of knowing about knowing. The essential purpose of metacognitive activities is to find ways in which to enhance learning and memory. Generally, this involves five distinct, but overlapping strategies, including: (1) rehearsal, (2) elaboration, (3) organization, (4) comprehension-monitoring, and (5) affect monitoring.

There are specific things that, as teachers, we can do to help students remember what they learn. These include: (1) getting and holding attention, (2) highlighting important information, (3) pointing out relationships between old and new knowledge, (4) providing opportunities for repetition and review, and (5) enhancing derivation of meaning from learning.

Information-processing theory focuses basically on memory processes, not on learning per se, although the two are very much related. Although information-processing theory has primarily grown from the work of cognitive psychologists, it nonetheless is a generic framework within which any particular theory of learning might fit. In Chapter 7, we turn our attention to two theoretical positions on how to enhance learning, each of which also has its own views on how to help students process information.

STUDY AND REVIEW QUESTIONS

1. What does it mean when we talk about information being encoded?
2. Can you explain why human information processing is frequently compared to the way in which a computer functions?
3. If someone asked you how the sensory-register component of the human information-processing system differed from the short-term memory component, how would you respond?
4. Why is attention so important in the sensory-register component?
5. Can you explain why the role of perception is so critical at the sensory-register stage of information-processing?
6. What are the basic functions of short-term memory?
7. How does short-term memory differ from long-term memory?

8. If someone asked you how you use "chunking" to help yourself remember, what examples could you give?
9. What are the main functions of episodic memory, semantic memory, and procedural memory? What are some examples of each of these from your own life?
10. What is the basic idea behind the "levels-of-processing" theory?
11. How does knowledge of the "executive skills" used in metacognitive processing help us understand how to make information-processing more efficient?
12. If you were asked to make a presentation to teachers on how to translate information-processing strategies into classroom teaching practices, what would you say?
13. Why do people forget?
14. If you were asked for suggestions about how to enhance long-term memory, how would you reply?
15. Students who use the PQ4R system are more likely to retain what they read than students who do not. Can you explain why by linking your response to the information-processing theory?

REFERENCES

Adams, A., Carnine, D., and Gersten, R. "Instructional Strategies for Studying Content Area Texts in the Intermediate Grades." *Reading Research Quarterly,* 1982, *18,* pp. 27–53.

Anderson, J. R. *The Architecture of Cognition.* Cambridge, MA: Harvard University Press, 1983.

Anderson, J. R. *Cognitive Psychology and its Implications,* 2nd ed. San Francisco: Freeman, 1985.

Atkinson, R. G., and Shiffrin, R. M. "Human Memory: A Proposed System and Its Control Processes." In K. W. Spence and J. T. Spence (Eds.), *The Psychology of Learning and Motivation,* Vol. 2. New York: Academic Press, 1968.

Baddeley, A. *Human Memory: Theory and Practice.* Boston: Allyn & Bacon, 1990.

Bower, G. H. "Mood and Memory." *The American Psychologist,* 1981, *36,* pp. 129–148.

Bower, G. H., Clark, M. C., Lesgold, A. M., and Winzenz, D. "Hierarchical Retrieval Schemes in Recall of Categorized Word Lists." *Journal of Verbal Learning and Behavior,* 1969, *8,* pp. 323–343.

Bower, G. H., and Karlin, M. B. "Depth of Processing Pictures of Faces and Recognition Memory." *Journal of Experimental Psychology,* 1974, *103,* pp. 751–757.

Chang, T. M. "Semantic-Memory: Facts and Models." *Psychological Bulletin,* 1986, *99,* pp. 199–220.

Combs, A. W., Richards, A. C., and Richards, F. R. *Perceptual Psychology: A Humanistic Study of Persons.* Lanham, NY: University Press of America, 1988.

Conway, M. "In Defense of Everyday Memory." *American Psychologist,* 1991, *46,* pp. 19–26.

Cooper, G. *Squad Helps Dog Bite Victim.* (Edited by *The Columbian Journalism Review.*) New York: Doubleday, 1980.

Craik, F. I. M. "Human Memory." *Annual Review of Psychology,* 1979, *30,* pp. 63–102.

Craik, F. I. M., and Lockhart, R. S. "Levels of Processing: A Framework for Memory Research." *Journal of Verbal Learning and Verbal Behavior,* 1972, *11,* pp. 671–684.

Flavell, J. M. *Cognitive Development,* 2nd ed. Englewood Cliffs, NJ: Prentice Hall, 1985.

Gagné, R. M. *The Conditions of Learning and Theory of Instruction,* 4th ed. New York: Holt, Rinehart and Winston, 1985.

Gagné, R. M., and Driscoll, M. P. *Essentials of Learning for Instruction,* 2nd ed. Englewood Cliffs, NJ: Prentice Hall, 1988.

Garner, R., and Alexander, P. A. "Metacognition: Answered and Unanswered Questions." *Educational Psychologist,* 1989, *24,* pp. 143–158.

Groves, P. M., and Rebec, G. V. *Introduction to Biological Psychology,* 3rd. ed. Dubuque, IA: Brown, 1988.

Hamilton, R. J. "A Framework for the Evaluation of the Effectiveness of Adjunct Questions and Objectives." *Review of Educational Research,* 1985, *55,* pp. 47–86.

Hoddes, E. "Does Sleep Help You Study?" *Psychology Today,* 1977, June, p. 69.

Houston, J. P. *Fundamentals of Learning and Memory,* 3rd ed. New York: Academic Press, 1986.

Kent, E. *The Brains of Men and Machines.* New York: McGraw-Hill, 1981.

Klatzky, R. *Memory and Awareness: An Information-Processing Perspective.* New York: Freeman, 1984.

Klatzky, R. L. *Human Memory; Structures and Processes,* 2nd ed. San Francisco: Freeman, 1980.

Kosslyn, S. M. "The Medium and The Message in Mental Imagery: A Theory." *Psychological Review,* 1981, *88,* pp. 46–66.

Lindsay, P. H., and Norman, D. A. *Human Information Processing: An Introduction to Psychology,* 2nd ed. New York: Academic Press, 1977.

Manning, B. H. *Cognitive Self-Instruction for Classroom Processes.* Albany: State University of New York Press, 1991.

Mayer, R. G. *The Promise of Cognitive Psychology.* San Francisco: Freeman, 1981.

Meyer, B. J. F., Brandt, D. M., and Bluth, G. J. "Use of Top-Level Structure in Text: Key for Reading Comprehension of Ninth-Graders." *Reading Research Quarterly,* 1980, *15,* pp. 72–103.

Miller, G. A. "The Magic Number Seven, Plus or Minus Two: Some Limits on our Capacity for Processing Information." *Psychological Review,* 1956, *63,* pp. 81–97.

Miller, P. H. *Theories of Developmental Psychology.* San Francisco: Freeman, 1983.

Norman, D. A. *Learning and Memory.* New York: Freeman, 1982.

Pavio, A. *Imagery and Verbal Processes.* New York: Holt, Rinehart and Winston, 1971.

Robinson, F. P. *Effective Study,* 4th ed. New York: Harper & Row, 1970.

Roitblat, H. L. *Introduction to Comparative Cognition.* New York: Freeman, 1987.

Rosenzweig, M. R., and Leiman, A. L. *Physiological Psychology.* Lexington, MA: Heath, 1982.

Sherry, D., and Schacter, D. "The Evolution of Multiple Memory Systems." *Psychological Review,* 1987, *94,* pp. 439–454.

Smith, F. *Comprehension and Learning: A Conceptual Framework for Teachers.* New York: Holt, Rinehart and Winston, 1975.

Sternberg, R. J. "Criteria for Intellectual Skills Training." *Educational Researcher,* 1983, *12,* pp. 6–12.

Thomas, E. L., and Robinson, M. A. *Improving Reading in Every Class: A Source Book for Teachers.* Boston: Allyn & Bacon, 1972.

Tulving, E. "Episodic and Semantic Memory." In E. Tulving and W. Donaldson (Eds.), *Organization of Memory.* New York: Academic Press, 1972.

Tulving, E. "How Many Memory Systems Are There?" *American Psychologist,* 1985, *40,* pp. 385–398.

Weinstein, C. F., and Mayer, R. F. "The Teaching of Learning Strategies." In M. C. Wittrock (Ed.), *Handbook of Research on Teaching.* New York: Macmillan, 1985.

SELECTED READINGS OF RELATED INTEREST

Baddeley, A. *Human Memory: Theory and Practice.* Boston: Allyn & Bacon, 1990. A fine sourcebook for those interested in knowing more on our current state of knowledge about memory functioning and ways to enhance memory effectiveness.

Gagné, R. M., and Driscoll, M. P. *Essentials of Learning for Instruction,* 2nd ed. Englewood Cliffs, NJ: Prentice Hall, 1988. A small paperback written for teachers that describes learning and ways to encourage it in an information-processing model.

Hamilton, R., and Ghatala, E. *Learning and Instruction.* New York: McGraw-Hill, 1994. Contains three excellent chapters related information-processing theory and its application to classroom settings.

Moely, B. E., Hart, S. S., Samtulli, K., Leal, L., Johnson, T., Rao, N., and Burney, L. "How Do Teachers Teach Memory Skills?" In J. Levin and M. Pressley (Eds.), *Educational Psychologist,* 1986, *21,* pp. 55–72. (Special issue on learning strategies.) A nice overview of activities and strategies that teachers can use to help students develop ways to strengthen their powers of retention.

Peterson, P. L. "Making Learning Meaningful: Lessons from Research on Cognition and Instruction." *Educational Psychologist,* 1988, *23,* pp. 365–374. A fine review of recent research related to what teachers can do to make learning more meaningful and, thus, more likely to be encoded into long-term memory.

Rosenweig, M. R. "Experience, Memory, and the Brain." *American Psychologist,* 1984, *39,* pp. 365–376. A somewhat technical article, but an excellent overview and review of a large body of research that shows how changing one's experiences can change brain chemistry and functioning, at least among lower animal forms.

Solso, R. L. *Cognitive Psychology,* 2nd ed. Boston: Allyn & Bacon, 1988. This basic text devotes itself solely to the explanation and elaboration of information-processing-in great detail.

7

Approaches to Classroom Learning and Learning Enhancement

CHAPTER OVERVIEW

IMPORTANT CHAPTER IDEAS

1. Learning is a process by which behavior is either modified or wholly changed through experience or training.
2. Cognitive approaches to learning involve a deductive process of working from the general to the specific.
3. Stimulus-response, or reinforcement, approaches to learning involve an inductive process of working from the specific to the general.
4. Bruner's discovery approach to learning, an outgrowth of cognitive theory, promotes the idea that learning is more apt to occur when students are encouraged to think intuitively, to make their own errors, and to find their own answers to tasks that are structured for exploration.
5. Those who promote discovery methods of learning encourage the learner to go beyond the information given to "discover" new information.
6. Students exposed to discovery methods do not necessarily learn more than students taught by other methods, but they are likely to have a more positive attitude about the experience.
7. A major strength of the discovery and the inquiry methods is that they promote learning through doing, which, in turn, promotes higher retention and a greater likelihood that learning will be transferred to other situations.
8. Ausubel's cognitive theory, called "reception learning," stresses the idea that learning is most likely to occur when new material is presented to students in an expository manner, a view that stresses the presentation of information by the teacher.

9. Gagné's learning processes and instructional events model is a cognitive view of learning, that closely complements the information-processing framework discussed in Chapter 6. Gagné stresses the quality, usefulness, and performance of students' learning and suggests nine specific "instructional events" to accomplish those goals.
10. Reinforcement approaches to learning concentrate on how learning can be shaped, controlled, and manipulated by reinforcing or rewarding desired behaviors or responses.
11. Punishment is very much deemphasized in reinforcement approaches, while positive reinforcement, administered contingently and intermittently, is highly promoted as a means of encouraging learning.
12. Programmed instruction and computer-assisted instruction are two technologies that use the basic principles of positive reinforcement to keep students involved in their use.
13. Anxious, low-achieving students, along with some who are disadvantaged or who have low aptitudes, are among those who have particularly benefitted from programmed learning and computer-assisted instruction.
14. Reinforcement methods have been criticized because some believe that these methods overemphasize extrinsic motivation and give the teacher too much control.
15. We are not likely to find any teacher using a pure form of either discovery or reinforcement methods; rather, it is the integration of both approaches into the classroom that promotes learning.
16. Research shows that there is a wide range of differences when it comes to individual styles and patterns of learning.
17. Diversity in learning style suggests that there must be different teaching methods if learning is to be successful.
18. Both discovery methods (emphasizing learning by doing) and reinforcement approaches (focusing on rewards) are helpful in promoting attention, elaboration, and organization, all prerequisites for successful information-processing.
19. There is no one best way to learn—there are many. What works well for each student is the best way.
20. As teachers, our primary task is to make our approaches to teaching and learning multifaceted so that what is best for each student is more likely to happen.

PROLOGUE

Learning is an interactive mix of intelligence, motivation, experience, psychological factors, and brain chemistry. It can be as simple as touching a hot stove and learning not to touch it again, as complex as trying to understand the theory of relativity and its application to the space program, or as confounding as trying to understand why people behave the way they do. Learning is an ongoing process of continual adaptation to our environment, assimilation of new information, and accommodation of new input to fit with prior knowledge. Usually, we say that learning has occurred when our behavior and/or attitudes have been changed or modified.

The essential purpose of this chapter is to briefly examine how two major theoretical positions—cognitive and behavioristic—explain how learning occurs and to review some approaches to learning that are associated with those positions. We also look at some of the various styles and patterns of learning that are exhibited by different students.

Let's begin with an important question.

WHAT IS LEARNING?

Although there are a number of definitions of learning, most psychologists and educators tend to agree that "learning is a process by which behavior is either modified or changed through experience or training." In this sense, learning refers not only to an outcome that is manifestly observable (e.g., learning to ride a bike, to divide with fractions, or to write a coherent sentence), but also to attitudes, feelings, and intellectual processes that may not be so obvious. Let's say, for example, that a smoker reads that a new study has proved conclusively that there is a powerful link between smoking and lung cancer. In spite of this new information, he or she continues to smoke. Should we conclude that learning has not occurred for this person? Not necessarily. Mere exposure to new information does not automatically lead to overt changes in behavior. Thus, we have to be sensitive to the more subtle and covert (hidden, masked) changes that may occur. We might note, for example, that there are differences in the smoker's intellectual behavior (the way he or she thinks about smoking) and his or her emotional behavior (the way he or she feels about smoking). At an intellectual level, we might hear the smoker deny the evidence ("The research isn't conclusive.") or rationalize his or her smoking ("It's better to smoke than to gain a lot of weight."). At an emotional level, we might observe that the smoker seems generally more nervous, uneasy, ambivalent, and perhaps even a bit guilty when he or she does smoke. From this, we might conclude that even though the smoker's *overt* behavior (smoking) remained the same, his or her *covert* behavior (feelings and attitudes about smoking) changed. Based on this evidence, we could legitimately infer that learning has indeed occurred. We do not see it in the act itself (smoking), but in the intellectual processing and the feelings associated with the act.

Learning can also be defined as *improvement* in behavior in the sense that, with time, we usually become more proficient at whatever it is we are learning. This does not necessarily mean, however, that one's behavior improves from the standpoint of desirability. On the one hand, a student could learn to be a clever con artist, a superb apple-polisher, and a person with a deep sense of inadequacy. On the other hand, a student could learn to be honest, straightforward, and confident in his or her ability.

HOW LEARNING OCCURS: COGNITIVE AND BEHAVIORISTIC VIEWS

Learning theories generally fall into two major groups: behavioristic theories (also known as stimulus-response theories) and cognitive theories (Bigge and Shermis, 1992). Theorists from both camps agree that learning results in a modification or change in behavior as a result of experience, but they disagree when describing (1) *how* learning occurs, and (2) how to best establish the conditions that maximize learning in the first place.

The question of what is learned is answered differently by each group of theorists. The behaviorist says that "habits," or specific ways of thinking or behaving, are learned. The cognitive theorist says that "cognitive structures," or more general ways of thinking, are learned. Both answers appeal to common sense. For example, when going from home to the grocery store, we probably activate specific ways of thinking and behaving so as to get to the store as quickly as possible. The behaviorist would say that our need for food (*stimulus*) caused us to go to the store (*response*) in order that we might purchase groceries (*reinforcement*). What we did, then, was to begin a chain of learned responses triggered by the stimulus (food)—the behaviorist is right. We repeated the same response pattern that we have used many times before when we had to go grocery shopping. However, from a cognitive theorist's point of view, we find our way to the store because what is learned are facts that enable us to deduce the best and quickest route to get there. Thus, if we can locate the grocery store from one starting point, we can find it from another because we know where the store is. We have, in other words, developed a *cognitive structure* in our minds that allows us to formulate general working principles, from which more specific deductive applications can be made.

A cognitive approach to learning is likely to be *holistic;* that is, it is a framework within which learning can be viewed on a *molar* basis, which gives us the opportunity to study the learning event intact. In this sense, learning is seen primarily as a *deductive* process of working from the general to the specific. The behavioristic or stimulus-response approach provides us with a framework for viewing learning on a *molecular* basis, which enables us to study the more specific, discrete components of each learning event. In this sense, learning is seen primarily as an *inductive* process, starting with the specific aspects of a learning situation and working toward its more general components.

A behavioristic approach to learning is concerned primarily with the observable and measurable aspects of human behavior, stimuli and responses, and with formulating rules that help explain the formation of relationships between these observable components of behavior. This approach is an outgrowth of the behavioristic model described in greater detail in Chapter 1. A cognitive approach to learning is concerned chiefly with such topics as decision making, information-processing, understanding, and insight as the means to more fully understanding how learning occurs.

Both Positions Have Value

Each of these theoretical views has something to offer. No single learning theory is comprehensive enough to explain or include all we need to know about how and why learning occurs. Cognitive learning theories help us understand the need for developing a broad cognitive structure in coping with specific learning tasks. Behavioristic theories help us to better define the conditions under which particular types of learning must be broken into smaller subunits. Another reason we need a multitheoretical approach to understanding learning is in response to the well-documented fact that people tend to develop individual cognitive styles and unique ways of organizing their experiences and learning (Ackerman, Sternberg, and Glasser, 1989). No one position can cover this vast range in individual differences.

Each of these two major theoretical positions has developed an approach to learning, which attempts to explain how learning occurs and how best to encourage it. An examination of the two positions reveals that each offers valuable information about the nature of learning and how to maximize its positive outcomes.

Let's first examine how learning is conceptualized from a cognitive theory point of view.

THE EVOLUTION OF LEARNING WITHIN A COGNITIVE FRAMEWORK

A critical component in any cognitive model of learning is the idea that, in order for meaningful learning to occur, the learner must be an active, involved participant in the process. This is not an idea that appeared overnight, but one that evolved slowly over time. Mayer (1992b) has suggested that our knowledge of learning processes has evolved along three levels of understanding, moving from learning as response acquisition, to learning as knowledge acquisition, to the current theory of learning as knowledge construction. Let's briefly examine this evolution and how it has influenced the cognitive psychologist's view of learning.

Learning as Response Acquisition

This view of learning dominated educational thinking during the first half of the twentieth century. Conclusions about how learning occurred were based largely on animal research, and required a huge leap of faith when it came to applying the findings to human learning. Based on how animals learned, human learning was seen as an essentially mechanistic process in which correct responses (answers) were weakened because rewards (e.g., teacher approval, good grades) were withheld. Within this more behavioristically structured educational setting, students were perceived as basically passive beings whose learning was orchestrated according to the rewards and punishments they experienced.

According to this perception of learning, the objective of instruction was to increase the number of correct answers generated by students. Within this framework, learning outcomes could be evaluated by measuring the amount of behavior change such as, for example, noting that students correctly solved four out of ten math problems on Monday and nine out of ten on Friday. Of course, it was not as simple as this, but the outcome illustrates the central thrust of the response acquisition view of learning, a view that concentrated mostly on students' responses to content and on ways to reinforce correct responses, and little on the way that students were thinking about (cognitively processing) the material to which they were exposed.

Learning as Knowledge Acquisition

The cognitive revolution of the 1950s and 1960s stressed knowledge acquisition as a new view of learning. Within this new theoretical framework, students became processors of the information dispensed by teachers. The focus shifted from how animals learn to how *humans* learn, and emphasis was placed on acquiring bodies of knowledge rather than on giving correct answers. According to this view of learning, the goal of instruction was to increase the amount of knowledge to which learners were exposed so that learning outcomes could be evaluated by measuring the amount of knowledge acquired. During this time, emphasis shifted from focusing on students' *responses* to new information to the broader interest in how students *acquired* knowledge, a move which has led cognitive psychologists to their current state of understanding about learning.

Learning as Knowledge Construction

As cognitive theory matured in the 1970s and 1980s to its current status, the emphasis changed from knowledge acquisition to knowledge construction. This happened primarily because educational psychologists began to do more research on how, and under what kinds of conditions, learning occurs in an actual classroom setting. It was a tremendous leap from the view of learning proposed earlier in this century that tried to generate principles of human learning based on lower animal studies. Thus, as we have come to understand more about how human learning occurs, the view of the learner has changed from that of a mere recipient of knowledge to that of a *constructor* of knowledge, a person capable of controlling his or her own cognitive processes during learning. Within this framework, increasingly more credit is given to students for being able to make sense of and interpret new information in light of what they already know. Learning is not merely *responding* to new information, nor is it just *acquiring* new information; it is also *constructing* new knowledge. The teacher's job is not only that of rewarding correct responses or dispensing information, but it also involves the more demanding task of helping students cognitively process new material in meaningful ways in order to encourage its storage in long-term memory.

COGNITIVE MODELS OF LEARNING

A basic tenet central to cognitive models of learning is the idea that the learner is an active processor of information who is trying to make sense of the information presented. This is in marked contrast to the behavioristic view of the learner as a passive recipient whose learning is automatically shaped by practice and reinforcement (Mayer, 1992a). Whereas behavioristic approaches to learning focus on ways to elicit correct responses that are immediately reinforced, cognitive approaches to learning are more concerned with ways to help students become more effective processors of information. In order to better understand how some of the basic tenets of cognitive psychology have been translated into instructional principles for enhancing classroom learning, we now turn our attention to three theorists who have been prominent in advancing the cognitive point of view: Jerome Bruner (Discovery Learning), David Ausubel (Reception Learning), and Robert Gagné (Learning Processes and Instructional Events).

Jerome Bruner: Discovery Learning

Bruner (1971, 1983) has been a leading proponent of the discovery method, arguing that this method of learning leads to a type of understanding that is not only more exciting to students but also very likely to increase their self-confidence and self-reliance. Actually, learning by discovery implies just that: learning by *discovering* the solution.

The basic idea behind this method is to give students a wide variety of examples of certain facts and information and to encourage them to discover the answer, or the underlying rules or principles. This is quite consistent with a cognitive approach to learning because, as noted by Divesta (1987), "The emphasis is on the total instructional event of which the learner is a part. The situational demands, the characteristics of the learner, the task demands, the purposes of the learner, and so on *interact* to determine the quality and texture of the event, such as a teaching or learning episode" (p. 208).

Theorists who favor this approach contend that what is learned by way of this method is remembered better and is more accessible for use in other learning situations because the student is an active, searching, experimenting person in the learning process.

What follows are some examples of the discovery method of learning (some refer to it as the "inquiry method") as it might be thought of, or done, in its pure form. It is important to recognize at the outset that we are not likely to find applicative purity in actual classroom situations. Occasionally, you may see a virtually untouched version, but in daily classroom life discovery methods are usually mixed with more *expository* teaching techniques, which involve teachers giving facts, explanations, and specific ideas. Reading this chapter, for example, is an example of expository learning in the sense that you are presented with facts and ideas that are already organized (one hopes) in a meaningful way. You do not have to discover them, because they are already there. You might, however, make many discoveries for yourself about how to *use* this information in meaningful ways.

To the extent that discovery or inquiry teaching and learning is used, what we examine next are some of the basic ingredients needed to make it work.

Learning by Doing Is Emphasized

The idea behind this approach goes back as far as John Dewey's early notions about the importance of "learning by doing," and of the necessity of encouraging students to solve their own problems within a broad "field of possible solutions," and thus to arrive at their own answers. As Dewey (1903) wrote:

> The child cannot get power of judgment excepting as he is continually exercised in forming and testing judgment. He must have an opportunity to select for himself, and then to attempt to put his own selections into execution that he may submit them to the only final test, that of action. Only thus can he learn to discriminate that which promises success from that which promises failure; only thus can he form the habit of relating his otherwise isolated ideas to the conditions which determine their value. (p. 27)

Intuitive Thinking Is Encouraged

Whereas analytical thinking is precise, methodical, and planned, intuitive thinking is more spontaneous and unplanned, the kind of cognitive processing that takes place without evident rational thought or inference. As Bruner (1960) described it:

> Intuitive thinking characteristically does not advance in careful, well-defined steps. . . . Usually intuitive thinking rests on familiarity with the domain of knowledge involved and with its structure, which makes it possible for the thinker to leap about, skipping steps and employing short cuts in a manner that requires a later recheck of conclusions by more analytic means, whether deductive or inductive. (pp. 55–56)

A Certain Amount of Structure Is Necessary

"Structure," as defined here, consists of the fundamental ideas, relationships, and patterns of the subject matter; that is, the essential information. With the discovery method, learning is regarded primarily as the rearrangement of thought patterns and the perception of new relationships within the existing structure of the subject matter. However, before this can happen, there has to be a certain amount of structure in order for discovery learning to occur. From Bruner's (1960) view, structure is important for at least four reasons:

1. Understanding the fundamentals makes a subject more comprehensible.
2. Unless detail is organized in a structured pattern, it is rapidly forgotten.
3. An understanding of fundamental principles and ideas appears to be the main road for adequate transfer.
4. Structure permits a person to narrow the gap between elementary and advanced knowledge.

A certain amount of structure gives students a framework within which they can integrate and comprehend new information and ideas. Structure helps students establish a relationship between their existing information and new information so that "knowledge" is reintegrated and updated. In this way, content is not only an array of facts to be absorbed, but also something that has structure (namely, a way of organizing facts in light of concepts and principles).

7.1 When Structure Is Missing

Perhaps you can get a better idea of what it's like when structure is missing by imagining the following scenario. Suppose that you have a psychology instructor who assigns a psychology text and gives these instructions: "Read this book. Discover as much as you can about human behavior. Learn as much as you can about your own behavior." For most students this would be a frustrating assignment. Why do you suppose it would be too frustrating? What is missing? What other kind of information would you like to have? To put the question more broadly, what kind of structure would you like to have for an assignment of this sort? How would it be helpful to you?

An Example of Discovery Learning

As you read the following example of how discovery learning takes place in a classroom setting, keep in mind that the ultimate aim of the discovery approach is to attain a general understanding of the structure of a subject matter that permits other knowledge to be related to it in a meaningful way (Bruner, 1983). Bruner (1966) cites numerous examples of how discovery learning works in practice. In one illustration, students in a fifth-grade geography class were given simple outline maps showing rivers and lakes, along with short notes about natural resources. Each student's task was to predict where major cities, railroad lines, and highways were likely to be located. As Bruner noted, this was presenting geography not as a set of knowns, but as a set of unknowns. As you can see, it was not the purpose of this lesson to transmit facts about geography. Indeed, for the duration of this learning experience, students were encouraged to exercise their intuitive thinking and analytic powers to draw inferences from the data.

Understandably, these students made some errors in drawing conclusions. From a discovery point of view, such errors, far from being fatal, can be highly instructive. If students are to avoid making the same mistake again, they need to know where their logic was faulty the first time, rather than simply to memorize a different answer. They also need a classroom climate that tolerates wrong hypotheses and incorrect answers—where they are not punished for being wrong.

Learning to form concepts is a vital cog in the machinery of the discovery approach. By forming concepts we are able to organize vast amounts of information into meaningful units that can be grouped together because they are similar in some way. Consider color: although there are 7.5 million discriminable shades of colors, by categorizing these colors in a dozen or more color concepts, we manage to deal with this diversity rather well.

Being able to form concepts makes it possible for people to demonstrate what Bruner (1973) calls the most characteristic aspect of mental life—the ability to go beyond the information given. The students in the fifth-grade geography class mentioned previously, for example, had to go beyond the information they could see in order to discover where the major cities might be found.

7.2 How I Learned About Topspin Return in Physics Class

I remember a marvelous discovery I made in a tenth-grade physics class when the teacher demonstrated how the air pressure decreased on the bottom side of a ball rotating in a counterclockwise direction, thereby causing it to drop more quickly. Being a fledgling tennis player, it occurred to me that this principle, if applied to my somewhat shaky game, might be an invaluable asset in keeping the ball in bounds. Thus, before any tennis instructor ever explained it to me, I discovered the wonderful aerodynamic advantage to putting topspin on one's return, which I labored to learn over many months of flailing and out-of-bounds smashes. The advantage of discovering something on one's own is that it tends to be more readily retained. Can you think of a discovery incident in your life?

How Effective Are Discovery Methods?

I refer to discovery "methods" because there are many ways to approach teaching or learning within a discovery or inquiry framework. There is, for example, a distinction between *discovery learning* and *guided discovery.* The difference between the two is that in guided discovery the teacher systematically provides hints and leading questions that keep students on track, whereas in pure discovery, students discover without aid. For example, if Bruner had wanted to make his pure discovery learning in geography a more guided discovery experience, the teacher would have asked leading questions such as, "Do you think there would be more advantages to locating near large rivers?" or "Would the terrain influence whether a city would develop there?" The teacher might have dropped such hints as, "Being centrally located might make a city accessible to many marketplaces," or "Building a city near the mouth of a river could provide a source of power."

We are not likely to find many instances of pure discovery techniques either in actual classrooms or in research designed to test discovery methods. Some research separates pure and guided discovery learning, but much of it seems to be more a blend of the two. Interestingly, whether research focuses on pure or on guided discovery, the results are about the same.

In an early study, Gagné and Brown (1961) found that students who learned to solve a series of arithmetic problems under a guided discovery method required more time to learn than students who were in the expository-method group. However, students in the guided discovery group performed much better than expository group students on tasks requiring them to use their knowledge in applied ways.

In a later study, Selim and Shrigley (1983) found that a group of fifth-grade students taught by the discovery method scored higher on a science test emphasizing recall and retention than another matched group taught by expository methods. The discovery students also had more positive attitudes about science. In another study, one group of high school social studies students was taught a two-week unit by a tightly structured expository-instruction strategy and another group by the more open-ended discovery method. The students in the expository-instruction group performed better on objective and subjective tests requiring application of knowledge, whereas the discovery students did better on tests requiring evaluative judgments. In a study measuring attitude, Fielding, Kameenui, and Gersten (1983) found that students also considered the discovery methods more challenging.

As you can see, the results are mixed. Although there is no clear evidence to suggest that the students who experience discovery methods learn any more (or less) than those who are exposed to expository modes, there is evidence to indicate that discovery students may feel more positive about their learning experiences. It seems wise to suggest that teachers include opportunities for discovery learning whenever it is important that students be able to apply, and not just understand, the principles they are studying.

Suggestions for Promoting Discovery Learning

When students learn by discovery, they assemble new ideas and information in a way that makes the knowledge gained more self-acquired than merely given. Six suggestions chosen from a number of sources (Bruner, 1966; Carin and Sund, 1985; Jacobsen et al., 1985; Wilcox, 1987) that can help students learn by discovery are as follows:

1. *Expose students to warm-up exercises.* Short practice sessions prepare students for indirect, discovery-type sessions. Students are given responsibility for asking questions, rather than answering them, as is more typical of expository learning. For example, "Twenty Questions" is a fun warm-up that students like, particularly the elementary level. Students are given a riddle and must solve it by asking the teacher only yes-or-no questions. An example might be: "The person who made it didn't want it. The person who bought it didn't need it. The person who used it didn't know it, what is it?" The answer: A coffin. Public interviews are also good ways to warm up a class. A student is selected to be interviewed and role-plays a famous person. The rest of the class tries to figure out who it is by asking questions about the person's life and experiences, which the role-playing student answers as best as he or she can. The idea is to help students get into a mind-set that encourages exploration and more intuitive, open-ended thinking. When beginning the actual discovery lesson, the following methods can be helpful.

2. *Emphasize contrasting features.* For example, what is the difference between humans and animals? between modern and prehistoric humans? between adults and children? between fruits and vegetables? and so on. In this way, you can help students begin to see the differences between subjects that are similar, and the similarities between subjects that are different.

3. *Encourage students to make intuitive guesses using information they already know.* For example, ask students to develop hunches about where a large airport might be built in relation to a large city, and then discuss the suggestions in terms of why they may, or may not, be feasible ideas. Rather than define a particular word, ask students to try to find what it means by looking at the word in context. By using what is available, help students to go beyond what is known in order to generate new ideas.

4. *Ask questions and let students try to find the answers.* The following questions are examples: Why is it easier for a light person to run faster and farther than a heavy person? Why does water boil? Why is it hard to remember events or ideas that are not meaningful? Help students to reason, visualize, and/or work analytically toward possible solutions.

5. *Stimulate awareness by encouraging students to consider consequences.* Ask questions such as the following: How can savings accounts be important? What would happen if there were no schools? What might happen if children were given adult status at age 10? Help students anticipate and see for themselves that all behavior has long-term implications and consequences.

6. *Encourage learning through doing and actual involvement.* Have students develop a social system and a hierarchy of authority in their classroom in order to better understand how and why early social systems developed. Wherever feasible, help students learn what works and what does not from their personal experiences.

Some Cautions About the Use of Discovery Methods

Discovery methods are not always appropriate nor do they always work. They have strengths, but shortcomings as well. Two in particular to keep in mind are:

1. *Discovery methods are not appropriate for all students.* There is the possibility that interpersonal difficulties can occur when the discovery method is used. For example, some students may become frustrated and even angry if teachers refuse to tell them what they obviously know. This is particularly likely to be the case for highly anxious and compulsive students, who do their best work in more structured, teacher-directed classes, where they are told what, when, and how much to learn.

There is evidence suggesting that discovery techniques might not always be appropriate for primary-grade pupils or students of any age who come from disadvantaged environments. Many of these students, for example, seem to want, need, and respond best in learning situations in which teachers give brief assignments, provide active instruction, and offer immediate feedback (Bennett et al., 1976; Good and Brophy, 1994). Rosenshine's (1976) review of research suggests that disadvantaged youth might not do very well with discovery learning because they frequently lack the background or self-confidence to make many discoveries on their own.

2. *Not all subjects fit the discovery mode.* Discovery learning may not work for some subjects. For example, Francis (1975) found that first-, third-, and sixth-grade students learned both simple and complex concepts more quickly and easily when taught by lecture methods rather than when taught by discovery methods. The learning gains of students taught with lecture methods was greater not only on memory tests, but also on transfer tests.

As mentioned earlier, research findings related to the efficiency and effectiveness of discovery or inquiry methods of learning are mixed, which is not surprising when you consider the complex interactive mix of student, teacher, and subject matter. In addition, not all subjects lend themselves to the discovery mode because of their factual nature and structural complexity, such as chemistry or geometry.

The shortcomings and criticisms of discovery learning examined here do not mean that this method is an ineffective or inappropriate method of teaching, but they do suggest that discovery might not be effective in certain subjects and with certain kinds of students. As with any instructional mode used to facilitate learning, it can lose its effectiveness if used too often.

David Ausubel: Reception Learning

Whereas Bruner proposes that students learn best by discovering facts and concepts for themselves, Ausubel (1963, 1977) argues that learning is likely to be enhanced when concepts, facts, and principles are presented to them. Central to Ausubel's approach is *expository teaching* (exposition means explanation), which is a teacher-planned, systematic presentation of meaningful information. A basic task of the teacher is to present the subject matter in ways that encourage students to make sense of it by relating the new information to what they already know, as opposed to memorizing it in rote fashion. Ausubel's approach, similar to Bruner's, involves the idea that learning in schools should involve organized bodies of knowledge structured around key concepts. However, whereas Bruner's emphasis was on guiding students to structure the lesson content themselves, Ausubel believed that this was the teacher's job and developed a conceptual framework around which teachers could structure the content for students, hence the stress on expository teaching (Ausubel, Novak, and Hanesian, 1978).

Although the role of teacher is quite different in discovery learning and reception learning, the two approaches do share some common ideas. First, both approaches emphasize the importance of actively involving students in the learning process. Second, both try to include students' prior knowledge in the assimilation of new learning. Third, both approaches recognize that knowledge is not static and that it continually changes (knowledge is updated, modified, and revised) once it is inside the learner's mind.

Three Basic Stages of Reception Learning

1. *Utilization of advance organizers.* Advance organizers provide a mind-set for the material to be presented. Ausubel (1980) defined an advance organizer as an abstract, general overview of the new information to be learned that occurs in advance of the actual learning. The chapter overview that occurs at the beginning of each chapter in this text is an example of an advance organizer in the sense that it gives you an idea of what to expect in the chapter ahead. Another example might be a high school social studies teacher who, prior to launching into a unit related to how religious values can sometimes be reflected in political decision making, encouraged her eleventh-grade students to discuss how their own religious convictions may be reflected in preferences for one political party over another. It was a robust discussion and set the stage nicely for more formal study.

Basically, organizers serve three purposes: (1) they direct attention to the main ideas or the central theme of the material to be studied, (2) they highlight relationships among ideas to be learned, and (3) they remind students of relevant information they already have. Research has shown that the use of advance organizers has a consistent, moderate, and generally positive effect on learning (Corkill et al., 1989). Advance organizers have proven to be most helpful in enhancing learning when the material is quite unfamiliar, complex, or difficult (Mayer, 1984).

2. *Presentation of material to be learned.* The second stage is at the core of reception learning, and involves a variety of teaching-learning methods that highlight the expository approach of this point of view. Thus, new material is presented by means of lectures, discussions, films, videotapes, and a variety of student tasks. There is a particularly strong emphasis on keeping student attention, as well as a need for material to be well organized so that it fits the structure or mind-set created by the advance organizers. For example, having seen the advance organizer in the form of the chapter overview at the beginning of this chapter, it is important that the contents of this chapter be consistent with the expectations created by that overview. When presenting material in this second stage, it is helpful to do so within the confines of a process called "progressive differentiation," which is basically a step-by-step procedure from general concepts to specific information, illustrative examples, and contrasts between old and new information and ideas (Ausubel, Novak, and Hanesian, 1978).

It is often helpful to begin with material that is relatively simple and clear when teaching a new unit. For example, an English teacher wishing to help students learn new punctuation skills may start by exposing them to new simple paragraphs that use essentially periods and commas, and then introduce them to progressively more difficult paragraphs that use increasingly complex forms of punctuation. The teacher would also want to contrast the differences between, for example, commas, semicolons, and colons, and in the process, give students plenty of opportunities for writing paragraphs that involve different forms of punctuation. The idea is to go from material that is general and simple to material that is more specific and complex.

3. *Reinforcing the cognitive structure.* In the third stage of the lesson, it is important that the teacher helps the students make connections between the structure laid out at the beginning of the lesson and the new information to which they have been exposed. For example, the English teacher in the previous example might have the students go back to the simple paragraphs that used just commas and periods and ask students to rewrite them in such a way that involved more complex forms of punctuation. It is one of several methods of evaluating students' knowledge of new material. In addition, stage three is the point at which students are given the opportunity to ask questions that extend their understanding beyond the boundaries of the lesson.

7.3 Setting the Stage for Reception Learning in Your Own Area

Imagine for a moment that you are beginning a unit in a content area of your choosing. You have seen how the three stages of reception learning involve using advance organizers, presenting the material, and then reinforcing the cognitive structure or learning that has occurred. If you had to present a lesson plan that incorporated these three steps, what would it look like? What would you do? How would you do it?

Robert Gagné: Learning Processes and Instructional Events

Robert Gagné (1977, 1984) (Gagné and Driscoll, 1988) is a cognitive psychologist who has developed a paradigm for learning that closely matches the information-processing model discussed in Chapter 6. Whereas Bruner is concerned about whether students learn by discovery and Ausubel about whether students are receiving the material to be learned in a meaningful way, Gagné is more concerned with the quality, permanence, and usefulness of their learning. In order for this to occur, Gagné has suggested that certain learning processes, each of which is associated with a particular instructional event, must occur in order to encourage useful, permanent learning.

Figure 7.1 presents an outline that shows the relationship between the steps in the learning process, the instructional events associated with each process, and an example of how each step might be activated in a classroom. The example in Figure 7.1 of an eighth-grade class exploring the concept of democracy is not a topic that could be discussed in a single lesson, but rather, is an illustration of the major activities that could be associated with each instructional event over a period of time. There are many other possibilities. The examples cited in Figure 7.1 are meant to be suggestive, not exhaustive.

As you can see in Figure 7.1, the instructor's first task is to *gain students' attention.* The next step is to establish an expectancy for learning by letting the students know what the *learning objectives* are and perhaps raising some questions that pique their curiosity. Once students are paying attention and have an expectancy for learning, the instructor can help the students relate what they already know to the material to be learned. Although this is not always possible to do in a meaningful way, it can be quite helpful in making connections between old and new information; for example, I know a high school history teacher who illustrates the truth in the adage, "history repeats itself," by giving examples of historical and contemporary events that share similarities. Once students *recall prior knowledge* to their working memories, the instructor then *presents the new material,* highlighting important aspects and key features. At this point, students should have the new material in their short-term or working memories, which means they are ready to process the information and move it into long-term memories. The teacher's part at this juncture is to *provide learning guidance and direction,* which can range from

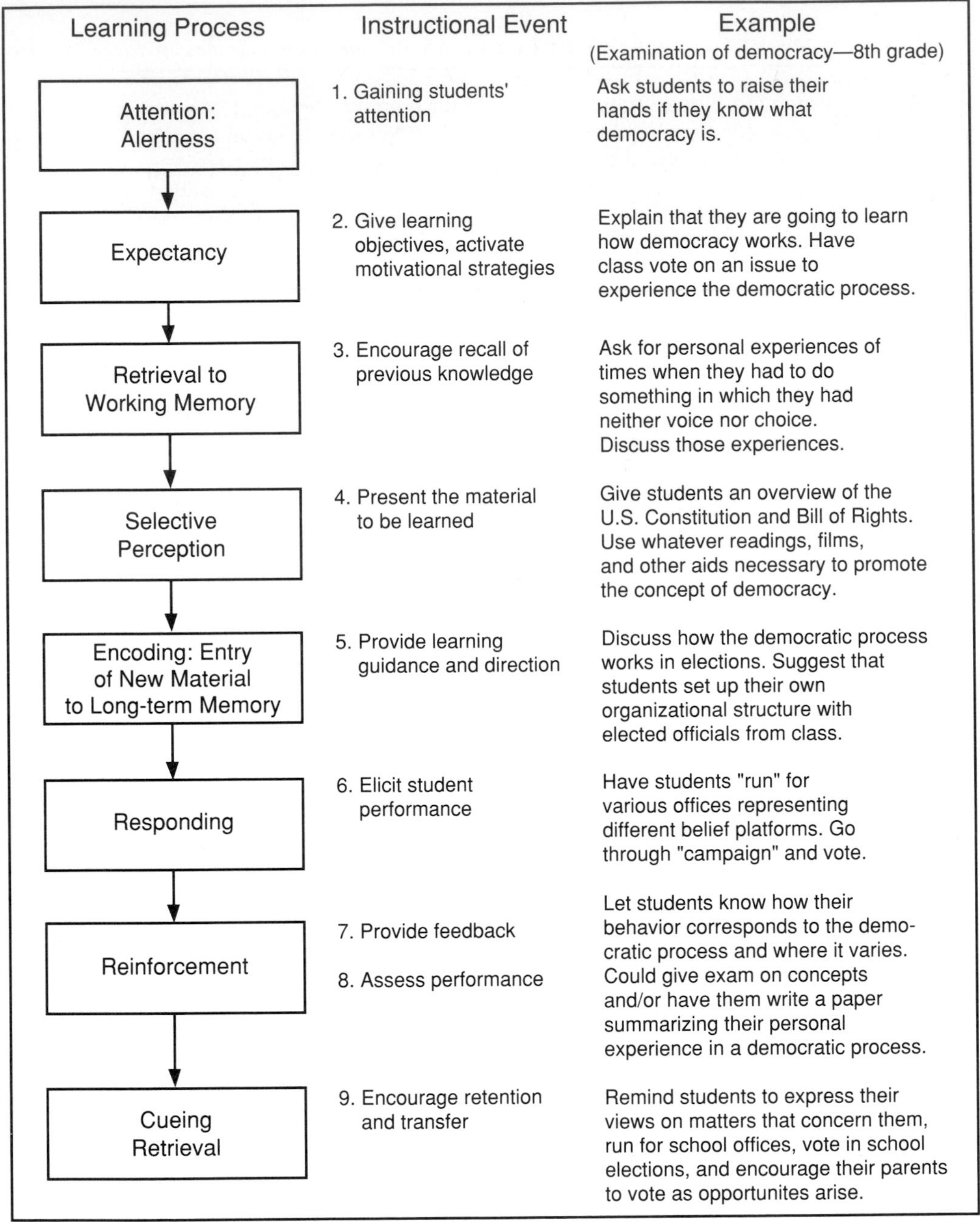

Figure 7.1. RELATION OF LEARNING PROCESSES TO INSTRUCTIONAL EVENTS.

(Adapted from THE CONDITIONS OF LEARNING AND THEORY OF INSTRUCTION, Fourth Edition by Robert Gagné, copyright © 1985 by Holt, Rinehart and Winston, Inc., reproduced by permission of the publisher.)

giving lectures and explanations to arranging guided discovery experiences, showing films, and/or going on field trips. The possibilities are endless.

The next step is to create opportunities to *elicit performance.* This enables students to demonstrate their understanding of the material. The nature of the responses enables teachers to *provide feedback* and to *assess performance,* all of which are reinforcements of the learning process. Finally, to ensure that *new knowledge* can be retrieved from long-term memory, teachers should have students practice applying this information in new situations. Practice and review are the best ways to *encourage retention and transfer.*

7.4 Using the Best of All Three Approaches

Assume, for the sake of this exercise, that you have been asked to put together a lesson plan that incorporates the important features in each of the three approaches to learning as advocated by Bruner, Ausubel, and Gagné. How would you devise such a plan? What would you include that reflects the basic ideas of each theorist?

A BEHAVIORIST MODEL: ENCOURAGING LEARNING THROUGH REINFORCEMENT

You may recall from our discussion in Chapter 1 that behavioristic psychology is a theoretical position that focuses attention on experience, behavior, and action and reaction. The use of reinforcement methods is a major means of encouraging learning within a behavioristic framework. Essentially, the purpose of these methods is to reinforce (reward) correct answers and proper behavior so that the likelihood of the desired responses being repeated increases.

B. F. Skinner (1984, 1987) has been the foremost contemporary exponent of learning within a reinforcement framework. With the intention of describing learning and behavior from an observer's point of view, Skinner concentrated almost exclusively on how learning can be shaped, controlled, and manipulated by reinforcing or rewarding specific desired behaviors or responses. As Skinner saw it, there are two types of responses in learning situations—*respondent* and *operant.* Respondent behaviors are elicited by specific stimuli in the environment of which we are a part. The fact that you are responding to this book by reading, turning the pages, and thinking about the ideas is an example of respondent behavior. It is called "respondent behavior" because it occurs in response to a stimulus, in this case, a book. Operant behaviors, in contrast, are a larger and more important class of behaviors not elicited by any known stimuli, but simply *emitted* by a person. They are called "operant behaviors" because, in a sense, they are simply operations that we perform in our ongoing behavior.

Reinforcing Operant Behaviors

Skinner was particularly concerned with operant behavior, which is associated more with responses than with stimuli. In a school situation, students emit responses to their environment, and these responses, if reinforced, tend to be repeated. Let's say, for example, that I am a student in your class, and initially I spend a lot of time looking down because I feel shy and intimidated. You are sensitive to my feelings, so the first time we make eye contact, you smile at me. I start to feel a little more relaxed, and begin to look up more often. Each time you see me do this, you smile. Pretty soon I am looking up and around more frequently, and as often as possible you meet my gaze with a warm look. Eventually, I am not only able to look at you and others, but also to participate in class. Thus, because you responded to a naturally occurring behavior (my looking up at you periodically) by reinforcing (rewarding) me with a smile and a warm look, you were able to help me be more relaxed and less shy. In this way, an operant behavior—my looking at you—has been reinforced, and I have been, in the language of behavioristic theory, "conditioned" to do this more often. If you had not rewarded my looking up behavior the way you did, chances are good that I would continue to look down, avoid eye contact, and wallow in my shy feelings.

Various psychologists, in particular, Alberto and Troutman (1986) and Wielkiewicz (1986), have attempted to extend the idea of operant conditioning to classroom learning in practical ways. One basic strategy they suggest to teachers is to ignore, insofar as is possible, all undesired (inappropriate, improper) behavior and to reward, instead, whenever desired (proper, correct) behavior is present. For example, if John is misbehaving, the teacher praises his classmate, Janet, who is seated near him and doing her work. John hears Janet being praised (rewarded), and he decides that he would like to be praised as well. If and when this happens, the teacher must be sure to praise, acknowledge, or otherwise reward John's improved behavior. The basic principle is to ignore the behavior that is operating negatively, thereby discouraging and, it is hoped, extinguishing it, while rewarding and reinforcing the behavior that is operating positively.

7.5 Some Reinforcement Research for You to Try

There are methods you can use to try the operant principles discussed here. For example, think of a person with whom you have an ongoing relationship. Perhaps there is a behavior that you would like to see that person exhibit more frequently. Rather than paying so much attention to what that person does that you do *not* like, focus more on what you *do* like. Whenever you see the desired behavior, acknowledge and reinforce it. Try this method for at least a week. Discover for yourself if positive reinforcement works.

An interesting classroom experiment by Kirby and Shields (1972) gives us a good example of how positively reinforcing operant behavior works. In order to help Tom, a 13-year-old boy, increase his rate of working arithmetic problems, he was placed in a positive reinforcement program. At first, the teacher gave Tom a page of multiplication problems and a twenty-minute period to solve as many as possible. The teacher corrected and returned the problems the next day without comment in order to get Tom's baseline rate for solving problems. During this period, Tom correctly finished an average of one-half of a problem for every minute of work.

The teacher then had Tom work on only two problems at a time and turn them in for correction. The problems were immediately corrected, and Tom was strongly praised when he did them correctly ("That's great! You got them right!"). This procedure of grading and praising two problems at a time was repeated throughout the twenty-minute work period for two days. Then Tom was asked to complete four problems, eight problems, and sixteen problems. During this time, Tom correctly completed 1.5 problems per minute, a gain of 300%. At the same time, the percentage of time he spent attending to his work rose from 50% to 100% during the reinforcement phase. Interestingly, the rate of correct responses fell when the reinforcement was discontinued for experimental reasons, but went up again when reinstituted.

7.6 Are Operant Reinforcements Manipulative?

There are times when teachers' behavior, as described in Tom's case, is seen as manipulative—in a negative sense. Trying to change a child's behavior through conditioning may be seen as designed, contrived, insincere, and by some, unethical. If you were asked whether it is appropriate and ethical for teachers to use operant reinforcement strategies to modify students' behavior, how would you respond?

Behavioristic approaches to learning show little concern about motivation or the need to infer internal processes (Gredler, 1992). Behavior reinforcement seems to be taken for granted as common sense. Food is reinforcing to a rat or a pigeon, and knowledge of correctness is reinforcing to a student in school. The fundamental idea behind operant learning is to elicit the correct responses so that they can be rewarded in a positive manner, which brings us to an important point about the behavioristic position regarding learning.

Punishment Is Deemphasized

Although punishment (e.g., teacher sarcasm or ridicule, public disapproval by the teacher, teacher's negative comments on an exam paper, etc.) can modify or change behavior, it can also lead to unnecessary problems. For example, punishment is likely to be associated with the giver rather than with the response to be extinguished. In addition, punishment does not necessarily tell students what the right response is, nor encourage students to want to make the correction. On the whole, operant conditioning in the classroom is most effective when rewards are emphasized. Students' reactions to punishment are typically more variable, less predictable, and more likely to reflect anger and resentment than their reactions to reward (Kazdin, 1989; Wielkiewicz, 1986).

Negative Reinforcement, Positive Reinforcement, and Punishment: How They Differ

Negative reinforcement is frequently confused with punishment and even with positive reinforcement. Therefore, we must make careful distinctions among the three concepts.

Positive reinforcement follows behavior; for example, if I give you the correct answer, behave the way I am supposed to, or remember to hand in my assignment, and you commend my effort, praise my work, or tell others what a good student I am, you are using positive reinforcement. I behave in a particular way; you like it; and you reinforce it with a rewarding response (i.e., a smile, praise, extra credit, and so on). If I interpret the responses as rewards, I am encouraged to behave in similar ways in the future.

The aim of negative reinforcement is the same; namely, to increase the likelihood of desired behaviors. The method, however, is different. Instead of a positive stimulus being presented, *an aversive stimulus is removed when the desired behavior is obtained.* For example, let's say that I am a student in your class, and I am having trouble learning how to correctly spell a list of words. You say to me that I will have to stay after school for fifteen minutes each day until I learn the words. On the third day, I finally spell all the words correctly and you allow me to leave with my classmates. This is an illustration of negative reinforcement: an aversive stimulus (staying after school) is removed when the desired behavior (spelling the words correctly) is obtained. The major difference between positive and negative reinforcement is that with positive reinforcement one behaves appropriately (does what is expected, learns) in order to obtain a reward; with negative reinforcement, one behaves appropriately in order to avoid unpleasant consequences.

Consider how this works in a classroom situation from an example suggested by Walker and Shea (1980). You are a high school English teacher and have just assigned thirty pages of reading for class tomorrow. There is groaning and complaining among the students (homework is an aversive stimulus for many of them). You also want them to complete an important assignment before class is over, but you notice that many students are inattentive and wasting time. To motivate them, you announce that they will not have to do the reading assignment for tomorrow if they finish the class assignment today.

You look around, and everyone is busy with the work they need to finish. This is an example of negative reinforcement: you remove something aversive (tomorrow's reading assignment) in order to get the behavior you desire—in this case, completion of the class assignment.

Whereas negative reinforcement is relief from an unpleasant or painful situation (e.g., it would no doubt be a relief for students not to have to stay after school), punishment is the experience of an unpleasant consequence following the behavior. For instance, if you, as the teacher in the "spelling words" example cited previously, had embarrassed me in front of the class for misspelling words, or made me stay after school for thirty minutes to practice spelling, this would simply be punishment. It would even more clearly be a punishment situation if you made me stay the full thirty minutes in spite of my spelling all the words correctly in the first five minutes. Remember, with negative reinforcement, the unpleasant consequences are removed when the desired behavior is achieved. With punishment, however, one still suffers the consequences regardless of whether the desired behavior is obtained. (This reminds me of an incident that occurred when I was about 9 years old. I "borrowed" a dollar from my mother's purse. Unbeknownst to me, she saw me take it, alas, and I was informed that my father would deal with this when he came home. I returned the dollar, apologized profusely, and pleaded for mercy. Although the desired behavior was obtained—my mother did get the dollar back—I still got a long lecture and was sent to my room by my not-too-sympathetic father. That is punishment.) Figure 7.2 presents some typical examples of rewards and punishments found within the larger context of society.

7.7 Your Own Experience with Reward and Punishment

As you think about your past and current school and home experiences, what are some examples you can recall that illustrate the effects of positive or negative reinforcement, or punishment? What relationships do you see between your academic achievement, particularly during elementary and high school, and the type of reinforcements (or punishments) you received? How do you suppose your personal history with reinforcements or punishments will influence your interactions with students?

Positive reinforcement is by far the most potent method for encouraging not only more learning, but also more learning that is resistant to forgetfulness (Glasser, 1990; Klein, 1987). Negative reinforcement encourages learning that is less permanent, but tends to lead to more negative associations related to the setting in which the learning occurred. Sometimes negative reinforcement is inadvertently used in such a way that it strengthens undesirable behavior.

REWARD	PUNISHMENT
If you expend your energy the way we want you to, you will get . . .	If you do not, you will get . . .
Business	
A job	Fired
Advancement	No promotion
Salary increases	No raises
Prestige	No recognition
Security	Insecurity
Religious Order	
Acceptance	Nonacceptance
Participation	Excommunication
Salvation	Damnation
Heaven	Hell
Educational Institutions	
Acceptance	Nonacceptance
Advancement	Nonadvancement
Graduation	Expelled
Higher degrees	No degrees
Chance for a better job	Poorer job
Political Institutions	
Participation	Ineligibility
Appointment	Passed over
Elected	Defeated
Deification	Obscurity
Military	
Accepted	Not accepted
Promotion	Passed over
Permanent rank	Temporary rank
Medals and honors	Court martialed
Retirement at rank	Dishonorably discharged
Social and Fraternal	
Acceptance	Blackballed
Exposure to others	Excluded
Committee work	No appointment
Officer position	No elected office
Retirement banquet	Expulsion

Figure 7.2. EXAMPLES OF REWARD AND PUNISHMENT SYSTEMS WITHIN A LARGER SOCIETAL CONTEXT.

7.8 Can You Figure This Out?

For the fourth time, Elizabeth has successfully whined her way out of taking a particular course, while Johnny has once again apologized to avoid experiencing the consequences of his misbehavior. How would you explain these as examples of negative reinforcement? Asked another way, *why* are they examples of negative reinforcement?

The Advantage of Contingency Reinforcements

Contingency reinforcement means that the reinforcement depends on certain conditions. When we say, "You will earn one good behavior point for each class session that you get to on time," or "I'll let you go to the museum with the others if and only if you promise to finish this assignment at home," we are making the reinforcement (the bonus point, or the museum trip) contingent on a particular response (getting to class on time, or completing a homework assignment).

The *Premack Principle* is a variation of the contingency-reinforcement idea that results from the work of Premack (1965). Basically, it is built on the idea that more frequent behavior can be used to reinforce less frequent behavior. That is, a behavior with a higher probability of occurrence can be used as a reinforcer for a behavior with a lower probability of occurrence. Parents and teachers use this principle constantly, although not always consciously: A child is allowed to have dessert *after* eating vegetables; a student is permitted to read comic books *after* completing an assignment. The teacher who says, "Let's go to recess now, so we'll be ready to settle down to your science lesson," or "Stop fooling around, and practice your spelling words," has missed the point. The idea is to use the *more* desirable (from the students' point of view) activity to motivate students to be involved in the *less* desirable activity. It would probably work better for the teacher to say, "Let's work a little now on the science unit, and then you can go out to play," or "Let's work on our spelling words for fifteen minutes, and *then* you can have free time."

Homme and Tosti (1965) offer the following example to show how, unlikely as it might seem, *misbehavior* can be used as a reinforcement to encourage *desired* behavior. Notice that the example also incorporates the operant-behavior idea already discussed.

A child is seated at the dinner table. Dinner is served. The other members of the family are eating. The child, however, does not eat. She plays with her shoes. The usual way to solve this problem is obvious: "Stop playing with your shoes! Eat your dinner!"

"Playing with shoes" is a high-frequency behavior and eating is a low one. When the problem is viewed this way, the contingency manager says, "Eat one bite of potatoes, then play with your shoes some more." It may be startling to spectators, but the latter method worked. Instead of having an emotional scene, with both parent and child upset, the contingency manager has a child cooperating in a gamelike atmosphere. What stimulus set off the playing-with-shoes operant in the first place? It is impossible to say. But it does not matter. If this higher frequency operant follows a lower frequency one, the latter will get strengthened. (p. 15)

7.9 Can You Think of Some Premack Examples?

Basically, the Premack Principle rewards students for doing the things they might not want to do with activities they *do* want to do. Now that you are aware of how it works, what examples from your own experience can you think of that illustrate this principle in action? Perhaps there are some things you remember your parents doing.

Intermittent Reinforcements Work Well

It is important to note that it is not necessary to reinforce every satisfactory response or correct answer in order to get positive results. Overviews of research in this area show rather clearly that whether it is animals or persons, both seem to work harder if they are reinforced only intermittently (Bigge and Shermis, 1992; Bower and Hilgard, 1981; Gredler, 1992). If, let us say, you were praised for making a contribution every time you opened your mouth in class, you very likely would grow insensitive, or at least indifferent, to subsequent compliments because they were so frequently and indiscriminately dispensed. Positive reinforcement, in whatever form, usually means more and has a greater impact if it is discriminately given and not too easily won.

The Best Strategy Is To Use a Variety of Reinforcements

We all like to be positively reinforced. Rewards arouse good feelings about ourselves, our work, and usually about those doing the rewarding. As noted by Hall and Hall (1980), the list of possible reinforcers is endless. There are, for example, *verbal reinforcers* (praise, encouragement), *physical reinforcers* (touches, pats, hugs), *nonverbal reinforcers* (smiles, winks, warm looks), *activity reinforcers* (being allowed to play games or listen to records), *token reinforcers* (points, chips, stars), and even *consumable reinforcers* (cookies, fruit, sugarless soft drinks). Positive reinforcement, although generally effective, is tricky. What works for one student may not work for another.

Some students respond best to tangible rewards (such as prizes, money, food, or tokens) that can be exchanged for something desired, while other students respond to less tangible, social rewards (such as praise, grades, honors, status symbols, or attention from peers or teachers). Benowitz and Busse (1970), for example, found that rewards involving small trinkets, toys, and other attractive items desired by children led to greater learning among some of the children than was produced by oral reinforcements such as, "Good work, Robert," "Fine job, Joni," and so forth. In contrast, the research done with young children by Anderson, Manooglan, and Reznick (1976) led them to conclude that some of the youngsters in their study showed less of an interest in drawing activities—an activity young children usually find naturally appealing—when given small monetary rewards than when the reinforcement was in the form of adult responsiveness and interest. Evaluation of research related to the effects of reinforcement consistently points to a wide range of differences in human responsiveness to the vast menu of positive reinforcements available (Klein, 1987; Logan and Gordon, 1981). You can see how necessary it is to know each student as an individual so that teachers know which kind of reinforcement to use with particular students.

7.10 Do Some Reinforcements Work Better for You than Others?

What kind of positive reinforcement do you respond to most favorably? Do you prefer the more tangible rewards, or are you particularly responsive to verbal reinforcements? Consider the instructors you currently have for various classes. What kinds of reinforcements do they use? How would you describe the effects of those reinforcements on your behavior?

In summary, reinforcement methods used to encourage learning stress the importance of both the quantity and quality of extrinsic rewards. This viewpoint assumes that the primary motive for learning lies outside the student. Learning occurs and teaching succeeds, according to reinforcement theory, when desired behavior has been adequately rewarded. A teacher can control and direct learning by providing reinforcement (usually approval or praise) when the student's behavior is consistent with the objectives the teacher is seeking to accomplish. Conversely, a teacher can undermine his or her own efforts by inadvertently reinforcing (through giving attention, sympathy, or whatever) when a student engages in behavior contrary to the teacher's goals.

The Keller Plan: Systematic Use of Reinforcement Concepts

F. S. Keller (1968), a colleague of Skinner's, developed an approach to individualizing instruction that does not use any special materials or machines. Commonly referred to as the *Personalized System of Instruction* (PSI), it is an approach to learning that uses basic behavioristic principles such as specific goals, small steps, and immediate feedback, and combines them with lectures, demonstrations, and tutoring.

The idea behind PSI is to break course readings into small units, each with specific goals and study guides. The typical format is for students to study the unit until they believe that they thoroughly understand it, and then to take a short test. Immediately after it is finished, the test is scored (frequently by a student who already passed the unit). If the students score was at least 80% or better, he or she is given the next unit. If the student misses the 80% mark by only one or two answers, the proctor calls his or her attention to the parts of the unit that should be reread. The student is given thirty minutes to do so, and then is tested again. If he or she misses the 80% mark by four or more questions, the student is advised to study more intensely and to take the exam again at a later date. Students who pass the first three units have the privilege of attending a lecture or demonstration, which is designed to be a source of motivation and, most important, reinforcement. Grades depend on the number of units successfully completed and, perhaps to a lesser extent, on midterms and final examinations.

Thus, a reinforcement format—establishing specific goals, attempting to attain them in small steps, and rewarding correct responses (along with helping those who gave incorrect responses)—serves as an overall framework for the promotion of learning.

Evaluations of the effectiveness of Keller's PSI approach have been mixed. For example, in a review of about fifty studies (Bangert, Kulik, and Kulik, 1983), it was found that students in grades six through twelve who were taught by the PSI method scored about the same on classroom exams as students taught by more conventional methods. At the college level, however, similar comparisons indicate that the PSI method not only leads to higher scores, but also indicates that students enjoy the experience more than those in conventional classes (Kulik, Kulik, and Cohen, 1979). Findings such as these suggest that students below college level might both want and need more student–teacher interaction than the PSI affords.

Reinforcement Without Teachers: Programmed Learning and Computer-Assisted Instruction

Programmed instruction is designed to be a self-instructional package in which a particular topic has been organized in a carefully planned sequence that requires learners to respond to questions or statements by filling in blanks, selecting from a series of possible answers, or solving a problem. Immediate feedback occurs after each response, thus invoking the operant-conditioning principle. It is an approach to learning that has been incorporated into programmed books, computers, and teaching machines. Teaching machines are nearly extinct, at least in schools. However, smaller, less complex versions of them—the type that tell children their spelling or arithmetic is correct or wrong—are available in toy stores.

Reinforcing correct responses is the basic principle in programmed instruction. That is, each correct answer provides students with the immediate gratification of "I'm right" and is the impetus to go on to the next step. Figure 7.3 shows a sample page from a programmed learning textbook. You can see

Only an __________ can modify a verb.	adverb
Many adverbs end in __________.	ly
When they modify the verb, these adverbs usually tell us something about the __________ of the verb.	action
Adverbs ending in __________ seldom modify linking verbs.	ly
Do they often modify verbs of action?	yes
Some of the following sentences contain linking verbs. The others contain verbs of action.	
The linking verbs are followed by objectives that modify the __________ of the sentence.	subject
The verbs of action are followed by adverbs ending in ly which modify the __________.	verb
In each sentence select the correct form of the adjective or adverb:	
A rose smells—sweet/sweetly.	sweet
This food tastes—bad/badly	bad
The professor speaks—rapid/rapidly.	rapidly
You sing—good/well.	well
He felt—quick/quickly—for the door knob.	quickly
He polished—vigorous/vigorously.	vigorously
The play ended—happy/happily.	happily
The snake struck—vicious/viciously.	viciously

Figure 7.3. AN EXAMPLE OF A PROGRAMMED LEARNING TEXT. Students cover the right-hand side of the page and look at it only when they want to check their answers for the exercises on the left.

that students get instant feedback on how they are doing, which makes it possible for them to change erroneous responses to the more gratifying correct responses. The objective of programmed instruction is to improve learning by: (1) breaking the topic into small units, (2) forcing students to respond to these small units, (3) providing immediate knowledge of results, and (4) allowing students to go at their own pace.

Basically, there are two kinds of programs—the linear model developed by Skinner (1954) and the branching format developed by Crowder (1961). As you might suspect, Skinner's *linear program* is based directly on operant-conditioning principles. Figure 7.3 is an example of a linear format. It is a program that all learners move through in exactly the same sequence, and yet it provides for individual differences by allowing students to go through at their own rate. It operates on an operant-conditioning model in that the arrangement of material in the program leads the student to make a correct response, which is, in itself, a reinforcement for that response. Linear programs have always been touted for their ability to give students immediate knowledge of results, which is a time-tested way for effectively promoting learning.

Branching programs are designed in such a way that it is possible for students to go through them at their own rates. Students who give all correct answers go through in the shortest time. Students who give incorrect answers at any point along the way literally "branch out" from the mainstream questions to receive some additional information. Whereas in linear programming students choose their own answer, in branching programming they choose from among alternatives. For example, after responding correctly to question one from a source using a branching program format, you might read (or hear, if using an audiocomputer), "That's good. Now go on to number four." However, if your response is incorrect to number one, you might read (or hear), "Oops, that's not quite right. Do questions two and three and we'll try again."

Linear and branching programs are not so different that they cannot be used in combination. Both, as you see, utilize the ideas of immediate feedback and much positive reinforcement. There is, however, considerable debate as to how reinforcing it is to simply get the right answer and to be told so by a book or machine.

7.11 If You Had To Make a Parental Choice . . . ?

For the sake of discussion, assume that you are a parent and that you have the choice of either sending your junior high school youngster to a special science class twice a week where he is taught by an adequate, but not great, teacher or to a section that has outstanding programmed instruction books. Which would you choose? How would you justify your choice?

Alvin Toffler (1970) warned us about the coming revolution in computers and, in 1980, he announced that it was upon us. Indeed, futurist Toffler sees this as the third wave in a series of monumental changes in human history. First, there was the agricultural revolution, then the industrial revolution, and now the computer revolution. It remains for history to tell us how greatly the third revolution will change the various basic components of modern life. The discovery of the silicon chip has made it possible to produce processing units so small that computers called "microcomputers" can be carried in one's pocket. Increasingly, computers of all sizes are becoming less expensive and easier to operate. They are becoming, as computer advertisers are fond of saying, more "user friendly."

Basically, computer-assisted instruction (CAI) involves the use of computers as tutors to present information, give students opportunities to practice what they learn, evaluate student achievement, and provide additional instruction when needed. It is a sort of ultrasophisticated teaching machine designed to present *programs*, or lessons, with or without a teacher's assistance.

In many ways, CAI is an attempt to use behavioral principles in a more efficient way than programmed instruction has traditionally done with textbooks and teaching machines.

Among the benefits associated with computer usage in the classroom is the flexibility it affords teachers, especially in terms of helping them respond to the individual needs of students. As with programmed tests, students can spend as much time as needed to master a task, either moving through the material quickly when it is easily grasped or taking more time with difficult topics. Examples of the more common classroom usages of computers include the following:

1. *Drill and practice.* Computer programs designed for this purpose are structured to help students in a variety of areas, such as math, spelling, reading, grammar usage, and any other subject in which they have to master fundamental facts. Computers used in this way resemble a teaching machine in that they present a stimulus, elicit a response, and reinforce the behavior.

2. *Tutorial teaching.* A major difference between computers used for drill and as a tutorial is that new material can be introduced. In a sense, the computer acts as a one-on-one instructor. As is the case for programmed books, computers can present the material in either linear or branching form, each of which works in the same way as explained previously for their programmed text versions.

3. *Problem solving.* In an effort to involve higher cognitive processes, sophisticated programs have been developed to involve students in solving a wide range of problems that involve memory skills, creative thinking, and the use of various learning strategies. Problem-solving programs are not in wide use yet, but where they are used, students' motivation is usually high (Kulik and Kulik, 1991). Which brings us to an important question.

How Successful Are Programmed Learning and Computer-Assisted Instruction?

Reviews of hundreds of comparisons of the effectiveness of programmed instruction to that of conventional teaching (Bangert, Kulik, and Kulik, 1983; Kulik, Cohen, and Ebeling, 1980) have found that students who used programmed materials did about as well (sometimes better) on achievement tests than those who did not use them. It is worth noting that particular *types* of students tend to respond more favorably to various aspects of programmed instruction than others. For example, it has been found that low-achieving and very anxious students often benefit from programmed instruction, perhaps because it is clear, organized in small steps, and allows students to repeat parts they do not understand the first time through (Tobias, 1982).

Research related to the effectiveness of CAI also shows mixed results. An analysis (Kulik, Bangert, and Williams, 1983) of about fifty studies involving sixth- to twelfth-grade students showed that those exposed to CAI scored slightly higher on exams than students taught in conventional ways. In particular, disadvantaged and low-aptitude students were helped by CAI. Research (Atkinson, 1984; Tobias, 1985) has shown that CAI methods are likely to be most useful when used in conjunction with regular classroom instruction.

In their meta-analysis of 254 studies involving students from kindergarten age to adults, Kulik and Kulik (1991) found that CAI raised final examination scores in a typical study from approximately the 50th percentile to the 62nd percentile. Interestingly, the CAI was most effective when the duration of students' exposure to it was four weeks or less and less effective when students were exposed to CAI for several months or longer. It may be that, after a certain point, the novelty begins to wear off and the original motivational incentive that was there in the beginning loses its effectiveness.

I think it is safe to say that modes of instruction that incorporate operant conditioning and positive reinforcement have value and contribute to the learning process. They are not a panacea, but where used to supplement regular classroom instruction, they offer another way of reaching the broad range of individual differences that confront every teacher. Ultimately, however, it is the human touch, not the electronic one, that contributes the most to creating a positive learning experience.

Some Cautions About the Use of Reinforcement Methods

A major caution about the use of reinforcement methods is related to the idea that they give the teacher a great deal of power and control over both the student and the student's curriculum. The teacher establishes the objectives, determines which student behaviors to reinforce, and then evaluates students to see how well they have met these predetermined objectives. While some people say that this is exactly the way teaching and learning should be, others fear that reinforcement strategies encourage students to follow in blind obedience, an obedience that is conditional to the authority of the teacher. In addition to the possibility that the teacher may exercise too much control, there are at least two other cautions about the use of reinforcement methods: (1) extrinsic motivation may overemphasized, and (2) humans have unpredictable responses. Let's briefly examine each of these.

Extrinsic Motivation May Be Overemphasized

Maslow (1977) has been as straightforward as anyone in pointing to some cautions when it comes to relying too heavily on reinforcement methods:

> [Reinforcement methods encourage] extrinsic learning, i.e., learning of the outside, learning of the impersonal, or arbitrary conditioning . . . of arbitrary meanings and responses. In this kind of learning, most often it is not the person himself who decides, but rather a teacher . . . who says, "I will use a buzzer," "I will use a bell," "I will use a red light," and most important, "I will reinforce this but not that." In this sense the learning is extrinsic to the learner, extrinsic to the personality, and is extrinsic also in the sense of collecting associations, conditionings, habits or modes of action. It is as if they are possessions which the learner accumulates in the same way that he accumulates keys or coins and puts them in his pocket. They have little or nothing to do with the actualization or growth of the peculiar, idiosyncratic kind of person he is. (p. 1)

Maslow's speculative fears are not without empirical support. Thomas (1980) reviewed a large number of studies concerned with the relationship between external and internal sources of motivation and concluded that when students learn to rely on the teacher for their source of reinforcement, instructional effects might not transfer to new situations. In other words, when the teacher becomes too much of an extrinsic motivator, the sort of self-propelled intrinsic motivation that supports out-of-class learning is delayed or prevented. Bates (1979) concluded from a somewhat similar review of research that when extrinsic rewards are routinely given, interest in an activity declines. This is not so much a criticism of extrinsic sources of motivation per se as it is about the *frequency* with which they are used. Extrinsic rewards given routinely and as a matter of course lose their effectiveness, something that Lepper and Chabay (1985) point to as a possibility when extrinsic rewards are overemphasized.

Human Responses Are Unpredictable

Brookshire's (1970) interesting discussions about learning pointed out some of the complications associated with the application of reinforcement principles to human learning. For example, in a task in which an animal or a human is confronted with a problem involving two levers or two buttons to press, the experimenter can arrange conditions so that pressing the right-hand lever is reinforced, at random, 70% of the time. The reinforcement might be food; a toy, in the case of a child; or money, in the case of an adult. Under these circumstances, the rational approach that would deliver the maximum number of reinforcements would be to press the right-hand lever, which is exactly what animals other than humans do. When humans are faced with such a problem, they will usually settle into pushing the right-hand lever 70% of the time and the left-hand lever 30% of the time, even though they get fewer reinforcements than they would if they stayed with the right-hand lever. Brookshire points out that the human behavior differed from other animals' because humans persisted in the belief that the problem was solvable and that, if they could find the right system, then they would get a reinforcement every time they pushed the lever. Other animals do better than humans because they do not try to outsmart a random system. They simply make the correct response and, in the majority of cases, get rewarded, which is the basis of any successful reinforcement method.

The application of reinforcement principles is not as predictably positive as it may sound. Humans are vastly complex organisms whose reactions to their environment are more than a series of conditioned responses. First, humans have a will (also referred to as determination or stubbornness). They can say, "I will not do it your way, no matter what you do." They also have a brain that is capable of seeing beyond the response and into the act itself. They can say, "Yes, I can see you want me to do it that way, but I see other alternatives."

COGNITIVE AND REINFORCEMENT METHODS ARE NOT MUTUALLY EXCLUSIVE

Both discovery and reinforcement methods can be used to facilitate and encourage classroom learning. We need not view these as either/or choices. Both have merits and strengths, and we can use the best that each has to offer.

Consider an example of both approaches at work in a fourth-grade classroom. The teacher had broken her class of twenty-five students into groups of five (a manageable size, so that everyone can talk). During their math lesson that morning, she and her students had been working on multiplication. She was interested in having her students develop an understanding of why multiplying was a shortcut for adding, but she wanted them to discover that for themselves. When they were in small groups, she said to them, "You know how to add, and we've just learned about multiplication. Now take what you know about these two processes and try to figure out how they are related." The students busied themselves with the assignment and as various groups came up with the answer, the teacher praised both their effort and their work with words, smiles, and occasional touches as she circled among the groups. If a group's reasoning was not correct, she simply pointed it out, suggested a new tack, gave them an encouraging word, and left them to continue working on the problem. Eventually, the entire class found the relationship between the two processes, and when the class came back as a total group, she told them how pleased she was with the work they had done. There were a lot of smiles from the students.

In all of this, the teacher was an active, guiding, praising adult. She took two processes, addition and multiplication, and asked her students to see how they were related, which, in Piagetian terms, required that they *assimilate* new information and accommodate it in light of existing knowledge. This is central to cognitive approaches to learning. The teacher began with a problem the students could handle, particularly with the help of some group thinking, encouraged them to keep trying when they struggled, and praised both their efforts and their correct answers when they finished. This is an example of combining the best of cognitive processing and positive reinforcement.

The best way to evaluate the two learning methods (discovery and reinforcement) is to talk to teachers and to watch them in action. It would be good if you could do this in a public or private school setting, but you can also learn a great deal just by observing your professors and instructors with an eye on how they encourage learning through cognitive and/or reinforcement approaches. How do they do it? What types of responses do they get? How do the students seem to feel about these professors' classes. How do *you* feel?

STYLES AND PATTERNS OF LEARNING VARY AMONG STUDENTS

Just as there are individual differences in height, weight, metabolism, personal interests, and other human characteristics, there are also differences among students when it comes to how they learn, the rate at which learning occurs, and the cognitive styles they prefer for learning new material (Curry, 1990; Dunn, 1990; Keefe, 1987; Reiff, 1992). We are beginning to realize that in order to assist each pupil and to capitalize on his or her natural inclination to understand, we must first be able not only to diagnose his or her style of learning, but also to accept it. There are many styles of learning, and there is no evidence to suggest that one is better than another. What is better is the style that fits each person most comfortably; what is not better is to try to fit a person into a learning mode that seems alien and uncomfortable. Once we accept and appreciate the idea that there are different ways of learning, each valid for particular students, then we see the importance of varying our approaches to teaching in order to accommodate different learning styles.

Three Basic Learning Styles: Visual, Aural, and Physical

Each person develops a particular style or preference for approaching new learning. Reissman (1977), for example, has suggested that there are three general learning styles that can be categorized principally as *visual* (reading), *aural* (listening), or *physical* (actively doing things). Some persons believe they learn best by listening to lectures, tapes, or discussions. Others find their learning is facilitated by reading, reviewing notes, scanning books, and so on. Some believe they learn more through active physical involvement, such as performing chemistry experiments rather than reading about them, or actually practicing on a pocket calculator rather than reading how to use one in a manual. It would not be true to say that any one mode is better than the other, but it would be accurate to say that each of us has a preference. Along these lines, Reissman (1977) has observed that

> Each classroom is likely to include students whose styles of learning vary widely. Although teachers cannot cater completely to each student's particular style, they can

> attempt to utilize the strengths and reduce or modify the weaknesses of those in their classes.
>
> An individual's basic style of learning is probably laid down early in life and is not subject to fundamental change. For example, a pupil who likes to learn by listening and speaking (aural style) is unlikely to change completely and become an outstanding reader. I am not suggesting that such a pupil will not learn to read and write fluently but rather that his or her best, most permanent learning is likely to continue to come from listening and speaking. (pp. 14–15)

In the interest of effective motivation, it is important to be sensitive to each student's learning style. If, for example, some students seem to learn best by reading, you might want not only to suggest books to them, but also to call on them more often in class to encourage them to experience more physical or verbal learning. (Some students even *hope* to be called on because they lack confidence to raise their hands.) Conversely, you might find it beneficial to encourage the more physical and aural students to read more. Once we identify and become aware of each student's particular style of learning, we can build on that style, along with helping him or her experience other modes of learning.

7.13 What Is Your Preferred Learning Style?

Notice that the key word here is *preferred.* Most people are able to learn new material with any one of the three styles we have discussed, but they usually prefer one over the other two. Some students learn best by listening to lectures and/or tapes and so would probably do their best learning in an aural mode. Others like to read and in other ways assimilate information with their eyes. Still others prefer as much of a hands-on, personal approach as possible and would be among those who learn through actual physical involvement, such as might be associated with lab work, field trips, or internship settings. What is *your* preferred mode of learning? How is that mode reflected in the courses you like most and in the way you study?

Four Characteristic Learning Patterns

When we talk about styles of learning, this has reference to *how* people learn. A person's learning pattern has more to do with the way one behaves during the learning experience. A learning pattern, then, refers specifically to a person's characteristic way of behaving when confronted with a problem to solve or resolve. After reviewing the work of many investigators who had studied learning, Rosenberg (1968) found that most of them more or less agreed on the existence and description of four general learning patterns. Rosenberg was struck by the consistency of these four patterns and labeled them the *rigid-*

inhibited, the *undisciplined*, the *acceptance-anxious*, and the *creative*. He is cautious to point out that we are dealing with *general categories* rather than with individuals. With this caution in mind, let us now turn our attention to a brief examination of each category in order to get a better understanding of how varied learning patterns can be.

Rigid-Inhibited

Students with a proclivity for this style of learning do best when given very precise directions and rules to follow. They tend to be those students who are tense, nervous, and generally on edge about one thing or another. The rigid-inhibited student learns best when directed by the teacher. I have observed, for example, that students who fall into this category tend to be somewhat uncertain and anxious when it comes to making their own decisions. If students are given an open-ended assignment as broad as writing a paper on any course-related topic that interests them, the rigid-inhibited ones are typically the first to ask questions such as the following: "What kind of paper do you want me to write?", "How long should it be?", "Should I typewrite, or can I handwrite?", "Can you give me an idea for a topic?" You can see the need for structure and direction in these questions.

Undisciplined

Students reflecting this pattern, particularly younger ones, tend to be what the label indicates—undisciplined. Their behavioral characteristics include: a refusal to do what is asked; an inclination to throw tantrums; a tendency to be destructive, lie, steal, and get into fights; and an inclination to speak to the teacher with disrespect. They frequently do not finish their work and have low tolerance for frustration. Like the rigid-inhibited student, they do better when their work is structured and when they know exactly what is expected of them. In addition, they usually function best when the teacher is firm. Because they lack inner controls of their own, they must rely more on the teacher for control.

Acceptance-Anxious

The need for approval and acceptance dominates the acceptance-anxious learner. These students are more concerned about what others think of their school performance than they are with the schoolwork itself. Most of all, they are fearful of being judged negatively. They are forever thinking, "Am I going to get this right? Probably not; what'll happen to me when I get it wrong? Will the teacher get mad? Will the other kids laugh at me? Will my mother and father hear about it?"

Acceptance-anxious students cannot easily incorporate the idea of being wrong, and they are inclined to worry excessively about whether they are pleasing others. Such students do their best with teachers who are warm and accepting; they feel their greatest tension and frustration with teachers who use a harsh, authoritarian manner, which increases their anxiety, and nothing interferes with learning more than high anxiety.

Because dependency comes easily for acceptance-anxious students, it is important for teachers to emphasize the importance of self-evaluation over the evaluation of others. Rather than say, "I think you have done a fine job," it would be wise, from time to time, to say things such as, "You have done a fine job, don't you think?" or "You must really feel pleased with that effort." It is particularly important for this type of student to feel free to make mistakes without fear of ridicule, derision, or embarrassment.

Creative

Students with this pattern are typically confident, capable of objectively evaluating their performance, and inclined to think divergently. Anxiety, rather than immobilizing them, spurs them to even greater achievement. They enjoy competition and solving their own problems, and jump at opportunities to use their imaginations. The "creative-pattern" very much likes to do the sort of open-ended paper described earlier, in which students are free to write on any topic that interests them.

Whereas students fitting the first three learning patterns learn best by authority, the creative student learns best by exploring, testing the limits, searching, manipulating, and playing. E. P. Torrance (1972), a psychologist noted for his work with creative students, has made the following observation about the need for a special type of environment in which to encourage students with creative learning patterns:

> The cat and the creative child both need a responsive environment more than a stimulating one. Many teachers and parents ask, "What can we do to stimulate creativity?" It is not necessary to stimulate the creative child to think creatively, although it may be necessary to provide a stimulating environment for the child who prefers to learn by authority and the child whose creativity has been suppressed for a long time. With the creative child, adults need largely to avoid throwing off course the child's thinking processes, guiding him by providing a responsive environment. It is my belief that this approach will lead to the controlled kind of freedom that seems to be necessary for productive, creative behavior. In defending the possible consequences of this approach, I point to the fact that the dogs in our neighborhood are kept on leashes so that they will remain under control. No one would think of placing a leash on any of the cats in this same neighborhood.
>
> A responsive environment is something quite different from what is commonly termed a "permissive atmosphere" or a "Laissez-faire" environment. A responsive environment requires the most alert and sensitive kind of guidance and direction. It

involves absorbed listening, fighting off criticism and ridicule, stirring the unresponsive, and deepening the superficial. It requires that each honest effort to learn is met with enough reward to ensure continued effort. The focus is on potential rather than on norms. (pp. 88–89)

These four patterns are not categories into which a student is locked forever. Research on learning does not, for example, support the idea that students who reflect rigid-inhibited or undisciplined patterns are *always* that way. For one thing, a student's pattern for learning can vary with the subject area. A student might feel rigid and inhibited in a math class, but display a creative pattern in English class. The pattern can also vary with the teacher. One teacher, by virtue of his or her personality, may be so lax and open-ended that students fall into the undisciplined mode. Another teacher might be so cold and domineering that students fall into the acceptance-anxious pattern. A student's learning pattern is not only an action dictated by his or her personality characteristics, but also a reaction triggered by the teacher and/or the subject matter.

7.14 Consider Your Own Learning Pattern

When you think about your own pattern of learning, where does it tend to fall? Do you see yourself moving in and out of different patterns depending on the teacher and subject matter? What implications do you see here for your work as a teacher?

Thinking Styles: Impulsive and Reflective

Just as there are differences among people in learning patterns and styles, so, too are there differences in how people think and conceptualize. Kagan (1965), for instance, has shown that some students are characteristically impulsive thinkers while others are characteristically reflective. Impulsive students operate in a fast conceptual tempo in the sense of being among the first to respond to a question, even if their response is wrong. Reading difficulties, notes Kagan, are not infrequently the consequence of an impulsive conceptual tempo that moves so rapidly that the learner skips words, overlooks letters, and, as a result, fails to grasp either the meaning or sounds of words as quickly as other students.

Reflective students, however, are slower to respond, preferring to evaluate alternative answers and to give correct responses rather than quick, erroneous ones. Indeed, when tests of reading and inductive reasoning were administered in the first and second grades, impulsive students made more errors than reflective students. As a behavioral characteristic, impulsiveness appears early in one's life, is reflected in a wide variety of situations, and is a relatively permanent and general trait.

Impulsiveness can be psychologically harmful to a student if he or she is punished excessively and made to feel bad by peers and teachers. If this happens over a long span of time, Kagan (1965) warns:

> [Students like this] will become alienated from the educational process. I have seen too many teachers respond with harsh sarcasm to the child who offers incorrect answers quickly, but praise the child who offers correct answers quickly. This attitude communicates to the child the value that teacher places upon speed of response and handicaps the impulsive child with average ability. (p. 159)

Conceptual Styles: Analytic and Thematic

Kagan (1965) also found that some students conceptualize *analytically* and others *thematically.* Whereas analytic students pay greater attention to the smaller details of a problem, thematic students respond to the problem as a whole. These styles are just as permanent and generalized as impulsiveness and reflectiveness.

Awareness of these various styles of conceptualization can assist us in comprehending the wider range of individual differences in the way students think about problems and conceptualize new material. This, in turn, can help us to understand why individual students respond in individual ways to various approaches to teaching.

IMPLICATIONS FOR TEACHERS

An awareness of the differences in learning styles and ways of thinking can be enormously helpful to us in our work as teachers. Recognizing, for example, that some students blurt out the first thing that comes into their minds, thereby frustrating the more reflective students still in the process of formulating careful responses, a teacher might want to require everyone to reflect on the question before responding. The teacher can also suggest a type of informal rotation plan for recitation. Understanding that some students flourish best within the global framework of the discovery approach enables a teacher to take individual differences in learning styles into account when developing expectations and lesson plans.

Analytic students, for instance, might feel uncomfortable working for extended periods within a more open-ended discovery framework, but do nicely with a specific task that demands analysis and closure. Thematic students, who tend to think more in terms of the big picture, might get easily bored with specific step-by-step assignments, but work enthusiastically on open-ended assignments that allow for more divergent thinking. Although it is not always possible to match our approaches to teaching with students' preferences for learning, there is a nice feeling of being in sync when what we do as teachers corresponds to what our students do best as learners.

You recall from our discussion about information processing in Chapter 6 that *attention, elaboration,* and *organization* are three key learning strategies for enhancing long-term memory. Let's review them. First, we must pay *attention* in order for new information to be processed and made sense of. Second, it is necessary to *elaborate* on new material so that meaningful connections can be made between it and more familiar material. Third, new material must be *organized* in such a way that relationships can be more easily perceived between similar and dissimilar items. Although the details of these processes are spelled out in Chapter 6, this brief review draws your attention to how both cognitive learning models and reinforcement approaches to learning can facilitate information-processing activities.

When teachers operate within Bruner's discovery framework, learning by doing is accentuated, which, with students of all ages, is a time-tested way of keeping their attention. By encouraging students to discover the answers for themselves, to make intuitive guesses, and to consider the consequences of their choices, we are encouraging them to elaborate and to go beyond simple memorization and rote-learning. Discovery approaches force students to impose a structure on the material so that it makes sense.

Ausubel's reception learning demands that teachers organize their material so the students can make sense of it. Hence, there is a heavy emphasis on preparing the students with advance organizers and structured presentations that are designed to get the students' attention and then, through a process of progressive differentiation, lead them from general concepts to specific information, which is an important part of helping students develop a cognitive understanding of the material.

Gagné's learning model, built as it is around a series of "instructional events," follows closely the steps in learning found in the information-processing model. As with all cognitive theories, there is a heavy emphasis placed on getting (and keeping) students' attention, helping them relate new material to previous knowledge, and giving feedback so meaningful connections can be made in long-term memory.

An awareness of reinforcement approaches alerts us to when, and how, to use positive reinforcement, which is a powerful way not only to get attention, but to keep attention focused. A basic idea underlying reinforcement approaches is that of organizing new material in such a way that it can be assimilated in a series of steps, thus providing opportunities for rewarding or reinforcing students as they move along a learning continuum.

EPILOGUE

Learning is a complex phenomenon that usually leads to some type of modification or wholesale change in behavior as a result of experience. The changes might be in overt behavior or in attitudes, beliefs, or values.

Cognitive theories and stimulus-response theories represent two major theoretical views of learning. Each has its own way of describing how learning occurs and how best to encourage it. Cognitive theory says that what is learned are "cognitive structures," or more general ways of thinking. Behavioristic theory suggests that what we learn are "habits," or specific ways of thinking or behaving. It has not been our purpose in this chapter to promote one theoretical position over the other. Both have their strengths and their weaknesses. Cognitive or inquiry methods of teaching and learning are an outgrowth of behavioristic theory. In broad terms, from cognitive models of learning we learn that it is important to pay attention to how students process information and to present new material in such a way that they are able to construct meaningful cognitive structures to help them understand, not just memorize. From cognitive methods, we learn strategies for helping students understand concepts and derive meaning from new information. From reinforcement methods we learn how and when to accentuate the positive.

Just as there are different approaches to learning, there are also different styles. Some students, by virtue of their experience, background, personal inclination, and perhaps, heredity, are rigid learners. They like precise directions and learn best when they know exactly what is to be done. Others need a lot of approval and acceptance, and do their best in a noncritical atmosphere. Others are creative-divergent individuals so caught up in their own pursuits that routine assignments bore them. They do best when given a lot of opportunity to creatively explore their own interests. People learn in various ways. With this simple truth in mind, good teachers work hard at developing individualized expectations and flexible teaching/learning plans.

Learning is most likely to occur when there is sufficient diversity in a teacher's approach to learning so as to keep reasonable pace with ongoing shifts in content, attention, and student interest.

In Chapter 8, we turn our attention to some ideas and strategies for one of the biggest challenges facing teachers, motivating students.

STUDY AND REVIEW QUESTIONS

1. How is learning usually defined?
2. What are the two major camps into which theories of learning usually fall? How do these two camps basically differ from each other?
3. Explain how cognitive methods of learning differ from behavioristic methods.
4. If a parent asked you how discovery methods worked in a classroom, how would you respond?
5. What are the major differences between Ausubel's "reception learning" and Gagné's "instructional events" approaches to learning?
6. Give an example of how the reception learning and instructional events models of learning work in the classroom.

7. What are some of the major advantages and disadvantages associated with both discovery and reinforcement approaches to learning?
8. How do negative reinforcement, positive reinforcement, and punishment differ from one another? Give some examples of how each might be used by teachers.
9. Why is it that reinforcements or rewards given contingently and intermittently work better than rewards given unconditionally and consistently?
10. How would you describe the role of the teacher in discovery learning? In reinforcement learning?
11. What three basic styles of learning can usually be observed among a group of students? How does each style operate?
12. What are the basic learning differences between impulsive and reflective learners? Between analytic and thematic learners?
13. Explain why no one approach to *and* for learning works best.

REFERENCES

Ackerman, P. L., Sternberg, R. J., and Glasser, R. (Eds.) *Learning and Individual Differences.* New York: Freeman, 1989.

Alberto, P. A., and Troutman, A. C. *Applied Behavior Analysis for Teachers,* 2nd ed. Columbus, OH: Merrill, 1986.

Anderson, R., Manooglan, S., and Reznik, J. S. "The Undermining and Enhancing of Intrinsic Motivation in Preschool Children." *Journal of Personality and Social Psychology,* 1976, *34,* pp. 915–922.

Atkinson, M. L. "Computer-Assisted Instruction: Current State of the Art." *Computers in the Schools,* 1984, *1,* 91–99.

Ausubel, D. P. *The Psychology of Meaningful Verbal Learning.* New York: Grune and Stratton, 1963.

Ausubel, D. P. "The Facilitation of Meaningful Verbal Learning in the Classroom." *Educational Psychologist,* 1977, *12,* pp. 162–178.

Ausubel, D. P. "Schemata, Cognitive Structures, and Advance Organizers. A Reply to Anderson, Spiro, and Anderson." *American Educational Research Journal,* 1980, *17,* pp. 400–404.

Ausubel, D. P., Novak, J., and Hanesian, H. *Educational Psychology: A Cognitive View,* 2nd ed. New York: Holt, Rinehart and Winston, 1978.

Ausubel, D. P., and Robinson, F. *School Learning: An Introduction to Educational Psychology.* New York: Holt, Rinehart and Winston, 1969.

Bangert, R. L., Kulik, J. A., and Kulik, C. C. "Individualized Systems of Instruction in Secondary Schools." *Review of Educational Research,* 1983, *53,* pp. 143–158.

Bates, J. A. "Extrinsic Reward and Intrinsic Motivation: A Review with Implications for the Classroom." *Review of Educational Research,* 1979, *49,* pp. 552–576.

Bennett, N., Jordan, J., Long, G., and Wade, B. *Teaching Styles and Pupil Progress.* Cambridge, MA: Harvard University Press, 1976.

Benowitz, M. L., and Busse, T. V. "Material Incentives and the Learning of Spelling Words in a Typical School Situation." *Journal of Educational Psychology,* 1970, *61,* pp. 24–26.

Berry, J. W. "Comparative Studies of Cognitive Styles." In R. J. Samuda and S. L. Woods (Eds.), *Perspectives in Immigrant and Minority Education.* Lanham, MD: Houghton Mifflin, 1983.

Bigge, M. L., and Shermis, S. S. *Learning Theories for Teachers,* 5th ed. New York: HarperCollins, 1992.

Bower, G. H., and Hilgard, E. R. *Theories of Learning,* 5th ed. Englewood Cliffs, NJ: 1981.

Brookshire, K. H., "Quantitative Differences in Learning Ability and Functions." In M. H. Marx (Ed.), *Learning Interactions,* New York, Macmillan, 1970.

Bruner, J. S. *The Process of Education.* New York: Vintage Books, 1960.

Bruner, J. S. *Toward a Theory of Instruction.* New York: Norton, 1966.

Bruner, J. S. *Beyond the Information Given: Studies in the Psychology of Knowing.* New York: Norton, 1973.

Bruner, J. S. *In Search of Mind: Essays in Autobiography.* New York: Harper & Row, 1983.

Carin, A. A., and Sund, R. B. *Teaching Science Through Discovery,* 5th ed. Columbus, OH: Merrill, 1985.

Corkill, A. J., Glover, J. A., Bruning, R. H., and Krug, D. "Advance Organizers: Retrieval Hypotheses." *Journal of Educational Psychology,* 1989, *81,* pp. 43–51.

Crowder, N. A. "Characteristics of Branching Programs." In A. A. Lumsdaine and R. Glaser (Eds.), *Teaching Machines and Programmed Learning.* Washington DC: National Education Association, 1961.

Curry, L. "A Critique of the Research on Learning Styles." *Educational Leadership,* October, 1990, pp. 50–56.

Dewey, J. *Ethical Principles Underlying Education.* Chicago: University of Chicago Press, 1903.

Divesta, F. J. "The Cognitive Movement and Education." In J. A. Glover and R. R. Ronning (Eds.), *Historical Foundation of Educational Psychology.* New York: Plenum, 1987.

Dunn, R. "Rita Dunn Answers Questions on Learning Styles." *Educational Leadership,* October, 1990, pp. 15–21.

Fabun, D. *On Motivation.* Beverly Hills, CA: Glencoe Press, 1968.

Fielding, G. D., Kameenui, E., and Gersten, R. "A Comparison of an Inquiry and Direct Instruction Approach to Teaching Legal Concepts and Applications to Secondary Schools." *Journal of Educational Research,* 1983, *76,* pp. 287–293.

Francis, E. "Grade Level and Task Difficulty in Learning by Discovery and Verbal Reception Methods." *Journal of Educational Psychology,* 1975, *67,* pp. 147–150.

Gagné, R. *The Conditions of Learning,* 3rd ed. New York: Holt, Rinehart and Winston, 1977.

Gagné, R. "Learning Outcomes and Their Effects." *American Psychologist,* 1984, *39,* pp. 377–385.

Gagné, R. M., and Brown, L. T. "Some Factors in the Programming of Conceptual Learning." *Journal of Experimental Psychology,* 1961, *62,* pp. 313–321.

Gagné, R., and Driscoll, M. P. *Essentials of Learning for Instruction,* 2nd ed. Englewood Cliffs, NJ: Prentice Hall, 1988.

Glasser, R. "The Reemergence of Learning Theory within Instructional Research." *American Psychologist,* 1990, *45,* pp. 29–39.

Good, T. L., and Brophy, J. E. *Looking in Classrooms,* 6th ed. New York: HarperCollins, 1994.

Gredler, M. E. *Learning and Instruction,* 2nd ed. New York: Macmillan, 1992.

Hall, R. V., and Hall, M. C. *How to Select Reinforcers.* Lawrence, KS: M&M Enterprises, 1980.

Homme, L. E., and Tosti, D. T. "Contingency Management and Motivation." *National Society for Programmed Instruction Journal,* 1965, *4,* pp. 14–16.

Jacobsen, D., Eggen, P., Kauchak, D., and Dulaney, C. *Methods for Teaching: A Skills Approach,* 2nd ed. Columbus, OH: Merrill, 1985.

Kagan, J. "Impulsive and Reflective Children: Significance of Conceptual Tempo." In J. D. Krumboltz (Ed.), *Learning and the Educational Process.* Chicago: Rand McNally, 1965.

Kazdin, M. *Behavior Modification in Applied Settings,* 4th ed. Pacific Groves, CA: Brooks/Cole, 1989.

Keefe, J. *Learning Style Theory and Practice.* Reston, VA: National Association of Secondary School Principals, 1987.

Keller, F. S. "Good-bye Teacher . . ." *Journal of Applied Behavior Analysis,* 1968, *1,* 79–88.

Kirby, F. D., and Shields, F. "Modification of Arithmetic Response Rate and Attending Behavior in a Seventh-Grade Student." *Journal of Applied Behavior Analysis,* 1972, *5,* pp. 79–84.

Klein, S. B. *Learning: Principles and Applications.* New York: McGraw-Hill, 1987.

Kulik, C. C., and Kulik, J. A. "Effectiveness of Computer-Based Instruction: An Upgraded Analysis." *Computers in Human Behavior,* 1991, *7,* pp. 75–94.

Kulik, J. A., Bangert, R. L., and Williams, G. W. "Effects of Computerized Teaching on Secondary School Students." *Journal of Educational Psychology,* 1983, *75,* pp. 19–26.

Kulik, J. A., Cohen, P. A., and Ebeling, B. J. "Effectiveness of Programmed Instruction in Higher Education: A Meta-Analysis of Findings." *Educational Evaluation and Policy Analysis,* 1980, *2,* pp. 51–64.

Kulik, J. A., Kulik, C. C., and Cohen, P. A. "A Meta-Analysis of Outcome Studies of Keller's Personalized System of Instruction." *American Psychologist,* 1979, *34,* pp. 307–318.

Lepper, M. R., and Chabay, R. W. "Intrinsic Motivation and Instruction: Conflicting Views on the Role of Motivational Processes in Computer-Based Education." *Educational Psychologist,* 1985, *20,* pp. 217–230.

Logan, F. A., and Gordon, W. C. *Fundamentals of Learning and Motivation,* 3rd ed. Dubuque, IA: Brown, 1981.

Maslow, A. H. "Some Differences Between Extrinsic and Intrinsic Motivation." In D. E. Hamachek (Ed.), *Human Dynamics in Psychology and Education,* 3rd ed. Boston: Allyn & Bacon, 1977.

Mayer, R. E. "Twenty-Five Years of Research on Advance Organizers." *Instructional Science,* 1984, *8,* pp. 133–169.

Mayer, R. E. *Educational Psychology: A Cognitive Approach.* Boston: Little, Brown, 1987.

Mayer, R. E. "Cognition and Instruction: Their Historic Meeting within Educational Psychology." *Journal of Educational Psychology,* 1992a, *84,* pp. 405–412.

Mayer, R. E. "Guiding Students' Cognitive Processing of Scientific Information." In M. Pressley, K. Harris, and J. Guthrie (Eds.), *Promoting Academic Competence and Literacy: Cognitive Research and Instructional Innovation.* San Diego, CA: Academic Press, 1992b.

Premack, D. "Reinforcement Theory." In D. Levine (Ed.), *Nebraska Symposium on Motivation.* Lincoln, NE: University of Nebraska Press, 1965.

Reiff, J. *Learning Styles.* Washington DC: National Education Association, 1992.

Reissman, F. "There is More than One Style for Learning." In D. E. Hamachek (Ed.), *Human Dynamics in Psychology and Education,* 3rd ed. Boston: Allyn & Bacon, 1977.

Rosenberg, M. B. *Diagnostic Teaching.* Seattle: Special Child Publications, 1968.

Rosenshine, B. "Classroom Instruction." In N. L. Gage (Ed.), *The Psychology of Teaching Methods.* The 75th Yearbook of the National Society for the Study of Education, Part I. Chicago: University of Chicago Press, 1976.

Selim, M. A., and Shrigley, R. L. "Group Dynamics Approach: A Sociological Approach for Testing the Effect of Discovery and Expository Teaching on the Science Achievement and Attitude of Young Egyptian Students." *Journal of Research in Science Teaching,* 1983, *20,* pp. 213–224.

Skinner, B. F. "The Science of Learning and the Art of Teaching." *Harvard Educational Review,* 1954, *24,* pp. 86–97.

Skinner, B. F. "The Shame of American Education." *American Psychologist,* 1984, *39,* pp. 947–954.

Skinner, B. F. "Whatever Happened to Psychology as the Science of Human Behavior?" *American Psychologist,* 1987, *42,* pp. 780–786.

Skinner, B. F. "Can Psychology Be a Science of Mind?" *American Psychologist,* 1990, *45,* pp. 1206–1210.

Thomas, J. W. "Agency and Achievement: Self-Management and Self-Regard." *Review of Educational Research,* 1980, *50,* pp. 213–240.

Tobias, S. "When Do Instructional Methods Make a Difference?" *Educational Researcher,* 1982, *11,* pp. 4–10.

Tobias, S. "Computer-Assisted Instruction." In M. C. Wang and H. J. Walberg (Eds.), *Adapting Instruction to Individual Differences.* Berkeley, CA: McCutchan, 1985.

Toffler, A. *Future Shock.* New York: Random House, 1970.

Toffler, A. *The Third Wave.* New York: Morrow, 1980.

Torrance, E. P. "Different Ways of Learning for Different Kinds of Students." In D. E. Hamachek (Ed.), *Human Dynamics in Psychology and Educators,* 2nd ed. Boston: Allyn & Bacon, 1972.

Walker, J. E., and Shea, T. M. *Behavior Modification: A Practical Approach for Educators,* 2nd ed. St. Louis: Mosby, 1980.

Wielkiewicz, R. M. *Behavior Management in the Schools: Principles and Procedures.* New York: Pergamon Press, 1986.

Wilcox, R. T. "Rediscovering Discovery Learning." *The Clearing House,* October, 1987, pp. 53–56.

SELECTED READINGS OF RELATED INTEREST

Driscoll, M. P. *Psychology of Learning for Instruction.* Needham Heights, MA: Allyn & Bacon, 1994. This is a cognitively oriented text that focuses on learning and instruction. Specific applications of learning theories are discussed and applied to a broad range of educational settings.

Foster, S. T. "Ten Principles of Learning Revised in Accordance with Cognitive Psychology." *Educational Psychologist,* 1986, *21,* pp. 235–243. Ten principles of learning that have been taught to teachers at all levels are revised in terms of modern cognitive psychology and presented in terms of their implications for teachers.

Gredler, M. E. *Learning and Instruction: Theory into Practice.* New York: Macmillan, 1992. A quite readable little book that exposes the reader to the major theories of learning and how their principles can be translated into classroom practices.

Keefe, J. *Learning Style Theory and Practice.* Reston, VA: National Association of Secondary School Principals, 1987. A fine overview of what is currently known about learning style theory and its application to classroom practices.

Reiff, J. *Learning Styles.* Washington DC: National Education Association, 1992. A short pamphlet (39 pages), but it gives an overview of what research is teaching us about the identification of different learning styles.

Schunk, D. *Learning Theories: An Educational Perspective.* New York: Macmillan, 1991. Every chapter offers detailed examination of learning principles applied to educational settings. Connections between theory and practice are clearly demonstrated.

8

Motivational Dynamics and Human Learning

CHAPTER OVERVIEW

IMPORTANT CHAPTER IDEAS

1. Ability is a reflection of what one *can* do; motivation is an indication of what one *wants* to do.
2. Although we are never unmotivated, we are not necessarily motivated in the same way, for the same reasons, or in the same direction.
3. Extrinsic motivation pushes us from the outside; intrinsic motivation pushes us from the inside.
4. Extrinsic motivators are most useful in getting the motivational machinery started; intrinsic motivation is usually necessary to keep it going.
5. Generally, praise is a more powerful motivator than either criticism or reproof on work performance; praise that is specific and contingent on actual success works best.
6. Praise given indiscriminately is not likely to have much credibility.
7. Success experiences tend to enhance motivation for learning, while failure experiences impair it, although students with high self-concepts and high need-achievement are sometimes motivated to work harder *following* poor performance.
8. Students who experience too much failure tend to set their sights either so low that no hazard is involved or so high that success is impossible.
9. Success-oriented students are likely to attribute their successes to internal reasons such as effort and ability, while failure-oriented students are inclined to attribute whatever successes they have to external factors such as luck, task difficulty, or other people's actions.
10. Problems of motivation occur when students attribute their failures to causes that they perceive as internal, stable, and uncontrollable.
11. How "certain" a student is of his or her self-esteem is a critical variable in whether a success or failure experience is believed and incorporated into his or her self-concept.
12. Confident students with high self-esteem both want and need a high level of personal and intellectual challenge.
13. Competitive conditions are not universally bad; some students do their best work under these circumstances.
14. Generally, cooperative, as opposed to competitive, approaches to learning are viewed by students as more positive, pleasant, and interpersonally enhancing, although cooperative efforts are not necessarily associated with greater learning or higher motivation. Used appropriately, both approaches have value in enhancing motivation.
15. The ability to motivate students is not a gift given to a chosen few; it is the result of hard work and careful planning.

PROLOGUE

Motivation is one of the great puzzles and great challenges of education. Every teacher has confronted that universal question: How can I motivate my students to learn, to *want* to learn, and to study so learning can happen? It is an important question and, like many important questions that encompass a broad spectrum of human behavior, there is neither a single answer nor a simple one. Although it would simplify a teacher's life considerably if there were one reasonably simple formula or strategy that would motivate all students in more or less the same way, the reality of the vast range of individual differences makes this impossible. Thus, we are better off at the onset if we simply accept the idea that what turns some students on is the very thing that turns others off; that what motivates Joni might discourage Jami; that what excites Mary might bore Marty. When we accept the idea that motivation—especially motivation for school learning—is a complex blend of personal life histories, attitudes, aspirations, and self-concepts, we are closer to using effectively what research and experience is telling us about how to improve both our teaching and learning practices.

Some questions we will seek to answer in this chapter are: How do intrinsic and extrinsic motivation differ? How does a student's own attributions regarding success or failure influence motivation? How can teacher praise be used more effectively as a motivator? How is motivation affected by success and failure? Why do some students tolerate failure experiences better than others? Does classroom competition help or hinder motivation? These are a few of the major questions we're going to examine in this chapter. Let's begin with a logical first question.

WHAT IS MOTIVATION?

Who among us has not had the experience of knowing there were at least half a dozen things that needed to be done—a term paper to write, an exam to prepare for, a pile of laundry to be washed, a letter to be written, and so forth—but felt absolutely no motivation to do any of it? Perhaps this is why motivation is sometimes referred to as the "go" of personality, in that its absence usually reduces most normal people to a state of listlessness and apathy. Although motivation cannot be seen directly, it can be inferred from behavior we ordinarily refer to as "ability." Ability refers to what an individual *can* do or is *able to do*, and motivation (or lack of it) refers to what a person *wants* to do. Motivation and ability may or may not go together. For example, a low grade on an exam might not be so much a reflection of low ability as of low motivation. In another case, a high grade on an exam might not be so much a reflection of exceptional ability as of high motivation, and, therefore, the willingness to work extra hard in an effort to do well. Generally, what a person in any grade in school, or any station in life, *wants to do* can be a powerful force in achieving his or her goals.

You might think of motivation as being the engine that powers and directs behavior. The key to that engine is in the hands of each individual. In school situations, some students are very good at turning their own keys and starting their own engines, and other students need help from the outside. As we progress through this chapter, we will try to understand more about why these differences exist.

Motives Trigger Motivation

Motives are related to motivation in the sense that they refer to the needs or desires that cause us to act—to feel motivated—in the first place. Motives serve three important functions: (1) energizing us (i.e., turning the key and starting the motivational engine); (2) directing us (i.e., pointing us in a particular direction); and (3) helping us to select the behavior most appropriate for achieving our goals. The feeling of being motivated, then, is a psychological state that is the consequence of a person's having activated his or her motives. Although a person might have similar motives for, say, success or achievement, how those motives are expressed in actual behavior varies greatly from one person to the next. For example, one student, motivated by a need to do well in all of his courses, puts in long, hard hours of diligent study, while another student, with similar motivation, pays to have his term papers written for him; one man, motivated to earn extra money, works overtime, while another man, with a desperate need for money, robs a gas station.

Human motivation is a complex issue that involves not only what one wants to do, but also the appropriateness of that want. Despite the complexity of motivation, one fact remains certain . . .

People Are Never Unmotivated

When motivation is looked at from the perspective of the person doing the behaving, that person is never unmotivated. Each of us, no matter who we are or what we do, is motivated to maintain and, if possible, enhance feelings of self-worth. This idea has been expressed in a variety of ways by psychologists over the years, some of whom were mentioned in Chapters 1 and 2. For David McClelland (1985), motivation is associated with a need for achievement; for Atkinson and Raynor (1978), motivation stems from a need to avoid failure; for Maslow (1987), motivation is triggered by any one of eight basic needs, ranging from the first, and most basic need, survival, to the need for self-esteem (which falls approximately in the middle of his scale), to the need for self-actualization and self-transcendence (which is at the top of his list); for Rogers (1962), motivation grows out of a need to be more fully functioning; for Covington (1984), motivation is fueled by the need to develop a basis for self-worth and to avoid feelings of shame; for Piaget (1983), motivation stems primarily from a need to make sense of the world, an effort leading to the assimilation of new knowledge and the accommodation of it with what is already known in order to maintain a state of mental equilibrium.

There is considerable overlap among these theories of motivation. For example, successfully satisfying the need for competence can lead to higher self-esteem and, possibly, self-actualization, which avoids failure and leads to fulfilling a need for achievement, which in turn, aids one's need for understanding—and so forth.

Motivation Can Be Either Toward Something or Away from It

Whether our motivation is toward something or away from it depends on our assessment of how well we will do. Motivation might be high and positive at the beginning of some experiences, but sometimes degenerates into a low energy force and negative feelings as time passes. Most kindergartners and first graders, for example, *start out* feeling excited about school. Unfortunately for many, it is a feeling soon lost as the original enthusiasm for schooling ebbs and wanes. For example, in an earlier survey on this issue, Flanagan (1973) found that although 41% of fourth-grade students reflected very high motivation for learning, this figure steadily declined in subsequent years until, in grade twelve, only 12% of students felt this way.

Like anyone else, students in school—at any level—do not stay motivated for long by experiences associated more with failure than with success. This does not mean they lose their motivation; it might mean that they lose their motivation only to go to school. Dropouts, for example, do not leave school because they have had too many success experiences or too many opportunities for enhancing personal adequacy and feelings of self-worth. They do drop out; however, when their failures exceed their successes, when their need to feel adequate is overwhelmed by feelings of inferiority and worthlessness. It is not surprising that reviews of dropout-related research reflect the idea that dropouts typically felt *better* about themselves *after* they have dropped out (Rumberger, 1987).

8.1 Have You Ever Been "Motivated" to Drop out of Something?

Think of something you have "dropped out" of in your life—a job, a club, a class, a friendship, an engagement, a marriage, or whatever was once meaningful to you. How would you explain your motivation to move away from one or more of these experiences? What was happening to your feelings of personal adequacy while you were still involved in these experiences? How did that change once you had dropped out?

Motivation, then, is an ongoing process. We might not all be motivated to do the same thing (which is one of a teacher's biggest problems), but we are never unmotivated. A challenge facing every teacher at every level of education is that of harnessing the motivational energy students bring to class so that it can be translated into positive learning experiences. In order to do this effectively, it is necessary to understand that motivation comes in two forms, an idea we turn to next.

Two Kinds of Motivation: Extrinsic and Intrinsic

When students work hard to win their parents' favor, gain teachers' praise, or earn high grades, we can rightly conclude that their motivation is primarily extrinsic; their reasons for work and study lie primarily outside themselves. If, however, students study because they enjoy the subject and desire to learn it, irrespective of the praise won or grades earned, this is an example of intrinsic motivation; the reasons for learning reside primarily inside themselves. A simple test of whether we are intrinsically or extrinsically motivated when we perform some task is the extent to which we feel independent of, or dependent on, the need for someone's approval at the completion of the task. Extrinsic motivation is fueled by the anticipation and expectation of some kind of payoff from an external source (e.g., a dollar for every A). Intrinsic motivation is fueled by one's own goals or ambitions (e.g., the payoff derived from one's own feelings of personal satisfaction or accomplishment). Intuitively, most of us recognize the value and importance of intrinsic motivation. It is self-starting, self-perpetuating, and requires only an inward interest to keep the motivational machinery going.

Extrinsic motivation is what most people have in the back of their minds when they think about what happens in everyday classroom situations. In this model, the teacher is assertive and the students are passive; students are shaped and molded by a variety of reward systems (e.g., praise, gold stars, the honor roll, special privileges), each of which reminds them that their reasons for doing the work are on the outside rather than on the inside. When carried to an extreme, this motivational model overpromotes the values of the teacher and underestimates the interest of the student.

Intrinsically motivated students are difficult to spot because even when they do class-related work as an end in itself, they usually receive some kind of payoff in the form of a grade, teacher approval, or recognition by peers. Thus, the myth is perpetuated that teachers always have to dangle a carrot in front of students' noses in order to motivate them to learn. As teachers, there will always be times when we find it necessary and appropriate to motivate our students extrinsically. Before we do, however, there are things we should know about the dynamics of extrinsic motivation.

Extrinsic Motivation Is Important—But Use It Cautiously

Extrinsic motivation can have a powerful effect on behavior. People work for a paycheck, not just because they like working. You work hard on a term paper to get as high a grade as possible, not just because you value the learning that comes from it.

8.2 How Important Are Extrinsic Motivators to You?

Reflect for a moment. How many things do you do simply for enjoyment? There are no grades involved, no payoffs, no rewards from an outside source; there is just the intrinsic value of the activity. How many things can you think of that you do primarily because of the payoff associated with those activities? If it were not for extrinsic motivators—teacher praise and grades being the most appreciated in school—what type of student do you suppose you would be? What do your own reflections tell you about the importance of extrinsic motivators in your life?

A major caution to be made about the use of extrinsic motivational strategies is that if students are preoccupied with rewards, they might not pay as much attention as they should to what they are supposed to be learning, and they might not appreciate the value of what they are learning. Research indicates that when external rewards are used excessively, we come to rely on rewards or payoffs as the reason for our behavior (Deci and Ryan, 1985). Money is an example of a powerful extrinsic motivator—either as an end in itself or for what it can purchase. This is fine, except that if students receive money for grades, eventually they might easily make money the reason for their behavior. That is, when intrinsically motivated students do something for money ("A dollar for every A," says Dad), their perception of the reason for doing it may shift from "I am doing it because I like it" to "I am doing it for the money." Because students are then performing for money (and therefore have less intrinsic motivation), they might stop performing or working when the monetary reward stops being given.

8.3 What About the Issue of Money for Grades?

Did you ever have the experience of being paid for good grades? If so, how did it affect you? If you were not doing very well and were told that if you did better you would be given a certain amount for every A and a certain amount for every B (or some such variation), how did that inducement influence you? If you were already doing well and got paid—either in money or special privileges—did that affect your work one way or the other? What is your feeling about paying students for good grades? Would you practice this with your children?

In addition, if students perceive themselves as completing assignments solely to obtain rewards, they may develop a "piecework mentality," or "minimum strategy," in which they concentrate on maximizing rewards by meeting minimum standards, rather than doing an excellent job as its own reward (Condry and Chambers, 1978). With this type of mind-set, students are inclined to write a 500-word essay assignment containing exactly 500 words, or to read only those parts of a text they are told will be on an exam, and not one page more. When teachers place tight limits on what they want (or will accept), and reward only those who stay within the boundaries, you can begin to see how and why rigid extrinsic reinforcers can encourage some students to adopt "minimum strategies."

There is still another caution related to the use of extrinsic motivation, and this has to do with the idea that if you pay, or otherwise reward, students to do something they would do anyway, they might end up no longer wanting to do it for its own sake.

Consider an example of how this principle works in an interesting piece of research done by Lepper and Greene (1975) with nursery school children. First, they noted which children in a nursery school setting enjoyed drawing pictures with felt pens. Second, the pens were removed from the classroom for two weeks, after which the children who had earlier shown an interest in drawing were brought, one at a time, into another room. The children were asked to make drawings with felt pens. One third of the children were promised a gold star and a red ribbon when they completed their drawing. Another third neither knew about nor received the award until they were finished with their drawings. A final third neither expected nor received any award. A week later, the felt pens were put on several tables around the room to see who would use them. A most interesting finding emerged: *children in the experiment who had been promised (and received) a gold star and red ribbon when they completed their drawing now spent only about half as much time drawing as they had at the time of the initial observation.* However, the children who had received no award, or who had unexpectedly received an award at the end of the experimental session, showed about the same amount of interest in the felt pens as they had originally.

What happened with the preschoolers who learned to expect a gold star and ribbon for their work might be somewhat similar to what sometimes happens to students who receive money for good grades—it is the reward that becomes important; the classes and learning become secondary.

Conversely, there is evidence to suggest that when verbal reinforcements are given as external rewards (e.g., "This is certainly a fine job," "I'm very pleased with this effort," "That's excellent, keep up the good work"), these rewards, apparently, are not so easily distinguishable from the intrinsic feelings of satisfaction one gets from doing a particular task (Deci and Ryan, 1985). If you complete a difficult and demanding project in which you were deeply involved, and your instructor says, "You have done a really nice job with this—excellent work!", the chances are good that the instructor's positive external evaluation will blend nicely with your intrinsic feelings of satisfaction. When this occurs, the inclination to perform a similar activity in the absence of external reward will be strengthened, which means that your intrinsic motivation has been increased.

Intrinsic motivation is the type of inner drive that we would most like to see in ourselves and in others. It propels us forward and onward with self-cycling energy fueled by its own curiosity and interest. However, in the real world we are not automatically energized to perform certain tasks, or to learn about certain topics. Sometimes, what it takes is an outside inducement—the possibility of a good grade or the threat of a failing one, the possibility of a positive experience or the threat of a negative one—to move us from an inactive to an active state.

It is clear that overstressing the use of extrinsic motivators can stifle intrinsic motivation. However, it is also clear that extrinsic motivators are sometimes necessary either to motivate students initially or to encourage them to explore a topic or field they might not know exists. Some examples include the following:

1. A fourth-grade teacher announces that next week there will be a spelling test (the extrinsic motivator). Already motivated students accept this as information and continue to study as they would anyway. Barely motivated students hear this as a motivational cue and study their spelling lists in order to get themselves ready. Perhaps two or three marginal students will do better than they expected and, as a consequence, will begin to feel a bit more intrinsically motivated.
2. A high school advisor suggests to several math whizzes that they take an English literature course, something they had hoped to avoid. They take the course and discover that they like it. During the next term, they take a follow-up course in English literature because of their new interest. What began as something done for extrinsic reasons (their advisor suggested they take the course) is now pursued for its own intrinsic value.

The use of rewards as extrinsic motivators has sometimes been found to *increase* intrinsic motivation, something that is likely to happen when the rewards are contingent on the *quality* of the performance as opposed to simply participating in an activity (Bates, 1979; Lepper, 1983). Extrinsic rewards are also likely to enhance intrinsic motivation when learning tasks are not very interesting (Morgan, 1984), or when the rewards are social, such as praise, rather than material (Deci, 1975). In each of these instances, extrinsic rewards are used to get the motivational machinery started, not to keep it going.

As discussed in Chapter 2, persons of all ages seek to satisfy a need for self-esteem and recognition. Extrinsic motivators, such as praise and words of encouragement, that are contingent on the quality of performance, or that are expressed when students are mired in what everyone agrees is a dull unit of study, can be a powerful form of recognition, a source of instant personal gratification that increases students' self-esteem. Consider the following two examples of how this works:

1. Ten-year-old Christopher is struggling with an assignment involving the conversion of fractions to decimals, something in which he is not very interested. The teacher wanders by and notices the *one* correct answer out of 10 problems and says: "Good work on this one, Chris. I bet if you look at the ones you missed, you'll see the idea involved." Chris beams and goes back to the task with renewed interest.
2. Fourteen-year-old Sandy is both feeling and looking very bored during a somewhat monotonous presentation about how various forms of city governments are run. Recognizing Sandy's lack of interest, the teacher asks Sandy what her opinion is about her own city's governmental structure. She replies with a thoughtful opinion. The teacher says, "I like the way you related your views to the current problems at city hall. It shows you've done some thinking about this." Sandy smiles inwardly and involves herself actively in the class.

Thus, two teachers helped two students to reinvolve themselves in class activities. Both students were recognized for what they did and for what was possible for them to achieve in the future; they were not punished for what they failed to do or for what was wrong with what they did. Recognition of this sort taps into the need for recognition and encouragement we all have, which can stir an interest and can lead to greater personal involvement. What might be boring becomes interesting when teachers pay as much attention to students as to a topic to be explored. When students feel important, the subject matter has a better chance of becoming important to them.

There are two working principles that we can extract from intrinsic versus extrinsic motivation research: (1) both types of motivation are important in the daily operations of classroom work; extrinsic motivators get things started when interest is lacking, and intrinsic motivation sustains learning itself; and (2) tangible rewards (e.g., gold stars, bonus points) are important extrinsic motivators, but a teacher's oral or written acknowledgments of a good job or fine effort are more likely to be incorporated in students' own feelings of satisfaction. This has the effect of encouraging the self-perpetuating energy behind intrinsic motivation.

8.4 How Has a Teacher Helped Your Intrinsic Motivation?

Can you think of some recent examples of instructors you've had and things that they have either said or written that have served to spark, or perhaps strengthen, your intrinsic interest in a particular subject area? What effect did the feedback have on your attitude about the class? About the topic? About the instructor? About yourself?

PRAISE AND CRITICISM: THEIR MOTIVATIONAL EFFECTS

Imagine that you have just had a class paper returned and at the end of it your instructor has written: "A really fine analysis of two teaching approaches. I like the way you translated the ideas of behaviorism and cognitive psychology into practical uses for classroom teachers. Keep up the good work." It is not difficult to see why you might puff with pride and feel a gush of enthusiasm. When appropriately and genuinely given, praise can be the sort of extrinsic validation that encourages the self-perpetuating intrinsic motivation we have just discussed.

As a general rule, praise is a more powerful motivator than criticism when trying to enhance students' work performances. For example, in Hurlock's (1925) early and now classic experiment to determine the relative effectiveness of praise and criticism, 100 fourth- and fifth-grade children were placed in four groups matched on the basis of intelligence and arithmetic skills. A 15-minute daily practice period in addition problems, which included tests, was given to the groups for five consecutive days. Members of group 1 were regularly praised for the quality of their work, were called by name, and were encouraged to improve. Those in group 2 were scolded for their errors, carelessness, and failure to improve. Group 3 was ignored; these students heard some of their classmates praised and others reproved, but they themselves went virtually unnoticed. Group 4, which acted as a control, was placed in a separate room and given no motivation.

At first, groups 1 (those praised) and 2 (those criticized) were stimulated to greater effort than either group 3 or 4. However, after the second day, group 2 declined markedly in achievement, while group 1 steadily and consistently continued to improve. Group 2, however, made greater gains than group 3 (those ignored) throughout the experiment. Apparently, being negatively criticized or being admonished is interpreted as signs of rejection, and is better than no recognition. (If you are thinking that what Hurlock did to the students in group 2 was fairly harsh, and perhaps even emotionally upsetting to some, you might be right. New ethical standards require that all researchers, in all fields, who use human subjects must meet ethical criteria designed to protect the participants from the possibility of psychological or physical damage. Hurlock probably could not have done his research—at least not in the way he did—in today's world.)

Caution: Students Respond Differently to Praise or Criticism

The effects of praise and criticism on motivation and learning are not as simple and clear-cut as Hurlock's (1925) results might indicate. Other research has indicated that the effects of praise and criticism are related to personality differences as well. For instance, students tend to respond to praise differently depending on whether they are more inclined to be introverted (i.e., quiet and shy) or extroverted (i.e., outgoing and confident) (Forlano and Axelrod, 1937; Leith and Davis, 1969; Thompson and Hunnicutt, 1944). The major conclusions drawn from these studies indicate the following:

1. When introverts and extroverts are grouped together (as in the case in all classrooms), either praise or criticism is more effective in increasing the work output of pupils than no external incentives. (Again, this is evidence that negative recognition is better than no recognition.)
2. If repeated often enough, praise increases the work output of introverts until it is significantly higher than that of introverts who are criticized or extroverts who are praised.
3. If repeated often enough, criticism increases the work output of extroverts until it is significantly higher than that of extroverts who are praised or introverts who are criticized.

Introverts tend to achieve a higher level of performance when praised, and extroverts tend to respond best when their work is more critically evaluated. The question is why. One reason might be the differing relationship styles of introverts and extroverts. Because the more introverted students relate best to their inner world of feelings and reflections, praise might be what helps them to relax their inhibitions and that encourages in them the necessary confidence to engage in more open, risk-taking behavior. Extroverted students, however, related best to the outer world of people and events and, apparently, are inclined to work harder when they feel that their relationship with the outside world is threatened by their subpar performance. When criticized, the extrovert student might think in a manner that says, "Wow, I'd better get busy and win back approval." A criticized introvert's thinking says, "Well, I blew it again. I guess the thing to do is for me to be quiet and take as few risks as possible."

8.5 What Is Your Style?

Would you say you are more introverted (i.e., quiet, inward, like being alone) or more extroverted (i.e., social, outgoing, enjoy being with others)? When you think about your personality style in relation to these two personality types, what resemblances do you see between the kind of person you are in relation to introversion and extroversion and your responsiveness to either praise or criticism from teachers? How closely do your personal experiences match those cited in the previously mentioned research?

We must be careful not to assume that there is a clear and obvious distinction in the reactions of introverted and extroverted students to praise and criticism. Behavior is never so simple that it can be reduced to black-and-white reactions. Although it seems to be generally true that introverts respond favorably to praise, some of the more introverted, quiet students might have a very healthy and positive self-concept of their academic ability, and are quiet not because they are fearful and need encouragement to draw them out, but because they are quietly confident and certain of themselves.

In research on another personality dimension (Lefcourt 1982; Lintner and Ducette, 1974), an *external locus of control* (i.e., an orientation directed toward the external world) tends to be more responsive to praise than students with an *internal locus of control* (i.e., an orientation directed inward). This is consistent with research by Witkin, Moore, Goodenough, and Cox (1977), who found that "field-independent" persons (i.e., those whose perceptions are organized from within) are less responsive to praise than "field-dependent" persons (i.e., those whose perceptions are strongly influenced by external circumstances).

Why should this be? It may well be that students—and people in general—who are more tuned into their own inner world of thoughts and feelings have less need for external validation. (The emphasis here is on *less*, as everyone has some need for praise and affirmation.) It may also be that when one is motivated internally, praise is more likely to be viewed as an intrusion or manipulation, or both.

Meaningful Praise Is Given Discriminately

Research related to the use of praise in classroom situations has made it clear that, in order to use praise and criticism wisely, we have to pay attention to how it affects individual students (Brophy and Good, 1986). You will find that some students respond eagerly to praise given for relatively minor accomplishments, and other students are motivated only by praise for genuinely noteworthy accomplishments related to their high ability. Research suggests that students of low socioeconomic status (SES) and low ability tend to respond positively to praise of all types because of their frequent encounters with failure (Ascione and Cole, 1977; Good, Ebmeir, and Beckerman, 1978). (So, too, do students in the first two or three grades of elementary school, who are still adult-oriented and looking for adult approval.) However, high SES students of high ability are less responsive to praise that is designed primarily to make them feel good because they already feel good. Praise that works best for better students is the type that is contingent on success and includes a credible connection between success and effort (not just ability). A struggling student might be satisfied to hear something such as, "You've worked very hard on this assignment, Tommy. I know you have the ability to do a good job." A high-achieving student is likely to respond favorably to a comment such as, "I have a feeling you can improve on this, Tammy. Work on developing this idea more fully."

In order for praise to have its greatest impact, there has to be the feeling that: (1) *it is not automatic and totally unconditional;* (2) *that not everyone receives it all the time;* (3) *that it fits the occasion;* and (4) *most importantly, that it fits the student.*

How Praise and Criticism Are Expressed Makes a Difference

The words used and the way they are expressed can make a big difference in whether a teacher's feedback is interpreted as praise or criticism by students (Anderson, White, and Wash, 1966). For example, a distinction should be made between constructive criticism given by a friendly teacher in a spirit of helpfulness ("That is an interesting idea, Helen, and one that is original. I wonder if you can think of some practical ways to fit it into the framework of our discussion.") and destructive put-downs—under the guise of constructive criticism—sometimes hurled at students by frustrated teachers ("Helen, that's an interesting idea, but frankly I don't see how it is relevant to our concerns."). Constructive criticism opens the door to further thinking by suggesting possibilities, and pointing to new directions. Destructive criticism closes the door to further thinking by reducing the idea and attacking the person.

This discussion reminds me of an experience in a class I had while a freshman in college. Although it might not seem a particularly significant event, at the time, it seemed so to me. I was not altogether confident of either myself or my abilities in the class. The professor was a man I admired immensely. He was a sensitive, warm, yet no-nonsense type who praised and criticized and approved and disapproved as the situation warranted. I was not one of the more vocal students in class, but I did contribute occasionally, although, I must admit, not fearlessly. I remember one class in particular in which, after I had made a contribution to the discussion, the professor commented on the insightfulness of my comment and patted my shoulder approvingly as he walked by my desk. I felt enormously good about that incident, and I distinctly remember having felt generally more confident about contributing after that day. Praise or approval can be communicated in many ways—not just orally. The instructor's brief pat on my shoulder is an example of how nonverbal approval can underscore and strengthen what words alone might not be able to accomplish. A nod, a smile, or merely stopping long enough to take a good look at what is being done, can express a worthwhile sentiment. There is a growing body of research to support what many people know intuitively and experientially, which is that a person's tone of voice, facial cues (Laird, 1984), and use of touch (Abramson, 1985; Older, 1982; Willison and Masson, 1986) can have a powerful effect on another's feelings about himself or herself, about others, and about their relationships.

The use of encouragement, which is a slightly shaded version of praise, is relevant here. Whereas praise underscores the worth of the task completed, encouragement focuses on a person's potential for completing that task. Praising statements, for example, might be on the order of, "You have done a fine job on that assignment," or "This is really a big improvement over last week's test." Encouraging statements might be, "Work hard on this assignment. I know you can do it," or "Pay close attention to this section of the book, and I bet you can make a big improvement on last week's test."

This distinction between praise and encouragement is important as we look for ways to help students encourage them, actually—to reach their individual potential.

8.6 How Powerful Are Touches and Smiles?

If so inclined, you can conduct some interesting "experiments" in the laboratory of your daily life. For example, make an effort to go through half of a day not smiling and not touching anyone. Don't hole up in your room, just withhold these nonverbal modes of communication. For the other half of the day, go out of your way to smile, and when it feels natural, use touch as another means of communication and contact. There are many variations of this suggestion. Do what feels comfortable to you. What differences, if any, do you notice in people's behavior? What are you learning about how your mode of communication affects relationships?

Among other things, effective praise is personal and specific. When Steve Kemp was an 11-year-old in Highland Park, California, and about to leave sixth-grade for junior high school, he asked his teacher to sign his autograph book. In it, his teacher wrote:

Steve—
This has been some year for me, looking at your mischievous smile every morning. You are a person who has learned to use his talents of scholarship, leadership, and sportsmanship. With these qualities I know you will lead a happy and successful life. You've been a good inspiration to many people. Never stop. Much luck in your new school with new-found friends and in your sports. I hope to read about you in the sports section of the paper in a few years. I'm very proud of you.

Mrs. Jamile

Steve Kemp did, indeed, end up on the sports pages, playing outfield in all-star fashion for three major league baseball clubs. That must have been a very meaningful note for him, because after all these years, he still has it among his prized possessions.

A characteristic of *personalized* feedback is that it is specific to a person. Note, for example, that Mrs. Jamile remembered Steve Kemp's "mischievous smile," not just any old smile. She pointed to specific talents—scholarship, leadership, and sportsmanship—not just to talents generally. Note, too, her very specific reference to his athletic skills, something he had evidently clearly established at that young age. When feedback is specific, it is more believable because students *know* teachers are talking *about* them and *to* them and not about everyone in general. Table 8.1 distinguishes between effective and ineffective praise.

Praise Is a Potent Motivator

Generally, praise is an all-purpose, motivational fuel. It helps some students in getting their motivational engines started, and it assists others in keeping them running smoothly. Research not only shows that more learning goes on when students are praised (Brophy and Good, 1986, Deci and Ryan, 1985; Koestner, Zuckerman, and Koestner, 1987), but also that the effects of being praised (or criticized) in one subject might transfer, in terms of impact on academic achievement, to one's performance in other subject areas (McMillan, 1976). If you receive kind words of praise from your psychology professor (or harsh words of criticism), it would not be surprising if this affected your perform-

Table 8.1. DISTINCTIONS BETWEEN EFFECTIVE AND INEFFECTIVE PRAISE

Praise that Tends to Be More Effective in Increasing Motivation and Enhancing Self-Concept	*Praise that Tends to Be Less Effective in Increasing Motivation and Enhancing Self-Concept*
1. Is given contingently (i.e., is linked to a particular accomplishment or task completion [e.g., "Nice going, Janice, you did just as required by the assignment"])	1. Is given randomly or indiscriminately (i.e., is not necessarily connected to particular task completion or accomplishment (e.g., general comment: "You always do good work, Janice")
2. Identifies the particulars of an accomplishment (e.g., "Well done, Randy, your spelling score improved by three points")	2. Tends to be restricted to global positive reactions (e.g., "Good job on the spelling test, class")
3. Reflects spontaneity, variety, and other signs of credibility; suggests clear attention to a student's accomplishment (e.g., teacher behaviors that are a mix of nonverbal approval behaviors—nods, smiles, touches—and statements that give immediate attention to a student's performance)	3. Shows a bland uniformity that suggests a conditioned response made with minimal attention to the student's accomplishment (e.g., teacher uses similar words, phrases, or gestures to praise performance regardless of what it was or who did it)

Continued

Table 8.1. *Continued*

Praise that Tends to Be More Effective in Increasing Motivation and Enhancing Self-Concept	*Praise that Tends to Be Less Effective in Increasing Motivation and Enhancing Self-Concept*
4. Rewards attainment of specified performance or effort criteria (e.g., "Excellent idea, Betty. I like the way you related it to our discussion")	4. Rewards mere participation, without consideration of performance processes or outcomes (e.g., "You really involved yourself in this discussion, Betty")
5. Gives information to students about their competence or the value of their accomplishments (e.g., "Your math skills have really improved, Debbie, and that will be very helpful to you in your next math class")	5. Either provides no information about competence at all or gives students information about their status (e.g., "You ranked about in the middle of the math test, Debbie")
6. Helps students to better appreciate both their thinking about problem solving and the work they invest (e.g., "I know you worked hard, Mary, and just look at the fine job you ended up with")	6. Encourages students to compare themselves with others in a competitive way (e.g., "You did not work as hard as Fran did, Mary, but I know you can do better if you do your homework like she does")
7. Uses student's prior performance as a measuring rod for describing present performance (e.g., "Good work, you have improved your score on each of the last two tests")	7. Uses the performance of peers as the measuring rod for describing student's present work (e.g., "Good work, you got 10 right—that's only two less than Billy and Sharon got")
8. Is given in recognition of a noteworthy effort or success at difficult (for *this* student) tasks (i.e., makes a point to give something a little extra to a particular student when something especially difficult has been tried or completed)	8. Is given without regard to the effort expended on the meaning of one accomplishment (i.e., although a particularly difficult task has been accomplished, teacher treats it as an ordinary accomplishment)
9. Attributes success to effort and ability, implying that similar successes can be expected in the future (e.g., "Great job, Tom. Your hard work and good thinking really shows here, as I'm sure it will on your next assignment")	9. Attributes success to ability alone or to external factors such as an easy task or luck (e.g., "Great job, Tom. Your brains really show on this project," or "Great job, Tom, you really had luck on your side this time")
10. Encourages intrinsic attribution—students believe that they expend effort on the task because they enjoy the task and/or want to develop new task-related skills (i.e., the kind of praise that says, in effect, "You are successful because you have it in your power to learn and to be good at something")	10. Encourages extrinsic attribution—students believe that they expend effort on the task for external reasons—to please the teacher, come in first, win an award, and so forth—(i.e., the kind of praise that says, in effect, "You've done a good job when you please me and/or finish ahead of the others")

From Brophy, J. "Teacher Praise: A Functional Analysis." *Review of Educational Research,* 1981, *51*: pp. 5–32.

ance in your English literature class for better or for worse, depending on what you had received.

A fact of school life is that not all students are motivated before they learn. This does not mean that they cannot become motivated *while* they learn. Both research and experience have shown that judicious and appropriate use of praise and constructive criticism can facilitate the learning process. Most of us cannot get enough compliments. Our egos are never so intact that a niche cannot be found in which to plug a little praise. However, praise, by its nature, is highly biodegradable and dissolves quickly after it is received, which is why each of us, no matter what our age or station in life, can always use more of it.

8.7 Try a Little Praise and See What Happens

For the next couple of days, make a deliberate effort to include honest praise as part of your daily interactions with various people. Try to zero in on things that people do or say that lend themselves to receiving genuine praise from you. If you're already the kind of person who praises a fair amount, make an effort to be very aware of how your praise affects people. You will want to pay particular attention to the ten characteristics of effective praise noted in Table 8.1. As you remain aware to the effects of praise, what are you learning?

Two other important variables related to motivational processes are the experiences of success and failure, which, like praise and criticism, can affect individual students in various ways.

THE EFFECTS OF SUCCESS AND FAILURE ON LEVEL OF ASPIRATION

A long time ago, the German psychologist Hoppe (1930) observed an aspect of behavior that each of us has undoubtedly seen in ourselves—the tendency to raise our goals after successes and to lower them after failures. By raising our aspirations upon meeting with success, we strive toward goals that are just a little higher, which promises growth in an upward direction. By lowering our aspirations following failure, we settle on goals that are more reachable, thereby helping us to avoid failure and experience some success. Of course, this does not always happen. Some persons continually set unrealistically high goals and inevitably fail, while still others set such low goals that they are unable to feel satisfaction from their accomplishments. There are any number of possible reasons for this, but the one most relevant to our discussion is the experience that people have had with success or failure in their lives.

A classic experiment conducted by Sears (1940) illustrates how this works, in this case with a population of elementary children. There were two groups of children, which included: (1) a "success" group, which had a consistent history of success in all academic subjects; (2) a "differential" group, consisting of youngsters with consistent records of success in reading, but with poor grades in mathematics. All of the children were given a series of twenty speed tests in reading and math. After the first trial, they were asked to estimate how long it would take them to do the next test. Then half of the children in each group were exposed to a "success condition" in which they were lavishly praised for their performance after most, but not all, of the remaining nineteen trials. The other half of the children in each group were exposed to a "failure condition" in which they were criticized for poor work after most, but not all, of the next nineteen trials. After each test, students were asked to estimate how long they thought it would take them to complete the next test.

It was found that one's experience with success or failure has a rather dramatic affect on level of aspiration. Students exposed to the failure condition showed much greater discrepancies between their estimated and actual performances than those in the success condition. They were also more variable in how they reacted; some tended to establish consistently lower goals, while others set impossibly high goals for themselves. Generally, students in group 1 (those with previous histories of academic success) were better able to cope with the experimental failures; their discrepancies and variability were less extreme. Interestingly, students with a previous history of failure, and who were in the success condition, also set realistic goals for themselves, although they had a tendency to predict that they would do better than they actually did.

Thus, this study, along with more current research (Bardwell, 1984; Haynes and Johnson, 1983) confirms Hoppe's (1930) ideas by underscoring the enormous effect that success and failure can have on aspirations. Success experiences tend to spur not just high, but realistic, aspirations about what is possible, irrespective of students' past history of success or failure. Conversely, repeated failure tends to cause students, particularly those with past histories of failure, to aspire to either unrealistically high, or dismally low, goals.

8.8 How Has Your Level of Aspiration Been Affected?

What experiences in your life can you think of that illustrate the effect of success or failure on your level of aspiration? In particular, what comes to mind when you think about this in relation to your academic experiences? How have your experiences with success and failure influenced your motivation and subsequent level of aspiration?

ATTRIBUTION THEORY: IMPLICATIONS FOR UNDERSTANDING MOTIVATION AND MOTIVATIONAL PROCESSES

Whether we succeed at something or fail at it, there is usually a need to understand why it happened. This is the role of attributions, which are basically efforts on the part of students—and people in general—to explain why certain life events happen the way they do. Weiner's (1979, 1984, 1990) work in attribution theory suggests that the four most commonly cited reasons that students use to explain why they did or did not do well on a task tend to include one or more of the following four possibilities: (1) ability, (2) effort, (3) task difficulty, or (4) luck. To explain a low grade on a biology test, for example, different students might make the following statements:

"I just don't understand how recessive genes are passed on." (Lack of ability)
"I didn't study near enough for that exam." (Lack of effort)
"That test was the hardest one yet." (Task difficulty)
"I made a lot of wrong guesses on the true–false part." (Lack of luck)

As you can see, each student attributes a different reason as the cause of not doing well. Weiner has observed that most of the causes to which students attribute their successes or failures occur in three different dimensions, which include (1) an internal or external dimension (inside or outside of the person), (2) a stable or unstable dimension (change or remain the same), and (3) a controllable or uncontrollable dimension (within the power of a person to control or not). For example, luck and task difficulty are seen as external to a person and uncontrollable because neither is anything that an individual can do anything about. Luck is viewed as unstable because it can change, but task difficulty is perceived as stable because the difficulty level is not likely to change. Table 8.2 provides an overview of the relationships found among the four attributions commonly used and the three dimensions in which each may fall.

Table 8.2. THE RELATIONSHIPS AMONG FOUR ATTRIBUTIONS AND THE THREE DIMENSIONS ON WHICH EACH MAY FALL

Focus of Attribution	*Locus of Control*	*Stability*	*Perceived Controllability*
Effort	Internal	Unstable	Controllable
Ability	Internal	Stable	Uncontrollable
Luck	External	Unstable	Uncontrollable
Task difficulty	External	Stable	Uncontrollable

Weiner has built a strong case for the idea that each of these three dimensions has important implications for understanding motivation. For example, the internal versus external dimension appears to be closely connected to feelings of self-esteem, pride, or confidence on the positive side, or feelings of guilt and shame on the negative side (Weiner, 1980). If, for instance, success or failure is attributed to internal factors (i.e., those things over which one has control), then success is likely to lead to pride and self-confidence, which will increase motivation. However, if failure is attributed to internal causes, then this could lead to feelings of anger and shame.

The stability dimension is tied closely to one's expectations about the future. If, for example, students attribute their success (or failure) to a stable factor such as ability, they are more likely to believe that they will probably succeed (or fail) on some similar task in the future. But if they attribute their performance to unstable factors such as effort or luck, they are likely to expect changes in the future when they have to perform similar tasks.

The control dimension is related to both future expectations and confidence. For example, a student who gets a good grade on a math exam and attributes that performance to controllable factors (e.g., careful thinking, effort), is likely to be proud of the accomplishment and to be more confident about taking future tests. However, if that student feels that the grade was largely the result of uncontrollable factors (e.g., a fluke, lucky guesses), then he or she is likely only to feel a deep sense of gratitude or perhaps to hope that the good fortune will continue.

How Attributions Affect Motivation

When students see themselves as basically capable people and attribute their failure experiences to lack of effort (i.e., an internal, controllable reason for their performance), they are usually in a good emotional position to determine strategies for doing better the next time. Motivation remains high, which is a positive, adaptive attitude that can lead to performing better, a sense of pride, and feelings of control (Ames, 1985).

The problems of motivation occur when students attribute their failures to causes that tend to be internal, stable, and uncontrollable. It is not surprising to find that students who feel like this rank high among the unmotivated. Apathetic resignation is a predictable reaction to failure if students believe that the causes are due to their own behavior (internal), are unlikely to change (stable), and are beyond their control to change for the better. To make motivational matters even worse for students like this, they are the very ones who do not seek help because they believe that there really is no way that they *could* be helped (Ames and Lau, 1982).

The Affect of Locus of Control on Attributions

A concept central to attribution theory is *locus of control* (Lefcourt, 1982; Rotter, 1990; Strickland, 1989). It is a concept that helps us understand why some students feel that they have more control over the events in their lives, or less, as the case may be. Students with an "internal locus of control" are those who believe that their school performance is due largely to their own efforts or abilities. Those with an "external locus of control" are more likely to believe that factors outside of themselves (e.g., luck, task difficulty, other people's actions) are responsible for how they perform in school. Basically, students with an *internal locus of control* will tend to explain (i.e., attribute) their school fortunes in terms of what *they* do, how *they* do, and how *they* are responsible, and students with an *external locus of control* will tend to explain their performance in terms of what *others* do and how *other* people, events, or circumstances are responsible for their successes or failures. Note that the differences between these two groups are in terms of what they *tend* to do. The differences are neither absolute nor malleable. There will always be times, for example, when students with a strong internal locus of control may blame the teacher for a poor test score or when students with a strong external locus of control will look within for an explanation of what happened on a test. The general tendency, however, will be for students with internal and external loci of control to explain their school performance in a manner consistent with their inner or outer orientation.

The locus of control idea has important implications for understanding the level of students' achievement and motivation. Research has shown, for example, that students with a high internal locus of control are likely to have better grades and test scores than do students of similar intelligence levels who are low in internal locus of control (Lefcourt, 1982; Messer, 1972; Nowicki, Duke, and Crouch, 1978). Still other research has shown that, next to ability level, locus of control is the most consistent predictor of a student's academic achievement (Brookover et al., 1979). The bottom line seems to be this: Students with an external locus of control—those who believe that doing well in school is due to luck, the teacher's whims, or other outside factors—are unlikely to be motivated to work hard. However, students with an internal locus of control—those who are convinced that success and failure are due primarily to their own efforts—are more apt to reflect the kind of motivation that leads to hard work and focused study. In reality, of course, how one performs in school is an outcome of both students' efforts and abilities (i.e., internal factors) and teacher behaviors, luck, and task difficulty (i.e., external factors). It is interesting to note that even in situations where success and failure have been rigged so that the outcomes are completely due to luck, students with a high internal locus of control will persist in believing that it was their own efforts that caused them to succeed or to fail (Lefcourt, 1982).

8.9 Do You Have an Internal or External Locus of Control?

What is your response to each of the following statements?

I more strongly believe that:

<A>	or	< B>	< A>	< B>
1. Promotions are earned through hard work and persistence.		Making a lot of money is largely a matter of getting the right breaks.		
2. I have noticed that there is usually a direct connection between how hard I study and the grades I get.		Many times the reactions of teachers seem haphazard to me.		
3. When I am right, I can convince others.		It is silly to think that one can really change another person's basic attitudes.		
4. I am the master of my fate.		A great deal that happens to me is probably a matter of chance.		

These are four items from a longer 29-item scale developed by Rotter (1966) for measuring the degree of a person's internal or external locus of control. Although a brief four-item scale will not allow you to arrive at any firm conclusions about yourself, they do give you an idea of the kind of thinking found to be associated with internal and external loci of control. The A column is for internal locus of control; the B column is for external locus of control.

How Attributions Affect Beliefs About Ability and Goal Setting

One of the most powerful attributions affecting motivation in school are students' beliefs about their abilities. These beliefs affect the goals students set for themselves, the attitudes they have about success and failure, and the motivational energy they are willing to invest in accomplishing their goals.

Adolescents and adults tend to use two basic views of ability. On the one hand, there is an *entity view,* which assumes that ability is an internal, stable, uncontrollable, personal possession. It is a characteristic that cannot be changed. One person may have more or less ability than another, but the amount each individual has is basically set. An *incremental view,* on the other hand, holds that ability is internal, but more unstable and controllable (Dweck and Bempechat, 1983). An incremental view is the more optimistic position because it offers the possibility that ability will be improved through practice, study, or hard work.

Through the early elementary grades, most students tend to believe almost exclusively in an incremental view of ability (Nicholls and Miller, 1984). That is, they tend to believe that smart people are those who try hard and that trying hard is what makes you smart. If you fail, this means you aren't smart *and* you didn't try hard. However, if you succeed, you must be a smart, hard worker (Stipek, 1993). Children are usually around 11 or 12 years old before they are able to differentiate among performance, ability, and effort. When they are able to see that differentiation, they see that someone who gets good grades without studying very hard must *really* be smart.

The kind of goals students set is strongly influenced by the kind of ability they attribute to themselves. Two broad categories of goals have been identified—*performance goals* and *learning goals* (Elliot and Dweck, 1988). Students oriented toward performance goals are concerned primarily about performance, an orientation that focuses their attention on how well they are doing in relation to others, on wanting to "look smart" and avoid seeming incompetent. In a sense, students in this category are more concerned with form than with substance. They tend to be very concerned about how they are being judged by others and are anxious to look good, hence the emphasis on performance. Students who orient their efforts toward learning goals seem to be different. Their primary motivation is to learn, to improve, and to increase their abilities and understandings no matter how many mistakes they make or how awkward they appear in the process. Table 8.3 provides an overview of the differences in perceptions and motivations between students with learning goals and those with performance goals.

It is instructive to note that students with an entity view of intelligence who lack confidence in their own abilities tend to set performance goals. They either set their goals so low that there is virtually no risk of failure or so high that no one, not even very bright students, could succeed. Although they are not able to take much credit for success when goals are low, they are able to avoid the stigma of failure, which they very much want to do. Even when they experience failure because their goals are unrealistically high, they are able to save face by pointing to how difficult the goals were and how few students achieved them.

Students with an incremental view of intelligence, however, tend to set learning goals and to look actively for ways to enhance their skills and understandings, since for them improvement is an indication of getting smarter.

8.10 How Would You Classify Your Goals?

When you think about your orientation to schooling and academic achievement, would you say that you are a person who leans primarily toward learning goals (primary emphasis on increasing competence) or toward performance goals (primary emphasis on avoiding failure and getting recognition)? If you were asked to explain how your goal orientation developed, how would you respond? How do your goals affect your motivation?

Table 8.3. DIFFERENCES IN PERCEPTIONS AFFECTING MOTIVATION BETWEEN STUDENTS WITH LEARNING GOALS AND THOSE WITH PERFORMANCE GOALS.

Student's Perceptions	*Those with Learning Goals*	*Those with Performance Goals*
Sees success as . . .	Improvement, progress	High normative performance, high grades
Places value on . . .	Effort/learning	Normatively high ability
Feels satisfaction when . . .	Working hard, feeling challenged	Doing better than others
Sees teacher oriented toward . . .	How students are learning	How students are performing
Views mistakes and errors as . . .	Part of learning	Anxiety-provoking
Focuses attention on . . .	Process of learning	Own performance compared to others'
Works hard in order to . . .	Learn something new	Out perform others, get high grades
Self-evaluation criteria tend to be . . .	Absolute, amount of progress	Normative, always compared to others

Adapted from Ames, C., and Archer, J. "Achievement Goals in the Classroom: Students' Learning Strategies and Motivation Processes." *Journal of Educational Psychology,* 1988, *80,* p. 261. Copyright 1988 by the American Psychological Association. Adapted by permission.

Self-Worth: The Link Between Attributions and Achievement Motivation

It is not surprising to find positive relationships among students' feelings of self-worth, their beliefs about ability, and their achievement motivation (Covington, 1984; Covington and Omelich, 1984, 1987). The work of Covington and his colleagues indicates that these factors are reflected in different ways by three types of students, who are described as *mastery-oriented, failure-avoiding,* and *failure-accepting.*

Mastery-oriented students have an incremental view of achievement, which allows them to see that ability can be improved, which, in turn, encourages them to set learning goals in order to increase their competencies. Because they are not fearful of failure, they are able to set moderately difficult goals and take the kind of risks that enable them to feel good about their successes and enhance their feelings of self-worth. In addition, they assume more of the responsibility for their own learning, something that is consistent with their inclination to attribute success to their own effort. As a package, behaviors of this sort usually lead to persistent, successful learning that is self-reinforcing (Alderman, 1985; Stipek, 1993).

Failure-avoiding students tend to embrace an entity view of ability and thus are more apt to set performance goals, which focus on looking good and avoiding failure. These students have a shaky sense of their own competence and self-worth and, as a consequence, take few risks to expand their intellect. Another group of students who fall into their group are those who have experienced some successes but also numerous failures. They tend to vacillate between working very diligently and working only cursorily, and between setting very low goals and setting unrealistically high goals. In a word, they are unpredictable.

Over time, failure-avoiding strategies, such as lack of effort, procrastination, inconsistent goal setting, and feeble excuses, are self-defeating and eventually lead to failure, which is what these students are trying to avoid. Students fitting this mold are the ones who give up and become, ultimately, *failure-accepting students,* inwardly convinced that their problems are due to lack of ability and that there is no hope of change.

Figure 8.1 provides you with an overview of the differences in motivations and attitudes between mastery-oriented and failure-oriented students. The focus of this discussion is the kind of overriding attitude that many students seem to have about school and their perceptions of probable success in academic matters. Some students carry with them a generalized attitude that enables them to feel reasonably confident about their academic possibilities. Others carry the more general feeling that they are not very capable in anything. Still others have a positive attitude about their abilities in some subject areas, but a negative attitude about their talents in other subject areas. Each student has his or her own blend of positive and negative self-perceptions, and some are decidedly more extreme than others. The ones we worry about the most are those who walk around with many negative attributions about themselves and their possibilities.

Strategies for Helping Students to Develop Positive Attributions

It is one thing to be aware of the fact that there are certain students who function as their own worst enemies because of their negative attitudes and self-defeating behaviors; it is another to know what to do about this when we see it. The following are suggestions that might help students to develop healthier attributions and to feel more motivated in school.

1. Simply telling students to "try harder" is not very effective. Students who are not doing well need to see evidence that effort on their part can pay off, that they can improve, and that their academic performance can change. Schunk (1982, 1985) has shown, for example, that when teachers show students the connection between past efforts and accomplishments in relation to current progress, students tend to perform at a higher level. It is as if they can actually see that effort *does* make a difference and so are inclined to try harder because there is evidence of a payoff. A way of helping

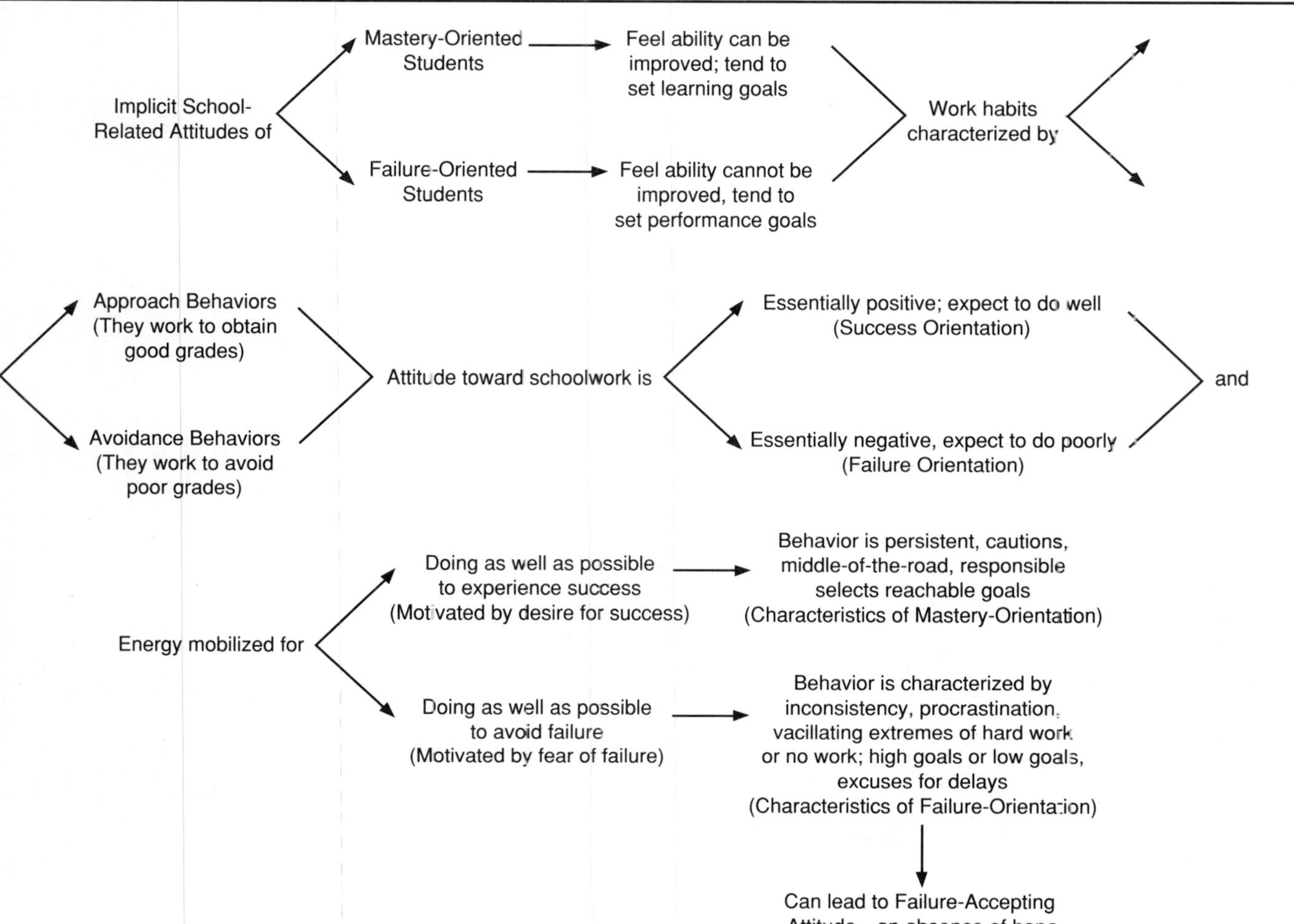

Figure 8.1. DIFFERENCES IN MOTIVATIONS AND ATTITUDES BETWEEN MASTERY-ORIENTED AND FAILURE-ORIENTED STUDENTS.

students see the evidence is to return work they have handed in with specific feedback for improvement and then to revise students' grades when improvements are made.

2. Remember that students' individual perceptions of success lie at the center of attribution theory and its variations. When effort is perceived as related to success and achievement, motivation increases. However, when students believe that lack of ability is the reason for failure and that ability is something over which they have no control, motivation decreases. A way to help students see that effort can make a difference is to praise students for effort as a personal characteristic rather than the effort itself. For example, it is preferable to say something like, "You are a really hard-working student, Tom" rather than, "The hard work you put in really shows." In the first case, we are praising the student, thereby emphasizing that Tom is in charge of the effort. In the second case, we are praising the effort and in a subtle way deemphasizing the control Tom had over the effort.

3. Deemphasize luck as a factor in students' achievement and emphasize ability as what really counts. The more students can see the tangible results of their efforts, the less likely they are to attribute their success to chance or luck. One of the best ways of doing this is by giving students tasks that allow them to succeed, and helping them to see that their successes are due to ability and working hard, not to luck.

4. Help failure-avoiding students to set realistic goals. This is such a simple and obvious strategy and yet it is easy to overlook. Frequently, students who do the poorest in school are the same ones who are likely to set unreachable goals for themselves. It is better to say to a student of moderate ability that you feel confident that his hard work will earn him a good grade (leaving it to him to determine what "good" is) than to tell him that you are sure he could get an A. Goals must be reasonable as well as reachable.

5. There is research to show that attributions *can* change—that students can alter their beliefs about what they can control in the world. A good example of this can be found in the results obtained by DeCharms (1984), who set up a special program to help inner-city elementary school children improve their achievement motivation. This program emphasized the idea of treating students as "origins" rather than as "pawns," which was part of an overall effort to help them think of themselves as "originals," masters of their own fate. Consistent with this idea, the students were taught to take responsibility for their behaviors, shown how to choose realistic goals, instructed how to achieve those goals, and so forth. Students who completed this program showed more substantial increases in achievement when compared to students who did not have this training; they had fewer absences; and, as shown in a follow-up

study, they were more likely than untrained students to graduate from high school.

Other studies have found that failure-accepting attitudes can be changed for the better by efforts on the part of teachers to communicate the idea that it is more likely to be lack of effort than lack of ability that leads to poor performance (Fosterling, 1985; McCombs, 1984). Similarly, Schunk (1983, 1985) found that students who received feedback from teachers suggesting that their past successes or failures were attributable to effort did better academically than students who received no feedback.

Thus, a powerful and effective way to help students develop and maintain positive self-attitudes so they can develop more of a mastery-level orientation is to communicate the idea that effort is something over which they have great control. In addition, it is important that students find out for themselves that effort *can* lead to improved performance and positive teacher feedback.

6. Help students feel worthwhile, adequate, and successful during the many interactions that occur daily. A verbal reward here, a positive comment there, a receptive and warm smile, and a friendly touch when it seems appropriate are ways of communicating the idea to a student that he or she is worthwhile and "successful" as a person. When students feel a sense of personal success, they are more likely to set realistic goals because they do not have to "prove" something to themselves (and others).

7. Prepare and assign tasks that have various levels of difficulty built into them. A fifth-grade teacher assigns book reports, but she is careful to assign somewhat easier books to students struggling with reading, and more difficult books to those with grade-level or advanced reading skills. This was not something publicly announced, but quietly done. Do not guarantee success (or the success will be meaningless), but look for ways to help make it possible.

8. Look for behaviors to praise, but make it honest praise. Give constructive criticism where, and when, necessary.

9. When dealing with high-achievement-motivation students, providing them with tasks and problems that offer opportunities for a mix of failure and success is most likely to sustain their high motivation. They need to be challenged, and will work hard when success is available, but not easily won.

10. When dealing with low-achievement-motivation students, providing them with tasks and problems that provide mainly successes, particularly during the early phases of new learning, is more likely to keep them interested. They usually have had more failures in their school experiences than most students, and need a lot of early success in new learning situations to feel confident enough to continue.

8.11 Remember the Teacher Who Made a Positive Difference?

> You may find it instructive to think back over your school history for a moment. Can you think of a teacher who had a big impact on you at a time when you really needed it? Do you recall how it changed your attitudes about yourself and possibly about school for the better? Do you see yourself being that kind of teacher?

SELF-ESTEEM: ITS EFFECTS ON SUCCESS AND FAILURE EXPECTATIONS

A general truism about human nature is that the ways in which any of us behaves or achieves is more or less consistent with how we see ourselves as individuals (Epstein, 1980; Hamachek, 1992; Strube and Roemmele, 1985). Just as some individuals develop success-oriented personalities and look for ways to succeed, there are others who develop failure-oriented personalities and find ways to do poorly (Covington, 1984; Reynolds, 1980). According to theories of self-consistency, persons who view themselves as failure types tend to reject their successes because these experiences "just do not fit" the way they see themselves. In a similar way, persons who view themselves as success types tend to reject their failures because, as in the case above, these experiences "just do not fit" the way they see themselves (Brim and Kagan, 1980; Lecky, 1945). There are, however, some instances in which the positive effects of an *unexpected* success (e.g., a smile of approval, a good grade, a pat on the back) can make even a failure type feel good. In other instances, however, no matter how good or unexpected the success, many failure-oriented persons will still reject outcomes that are inconsistent with their negative self-concepts.

The important question is this: What determines which experiences—success or failure—will be dominant over the other? In an effort to answer this question, psychologists have begun looking at how our feelings about ourselves influence our readiness to incorporate, or "believe," our successes or failures.

In one study, a team of researchers found that subjects with low self-esteem who resisted the researchers' attempts to lower their self-esteem further proceeded to participate even more vigorously in the experimental task (Pepitone et al., 1969). These were subjects who could easily be made to feel more negative about themselves. At the same time, another group of subjects with low self-esteem did not resist the researchers' efforts to lower self-esteem and behaved in a listless manner consistent with their negative self-images. Coopersmith (1967) found somewhat similar results in his discovery of two behavior patterns among boys with low self-esteem. In one group were boys who had low self-esteem but who were nonetheless held in high esteem by their peers and teachers. The overt behavior of these boys reflected high achievement and a strong desire for improvement. It was almost as if their low self-appraisal had put them in a state of hyperreadiness for praise and success.

Conversely, there was another group of boys who did not strive to achieve and, in fact, seemed to be locked into a self-perception of failure.

Self-esteem appears to have a strong affect on whether we "believe" a success or failure experience. The question remains: What determines what an individual believes? An interesting study by Marecek and Mattee (1972) might provide some answers. In their investigation, it was hypothesized that persons with low self-esteem might differ in the certainty of their self-appraisal and that, perhaps, certainty about a low self-appraisal is a critical factor in determining whether persons with low self-esteem will allow themselves to be buoyed by success or will reject it in favor of remaining consistent with their failure images. The thinking was that if we are *certain* about our self-esteem, we will be more likely to maintain the status quo. Conversely, if we are *uncertain* about our low self-appraisal, we might be more open to success experiences. If we are uncertain, it might suggest that we do not quite believe that our negative self-feelings stem from intrinsic, immutable qualities. Furthermore, this state of uncertain self-appraisal might leave those of us who are deprived of success "hungry" for success experiences that will help us reject our past failure experiences.

Self-Esteem Certainty: Effects on Motivation

To explore the relationship between self-esteem certainty and motivation, Marecek and Mattee (1972) examined the interplay of high and low self-esteem and high and low certainty of self-esteem in a study involving seventy-two college-age subjects. Those with high and low self-esteem were psychologically evaluated to determine the amount of certainty attached to their self-appraisal, and then asked to perform a task in which the outcome was either produced by their own effort or determined by chance. Halfway through the task, all individuals were led to believe that their performance to that point was highly successful. It was predicted that the subjects' reactions to success would depend not only on their self-appraisal, but also on the amount of certainty invested in that appraisal, and on the perceived self-responsibility for the success outcome. There were four groups, which consisted of those who were: (1) high in self-esteem and certain of it, (2) high in self-esteem and uncertain of it, (3) low in self-esteem and certain of it, and (4) low in self-esteem and uncertain of it. The following four key findings emerged from the data:

1. Persons high in self-esteem and certain of it were inclined to accept their successes whether the successes were self-determined or obtained by luck. In fact, they were even a bit blasé about it, probably because success experiences were neither strange to them nor inconsistent with their expectations. Their motivation for achievement, which was high initially, remained the same.

2. Persons high in self-esteem and uncertain of it were positively affected by success whether it was obtained by luck or by self-determined effort. In other words, they welcomed success because it enabled them to fortify their tenuous, high-status position, and because it substantiated their precarious, high self-appraisal.
3. Persons low in self-esteem and certain of it tended to reject their success experiences (in order to be consistent with their failure image), but were inclined to be positively affected and motivated by successes they saw as determined by luck or fate. Indeed, one of the interesting results of the study was that this group made the greatest improvement in its performance under the second half of the experimental conditions. This verifies an earlier study by Mattee (1971), in which he found that even persons with deeply rooted and chronically low self-esteem will enthusiastically embrace a successful outcome if they believe it has more to do with luck than with skill.
4. Persons low in self-esteem and uncertain of it tend to accept success no matter what form it takes, particularly because they are unconvinced of their low self-appraisals and are eager for any evidence to the contrary.

Teacher Behaviors that Build Students' Self-Esteem

It seems fairly clear that neither a success nor a failure experience by *itself* can explain the motivational consequences that follow it. We also have to consider the level and certainty of a student's self-esteem in order to encourage high motivation and greater risk-taking behavior. There are at least three implications for teaching practices that might be of some value in enhancing student motivation.

1. *High-self-esteem students must be challenged.* Confident high-self-esteem, high-need-achieving students not only want, and can tolerate, a higher level of intellectual and personal challenge, but in fact need to be more critically challenged and pushed in order to reach the upper limits of their abilities. Just as both average and somewhat marginal students need a teacher who will not push them too fast, too soon, so do above-average students need a teacher who does not indiscriminately praise everything they do. Sometimes, one of the finest compliments a teacher can give a student is to say something such as, "You know, Richard, I really think you can do better work than this." This is not something one would want to say to students who have tried their hardest and have given you their best efforts, but it might be an observation appropriately shared with students who are giving you less than their best efforts, and both you and they know it. Suggesting to students that they can probably improve their performance communicates two things: (1) that you have *faith* in their capacity to do better, and (2) that they have the *ability* to do better. Both elements can serve as strong motivators.

2. *Offer a variety of ways to achieve success.* Both students with low self-esteem and students with high self-esteem who are uncertain about their self-appraisals are inclined to respond favorably and eagerly to success experiences, whether they are gained through their own efforts or through a lucky break. In either case, a teacher can hardly go wrong by making success experiences, with various degrees of difficulty, as available as possible. For example, a high school English teacher I know is fond of giving daily, short quizzes on homework assignments. Some of these quizzes are exceptionally difficult, and only the very best students do well on them, and other quizzes are only moderately difficult, and most students do well on them. A third type of quiz he gives contains a range in difficulty, from the very easy to the very difficult question, so that each of his students can experience success at his or her level. Because practically all students have an opportunity to sample the fruits of success in his class, virtually all of the students who take his class enjoy being there and learn quite a bit about English.

3. *Short-circuit the "I can't" cycle with ample praise over time.* Probably one of the most important findings growing out of research dealing with certainty of self-esteem is the indication that we can interrupt the vicious cycle in which students with low self-esteem confirm their low self-images by: (1) avoiding experiences that might otherwise help them view themselves more positively; and (2) disbelieving their successes when they occur, thereby maintaining their low self-esteem. Remember that even students certain of their low self-esteem respond favorably to success if they can believe their own ability did not have too much to do with it. Although it might sound strange, some people really do find it difficult to believe that whatever successes they have are due to their ability or intelligence. Usually, they have had many failures in the past and/or they have been made to *feel* like failures. Either way, success is difficult for them to handle because they are not used to it and do not know how to handle it, and because it establishes a precedent that they fear they might not be able to live up to. This processing is done largely at an unconscious level. It is not very often that we hear anyone admit that he or she is a failure-oriented person. The feeling might not be there in words, but it is there in behavior. It is a deeply buried attitude that takes time to change.

As teachers, we can encourage this change in many ways. We can praise the student with low self-esteem publicly, being careful not to overdo it and thereby reduce our credibility (e.g., "That's an interesting idea, Betty. I hadn't thought of it that way before."). We can look for strengths to comment on in papers and examinations (e.g., "This is a well-expressed paragraph, Joe." "You did well on this part of the exam, Sue."). We can also be sensitive to experiences the student with low self-esteem might have outside of the classroom, whether on the playground or in extracurricular activities (e.g., "You can really sock that ball, Bill.", "I hear you had an interesting idea for the Science Club fair, Joan. I'm sure you must be pleased."). It does not matter that students with low self-esteem might initially deny any credit for a successful effort. The point is that over a long enough period, encouraging feedback might help them develop self-appraisals that are slightly more positive, thereby making greater degrees of personal credit for success acceptable to them.

As soon as such a positive, escalating cycle is initiated, we can, I think, reasonably assume that self-esteem will be enhanced gradually until students are able to evaluate themselves at least a bit more positively. Nothing succeeds like success, and understanding the subtle dynamics between one's self-esteem and the acceptance of success experiences can help us to assist students to both maintain and enhance their motivation for learning and achievement.

8.12 What a Teacher Says Can Have a Big Impact

> About three weeks before my doctoral comprehensive exams, I expressed my considerable apprehension about those exams to my advisor. His response was, "You know, Don, when you pass those exams you will look back and wonder why you worried so much." I heard basically one word. He did not say *if,* but *when,* which I readily interpreted as meaning he believed I could do it. I felt not only more motivated, but also 10 feet taller. After all these years I still remember the interaction. Have you ever had an experience in which a teacher's feedback gave you new hope and renewed energy?

COMPETITION AND COOPERATION: EFFECTS ON MOTIVATION

By definition, *competition* refers to a contest between rivals, *Webster's* dictionary says, "as if for a prize." *Cooperation,* however, refers to an association with another, or others, for mutual, or common, benefit.

Some people say that competitive approaches bring out the best in students, and others champion cooperative approaches. Johnson and Johnson (1994) have noted that "myths" have developed about the virtues of competition and the evils of cooperation. Five common myths about competitive approaches are expressed in the following:

1. Our society is highly competitive, and students must be educated to succeed in a "survival of the fittest" world.
2. Achievement, success, outstanding performance, superhuman effort, the rise of the great leader, drive, ambition, and motivation depend on competing with others.
3. Competition builds character and toughens the young for life in the real world.
4. Students prefer competitive situations.
5. Competition builds self-confidence and self-esteem.

Six myths about the alleged evils of cooperative approaches could be expressed in the following ways:

1. When cooperation is used, students work together, and the student who wants to work by himself or herself is forbidden to do so.
2. Cooperation among students will enslave the gifted while giving the less gifted a "free lunch."
3. Students who do not contribute to the group's work, or who in some way reduce the group's performance, will be punished.
4. Many students will (through apathy) do no work, learn nothing, and yet receive the benefits of the work of other students.
5. Cooperative goal structures will result in students' doing the things they are good at and never working on skills and knowledge that are difficult for them.
6. If students work together cooperatively they will lose their individual identities because the group will force them to conform to its standards.

8.13 Competition or Cooperation? Which Do You Prefer?

How do you feel about being in competitive situations? Do you find yourself doing better in those circumstances, or do you become tense and do less than your best? If you had your choice between working with a group where everyone received the same grade (a common group grade), or working by yourself competing against others, which would you choose? Why? What does your choice suggest about how you view cooperative and competitive motivational techniques as a teacher?

What works best as a motivational strategy in classroom situations—competitive situations or cooperative efforts? Let's turn our attention to what research says about this.

Competition as a Motivational Strategy

Competition can add excitement and incentive to almost any activity you can imagine—a tennis match, football game, hog-calling contest, or classroom exam. It can be either individual (i.e., each person competes against everyone else) or group (i.e., people are divided into competing teams) competition. Ordinarily, classroom competition revolves around test scores, grades, or other performance measures. It is also possible to add competitive features to ordinary instruction by including activities such as debates, simulation games, or argumentative essays (Keller, 1992).

It is difficult—in fact, almost impossible—to find anything in the educational or psychological literature that applauds the virtues of competition as a motivator. Although competition creates winners, it also creates losers (many more losers, proportionately, than winners), which is why it creates so many problems in schools. Students whose test scores rank near the bottom on a test can suffer at least temporary embarrassment or even humiliation, and those whose grades are *consistently* near the bottom can experience more permanent losses in confidence, self-concept, and certainly any zest they might have for learning (Ames, 1984).

This is not a plea for discarding competitive elements altogether. Schools must prepare students to live (and compete) in the real world. Even if we tried, it would not be possible to eliminate competition in classroom settings. It is, however, possible to use our awareness of the effects of competition so that we can use it constructively and avoid its destructive features.

Examples of Destructive Competition

Dealing wisely with individual differences means, first, recognizing the destructive effects of competition when it is misused. Examples of destructive competition are numerous; the following are three true instances to descirbe this type of competition.

1. A fifth-grade science teacher has each of her thirty-one students read his or her most recent test score aloud in class so that she can record that score and its corresponding grade in her grading book. On top of that, she announces out loud the grade equivalent of each score. This is very rewarding for the top students and very sad (and punishing) for lower students. This is destructive competition at its worst, because if you did not do well, the whole class knows.

2. A high school history teacher posts the grades of his exams by name, score, and letter grade on his classroom door, which, as he says, "lets the kids know how they're doing and gets the low scorers off their fannies." This might be fine in some cases, but what of the low scorers who did the best they could? Besides, why should one's performance in history class become a topic of invidious comparison and idle social conversation, particularly among high school students who are not particularly noted for merciful judgments of one another?

3. A junior high English instructor hands back both exams and term papers in chronological grade order, announces the grade associated with each new grade category, and then calls students one at a time to retrieve their papers. Again, this is a primitive reward–punishment system in action.

Approaches such as the above are destructive for the following reasons:

1. Learning is deemphasized because the primary goal is to be better than others. Thus, learning is seen as a means to an end, not as an end in itself.

2. Only a few students can feel satisfied and rewarded. Public disapproval or failure is often worse than that experienced privately because now students

have to be concerned not only about their lack of performance, but their possible loss of approval and acceptance as well. It is difficult enough to improve one's effort without having his or her social image to worry about, too.

3. When performance is consistently reported in terms of relative position, what frequently happens is that, for many students, quality deteriorates, experimentation and risk taking decrease because of the fear of failure, and general improvement is discouraged. Remember, there can be little, if any, improvement if we do not try, and experience some success in doing, those things we thought we could not do.

Examples of Constructive Competition

The very nature of competition means that someone wins and someone loses. There are, however, ways of reducing the sting of losing without diluting the healthy features of competition. Consider the following examples:

1. Encourage each student to compete against himself or herself as much as possible. On a term paper a teacher might write, "Pretty good work here, Chuck. Perhaps next time you can write a stronger concluding statement." Another teacher might write on a C+ exam, "This is not at all bad, Cindy. I'm pleased with your effort. Let's see if you can top this next time." In these instances, we are not requested to match the record of the brightest student in class, but challenged only to beat our own previous performance. True, both the term paper and the exam were graded competitively against the entire class, *but the emphasis in each case was on the student's topping himself or herself.* That is the difference.

2. Keep grades confidential. The implications of this should be self-evident. How students do at any level is their own business. It should be their choice to divulge grades, not the teacher's.

3. Try to give every student a chance for success by arranging situations and recognizing experiences in which students of various abilities can be acknowledged for their best efforts. For example, put up examples of not just the best ideas for or contents in papers but the *neatest* papers and the *best organized* papers. In addition, a teacher could make a special effort to recognize behavior such as punctuality and dependability and to give special acknowledgment for skill in arts and crafts, special interests, music, and hobbies. If students know for sure that there are some things they can do well, and they themselves are appreciated, the things they *cannot* do as well might not be as forbidding.

A fourth-grade teacher I know has a knack for turning otherwise dull class activities into interesting games in which all students have a chance to experience success. One such game is called *Spelling Baseball,* which is done very simply be dividing the class into two, approximately equal, teams and "pitching" each player a spelling word. Each time a player spells a word correctly, his or her team is awarded a base. Four bases equal one run, and each misspelled word is an out. No team member is ever eliminated, and the pressure is reduced considerably. If a particular student makes too many outs, the teacher simply feeds him or her a slow ball in the form of an easy word at his or her next time at bat. Also, the teacher uses a new arrangement of players for each game to minimize the possibility of intense team rivalries. There are no prizes for winning—just the score and whatever naturally good feeling might accompany it. The students love the game, and the teacher has fun, too.

Another thing that can be done is to arrange simulated quiz programs, which are usually conducted during times when material is being reviewed for an examination. Again, equal sides are chosen and each side gets so many points for a right answer given to the teacher, or "the quizmaster," as he or she is called. Students who are a bit slower are asked somewhat easier questions so that, again, everyone has an opportunity for success. A variation of both games is to have groups of at least three students work together so that each "team" is actually composed of four groups of three students. Thus, within a modified competitive framework, students can also have the experience of cooperating.

Competition is here to stay: Watch any group of children of any age and you have an idea of how quickly and easily a competitive element is added to their activities. There are two important differences, however, between the recreational competition that emerges naturally in social interactions and the competition that is embedded in many classroom activities: (1) in their own competitive activities, the youths involved can choose whether they want to be a part of it; and (2) if they do choose to be a part of it, they can get out at any time.

In sum, when thinking about using competitive elements in our classrooms, we need to be aware of the risks, and keep them to a minimum by making sure that everyone has a fair chance of winning, that attention is focused on the task efforts rather than on performance comparisons, and that, in general, the emphasis is on the positive outcomes, not the negative consequences (e.g., those finishing near the top are congratulated but those finishing further down the list are not criticized, and the accomplishments of the class as a whole, not just the high performers, are recognized).

8.14 What Are Your Experiences with Classroom Competition?

What are some examples of destructive and constructive classroom competition that you've experienced? What effects—for better or worse—did they have on you?

There are three types of goal structures (i.e., ways in which students relate to one another and to the teacher during the learning process) within which teachers can work (Johnson and Johnson, 1994):

1. *Individualistic*—one student's achievement of a goal is unrelated to other students' achievement of the goal (e.g., working individually on a specific area of weakness with the individual's grade based on his or her own progress)
2. *Competitive*—students work against one another to achieve goals that only a few can attain
3. *Cooperative*—students work together toward each shared goal

Table 8.4 describes the interaction differences among group members in each of these types of goal structures. Notice how much more interaction,

Table 8.4. INTERACTION AMONG GROUP MEMBERS IN THREE TYPES OF GOAL STRUCTURE

Cooperative	*Competitive*	*Individualistic*
High interaction	Low interaction	No interaction
Effective communication and information exchange	Misleading or threatening, communication and information exchange, or none at all	No interaction
Facilitation of others' productivity; helping and sharing	Obstruction of others' productivity	No interaction
Peer influence toward productivity	Peer influence against productivity	No interaction
High utilization of other members' resources	Low utilization of others' resources	No interaction
High divergent and risk-taking thinking	Low divergent and risk-taking thinking	No interaction
High emotional involvement in and commitment to productivity by all members	High emotional involvement in and commitment to productivity by the few members who have a chance to win	No interaction
High acceptance and support among members	Low acceptance and support among members	No interaction
High trust among members	Low trust among members	No interaction
Problem-solving conflict management	Win-or-lose conflict management	No interaction
Division of labor possible	Division of labor impossible	No interaction
Decreased fear of failure	Increased fear of failure	No interaction

Adapted from Johnson, D. W., and Johnson, F. P., *Joining Together: Group Theory and Group Skills.* 2nd ed. Englewood Cliffs, NJ: Prentice Hall, 1982.

mutual help, trust, and decreased fear of failure there is among those in cooperative groups. These conditions, among others, are some of the reasons research comparing cooperative, competitive, and individualized learning so overwhelmingly leads many to favor cooperative learning modes. Sharing mutual goals in a psychologically supportive framework seems to give students in cooperative modes more energy for assimilating new information because there is less need to protect their egos. Does this mean we should throw out competitive features altogether? Not at all, as we shall see.

Cooperative Learning Approaches: Some Examples

One popular approach to cooperative learning, called the *Learning Together* model, was developed by Johnson and Johnson (1985). It is an approach in which students work together in four- or five-member heterogeneous groups on assignment sheets. The idea is to have students of various abilities, races and ethnicities, as well as both sexes, work together. Each group hands in a single, cooperatively produced assignment and is praised (i.e., rewarded) for its performance and for working well together.

There is also a model called *Group Investigation* developed by Sharan and his colleagues (1984), in which students form their own two- to six-member groups to work together using cooperative inquiry, group discussion, and cooperative planning and projects. Subtopics of a larger unit are taken by each group. Eventually, each group presents its findings to the entire class and is evaluated on the quality of its report.

Another approach is known as *Teams-Games-Tournament* (DeVries, Slavin, and Fennessey, 1980), which is a format that calls for students to work together in four- to five-member heterogeneously grouped teams to help one another learn the material and to prepare for competitions against other teams. For the tournaments, students are assigned to three-person tables consisting of students from other teams who are similar in achievement. Each table then competes at academic games covering the content taught that week and practiced during team meetings. This simplified description of the *Teams-Games-Tournament* concept illustrates how both cooperation *and* competition can be part of the process.

Advantages and Disadvantages Associated with Competition and Cooperation

Cooperative and competitive conditions involve at least two aspects: (1) the motivational factor, or the individual's need to achieve under the two conditions; and (2) the procedural factor, or the relative effectiveness of either one or the other in the attainment of goals. In addition, the nature of the task to be accomplished will often determine whether competition or cooperation will be most effective. Cooperative efforts are particularly appropriate for tasks in which collective effort is an important prerequisite to solving a particular problem (Johnson and Johnson, 1994).

However, some research indicates that cooperation can be superior to cooperative approaches when a task is relatively simple (e.g., adding or subtracting), or when sheer quantity of work is derived on a mechanized or skill-oriented task that requires little, if any, help from another person (e.g., cutting blocks of wood in a shop class, mixing chemicals in a chemistry lab, learning specific physical skills in a physical education class) (Michaels, 1977; Okun and DiVesta, 1975).

In addition, Sharan and Sharan's (1989/90) and Slavin's (1987, 1990) analyses of studies related to cooperative approaches suggest that when learning goals are interpersonally oriented, such as increasing mutual concern among students or developing positive race relations in desegregated schools, cooperative strategies, either on a one-to-one or small-groups basis, work best. Students probably would not learn much about empathy or positive race relations if they were competing with one another for the highest scores on tests designed simply to test their knowledge of empathy or ethnic group differences. Similarly, other research indicates that when tasks are more complex (e.g., solving story math problems or recalling specific information such as names and dates), cooperation results in higher achievement than does competition (DeVries and Edwards, 1974).

Conversely, research data indicate that students might be more motivated to perform at a higher level under competitive circumstances. Clifford (1972), for example, demonstrated this in her experiment in which fifth-grade students were placed into three groups and then given a vocabulary test. The two groups that competed for a reward—one to win candy and the other to be the leaders in a game—performed better than the group that was not competing for any reward. (Note that *groups* were competing, which is a safer form of competition, because no *one* person has to lose; losing, like winning, can be shared.)

Although students might sometimes perform at a higher level under competitive circumstances, Johnson and Johnson (1994) found that high levels of anxiety (too much of which can interfere with performance) are much more likely to be associated with competitive classes than with those that are more cooperatively structured.

Torrance (1965) reported that competition is effective in the stimulation of creative thinking. He notes, for example, a "fairly consistent tendency" for students performing creative thinking tasks under competitive conditions to excel more than those who work in a noncompetitive situation, with the former producing a much larger number and a greater flexibility of responses. This is further supported by research whose findings suggested that group members were more highly motivated and more productive under both individual and intergroup competition than in a purely cooperative condition in which individuals cooperated without their group competing with other groups (Julian and Perry, 1967).

Sometimes, cooperative approaches seem better motivators, while at other times, competitive strategies work best. *Both* cooperative and competitive approaches can enhance motivation and, in some instances, raise achievement in particular subjects. It is not as if one approach is all right and the other is all wrong. It depends on when each is used and for what purpose.

Implications for Teachers

One's feelings about the effects of competitive and cooperative teaching and learning strategies are probably related to each individual's personal experiences in those situations. This is both inevitable and normal. However, rather than impose our own personal preferences, it is important that we keep our students in mind. Some students need, and want, a competitive atmosphere in order to do their best. Still others need the more relaxed climate that cooperative activities provide. In any classroom, there rightfully should be a place and an opportunity for both types of activities, but not one to the exclusion of the other. Both have a place, and just because we might not have had the experience of performing very well under competitive circumstances, this is no reason to stereotype all competitive activities as bad. Conversely, just because we might have had the experience of doing well under competitive conditions and, in fact, reached peak performances, does not mean that competition does that for all people. Competitive approaches, like cooperative methods, can be positive or negative motivators depending on how they are used. It is a balance we seek.

EPILOGUE

Just as there is more than one way for learning to occur, there is more than one way to stimulate and enhance student motivation. Some students, we know, are driven by strong inner drives to learn and achieve, and others function best when working for reasons or goals that are outside, or extrinsic to, their inner states. Some students are spurred on by praise and other expressions of positive reinforcement; others work hardest when their work is more critically appraised.

Students who experience more successes than failures in their school histories are more likely to set reasonable, reachable goals and to be among those students who are motivated to do well. As a group, they have been referred to as *mastery-oriented students* because they see ability as something that can be improved, a belief that enables them to take more responsibility for their own learning.

Students who experience excessive failure tend to be unpredictable. Referred to as *failure-avoiding students,* their motivation is to avoid failure, which translates into behavior that vacillates between working hard and working hardly at all, and setting very low or unrealistically high goals. Failure-avoiding students are inclined to credit whatever successes they have to external factors, such as luck, fate, or an easy exam; success-oriented students are more likely to credit their successes to internal factors, such as ability and effort.

Self-esteem is an important personal variable in considering the relative impact of a success or failure experience on a student's motivation. Not only is self-esteem important, so, too, is the "certainty" of a student's beliefs about his or her high or low self esteem.

The merits of a competitive over a cooperative, or vice versa, classroom are part of an ongoing debate; proponents of each see value and worth in their respective approach. Because learning occurs in so many ways for so many types of students, there is a place and purpose for each process in the classroom at every level.

It is not easy to assess the degree to which students are motivated. Classrooms are not neatly divided into the sleepers and the hand wavers. Sometimes, the most involved students are the ones who say hardly a word, but who, in actuality, are engrossed in ideas and thoughts related to what is happening. They are not unmotivated, but merely quiet. Involvement and detachment are not permanent conditions. More accurately, they are fleeting psychological states that can, and often do, come and go in a twinkling of an eye. The girl who was furiously waving her hand a few minutes ago is now daydreaming as she looks out the window. The bored-looking boy is now the one actively engaged in class discussion. The ceiling gazer is now looking directly at the teacher with an expression of interest. And so it goes. The kaleidoscope of motivational postures is in constant flux. Wise teachers realize that the best way to keep students interested and motivated is to praise liberally, but selectively and contingently, and to be well prepared for, and enthusiastic about, their teaching.

In summary, classroom motivation and human learning is a three-dimensional process that includes the content at hand, the student, and the teacher. Each plays a part. Motivating students is not a gift reserved only for the super teacher with built-in charisma; it is, rather, the consequence of hard work, careful planning, and a deep concern for the ultimate expression of growth potential in each student.

STUDY AND REVIEW QUESTIONS

1. Why is it important for teachers to understand (and appreciate) the idea that students are never unmotivated?
2. What is the difference between intrinsic and extrinsic motivation? Can you give examples of each?
3. As teachers, why should we use extrinsic motivators cautiously?
4. Can you explain why extrinsic motivators can sometimes shut down intrinsic motivation?

5. Why is it that praise given contingently is more effective than praise given indiscriminately?
6. What is one of the basic differences between effective and ineffective praise?
7. Repeated failure is associated with setting levels of aspiration that are either unrealistically high or dismally low. Can you explain why this sometimes happens?
8. Can you explain why students with an incremental view of intelligence are more likely to set performance goals than learning goals?
9. Why are students with an external locus of control less likely to be motivated to work in school than those with an internal locus of control?
10. How does attribution theory help us understand students' motivations?
11. Explain how high or low self-esteem certainty affects motivation.
12. What can teachers do to raise self-esteem?
13. What are the major problems associated with using competition as a motivational strategy?
14. What advantages are connected with using both competitive and cooperative learning modes as motivational tools?

REFERENCES

Abramson, D. M. "Therapeutic Touch." *New Age,* 1985, June, pp. 43–47.

Alderman, M. K. "Achievement Motivation and the Preservice Teacher." In M. Alderman and M. Cohen (Eds.) *Motivation Theory and Practice for Preservice Teachers.* Washington, DC: Eric Clearinghouse on Teacher Education, 1985.

Ames, C. "Attributions and Cognition in Motivation Theory." In M. Alderman and M. Cohen (Eds.), *Motivation Theory and Practice for Preservice Teachers.* Washington, DC: Eric Clearinghouse on Teacher Education, 1985.

Ames, C. "Competitive, Cooperative, and Individualistic Goal Structures: A Cognitive-Motivational Analysis." In R. Ames and C. Ames (Eds.), *Research on Motivation in Education. Vol. 1: Student Motivation.* New York: Academic Press, 1984.

Ames, R., and Archer, J. "Achievement Goals in the Classroom: Students' Learning Strategies and Motivation Processes." *Journal of Educational Psychology,* 1988, *80,* p. 261.

Ames, R., and Lau, S. "An Attributional Analysis of Student-Help-Seeking in Academic Settings." *Journal of Educational Psychology,* 1982, *74,* pp. 414–423.

Anderson, H. E., White, W. F.., and Wash, J. A. "Generalized Effects of Praise and Reproof." *Journal of Educational Psychology,* 1966, *57,* pp. 619–173.

Ascione, F., and Cole, P. "Are Nurturance and the Satiation of Social Reinforcers Equivalent Operations?" *Journal of Psychology,* 1977, *96,* pp. 223–233.

Atkinson, J. W. and Raynor, J. O. *Personality, Motivation, and Achievement.* Washington, DC: Hemisphere, 1978.

Bardwell, R. "The Development and Motivational Function of Expectations." *American Educational Research Journal,* 1984, *21,* pp. 461–472.

Bates, J. A. "Extrinsic Reward and Intrinsic Motivation: A Review with Implications for the Classroom." *Review of Educational Research,* 1979, *19,* pp. 557–576.

Brim, O. G., and Kagan, N. (Eds.). *Constancy and Change in Human Development.* Cambridge, MA: Harvard University Press, 1980.

Brookover, W., et al. *School Social Systems and Student Achievement.* New York: Praeger, 1979.

Brophy, J., and Good, T. "Teacher Behavior and Student Achievement." In M. Wittrock (Ed.), *Handbook of Research on Teaching.* New York: Macmillan, 1986.

Brophy, J. "Teacher Praise: A Functional Analysis." *Review of Educational Research,* 1981, *51,* pp. 5–32.

Clifford, M. M. "Effects of Competition as a Motivational Technique in the Classroom." *American Educational Research Journal,* 1972, *9,* pp. 123–137.

Condry, J., and Chambers, J. "Intrinsic Motivation and the Process of Learning." In M. Lepper and D. Greene (Eds.), *The Hidden Cost of Reward: New Perspectives on the Psychology of Human Motivation.* Hillsdale, NJ: Lawrence Erlbaum, 1978.

Coopersmith, S. *The Antecedents of Self-Esteem.* San Francisco, CA: Freeman, 1967.

Covington, M. V. "The Self-Worth Theory of Achievement Motivation: Findings and Implications." *Elementary School Journal,* 1984, *85,* pp. 5–20.

Covington, M. V., and Omelich, C. L. "An Empirical Examination of Weiner's Critique of Attribution Research." *Journal of Educational Psychology,* 1984, *76,* pp. 1214–1225.

Covington, M. V., and Omelich, C. L. "I Knew It Cold Before the Exam: A Test of the Anxiety-Blocking Hypothesis." *Journal of Educational Psychology,* 1987, *79,* pp. 393–400.

DeCharms, R. "Motivation Enhancement in Educational Settings." In R. Ames and C. Ames (Eds.), *Research on Motivation in Education.* New York: Plenum, 1984.

Deci, E. L. *Intrinsic Motivation.* New York: Plenum, 1975.

Deci, E., and Ryan, R. *Intrinsic Motivation and Self-Determination in Human Behavior.* New York: Plenum, 1985.

DeVries, D. L., and Edwards, K. J. *Cooperation in the Classroom: Towards a Theory of Alternative Reward-Task Classroom Structures.* Paper presented at the annual meeting of the American Educational Research Association, Chicago, 1974.

DeVries, D. L., Slavin, R. E., and Fennessey, G. M. *Team-Games-Tournament: The Team Learning Approach.* Englewood Cliffs, NJ: Educational Technology Publications, 1980.

Dweck, C. S., and Bempechat, J. "Children's Theories of Intelligence: Consequences for Learning." In S. Paris, G. Olson, and H. Stevenson (Eds.), *Learning and Motivation in the Classroom.* Hillsdale, NJ: Erlbaum, 1983.

Elliot, E. S., and Dweck, C. S. "Goals: An Approach to Motivation and Achievement." *Journal of Personality and Social Psychology,* 1988, *54,* pp. 5–12.

Epstein, S. "The Self-Concept: A Review and the Proposal of an Integrated Theory of Personality." In E. Staub (Ed.), *Personality: Basic Concepts and Current Research.* Englewood Cliffs, NJ: Prentice Hall, 1980.

Flanagan, J. C. "Education: How and for What." *American Psychologist,* 1973, *28,* pp. 551–556.

Forlano, G., and Axelrod, H. C. "The Effect of Repeated Praise or Blame on the Performance of Introverts & Extroverts." *Journal of Educational Psychology,* 1937, *28,* pp. 92–100.

Fosterling, F. "Attribution Retraining: A Review." *Psychological Bulletin,* 1985, *98,* pp. 495–512.

Good, T., Ebmeir, H., and Beckerman, T. "Teaching Mathematics in High and Low SES Classrooms: An Empirical Comparison." *Journal of Teacher Education,* 1978, *29,* pp. 85–90.

Hamachek, D. *Encounters with the Self,* 4th ed. Fort Worth: Harcourt Brace Jovanovich, 1992.

Haynes, N. M., and Johnson, S. "Self-and Teacher-Expectancy Effects on Academic Performance of College Students Enrolled in an Academic Reinforcement Program." *American Educational Research Journal,* 1983, *20,* pp. 511–516.

Hoppe, F. "Erfolg and Misserfolg." *Psychologische Forschung,* 1930, *14,* pp. 1–62.

Hurlock, E. B. "An Evaluation of Certain Incentives Used in School Work." *Journal of Educational Psychology,* 1925, *16,* pp. 145–159.

Johnson, D. W., and Johnson, R. T. "Cooperative Learning and Adaptive Education." In M. C. Wang & H. J. Walberg (Eds.), *Adapting Instruction to Individual Differences.* Berkeley, CA: McCutchan, 1985.

Johnson, D. W., and Johnson, R. T. *Learning Together and Alone: Cooperative, Competitive, and Individualistic Learning,* 4th ed. Needham Hts, MA: Allyn and Bacon, 1994.

Johnson, D. W., and Johnson, F. P. *Joining Together: Group Theory and Group Skills,* 2nd ed. Englewood Cliffs, NJ: Prentice Hall, 1982.

Julian, J. W., and Perry, F. A. "Cooperation Contrasted with Intra-Group and Inter-Group Competition." *Sociometry,* 1967, *5,* pp. 9–24.

Keller, J. M. "Motivational Systems." in H. D. Stolovitch and E. J. Keeps (Eds.), *Handbook of Human Performance Technology.* San Francisco, CA: Jossey-Bass, 1992.

Koestner, R., Zuckerman, M., and Koestner, J. "Praise, Involvement, and Intrinsic Motivation." *Journal of Personality and Social Psychology,* 1987, *53,* pp. 383–390.

Laird, J. D. "The Real Role of Facial Response in the Experience of Emotion: A Reply to Tourangeau, Ellsworth, and Others." *Journal of Personality and Social Psychology,* 1984, *47,* pp. 909–917.

Lecky, P. *Self-Consistency: A Theory of Personality.* New York: Island Press, 1945.

Lefcourt, H. M. *Locus of Control: Current Trends in Theory and Research,* 2nd ed. Hillsdale, NJ: Erlbaum, 1982.

Leith, G., and Davis, T. "The Influence of Social Reinforcement on Achievement." *Educational Research,* 1969, *2,* pp. 132–137.

Lepper, M. R. "Extrinsic Reward and Intrinsic Motivation: Implications for the Classroom." In J. M. Levine and M. C. Wang (Eds.), *Teacher and Student Perceptions: Implications for Learning.* Hillsdale, NJ: Erlbaum, 1983.

Lepper, M. R., and Greene, D. "Turning Play into Work: Effects of Adult Surveillance and Extrinsic Rewards on Children's Intrinsic Motivation." *Journal of Personality and Social Psychology,* 1975, *31,* pp. 479–486.

Lintner, A. C., and Ducette, J. "The Effects of Locus of Control, Academic Failure and Task Dimensions to Praise." *American Educational Research Journal,* 1974, *11,* pp. 231–239.

Maracek, J., and Mattee, D. R. "Avoidance of Continued Success as a Function of Self-Esteem, Level of Esteem Certainty, and Responsibility for Success." *Journal of Personality and Social Psychology,* 1972, *22,* pp. 98–107.

Maslow, A. H. *Motivation and Personality,* 3rd ed. (Rev. by R. Frager, et al.) New York: Harper & Row, 1987.

Mattee, D. R. "Rejection of Unexpected Success as a Function of the Negative Consequences of Accepting Success." *Journal of Personality and Social Psychology,* 1971, *17,* pp. 332–341.

McClelland, D. *Human Motivation.* Glenview, IL: Scott, Foresman, 1985.

McCombs, B. L. "Processes and Skills Underlining Continuing Motivation to Learn: Toward a Definition of Motivational Skills Training Interventions." *Educational Psychologist,* 1984, *21,* pp. 379–398.

McMillan, J. H. "Factors Affecting the Development of Pupil Attitudes Toward School Subjects." *Psychology in the Schools,* 1976, *13,* pp. 322–325.

Messer, S. "The Relation of Internal-External Control to Academic Performance." *Child Development,* 1972, *43,* pp. 1456–1462.

Michaels, J. W. "Classroom Reward Structures and Academic Performance." *Review of Educational Research,* 1977, *47,* pp. 87–98.

Morgan, M. "Reward-induced Decrements and Increments in Intrinsic Motivation." *Review of Educational Research,* 1984, *54,* pp. 5–30.

Nicholls, J. G., and Miller, A. "Conceptions of Ability and Achievement Motivation." In R. Ames and C. Ames (Eds.), *Research on Motivation in Education. Vol. 1: Student Motivation.* New York: Academic Press, 1984.

Nowicki, S., Duke, M. P., and Crouch, M. P. D. "Sex Differences in Locus of Control and Performance under Comparative and Cooperative Conditions." *Journal of Educational Psychology,* 1978, *70,* pp. 482–486.

Older, J. *Touching Is Healing.* New York: Stein and Day, 1982.

Okun, M. A., and DiVesta, F. J. "Cooperation and Competition in Coaching Groups." *Journal of Personality and Social Psychology,* 1975, *31,* pp. 615–620.

Pepitone, A., et al. *The Role of Self-Esteem in Competitive Behavior.* Unpublished manuscript, University of Pennsylvania, 1969.

Piaget, J. "Piaget's Theory." In P.H. Mussen (Ed.), *Carmichael's Manual of Child Psychology,* Vol. 1. New York: Wiley, 1983.

Reynolds, W. M. "Self-Esteem and Classroom Behavior in Elementary School Children." *Psychology in the Schools,* 1980, *17,* pp. 273–277.

Rogers, C. R. "Toward Becoming a Fully Functioning Person." In A. W. Combs (Ed.), *Perceiving, Behaving, Becoming.* Washington, DC: Association for Supervision and Curriculum Development, 1962.

Rotter, J. B. "Generalized Expectancies for Internal Versus External Control of Reinforcement." *Psychological Monographs,* 1966, *80,* (609).

Rotter, J. B. "Internal Versus External Control of Reinforcement: A Case History of a Variable." *American Psychologist,* 1990, *45,* pp. 489–493.

Rumberger, R. W. "High School Dropouts: A Review of Issues and Evidence." *Review of Educational Research,* 1987, *57,* pp. 101–121.

Schunk, D. H. "Effects of Effort Attributional Feedback on Children's Perceived Self-Efficacy and Achievement. *Journal of Educational Psychology,* 1982, *74,* pp. 548–558.

Schunk, D. H. "Reward Contingencies and the Development of Children's Skills and Self-Efficacy." *Journal of Educational Psychology,* 1983, *75,* pp. 511–518.

Schunk, D. H. "Social Comparison, Self-Efficacy, and Motivation." In M. Alderman and M. Cohen (Eds.), *Motivation Theory and Practice for Preservice Teachers.* Washington, DC: Eric Clearinghouse on Teacher Education, 1985.

Sears, P. S. "Levels of Aspiration in Academically Successful and Unsuccessful Children." *Journal of Abnormal Social Psychology,* 1940, *35,* pp 498–536.

Sharan, S., et al. *Cooperative Learning in the Classroom: Research in Desegregated Schools.* Hillsdale, NJ: Lawrence Erlbaum, 1984.

Sharan, Y., and Sharan, S. "Group Investigation Expands Cooperative Learning." *Educational Leadership,* 1989/90, *47,* pp. 17–21.

Slavin, R. "Cooperative Learning: Can Students Help Students Learn?" *Instructor,* 1987, *96,* pp. 74–76, 78.

Slavin, R. E. *Cooperative Learning: Theory, Research, and Practice.* Englewood Cliffs, NJ: Prentice Hall, 1990.

Stipek, D. J. *Motivation to Learn,* 2nd ed. Boston: Allyn and Bacon, 1993.

Strickland, B. R. "Internal-External Control Expectancies: From Contingency to Creativity." *American Psychologist,* 1989, *44,* pp. 1–12.

Strube, M. J., and Roemmele, L. A. "Self-Enhancement, Self-Assessment, and Self-Evaluative Choice." *Journal of Personality and Social Psychology,* 1985, *49,* pp. 981–993.

Thompson, G. G., and Hunnicutt, C. W. "The Effect of Praise or Blame on the Work Achievement of 'Introverts' or 'Extroverts.'" *Journal of Educational Psychology,* 1944, *35,* pp. 257–266.

Torrance, E. P. *Rewarding Creative Behavior.* Englewood Cliffs, NJ: Prentice Hall, 1965.

Weiner, B. "A Theory of Motivation for Some Classroom Experiences." *Journal of Educational Psychology,* 1979, *71,* pp. 3–25.

Weiner, B. "History of Motivational Research in Education" *Journal of Educational Psychology,* 1990, *82,* pp. 616–622.

Weiner, B. "Principals for a Theory of Student Motivation and Their Application within an Attributional Framework." In R. Ames and C. Ames (Eds.), *Research on Motivation in Education,* Vol. 1. New York: Academic Press, 1984.

Weiner, B. "The Role of Affect in Rational (Attributional) Approaches to Human Motivation." *Educational Researcher,* 1980, *9,* pp. 4–11.

Willison, B. G., and Masson, R. L. "The Role of Touch in Therapy: An Adjunct to Communication." *Journal of Counseling and Development,* 1986, April, pp. 497–500.

Witken, H., et al. "Field-Dependent and Field-Independent Cognitive Styles and Their Implications." *Review of Educational Research,* 1977, *47,* 1–64.

SELECTED READINGS OF RELATED INTEREST

Good, T. L., and Brophy, J. E. *Looking in Classrooms,* 6th ed. New York: Harper & Row, 1994. This is an excellent book about all aspects of classroom life, with a particularly good chapter about motivation.

McClelland, D. C. *Human Motivation.* Glenview, IL: Scott, Foresman, 1985. This book addresses the broad sweep of human motivation with particular emphasis on individual differences in human motivation.

Raffini, J. P. *Winners Without Losers: Structures and Strategies for Increasing Student Motivation.* Needham Hts, MA: Allyn and Bacon, 1993. You will find this a helpful resource of practical suggestions and strategies for dealing with problems of student apathy and motivating students to learn.

Reiff, J. C. *Learning Styles.* Washington, DC: National Education Association, 1992. This is a short, readable paperback that takes the reader beyond research with practical suggestions for creating a classroom that benefits from positive learning styles.

Stipek, D. J. *Motivation to Learn: From Theory to Practice,* 2nd ed. Boston: Allyn and Bacon, 1993. This book provides readers with a thorough understanding of motivation theories and an appreciation for their applications to classroom settings.

Tomlinson, T. M. (Ed.). *Motivating Students to Learn: Overcoming Barriers to High Achievement.* Berkeley, CA: McCutchan, 1993. This book explores new developments in theory, practice, and programs that promise to boast the quality and quantity of academic effort among students of all ability levels and backgrounds; it is especially relevant for teachers.

9

Self-Concept Dynamics and Teacher Expectations as Related to Learning

CHAPTER OVERVIEW

IMPORTANT CHAPTER IDEAS

1. Self-concept is an expression of how people *think* of themselves; self-esteem is the barometer of how they *feel* about themselves.
2. Some students do poorly in school more because of a low self-concept than because of low intelligence.
3. Self-concept and behavior are interactive and reciprocal; each influences the other.
4. Global measures of self-concept of ability are not as good at predicting academic achievement as are more specific measures of self-concept of ability related to particular subject areas (e.g., math self-concept, English self-concept).
5. Self-concept and self-esteem are determined in part by how we see ourselves in comparison to those similar to us.
6. Low self-esteem students have a tendency to set goals for themselves that are either too high or too low; these students are unpredictable.
7. Children's experiences in elementary school—for better or worse—significantly shape the subsequent direction of their attitudes toward themselves as learners, specifically, and toward school, generally.
8. Those who drop out of high school tend to have had a disproportionate number of failure experiences in their early school experiences.
9. It is not possible to say for certain which comes first—a high self-concept or high achievement. It is possible to say that the relationship is reciprocal; a change in one effects a change in the other.
10. A positive self-concept is a necessary, but not a sufficient, condition for achievement.
11. High and low self-concept students are distinguished from each other as much by their differences in behavior as by their differences in motivation—students with high self-concepts are more motivated by their expectations for success, and students with low self-concepts by their fear of failure.
12. Helping students to develop a sense of their own power to make things happen as a result of new skills and/or knowledge is one of a teacher's most important contributions to students.
13. All things being equal, students have a better chance to do well in school when teachers have positive, but realistic, expectations for them.
14. A self-fulfilling prophecy is the outcome of acting on false beliefs and behaving as if they were true.

15. Teachers communicate their expectations through a complex network of verbal and nonverbal cues.
16. Students can be helped to feel better about themselves by periodically being challenged by teacher expectations that take them beyond the "safety" of their own choices.
17. Positive, realistic expectations not only represent a belief in students' adequacy, but relay the message that students have the ability to do what is required.
18. Expectations are powerful, self-perpetuating attitudes for students as well as teachers because expectations guide both perceptions and behavior.

PROLOGUE

Self-concept is the connecting link between one's knowledge and one's performance. It is the bridge between what we know and how well we perform, whether it is on a math test or in a tennis match. It is not surprising to find that self-concept dynamics and learning are linked. How students *feel* about their outcome possibilities can have a considerable influence on whether or not positive possibilities are realized. If Daniel, who we know has an above-average IQ, concludes that he is going to have trouble in math because "I'm just not good at numbers," chances are very good that Daniel will have difficulty in math. If Diane, who we know has a somewhat average IQ, says, "I'm looking forward to math. I feel I can do pretty well in that subject," chances are fairly good that Diane will, all things being equal, do rather well in math. Classroom observations and research are helping us to understand that how persons perform in school—or anywhere else, for that matter—depends not only on what they are *actually* capable of doing, but also on what they *believe* they are capable of doing.

The self consists of two basic components—concepts and feelings. We know we have particular qualities, but, equally important, we have certain feelings about those qualities. For example, we might know that our measured IQ is, say, 120, but unless we have the self-confidence and necessary belief in ourselves to do the things that are possible within our abilities, our 120 IQ is a practically useless possession. What we have by way of personal attributes is far less important than how we feel about those attributes.

In this chapter, we turn our attention to some important questions related to self-concept and learning. What is self-concept? How is it related to self-esteem? What effect does school failure have on self-concept? How are self-concept and level of aspiration related? Which comes first—a positive self-concept or high achievement? What part do teachers play in shaping a student's concept of self? What can teachers do to encourage the development of healthy self-attitudes? These and related questions are addressed in this chapter. We will turn our attention, first, to four important psychological constructs.

SELF, SELF-CONCEPT, SELF-ESTEEM, AND PERSONALITY

Self, self-concept, self-esteem, and personality are terms that overlap to some extent with each other, with each referring to a particular component of our total being. The *self,* as it is used here, refers to our sense of personal existence; it is that part of ourselves of which we are consciously aware. *Self-concept* is our idea of personal identity; it refers to the cluster of perceptions and attitudes we have about ourselves at any given moment. Another way of looking at self-concept is as an expression of the way we have come to think about ourselves. Thus, out of our awareness of ourselves grows the idea (or concept) of the type of person we perceive ourselves to be.

Whereas self-concept is the *cognitive* part of self-perception, self-esteem is the *affective* dimension of self-perception. That is, not only do we have *ideas* about who we are, we also have *feelings* about who we are. Self-concept is the purely descriptive aspect of our self-perceptions; for example, we might say, "I am a student," "I weigh 170 pounds," or "I have many friends." These are descriptive statements that can be verified. Self-esteem, however, is the evaluative component of our self-perceptions and is reflected in statements such as, "I am an excellent (or average or poor) student," "My weight is ideal," or "I am a friendly person." The descriptive statement "I am a student" is part of self-concept, but is not necessarily relevant to self-esteem; the statement "I am an excellent student," however, clearly is relevant to self-esteem. Self-esteem, then, is constructed of our evaluations of the things we do, of who we are, and of what we achieve in terms of our private assessment of the goodness, worthiness, and/or significance of these things. Self-esteem refers quite literally to the extent to which we admire or value the self. Out of all of this emerges what is commonly referred to as *personality.* You can begin to see why personalities differ so greatly among individuals. Individuals have distinct levels of awareness of the self (of themselves as total beings); distinct ideas (self-conceptions) about their awareness; distinct levels of self-esteem and, as a consequence, distinct feelings about themselves as individuals and distinct ways of projecting themselves to others.

SELF-CONCEPT AND BEHAVIOR ARE INTERACTIVE AND RECIPROCAL

There is a dynamic interaction between the way we think about ourselves and the way we behave. The way we see ourselves is constructed from a private conception of the "sort of person I am," which is then acted out in behavior (Hamachek, 1992). If Amy sees herself as strong and not easily pushed around, she might stand up for herself assertively; if Andrew sees himself as inadequate compared to most others, he might behave timidly and find himself bullied by others; if Brian sees himself as a reasonably successful student, he probably makes an effort to meet class deadlines, comes to class prepared, and studies carefully for exams; if Barbara views herself as a somewhat marginal, below-average student, she might do things such as hand in assignments late, seldom prepare for class, and cram the night before an exam.

The relationship between self-concept and behavior is interactive and reciprocal. Self-concept influences behavior, but so too does behavior influence self-concept. For example, Nicole, a high school junior, wanted to do at least B work in her geometry class, but had the haunting suspicion that she just was not smart enough to do it. Her performance in that class was consistently around the C+ level. She decided to take a risk and study harder than she ever had before for the last two tests. (She changed her behavior.) What was the result? She received an A− and a B+, which gave her a B average in geometry for the 10-week marking period. Her self-concept of ability in that class changed in the direction of greater confidence. She received a B in geometry in the next grading period as well. Raw ability was missing, perhaps, but what was not missing was the willingness to compensate for that with extra effort. The result was that not only did she know more about geometry by studying extra hard, but also that she developed a more positive self-concept and higher self-esteem than she had had previously. By changing her behavior (i.e., she prepared more diligently), Nicole improved her self-esteem.

The influence of behavior on self-concept does not always work as neatly and positively as in Nicole's case. Negative outcomes are possible as well. Persons who are reasonably confident and have high self-esteem may find themselves doubting their abilities or questioning their skills after receiving a couple of low grades on exams, or fumbling the ball or striking out in several key instances. If individuals such as these were to stop trying as hard suddenly because they doubted their ability to be successful, then it is likely that over time they would be less and less successful, which would further erode the confidence they had in the first place. It is in ways such as these that self-concept and behavior are interactive and mutually reinforcing.

9.1 How Has Your Self-Concept Been Affected?

Sometimes the things we do or the way we perform influences how we feel about ourselves. Similarly, there are times when the way we feel about ourselves affects how we perform. What examples come to mind from your experiences as a student that illustrate how each of these possibilities works in school situations?

SELF-CONCEPT IS HIERARCHICAL AND MULTIDIMENSIONAL

Although it would simplify matters to be able to think about self-concept as a single global intrapsychic construct that governed all aspects of one's school-related behaviors, it is somewhat more complicated than that. As a result of a series of studies and analyses by Marsh (1990a, 1990b) and Marsh and Shavelson (1985), four components of school self-concept have been identified: (1) general self-concept, (2) nonacademic self-concept, (3) academic English self-concept, and (4) academic mathematics self-concept. General self-concept refers to our overall integration of the various components of the self; it helps determine the course of our more general everyday behavior. For students—and perhaps to others—general self-concept is organized along nonacademic and academic lines, while English and math are associated with academic self-concept.

Figure 9.1 provides you with a visual conceptualization of how self-concept and its various facets are configured. You can see that one's nonacademic self-concept includes components such as physical ability and appearance and peer and parent relationships; academic, English self-concept includes compo-

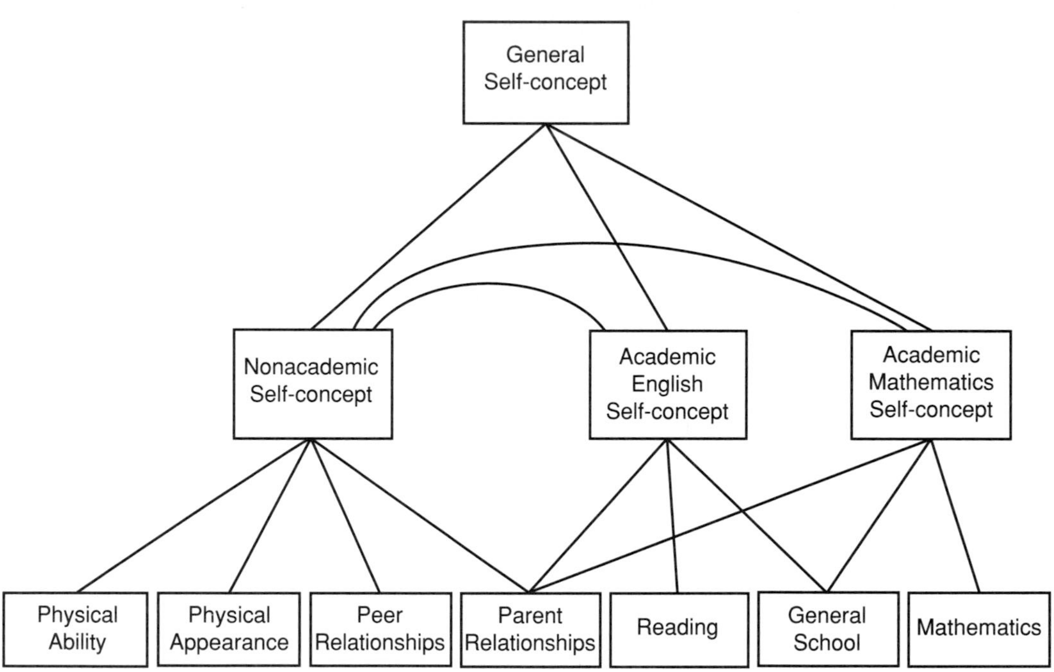

Figure 9.1. CONCEPTUALIZATION OF SELF-CONCEPT SHOWING ITS HIERARCHICAL AND MULTIFACETED ORGANIZATION

(From H. W. Marsh, "A Multidimensional, Hierarchical Model of Self-Concept: Theoretical and Empirical Justification." *Educational Psychology Review,* 1990, *2,* p. 90. Reprinted with permission of Plenum Publishing Corporation and the author.)

nents such as parent relationships, reading, and general school performance. The fourth facet, academic, mathematics self-concept, represents the components of parent relationships, general school performance, and mathematics. The hierarchical configuration in Figure 9.1 suggests how the various components and facets of self-concept are related to each other. For example, English self-concept and nonacademic self-concept are positively correlated with each other, as are mathematics self-concept and nonacademic self-concept. This suggests that as one's self-concept strengthens or weakens in one of these areas, it is likely to go up or down in the other as well. Note, however, that there is no line connecting English self-concept to math self-concept, which suggests that these two facets of self concept are nearly uncorrelated. What this means is that a person could have a rather low self-concept when it comes to mathematics ability but still have a fairly high self-concept in areas involving English skills. Or, a student could have a fairly low self-concept when it comes to mathematics and English skills, but still have a positive general self-concept because his or her nonacademic self-concept was high enough to compensate for the math and English deficiencies. This might be the case for a student who had a low self-concept when it came to math or English but whose nonacademic self-concept was especially high in the areas of physical ability and peer relationships. A gifted athlete, for example, might have a positive general self-concept even though his or her self-concept in mathematics or English is low.

What affects one area of a person's self-concept may or may not affect other areas. Self-concept is not composed of just one thing, rather it is constructed from various skills, deficits, strengths, and experiences, which as a package comprise our more global perceptions (i.e., general self-concept) of who we are and what we can do. Because one's general self-concept is constructed from so many factors, measures of general self-concept tend not to be very good predictors of achievement in specific school subjects (Marsh, Byrne, and Shavelson, 1988; Shavelson and Marsh, 1986).

An example may make this clearer. If we were to measure a man's general physical strength and agility and find that he was above average in those areas, we could make some general predictions about his athletic prowess. However, it would be difficult for us to predict the *particular* athletic event(s) he would be best at from these measurements. In order to do this, we would need at least two additional pieces of information: (1) his own assessment of ability in specific areas, and (2) more specific measures of his skills in those areas. Knowing only that a man is above average in physical strength tells us nothing about how the strength can or will be used; nor does it say anything about the events that have contributed to his development of physical strength. Similarly, predicting achievement in specific content areas is difficult when we know about a student's general self-concept only. If we know that a student has, for example, a high positive general self-concept, this tells us only that, in relation to other students, it is at the very least above average. It tells us nothing about whether that self-concept is related to particular academic and nonacademic talents, nor will it tell us anything about the experiences (academic and nonacademic) that have contributed to its development.

By conceptualizing one's school self-concept as having various facets and being arranged in a hierarchical manner, as in Figure 9.1, you can begin to see how various people and experiences can influence the different facets of self-concept. As pointed out in Marsh's (1990a) review of literature related to this idea, we are more likely to obtain a reliable reading about the relationship between self-concept and achievement by paying attention to students' specific self-concepts in specific academic and nonacademic areas.

9.2 Is Your Academic Self-Concept Higher in Certain Subjects?

Although some students have a positive self-concept of ability in practically all of the courses they take, others find that their positive self-concepts in certain subject areas help make courses in which they are weaker at least more bearable. Have you had experiences where you felt woefully inadequate in certain courses but very capable and competent in others? What effect did experiences like this have on your more general feelings about yourself? What implications can you draw from this for your work as a teacher?

SELF-ESTEEM IS AFFECTED BY ONE'S COMPARISON OF SELF WITH OTHERS

How we feel about ourselves is influenced strongly by how we compare ourselves with others. In a famous passage illustrating this idea, William James (1890) noted insightfully:

> I am not often confronted by the necessity of standing by one of my empirical selves and relinquishing the rest. Not that I would not, if I could, be both handsome and fat and well-dressed, and a great athlete, and make a million a year, be a wit, a bon-vivant, and lady-killer as well as a philosopher, a philanthropist, statesman, warrior, and African explorer, as well as "tone-poet" and saint. But the thing is simply impossible. The millionaire's work would run counter to the saint's; the bon-vivant and the philanthropist would trip up each other; the philosopher and lady-killer could not keep house in the same tenement of clay . . . to make any of them actual, the rest must more or less be suppressed . . . So the seeker of his truest, strongest, deepest self must review the list carefully, and pick out the one on which to stake his salvation. All other selves thereupon become unreal, but the fortunes of this self as real. Its failures are real failures, it triumphs, carrying shame and gladness with them . . . I, who for the time have staked my all on being a psychologist, am mortified if others know more psychology than I. But I am contented to wallow in the grossest ignorance of Greek. My deficiencies in that give me no sense of personal humiliation at all. (p. 91)

It is clear from the preceding quotation that how James felt about himself depended, in large measure, on how he viewed his own efforts in relation to others *who also backed themselves as psychologists.* In other words, our feelings of self-worth and self-esteem grow, in part, from our perceptions of ourselves in comparison to others whose skills, abilities, and aptitudes are similar to our own.

Mettee and Riskin (1974) found some interesting experimental evidence for this by pitting pairs of college women against each other in written tests. After revealing the results of the tests, they asked each woman whether or not she liked her partner. To their surprise, they found that the woman who was decisively beaten by her partner tended to like that partner. However, the woman who was only marginally defeated generally disliked her partner. The probable reason for this outcome is that the woman who was defeated by a wide margin did not really compare herself to her competitor, because she saw the other person as too different from herself for comparison. The woman who was defeated by only a slight margin perceived herself as defeated by her competitor. This threatened her self-esteem, and in defense she developed a strong dislike for her competitor. Thus, the *most accurate, and hence, most potent, comparison information is derived from persons who are similar to us.* When we perceive others as greatly dissimilar, they are perceived as incomparable. This comparable–incomparable distinction allows us to screen out negative information about ourselves because the only information that really "counts" comes from comparable people, an idea that has support from other research (Harter, Whitesell, and Kowalski, 1992; Tesser and Campbell, 1980; Wheeler and Miyake, 1992, Zanna, Goethals, and Hill, 1975).

Comparisons—quietly, subtly, unobserved—go on all the time. C students tend to compare themselves to other C students, and A students compare themselves to other A students. The point is, most of us "back" ourselves to be at least as good as most others in one or two areas, and the reference group we use for purposes of comparison tends to be more like us than unlike us. We might add, too, that this comparable–incomparable defense system is used to protect us from the achievements of persons we regard as inferior. For example, if we are outperformed by somebody we perceive as far inferior to ourselves, the performance can be dismissed as an isolated incident. Self-esteem is not likely to suffer much because of a tendency to consider the inferior person too far below us for comparison.

The groups with whom we compare ourselves play an important part in helping us sort through how we feel and think about ourselves. As high self-esteem usually comes from being able to do one or two things at least as well as, if not a trifle better than, most other people, it would be difficult to maintain, not to mention enhance, self-esteem if we compared ourselves with persons who were obviously either too superior or too inferior to ourselves in accomplishment. In the first case, it is a losing battle; in the second case, it is a hollow victory.

9.3 What Kinds of Comparisons Do You Make?

> Can you think of two or three things at which you "back" yourself to be good? Have you noticed how important it is to find out how others have done on a particular task before you're able to decide how well you've done? What conditions are necessary before you can feel positive about how you've done in relation to others?

LEVEL OF ASPIRATION AND SELF-ESTEEM ARE INTERRELATED

What we set as our personal levels of aspiration have an important impact on our feelings of self-esteem because they help establish criteria for success or failure. What is a success, or enhancing experience, for one can be a failure, or deflating experience, for another. Consider two examples of how this might work. Jeffrey received a C in a course that he regarded as particularly difficult. However, that C grade was consistent with his personal expectations and level of aspiration, and he felt it was a minor, if not a major, success. At the same time, Jessica, who also received a C in the course, viewed this as a failure experience because her expectations and level of aspiration were not lower than a B. Jeffrey maintained his self-esteem because the C grade represented at least an even return on his personal investment. Jessica, however, lost a measure of self-esteem *because the return was less than her personal investment.* By starting out with differing amounts of personal investment, Jeffrey and Jessica had differing expectations for a personal return in order to maintain their original level of self-esteem. In a similar vein, both could have *enhanced* their self-esteem if they had received grades that *exceeded* their original level of self-esteem.

The relationship between level of aspiration and self-esteem is a tricky one. When self-esteem is low, students (and others) have a tendency to set their sights either too high or too low. Students with low self-esteem are somewhat unpredictable when it comes to goal setting, which is a major reason why, as teachers, we need to work even harder with students whose self-worth is insecure. We need to help them develop realistic levels of aspirations. Another way to look at this is in terms of helping students—both those with high and with low self-esteem—to develop realistic expectations of return given their particular capacities for investment.

HISTORY OF SUCCESSES AND FAILURES AFFECTS LEVEL OF SELF-ESTEEM

Although our levels of aspiration determine to a large extent what we interpret as failure or success, and hence what either adds to or subtracts from our self-esteem, another factor worth considering is our history of successes and failures. To fail at something is more tolerable, and less likely to threaten our self-esteem, if we have had a history of success in that particular endeavor. For example, a girl who has had many boyfriends is not likely to sour on boys if she loses one, but a girl who has few boyfriends might; a team with a 10–0 record is not likely to give up on the season after losing the eleventh game, but a 0–10 team might; a student with a long string of above-average grades is not likely to quit school if he fails his first course, but a below-average student who fails his fifth course might. In other words, the impact of falling short of one's personal aspirations is less self-deflating if one's list of successes in that endeavor exceeds the tally of failures.

Most of us keep an ongoing emotional balance sheet on which we record our successes and failures. Our view of ourselves is lowered, and feelings of self-esteem reduced, when personal debits (i.e., failures, losses) are greater than personal assets (i.e., successes, gains). Conversely, self-concept is raised, and self-esteem elevated, when our emotional ledger reflects more in the way of assets than debits.

Unfortunately, not all students are able to taste the fruits of success, and, in fact, are so dominated by the fear of failure that their entire lives are altered by the fear of failure and its consequences. They too easily become the "failure-oriented" students we discussed in Chapter 8 whose goal setting is unpredictable and whose work habits are inconsistent. It is an orientation to schooling, and eventually, to life that causes some students to believe that they are simply doomed to do poorly. It is an orientation rooted in attitudes about success and failure that goes back as far as the elementary school years, an idea we turn to next.

9.4 How Is Your Self-Esteem These Days?

Reflect a moment. In just this past week, what have you recorded in the debit and asset columns of your emotional ledger? Does one column exceed the other, or are they approximately equal? How has your self-esteem been affected by the mental arithmetic of the past week? Can you think of any particular classroom instances that have affected one side of the ledger or the other? How has your self-esteem affected your academic work for better or worse?

THE IMPORTANCE OF SUCCESS IN THE EARLY YEARS

The years from 5 to 12—from kindergarten through sixth grade—are crucial years in children's development. It is during these years that children begin to test themselves, expand their range further from home, and be exposed to increasingly more complicated challenges. Learning, which during their preschool years was random and informal, becomes more systematic and organized during these years. Not only are there more experiences in which to take part, but there are increased demands to *remember* those experiences, which can range all the way from learning the alphabet, to learning to read, add, subtract, spell, and write coherent sentences. What happens in these early years is central to all subsequent schooling, not just in terms of basic knowledge but in terms of basic attitudes about themselves. These are years when the footings of children's self-concepts are either firmly established in experiences of success, accomplishment, and pride in themselves, or planted in shifting sands of self-doubt, failure, and feelings of worthlessness. There are at least three good reasons for these possible outcomes.

1. *Elementary-age children's self-esteem is incomplete and impressionable.* Children at this age are in the early phases of forming their concepts of self. This does not mean that they have no sense of identity whatsoever, but it does suggest that *their sense of who they are and what they can do is incompletely formed.* Characteristically, elementary-age youngsters are malleable and impressionable. They are ready not only to please adults but also to *believe* them as well. Indeed, what adults say about them or how they evaluate either their person or performance is incorporated more readily, more easily, and more uncritically than at any other developmental stage. The feedback children receive from peers and adults—particularly significant adults like parents and teachers—is likely to have a greater impact because a child this age is still developing and incomplete, is more open to input, and, thus, is more susceptible to influence.

2. *Elementary-age children have immature defenses. They are vulnerable.* Youth this age are not well defended psychologically. In the absence of a consolidated and reasonably well-integrated self-image, they are less likely to use active and assertive mechanisms such as denial or projection in order to protect themselves from ego-damaging experiences and more likely to use the passive and more primitive mechanism of regression, which allows them to stay at a safer and more dependent level of development. (Indeed, whether in children or adults, regressive behavior is not an uncommon phenomenon following failure experiences.) In order to use a defense mechanism, one first has to have a reasonably well-defined self. Elementary-age children are not totally incapable of compensating for their failures by displacing their anger or projecting blame for poor work on the teacher. It is a matter of degree. If a second grader fails a spelling test, he is more likely to "believe" that mark (i.e., incorporate it, internalize it) than a twelfth-grade student with a positive view of herself and a history of doing well in school, who fails a geometry test. The twelfth grader can blame her performance on a fluke, deny its importance, rationalize her lack of study, or project it on her teacher. As long as her performance is inconsistent with her concept of self, she can defend herself against the loss of self-esteem. The second grader, however, does not yet have a well-defined self with which he can or must be consistent. Hence, whether it is a failure or a success,

elementary-age children can offer far less resistance to impact and will be much less critical recipients of its place in their evolving sense of self.

3. *Elementary-age children are still in the "industry versus inferiority" stage.* As noted in greater detail in Chapter 2, the 6- to 12-year-old age group represents a growth phase that Erikson (1980) has referred to as the "industry versus inferiority" stage. This is a time in children's growth and development when they naturally learn to be either industrious, productive, and autonomous, or inferior-feeling, withdrawn, and dependent. The major change of this period, as Erikson sees it, is the development of a sense of inadequacy and inferiority in children who do not receive recognition for their efforts. Again, we are reminded of how incredibly important a teacher's feedback is to children at this point in their development.

9.5 What Were Your Elementary School Years Like?

What about your own elementary school experiences? What kind of academic foundation did you establish in those years? Did you have some particular success (or failure) that made an unusual impact? How did those experiences affect your work as a student? What relationships do you see between your experience as an elementary school student and the growth of your overall self-concept of ability? What does this suggest to you for your own work as a teacher?

Elementary School Failures Are Related to Later School Problems

At this time in American education, there is increasing attention being given to the back-to-basics movement. Core curricula are being restored, and teachers are being encouraged to toughen up both their expectations and standards. On the plus side, this wave of national pressure for increased achievement will no doubt shake some students out of their lethargy as they strive to meet higher demands. Students with fairly positive self-concepts have a tendency to respond favorably to new challenges and higher demands. On the negative side, this same wave might doom other students—by virtue of lower self-esteem, lower intelligence, less opportunity for learning, or some combination of these factors—to increased failure at the very time in their development when it affects them most. Research that has explored the effects of early failure experiences points clearly to the cumulative negative impact of these experiences over time (Eckstrom, Goertz, Pollack, and Rock, 1986; Mann, 1986). These cumulative effects usually result in lower self-esteem, a more negative attitude toward school, and a generalized attitude that "school is not for me" (Sagor, 1988; Stern and Catterall, 1985).

It is not surprising that a large number of high school students who drop out of school have had many failure experiences early in their academic lives. Consider some of the data:

1. More than 1200 students in grades 6 and 7 from fourteen representative schools in a North Carolina study were investigated to differentiate between repeaters and nonrepeaters (Godfrey, 1971). Results showed that those who had been retained were reading at a 6.8 grade level; those repeating one grade scored a 5.2 level. On mathematics achievement, nonrepeaters averaged in the 27th percentile; those repeating one grade were in the 10th percentile; and those repeating two or more grades dropped to the 5th percentile. Failing was also found to have a strong influence on a student's feeling of self-worth. For example, on all of the subscales of the *Tennessee Self-Concept Scale,* students who repeated grades scored lower than those who had not. Students repeating two or more grades scored far below the mean subscale.

2. More than 74% of the dropouts in one school system repeated at least one grade as compared to only 18% among students who graduated from high school (Hall, 1964).

3. Eckstrom and his colleagues (1986) found, in their review of data from a national longitudinal dropout study, that one third of those who dropped out said they did so because they did not like school as a result of negative experiences, and another one third specifically cited poor grades as their reason for leaving.

4. In an earlier investigation of the long-term effects of early school failure, Dillon (1949) found that of 2000 children who began first grade at the same time in the same school system, 643 dropped out before completing high school. All but five of these dropouts, 638, or 99%, had been retained in the first grade. As a combined total, these 643 students failed a total of more than 1800 grades during their first 6 years of school. On average, this means that each dropout failed every other year for 6 years.

Dropping Out: A Possible Consequence of Too Much Failure and Low Self-Esteem

Usually, when we discover that we are not very good at something we either reduce the time we put into it or we cease doing it altogether. To continue is too painful because it reminds us of a failing or shortcoming we would prefer to forget. Most of us can live with our various shortcomings if we can experience at least some success periodically in areas that are more central to our self-esteem. For example, doing reasonably well in school or work, which may be more central to our feelings of self-worth, makes it possible for us to do other things less well (e.g., sing, dance, play tennis, golf) without losing our self-esteem. It is, likely, however, that people who do those things for a living might experience dips in self-esteem if they suddenly find themselves not singing, or dancing, or playing tennis or golf as well as they had. For them, those activities *would* be more central to their feelings of self-worth. If their skills decreased significantly enough, they probably would stop doing what they were doing and go on to something more rewarding.

Basically, this is exactly what happens to the millions of dropouts who, because of their many failures and commensurate feelings of low self worth, terminate their education. Schooling *is* central to their lives. When that is not going well, there is nothing that can be put in its place. It is not particularly surprising that the results of a nine year study of more than 1600 males from grade 10 onward showed that the average level of self-esteem of those who eventually dropped out was consistently lower than that of all other students (Bachman, O'Malley, and Johnson, 1978). And perhaps it is also not surprising to find, as Bachman and O'Malley (1977) did in a four-year study, that dropouts' self-esteem got *higher* after they were out of school. Like any of us who experience too much failure in what we are doing, leaving it and going on to something else usually helps us to feel better. It is sad but true that some students' sense of self-worth improves, at least temporarily, *after* they drop out of school. Not all dropouts, of course, leave school because of failure to do well. Some leave because they are bored, angry, beset with personal problems, or have low intelligence, or some combination of these factors. As pointed out by Fine and Rosenberg (1983), approximately one fifth of all dropouts can be classified as gifted. Most, however, leave to escape the painful cumulative effects of repeated failure experiences (Eckstrom et al., 1986; Kagan, 1990).

9.6 Have You Ever "Dropped Out" of Something?

You might have a better understanding of why certain students drop out of school by reflecting on experiences, events, organizations, and even relationships that you "dropped out of." What was your motivation for not staying with whatever it was you chose not to participate in any longer? How was your self-esteem affected *prior* to leaving? After? What can you learn from your own experiences about why some students drop out?

Self-Concept Directions and Achievement Potentials Are Formed Early

The dropout problem is one of enormous proportions. The overall national average is approximately 25% (Finn, 1991). More than four million young people between the ages of 16 and 24 drop out of school, which is 13% of this age group. In large urban areas, this number jumps to somewhere between 40% and 60% (Hahn, 1987). The numbers are staggering, not to mention the economic and social problems created by incompletely educated young men and women trying to succeed in an increasingly more knowledge-oriented, technologically based world.

Leaving school early is one very explicit and dramatic consequence of failures that occur too early and too frequently. What we have not mentioned are those hundreds of thousands of children who are victimized by excessive early school failures but who do not choose so dramatic an exit. Rather, they persist through school, suffering quietly and inwardly, and eventually graduate into a competitive society that demands not only a reasonable level of competence in some kind of work but also a certain degree of confidence in one's ability to do it. Although we can take collective pride in the fact that the United States has the highest stay-in-school rate in the world, the reality is that thousands of young people graduate after 13 years of school feeling somewhat helpless, hopeless, and defeated. Feelings like these, whether among those who drop out because they cannot tolerate more failure or among those who stay in school and suffer through it, start during the elementary years.

For example, although studies indicate that approximately 70% of all dropouts complete at least a ninth-grade education, there is increasing evidence that negative attitudes about school and thoughts of leaving it begin early in a child's school experiences. Following an extensive review of research literature related to the dropout problem, Peck, Law, and Mills (1987) noted that dropouts "at an early age, develop a poor self-concept and a high level of insecurity about their ability to learn easily or do well in school" (p. 8). Experiences of success and/or failure during the early years apparently can have a significant impact on the self-perceptions of elementary-age youths.

Findings of longitudinal research indicate that a critical period for the formation of abilities and attitudes for school learning occurs, or is set or stabilized, between the ages of 5 and 9. For example, Bloom's (1964) analysis suggests that adolescent or adult intelligence is approximately 50% stabilized or predictable by the first grade, whereas adolescent *achievement* in school is predictable to the same extent only at age 9, or about the end of grade 3. This means that factors that contribute to school achievement other than intelligence are to a considerable extent stabilized during the first three grades. In large measure, these factors are sheer skill factors, which are cumulative in nature. If children have more skills in the first grade, they accumulate further skills in the second, and more in the third, and so forth. However, as noted by Kohlberg, LaCrosse, and Ricks (1972), "in large part . . . this stabilization of school achievement is based on the stabilization of factors of interest in learning, attention, and *sense of competence.*"

All of this research points to the fact that early establishment of a positive or negative attitudinal set can influence, for better or worse, subsequent school achievement. Children's feelings about their ability to do schoolwork (i.e., their sense of competence) are rooted in their early school experiences, and these determine, to a great extent, both the intensity and direction of their emerging self-conceptions of ability. Which bring us to an important consideration.

Four Reasons Early School Successes Are Crucial

It is clear that early school failure experiences have lasting effects. The earlier they occur, the more likely they will be incorporated in children's concepts of their academic ability and their sense of personal worth. Experiencing as much success as possible in the elementary years is important for at least four basic reasons: (1) subsequent success is not only easier to build onto early success, it seems more possible to the student; (2) early success gives children not only a sense of competence and accomplishment, but a precedent with which they can strive to be consistent; (3) early school success makes any later school failures more bearable because they are more likely to occur within a consolidated self-esteem buttressed by achievement and fortified by personal accomplishment; and (4) early school successes help students develop the kind of positive mental image of themselves with which they can strive to be consistent.

This last point is particularly important because it underscores what social science researchers have shown to be true about human behavior. We tend to behave in reasonably consistent and stable ways, which means that once our image of ourselves is fixed in our minds, we tend to behave (and achieve) in a manner that is more or less in line with that image (Brim and Kagan, 1980; Hamachek, 1992; Ozer, 1986; Underwood and Moore, 1981).

SELF-CONCEPT AND SCHOOL PERFORMANCE ARE OFTEN LINKED

Whether conscious of it or not, we each have a mental blueprint of the type of person we are. It is a blueprint consisting of a system of interrelated ideas, attitudes, and values that are influenced by our past experiences, our history of successes and failures, and the way other people have responded to us particularly during our formative years. We each develop a consolidated framework of beliefs about ourselves, and proceed to live and perform in a manner that is consistent with that framework. In short, we "act like" the sort of person we perceive ourselves to be. Indeed, it is extremely difficult to act otherwise, despite a strong conscious effort and exercise of willpower.

9.7 Can You Behave Differently Than the Person You Are?

If you would like to experience how difficult it is to be anyone but yourself, you might find it informative to make a deliberate effort for just one day to behave in a way that is different from how you see yourself. If you see yourself as quiet and shy, make an effort to behave more talkatively and assertively (or the other way around, if you see yourself as gregarious). In other words, pick what seems to be a dominant characteristic in yourself and try to be its opposite. What do you think you will learn?

Behavior Is Often Consistent with Self-Perceptions

It seldom occurs to students that their academic trouble lies in their own evaluations of themselves. If you tell struggling students that they only "think" they cannot grasp algebra, for example, they might very well give you a "Who are you trying to kid?" look. In their own way, they might have tried again and again, but still their report cards tell a different story. A request (more often a demand or admonishment) destined to fall on deaf ears is the one parents and teachers frequently make of some students: "Study harder." This is fine for students who already have high self-concepts and high needs for achievement, because they are likely to respond to the challenge in order to produce at a level consistent with their self-images. However, for students whose self-pictures are that of being poor students, the impact is lost. As a low-concept, low-achieving ninth-grade girl once told me, "Study? Ha! Why should I study to fail?" This student was not aware that her frustrations with failure had already set the wheels in motion for her to behave in ways that were consistent with a failure self-image. Again, we need to remind ourselves that this consistency is not always voluntary or deliberate, but compulsive, and generally unconsciously motivated.

It is important to remember the effects of self-consistency because it will help us understand better the relationship between school performance and self-concept. *As soon as students "lock in" on a perception of what they are, and are not, able to do, it is difficult to shake them from it, particularly if the perception has time to root itself into a firmly established belief.* The findings from a study done by Lepper, Ross, and Lau (1986) with fifty-two male and female high school students illustrates this principle. The format of the study was set up (rigged, actually) in such a way so that approximately half of the students were successful solving a set of math problems while the other half failed. The important aspect of this study is that those students who failed persisted in their negative self-evaluations even when it was made clear to them that their failures were due to clearly inferior instruction. Although the investigators expected failing students, in particular, to grasp at any reasonable explanation for their seemingly poor performance, they did not do so. The researchers concluded their report with an ominous warning:

> The practical implications of the present studies seem relatively clear. Overcoming the pernicious effects of early school failures on students' self-perceptions and attitudes may indeed prove a difficult assignment. Simply demonstrating to a child, even in a clear and concrete fashion, that his or her poor performance may well have been the consequence of an inept or biased teacher, a substandard school, or even prior social, cultural, or economic disadvantages may have little impact on his or her feelings of personal competence or potential. If the student's beliefs are translated, as well, into a selective avoidance of related subjects or tasks in the future—as in the present experiment where failure subjects showed less optimism and enthusiasm about the inclusion of related materials in the curriculum—opportunities for subsequent enlightenment

may be precluded, and negative views about one's abilities may become self-fulfilling. (p. 490)

9.8 How About Your Own Self-Perception?

When you think about it consciously, what kind of academic self-perception would you say you have "locked in on"? What kind of influence would you say that perception has had on how you function as a student and how you feel about your abilities? How would you describe the relationship between your self-concept as a student and your achievement? What can you learn from this self-examination that may help you function more effectively as a teacher?

In any discussion involving self-concept and academic achievement, the old chicken or the egg question invariably arises . . .

WHICH COMES FIRST—A POSITIVE SELF-CONCEPT OR HIGH ACHIEVEMENT?

Although one might argue that students would first have to do well in school in order to possess a positive self-image about their academic abilities, it could also be argued that a positive self-image must precede doing well in school. There is ammunition for both sides of the debate.

On The Side of Self-Concept Preceding Achievement

Consider first some of the evidence on the side of those who argue that a positive self-concept precedes doing well in school. For example, in an early study by Wattenberg and Clifford (1964), evidence was found suggesting that a negative self-image may affect a skill as basic as reading before children even enter first grade. In a sample that included 128 kindergarten students in two schools, intelligence, self-concept, ego strength, and reading ability were measured in all of the students when they were in kindergarten and then again when they finished second grade. It was found that measures of self-concept and ego strength made at the beginning of kindergarten were more predictive of reading ability two and one-half years later than were measures of intelligence. In other words, the self-attitudes of kindergarten students were a more accurate indication of their potential reading skills than intelligence test scores. However, we cannot assume from this finding that there is no relationship between mental ability and reading achievement. All that we can safely conclude is that a measure of kindergarten students' self-concept and ego strength may be a good predictor of how they might fare in their reading skills by the third grade. Also, a 5-year-old's verbal skills are usually not sufficiently developed to be measured with great accuracy, which may be one reason that

Wattenberg and Clifford found a low relationship between intelligence and later reading achievement.

A study a year later by Lamy (1965), investigating the relationship between kindergarten children's perceptions of themselves and their subsequent reading in the first grade, demonstrated similar results. Her findings led her to suggest that not only do children's self-perceptions give as good a prediction of later reading achievement as intelligence test scores, but that children's self-concepts may be causal factors in their subsequent reading achievement.

Other evidence for the idea that a positive self-concept precedes high achievement was revealed in a study involving 53 children in two elementary classrooms. A major finding was that students who began with high self-concepts not only spent more time working on school-related tasks than students with low self-concepts, but they were also more likely to be among those who *improved* their self-images by getting things done, something referred to as a "positive feedback loop" (Shiffler, Lynch-Sauer, and Nadelman, 1977).

There is also evidence showing that doing well academically is preceded by a high self-concept for high school students, as well. For example, Felson's (1984) analysis of self-concept and school achievement data collected during the 10th, 11th, and 12th grades for 2213 high school males showed a consistent positive relationship between self-concept of ability and grade point average in the 11th and 12th grades. In other words, those students who perceived themselves as capable were more likely to be among those with a higher grade point average, an outcome due, in part, to what Felson saw as differences in effort. In his words, "Students who believe they are smart apparently work harder than students with less favorable self-appraisals and this effort results in higher grades" (p. 950).

Let us be clear in understanding that a positive or negative self-concept does not *cause* high or low achievement. What we can say is that one's self-concept can affect achievement. This affect can work in one of two ways, depending on the nature of one's self-concept. First, the more ability students attribute to themselves, the greater their estimation of the probability of success if they work hard. To put it differently, students whose self-concept of ability is high may expect greater payoffs from their efforts and work harder to obtain them. Second, students with low self-appraisals are more likely to expect low achievement (if not failure) and, as a result, are less inclined to work hard because to do so and fail could be a severe blow to their already shaky self-esteem. (Have you ever experienced a time in your life, for example, when you felt a great eagerness to prepare for something that you just *knew* you probably would not do well?)

On the Side of Achievement Preceding Self-Concept

On the other side of the argument, Kifer's (1975) longitudinal study of students from grades two to eight, which investigated how school achievement performance and personality characteristics, including self-concept, are related over time and over a series of tasks, revealed that successful achievement precedes a positive self-concept. On the basis of his findings, Kifer argues that success or failure of and by itself is not sufficient to explain changes in self-concept. Rather, it is the *pattern* and *consistency* of success or failure and the *accumulation* of those experiences that affect an individual's self-concept. He found, for example, that the relationship between self-concept and achievement became stronger and more robust as success or failure became prolonged and as a consistent pattern of accomplishments (or lack of accomplishments) emerged.

Other studies, such as Bridgeman and Shipman's (1978) longitudinal investigation of 404 children from the time they were in preschool through third grade, and Calsyn and Kenny's (1977) analysis of a 5-year investigation of 556 high school students both found that a student's academic self-concept was more likely to be influenced by academic achievement than the other way around, a finding also supported by Kelly and Jordan's (1990) study of 197 male and female eighth-grade students. Bachman and O'Malley (1986) came to a similar conclusion in their longitudinal investigation of relationships between academic achievement and self-esteem of more than 1400 males followed from approximately age 15 to 23. In their words, ". . . it is the actual abilities, not the self-concepts that make the difference" (p. 45). In response to the important question of which pathway actual abilities take to shape self-concepts, Bachman and O'Malley offer the following response:

> Our findings clearly show that one pathway is via classroom grades. But the findings also show that even more of an impact of actual ability on self-concepts occurs independent of grades (such as) personal communications from teachers (e.g., "You are much brighter than these grades reflect"), comments from parents (perhaps along similar lines), information from other significant adults, and in many cases direct knowledge about performance on standardized tests of ability. (p. 45)

This, then, is a sampling of the evidence that each side offers when debating the question of which comes first, a positive self-concept or high achievement. One of the reasons the answer to this question is equivocal has to do with differences in the methodologies used by researchers in this area. A second reason has to do with the fact that relationships between self-concept and academic achievement can, as pointed out by Hansford and Hattie (1982), vary with age, self-concept definition, and measure of academic performance.

On the Side of Both Sides

Does this mean that because no consistent causal relationship is found between self-concept and academic achievement that the self-concept idea has no validity? Not at all. Although it is not possible to specify which came first, good schoolwork or high self-regard, it does not seem unreasonable to suggest that *each is mutually reinforcing to the other to the extent that a positive (or negative) change in one facilitates a commensurate change in the other.* If, for example, Robin, a fifth-grade student with low self-esteem begins school with negative expectations for her chances of success but experiences some small triumphs and a few large successes now and then, chances are fairly good that she will begin to feel more confident in her abilities. In this case, achievement leads to a more positive self-concept. Have you ever had the experience of taking a difficult course in which you did not expect to fare well (your self-concept was shaky), but you earned a high grade? Chances are that your high grade enhanced your self-concept in that area, particularly if you were able to attribute your success to your own effort and knowledge, rather than to luck and good fortune.

As an example the other way, consider Robert, a 10th grader with high self-esteem who takes a geometry course taught by a teacher with a reputation for being tough and demanding. Although some students wilt in the face of the pressures they feel, Robert remains firm in his conviction that he can handle the materials. A below-average grade on the first exam only firms his resolve to do better on subsequent tests. So he studies even harder and receives progressively better scores on other exams. Because his self-concept of ability to do math is fairly high to begin with, his initial brush with low achievement does not depress his efforts but motivates him to work harder. In this case, a positive self-concept preceded high achievement and was a source of internal motivation to try harder even in the face of a below-average performance. Of course, if Robert were to experience enough subpar performances, then we might expect that his own estimate of ability would begin to decline. Nothing in the research literature suggests that a high self-concept person is forever immunized to the effects of failure when failure is excessive and consistent.

As a general rule, however, a person with low self-concept will tend to give up more easily following failure experiences. An individual with a higher self-concept, however, will tend to put more effort into improving what needs to be improved when things do not go well. Fortunately, the chicken or the egg question is more academic than practical. The important thing is that self-concept and achievement are interactive and reciprocal forces, each with the potential to affect the other in positive or negative ways.

9.9 How Has Your Self-Concept Fared?

What about your own case? Have you ever had an experience in school where you started out with low confidence—a low self-concept, actually—only to experience success almost in spite of yourself? What effect did that have on your self-concept? Or perhaps you have experienced the other side of the coin—a time when you encountered failure after beginning with high confidence. How did that affect your self-concept of ability?

When a low self-concept is the problem, there is a particular kind of psychological medicine that is almost guaranteed to help.

SUCCESS: ANTIDOTE FOR A NEGATIVE SELF-CONCEPT

Success, self-esteem, and a positive self-concept are very closely related. Success, for most people, is an affirming, positive happening that feeds egos and fuels motivation. It helps people in two ways: (1) They can feel good about themselves (i.e., internal reward) because they have accomplished something successfully, and (2) it provides an opportunity for significant others to respond positively and favorably (i.e., external reward) to the person behind the accomplishment. Success has a decided influence on students' behavior and on how they feel about themselves. For example, Yarworth and Gauthier (1978) found, in their study involving 450 high school students, that students with high self-concept took more risks, and, as a result, experienced more success, which helped enhance their positive feelings. Low self-concept students, however, were more wary about the possibilities of success and took fewer chances, thereby reducing their opportunities for success, thus reinforcing their negative mind-set about themselves. You can see the reciprocal influence of self-concept and achievement at work.

In his investigation involving 197 college freshman, Borislow (1962) found that even though certain students began their studies with what seemed to be a somewhat indifferent and unmotivated "I don't care if I do well or not" attitude, doing poorly still had a decidedly negative effect on their self-attitudes. A person may act as if failure does not really matter, but in the final analysis, it *does* matter. Losing or doing poorly may "build character," as coaches are fond of saying, but it does not build confidence. Just as success is likely to breed a feeling of success, so does failure breed a feeling of failure.

Dyson's (1967) study investigating the relationships between self-concept and ability grouping among seventh-graders illustrates the point about the power of success. Among other things, it was found that high-achieving (high success) students reported significantly higher self-concepts than low-achieving (low success) students, regardless of the type of grouping procedures utilized in the academic program. Noteworthy in Dyson's final observation:

> If there is one particularly significant result growing out of this research, it is that "nothing succeeds like success." This is not a new understanding, as the old cliche indicates. The work reported here does, however, re-emphasize the importance of success in the learning situation as a contribution to positive psychological growth and it indicates that this feeling of success is probably more crucial in its effect on the student's self-concept than how an individual is grouped for instruction. (p. 404)

When considering the relationships between self-concept and achievement, an important principle becomes evident.

A POSITIVE SELF-CONCEPT IS NECESSARY BUT NOT ENOUGH

In a research effort designed to investigate the relationship between self-concept of ability and academic performance of more than 1000 male and female students from the time they started seventh grade and completed 10th grade, Brookover and his associates (1965, 1967) found that self-concept was a significant factor in achievement at each grade level studied. In the final phase of this study, the following important observation was made:

> The correlation between self-concept of ability and grade point average ranges from .48 to .63 over the six years. It falls below .50 only among boys in the 12th grade . . . In addition, the high correlation between perceived evaluations and self-concepts tends to support the theory that perceived evaluations are a necessary and sufficient condition for (the growth of a positive or high) self-concept of ability, but (a positive) self-concept of ability is only a necessary, but not a sufficient condition for achievement. The latter is further supported by the analysis of the achievement of students with high and low self concepts of ability. This revealed that although a significant proportion of students with high self-concepts of ability achieved at a relatively lower level, practically none of the students with lower (less positive) self-concepts of ability achieved at a high level. (Brookover at al., 1965, pp. 142–143)

This research is important for two reasons. First, it underscored the influence that significant others (i.e., emotionally important people like parents and teachers) can have in the self-concept of developing youths, a finding later supported by Bachman and O'Malley's (1986) study of more than 1400 high school age males, which was mentioned previously. These findings remind us that children's self-concepts are molded, in part, during this long immersion in an interpersonal stream of reflected appraisals from people important to them. Second, this research supports the idea that it takes more than a positive self-concept to achieve and perform well academically; it also takes motivation, determination, and the help of emotionally supportive people, especially parents and teachers.

The bottom line is that *the possession of a high self-concept does not cause high academic achievement;* it does, however, play a vitally important supporting role. Remember, a person could have a positive self-concept that is sustained and nurtured by success in nonacademic pursuits—athletics, extracurricular activities, peer group popularity, creative expression in the arts, and so forth. This same person might be an average student academically, but retain his or her high self-concept status because it is nurtured and reinforced in nonacademic areas. Here we have an example of a person who has a high self-concept but now is doing only average work academically, which illustrates the idea that a high self-concept does not necessarily *cause* high achievement. When we think about self-concept as being multidimensional and arranged hierarchically, as in Figure 9.1, then it can be more readily seen how a student could be rather successful in one area, but not very successful in two or three or more areas and *still* have a relatively high self-concept. Although it is possible to do average and even below-average work academically and still have a fairly high self-concept, it is far more difficult to have a low self-concept of ability and expect to do well academically.

BEHAVIORAL DIFFERENCES BETWEEN STUDENTS WITH HIGH AND LOW SELF-CONCEPT

Table 9.1 represents an effort to identify some of the more common behavior patterns that various research efforts have identified as those that tend to distinguish between students with high and low self-concepts of ability. Sev-

Table 9.1. TEN BEHAVIORS COMMONLY ASSOCIATED WITH HIGH AND LOW SELF-CONCEPT OF ABILITY STUDENTS

Students with a high, positive self-concept of ability tend to be:	*Students with a low, negative self-concept of ability tend to be:*
1. Intellectually active—explore, probe, ask questions, get excited about learning new things	1. Intellectually passive—do not ask many questions, and seem unenthusiastic about learning new things
2. Motivated to do as well as possible to get good grades; actively look for ways to be successful	2. Motivated to do as well as possible to avoid poor grades; actively look for ways to avoid falling
3. Involved in class discussions; not afraid to express themselves	3. Quiet during class discussions, seem afraid to express their ideas
4. Among those who, when given a choice, sit near the front of a room	4. Among those who, when given a choice, sit near the back of a room
5. Among those who attribute their successes to hard work, effort, and ability on their part	5. Among those who attribute their success to luck, fate, or some other outside source
6. Among those who attribute their failures to a fluke, unlucky break, or other outside sources	6. Among those who attribute their failures to lack of ability, lack of know-how, or low intelligence
7. Among those who set realistic, reachable goals for themselves, making success more possible	7. Among those who set unrealistic, unreachable goals for themselves, making success less possible
8. Among those who are willing to ask for help; are able to admit not knowing without embarrassment	8. Among those who are not willing to ask for help; seem to have problems admitting they do not know something
9. Among those who do their work when it is to be done; assignments are handed in on time	9. Among those who procrastinate doing their schoolwork; assignments due are frequently late
10. Among those who are able to take modest pride in their own abilities, but are not pushy or overbearing	10. Among those who try to bluff others into believing that they know more than they really do; can be overbearing

eral research sources were particularly helpful in identifying those differentiating behaviors (Byrne, 1986; Chiu, 1987; Coopersmith, 1967; Findley and Cooper, 1983; Hogan and Weiss, 1974; Hoge and Luce, 1979; Marsh, 1984; Maw and Maw, 1970; Rotherham, 1987; Schunk, 1983). I am not suggesting that we will always find the students with high self-concepts on one side and the students with low self-concepts on the other, but overall we are likely to find the higher students doing things that reflect their self-confidence and lower students behaving in ways that reveal their self-doubts. Students with high and low self-concepts are distinguished from each other as much by their differences in behavior as by their differences in motivation—highs being more motivated by their expectations of success and lows by their fear of failure.

STRATEGIES TEACHERS CAN USE TO ENHANCE SELF-CONCEPT AND SCHOOL ACHIEVEMENT

At every grade level, students come to school with preconceptions about themselves and their abilities. As we have already seen, successful students are typically characterized by self-confidence, self-acceptance, and feelings of adequacy and personal competence, while less successful students are more apt to be distinguished by their feelings of uncertainty, low self-regard, self-derogatory attitudes, and inferiority feelings. Students with high self-esteem have the types of feelings about themselves and positive attitudes we would like to see in all of our students. However, this is the real world, and part of its reality is the fact that some students are very negative about themselves and their abilities. Are there specific things a teacher can do to help students with low self-concepts to feel better about themselves as part of an overall effort to raise achievement? Let's turn our attention to some ideas for doing this.

Help Students Develop Specific Skills

We have already made the point that self-concept and achievement are interactive and reciprocal. When one goes up, it is likely that the other will, too. This is no better illustrated than in Bachman and O'Malley's (1986) analysis of educational and psychological data collected for more than 1400 males five years after their high school graduation. One of their clearest findings was that it was the actual abilities and skills of these young men, rather than their self-concepts, that had the biggest impact on their educational and occupational outcomes five years after graduation. This does not mean that their self-concepts of ability did not play an important part at earlier, more formative, stages of their development. It does suggest, however, that having tangible and real skills and abilities are important working cogs in the psychological machinery that makes it possible for persons to move onward and upward.

A good way to promote this process is to . . .

Point Out Students' Abilities and Talents

In an effort to find out how teachers influence students to feel either positively or negatively about their abilities and potentials, Staines (1958) set up a research format designed to answer the following questions:

1. What part do teachers play in the development of the child's self?
2. Can teachers change a student's self-picture?
3. If they can, what methods of teaching produce what types of self-pictures?
4. Is it possible to make distinctions among teachers in terms of the frequency and type of comments they make about a student's self?

The basic assumption of the study was that because teachers are an important aspect of students' emotional world, it is likely that they can have an important influence on students' self-concepts.

In order to test this assumption, two elementary classes were matched for age, intelligence, and socioeconomic status. In one class, teacher A deliberately set out to assist students to view themselves as planning, purposeful, discriminating, responsible, and accountable individuals. It was considered important that students test their purposes by carrying them through, see themselves as adequate and causal (i.e., persons who can *make* things happen), and, at the same time, differentiate between their strengths and weaknesses. In order to facilitate these goals, teacher A made it a point to get to know each student and to familiarize himself with the general area of self-concept dynamics, and how these dynamics were related to behavior. In class, the teacher was likely to make comments such as the following, all designed to help students toward more positive views of themselves, while at the same time assisting them to be realistic about their abilities.

1. "Randy, you're tall, help me with this."
2. "Jane, you know, you're very good at solving addition problems."
3. "Good boy! Look at this, everyone!"
4. "Sally, you seem to do better in arithmetic than English."
5. "That's a good idea, Debbie, it helps us see how these two problems are related."
6. "I like the way you volunteered in class today, Dan, you really helped our discussion to move along."
7. "Jane, you have really good coordination. Have you thought of trying out for the softball team?"
8. "You're a fine one, you are."

Note the emphasis on highlighting specific strengths, assets, and skills; on helping the student sort out his or her strengths and weaknesses; and, as in the last statement, on commenting on the student's worth as a total, or "whole," person.

Teacher B was judged an equally effective teacher, but his techniques were more along the line of traditional teaching (i.e., content-oriented, telling and testing), and not adapted to fit within a framework that explicitly considered strategies for self-concept enhancement.

When the twelve-week experimental period was concluded, data from teacher B's class indicated that traditional, high-pressure teaching—with vigorous personal emphasis, great stress on correctness and on the serious consequences of failure, and constant emphasis on passing examinations—leads to greater insecurity. Concerning achievement, the students of teacher A reflected slightly higher average improvement in standardized reading and number tests than the students of teacher B. If it is objected to that a teacher cannot spend time assisting students toward a more positive, healthy attitude for fear of shortchanging them in the way of content, here is some evidence to suggest that at least equally good academic results can be obtained while helping students to see themselves in a more positive light. Feedback of this type serves another important function. It gives students some external criteria from which to gauge how well they are doing and what needs to be improved.

When it comes to feedback, there is something else that teachers can do. As teachers, one of the most important contributions we make to our students' growth is in helping them develop a sense of their own power when it comes to using their skills and/or knowledge to effect positive changes in their lives. A high school English teacher of mine used to end every class with this query for us to think about: "This is what we learned today. (She would give us a summarized version). Now how will you use this knowledge to behave more intelligently?" For the last ten minutes of practically every class, we talked about how we would use what we had learned. The discussion helped us to "set" the new information in our minds, and it encouraged us to be pragmatically realistic about how we really could, or should, be "more intelligent" because of what we had just learned about sentence structure or Shakespeare.

9.10 How Have Teachers Encouraged You to Use Your "Power"?

Can you think of some teachers you've had who, like my English teacher, helped you to develop a sense of intellectual "power" so you could actually use the knowledge you had assimilated or the skills you had learned? What, specifically, did they do that encouraged you to put your knowledge to use?

Use Praise, But Do So Appropriately

There are at least five basic principles to keep in mind regarding the use of praise:

1. As a general rule, praise is a more powerful motivator than either criticism or reproof.
2. Praise does not affect all students in the same way; for example, bright students with high self-concepts frequently work harder when their ideas are challenged and gently criticized. (They *want* to show you that they can do it.)
3. Praise is not just what is said but *how* it is said.
4. Effective praise tends to do at least three things. It (1) communicates how you feel about the performance, (2) communicates something about how well the student has done, and (3) encourages the student to evaluate his or her own performance. These are not necessarily communicated all at one time, but if they were, a praising remark might sound like this: "I feel really good about your performance (or effort) because you have made such a nice improvement over your last try. How do you feel about what you have accomplished?"
5. Honesty is important. Only praiseworthy performances or effects should be praised.

Develop Positive Expectations—Believe Students Can Do It

Predicting rain or sunny skies does not affect tomorrow's weather, but a Harris poll predicting victory or defeat for a particular political candidate can have a definite effect on the outcome. Betting on the flip of a coin doesn't change the odds, but letting an athlete know that you have bet on him or her can considerably affect his or her performance. When Roger Bannister began training for the four-minute mile, hardly anybody believed it could be done. Bannister himself wasn't sure, but he is quoted as having said many times, "I knew my trainer believed in me and I couldn't let him down." Thus, in 1954 he became the first person in the world to break the four-minute barrier with a 3.59.4 mile, something that today is done routinely by top runners in competition. Charles E. Wilcox, former General Motors president, was fond of saying that one of the differences between good bosses and poor bosses is that "good bosses make their workers feel that they have more ability than they think they have so that they consistently do better work than they thought they could." Hundreds of years ago, Goethe observed, "Treat people as if they were what they ought to be and you help them to become what they are capable of being."

The essence of these quotations is that one person's expectancy of another person's behavior somehow comes to be realized—not always, but enough so that increasing attention has been given in recent years to the way in which self-fulfilling prophecies work in the classroom. Eliza Doolittle, who was changed from an awkward cockney flower girl into an elegant lady in George Bernard Shaw's famous play, *Pygmalion,* described the process involved quite simply: "the difference between a lady and a flower girl is not how she behaves, but how she is treated." Although it does not work quite as simply in the classroom, there is increasing evidence to suggest that perhaps one difference between poor students and good students is not how they behave, but how they are treated. Like Eliza, students in school—whether in first grade or twelfth—have a tendency to perform as they are expected to perform. Rosenthal and Jacobson's (1968) bombshell book *Pygmalion in the Classroom* reported the first major research showing that a teacher's positive expectations can influence students' school achievement. Here is what they did.

Within each of six grades in a particular school were those classrooms in which children performed at above-average, average, and below-average levels of scholastic achievement. In each of these classes, an average of 20% of the children were identified to the teachers as having scores on the *Test for Intellectual Blooming,* which suggested that they would show unusual academic gains during the year. Actually, the children had been picked at random from the total population of children taking the same test. Eight months after the experimental conditions were instituted, all children were retested with the same test. What were the results?

For the school as a whole, those children from whom the teachers had been led to expect greater intellectual gain showed significantly greater gain in test score than did other children in the school. In fact, the lower the grade level, the greater the test-score gain. Apparently, *teachers interacted with the "brighter" children more positively and more favorably, and the children responded in kind by showing greater gains in test score.* Why should there be more change in the lower grades? One reason is that younger children are generally more malleable, less fixed, and more capable of change. A second possibility is that younger, "newer" elementary school children do not have firmly established reputations that can be passed on from one teacher to the next. Perhaps as students move from one grade to the next, their reputations—for better or worse—precede them, which colors both teachers' perceptions of, and expectations for, their behavior and academic performance. Thus, new students might show more expectancy effects because they have not been stereotyped by reputations passed on from teacher to teacher, which is in fact what Raudenbush (1984) found in his review of eighteen experiments on induced teacher expectations. Effects were stronger in grades one and two than in grades three through six. They became strong again at grade seven, the first year of junior high for most students.

9.11 Have You Ever Been Affected by a Teacher's Expectations?

As you think about expectations and how they may effect students' achievement, can you think of some examples from your own school experience when teachers' expectations had a bearing—for better or worse—on how you performed?

Induced Versus Natural Expectations

It is important to note that the types of expectations reported by Rosenthal (1968, 1973, 1974), and reviewed by Raudenbush (1984), were what are called "induced expectations." That is, they were expectations created, or "induced" in the minds of teachers by leading them to believe that particular students with whom they would work had unusually high learning potential, when, in fact, those students had been selected randomly. Believing these students to have unusual potential, teachers presumably communicated their positive expectations in a variety of ways, which helped these students to increase their achievement levels. Other studies have arrived at similar results (Babad, Inbar, and Rosenthal, 1982; Guttman and Bartel, 1982). What happens, however, when teachers form their *own* expectations based on their *own* experiences?

Seaver (1973) studied teachers' "natural expectancies" by analyzing the performance of twenty-seven elementary-age students who had older siblings precede them in school by no more than three grade levels, and who had the same teacher as the younger siblings. Seaver reasoned that teachers who had taught a student's older brother or sister would have a built-in expectancy for the younger child; high if the older child did well, and low if he or she did poorly. In addition, the school environment provided a natural control group of students whose older siblings had different teachers. It was found that teacher expectancies did, indeed, make a difference. When the older sibling's performance had been high, the performance of children in the high-expectancy group was higher than that of the control group on eight measures of academic achievement. When the older sibling's performance had been low, the expectancy group scored lower than the controls on seven of the eight tests. Research shows us what we might always have suspected: the reputation that older siblings establish in school gets passed on to their brothers and sisters, and teachers tend to expect—and therefore get—from the younger members of a family what they had learned to expect from the older members.

Additional support for the power of natural expectancies comes from an investigation by Palardy (1969), who found that if first-grade teachers believed boys would achieve as well as girls in reading, the boys did, in fact, perform better than boys with teachers who believed girls were better readers. Another study in this vein found that elementary-level teachers have a tendency to overestimate the IQs of girls and underestimate the IQs of boys (Doyle,

Hancock, and Kifer, 1971). The revealing aspect of this is that even though there was no actual IQ difference between boys and girls, the girls showed higher reading achievement. Not only that, *but within both sexes, the children whose IQs had been overestimated by teachers showed higher reading achievement.* Remember, actual IQ is not the important factor here. What seems to make a difference is a teacher's perceptions or beliefs about a particular student's IQ, which in turn sets in motion particular expectancies.

Teacher expectations can be a powerful force in shaping students' behavior and in influencing achievement outcomes, which brings us to an important question.

WHAT IS THE PSYCHOLOGY BEHIND TEACHER EXPECTATIONS?

A teacher's expectations of any given student's academic performance is an essentially private prediction about a student's potential for achievement based on what is currently known about the student. Although these expectations are not necessarily conscious, they nonetheless can act as powerful mediators between how students feel about themselves and how they perform academically. Before a student ever enters a classroom, he or she has been subjected to a myriad of inputs that have shaped his or her self-concept, behavior, and achievement attitudes in particular directions. Acting on the information that is before them, real or imagined—perhaps a bit of both—teachers develop expectations of how well or how poorly particular students will do in their classrooms. It is a continuous cycle of inputs and outputs. Figure 9.2 will give you an idea of the complexity of that cycle. Notice the many input variables that influence who a student is as a total person. These input variables influence a teacher's expectations, which influence how a teacher interacts with any given student, which, in turn, affects how the student responds to the teacher, and the cycle begins.

How Expectations Can Become Self-Fulfilling Prophecies

Johnny Carson made a joke on the "Tonight Show" several years ago about supplies of toilet paper being tight. There really was no shortage—until Carson's joke. In a matter of days, toilet paper became a rare commodity. Americans, believing Carson was serious, bought every roll of toilet paper they could get their hands on. Soon, a lot of persons had several month's supply of toilet paper—but stores had virtually none.

Embedded in this Carson caper is a natural example of a self-fulfilling prophecy. As defined many years ago by Robert Merton (1948), who was the first to use the term, a self-fulfilling prophecy begins with a false definition of a situation, which in turn engenders behavior that brings the situation into conformity and the expectation. Thus, an erroneous expectation (there would

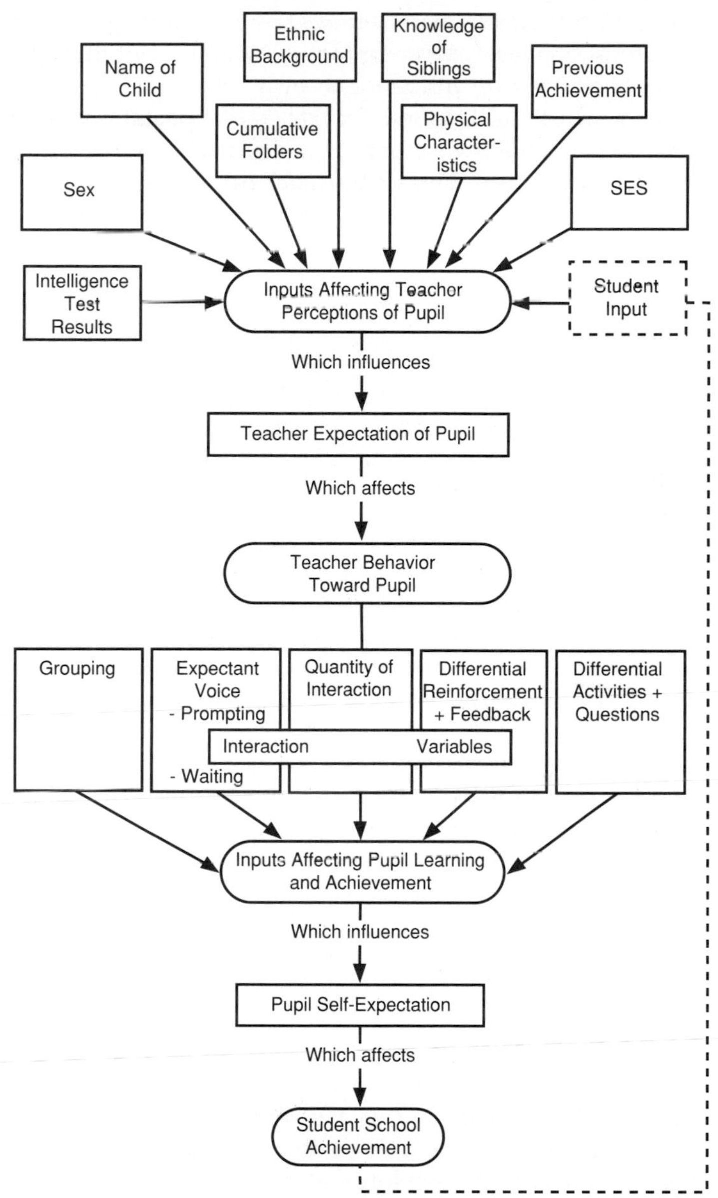

Figure 9.2. THE BEHAVIORAL CYCLE OF PUPIL BEHAVIOR, TEACHER EXPECTATIONS, AND STUDENT ACHIEVEMENT

(From Braun, C. "Teacher Expectations: Sociopsychological Dynamics." *Review of Educational Research,* 1976, *46,* p. 413. Copyright © 1976 by the American Educational Research Association. Adapted by permission of the publisher.)

be a shortage of toilet paper) led to behavior (panic buying) that caused the expectation to come true.

Although merely wishing for something is not likely to make it come true, our expectations do influence the way we behave, and the way we behave affects how others respond. In fact, the expectations we have of others can cause us to interact with them in a way that leads them to respond just as we thought they would. This justifies our original expectations (predictions), and thus is born a self-fulfilling prophecy.

9.12 How Do You Suppose You Would Respond?

Consider carefully the examples in this box and your probable responses to each scenario. Suppose you were thinking about taking a course from an instructor you knew nothing about, and wanted to talk to him about course requirements and other related aspects of his class. You ask a friend about him and you are told: "Kimbal is a terrific person. He knows his stuff; he has a sense of humor; he's a warm person, and he's easy to talk to—someone you'll like." If you heard this about Mr. Kimbal, how do you think you would respond to him when meeting him for the first time? However, suppose your friend had said: "You're thinking of taking a course with Kimbal? Well, I'd be careful if I were you. It's hard to feel comfortable with him. He seems so . . . well, cold and abrupt. I never had the feeling that he enjoyed talking to people." If you hear this about Mr. Kimbal, how do you think you would react to him when meeting him for the first time?

If you are like most people, your response to Mr. Kimbal would be quite different, depending on which of these contrasting characterizations you had heard. If you had heard the first description, you probably would look forward to your visit with him; you might tell him that you had heard he was a fine instructor and someone with whom students liked to talk. You might also say that you were looking forward to taking his course and ask if he would tell you a bit about it. If, however, you had heard the second description, you might approach your appointment with apprehension and hesitancy. You might look somewhat more serious and guarded, and you might present yourself to him in a more formal, businesslike manner.

Now, turn the scenario around and put yourself in Kimbal's shoes. He knows nothing about you as a person and reacts solely on the basis of his impressions of you during that initial meeting. Consider for a moment how he might respond to the person you present in the two approaches previously described. Learning from you, in the first instance, that you heard he was a fine instructor, that students liked him, and that you were looking forward to taking his class, it is likely that he would feel good about himself and you. Your behavior might help him feel comfortable with you, and perhaps even more willing to spend a little extra time answering your questions. What you see in his behavior would tend to confirm what you thought about him initially.

How do you think Kimbal might respond if you approached him somewhat nervously and formally, as in the second instance? No doubt, he would respond in kind. If he were not already a somewhat nervous and formal person, he might soon become one. Sensing your cautious mood, he might feel that you really didn't want to spend a lot of time with him, or he might even feel that you don't like him. In light of your behavior, he might conclude that attempts at small talk would be risky, so he would give you the information you wanted, you would be on your way, and you would think to yourself, "My friend was right—he *is* cold; he really *doesn't* enjoy talking to people."

You can see in the previous examples that a self-fulfilling prophecy is not the outgrowth of an expectation; rather, it is an outgrowth of the behavior that the expectation produces. This behavior has an effect on other persons, which increases the likelihood that they will act in expected ways.

When thinking about the ways in which expectations work in a classroom setting, we need to remember that it is the constant interplay between expectations and behavior that finally converts an erroneous expectation into a self-fulfilling prophecy. Although every self-fulfilling prophecy begins with an expectation, *it is the behavior that this expectation produces, not the expectation itself, that brings about a self-fulfilling prophecy.* Good and Brophy (1994) have suggested a six-step model to help us understand how teachers' expectations can become self-fulfilling prophecies.

1. Early in the school year, teachers form expectations of their students, which are shaped by their knowledge gained from school records and personal observations. Some of these expectations are appropriate and others are not. These initial impressions are relatively rigid and are resistant to change even in the face of contradictory evidence.
2. Students are treated in accordance with teachers' expectations of them.
3. Other things being equal, a student's response to teacher behavior will be reciprocal (e.g., teacher warmth will lead to student warmth; teacher coldness or hostility will lead to student withdrawal or hostility; and so forth).
4. If the teacher treatment is consistent over time, and if students do not resist its impact, it might begin to affect their self-concepts, aspirations, motivation, and interpersonal relationships.
5. Students' behavior will generally complement and reinforce teachers' expectations, which encourages teachers to act on their original expectations more forcefully, and which causes students to conform to these expectations more than they might have otherwise.
6. The ultimate effect of expectations is that students with high expectations will be led to achieve at, or near, their potential, and students with low expectations will fall short of gaining as much as they could have if taught in another manner.

As you see, the process is cyclical. It begins with an expectation that might, or might not, be accurate; the teacher responds to the expectation; the student responds, in kind, to the teacher; the teacher's expectation is reinforced; the teacher behaves with greater conviction; the student, if susceptible to the teacher's input, performs in a manner that validates the teacher's original expectation. Thus, the cycle is completed.

According to Good and Brophy (1994) the effects of a self-fulfilling prophecy can occur with teacher expectations only if all elements of the model are present. For example, a teacher might have particular expectations, but not communicate them consistently, or might change them. Another reason a teacher's expectations might not become self-fulfilling is that the students might steadily resist the effects of those expectations. I have heard many accounts from students who said that they were subjected to teachers' negative expectations, but refused to bend. As one senior-year college student expressed it, "I had a math teacher who told me more times than I can count that I was one of his 'slower' students and that I might want to consider going to a trade school to learn a specific skill rather than to college, which was my dream. On more than one occasion I remember thinking, 'you are wrong and I will show you.' "

9.13 Have You Ever Resisted a Negative Expectation?

> Have you ever had any experience with a teacher who communicated to you the idea that you probably would not do well in a particular course, task, or vocation, and because of his or her negative expectations you were even *more* determined to succeed? Some students might give up in the face of feedback like this. How would you explain your determination not to, if you were a person who resisted? What can you take from this experience to enhance your wisdom as a teacher?

How Are Positive Expectations Communicated?

The actual mechanics by which teacher expectations are communicated are complex. The words spoken are important, of course, but so, too, are the subtle nuances built into the interactions between teacher and student (e.g., tone of voice, facial expression, posture, other types of body English. Chaiken, Sigler, and Derlega (1974) zeroed in on nonverbal cues in order to study how teachers' expectations are actually transmitted. They found that teachers anticipating superior performance from their students engaged in more positive nonverbal behaviors (e.g., smiling, leaning toward the student, making eye contact, nodding affirmatively) than teachers with either no expectations or with low expectations for performance. These results strongly suggest that even when teachers do not tell students outright what the world anticipates from them, the message is still there in subtle, but potent, ways.

In an effort to explain how positive expectations are communicated, Rosenthal (1974) has proposed a "four-factor theory" of the influences that are likely to encourage students to do well. As Rosenthal sees it, when teachers have positive expectations, they tend to do the following:

1. Give more positive feedback to their special students about their performance (feedback factor).
2. Give their special students more opportunities to respond to questions (output factor).
3. Create a warmer social-emotional mood for their special students (climate factor).
4. Teach more, and more difficult, material to their special students (input factor).

You might find it useful to think of the acronym FOCI as an aid to remembering how you can channel your efforts toward positive expectations.

F—eedback, give more positive
O—utput, give more opportunities for student
C—limate, create a warm, inviting
I—nput, give students more

All of these factors interact in such a way as to create a more positive and facilitating learning environment for students for whom teachers have high, positive expectations. It is easy to see why some students might flourish, and others might not.

How Are Negative Expectations Communicated?

The transmission of low expectations is a subtle packaging of words, gestures, and decisions that, when received by particular students on a daily basis, have the cumulative effect of influencing their work in a negative direction. Teachers are usually *unaware* of the things they do or say that communicate low or high expectations. In that there are frequently, but not always, messages that are communicated outside awareness, there is practically no opportunity for modifying negative messages. Hence, there is an advantage to developing a conscious awareness of the types of teacher behaviors that convey negative or positive expectations to students.

Good and Brophy (1994) reviewed a large body of research related to things teachers do that reflect different treatment of high and low achievers. The following are 15 teacher behaviors that might help perpetuate the cyclical nature of negative, self-fulfilling prophecies:

1. Waiting less time for low achievers to answer questions
2. Giving low achievers answers, or calling on someone else rather than helping low achievers over the rough spots (thus, low achievers have fewer chances to be successful)

3. Rewarding inappropriate behavior or incorrect answers by low achievers (which might make them feel embarrassed rather than helped)
4. Criticizing low achievers more often for failure
5. Praising low achievers less frequently than highs for success
6. Failing to give feedback to the public responses of low achievers
7. Paying less attention to low achievers, and interacting with them less frequently
8. Calling on low achievers less often to respond to questions, even when they volunteer
9. Seating the low achievers further from the teacher (with the possible nonverbal message being, "You are not important")
10. Demanding less work, effort, and appropriate responses from low achievers (with the possible inference by low achievers being, "I really must be dumb")
11. Interacting more with low achievers privately than publicly, and monitoring their activities more closely (This might underscore fears low achievers have about really needing help if that much special attention is required.)
12. Giving low achievers, but not high achievers, the benefit of the doubt in borderline cases when grading or giving assignments
13. Giving briefer, and less informative, feedback to questions asked by low achievers
14. Having less friendly interaction with low achievers, including less smiling and other nonverbal indicators of support and responsiveness
15. Showing less acceptance of low achievers' ideas

Note that practically all of these actions have direct effects on students' opportunity and motivation to learn. The fact that teachers criticize low achievers more often for failure, and praise them less often for success, is bound to have a negative effect on their motivations. If low achievers are provided with less information, and given less feedback than high achievers, this makes it even more difficult for the low achievers to progress. It can be a vicious cycle.

Good and Brophy (1994) suggest that we keep the following three cautions in mind when thinking about how teachers communicate low expectations:

1. There are vast differences among teachers in how much they dispense differential treatment to students for whom they have various expectations.
2. Treatment differences are sometimes caused more by the student than by the teacher. For example, if low achievers choose not to be involved, it will be difficult for teachers to respond to them as often, and if their contributions are of lesser quality, teachers might find it difficult to use low achievers' ideas as frequently as they do those of high achievers.

3. Some forms of what appears to be differential treatment might actually represent sound, individualized instruction. For example, because low achievers do require more structuring of their activities and closer monitoring of their work, it might be argued that it makes good instructional sense to have more frequent private conversations with them or to ask them easier questions. We should not assume that the expressions of differential treatment previously described are necessarily harmful or inappropriate. What we observe in any given moment in a classroom is not enough to allow us to know whether what we saw is healthy or unhealthy or excellent teaching or poor teaching. No single interaction or classroom event dooms students to failure or propels them to success. It is the cumulation of many similar events and interactions that can make a difference to a student—for better or worse. Being called on less often than others during a particular day probably doesn't make that much difference to any student; not being called on for days, or even weeks, probably will make a difference. Getting an earful of criticism in a particular class occasionally is not likely to destroy any student's motivation for learning permanently; hearing constant criticism in many classes very likely could. It is the effect over time that takes the greatest toll.

9.14 The Effect of Success and Failure Can Be Cumulative

As you reflect on your life as a student, what examples come to mind that show the cumulative effect of particular success or failure experiences that you have had? Did you ever have an experience in school that represented a type of turning point for you? What happened? Why was it so important to you? What part did the teacher play? What can you take from this experience to help you become a better teacher?

DO TEACHER EXPECTATIONS REALLY MAKE A DIFFERENCE?

Although Rosenthal's (1973) original expectancy research has been criticized by some researchers (Elahoff and Snow, 1970; Gephart, 1970; Wineburg, 1987) for shortcomings in design and methodology, none of these criticism denied the possibility that teacher expectations can be an important variable in students' learning. Not all research supports the expectancy phenomenon, but much of it does. For example, Rosenthal (1973) reviewed 242 studies and found that 84 of them reported that teachers' expectations made a significant difference in how subjects performed in various situations. Eighty-four might not seem like large number of supporting studies, however, if we apply the rules of statistical significance to the number, we might expect that only approximately 5% of those 242 studies (approximately twelve) to have agreed with chance prediction alone. The fact that we have eighty-four, seven times more than chance would dictate, suggests that expectations do indeed affect performance in particular circumstances. Several large-scale reviews of expectancy research tend to confirm this conclusion (Braun, 1976; Cooper, 1979; Good and Brophy, 1994).

When used positively by aware teachers, expectations can perform another function that we have not mentioned yet. Positive, reasonable, and fair expectations can play a part in stretching students beyond the safety of their own choices.

The word "safety" is used because evidence indicates that when persons do only as they choose to do, they feel less successful and competent, even if they succeed, than those who accomplish a task that they did not choose and that represents another person's expectations.

Luginbuhl (1972) has noted, for example, that if persons succeed at a problem they chose from a number of problems, their feeling of success can be blunted by the knowledge that *they influenced the situation to make success more possible.* It might not be wise for a teacher to permit students to have their own way (e.g., choose the number or types of books to read, the type of paper to write) *all the time.* Living up to a teacher's expectations (e.g., writing a report on an assigned topic, getting it done and handed in on time) is another way students can feel successful and thereby add to their feelings of competence and self-esteem.

Clearly defined teacher expectations can serve as an important framework for student self-evaluation. For instance, if an elementary school child is supposed to keep quiet when someone is talking, and does, he *knows* he is successful. If a high school student knows she is expected to participate, and she does, she knows she tried her best. If she is supposed to have a book report in by Friday noon, and she does, she knows she successfully lived up to an expectation. In other words, the existence of teacher expectations can leave students with the feeling that a definition of their school environment is possible and that the world does impose restrictions and make demands that they can learn to handle on a daily basis.

Expectations perform another important function. They not only represent a belief in students' adequacy, but they also relay the message that students have the ability to do what is required of them. When set at reasonable levels, expectations represent a vote of confidence.

Do teacher expectations make a difference? On the basis of the evidence, I think they definitely do. There is no magic in this. Students will not do better or work as hard as they are able just because the teacher "expects" or "believes" that they can do good work. A teacher's expectations of, or beliefs in, a student's adequacy will probably not make a whit of difference unless those beliefs were explicitly expressed in teacher behavior that was supportive, encouraging, and functionally helpful. All in all, it appears that teachers see what they expect to see, and the pupil sees what the teacher sees.

9.15 Expectations Are All Around Us

If you look around, you might see examples of how expectations work in areas of your life outside the classroom. What about the expectations your parents had of your behavior and achievement in school? Does your loved one or roommate have expectations of you? Do you of him or her? How are those expectations communicated? How has your behavior been influenced? In what ways have you influenced the other person?

A WORD OF CAUTION ABOUT EXPECTATIONS

There is nothing mystical about how a teacher's expectations work, and the influence these expectations can have on student behavior and performance. If students strive to live up to teachers' expectations, it will be not only because the expectations are reasonable, but because of an interpersonal relationship in which teachers are viewed as persons who are basically trustworthy, friendly, warm, and sure of themselves. Students, particularly at the elementary level, are eager to please, and will work hard to meet expectations if they like the teacher and are sure that the teacher likes them.

Expectations are powerful, self-perpetuating attitudes for students as well as teachers because expectations guide both perceptions and behavior. When we expect that something will happen in a particular way, the likelihood of that "something" happening is far greater than if we did not have such an expectation. For example, if Michael anticipates teaching to be a drag, and boring, and Michelle looks forward to teaching because it is a challenge and seems exciting, is it difficult to predict which of the two will find the most reward in his or her work?

If, at the beginning of a new school year, one of David's ninth-grade teachers is told that he is "difficult to manage" because he is "so restless," and another is given information suggesting that he will "be a challenge" because he is "so intellectually curious," is it difficult to predict which teacher will see a problem and which teacher will see potential? Thus, expectations not only cause us to notice some things and to fail to notice others, they affect the way we *interpret* what we notice, something we need to be conscious of in our interactions with others.

EPILOGUE

Probably no thirteen-year span is more critical in shaping attitudes about oneself—particularly feelings of adequacy and competence—than that between ages 5 and 18. These are the years—the formative years—when growing children and developing adolescents incorporate and refine the attitude that says, "I can," or the one that says, "I can't." The role of the school in the development and change of self-concept is enormous. It dispenses praise and reproof and acceptance and rejection on a colossal scale. Indeed, school provides not only the stage on which much of the drama of a young person's formative years is played, but houses the most critical audience in the world—peers and teachers. It is here, in the face of their severest critics, that students are likely to be reminded repeatedly of either their failings and shortcomings or of their strengths and possibilities.

If we were to pick out a time in children's lives that is probably the most crucial in shaping their feelings of academic competence and intellectual adequacy, it would be the elementary school years. It is during these years that children are most susceptible to the emotional consequences of success or failure precisely because their sense of who they are and what they can do is incompletely formed. If children experience more failures than successes in elementary school, they can develop the sort of negative self-attitudes that lead to defeatism, despair, and hopelessness, none of which are good predictors of later academic success or healthy adjustment during the adult years.

Research evidence does not permit us to say that a high self-concept will automatically lead to high achievement, but it does allow us to conclude that high achievement rarely occurs in the absence of a reasonably high self-concept. Although we cannot say definitely which comes first, good schoolwork or high self-regard, we can say that they are mutually reinforcing to the extent that a positive change in one encourages a positive change in the other.

Although a student's self-concept expands and takes shape during the elementary years, it is important to keep in mind that it can be reshaped, redirected, and modified—for better or worse—during the junior high and high school years. No matter what the grade level—kindergarten or college—teachers are a potent source of feedback for students' feelings about themselves. A child ridiculed at the blackboard in front of his buddies by an insensitive teacher might learn that it is better not to raise his hand, that maybe he is not as capable as other kids. A quiet, uncertain adolescent praised in the presence of her classmates for a contribution she made might learn that speaking out, that taking a risk now and then, is not so dangerous after all.

All in all, what happens to children as they go through school must certainly rank as one of the most important experiences in their lives. Depending on what happens at school, students learn that they are able or unable, adequate or inadequate. One's concept of self is learned, and what is learned can be taught. The question is not whether we approve of teaching for a positive sense of self in school settings, but whether the effects of schooling are positive or negative. School is likely to be a positive experience that encourages healthy self-attitudes to the extent that we concentrate on students' strengths, praise their best efforts, and establish fair and consistent expectations for performance.

STUDY AND REVIEW QUESTIONS

1. How would you describe the difference between self-concept and self-esteem?
2. The point was made that self-concept and behavior are reciprocal and interactive. Can you explain what this means, and why it is so?
3. Why is it that global measures of self-concept are not very good predictors of achievement in specific school subjects?
4. Can you explain why the most accurate and, hence, the most potent comparison information is derived from persons similar to us?
5. Explain why it is so important for all children to experience as much success as possible in elementary school. If their failures outnumber their successes, what are the possible consequences?
6. What does research suggest about the relationship between self-concept and school achievement? How would you describe the strength of that relationship?
7. Which comes first—a high self-concept or high achievement?
8. The point was made that a positive self-concept is a necessary, but not a sufficient, condition for achievement. Can you explain why this is the case?
9. What are four or five behavioral differences that tend to distinguish between students with high and low self-concept?
10. Discuss at least three strategies teachers can use to help students enhance their self-concepts and increase school achievement.
11. What is a self-fulfilling prophecy?
12. How would you describe the relationship between expectations and self-fulfilling prophecy?
13. Explain the difference between "induced" teacher expectations and "natural" expectations? How are each formed?
14. Using the six-step model proposed by Brophy and Good, give an example of how a teacher's expectations can become a self-fulfilling prophecy.
15. Rosenthal has proposed a "four-factor" theory to explain how positive expectations are communicated. What are those four factors, and how does each work?
16. Fifteen teacher behaviors associated with the communication of low expectations were cited and briefly discussed. Recall seven or eight of them and explain *why* those behaviors are associated with low expectations?
17. When thinking about how teachers communicate low expectations, there are at least three cautions to keep in mind. What are they?

18. Why is it that if students only do what they choose to do that their self-concepts might not be enhanced? Conversely, if students meet fair and reasonable teacher expectations, their self-concepts might be more positive. How would you explain this?

REFERENCES

Babad, E. Y., Inbar, J., and Rosenthal, R. "Teachers' Judgment of Students' Potential as a Function of Teachers' Susceptibility to Biasing Information." *Journal of Personality and Social Psychology,* 1982, *42,* pp. 541–547.

Bachman, J. G., and O'Malley, P.M. "Self-Esteem in Young Men: A Longitudinal Analysis of the Impact of Educational and Occupational Attainment." *Journal of Personality and Social Psychology,* 1977, *50,* pp. 365–380.

Bachman, J. G., and O'Malley, P.M. "Self-Concepts, Self-Esteem, and Educational Experiences: The Frog Pond Revisited (Again)." *Journal of Personality and Social Psychology,* 1986, *35,* pp. 35–46.

Bachman, J. G., O'Malley, P. M., and Johnson, J. *Adolescence to Adulthood: Changes and Stability in the Lives of Young Men.* Ann Arbor: University of Michigan, Institute for Social Research, 1978.

Bloom, B. S. *Stability and Change in Human Characteristics.* New York: Wiley, 1964.

Borislow, B. "Self-Evaluation and Academic Achievement." *Journal of Counseling Psychology,* 1962, *9,* pp. 245–254.

Braun, C. "Teacher Expectations: Sociopsychological Dynamics." *Review of Educational Research,* 1976, *46,* pp. 185–213.

Bridgeman, B., and Shipman, V. C. "Preschool Measures of Self-Esteem and Achievement as Predictors of Third-Grade Achievement." *Journal of Educational Psychology,* 1978, *70,* 17–28.

Brim, O. G., and Kagan, J. (Eds.). *Constancy and Change in Human Development.* Cambridge, MA: Harvard University Press, 1980.

Brookover, W. B., Erickson, E. L., and Joiner, L. M. *Self-Concept of Ability and School Achievement Relationship of Self-Concept to Achievement in High School* (Educational Research Series No. 36). East Lansing, MI: Educational Publication Services, 1967.

Brookover, W. B., LePere, J. M., Hamachek, D., Thomas, S., and Erickson, E. L. *Self-Concept of Ability and School Achievement, II.* East Lansing, MI: Educational Publication Services, 1965.

Byrne, B. M. "Self-Concept/Academic Achievement Relations: An Investigation of Dimensionality, Stability, and Causality." *Canadian Journal of Behavioral Science,* 1986, *18,* pp. 173–186.

Calsyn, R. L., and Kenny, D. A. "Self-Concept of Ability and Perceived Evaluation of Others: Cause or Effect of Achievement?" *Journal of Educational Psychology,* 1977, *69,* pp. 135–145.

Chaiken, A., Sigler, E., and Derlega, V. "Non-Verbal Mediators of Teacher Expectancy Efforts." *Journal of Personality and Social Psychology,* 1974, *20,* pp. 144–149.

Chiu, L. H. "Development of the Self-Esteem Rating Scale for Children (revised)." *Measurement and Evaluation in Counseling and Development,* 1987, April, pp. 36–41.

Cooper, H. M. "Pygmalion Grows Up: A Model for Teacher Expectation Communication and Performance Influence." *Review of Educational Research,* 1979, *49,* pp. 389–410.

Coopersmith, S. *The Antecedents of Self-Esteem.* San Francisco: Freeman, 1967.

Dillon, H. A. *A Major Educational Problem.* New York: National Child Labor Committee, 1949.

Doyle, W. G., Hancock, G., and Kifer, E. *Teacher's Perceptions: Do They Make a Difference?* Paper presented at the American Education Research Association annual meeting, Chicago, 1971.

Dyson, E. "A Study of Ability Grouping and Self-Concept." *Journal of Education Research,* 1967, *60,* pp. 403–405.

Ekstrom, R. B., Goertz, M. E., Pollack, J. M., and Rock, D. A. "Who Drops Out of School and Why? Findings from a National Study." *Teachers College Record,* 1986, *87,* pp. 356–373.

Elahoff, J. D. , and Snow, R. E. *A Case Study in Statistical Inference: Reconsideration of the Rosenthal-Jacobson Data on Teacher Expectancy* (Tech. Rep. No. 15). Stanford: Stanford Center for Research and Development in Teaching, Stanford University, 1970.

Erikson, E. H. *Identity and the Life Cycle.* New York: W. W. Norton, 1980.

Felson, R. B. "The Effects of Self-Appraisals of Ability on Academic Performance." *Journal of Personality and Social Psychology,* 1984, *47,* pp. 944–952.

Findley, M. J., and Cooper, H. M. "Locus of Control and Academic Achievement: A Literature Review." *Journal of Personality and Social Psychology,* 1983, *44,* pp. 419–427.

Fine, M., and Rosenberg, P. "Dropping Out of High School: The Ideology of School and Work." *Journal of Education,* 1983, *165,* pp. 257–272.

Finn, J. D. "How to Make the Dropout Problem Go Away." *Educational Researcher,* 1991, January–February, pp. 28–30.

Gephart, W. J. "Will the Real Pygmalion Please Stand Up? *American Educational Research Journal,* 1970, *7,* pp. 473–475.

Godfrey, E. *North Carolina Education,* 1971, October, II, pp. 10–11, 29.

Good, T. L., and Brophy, J. E. *Looking in Classrooms,* 6th ed. New York: HarperCollins, 1994.

Guttman, J., and Bartel, D. "Stereotypic Perceptions of Teachers." *American Educational Research Journal,* 1982, *19,* pp. 519–528.

Hahn, A. "Reaching Out to America's Dropouts: What to Do?" *Phi Delta Kappan,* 1987, December, pp. 256–263.

Hall, J. A. *A Study of Dropouts.* Miami: Dade County Public Schools, Department of Research and Information, 1964.

Hamachek, D. *Encounters with the Self,* 4th ed. Fort Worth: Harcourt Brace Jovanovich, 1992.

Hansford, B. C., and Hattie, J. A. "The Relationship Between Self and Achievement/Performance Measures." *Review of Education Research,* 1982, *52,* pp. 123–142.

Harter, S., Whitesell, R., and Kowalski, P. "Individual Differences in the Effects of Educational Transitions on Young Adolescents' Perceptions of Competence and Motivational Orientation." *American Educational Research Journal,* 1992, *29,* pp. 777–807.

Hogan, R., and Weiss, D. S. "Personality Correlates of Superior Academic Achievements." *Journal of Counseling Psychology,* 1974, *21,* pp. 144–149.

Hoge, R. V., and Luce, S. "Predicting Classroom Achievement from Classroom Behavior." *Review of Educational Research,* 1979, *49,* pp. 479–496.

James, W. *Principles of Psychology.* I. New York: Holt, 1890.

Kagan, D. M. "How Schools Alienate Students at Risk: A Model for Examining Proximal Classroom Variables." *Educational Psychologist,* 1990, *25,* pp. 105–125.

Kelly, K. R., and Jordan, L. K. "Effects of Academic Achievement and Gender on Academic and Social Self-Concept: A Replication Study." *Journal of Counseling and Development,* 1990, *69,* pp. 173–177.

Kifer, E. "The Effects of School Achievement on the Affective Traits of the Learner." Paper presented at the annual meeting of the American Educational Research Association, New Orleans, 1975.

Kohlberg, L., LaCrosse, J., and Ricks, D. "The Predictability of Adult Mental Health from Childhood Behavior." In B. B. Wolman (Ed.), *Manual of Child Psychopathology.* New York: McGraw-Hill, 1972.

Lamy, M. W. "Relationship of Self-Perceptions of Early Primary Children to Achievement in Reading." In I. J. Gordon (Ed.), *Human Development: Readings in Research.* Glenview, IL: Scott, Foresman, 1965.

Lepper, M. R., Ross, L., and Lau, R. R. "Persistence of Inaccurate Beliefs About the Self: Perseverance Effects in the Classroom." *Journal of Personality and Social Psychology,* 1986, *50,* pp. 42–491.

Luginbuhl, J. E. R. "Role of Choice and Outcome on Feelings of Success and Estimates of Ability." *Journal of Personality and Social Psychology,* 1972, *22,* pp. 121–127.

Mann, D. "Can We Help Dropouts: Thinking About the Undoable." *Teachers College Record,* 1986.

Marsh, H. W. "A Multidimensional, Hierarchial Model of Self-Concept: Theoretical and Empirical Justification." *Educational Psychology Review,* 1990a, *2,* pp. 77–172.

Marsh, H. W. "Relations Among Dimensions of Self-Attribution, Dimensions of Self-Concept, and Academic Achievement." *Journal of Educational Psychology,* 1984, *76,* pp. 1291–1308.

Marsh, H. W. "The Influence of Internal and External Frames of Reference on the Formulation of English and Math Self-Concepts." *Journal of Educational Psychology,* 1990b, *82,* pp. 107–116.

Marsh, H. W., Byrne, B. M., and Shavelson, R. J. "A Multifaceted Academic Self-Concept: Its Hierarchial Structure and Its Relation to Academic Achievement." *Journal of Educational Psychology,* 1988, *80,* pp. 366–380.

Marsh, H. W., and Shavelson, R. J. "Self-Concept: Its Multifaceted, Hierarchial Structure." *Educational Psychologist,* 1985, *20,* pp. 107–123.

Maw, W. H., and Maw, E. H. "Self-Concepts of High- and Low-Curiosity Boys." *Child Development,* 1970, *70,* pp. 169–175.

Merton, R. K. "The Self-Fulfilling Prophecy." *Antioch Review,* 1948, *8,* pp. 193–210.

Mettee, D., and Riskin, D. "Size of Defeat and Liking for Superior Ability Competitions." *Journal of Experimental Social Psychology,* 1974, *10,* pp. 333–351.

Ozer, D. J. *Consistency in Personality: A Methodological Framework.* New York: Springer-Verlag, 1986.

Palardy, M. J. "What Teachers Believe, What Children Achieve." *Elementary School Journal,* 1969, *69,* pp. 370–374.

Peck, N., Law, A., and Mills, R. C. *Dropout Prevention: What We Have Learned.* Eric Counseling and Personnel Services Clearing House, Ann Arbor, The University of Michigan, 1987.

Raudenbush, S. "Magnitude of Teacher Expectancy Effects on Pupil IQ as a Function of the Credibility of Expectancy Induction: A Synthesis of Findings from 18 Experiments." *Journal of Educational Psychology,* 1984, *76,* pp. 85–97.

Rosenthal, R., and Jacobson, L. *Pygmalion in the Classroom.* New York: Holt, Rinehart, and Winston, 1968.

Rosenthal, R. *On the Social Psychology of the Self-Fulfilling Prophecy: Further Evidence for Pygmalion Effects and Their Mediating Mechanisms.* New York: MSS Modular Publications, 1974.

Rosenthal, R. "The Pygmalion Effect Lives." *Psychology Today,* 1973, September, p. 60.

Rotherham, M. J. "Children's Social and Academic Competence." *Journal of Educational Research,* 1987, *80,* pp. 206–211.

Sagor, R. "Teetering on the Edge of Failure." *Learning,* 1988, April, pp. 29–33.

Schunk, D. H. "Goal Difficulty and Attainment Information: Effects on Children's Behaviors." *Human Learning,* 1983, *25,* pp. 107–117.

Seaver, W. B. "Effects of Naturally Induced Teacher Expectancies." *Journal of Abnormal and Social Psychology.* 1973, *28,* pp. 333–342.

Shavelson, R. J., and Marsh, H. W. "On the Structure of Self-Concept." In R. Schwarzer (Ed.), *Anxiety and Cognitions.* Hillsdale, NJ: Lawrence Erlbaum, 1986.

Shiffler, N., Lynch-Sauer, J., and Nadelman, L. "Relationship Between Self-Concept and Behavior in Two Informal Elementary Classrooms." *Journal of Educational Psychology,* 1977, *69,* pp. 349–359.

Staines, J. W. "The Self-Picture as a Factor in the Classroom." *The British Journal of Educational Psychology,* 1958, *28,* pp. 97–111.

Stern, D., and Catterall, J. "Reducing the High Dropout Rate in California: Why We Should and How We May." In D. Stern, J. Catterall, C. Alhadeff, and M. Ash (Eds.), *Report to the California Policy Seminar on Reducing the Dropout Rate in California.* Berkeley: University of California School of Education, 1985.

Tesser, A., and Campbell, J. "Self-Definition: The Impact of Relative Performance and Similarity of Others." *Social Psychology Quarterly,* 1980, *43,* pp. 341–347.

Underwood, B., and Moore, B.S. "Sources of Behavioral Consistency." *Journal of Personality and Social Psychology,* 1981, *40,* pp. 780–785.

Yarworth, J. S., and Gautheir, W. J. "Relationship of Student Self-Concept and Selected Personal Variables to Participation in School Activities." *Journal of Educational Psychology,* 1978, *70,* pp. 335–344.

Wattenberg, C., and Clifford, C. "Relation of Self-Concept to Beginning Achievement in Reading." *Child Development,* 1964, *35,* pp. 461–467.

Wheeler, L., and Miyake, K. "Social Comparison in Everyday Life." *Journal of Personality and Social Psychology,* 1992, *62,* pp. 760–773.

Wineburg, S. S. "The Self-Fulfillment of the Self-Fulfilling Prophecy." *Educational Researcher,* 1987, December, pp. 28–37.

Zanna, M. P., Goethals, G. R., and Hill, J. F. "Evaluating a Sex-Related Ability: Social Comparison with Similar Others and Standard Setters." *Journal of Experimental Social Psychology,* 1975, *11,* pp. 86–93.

SELECTED READINGS OF RELATED INTEREST

Beane, J. A., and Lipka, R. P. *Self-Concept, Self-Esteem, and the Curriculum.* Columbia University: Teachers College Press, 1986. This volume represents an effort to blend educational psychology and curriculum planning with a focus on self-concept and self-esteem. It includes excellent discussions on how self-perceptions are related to school achievement and implications for curriculum planning.

Borba, M. *Esteem Builders: A K–8 Self-Esteem Curriculum for Improving School Achievement, Behavior, and School Climate.* Rolling Hills Estates, CA: Jalmar Press, 1989. This volume is rich with ideas for building a curriculum and developing a kind of climate that encourages the development of positive attitudes about oneself and learning.

Brinthaupt, T. M., and Lipka, R. P. (Eds.). *The Self: Definitional and Methodological Issues.* New York: The State University of New York Press, 1992. For those interested in exploring self and self-concept issues more deeply, this book, although somewhat technical, is a fine reference source.

Canfield, J. *Self-Esteem in the Classroom: A Curriculum Guide.* Rolling Hills Estates, CA: Jalmar Press, 1982. A comprehensive resource guide containing more than 200 activities for all grade levels, plus 79 activities specifically for elementary use, this book also includes a discussion explaining the relationship between self-concept and school achievement.

Canfield, J., and Siccone, F. *101 Ways to Develop Self-Esteem and Responsibility.* Needham Heights, MA: Allyn and Bacon, 1993. This book is a veritable gold mine of practical ideas, exercises, and suggestions that teachers can use in their everyday activities to help students perform better in school and enhance their self-esteem.

Canfield, J., and Wells, H. C. *One Hundred (100) Ways to Enhance Self-Concept,* 2nd ed. Needham Heights, MA: Allyn and Bacon, 1994. This is a new edition of a tremendously successful book—30 printings in 16 years. The authors have collected a fresh and appealing collection of activities and examples of how teachers can build a validating, success-oriented classroom community.

Purkey, W. W. *Inviting School Success: A Self-Concept Approach to Teaching and Learning,* 2nd ed. Belmont, CA: Wadsworth, 1984. Compared to other approaches to teaching that describe teachers as managers, motivators, shapers, or guides, this book defines the teacher as an *inviter,* in the sense of inviting students to see themselves as able, valuable, and self-directing.

10

Assessing Learning Outcomes

CHAPTER OVERVIEW

IMPORTANT CHAPTER IDEAS

1. *Measurement* of students' learning is a way of answering questions such as, "How much do they know?" and "How high is their achievement?"
2. *Evaluation* of students' learning is a way of assessing "how well" or "how satisfactorily" they have performed.
3. Formative evaluation is concerned with "how *are* we doing?"; summative evaluation is concerned with "how *did* we do?"
4. Instructional objectives define what is to be learned, which in turn determines what is to be evaluated.
5. There are three major domains of objectives: cognitive, affective, and psychomotor.
6. A good test has both reliability and validity, but cannot be reliable unless it is valid.
7. Measures of central tendency are useful score interpreters because they reflect the point at which a group of scores tends to cluster or center.

8. Range, percentile rank, and standard deviation are useful in understanding test scores in relation to the total distribution of scores.
9. A test's standard error of measure alerts us to the fact that scores are not exact and that they can always vary because of some type of measurement error.
10. Criterion-referenced testing is an approach to measurement in which each student is tested against an objective criterion.
11. Mastery learning is associated with criterion-referenced measurement and is built on the assumption that most students can master what is taught if given enough time.
12. A major argument against mastery approaches to learning and evaluation is that too much of a teacher's time is spent on corrective instruction, which, while benefiting slower students, holds up the faster ones.
13. A major argument in favor of mastery approaches is that, theoretically at least, all students can demonstrate the same level of learning if given enough time to do so.
14. Norm-referenced testing is a way of telling how well students have done in a specified amount of time when compared to other students.
15. The specific types of tests teachers use is determined to some extent by what they wish to measure.
16. Standardized tests are different from teacher-made tests in that they are commercially prepared to measure knowledge in specific content areas, standardized on large groups of students, and used to compare students' performances in one school, city, or state, with another. They are helpful in diagnosing and evaluating students for placement in special education or special ability groups.
17. Authentic assessment is a new movement in measuring students' progress that asks them to apply their school-acquired knowledge and skills in ways that approximate actual life circumstances.
18. Portfolios and exhibitions are being used more frequently as methods for assessing students' progress.
19. There is no "best" way to measure students achievement; rather, the best advice is to use a variety of approaches.
20. Although the grading system will probably never be perfect for all students, it can be fair when used wisely and humanely.

PROLOGUE

Where there is teaching and learning, there must be a fair way of assessing the kind and amount of learning that has occurred. Measuring the extent of students' learning and evaluating the merits of it are two of the more important and difficult aspects of being a teacher.

Evaluation is part of everyday living. It helps us to know our strengths and to identify our weaknesses. Assessing student progress is not an easy task. It involves a delicate balance of subjective feelings and objective evidence. However it is done, it is an important part of every teacher's life.

Creating exams, grading papers, assigning grades, and so forth do not have to be mechanical and dehumanizing activities. They can be honest, humane efforts to help students recognize their limitations and identify their strengths. Like most everything else in life, there are better ways and bad ways for doing this. In order to help you to select the better ways, this chapter provides an overview of some of the basic ideas and concepts related to sound measurement and evaluation practices.

How do measurement and evaluation differ? What is the difference between a reliable test and valid one? What are the common measures of central tendency? How does norm-referenced testing differ from criterion-referenced testing? What are the advantages and disadvantages of various types of teacher-made tests? How do standardized tests differ from teacher-made tests? What are some of the major issues associated with grading and reporting? What are some alternative grading system possibilities? These and related questions are addressed in this chapter.

MEASUREMENT AND EVALUATION: DIFFERENT BUT RELATED

Although the terms *measurement* and *evaluation* are used loosely and, frequently, interchangeably, they refer to distinct processes. The term *measurement* refers to a process of determining the extent, dimensions, or quantity of something. In education, measurement procedures refer to the use of objective tests that yield quantitative data. A measurement is relatively objective and impersonal, and addresses itself to such questions as "How much do students know?" and "How high is their achievement?"

Evaluation is a different process in the sense that it involves a qualitative judgment of "how well" or "how satisfactorily" a student has performed. Evaluations are usually subjective, personal, and difficult to define with a high degree of precision. Thus, to evaluate something means to place a value on it based on previously determined standards. When you give your students a test that yields a particular score, the score represents a measurement. When you decide what grades to assign to those scores, you have made an evaluation. Thus, we can say that the score from a test represents a measurement, and the interpretation concerning the meaning and value of that score represents an evaluation.

Formative and Summative Assessment

Basically, formative assessment is the kind that is used to help guide teachers in planning and to help guide students in identifying areas of weakness. One kind of formative assessment is with the use of a *pretest*, which gives both the teacher and the students an idea of how much is already known. And sometimes formative tests of various kinds are given during the course of instruction in order to isolate areas in which students are having more trouble.

Usually, tests of this kind are not scored for measurement purposes, but are used as diagnostic tools to find out where more assistance is needed. You might say that formative assessment allows the teacher and the student to *form* some tentative ideas about the nature of the progress being made.

The major function of summative evaluation, however, is to determine the overall status of learning and achievement at the conclusion of an instruction unit. Usually, this type of feedback is the byproduct of a final examination and/or final paper. Compared to formative evaluation, there is greater finality associated with summative evaluation. It is one thing to do poorly on a short quiz that can be made up (or brought up) on other quizzes, it is quite another to fall short of one's best on a final test; there is only one final exam. You might say that summative evaluations *sum up* one's overall progress.

In order to measure how much students have learned, and to evaluate how well they have performed, it is necessary first to specify what we hoped they would learn in the first place, an idea we turn to next.

10.1 Which Would You Say Is More Important?

Assume that a principal who is interviewing you for a staff position asks you the following question, "What kind of assessment would you want to use more frequently with your students—formative or summative?" How would you respond? Why would you respond the way you do?

ASSESSMENT PREREQUISITES: DEFINITION OF GOALS AND OBJECTIVES

Two basic questions must be answered before we can assess students' learning: (1) "Why is this subject matter being offered in the first place?"; (2) "What do I want my students to learn from this subject matter?" When we are able to answer these questions in at least a general sort of way, we can begin to be more specific about what the objectives and goals should be. Usually, these goals and objectives can be broken into three major classes, which are the following:

1. *Informational goals and objectives* include learning and mastering such things as names, dates, technical terms, rules, definitions, principles, concepts, and formulae.
2. *Proficiency goals and objectives* include learning to write legibly; using the school library; presenting a reasonably clear, coherent oral report in class; or even swimming 100 yards without stopping.
3. *Attitudinal goals and objectives,* a more difficult area of evaluation, involve aesthetic values, personal preferences, and individual tests. It would include such objectives as encouraging an appreciation for reading or for the contributions of political and scientific figures, pride in one's social heritage, and loyalty to certain democratic ideals.

Almost all educational psychologists and teachers agree that objectives are important. There is, however, disagreement about how specific they should be. It has been argued by some educational psychologists (Hopkins and Antes, 1985; Payne, 1992) that there are many advantages to formulating and stating very explicitly objectives based on observable performance. The argument in favor of specific behavioral objectives is that: (1) teachers will know more clearly what to teach to achieve those objectives, (2) objectives can serve as neon-bulbed guidelines to assist students directly toward their mastery, and (3) specific objectives can be utilized as the basis for constructing examinations to evaluate how well and to what extent the objectives have been accomplished. Some examples of objectives of this type might be the following:

1. The student should be able to add and subtract fractions associated with three-digit numbers.
2. The student should be able to discuss four major political-social causes of the Civil War.
3. The student should be able to park a regular-sized sedan in a space of fourteen feet, no more than six to eight inches from the curb. He or she should do this in thirty seconds, using no more than four changes of gear.

Objectives described in terms similar to those above are called *behavioral objectives.* They describe the desired *outcomes* in terms of specific acts or behaviors. They indicate the *conditions* or *context* (e.g., *three*-digit fractions, *four* political-social causes, *regular sized* sedan in a *fourteen* foot space) under which the behavior should occur.

Not all, however, would agree that highly specific behavioral objectives are a good idea. Ebel (1972), for example, has suggested that there are hazards associated with drawing up specific objectives.

> Defining educational objectives in terms of desired behavior . . . appears to assume that despite the highly complex and rapidly changing world in which we live, a teacher can know ahead of time how the scholar ought to behave in a given set of circumstances. It also seems to assume that the teacher is entitled to prescribe in his behavior for him. . . . It seems important to suggest strongly that the proper starting point of educational planning in a democracy is not the kind of behaviors present adults desire future adults to exhibit but rather the kind of equipment that will enable them to choose their own behaviors intelligently. (pp. 62–64)

No one argues that behavioral objectives are not important at all. There is wide agreement that they are necessary in order to know where to begin a learning experience, how to assess it along the way, and where to conclude it. Some curriculum areas, such as math and science, might demand more specific objectives to reflect the more exact nature of the content. Other curriculum areas, such as social science, art, literature, and English composition, might tolerate more general objectives because of the more relative nature of the content.

10.2 How Do You Feel About Instructional Objectives?

How specific do you think objectives should be? As a student, would you prefer to be confronted with specific objectives that leave no doubt as to what you are to learn and be tested on, or would you prefer more general objectives that allow you more latitude for a voice and choice in your learning? When you think about what you will be teaching and the level at which you will teach, do you think specific or more general instructional objectives will be appropriate? Why?

OBJECTIVES COME IN THREE DOMAINS: COGNITIVE, AFFECTIVE, AND PSYCHOMOTOR

Behavioral objectives can usually be classified under one of three domains of objectives—cognitive, affective, and psychomotor. A distinct taxonomy, or classification scheme, has been published for each of these domains, which can be enormously useful in helping one decide not only what objectives to include in an instructional program, but how to teach those objectives in meaningful ways. Bloom, Englehart, Furst, Hill, and Krathwohl (1956) developed the taxonomy for the cognitive domain; Krathwohl, Bloom, and Masia (1964) for the affective domain; and Harrow (1972) for the psychomotor domain.

Within the *cognitive domain* there are six levels of "knowing," for which there might be objectives. From the most simple means of knowing to the most complex, the six levels fall in this order:

1. *Knowledge:* The ability to remember ideas, facts, and information (e.g., knowing the difference between measurement and evaluation).
2. *Comprehension:* The ability to receive information and make use of it (e.g., understanding that to "measure" performance is not to "evaluate" performance).
3. *Application:* The ability to use abstractions, rules, principles, ideas, and methods in particular situations (e.g., the ability to choose the proper testing procedure to measure student's learning in a given area).
4. *Analysis:* The ability to break communication into its constituent elements or parts (e.g., the ability to determine whether a testing procedure is a *valid* measure of students' learning).
5. *Synthesis:* The ability to work with pieces, parts, and elements, and to combine them to form a new pattern of understanding (e.g., the ability to discuss how using behavioral objectives relates to teaching from a behavioristic or a humanistic point of view).

6. *Evaluation:* The ability to make quantitative or qualitative judgments about the extent to which materials, methods, or ideas satisfy given criteria (e.g., the ability to judge the merits of using behavioral objectives as a means for facilitating self-concept enhancement; or the ability to decide whether allowing students to evaluate themselves is justified). Evaluation, presumably, is the highest level of cognitive activity.

The basic idea underlying the taxonomy of the *affective domain* is that inner growth takes place as persons grow aware of, and then adopt, attitudes, principles, codes, and sanctions that support their value judgments and guide their behavior. Thus, the steps in this process move from the least complex behavior of *receiving* to the most complex behavior of arriving at a *value* or *value complex*, in the following order. (The examples, remember, are merely some illustrations that I have attempted to relate to this particular chapter. They are by no means the only conclusions possible in any of these five categories.)

1. *Receiving:* Learners are merely sensitized to, or willing to receive or attend to, particular events or ideas (e.g., reading this particular chapter on measurement and evaluation and becoming alert to the various ways for using measurement principles).
2. *Responding:* Learners move from being merely passive recipients of specific inputs, to showing a willingness to respond by using the input in some way, to feeling, eventually, a sense of satisfaction in responding (e.g., learning about ways to evaluate students' learning, to trying some of those ways, to feeling good about the methods used).
3. *Valuing:* Learners progress from merely "knowing" about something to "valuing" it, seeing it as having worth (e.g., coming to accept evaluation procedures as worthwhile and valuable teacher practices that can help promote learning).
4. *Organization of values:* Learners organize a set of values (e.g., truth, wealth, altruism) into a system; they determine their interrelationships and then decide which ones will be passive or dominant (e.g., concluding that student learning can best be done with a criterion-referenced evaluation system, and showing a willingness to talk about, and even defend, that as a good system).
5. *Characterization by a value or value complex:* Here, people have not merely achieved all of the steps lower in the scale of internalization, they have acted in a manner so consistent with those values that they are now integrated into a total behavioral philosophy or world view. For example, as seen by others, people who have achieved this level will be viewed as behaving consistently across different situations because their *value complex* has been thoroughly integrated into their total personality. An instructor for instance, who believes that a criterion-referenced approach is fair and humane for students because it allows time for students to master material at their own pace, might argue the value or worth of that

approach for all classes, at all levels of education. It has become part of his or her *value complex* when thinking about education.

It is much more difficult to write objectives for the affective domain, particularly at the fourth and fifth levels. It is one thing to specify what students should know (i.e., cognitive objectives), but it is another, and somewhat more hazardous, thing to specify what students should *feel* or value.

10.3 Should Affective Objectives Be Part of Public Education?

Some people argue that affective objectives should have no place in children's education because they are too explicit about what students are supposed to feel about particular things, events, or ideas and about what they are supposed to value. For example, some have argued the affective values taught are too often those of "secular humanism" that indoctrinate children with only one point of view about life and living. What is your view on this topic? Is it possible *not* to teach values? Is there a way of resolving this debate?

The *psychomotor domain* is clear-cut and uncontroversial. Learners usually have to go through a particular sequence of steps, and to that end, objectives can be written to correspond to the following seven categories in the psychomotor domain:

1. *Perception:* This involves the use of sense organs to obtain cues that guide motor activity (e.g., learning to hold a tennis racket in a particular way for a forehand or a backhand volley).
2. *Set:* Perception of cues leads to a readiness or a "set" to take a particular action (e.g., getting one's feet in the right position to return a volley or to drive a golf ball).
3. *Guided response:* This happens in the early phases of learning a new skill that might include imitating the instructor, or making a series of trial-and-error attempts, after which the teacher gives feedback.
4. *Mechanism:* The concern here is with relatively simple performance acts in which learned responses have become habitual and are performed with a degree of proficiency. There is an effort here to improve the "mechanism" of the learned response and to move it to a higher level of proficiency (e.g., moving from a single somersault, tuck position dive to a smoother one with less splash).
5. *Complex overt response:* Concentration here is on the skillful performance of motor acts that involve more complex movement patterns than seen in number 4 (e.g., moving from a single somersault, tuck position dive to a double somersault, tuck position with a half twist).
6. *Adaptation:* This is concerned with skills so well developed that one can modify movement patterns to fit the special demands of the situation (e.g., not just returning the tennis ball, but putting "English" on it for backspin).

7. *Origination:* This refers to creating new movement patterns that emphasize creativity based on highly adaptive skills (e.g., creating a new dance step or a new musical composition requiring exceptionally fast keyboard transitions).

Developing objectives in physical education, dance, speech, acting, vocational education, and art can all be helped by considering this taxonomy. However, the psychomotor domain is not as easily put into a hierarchical order as are the cognitive and affective areas.

Having established objectives, the next thing step is to develop a good test.

WHAT ARE THE CHARACTERISTICS OF A GOOD TEST?

Whether we want to measure the distance to the moon, our weight, or school achievement, we must first be certain that the measuring instrument we use can be depended on for reasonably accurate results. In order to check this, we must ask two basic questions:

1. Is the measuring instrument valid (i.e., does it measure what it is supposed to measure?)?
2. Is the instrument reliable (i.e., does it give consistent results?)?

Test Validity Is Essential

To determine whether a test measures what it is supposed to measure, we must first have some idea of what we want to measure; that is, the value of having goals and objectives toward which we are teaching. If our goals and objectives are clear, then it is more possible not only to guide students' learning more effectively, but also to assess their learning with greater validity. When students complain, and often justifiably, that an exam covers material they were unprepared for, this might suggest that the test is not valid for the purpose for which it was intended. Students do not assess an exam in terms of the more abstract concept of validity, but they do react to a more personally sensed feeling of fairness. A wise teacher knows that if too many students take issue with an exam's "fairness," then either the exam was inappropriate for the goals and objectives it sought to measure, or the goals were not clearly explained initially.

Content Validity Is Important

There are several ways of looking at validity. One of these concerns content validity—the extent to which a test "covers" the content that is studied. When testing for achievement in a particular subject area, you can get an idea of the validity of a test by carefully examining its content and comparing that content with the things you want to test. If, for example, you wished to measure skill in solving math story problems, you would want to stay away from items that dealt primarily with number manipulation or addition.

It is possible that a test has content validity for one teacher, but not for another. If, for example, you are interested primarily in problem solving (e.g., figuring out square feet, square yards, or square roots), you might want a test in which the numerical computations are relatively easy. You could then regard this test as valid for your purposes. Another teacher, however, might be searching for a test that will determine depth of skill in doing numerical computations. If the test is limited to easy computation items, it is not valid for this objective.

In general, a good test provides measurement of a good sampling of content and is balanced with respect to coverage of the various parts of the subject.

Construct Validity Is Necessary

Construct validity is a second aspect of validity. It refers to all of the types of learning specified or implied in the objectives. For example, a test that measures only memory of specific facts would lack validity for the objectives that specify other learning goals. Knowledge of facts, for instance, is not the same as the understanding of ideas, and if all a test does is measure a student's memory of factual material, without giving that student a chance to synthesize and integrate ideas, then the test lacks construct validity for an objective that includes both types of testing. The definition of the nominal form of *construct* is something "constructed" by mental synthesis. If a test allows students to "construct" their responses in a manner that is consistent with what the objectives had prepared them for, we can say that the test has "construct validity."

Thus, test validity is specific to purpose, subject matter, objectives, and students; it is not a general characteristic. *Validity* is a relative term; there are degrees of goodness, as there are degrees of badness. Validity is taken into consideration by designing a test that will cover the subject adequately, will measure the types of learning indicated by objectives, and will be suitable for a particular group of students. A test's validity, whether it is a teacher-made classroom test or a standardized achievement test constructed by a testing firm, is the degree to which testing procedures and interpretations help us to measure what we want to measure. Measurement experts are in agreement about the idea that the most important quality to consider when constructing or selecting a test (or other evaluation instrument) is its validity (Gronlund and Linn, 1990; Mehrens and Lehmann, 1991).

Reliability Is Essential

One characteristic of a reliable test is that it gives consistent results. With repeated testing, students are likely to maintain about the same relative rank in their group each time they take a particular test.

It is nearly impossible to construct a totally reliable test. It is not very likely that students' performance on the same examination taken two days apart will be identical. There are at least three factors that can contribute to this variability in examination performance; they are the following:

1. Exams that are too easy or too difficult, or that encourage students to make widely divergent interpretations of the same questions, are not likely to yield highly reliable scores.
2. The stability of a student's ability to respond to the items on an examination changes. Most of us vary from hour to hour and from day to day in our intellectual alertness, physical energy, and emotional balance. Any one of these personal considerations can affect test performance appreciably, and thereby influence the reliability of the test results.
3. The consistency and objectivity of teachers who score the test are the last factor. If the scores teachers assign depend largely on their personal whims of the moment, rather than on standards applied equally to all papers or tests, then it is not likely that these scores will be reliable.

We might also note that a test can be reliable without being valid. For example, a 100-item multiple-choice mathematics test would very likely be an invalid test for measuring English proficiency. Nonetheless, if similar forms of this test were administered on two occasions to a group of students and yielded identical results, we would conclude that the test was reliable, although not necessarily valid. However, if a test is to be valid, it must also be reliable. That is, unless a test consistently measures what it is supposed to measure, we can never be certain that the results are accurate indications of what a student knows or has mastered.

10.4 How Can This Be?

A test can be reliable even if it is not valid, but it cannot be valid if it is not reliable. Think about that. Try to explain in your own words why this is so.

Reliability Increases with Longer Tests

Generally, the reliability of a test can be increased by increasing its length. For example, a student's performance, relative to other students, can be expected to fluctuate much less on a 100-item test than on a 10-item test, and less on a 10-item test than on a 5-item test. The presence of chance factors in a student's responses to questions are much greater when there are ten items involved than when 100 items are involved. Thus, the possibility of receiving a low score because of several very difficult questions, or a high score because of some lucky guesses, tends to be lessened on longer tests.

The principle at work is the same one we might use intuitively when considering a ballplayer's batting average. If a player's average were .500, but he or she had been to bat only ten times, we probably would not take that high average too seriously. We might easily conclude that at least a couple of those hits were either lucky or flukes. However, if that player's batting average were .500 after having batted 100 times, then we might take that average more seriously. We would probably be more willing to accept the .500 average as a reliable index of his or her batting skill because the "test" of the batter's hitting skills was longer, which makes the resulting batting average *less subject to flukes and lucky breaks.* The same applies to scores derived from longer, rather than shorter, tests.

Devising tests that are valid and reliable is an important first step. We turn our attention now to ways in which we can interpret and understand what test scores mean.

MEASURES OF CENTRAL TENDENCY: AIDS FOR INTERPRETING TEST SCORES

A measure of central tendency is a single value that describes average performance on a test. Measures of central tendency show us the score, or point, about which a group of scores tend to cluster or center. Those used most frequently are the *mean,* the *median,* and the *mode.* Let us briefly examine each of these.

Mean

An arithmetic mean is obtained by adding all scores together and dividing by the number of tests. Thus, the mean for six test scores of 40, 50, 65, 70, 75, and 80 would be 380 ÷ 6, or 63.3. When the word *average* is used without further definition, it is generally synonymous with mean.

Median

A median is defined as a point in a distribution that has an equal number of cases on both sides of it. It is the midpoint in a distribution above and below which 50% of scores lie. For example, given test scores of 11, 13, 19, 20, and 21, the median would be 19. This is easy enough to figure out when there are an odd number of test scores, as in the preceding example. However, when there are an even number of test scores of 15, 16, 18, 19, 23, 25, 25 and 30, the median would be 21(19 + 23 = 42 ÷ 2 = 21).

Mode

A third measure of central tendency, and one used rather infrequently, is the mode. Quite simply, a mode is that score in a group of scores that occurs most often. The mode of 80, 83, 83, 87, 92, and 97 is 83 because there are more 83s than any other score.

SCORE DISTRIBUTION DICTATES MEASURE OF CENTRAL TENDENCY TO USE

Test scores tend to be distributed around the average in a characteristic manner. That is, for most tests there is a tendency for more students to get average, or near average, scores than either very high or very low scores. Often, but by no means always, the test scores of large groups of students are distributed in a manner that, in mathematics, approximates a normal curve or forms a *normal distribution.* What this amounts to is a rough probability distribution that one might get by noting the number of times heads and tails come up when a coin is tossed twenty times in succession. The most common combination of results would be ten heads and ten tails. It would be highly unusual to get twenty heads or twenty tails in a row. If the frequency with which each possible combination of heads and tails were plotted on a line graph, a rough approximation of the normal distribution would be obtained. In Figure 10.1, note that when scores are normally distributed, the mean, median, and mode all fall at about the same point, and dissect the distribution into equal parts.

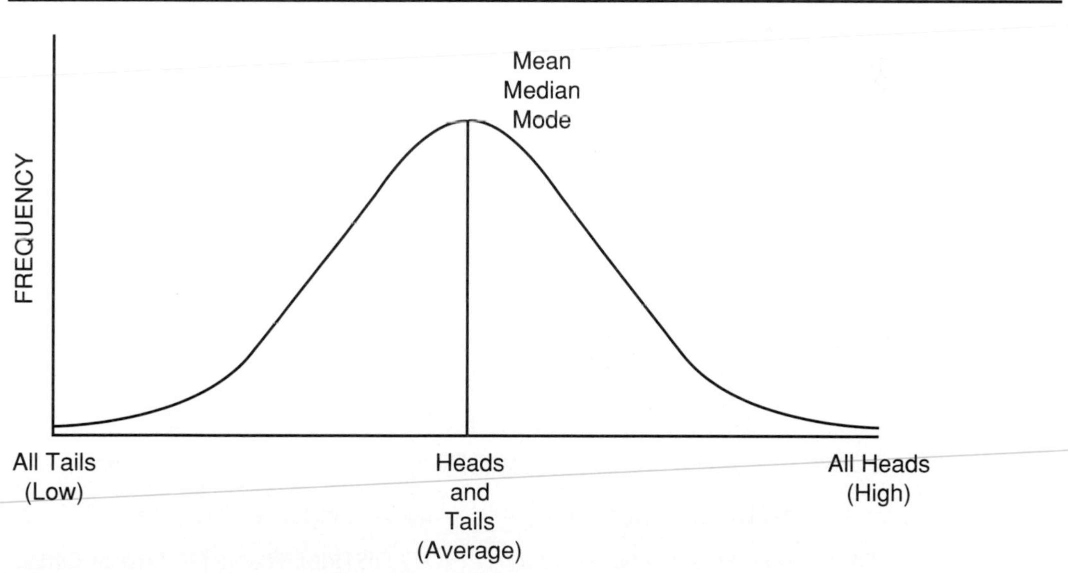

Figure 10.1. A NORMAL DISTRIBUTION CURVE.

10.5 Try a Little Experiment

> Take a coin and flip it twenty times. Keep track of the heads/tails ratio. How close does it come to approximating a normal curve of distribution?

Although there is reason to believe that in the total population many skills and abilities tend to be distributed in a form similar to a normal curve, in practice, this is not always the case. The reason for this is that a distribution of scores is dependent not only on the characteristic being measured, but on: (1) how it is measured, (2) the individuals being measured, and (3) a number of chance factors (e.g., mood, external factors, luck).

When scores are not normally distributed, they sometimes form a "skewed" distribution. High scores or low scores tend to be clustered together more than in a normal distribution, with remaining scores grouping at one end. Figure 10.2 will give you an idea of what a skewed distribution is. When a distribution is skewed toward one end or the other, the mean and the median will not be identical. The mean is likely to be pulled in the direction of the skewed portion, or toward the "tail," of the distribution. When this happens,

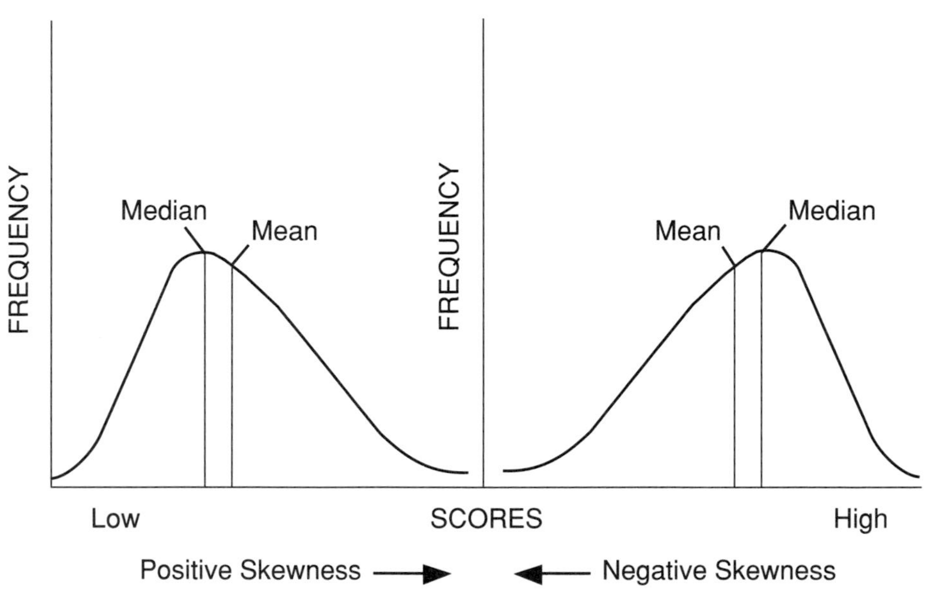

Figure 10.2. POSITIVELY SKEWED AND NEGATIVELY SKEWED DISTRIBUTIONS OF TEST SCORES.

extremely high scores will tend to raise the mean, and extremely low scores will tend to lower it. A very difficult test is likely to have a positively skewed distribution of scores, whereas a very easy one is likely to have a negatively skewed distribution.

Whenever a distribution of scores approximates the shape of a normal curve, the *mean* is our best indication of the central tendency of the scores. However, if the distribution is skewed in one direction or the other, the *median* is probably our indication of central tendency. The reason that the median is the preferable statistic to use in the case of distribution skewing is because extreme scores are ignored; therefore, it makes no difference how far they are from the center. The mean, however, is of such a nature that every score in a distribution affects it, and it is easily pulled in the direction of scores that severely deviate from the center.

In summary, then, the mean gives us the "average" score; the median provides us the midpoint score; and the mode is the score appearing most frequently.

RANGE, PERCENTILE RANK, AND STANDARD DEVIATION: SCORE INTERPRETATION AIDS

In describing and interpreting a group of test scores, it is often useful to indicate not only an average score, but how widely the test scores are spread out and how a particular score can be understood in relation to others.

The most simple measure of spread or dispersion is the *range,* which indicates the difference between the lowest score and the highest score in a group. For example, if the highest score of a test is 95 and the lowest is 40, the range is 55.

Probably the easiest way of making sense of scores, and one that is quickly understood by students and parents, is to establish percentile norms for the class and convert each student's score into an equivalent percentile rank. By definition, a *percentile rank* refers to the percentage of cases falling below a given score. To determine the percentile rank of particular scores, we would take the number of those who rank below each raw score *plus* one-half those who receive exactly the score in question, divide by the total number of persons in the group, and then multiply by 100. The formula for computing percentile ranks works as follows:

$$\frac{\text{Number of persons below a given score} + 1/2 \text{ of persons at score}}{\text{Total number of persons (N)}} \times 100 = \text{percentile rank}$$

To give you an idea of how this formula works, assume that the numbers shown as follows represent scores on a test of thirty students in a given class.

71	65	61	60	57	52
69	64	61	60	57	50
67	63	61	59	56	47
66	63	60	59	55	46
65	62	60	58	54	43

In order to determine the percentile rank of a score of 59, we would first note that eleven students have scores lower than this, and that two students have scores at 59. Therefore, substituting 30 to N in our formula, we would have:

$$\text{percentile rank} = \frac{11+1}{30} \times 100 = 40$$

Thus, 40 would be the percentile rank of a raw score of 59. This means that 60% of all students taking the test scored higher than 59.

Let us take another example, this time with a raw score of 64. We note that twenty-three students have scores lower than 64, and that only one student has a score of 64. The percentile rank of 64 is then:

$$\text{percentile rank} = \frac{23+.05}{30} \times 100 = 76.8$$

Thus, 76 would be the percentile rank of a raw score of 64, which means that only 24% of students taking the test scored higher than 64. (Note that when only one person obtains the raw score for which the percentile rank is being determined, we add one-half of one, or 0.5, to the number of persons below the score.)

10.6 Can You Figure These Out?

Using the scores shown for the thirty students on the previous page, what would the percentile rank be for a student with a score of 61 and another student with a score of 57?

Another common method of translating scores into equivalents that indicate where a student stands in a group utilizes the *mean* and the *standard deviation* as a basis for norms. The standard deviation is a measure of the amount of variability in a group of scores, which in a normal distribution of scores indicates how far one needs to go above and below the *mean* of a test to include a given percentage of all scores. (For example, one standard deviation above and below the mean includes, as you see in Figure 10.3, approximately 68% of all scores on a test.) This technique is not often used in the classroom. It is, however, frequently used to report test results of standardized achievement, personality, aptitude, and interest, which means that as a teacher you need at least a reading, if not a functional, understanding of its use. (If you are curious about the statistical procedures for working out the standard deviation of a group of scores, Mehrens and Lehmann [1991], or Payne [1992] would be useful references.)

If any normal distribution, about two-thirds of cases (or 68%) fall within one standard deviation above or below the mean, which suggests that there is a fixed relationship between where a score falls in a normal distribution and its distance from the mean. In Figure 10.3, you can see the approximate percentage of cases that correspond to each standard deviation unit. You can also see the corresponding percentile equivalents for each of the standard deviation units.

Regardless of how large or small the standard deviation is in any particular group of scores, it can be a useful reference point. For instance, in a normal distribution of scores, if we look at those that are one standard-deviation unit from the mean, we find ourselves directly at that point where the curve changes from convex to concave. If we go three standard-deviation units from the mean, we reach a point in the distribution that has less than 1% of the scores. Thus, it is possible to state in standard-deviation units how far each score is from the mean and to indicate where each one fits in the total distribution.

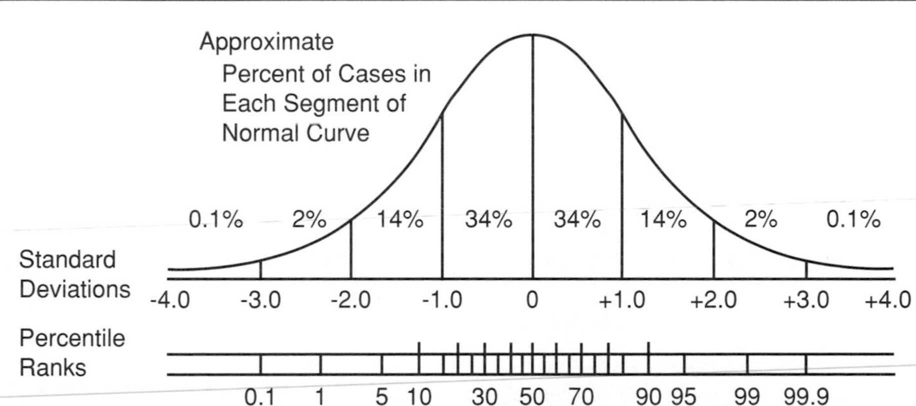

Figure 10.3. A NORMAL DISTRIBUTION CURVE SHOWING STANDARD DEVIATIONS AND PERCENTILE EQUIVALENTS.

NO TEST IS PERFECT—EACH HAS ITS OWN STANDARD ERROR OF MEASUREMENT

The practical importance of considering the standard error of measurement of a test is that it alerts us to the fact that scores are not exact, and that they can always vary because of some type of measurement error. The only type of error—or variation in scores on similar tests—that is "standard," and therefore measurable, is "sampling error." For example, suppose you want to find out how well your junior high school students can spell. There are, let us say, 200,000 words you might ask them to spell, but of that number, there are only 5000 they would ordinarily be asked to spell by junior high age. If you select 100 of these words at random, an accurate score on these words will give you an estimate of the percentage of the 5000 words the students should be able to spell. However, if you randomly choose 100 words for another test, you know that very few students will get the same score on both tests. This variation, as a result the sample that happens to be chosen, is what the standard error indicates.

Thus, the standard error tells within what limits scores can be expected to vary by pure chance *as a result of the selection of items.* When we add to that our own *bias* in selecting particular items, the *silly mistakes* we might make in writing test items and in scoring them, and the *external circumstances* (e.g., noise, sickness, interruptions, hot weather) that might affect students' responses, you can begin to see why there might be a large variation between two or more measures of a single ability.

If a student were to take the spelling test on more than one occasion, how much variance could we usually expect from test score to test score? Statisticians have calculated that any person's hypothetical distribution of actual scores is normally distributed, which means that 68% of the time, a person's actual score is within one standard error of measurement of his or her true score. The reason for explaining it in this way is that standard error of measurement is a particular form of standard deviation—the standard deviation of errors of measurement. You can get a visual idea of this concept by referring to Figure 10.3. You see that one standard deviation above and below the mean includes about 68% of the cases in a normal distribution of scores.

It has been determined by the Educational Testing Service (1962) that tests (true–false, multiple-choice, matching, and so forth) of varied lengths have a specific standard error of measurement, which are as follows:

Number of items	*Standard error*
<24	2
24–27	3
48–89	4
90–109	5
110–129	6
130–150	7

Let us say we give a test of 100 items. Looking at the table, we see that a test of that length has a standard error of five, which means that if we were to give different forms of the same test to the same students, two scores out of three (68%—one standard error) will lie within five raw-score points of the "true score" these students would attain if we continued testing with repeated random samples of items from the universe of items testing the same ability. Let us assume that Johnny received a score of 70 on a single administration of that 100-item test. With a standard error of five, this means that the chances are about 68 out of 100 that the true score was between 65 and 75 (70 plus or minus 5), which means that if Johnny took a retest, the likelihood is 68% that his score would fall somewhere in the 65 to 75 range.

This information can be particularly useful when deciding whether there is a true difference between scores by two students. For example, if Johnny has a 70 on a 100-item test, and Jeannie has a 74, there is probably not a real difference between the two scores because they lie in overlapping ten-point ranges. If, however, Jeannie receives a score of 80, we can with greater confidence point to a possible true difference between the scores because their ranges no longer overlap (e.g., 70 plus or minus 5 = 65 – 75 and 80 plus or minus 5 = 75 – 85).

If you look in the index of a textbook of elementary statistics, you might find as many as fifteen types of standard error; of scores, averages, differences, correlations, proportions, and so forth. They are all computed in their own ways and yield figures of their own orders of magnitude. However it is expressed, the standard score concept reminds us of an important statistical fact of life: No given score is sacrosanct or absolute; rather, it represents a range of possibilities, something we need to consider in our efforts to assess fairly the performance of our students.

The factors we have examined so far—validity, reliability, measures of central tendency, standard error of measurement, and so forth—are all very important to consider when setting up a testing program. A basic question remains, and it is one you will one day have to answer: What type of testing is most appropriate for your purposes? Let us turn our attention now to some of the options from which you can choose.

CRITERION-REFERENCED ASSESSMENT—EVERY STUDENT CAN PASS

The quantity of students' learning can be expressed in one, or both, of two ways: (1) as the amount, or extent, of learning in relation to what they could (or should) have learned; and (2) as the amount they learned in relation to those who learned less than they. The first uses *criterion-referenced* measurements, and the second method uses *norm-referenced* measurements.

How Criterion-Referenced Testing Works

In criterion-referenced testing, *each person is measured against an objective criterion.* Because there is no predetermined number of passes or failures, every student in class has a chance of passing. In this type of test, we do not ask where a student stands in relation to other students, but where he or she stands on a scale representing zero mastery to perfect mastery of a subject. In driver education, for example, we might decide that in order to pass the course a student must be able to park a car within so many inches of a curb, between two other cars so many feet apart, and within so many minutes or so many gear changes. How students perform in relation to other driver-education students does not matter. How they perform in relation to an objective and predetermined criterion does. If all students met the criterion, they would pass. Those who did not would repractice and retake the test until they did.

Mastery Learning and Criterion-Referenced Assessment

The use of criterion-referenced measurement stems from the belief that most students can learn (i.e., master) almost anything if given enough time. At the core of the criterion-referenced argument is the belief that if we can state our objectives in behavioral terms, the important consideration becomes an assessment of whether students have, in fact, achieved these objectives, rather than a concern for their position relative to other students. This is where "mastery test" comes into the picture, which is nothing more than a particular type of criterion-referenced test.

The mastery learning concept was triggered by an intriguing article by Carroll (1963), who argued that differences in student achievement (i.e., mastery) were not the result of inherent differences in learning potential (i.e., some students can master given material and others cannot), but of differences in the time needed to learn (i.e., some students take longer to master material, but they will master it if given enough time). The basic argument Carroll expressed can be seen in the following equation:

$$\text{Degree of learning} = \frac{\text{Time actually spent}}{\text{Time needed}}$$

Thus, Carroll's argument is that all students can master a particular curriculum if given enough time. As pointed out by Anderson (1985), the model assumes a trade-off between learning time and individual differences in mastery. This means that schools cannot have both fixed learning times and fixed mastery. Traditional approaches to schooling deal with this dilemma by establishing learning times and accepting individual differences in mastery levels. The mastery-learning model deals with it by establishing mastery levels and accepting individual differences in learning time (Guskey and Gates, 1986).

Within a mastery-learning model, students are required to work on a particular learning unit until they have achieved a specified, minimum level of achievement. When they do this, they are considered to have "mastered" the material. If they do not perform at a minimum specified level, then they are required to restudy the material covered in the test until they perform adequately (i.e., until they "master" the material).

The heart of mastery learning is the cycle of teaching, testing, reteaching, and retesting. Students are informed of the objectives of a given unit, and instruction is then geared to helping students achieve those objectives. At the conclusion of the unit, students receive some type of formative-evaluation tests designed to assess their level of mastery. Those who meet, or pass, the preset performance standards (usually 80% correct or better) are certified as having mastered the unit and are not required to do further work on it. These students will usually move on to another unit, or, more typically, will work on enrichment activities until the class as a whole is ready to move on to the next unit together. Meanwhile, students who failed to achieve mastery receive corrective instruction and additional practice time, and then are assessed again. Although these cycles of assessment and reteaching might go on indefinitely until all students reach mastery, in actual practice, the cycle usually ceases after the second test administration. Thus, in actual practice, most group-based mastery programs are a compromise between traditional programs that allow little, if any, extra time to slower learners and ideal mastery programs that allow unlimited time to all learners.

Arguments Opposing the Mastery Approach

A major problem associated with the mastery approach is that half, or more, of a teacher's instructional time is spent on corrective instruction with students who fail to reach the predetermined mastery level, which, although good for the slower students, holds up the faster students (Arlin, 1984; Slavin and Karweit, 1985).

Another problem associated with mastery learning is setting criterion for it (Hopkins, Stanley, and Hopkins, 1990; Shepard, 1979). That is, how *much* should students be required to know before passing? How *well* should students perform before "mastery" is acquired? Should the criterion be 100%, or would 80% be sufficient? Should it depend on the subject matter? In regard to these questions, Carroll (1971) points out that if a task is difficult, or depends on special aptitudes, there might be a number of students who *never* make it. For example, no matter how highly motivated some persons are, or how much time they put into it, they might never run 100 yards in ten seconds or become concert pianists or brain surgeons.

Arguments Favoring the Mastery Approach

A major argument for mastery testing is that it allows all students to demonstrate the same level of learning if given enough time. In this way, failure is virtually eliminated, and self-concept enhances. Bloom, Hastings, and Madaus (1971) put it this way:

> Mastery learning can be one of the more powerful sources of mental health. We are convinced that many of the neurotic symptoms displayed by high school and college students are exacerbated by painful and frustrating experiences in school learning. If 90% of the students are given positive indications of adequacy in learning, one might expect them to need less and less in the way of emotional therapy and psychological help. Conversely, frequent indications of failure and learning inadequacy are bound to be accompanied by increased self-doubt in the student. (p. 56)

Although the research findings related to benefits of mastery approaches are not unequivocal, two reviews of literature (Anderson and Burns, 1987; Good and Brophy, 1987) related to mastery learning have shown that it has been successful in increasing the percentage of students who successfully reach mastery criteria or basic objectives, an outcome that has been particularly noticeable for lower achievers. However, the mastery approach has not succeeded in reducing the time that slow learners need to learn (relative to the time needed by faster learners). On the positive side, slow learners do have more time to achieve some level of mastery. On the negative side, fast learners have to be delayed while slower learners catch up. Perhaps a reasonable compromise to this problem is to identify those achievement objectives that seem most essential, and, while allowing for greater variability of performance on objectives that seem less essential, see to it that all students master these objectives.

10.7 Which Objectives Would You Consider Really Important?

When you consider the subject(s) you will teach and the level at which you will be teaching, what learning objectives would you want *all* of your students to achieve? What are some examples of objectives that you consider less important, and on which you would be willing to tolerate more individual differences in performance?

Should you use criterion-referenced testing procedures? As you have seen, there are responses to that question. Before we address it more specifically, let us first take a brief look at another major approach to testing, and then compare the two in our search for guidelines that help determine which testing procedures to use, and when.

NORM-REFERENCED ASSESSMENT—NOT EVERYONE PASSES

Norm-referenced testing is the type with which most of us are familiar because it is the one most commonly used by teachers. It is a way of discriminating among individuals at all points along a continuum, and it is deliberately devised so that persons who have more aptitude, or who have learned more, will score higher on a test than those who have less aptitude, or who have learned less. The interpretation, then, of "how much" aptitude persons possess, or "how much" they have learned, is a normative one; it depends on how much aptitude others have, and on how much others have learned.

A primary difference between norm-referenced and criterion-referenced measurements is in the quantitative scales used to express how much, or how well, a person can do. In norm-referenced testing, it is appropriate to use the various measures of central tendency to locate the middle or average level of performance for a specified group of students. Our scale is then anchored somewhere in the middle of the distribution, and we report students' performance in relation to how they rank relative to others. We might say, "Your score is about average in relation to others in class," or "You exceeded more than 70% of your class." Such group *norms* are typically used when we need to give meaning to scores on intelligence tests and standardized tests of achievement. They are also used in teacher-made tests whenever the instructor "marks on the curve."

CHOOSING BETWEEN NORM- AND CRITERION-REFERENCED ASSESSMENT

Both norm- and criterion-referenced measurements are useful. Each has its place, and each can serve a particular purpose, depending on what a teacher's testing objectives are. If you want to discriminate between degrees of excellence or deficiency, or differentiate levels of proficiency in a given task, then norm-referenced testing is most appropriate. It tells us how well, or how poorly, a student is performing in relation to others.

If, however, you are less concerned with differential levels, ability, or skill, and more concerned with each student reaching a predetermined level of performance no matter how much time it takes, then criterion-referenced testing is appropriate.

One way to decide whether to use norm-referenced or criterion-referenced tests is to make a distinction between what Gronlund and Linn (1990) describe as objectives that are considered *minimum essentials,* and those that encourage *maximum development.* If we want our students to achieve specific, minimum essentials, then the amount of time they take to "master" them is probably less important than the fact that they do. Here, criterion-referenced testing is most appropriate. If you want to encourage maximum development (you would need to discriminate among those who achieve beyond a particular minimal level of mastery), then norm-referenced testing is probably most appropriate.

Norm-referenced versus criterion-referenced measurement is a question of which is most *appropriate* in light of the goals and purposes a teacher has in mind. The way most schools are currently organized, with the time of instruction constant and the degree of learning variable, norm-referenced testing is most prevalent. This does not mean that it is *appropriate* in all instances.

Ebel (1978) has suggested that there is a difference in the concept of learning implied by the two tests, which might be useful for us to know in choosing the measurement mode most appropriate for our purposes. Ebel states:

> If the primary goals of learning are to acquire a series of essential abilities, distinct from each other, few in number, and important enough individually to be specified separately, studied separately, then a criterion-referenced test is clearly the test that ought to be used. But if the substance of learning is an infinity of particulars, too numerous to be specified separately, too interdependent to be studied or mastered separately; if the goal of learning lies beyond acquisition to understanding; and if understanding results from coming to know the multitude of relationships among these particulars, then a (norm-referenced) test that probes for these relationships at as many different angles as possible is the kind of test ought to be used. (p. 4)

10.8 What Would Your Choice Be?

> When you think of the kind of evaluation that you will want to do, given what you will teach and to whom, would you be inclined to choose a norm-referenced or criterion-referenced approach? If asked why you made the choice you did, how would you respond? As a student, why do you prefer one approach over the other?

Whether one chooses to use norm-referenced or criterion-referenced tests, there remains the problem of creating good (i.e., fair, valid, reliable) exams—either essay or objective—to help us achieve our goals.

PLANNING AND CONSTRUCTING GOOD CLASSROOM TESTS

Regardless of the type of assessment format you use (norm-referenced or criterion-referenced), or what type of test you choose (essay or objective), it should be related to your course objectives. This will enable you to assess more accurately how well your students are progressing relative to what the course or unit is supposed to cover.

A good way to begin thinking about the type of test you want to use, and what you want the test to cover, is to do a content analysis of the course or unit material. This can be done simply by making an outline of the major ideas, general concepts, and specific knowledge associated with the objectives. Major *ideas* might include a list of complex ideas, principles, relationships, generalizations, and laws, which students should be able to explain in a page or more.

General concepts might include lists of terms and simple ideas, which students should be able to explain in a sentence or two. *Specific knowledge* might include a list of facts, dates, and names, which students should be able to recall or recognize. This is your starting point, and it brings you to a logical next step.

Choose the Test that Best Measures Your Objectives

The question of what type of test to use is determined to some extent by what it is you wish to measure. If one of your objectives were to have students understand major ideas and general concepts, it would be more appropriate to construct an essay test, or a short-answer test, or some combination of the two. If your objectives are more involved in having students absorb specific knowledge, it would seem more appropriate to construct some type of objective test. There are advantages and disadvantages to both essay and objective tests, and, as you no doubt know from personal experience, there are both good and bad tests of each type. As a teacher, you must use the advantages by constructing tests that are fair, valid, and reliable. Inasmuch as this is easier said than done, we're going to turn our attention now to some guidelines and suggestions for making that happen.

Preparing and Using Essay Exams: Factors to Consider

Measurement specialists (Hopkins, Stanley, and Hopkins, 1990; Mehrens and Lehmann, 1991; Payne, 1992) have detailed both the advantages and disadvantages of using essay tests as a means of assessing student progress. There are at least seven arguments that arise when citing the advantages for using an essay test.

1. It is relatively easy to construct and to administer.
2. It is adaptable to nearly all types of subject matter.
3. It offers a way of finding out how well a student can express him- or herself in writing.
4. It serves as a natural test of a student's ability to synthesize, integrate, and organize his or her ideas.
5. It permits a student to make subtle distinctions, inasmuch as he or she has no need to be satisfied with short, one- or two-word responses or flat-footed "yes" or "no," or "true" or "false," answers.
6. It offers less opportunity to guess, inasmuch as alternative responses are not neatly arranged for students to choose one at random.
7. It encourages students to prepare in such a way that synthesis and organization are stressed. Many students report that with essay test preparation, they are more likely to look for broad, general concepts, and for relations between concepts, rather than to memorize specific facts and isolated components.

There are also disadvantages to essay tests. Consider five that are frequently mentioned:

1. The subjectivity of scoring can adversely affect the reliability and validity of the test.
2. It can sample only a limited amount of subject matter.
3. It is laborious and time-consuming to grade.
4. The scoring can be influenced by irrelevant factors, such as handwriting and neatness, length, organization, and bluffing.
5. The scoring can also be influenced—for better or worse—by the scorer's frame of mind or physical state, and by time factors.

Mehrens and Lehmann (1991) suggest that in order for an essay question to approach being "good," it should establish the framework within which the student operates when answering the question. Ways for doing this include the following suggestions:

1. *Be specific about the area covered by the question.* Give the student an idea of what it is you are looking for. For example, the question "Discuss criterion-referenced testing" is so nonspecific and open-ended that thirty students might give thirty distinct responses. When specificity is lacking, so too is validity. A better question would be, "Explain why criterion-referenced testing may be a fairer procedure to use in elementary schools than norm-referenced testing."

2. *Use descriptive words.* Words such as *outline, select, define, classify, illustrate,* and *summarize* are fairly clear in their meaning. They describe for the student what he or she has to do, and thereby reduce ambiguity. Words such as *discuss, compare, explain,* and *contrast* are less clear, and might need to be defined further in order for the student to be certain what they mean in context. For example, the question "Explain what is meant by validity and reliability" is fairly vague as it stands. We can tap students' knowledge about validity and reliability by being more descriptive about what we want them to explain. An example of a better question, then, might be: "Explain how the validity and reliability of a test can affect the results and the interpretation of its results."

3. *Indicate the value of the question and the approximate time to be spent in answering it.* This is fairly self-explanatory. It simply helps students to gauge their time on each question in relation to the total time allotted for the test, and it helps them to decide where they should place their emphasis in responding to the various essay questions.

Scoring Essay Exams

Unquestionably, scoring essay exams is a very subjective process. Students do not expect perfection in a teacher, but they do look for fairness. The following four suggestions might help make the task of grading essay exams as precise, and as fair, as possible:

1. Prepare at least a broad outline of the major points, ideas, or concepts you feel should be included in the answer. This outline should reflect the objectives of the courses or unit studied.

2. Strive for consistency in grading. A teacher is human and, therefore, fallible. It is possible to be influenced by the first few papers read, and grade either too permissively or too harshly, depending on your initial mind-set. To minimize this possibility, it is wise to check your scoring criteria against the actual responses to be certain that the standards are being applied consistently.

3. Make an effort to judge the mechanics of expression separately from content. This is not to say that grammar and syntax are of no importance. They are. If you feel that the mechanics of expression are very important, then it is best to assign a percentage of a question's total value to such factors as legibility, punctuation, spelling, and grammar. In addition, make it clear to students that you are going to do this. As we have talked about in previous chapters, once students know what a teacher's expectations are, they are more likely to live up to them—or at least to try.

4. Avoid scoring essay papers while you are angry, down, or depressed. Inner feelings tend to get projected "out there," and if one is feeling angry or down while attempting to read essay exams, those feelings can be unconsciously projected into the scoring of them.

Preparing and Using Objective Exams: Factors to Consider

As with essay tests, advantages and disadvantages have also been noted for objective tests (Ebel and Frisbie, 1991; Mehrens and Lehmann, 1991; Payne, 1992). The following five major advantages are frequently cited as favoring objective exams as a means of assessing student progress:

1. It allows for a more comprehensive sampling of a broad range of subject matter.
2. It offers a greater economy of time in answering and scoring.
3. Its objectivity in scoring improves test reliability and ensures agreement regardless of who scores it.
4. The test items can be stated in simple language, and can be easily read.
5. It eliminates such external influences on scoring as how the scorer feels and the student's skill at bluffing.

Frequently cited disadvantages of an objective test include the following:

1. Test construction is generally tedious and time-consuming.
2. It might tend to overemphasize factual knowledge.
3. It might place undue emphasis on rote memorization.
4. It might encourage guessing, rather than thinking and problem solving.
5. It might be difficult, or even impossible, to adapt to some forms of subject matter.

Four Commonly Used Objective Exams

An objective test is "objective" insofar as different scorers can arrive at the same score. The answers are short, consisting of a single word, number, or phrase, which is precisely predetermined by the person constructing the test. Typical examples of objective tests are multiple-choice tests, true–false tests, matching tests, and completion-type tests.

Multiple-Choice Tests

Multiple-choice tests are probably the most highly regarded and widely used form of objective testing. According to Ebel and Frisbie (1991), they are:

> Adaptable to the measurement of most important educational outcomes—knowledge, understanding, and judgment ability to solve problems, to recommend appropriate action, to make predictions. Almost any understanding or ability that can be tested by means of any other form—short answer, completion, true–false, matching, or essay—can also be tested by means of multiple-choice items. (p. 154)

The following suggestions might be useful in writing effective multiple-choice items:

1. Write as many items as possible in question form. Not only does this reduce the possibility of copying the item directly from a textbook, it encourages specific thinking, and focuses on one important idea. An example:

   When is a test considered valid?
   a. When it is reliable
   b. When it does what it says it does
   c. When the scoring can be done objectively
   d. When it measures knowledge that is indirectly related to objectives
2. Include three or more alternatives for every stem. (The stem is the question or initial statement.) Four alternatives to choose from are preferable to three because it reduces the possibility of correctness by guess. For example, if students try to guess their way through an exam, the chances of guessing correctly with a four-choice item would be 25%, and with a five-choice item, 20%.

3. Make sure all incorrect alternatives (i.e., *distractors*) are credible and logical enough not to be dismissed as absurd by a student who does not know the correct answer. An example of implausible distractors:

   What is an important factor in New York City's development as an important seat of commerce?
   a. Its population of industrious citizens
   b. Its large foreign-born population
   c. Its excellent harbor facilities
   d. Its scenic setting, considered worth visiting

4. If the item stem is a statement, be sure that each distractor can fit as a grammatically correct ending. An example of distractors that do not fit grammatically:

   A biologist who studies the relationships between an organism and its environment is an:
   a. Structuralist
   b. Taxonomist
   c. Ecologist
   d. Ethnologist

   The appearance of the indefinite article an automatically rules out *a* and *b* as possible answers. This situation could be remedied by using a combination *a(an)* at the end of the stem or by having each of the distractors begin with a vowel.

5. Try to make all of the responses approximately the same length. Sometimes, novices in test construction unwittingly make their correct answer longer than the rest, and thereby provide a clue to the correct answer.

6. Be sure that distractors and correct responses have some homogeneity (i.e., they should be fairly similar in content or location). In the following example about the eye, other sense organs are incorporated, thus reducing the effectiveness of the item:

   What is the term for the part of the eye most sensitive to light waves?
   a. Retina
   b. Iris
   c. Cochlea
   d. Stapes
   e. Septum

   This question could be improved by using only parts of the eye, and thereby calling for finer discrimination:

   What is the term for the part of the eye most sensitive to light waves?
   a. Retina
   b. Choroid layer
   c. Iris
   d. Fovea centralis
   e. Lens

7. The responses "none of the above" or "all of the above" might be useful in items with only one possible answer, as in problems involving spelling or mathematical computation, but they should not be used in a "best answer" type of item because they are difficult to construct, particularly the "all of the above" variety, and take more time than measurement experts think is worthwhile.
8. If it is impossible to invent more than three plausible responses, do not waste time trying to create others.

True–False Tests

Linus, the blanket-loving little rogue in *Peanuts,* once observed: "Taking a true–false test is like having the wind at your back." There is by no means 100% agreement that true–false tests are all that easy, or even desirable, but the fact remains that they are widely used as a type of objective measure. The following are some practical ways of making *good* true–false tests:

1. Minimize the possibility of confusion by writing each item so that it contains only one idea.
   A poor item: A valid test is one that measures what it is supposed to measure, and a reliable one gives similar results with repeated administrations.
   A better item: A valid test is one that measures what it is supposed to measure.
2. Avoid the inclination to lift items directly from the text. This favors the student who has slavishly memorized the actual words of the assignment. It is better to create an item that calls for knowledge of the sense of a paragraph or larger unit.
3. Take care not to use words that make it possible for a student to respond correctly to an item when he or she knows nothing about the material. The words *all* and *always* and *no* and *never,* call for a "false" response, *sometimes* and *usually* a "true" response, and so forth. If, however, you are careful to distribute words of this nature equally among true and false items, the problem is eliminated.
4. Do not emphasize the trivial. To do so only encourages rote memorization.
   A poor item: Charles Darwin was born February 12, 1809.
   A better item: Charles Darwin was born early in the nineteenth century.
5. Avoid negative statements. Suppose, for instance, we say, "True–false tests are not limited to the testing of factual material." Because true–false tests do not have this limitation, the general idea is true. However, because of the ambiguity of the negative statement it is difficult to decide whether it is true or false. It would be clearer and more direct to say, "True–false tests test only factual material." Here the statement is false both generally and in its technical phrasing.

6. Attribute opinions or attitudes used as item content to some particular source so that students know you are not asking for a personal opinion.
   A poor item: All dreams are expressions of our repressed desires and frustrations.
   A better item: According to Freud, all dreams are expressions of our repressed desires and frustrations.
7. Construct the test so that there are roughly an equal number of true and false statements. These should be arranged so that there is no particular pattern of response.

Matching Tests

As the name implies, matching tests measure students' ability to match or associate related objects or ideas. Students are asked to match an item in one column with an item in a second column. For example:

In the left-hand column below are some basic "discoveries" associated with various psychologists and educators of our time. For each discovery, choose a name from the right-hand column and place the letter identifying it on the line preceding the number of the title. Each item may be used once, more than, once, or not at all.

1.	______	Self-actualization	a. Rogers
2.	______	The fully functioning person	b. Cattell
3.	______	The urge for competence	c. Wechsler
4.	______	Mastery learning	d. Maslow
5.	______	Crystallized and fluid intelligence	e. Freud
			f. White
			g. Carroll

Some general suggestions for constructing good matching tests include the following:

1. Make each matching exercise *homogenous* in the sense that all premises, and all responses, refer to the same type of thing. In the previous example, all of the names are of psychologists and/or educators, and each is associated with some sort of psychological and/or educational endeavor.
2. Be able to give a full, and logical, basis for your matching.
3. Avoid the "perfect matching" situation in which the number of premises on the left is equal to the number of responses on the right. If a student knows all of the associations except one, he or she will automatically get this by elimination.
4. Be sure that all responses are plausible distractors for each premise. If, for example, Hillary Clinton had been included in the right-hand column of our example, she would not have been a very plausible distractor.

Completion Tests

Completion items are statements with one or more missing words that must be provided by the student. The following items are simple examples of this form:

1. The process of determining the extent, dimensions, or quantity of something is called ______________ .
2. A normal curve is used in conjunction with ______________-referenced measurement.
3. What is the term for that group of scores that occurs most frequently in a distribution? ______________ .

Whatever form a completion item takes, its essential features are that the answers consist of only one or two words, and that these words are supplied by the student rather than selected by him or her from a list of alternatives. It is the type of item that is relatively easy to construct, particularly when compared with multiple-choice and matching items, because it does not require a list of plausible distractors. Another of its strengths (although not from a student's point of view) is that it offers little opportunity for guessing. Students either know the answer or they do not.

An inherent weakness of this type of testing is that a teacher can never anticipate all of the possibly correct answers that students might insert. Another weakness is that too much reliance on it can lead to an overemphasis on memorization of factual information.

Essay or Objective—Which Test Is Best?

Whether to use essay or objective tests is a question for which research does not point to a consistent answer. It appears that both essay tests and objective tests have value. Ebel and Frisbie (1991) have, for instance, concluded that:

> 1. Either an essay or an objective test can be used to measure almost any important educational achievement that any written test can measure.
> 2. Either an essay or an objective test can be used to encourage students to study for understanding of principles, organization and integration of ideas, and application of knowledge to the solution of problems. (p. 122)

10.9 How Are Your Experiences Shaping Your Attitudes?

In what ways do you suppose that your experiences as a test-taking student will influence your behavior as a test-giving teacher?

Perhaps the question to be asked is not which type of test is best, but the more complex question of which type of test is best for particular teacher, class, material, and conditions.

The best strategy for testing, as with other classroom activities, is probably to use a variety of approaches. Some students feel more comfortable with objective tests; others are more at home with the essay type. If the class is not so large as to make essay testing impractical, there can be no harm in using both types of examinations. No matter what you do, you can be sure that although you might please some students some of the time, you will never please all students all of the time. If a teacher gives an objective test, some students will say, "It doesn't let you express yourself." If an essay test is administered, some students will complain "It's so vague. How can we know what's expected?" The lot of a teacher is not an easy one.

STANDARDIZED TESTS: THEIR PURPOSE AND USE

Standardized tests differ from teacher-made tests in that they are commercially prepared by measurement specialists, and include a fixed set of questions with the same directions, timing, constraints, and scoring procedures. In addition, the publishers of standardized tests provide a reference, or *norm,* group of students who have already taken the test so that teachers and counselors can compare their students' performances with those of other students in the state or nation. Thus, it is possible to see how your students are doing in particular areas relative to others of a similar age or grade.

Achievement tests and *aptitude* tests are the two types of standardized tests most used in school evaluation programs. An aptitude measures a student's *aptness,* or potential, for success in learning generally, or in particular areas. Individual intelligence tests and group scholastic aptitude tests are the most widely used aptitude tests. The Scholastic Aptitude Test (SAT), for example, is widely used to predict a student's potential for college-level work.

The most common standardized tests used in schools are achievement tests. They are designed to measure how knowledgeable students are in specific content areas such as language usage, grammar, reading comprehension, computation, science, social studies, and mathematics.

Standardized tests are not meant to take the place of teacher-made tests, nor are they used for grading purposes. Basically, standardized tests serve three primary functions: (1) *selection and placement* (e.g., to help decide whether to place students in special education programs, or to assign students to "tracks" or ability groups); (2) *diagnosis* (e.g., to assist in the diagnosis of learning problems or academic strengths); (3) *evaluation* (e.g., to assess the overall progress of students and the effectiveness of teachers and schools). We see examples of this when we read reports of how students in particular schools are doing in comparison to those in other schools in the city, in the state, or, for that matter, across the nation.

A quick way to get information about any particular standardized test is from a series called the *Mental Measurement Yearbooks.* Formerly edited by Oscar K. Buros, and now done by psychologists at the University of Nebraska, these yearbooks contain reviews of every major test, with information about the strengths and weaknesses of each, as well as their appropriate age levels. Instructions for ordering the tests are also included.

GRADING AND REPORTING: ISSUES AND PROBLEMS

Grading and reporting are as much human problems as they are measurement problems. Whether it is a first-grade teacher, a high school chemistry instructor, or a college professor, the task of sitting in judgment—of placing a value on another person's performance—is an awesome responsibility. We can talk about "objectifying" our examinations and scoring procedures all we want, but in the final analysis, every teacher is involved in a very subjective process of assessing, grading, and reporting how well, or how poorly, a student has done during a given time period.

Reporting pupil progress is an almost universal happening. What varies is how it is done. Higher percentages of elementary, than of secondary, teachers use a report with either pass or fail, a written description of a pupil's performance, or a scheduled conference with parents. More secondary teachers than elementary teacher use classified letter scales (A–F) or percentage grades (Gronlund and Linn, 1990).

There is also evidence suggesting that elementary, junior high, and high school teachers view the *purpose* of grading differently. In Burton's (1983) investigation of this issue, more than one-half (52%) of the elementary teachers in the study said that their main reason for giving grades was that the school district required it. In their view, the evaluative functions of the grades were not that important. In addition, many of the elementary teachers felt powerless to do anything about the purposes of grading and tended to blame grading practices on college systems. Junior high and high school teachers, however, said that "informing students" was the most important reason for grading, that grades were a "service" to students, and that teachers "owed" it to students as part of their education.

To Grade or Not To Grade?

The business of grading is a touchy, emotional issue. Some argue that grades represent an important cog in the wheel of educational pursuit, others have advocated abolishing grades altogether. For example, Melby (1966), speaking from his experience as a high school principal, school superintendent, college professor, college dean, and university president, has observed the following:

> The marking system is irrelevant and mischievous. It is destructive. It destroys the self concepts of millions of children every year. Note the plight of the deprived child. He often enters school at six with few of the preschool experiences that the middle-class children bring to school. We ask him to learn to read. He is not ready to read. We give him a low mark—we repeat the low mark for each marking period—often for as long as the child remains in school. At the end of perhaps the ninth grade, the child drops out of school. What has he learned? He has learned he cannot learn. We have told him so several dozen times. Why should he think otherwise? (p. 104)

Melby may have a point, particularly in light of data showing that a larger percentage of lower grades are associated with more students skipping school and increased dropout rates (Moos and Moos, 1978; Trickett and Moos, 1974). These possibilities are even more likely with disadvantaged students (Wessman, 1972).

Melby's personal observations are supported to some extent by some tougher empirical data drawn from Gottfredson's (1982) 8-year longitudinal study of a nationally representative sample of 2213 young men from the time they were in 10th grade until they were five years out of high school. Among other things, Gottfredson found that students' sense of commitment to educational values was directly affected by their school performance; in her words:

> The grades students receive operate to mold their personalities. . . . Students react to grade failure by drawing away; they become resentful, detached, and anxious. They respond to school success by renewing commitment to conventional goals. . . . Continued focus on academic accomplishment and traditional reward structures will prohibit many individuals from ever experiencing success in school and will offer instead anxiety-provoking and alienating experiences. (p. 543)

That is one side of the issue. The other side is expressed by measurement experts Ebel and Frisbie (1991), who say:

> Grades are necessary. If they are inaccurate, invalid, or meaningless, the remedy lies less in de-emphasizing marks than in assigning them more carefully so that they more truly report the extent of important achievements. Instead of seeking to minimize their importance or seeking to find some less painful substitutes, perhaps instructors should devote more attention to improving the validity and precision of marks they assign and to minimize (their) misinterpretations. (p. 265)

The literature is replete with passionate articles for and against grades, and with research reports, some that support the traditional use and public reporting of grades, and some that conclude that grading will surely lead us into an educational wasteland studded with school failures. What can we do about the grading issue? We can continue as we have with our varied public reporting systems, or we can look for alternatives.

10.10 How Do You Feel About Grades?

How would you say the grading systems to which you've been subjected have affected your attitudes about school? About your abilities? How would you say that grades have helped you to be a better student? Or have they affected your learning negatively? Would you say that the grades you've received are an accurate reflection of your school ability? How would you explain your answer to someone who wanted to understand better what you meant?

ALTERNATIVE METHODS FOR ASSESSING STUDENT PROGRESS

Although there are impassioned pleas on the side of abolishing grades altogether, particularly because low grades tend to be associated with absenteeism, dropping out, and school failure, the situation is not so simple as it may appear on the surface. As an illustration of the complexity of this problem, Clifford's (1990, 1991) monumental review of research related to the effects of failure from several perspectives concluded with the observation that failure can have both positive and negative effects on subsequent academic performance, depending on the situation and the personalities of the students involved. So to think that by eliminating grading we would solve our problems with dropping out, absenteeism, and failure would probably be not only simplistic, but also ill-advised. However, there may be some alternative means of assessment that offer choices that might either supplement or replace the usual A, B, C grading system. Let's consider some possibilities.

Authentic Assessment: Performance in Context

One of the major criticisms of traditional classroom tests is that they assess low-level skills that have no equivalent in the real world. Students are asked to answer questions and solve problems that they will probably never encounter again. In addition, they are expected to do so alone while working under extreme time constraints, without the aid of any tools or resources. Critics of traditional testing and grading systems argue that the real world is not like this. Important problems require much reflection, take time to solve, and frequently involve the use of outside resources, consultations with others, and the integration of basic skills with creativity and higher-level thinking (Kirst, 1991; Wiggins, 1989a).

These kinds of criticisms have led to a movement in contemporary education called *authentic assessment,* which basically is an approach to testing that asks students to apply their school-acquired knowledge and skills as they would in real life. We wouldn't, for example, pass a student in driver education simply on his or her ability to pass a true–false test on the principles of safe driving; we would also want that student to demonstrate his or her knowledge and skill behind the wheel of a real car in actual road conditions. *That* is authentic assessment.

Wiggin's (1989a) has made the observation that if our instructional goals for students include skills and abilities such as speaking, writing, listening, creating, thinking critically, solving problems, and applying knowledge, then our assessments should ask students to speak, write, listen, create, think critically, solve problems, and apply knowledge appropriately. The point is further made that, as teachers, we must test these capabilities and skills that we regard as essential, and *test them in context*. As stated by Wiggins (1989b). "Make (tests) replicate, within reason, the challenges at the heart of each academic discipline. Let them be—authentic" (p. 41).

The focus on authentic assessment has led to an emphasis on *performance in context*. That is, just as driver education students are required to demonstrate that they can actually operate a car safely (perform in the *context* of real-life road conditions), students in school can be required to perform within the context of the subject matter or skill they are learning. For example, instead of checking answers to objective test questions that are removed from circumstances where the facts are needed, students are confronted with real problems. Facts are used in the context in which they apply; for example, students in an English class use the proper syntax to write forceful letters to their legislators regarding their feelings about an environmental bill being considered (or whatever bill about which they have convictions). As another illustration, students in a social science class, working individually or in pairs, contrast and compare various forms of city government to analyze the various ways that democratic principles are fostered and expressed in a free society and follow this up by interviewing members of their own city government. Rather then merely *selecting* the one and only correct answer for each item on an objective test, students *create* responses that involve analyses and critical comparisons, along with whatever graphs, diagrams, and narrative are needed to complete the task.

Thus, authentic assessment is a way to encourage students to use their knowledge—to perform, you might say, in ways that are more closely tied to and relevant to actual life circumstances.

Portfolios and Exhibitions: Other Examples of Performance in Context

Portfolios and exhibitions are two new assessment approaches that require performance in context. Because the two processes are so closely intertwined, these new assessment formats make it difficult to tell where instruction stops and assessment starts.

Essentially, a portfolio is a purposeful collection of work done by the student that reflects the efforts, progress, and achievements in one or more areas. Portfolios can include work in progress, work completed, revision, student self-analyses, and reflections on what the student learned (Paulson, Paulson, and Meyer, 1991).

Written work and even artistic pieces are commonly included in portfolios, but it is also common to find such things as diagrams, charts, graphs, peer and teacher comments, audio- or videotapes, lab reports, computer programs, outside evaluations, and anything that reflects one's learning in the area being assessed (Belanoff and Dickson, 1991). Portfolios have at least two advantages over traditional means of assessment: (1) It is possible to see a student's progress (or lack of it) over a time continuum, and (2) there is a greater array of evidence that is useful for more accurately diagnosing a student's strengths and weaknesses.

An exhibition is something like a performance test that has two additional components. First, it is public, which means that students putting together their exhibition must take an audience into account, which means, in addition, that communication and understanding are important. Second, an exhibition demands many hours of careful preparation, because it is the concluding experience of an entire program of study (Wiggins, 1989b). When, for example, a graduate student "defends" his or her thesis before a graduate committee and other interested onlookers; this represents a kind of "exhibition" of knowledge in the sense that it is public, communication and understanding are critical, and it requires long hours of preparation.

Figure 10.4 gives you a good idea of the sort of requirements and activities that go into making up an exhibition, at least as practiced by a high school in Racine, Wisconsin. Note that a portfolio, a research project, and oral presentations are all part of the requirements of an exhibition.

10.11 Where Would You Send Your Children?

Imagine for a moment that you are a parent of teenagers and that you have your choice as to whether to send your children either to a school where portfolios and exhibitions are used as a primary means of assessment or to a school where more traditional means of evaluation are used. Which school would you probably choose and what would your reasons be?

Alternative Grading Possibilities

Over the years, many ideas have been suggested for different ways of assessing students' school performance. Kirschenbaum, Simon, and Napier (1971) have suggested a number of alternative grading systems that might illustrate the range of options available beyond traditional systems.

The Rite of Passage Experience (R.O.P.E.) at Walden III, Racine, Wisconsin

All seniors must complete a portfolio, a study project on U.S. history, and 15 oral and written presentations before a R.O.P.E. committee composed of staff, students, and an outside adult. Nine of the presentations are based on the materials in the portfolio and the project; the remaining six are developed for presentation before the committee. All seniors must enroll in a yearlong course designed to help them meet these requirements.

The eight-part *portfolio,* developed in the first semester, is intended to be "a reflection and analysis of the senior's own life and times." The requirements include:

- a written autobiography,
- a reflection on work (including a resume),
- an essay on ethics,
- a written summary of coursework in science,
- an artistic product or a written report on art (including an essay on artistic standards used in judging artwork).

The *project* is a research paper on a topic of the student's choosing in American history. The student is orally questioned on the paper in the presentations before the committee during the second semester.

The *presentations* include oral tests on the previous work, as well as six additional presentations on the essential subject areas and "personal proficiency" (life skills, setting and realizing personal goals, etc.). The presentations before the committee usually last an hour, with most students averaging about 6 separate appearances to complete all 15.

A diploma is awarded to those passing 12 of the 15 presentations and meeting district requirements in math, government, reading, and English.

Note: This summary is paraphrased from both the R.O.P.E. Student Handbook and an earlier draft of Archbald and Newmann's (1988) *Beyond Standardized Testing.*

Figure 10.4. AN EXAMPLE OF THE COMPONENTS THAT COMPRISE AN EXHIBITION THAT MUST BE COMPLETED BY HIGH SCHOOL STUDENTS PRIOR TO GRADUATION.

(From Wiggins, G. "Teaching to the Authentic Test." *Educational Leadership,* 1989, *46,* p. 42. Reprinted with permission of the Association for Supervision and Curriculum Development.)

First, they make a distinction between *private evaluation,* which involves teachers, students, and parents working together in identifying strengths and weaknesses and in planning steps toward improved performance, and *public evaluation,* which is the summary data about the student made available to parties outside of the school and home. Because it is the information about a student that is made public that can be most damaging (or most helpful, I would think, if the student has done well) as far as future opportunities are concerned, eight alternatives to traditional grading practices are offered.

Written Evaluations

Written evaluations allow the teacher to describe in greater detail strengths and weaknesses and to discuss recommendations for improvement. The thinking is that these will be more meaningful to parents, admissions officers, and potential employers. (This is enormously time-consuming, which is a major argument against it).

Self-Evaluation Procedures

Self-evaluation procedures require students to evaluate their own progress, either in writing or in a conference with the teacher. These evaluations are then sent to parents, and are included in permanent records. There are no grades. (Again, there is the problem of the amount of a teacher's time this would take. Another problem, as Birnbaum [1973] has shown, is that poorer students tend to overestimate their performance, and better students tend to underestimate it, which can lead to serious distortion in evaluation validity.)

Give Grades, But Do Not Tell Students

There are systems where students receive grades as usual, but are not told. Rather, a strong, personalized advising system keeps students appraised of how they are doing, and gives them a clear perspective of where they stand in relation to peers. (It is difficult imagining either students or parents tolerating not being told. Honest, accurate feedback is a key prerequisite to learning.)

The Contract System

There are two ways to enact a contract system. One is to make a "contract" with an entire class as to the type, quantity, and ideally, quality of work the students will do, and then to assign a blanket grade to the entire class, which could be anywhere from A to F, depending on how well the contract was met. The other way is to make contracts with individual students that include the student's own agreement as to how his or her grade will be determined. (Individual contracts seem more fair and realistic. The teacher has to take special care to have uniform standards for what constitutes an A contract, a B contract, and so forth.)

The Mastery Approach (Performance Curriculum)

When the mastery approach to grading is used, the teacher establishes behavioral objectives; students work at their own pace in what amounts to an individualized course of study; and when a prescribed level of mastery has been reached, they pass with at least a C. If they choose, they can earn a B or an A by going on to a higher level of mastery in whatever the subject area happens to be. (As discussed previously, this has worked well for many teachers. It benefits slower students, but might hold back better ones.)

Pass/Fail Grading

When using pass/fail grading, teachers state at the beginning of a course their criteria for a passing grade, or teachers and students together decide on the criteria for a passing grade. Students who meet the criteria pass. Those who do not fail. Students who fail can redo the work if they desire. (This system reduces some students' anxiety about grades, but it does not distinguish between various levels of ability.)

Credit/No-Credit Grading

Credit/no-credit grading works exactly the same way as the pass/fail system, except that the categories are called "credit" and "no credit." The major difference is that "no credit" does not connote failing work, and is noted as "no credit" in transcripts. (As with the pass/fail system, student anxiety is reduced, but as discovered by Gold, Reilly, Silverman, and Lehr (1971), so, too, is student achievement.)

Blanket Grading

Blanket grading works like this: A teacher announces at the beginning of a term that anyone in the class who does the work will receive a blanket grade, which is anywhere from a C to an A. The teacher says, in effect, that anyone who achieves this minimum level of mastery will receive this blanket grade. (A major problem with this is that it reinforces a "minimum level of performance" mentality. Anxiety is reduced, but we need to keep this in perspective in light of what research (van der Ploeg, Schwarzer, and Spielberger, 1984) has shown repeatedly: although either too much or too little anxiety interferes with learning, a moderate amount helps keep students alert and motivated.

SOME TYPE OF GRADING SYSTEM IS NECESSARY

It seems decidedly true that our assorted grading systems are something less than perfect or 100% reliable. However, those who would toss out grades altogether are confronted with what Ebel (1974) has described as a logical dilemma:

> Those who claim that learning proceeds better in the absence than in the presence of systematic determinations of achievement encounter an interesting logical problem. They cannot provide evidence to support the claim without doing what they say ought not to be done. They must measure achievement to prove that learning is facilitated by not measuring achievement. It is impossible in principle to show that more will be learned when no attempt is made to determine how much has been learned. And there is something patently absurd in the assertion that the best progress will be made when no attention is paid to progress. (p. 2)

Grades that are fair, free from negative teacher bias, and based on observable performance related to learning objectives, are necessary. Grades that are unfair, distorted by negative teacher attitudes, and that have little, if any, relationship to learning objectives, are detrimental.

Students not only have a right to know, but want to know, how they are progressing academically in relation to their previous efforts, and in relation to their peers. Comparing oneself with one's past performance—in whatever it might be—and with others who have performed in the same area, is an important way of reality-testing the limits of one's talent and abilities.

Eliminating grades does not seem to be either a rational or constructive possibility. As teachers, we need to spend more time on improving the validity and precision of grades we give. In particular, we would do well to remember that in the end, regardless of the careful steps we take to make our assessment of students achievement truly objective, there will always be the inevitable human factors—personal feelings, subjective interpretations—involved in the giving and receiving of grades. A low grade given without compassion not only communicates the idea that a student may be lacking ability (which is difficult enough), but it also conveys the message that he or she may be short on worth, feedback guaranteed to kill motivation.

In the final analysis, it is not just the system we choose for assessment purposes, but how we administer that system on a person to person level that contributes more than we might realize to this enterprise we call education.

EPILOGUE

Measuring student achievement and evaluating learning are difficult, demanding tasks. Although it is sometimes said that tests and grades destroy, or at least interfere with, healthy, positive teacher–student relationships, there is no evidence I am aware of to support this on any broad scale. I suspect that it is more the nature of a teacher that makes a difference in the quality of teacher–student relationships than the nature of a grading system.

In order for classroom measurement and evaluation to have any chance of working fairly and equitably for all students, we have to be as clear as possible about our goals and objectives. It is impossible to construct a valid measurement instrument unless we are clear about what it is supposed to measure in the first place. Hence, the importance of objectives.

Two major approaches to measurement are criterion-referenced testing and norm-referenced testing. With the former, the major variable is time, with each student spending as much time as he or she needs to reach a predetermined level of "mastery." Criterion-referenced measurement is ideally suited to measuring achievement at the elementary-school level, inasmuch as it automatically takes into account the fact that differential growth rates cause vast differences in learning readiness.

Norm-referenced measurement, however, pits students against each other along a performance continuum from high to low. That is, students are assessed according to an established norm of what is high achievement or low achievement. In this system, there will always be some who fail. It is a system still too frequently used in elementary schools, and one that might encourage early feelings of failure in children who are too young and vulnerable to defend themselves.

Both objective tests and essay tests have a place and a purpose in classroom measurement. Which type is used should, again, relate to what your objectives are. Generally, an approach to student evaluation that includes a variety of measurement procedures is most likely to satisfy both ourselves and our students in our mutual quest for a productive and satisfying learning experience.

Portfolios and exhibitions are rapidly gaining favor as alternative methods for assessing students' performance. Both represent ways to make it more possible to assess a student's performance in context, which means that we are in a better position to assess not only what a student knows, but also what a student can do *with* what he or she knows.

STUDY AND REVIEW QUESTIONS

1. What is the distinction between measurement and evaluation?
2. Can you explain how summative evaluation differs from formative evaluation? How is each used?

3. Why is it important for teachers to specify their learning objectives?
4. How are effective, cognitive, and psychomotor objectives distinguished from one another? Can you give an example of each?
5. What does it mean to say that a test is valid? What does it mean to say that it is reliable?
6. Can a test be valid if it is not reliable? Why or why not?
7. How are measures of central tendency helpful in interpreting test scores?
8. Can you explain why it is that when test scores are skewed toward the high or low end of a scale that the median is our best measure of central tendency?
9. What does it mean when it is said that every test has a standard error of measurement?
10. How does a criterion-referenced measurement differ from a norm-referenced measurement?
11. Can you explain why it is that criterion-referenced, rather than norm-referenced, testing is associated with mastery learning?
12. What are the basic arguments for and against the mastery approach to learning and evaluation?
13. What factors should teachers consider when deciding which type of exam to use?
14. How do standardized tests differ from teacher-made tests? For what are standardized tests best used?
15. What are some of the arguments for and against grading?
16. If a parent asked you what "authentic assessment" was and how "performance in context" was related to it, how would you respond?
17. Can you explain why it is that approaches to student evaluation that include portfolios and exhibitions are linked to the idea of authentic assessment?

REFERENCES

Anderson, L. W. "A Retrospective and Prospective View of Bloom's 'Learning for Mastery.' " In M. C. Wang and H. J. Walbert (Eds.), *Adapting Instruction to Individual Differences.* Berkeley, CA: McCutchan, 1985.

Anderson, L. W., and Burns, R. B. "Values, Evidence, and Mastery Learning." *Review of Educational Research,* 1987, *57,* pp. 215–223.

Arlin, M. "Time, Equality, and Mastery Learning." *Review of Educational Research,* 1984. *54,* pp. 65–86.

Belanoff, P., and Dickson, M. *Portfolios: Process and Product.* Portsmouth, NH: Heineman, Boynton/Cook, 1991.

Birnbaum, R. "Academic Rip-Off." *Human Behavior,* 1973, March, p. 33.

Bloom, B. S., Englehart, M. B., Furst, E. J., Hill, W. H., and Krathwohl, D. R. *Taxonomy of Educational Objectives: Handbook I. Cognitive Domain.* New York: McKay, 1956.

Bloom, B. S., Hastings, J. T., and Madaus, G. F. *Handbook on Formative and Summative Evaluation of Student Learning.* New York: McGraw-Hill, 1971.

Burton, F. *A Study of the Letter Grade System and its Effects on the Curriculum.* ERIC Document No. 238143, 1983.

Carroll, J. B. "A Model of School Learning." *Teachers College Record,* 1963, *64,* pp. 723–733.

Carroll, J. B. "Problems of Measurement Related to the Concept of Learning for Mastery." In J. H. Block (Ed.), *Mastery Learning: Theory and Practice.* New York: Holt, Rinehart and Winston, 1971.

Clifford, M. M. "Students Need Challenge, Not Easy Success." *Educational Leadership,* 1990, *48,* pp. 22–26.

Clifford, M. M. "Risk-Taking: Empirical and Educational Considerations." *Educational Psychologist,* 1991, *26,* pp. 263–298.

Ebel, R. L. *Essentials of Educational Measurement,* 2nd ed. Englewood Cliffs, NJ: Prentice Hall, 1972.

Ebel, R. L. "Should We Get Rid of Grades?" *Measurement in Education,* 1974, *5,* pp. 1–5.

Ebel, R. L. "The Case for Norm-Referenced Measurements." *Educational Researcher,* 1978, *7,* pp. 3–7.

Ebel, R. L., and Frisbie, D. A. *Essentials of Educational Measurement,* 5th ed. Englewood Cliffs, NJ: Prentice Hall, 1991.

Educational Testing Service. *Short-Cut Statistics for Teacher-Made Tests,* 2nd ed. Princeton, NJ: Educational Testing Service, 1962.

Gold, R. M., Reilly, A., Silverman, R., and Lehr, R. "Academic Achievement Declines Under Pass-Fail Grading." *Journal of Experimental Education,* 1971, *39,* pp. 17–21.

Good, T. L., and Brophy, J. E. *Looking in Classrooms,* 4th ed. New York: Harper and Row, 1987.

Gottfredson, D. C. "Personality and Persistence in Education: A Longitudinal Study." *Journal of Personality and Social Psychology,* 1982, *43,* pp. 532–545.

Gronlund, N. E., and Linn, R. L. *Measurement and Evaluation in Teaching,* 6th ed. New York: Macmillan, 1990.

Guskey, T. R., and Gates, S. L. "Synthesis of Research on Mastery Learning." *Educational Leadership,* 1986, *43,* pp. 73–81.

Harrow, A. J. *A Taxonomy of the Psychomotor Domain: A Guide for Developing Behavioral Objectives,* New York: McKay, 1972.

Hopkins, C. D., and Antes, R. L. *Classroom Measurement and Evaluation,* 2nd ed. Itasca, IL: Peacock, 1985.

Hopkins, K. D., Stanley, J. C., and Hopkins, B. R. *Educational and Psychological Measurement and Evaluation,* 7th ed. Englewood Cliffs, NJ: Prentice Hall, 1990.

Kirschenbaum, H., Simon, S., and Napier, R. W. *Wad-Ja-Get? The Grading Game in American Education.* New York: Hart, 1971.

Kirst, M. "Interview on Assessment Issues with Lorrie Shepard." *Educational Researcher,* 1991, *20,* pp. 24–27.

Krathwohl, D. R., Bloom, B. S., and Masia, B. B. *Taxonomy of Educational Objectives: Handbook II. Affective Domain.* New York: McKay, 1964.

Mehrens, W. A., and Lehmann, I. J. *Measurement and Evaluation in Education and Psychology,* 4th ed. Fort Worth: Harcourt Brace Jovanovich, 1991.

Melby, E. O. "It's Time for Schools to Abolish the Marking System." *Nation's Schools,* 1966, *77,* pp. 102–105.

Moos, R. H., and Moos, B. S. "Classroom Social Climate and Student Absences and Grades." *Journal of Educational Psychology,* 1978, *70,* pp. 263–269.

Paulson, F. L., Paulson, P. R., and Meyer, C. A. "What Makes a Portfolio a Portfolio:" *Educational Leadership,* 1991, *48,* pp. 60–63.

Payne, D. A. *Measuring and Evaluating Education Outcomes.* New York: Merrill, 1992.

Shepard, L. A. "Norm-Referenced vs. Criterion-Referenced Testing." *Educational Horizons,* 1979, *58,*pp. 26–32.

Slavin, R. E., and Karweit, N. L. "Effects of Whole-Class, Ability Grouped, and Individualized Instruction on Mathematics Achievement." *American Educational Research Journal,* 1985, *22,* pp. 351–367.

Trickett, E., and Moos, R. "Personal Correlates of Contrasting Environments: Student Satisfaction with High School Classrooms." *American Journal of Community Psychology,* 1974, *2,* pp. 1–12.

van der Ploeg, H. M., Schwarzer, R., and Spielberger, C. D. (Eds.), *Advances in Test Anxiety Research,* Vol. 3. Hillsdale, NJ: Lawrence Erlbaum, 1984.

Wessman, A. "Scholastic and Psychological Effects of Compensatory Education Program for Disadvantaged High School Students: Project ABC." *American Educational Research Journal,* 1972, *9,* pp. 361–372.

Wiggins, G. "A True Test: Toward More Authentic and Equitable Assessment." *Phi Delta Kappan,* May 1989a, pp. 703–713.

Wiggins, G. "Teaching to the Authentic Test." *Educational Leadership,* 1989b, *46,* pp. 41–47

SELECTED READINGS OF RELATED INTEREST

Ebel, R. L., and Frisbie, D. A. *Essentials of Educational Measurement.* 5th ed., Englewood Cliffs, NJ: Prentice Hall, 1991. A classic in the measurement field, this book presents in a clear, in concise manner basic measurement and evaluation concepts. It is especially strong on the writing of test items.

Gronlund, N. E. *How to Make Achievement Tests and Assessments,* 5th ed. Needham Heights, MA: Allyn and Bacon, 1993. This book is a brief, practical guide for teachers to help them make better tests and assessment instruments. Content is presented in a simple, direct, and easily understood manner.

Hopkins, K. D., Stanley, J. C., and Hopkins, B. R. *Educational and Psychological Measurement and Evaluation,* 7th ed. Englewood Cliffs NJ: Prentice Hall, 1990. First published in 1941, the lasting power of this volume speaks to its acceptance over the years as an authoritative, respected book. It is especially strong in regard to the construction of classroom tests.

Oosterhol, A. C. *Classroom Applications of Educational Measurement.* New York: Macmillan, 1990. This book offers comprehensive coverage of all aspects of educational measurement, with a strong emphasis on integrating testing with teaching to improve classroom instruction.

Payne, D. A. *Measuring and Evaluating Educational Outcomes.* New York: Macmillan, 1992. This is a solid, basic text that presents in a clear and readable manner the basic principles associated with measuring and evaluating student progress; excellent examples are used throughout the text.

TOWARD BECOMING AN EFFECTIVE TEACHER AND ACHIEVING POSITIVE TEACHING OUTCOMES

Teachers can have an enormous impact on young lives. You undoubtedly could carry on at some length about several (or more) favorite teachers that you remember from your kindergarten through high school years. And you may have a few recollections of teachers that you would just as soon not think about. What is it about the good teachers we've all had that makes them good in the first place? Is it in their manner? Their personality? Their competence? Or are the qualities that make good teachers good so elusive and undefinable as to defy identification and assessment?

With questions of this sort in mind, our major objective of the next three chapters is to examine what it means to be a good teacher. Specifically, we will try to understand more deeply and fully what it is that makes a teacher "effective." In addition, we will look at why self-understanding seems to be such an important prerequisite for good teaching, along with some ideas that might facilitate your own search for self-knowledge. Finally, we will examine some rather specific strategies for helping to make teaching more meaningful, relevant, and lasting. As we do this, we will take into account social-class factors in order to keep in mind that what is meaningful and relevant to one student might not be to another.

In what basic ways do "good" teachers differ from "poor" teachers in their approach to students and subject matter? What impact do various teaching styles have on students' attitudes toward school and achievement? Why is flexibility such an important teacher quality? What are the practical applications of self-understanding for teachers? What are some ways to explore the psychological content of a curriculum? What should we take into consideration when teaching students from various social and ethnic backgrounds?

These are some of the questions to be discussed. You will find many more of a related nature in the three chapters ahead.

11

Psychology and Behaviors of Effective Teachers

CHAPTER OVERVIEW

IMPORTANT CHAPTER IDEAS

1. There is no "best" type of teacher or best type of teaching method, but there are "better" methods.
2. There are particular "patterns" of teaching behaviors that are associated with effective and ineffective teachers.
3. Being "tough" on students and holding them to high standards is more likely to work when expectations are combined with warmth and caring.

4. Teacher effectiveness, as measured by students' evaluations, is related—for better or worse—to a teacher's personality, a finding that holds true at all levels, including college.
5. A teacher's personality might influence student achievement for better or worse, depending on whether the characteristics are positive or negative.
6. Teacher enthusiasm is positively correlated with student achievement.
7. Good teachers are not perfect, in the sense of doing and saying the right thing all of the time; they are, however, fair.
8. Effective teachers tend to be more proactive than overactive.
9. Effective teaching is not just a matter of knowing; it is a matter of communicating what is known.
10. Good teachers are not only well-grounded in their subject area, but also have broad interests that enable them to relate other areas to their teaching.
11. Thorough preparation is a trademark of good teachers.
12. Effective teachers value academic achievement.
13. Assuming responsibility for students' learning is a characteristic of good teachers.
14. Effective teachers consider the needs and abilities of their students when planning instructional strategies.
15. Effective teachers are as concerned about increasing their students' self-esteem as they are about increasing their students' knowledge.
16. Students whose teachers are interested in knowing more about them tend to do better academically than students whose teachers do not know them as well.
17. Explicit teaching is a method used by effective teachers in subject areas that are well defined and structured (e.g., science, mathematics).
18. Effective teachers make sure that students have ample time (allocated time and engaged time) to accomplish their learning objectives.
19. Flexibility is among the most frequently used adjectives to describe the behavior of good teachers.
20. Being a flexible teacher does not mean that one is wish-washy; it does mean that one is able to use a variety of instructional modes to meet students' multiple needs successfully.

PROLOGUE

To the casual observer, teaching may appear easy; that is, until one begins to see the smaller units of behavior dynamics within the larger context of a functional classroom. There is a stunning array of behavior possibilities—some students are listening and learning, trying and studying, while others are in various stages of resisting and refusing, defying and dissenting. Classrooms are seldom neat and orderly places where students, like automations, move willingly from one activity to another with restrained enthusiasm. This does not mean that there is no order in the educational enterprise of individual classrooms, but it does suggest that events cannot always be predicted before they happen, or be easily controlled when they do. In the small, sometimes crowded, quarters of a classroom, events come and go with amazing rapidity, and it takes savvy and interpersonal competence to keep up with the shifting tides of instructional activities, students' needs, and one's personal goals. It has been estimated, for example, that in a single day, an elementary teacher might have 1000 interpersonal exchanges with students (Jackson, 1968). Secondary school teachers may interact with as many as 150 different students per day. This astonishing number of teacher–student interactions is one of the reasons that teaching is an incredibly demanding and complex task.

What sort of individual does it take to be an effective teacher under such trying circumstances? What qualities tend to distinguish "good" or "effective" teachers from the rest? The purpose of this chapter is to explore these questions in order to identify behaviors and personal qualities that contribute to making good teachers "good," and in the process determine what is required to be a competent, able teacher.

GOOD TEACHING IS DONE IN MORE THAN ONE WAY

Each of us can no doubt point to some subjective experiences with vastly different teachers over the years and conclude, on that basis alone, that it is very possible for two teachers to have different personal styles and different modes of instruction, and, yet, to be very similar in terms of their effectiveness. Empirical research points to a similar conclusion: there is no best way to be a good teacher. This is true at the elementary school level (Soar and Soar, 1978), at the junior high level (Evertson, Anderson, and Brophy, 1978), and at the high school level (Stallings and Hentzell, 1978). Although no single teaching behavior can be associated with effective instruction, McDonald (1975) has observed from his research with teachers that there are certain "patterns" of behaviors that distinguish between effective and ineffective teachers. As we work our way through this chapter, you will begin to see these patterns emerge as we look at three major dimensions of teacher behavior: (1) personality traits, (2) intellectual behaviors, and (3) instructional methods and interaction styles.

Good teaching is both an art and a science; it is done by an artist who is able to utilize to the fullest in a classroom the best scientific research on human resources and technological advances.

One of the best ways to learn how to do something, whether it be plumbing, quarterbacking, or teaching, is to observe and study carefully the behaviors of those who are successful at their craft. Research and experience have taught us a great deal about why successful teachers are successful, and even why some teachers are more effective than others with particular types of students. There is a great deal to be learned from the vast array of evidence. Although no one can tell you precisely what you must do to be a good teacher, there are nonetheless many excellent guidelines for you to follow as you develop, and grow into, your own unique teaching style.

When talking about effective teaching and effective teacher behavior, a question frequently asked is . . .

HOW ARE EFFECTIVE TEACHERS IDENTIFIED?

It takes more than armchair theorizing to decide exactly what it is that makes an effective teacher. In fact, researchers who study teacher behavior make a distinction between "good" teaching and "effective" teaching. Berliner (1987b), for example, makes the point that a teacher who begins class on time, reviews material with students, emphasizes important points, asks higher-order questions, and so forth, might be judged to be a "good" teacher irrespective of whether students are learning anything. In this sense, good (and poor) teaching is determined by particular values and standards of good practice, independent of effectiveness. The idea of effective teaching, however, is always linked to instructional outcomes. Thus, "effective" teaching is related more to students' academic performance, and "good" teaching is associated more with teachers' classroom behavior. Although it is important for researchers to distinguish between good teaching and effective teaching, for our purpose, we will use these terms interchangeably, recognizing that each component is reciprocal and part of a larger, and more holistic, picture of what it means to be a superior (or mediocre, or inferior) teacher.

How can we identify behaviors associated with good or effective teaching? Dunkin and Biddle (1974) and Good and Brophy (1994) have been instrumental in suggesting and designing research methodologies for answering that question. Here are some possibilities taken from their work:

1. Ask students, experienced teachers, principals, and college professors to list characteristics they associate with good teaching.
2. Choose several classrooms and do intensive case studies on them over a long time period, including in-depth interviews with students and teachers. Keep student performance records.
3. Observe a variety of classrooms, rate various teachers on specific traits, and then examine which traits are associated with teachers whose students are among the highly motivated and/or the highly achieving.
4. Identify teachers whose students consistently achieve at a higher level than other students; then carefully observe those successful teachers to see what they do.
5. Train teachers to use various strategies to teach the same lesson, and then determine which approach leads to the greatest student learning.

These are a few of the ways that teacher effectiveness research is conducted. When a teacher can be categorized as a good or effective teacher, it is because he or she is engaging in observable and specifiable behaviors that set him or her a cut above others. Although truly fine teaching can be a highly developed artistic skill, it is a skill that can be studied, understood, and shared with others. Not every artist can be made into a teacher, but most teachers can be made into something of a classroom artist once they are aware of the interactive and instructional options available to them on the palette of behavioral choices. Although it is difficult to define effective teaching with a high degree of specificity (there are just too many ways to be an effective teacher), it is possible to define effective teaching in broader terms. As Berliner (1987b) has suggested:

> I define an effective teacher as one whose students end up possessing at least the knowledge and skills judged to be appropriate for that particular type of student (say, fourth-graders, low-ability general mathematic students, or advanced biology students). In other words, effectiveness here simply means that teachers get most of their students to learn most of what they are supposed to learn. (p. 94)

For the most part, research efforts aimed at studying teacher effectiveness have attempted to probe one or more of the following three dimensions of teacher behavior: (1) personality traits, (2) intellectual characteristics, and (3) instructional approaches. We will consider each of these.

11.1 Some Observational Research for You to Do

Reading what research has to teach us about effective teaching and studying a variety of teaching strategies that seem to work are two ways to learn what is involved in good teaching. Another excellent way is to study carefully those teachers you currently have, and will have in the future, whom you regard as the best practitioners of their craft. What do they do that sets them apart? How do they talk, gesture, and illustrate ideas? Observe them carefully. What makes them so special? What is it they do that helps you to be a better student?

PERSONALITY TRAITS OF GOOD TEACHERS

The term *personality* is a global construct, one that typically refers to the entire person as seen by most others. When we talk about a person's personality, it is usually in reference to distinctive patterns of actions, thoughts, and emotions that characterize his or her overall behavior. Although he or she may not be aware of it, each person has one of these "personalities." It is an attribute of each of us that contributes to the emotional tone of our relationships and that makes us either easy or difficult to get along with, which is why personality considerations are so crucial for teachers and teaching. There is probably no other profession in which one's personality is such an important factor as in teaching, in that it contributes so significantly to the interpersonal medium within which learning occurs.

Personality is part of the interactive aspect of teaching. That is, in our interactions we not only communicate what we know, we telegraph who we are and what we are. This might not be such an important consideration in other professions, in that the contact between the "professional" and the client is typically brief and transitory. This is not the case for teachers and students. Here, contact is extended, and extensive, over long time periods, allowing the interactive aspects of the teacher–learner relationship to have a greater cumulative effect—for better or worse.

Warmth and Caring Tend To Stand Out

Edward H. Fitler Elementary School, an old building of dirty granite in working-class Philadelphia, is run by Principal William R. Crumley, Jr. He and his teachers insist that boys and girls (35% white, 45% black, the rest Hispanic and Asian) form orderly, separate lines when entering or leaving class; that they not eat, sing, or "play" on the school bus; and that they not wear gym shoes or blue jeans except for gym, on the grounds that these rules encourage self-respect and a conscious effort on the part of all children. In Crumley's words, "Hey, there's a no-nonsense thing going on here" ("Trying the Old-Fashioned Way," 1981).

It is no nonsense. Crumley and his staff emphasize the basics—reading, science, math, spelling, and writing (including fifteen minutes daily of penmanship). Students are not promoted unless they receive at least a C in math and reading. Parents have to pick up report cards. Parents and teachers must sign the one-hour homework lessons assigned to pupils four times a week. It is a tough school, but it works in a positive way. Less than 50% of Philadelphia's pupils reach, or surpass, the national median on standardized tests in reading, math, and language skills; at Fitler, 81% of its 450 students did so.

One obvious reason for Fitler's success can be attributed to the faculty's commitment to teaching. Less obvious is Crumley's pervasive attitude of caring for, and involvement with, students. He knows many of the students by name, knows most of their parents, and tries to make himself instantly available to any teacher. He believes in discipline and standards, but he also believes in combining those with justice and love. Teachers know this, and students see it in his behavior. Students are less likely to goof off when they know for sure that the teachers (and principals) in their lives care about them and show it. Fitler Elementary School is an example of that.

Students have always been astute observers of the personality characteristics of their teachers and they are in generally high agreement about what it is they like about teachers at a more personal level. For example, in an earlier research project, Witty (1967) found, from an analysis of more than 12,000 letters written in response to "The Teacher Who Helped Me Most," that the top-ranking personality traits associated with these teachers were the following: (1) cooperative, democratic attitude; (2) kindliness and consideration for the individual; (3) patience; (4) broad interests; (5) pleasant personal appearance and manner; (6) fairness and impartiality; (7) a sense of humor; (8) pleasant disposition and consistent behavior; (9) interest in pupil problems; and (10) flexibility.

More recent studies (Murray, 1983; Soar and Soar, 1979) support Witty's findings; that is, warmth, friendliness, and understanding are teacher traits most strongly related to positive students attitudes.

Sherman and Blackman's (1975) analysis of 1500 college students' evaluations of 108 men and women faculty members revealed further evidence of the relationship between personality and teaching effectiveness; the authors concluded:

> The evidence leans toward the importance of the personal characteristics of the cause of the perceived instructional effectiveness . . . A professor wishing to improve his perceived effectiveness may best begin on personal attributes rather than focus his energy on course functions and activities which, on the surface, seem more readily open to alteration. (p. 129)

In general, research points strongly to the idea that teachers who are warm and friendly tend to have students who like them and their class.

What happens when these personal qualities are related to the more rigid test of whether having them makes any difference in the actual performance of students?

Sears (1940) found positive correlations between the extent to which a teacher reflects a personal interest in, and willingness to listen to, students' ideas and the creativity shown by elementary-level students. Tikunoff, Berliner, and Rist (1975) found that second- and fifth-grade students of teachers who, among other things, were accepting, cooperative, and involved, showed greater learning gains in mathematics and reading than students whose teachers rated lower on these characteristics.

It is worth noting that while research with K–12 students suggests that a teacher's personality *might* influence student achievement in either a positive or negative way, this is less likely to be true for college students (Abrami, Leventhal, and Perry, 1982; Centra, 1977). Younger students' self-concepts are not fully consolidated, and their personalities are less well formed, which might be why they are more influenced by, and vulnerable to, teachers' personal qualities.

A word of caution: The studies we have considered in this section are all correlational; that is, they do not tell us that the particular aspects of a teacher's personality—warmth, friendliness, sense of humor, and so forth—*cause* positive student attitudes or student learning, or student creativity, only that the two variables are related to each other. There is nothing inherent in a teacher's personality that, by itself, promotes learning.

However, a teacher's personality does promote a positive or negative classroom climate. It can punctuate an emotional climate with what Purkey and Novak (1984) call an "inviting" or a "disinviting" tone. It is the difference between being in a classroom and feeling invited, important, and valued and feeling uninvited, unimportant, and not valued.

Because a teacher's personality is so much a part of everything he or she does, it is difficult to prove that it "causes" any changes in students' achievement and attitudes. There is, however, little question that this amorphous dimension of our being is a definite factor in every classroom that—for better or worse—sets an emotional tone to which students resonate in various ways.

11.2 How Are You Affected?

Some students are relatively indifferent to a teacher's personality; others are strongly affected in positive or negative ways. How are you affected? On a scale from 1 to 5, with 5 being very much so, where would you put the importance of a teacher's personality in terms of how it affects your attitude about learning and that teacher's class? What particular personality characteristics affect you most?

Enthusiasm Is Evident

Enthusiasm, like warmth, is one of those high-inference characteristics; that is, it is difficult to define objectively. Yet it exists and can have a powerful effect on the overall emotional climate of a classroom.

Enthusiastic teachers bring life and positive energy into a classroom, which are recognized in qualities such as alertness, intensity, vigor, and movement. They are capable of showing emotions such as joy, surprise, frustration, and delight. One researcher went as far as operationalizing enthusiasm to include behaviors such as demonstrative gesturing; using varied, rapid, and excited vocal delivery; using descriptive words (to add color and zest); opening one's eyes wider (to make them more lively), and an easy-going acceptance of students' ideas and questions (Collins, 1978).

Teacher enthusiasm consists of at least two basic components, which include: (1) a sincere interest in the subject, and (2) vigor and positive energy. Good teachers have these qualities. Teachers who are less dynamic, perhaps even shy, can compensate by funneling their enthusiasm through the subject matter, if not through their personalities. For example, a somewhat quiet fourth-grade teacher takes her class on frequent field trips, and has them thinking and talking about it as much as 2 weeks in advance. Before they visited the zoo, the students worked in small groups with each group being responsible for reporting on a particular animal, which included classifying an animal as either—in the students' terminology—an "eater" of other animals or an "eatee."

Enthusiasm can be shown in many ways. It does not necessarily mean that a teacher has to bounce around with endless energy. It can show itself in quieter, more subtle ways. If you think of enthusiasm as an essentially positive energy capable of both kindling and capturing attention, there are endless ways to express it. Consider the following account offered by Bereiter, Washington, Engetmann, and Osborn (1969), which reflects, I think, an enthusiasm, a positive energy that is conveyed in a more subtle, playful manner:

> When a good teacher pointed to a picture and said, "What's this?" she expected all children to respond. If they didn't respond, she would perhaps smile and say, "I didn't hear you. What's this?" By now all the children were responding. She would smile, cock her head and say, "I didn't hear you." Now the children would let out a veritable roar. The teacher would acknowledge, "Now I hear you," and proceed with the next task, with virtually 100% of them responding. Basically her approach was to stop and introduce some kind of gimmick if the children—all of them—were not responding or paying attention. She did not bludgeon the children, she "conned" them. It seemed obvious that they understood her rules; she would not go on until they performed. It seemed that they liked performing because when they performed well she acted pleased.

Does a teacher's enthusiasm make a positive difference in students' learning and attitudes? It seems to. For example, teachers who are trained to be more enthusiastic have students who are more attentive and involved in class, although they do not necessarily do better on classroom tests (Gillet and Gall, 1982).

Other researchers (Mastin, 1963; Rosenshine and Furst, 1973), however, have pointed to evidence suggesting that not only is teacher enthusiasm related to higher student achievement, but that students respond more favorably to material presented by enthusiastic teachers.

11.3 Are You an Enthusiastic Person?

> If five people who know you well were to rate your potential for being an "enthusiastic" teacher, in the sense of bringing life and energy to a classroom, how do you suppose they would assess that component of your personality?

Proactive Behaviors Are Well Developed

To be a proactive teacher is to be one who is essentially positive, flexible, democratic, and capable of setting reasonable goals for the class as a whole, and for individual students. Good and Brophy (1994) have noted from their research that teachers can be thought of as being on a continuum from *proactive* to *overreactive,* with the more effective teachers clustering toward the proactive end.

Overreactive teachers are those who have developed rigid, stereotyped ideas about their students based on past records or on first impressions of student behavior. For the most part, they tend to treat their students as stereotypes rather than as individuals. Perhaps not surprisingly, overreactive teachers are the most likely to have negative-expectation effects on their students; that is, they are more likely to be among those teachers who differentiate considerably in their treatment of high versus low achievers (Brattesani, Weinstein, and Marshall, 1984). The significance of this is that overreactive, highly differentiating teachers have been found to add 9% to 18% to the variance in student achievement beyond the level that could have been predicted from prior achievement (Monk, 1983). Although there is little evidence showing that even proactive teachers can raise the achievement of individual students by projecting positive expectations, there is considerable evidence indicating that overreactive teachers can minimize the possibility of student achievement by projecting low expectations.

The fact that proactive teachers do not necessarily raise the achievement levels of their students is not a negative indictment. It is simply an unfortunate fact of academic life that the most sizable teacher-expectation effects on student achievement tend to be negative, in which low expectations lead to lower achievement than might have been attained otherwise (Brophy, 1983).

11.4 Where Do You Fit?

Proactive teachers are those who tend to be open-minded, personally flexible, accepting of people and views different from their own, and free of strong prejudices. Overreactive teachers are inclined to be somewhat rigid, authoritarian, and subject to fairly strong prejudices. Given what you know about yourself and the way you relate to others, which of these two descriptions fits you most closely?

Humanness Is Apparent

The evidence is reasonably clear when comparing effective teachers and less effective teachers on the basis of personality characteristics. Effective teachers tend to be "human" in the fullest sense of the word. They have a sense of humor, a pleasant manner, and are viewed as friendly, fair, and enthusiastic by their students. As demonstrated by William R. Crumley, Jr., at the Fitler Elementary School, if the caring and personal touch are there, it is even possible to have tough, hard rules (some would say "authoritarian" rules) and still be a good teacher worthy of great respect.

As pointed out by Porter and Brophy (1987), there is nothing in the literature to suggest that a teacher has to excel at all times in the qualities associated with good teaching in order to be a good teacher. Being fully human does not mean being perfect, which, no doubt, is relieving information for most of us.

In fact, Morse and his coworkers (1961) found that there are many acceptable personality characteristics that can go into making a good teacher. From their interviews of students in grades 3 and 10, the researchers noted two major trends. For example, students tended to rate a teacher as good on such matters as "She helps us learn," even if she was considered tough, and "She cares about us," even if the lessons were somewhat confusing. Wide differences were found in the considerations students weighed in their judgments. However, should a teacher be too extreme in one dimension—for example, "mean" rather than merely "strict," or "chaotic" rather than merely "lax," or "arbitrary" rather than merely "quite demanding"—the student would more often than not overlook the teacher's more positive characteristics. In other words, a student's otherwise positive perceptions were frequently lost because of some overriding negative characteristic of the teacher that blocked his or her good points. The important point is that students were tolerant of a range of differences in a teacher's behavior unless the behavior became too extreme. Another way of looking at this is that a teacher does not have to have some type of perfect or unassailable personality to be regarded as an effective teacher—at least by students. Students do not expect perfection in teachers. They do, however, look for fairness, a personal quality consistently associated with good teachers.

Warmth, a sense of fairness, and humanness are important components of the psychology and behavior of effective teachers. Qualities of this type help teachers to be sensitive and empathic. Intellectual strength and subject-matter competence give teachers substance and depth, an idea we turn to next.

INTELLECTUAL CHARACTERISTICS OF EFFECTIVE TEACHERS

How much teachers know, their preparedness, the clarity of their presentations, how well they think on their feet, and how stimulating they are to their students are considerations that must be taken into account when looking at the intellectual dimensions of a good teacher. The part that cognitive and intellectual dimensions play in effective teaching is difficult to assess because they depend not only on how much a teacher knows, but on how well he or she can *communicate* what is known. There are at least six ways that we can think about and categorize the intellectual behaviors of good teachers.

Subject-Matter Knowledge Is Combined with Specific Instructional Skills

One of the important things that research on teaching has brought us is that being in command of one's subject matter, although absolutely necessary, is not, in itself, a sufficient condition to be an effective teacher. In addition to knowing the important facts, concepts, and procedures of their own academic discipline, effective teachers have the instructional savvy necessary to translate their knowledge into the curriculum—into assignments, explanations, lessons, questions, tests, examples, demonstrations, and other activities of teaching (Leinhardt and Greeno, 1986; Wilson, Shulman, and Richert, 1987).

Research is showing that expert teachers differ from novice and less effective teachers in much the same ways that expert physicists, physicians, or even chess players differ from novices in these fields (Good and Brophy, 1994; Leinhardt and Smith, 1985). Skilled, effective teachers, for example, work from integrated, underlying principles for action, which allows them to have access to richer and more elaborate strategies for coping with problems in teaching. As an illustration of this, one study found that effective math teachers could review a previous day's work with students in two or three minutes, compared to the fifteen minutes or so taken by less effective teachers (Leinhardt, 1986).

A word of caution: Subject-matter knowledge and action-system knowledge do not guarantee that one will be an effective teacher. As noted by Good and Brophy (1994).

> Even with both kinds of knowledge, however, some teachers may fail because they do not apply the knowledge they possess. Such teachers may have inappropriately low expectations for students' ability to learn or for their own ability to teach. Or, they may not be active decision makers. (p. 2)

No one ever said that being a good teacher is easy.

Careful Preparation Is a Trademark

Research related to effective teaching consistently suggests that, whether at the college level (Goldsmid, Gruber, and Wilson, 1977) or in the public schools (Davis and Thomas, 1989; Wright and Nuthall, 1970), effective teachers prepare thoroughly to carry out the responsibilities associated with their craft. It appears that good, or effective, teaching is not simply something that happens among a gifted few born with natural talents, but is, moreover, a consequence of hard work and thorough preparation. Teachers' intellectual preparedness is responded to positively by both gifted students and average students at all levels. For example, Milgram (1979) found in her research with 459 gifted and nongifted children in grades four through six that all children, regardless of level of intelligence or of creative thinking, sex, or age, valued the intellectual preparedness of teachers more highly than teacher creativity and personality. Milgram noted that girls emphasized personality more, and intelligence and creativity less, than boys, a finding she believes was consistent with the emphasis that girls place on desirable personal-social relations. Regarding gifted high school students, Bishop (1976) has reported that teachers who are judged successful by these students were characterized as being more intellectually prepared than less successful teachers. (Bishop did not compare the judgments of gifted versus nongifted students.)

Thorough preparation is indeed a trademark of good teachers. I am reminded here of the wisdom in an observation made to me while in graduate school by one of my psychology professors, Elton McNeil, in response to a comment I had made about how easy he made teaching psychology look. "That may be," he said, "but you have no idea of the number of hours I put into making it *appear* easy."

Organization and Clarity Are Well-Developed Qualities

Anyone who has ever been a student knows what it's like to sit through a presentation by a confusing, disorganized teacher. Not only is it likely to be a boring experience, but it is also difficult to stay attentive. When attention wanes, so too, does learning. It is not surprising, then, to find that teachers who are organized and who give clear presentations and explanations tend to have students who not only learn more but who rate their teachers more positively (Davis and Thomas, 1989; Hines, Cruickshank, and Kennedy, 1985; Land, 1987; Murray, 1983). The more complex the material, the more necessary it is for the teacher to present it as clearly and as systematically as possible. A teacher's clear and organized explanation does for a student's mind what a good lightbulb does for a dimly lit room—it cuts through darkness and shadows. Clarity makes its object more knowable, and thereby more understandable. There is the question of what constitutes complex material, in that what is complex to one person might be simple to another, and vice versa. Perhaps the best—or at least the safest—tactic is to approach each lesson as though your students were all in a dimly lit area of understanding and that your presentation or explanation was the light they needed for greater clarity. Those students who need a bit more light will turn toward you for greater illumination. Those who do not, will save it for a darker day.

11.5 How Organized Are You?

When you've had classes with teachers who lacked clarity in their presentations and who, in addition, seem unorganized, how did this affect your learning? How did it affect your feeling about the class generally and the teacher specifically? In the next several days, you may find it particularly revealing to pay close attention to your ability to be clear with people when trying to explain things. Is there anything about the way that you manage your life on a daily basis that may offer some clue as to your inclination (or lack of it) to be an organized teacher?

Greater Responsibility Is Assumed for Student Outcomes

Less effective teachers tend to see their students as mostly responsible for what they learn and how they behave. Effective teachers are different. They are more likely to believe that when there is a breakdown in the teaching/learning process both the teacher and the student must assess the situation and make adjustments. For example, it has been found that when effective teachers are confronted with students who have ongoing personal adjustment difficulties, they see these cases as problems to be corrected rather than merely endured (Brophy and Rohrkemper, 1988). Effective teachers work on building relationships with problem students, relying on special attention, socialization strategies (i.e., helping students to be involved with others), and, when necessary, the assistance of mental health professionals.

We can see an example of this positive teacher attitude at work in a specific content area. Research in secondary science classes has shown that low-aptitude students achieve more if their teachers accept responsibility for seeing that all students learn science than they do if their teachers attribute degree of science mastery primarily to ability and motivation factors residing solely within the students (Lee and Gallagher, 1986).

Less effective teachers are not as quick to assume this type of responsibility. Rather, they are more likely to turn the responsibility for dealing with students who are not learning, or who are in other ways presenting problems, over to persons such as the principal, school psychologist, or school counselor. In other instances, less effective teachers simply try to control their more difficult students through demands backed by threats of punishment (e.g., "You better get busy, young man.", "Your grade is going to suffer if this keeps up.").

11.6 Whose Responsibility Is It?

Consider the following statements:

1. The teacher's central responsibility is to teach, and it is the student's responsibility to learn.
2. Whether students learn anything depends primarily on the teacher; therefore, teachers are responsible for students' learning.
3. Usually, when students fail to learn, at least 51% of the reason for the failure is attributable to the teacher.
4. Usually, when students fail to learn, at least 51% of the reason for the failure resides in the students themselves.

Which of these statements (if any) do you agree with? What does your agreement suggest about your implicit ideas about the teaching/learning process?

Preparing Students for New Learning Is a Honed Skill

Effective teachers are particularly adept at preparing their students for the presentation of new material. For example, effective teachers, more so than less effective teachers, are likely to give students what are called *advanced organizers* in the form of study questions, or perhaps general overviews of short bits of relevant reading, prior to a complex learning task (Mayer, 1984). In addition, effective teachers are more likely to see to it that students understand what is expected of them, and why, which not only keeps students on track, but helps them to develop a sense of personal responsibility for their work (Anderson and Prawat, 1983). Sometimes teachers are vague about what they want students to learn. For example, in a study done by Duffy, Roehler, Meloth, and Vavrus (1986) an ineffective reading teacher began her lesson on using context in reading by saying, "Today we are going to learn about context. This skill will help you in your reading" (p. 206). This is a fairly general statement about what students are supposed to learn. Contrast that statement with what was expressed by a teacher judged to be more effective:

> At the end of today's lesson, you will be able to use the other words in a sentence to figure out the meaning of an unknown word. The skill is one that you will use when you come to a word that you don't know and you have to figure out what the word means. (p. 206)

Effective teachers are also more skilled at explaining "how" to do the work of particular lessons. Berliner (1987a), for example, found that an ineffective teacher might introduce a lesson on understanding words with prefixes by saying something like, "Here are some words with prefixes. Write the meanings of each in the blanks." A more effective teacher, by contrast, would be more likely to demonstrate (1) how to divide the words into a prefix and root, (2) how to determine the meaning of a root and the prefix, and (3) how to put the two meanings together in order to make sense of the whole word.

Another characteristic of effective teachers is their skill in giving verbal signals that indicate transitions from one topic to another with phrases such as "The next area we'll look at is . . . ," "Now let us turn our attention to . . . ," or "The second step we will consider is . . . " (Berliner, 1987b).

The point in preparing students for new learning is simple and basic: When they know clearly what the expectations and directions are, the energy that might ordinarily go into worrying about *what* to do is more likely to be given over to actually *doing* it.

Thoughtful Self-Examination Is Ongoing

When considering the intellectual behaviors of good teachers, the picture emerging from research features a command of content area(s), a willingness to organize and prepare carefully (behaviors that reflect a high value placed on academic achievement and learning), and a desire to carefully lay the groundwork that will enable all students to be prepared for new learning. Doing all of these things requires planning and foresight, which are characteristic behaviors of effective teachers. In a word, effective teachers are *thoughtful* about their practice. Porter and Brophy's (1987) review of teacher effectiveness research points to a number of reasons that effective teachers are good at what they do: (1) they take time for reflection and self-evaluation, (2) they monitor their instruction to be sure that the subject matter is meaningful and worthwhile, and (3) they accept responsibility for guiding student learning and behavior.

Accomplishing these goals requires thoughtful preparation. Good teachers are known for this, which is one of the reasons effective teachers are effective in the first place.

However important these qualities might be in contributing to a teacher's overall effectiveness, they are practically useless if they are not translated into learning that makes a difference, and into achievement that is real and lasting. Whether this occurs depends very much on a teacher's instructional methods and interaction style.

INTERACTION STYLES AND INSTRUCTIONAL METHODS OF EFFECTIVE TEACHERS

Effective teachers differ from less effective teachers not just in particular personality traits and specific intellectual behaviors, but in the way they teach and interact with students. For better or worse, how we, as teachers, "teach" makes a difference. It is not just what we do, but how we do it that matters. What is it that effective teachers do?

Effective Teachers Challenge and Encourage

Thousands of words are spoken and exchanged during any given day in class. By itself, a particular word has little meaning. However, when combined with other words, and delivered at a particular volume and with a particular inflection and intonation, words can chop down a confident bearing or firm up a shaky confidence, challenge and encourage students to go further, to not give up, or dishearten and discourage students to the point where trying further seems to them fruitless.

Research on teachers' talk has been being conducted for a long time. An early study by Barr (1929) is relevant because it underscores some important differences between good and poor teachers in terms of verbal feedback they give to students. Keeping detailed stenographic records and observation charts on forty-seven high school social studies teachers who were rated as superior in teaching skills, and comparing them with forty-seven social studies teachers who were rated below average, Barr was able to closely observe many teacher–student interactions. Some characteristic comments made by good teachers and poor teachers follow. As you read through them, try to "hear" inflection and intonation.

1. *Characteristic Comments Made by Ineffective, But Not by Effective, Teachers:* Are you working hard? Aren't you ever going to learn that word? Everyone sit up straight, please. I'm afraid you're confused. No, that's wrong. Oh, dear, don't you know that? Oh, sit down. Say something. . . . and so on, through nearly 100 expressions. (Note the overtones of frustration, futility, and impatience that are revealed.)

2. *Characteristic Comments Made by Effective, But Not by Ineffective, Teachers:* Aha, that's the idea. Are you going to accept that as an answer? I should like more proof. Do you suppose you could supply a better word? Can you prove your statement? Don't you really think you could? I'm not quite clear on that—think a moment. Let's stick to the question. My last question probably wasn't a good one. . . . (Note the emphasis on challenging students, on pushing and encouraging them to go beyond wherever they might be at the moment.)

11.7 How Teachers Say Things Makes a Difference

Although what teachers say is important, so, too, is how they say it. For example take the following statements and, simply by changing your inflection, make each one sound positive or negative: "Good job," "No, that's wrong," "Can you prove your statement?" "Let's stick to the question," "Say something," "Oh dear, don't you know that?"

Words might convey the message, but do you see how tone and inflection transmit the feelings behind the message?

Feedback Is Personalized, Discriminate, and Specific

Effective teachers are adept at giving feedback that is personalized, and that is specific to something that has been, or will be, accomplished. Whatever the form of feedback, instructional, directive, or praise, it is most effective when students are able to apply it directly to themselves.

We can see an example of how this works in the results of an interesting study with high school and junior high school teachers and students in which teachers graded objective tests taken by their students and then randomly assigned each paper to one of three groups (Page, 1958). Group 1 students were given back their papers with no comment except a mark. All of group 2 students were given a stereotyped, standard comment, from "Excellent," if their scores were high, to "Let's raise this grade." All C students, for example, received their marks with the notation, "Perhaps try to do still better." For those in group 3, teachers wrote a personal comment on every paper saying whatever they thought might encourage that particular student. On the next objective test, groups 2 and 3 outperformed group 1. Personalized comments had a greater effect than standardized comments, and even a very short standard comment written on a paper produced measurable achievement gains. *The greatest improvement was made by the failing students in group 3 who received encouraging personal notes on their papers.* This study points to the motivational implications of evaluating practices that go far beyond the simple indication of right or wrong answers.

Good and Brophy (1994) note that effective teachers give feedback that is: (1) tailored to particular students (rather than delivered to the entire class); (2) delivered in a straightforward, declarative sentence (rather than in gushy exclamations); and (3) given when someone really needs help or has done a particularly fine job (rather than delivered indiscriminately to either individual students or the class as a whole whether it is needed or not).

This last point is an important one, particularly when feedback takes the form of praise. Effusive teacher praise for essentially minor accomplishments causes both onlookers and recipients to conclude that the teacher feels sorry for the recipients because they are slower than the other students (Meyer et al., 1979), an outcome more likely to cause feelings of embarrassment than feelings of pride in accomplishment.

11.8 A Teacher's Feedback Can Make a Powerful Difference

As I write about various interactions that occur between teachers and students, I find myself frequently remembering experiences that occurred in my own schooling. I recall, for example, a psychology professor who gave me a B on my first research report and beneath the grade had written: "You can probably strengthen your next paper by spending more time on critiquing the methodology. I'm looking forward to seeing your ideas." I felt enormously encouraged. Can you think of some examples of teacher feedback that lifted your hopes and motivation?

Positive Rapport and High Expectations Are Practiced and Valued

The rapport—"relationship" or "bond"—that exists between teachers and students is the interpersonal medium within which teaching and learning occur. It can be good or bad, weak or strong; whatever it might be, it does make a difference—for better or worse. Research tends to support the idea that one of the reasons effective teachers are effective is because they are able to establish interaction styles characterized by positive rapport. How do they accomplish this? Research findings suggest the following three overlapping possibilities:

1. Slavin's (1987) review of research indicates that positive—rapport teachers have as their important overall goals the improvement of their relationships with students and the nurturing of students' self-esteem.

2. As suggested by Johnson, Skon, and Johnson's (1980) research, one of the ways they do this is to emphasize cooperation, rather than competition, in their classrooms, which usually results in a more positive learning experience for their students.
3. Another thing they do is emphasize the learning process, rather than its products (Slavin, 1990).

Activities of this variety might have the effect of creating classrooms that look more like cooperative enterprises than competitive contests, where both teachers and students are sensitive to the human components of the teaching/learning process, not just to the academic outcomes derived from it.

Does positive rapport result in better achievement? Good and Grouws (1975) found, in their study involving third and fourth graders, that the students' rapport-rating scores were both descriptive and predictive of their achievement; that is, the higher the rapport, the greater the achievement.

The process of positive rapport, coupled with high expectations, is no better illustrated than in the results of a study reported by Pedersen, Faucher, and Eaton (1978). In the process of looking at the long-term outcomes of fifty-nine adults who had attended a single school in a poor neighborhood, one bit of information recurred; among the individuals being studied, those who had a particular first-grade teacher (called Miss A in the study) were more likely to show IQ increases during elementary school, got better grades, finished more years of schooling, and were more successful as adults. Not one of Miss A's students whom Pederson was able to contact for interview (44 others were interviewed who had other first-grade teachers) was in the lowest level of adult success as defined in this study, despite the fact that most of the children in Miss A's classes came from poor, and often minority, families. Pedersen and his colleagues systematically ruled out other reasons for the success of Miss A's students. In race, religion, intelligence, and economic status, Miss A's pupils were similar to their schoolmates.

The reason for the difference was Miss A herself. She believed that all her students could learn, conveyed that message strongly to them, and got involved in the lives of her students in ways personally meaningful to them.

In the course of his research, Pedersen asked all of his subjects to name as many of their elementary school teachers as they could. Everyone who had Miss A for first grade remembered her. Most of those who had other first-grade teachers could not remember their teacher's name. Four of the subjects said Miss A was their first-grade teacher when, in fact, records showed she was not. Pedersen ascribed it to "wishful thinking."

Although this is only one study, and has a small number of subjects, the results are consistent with other research efforts we examined. Teachers who have a good rapport with their students, and who have high, but reasonable, expectations for them, can make a big difference for the better. As Pedersen et al. (1978) expressed it:

> If children are fortunate enough to begin their schooling with an optimistic teacher who expects them to do well and who teaches them the basic skills needed for further academic success, they are likely to perform better than those exposed to a teacher who conveys a discouraging, self-defeating outlook. (p. 11)

11.9 Do You Remember a Special Teacher?

Was there a particular teacher in your early school days you remember as having a particularly positive effect on you? What was that person like? What did he or she do that made a positive difference to you?

Sufficient Time Is Allowed for Learning

There are two components to time when considered in relation to classroom learning. There is *allocated time,* which teachers devote (i.e., allocate) to particular content areas on a given day; and there is *engaged time,* which is the actual time on-task that students spend on a particular subject.

There is wide variation among teachers in how they allocate their time to particular subjects. For example, in one study of seventy-five teachers in grades 2 through 6, it was found that an average of only 15 minutes per week was spent on science in second-grade classes (Ebmeier and Ziomek, 1983). Often there were differences in how instructional time was allocated to particular subjects, even between classes in the same grade in the same school. Berliner (1987a) notes that his research indicated allocated time ranges from 16 to 50 minutes a day in mathematics instruction, and from 45 to 137 minutes a day in reading instruction.

In many cases, teachers simply might not be aware of the discrepancies in time given to one subject over another. There is evidence, however, suggesting that some teachers, at least, allocate more time to their favorite content areas. For example, Schmidt and Buchmann (1983) found that teachers who enjoyed teaching reading more than writing stressed reading over language arts instruction, while teachers who enjoyed mathematics more than social studies allocated more time to mathematics. In fact, teachers who enjoyed teaching mathematics spent more than 50% more time teaching math than teachers who did not.

Research shows clearly that effective teachers allow sufficient allocated time and student-engaged time, or time on-task, for each subject. For example, classrooms generally range along a continuum from approximately 50% to 90% time on-tasks by students. Effective teachers are typically found at the higher end of that continuum (Berliner, 1987b). Their students are working on the tasks they are supposed to be working on from 75% to 90% of the time.

The relationship between allocated time and engaged time and teacher effectiveness is clear. If students in class A have been allocated forty hours worth of time for reading comprehension activities, and students in class B have been allocated ten hours for similar activities, is there any question which group of students will probably do better on reading comprehension tests? If teacher effectiveness is measured, in part, at least, by how much students learn, is there any question which teacher will be judged most effective?

When thinking about the relationship between allocated time and teacher effectiveness, Berliner (1987b) makes an important point:

> We seem to be saying that more allocated time is better. If this rule is not adhered to blindly, it is, within limits, often true. Certainly we must remember that more is better only up to some point. Beyond that point, "more" is bound to be boring. Nevertheless, effective teachers seem to keep the fact clearly in mind that some curriculum areas will never be learned if enough time is not allocated to them. For example, most of us could not translate .6667 into the fraction two-thirds (2/3) or into 667% if some teacher had not allocated enough time to learn these equivalencies in mathematics. (p. 978)

Perhaps one could argue that equivalencies of this type were learned not because there was ample time in school to do so, but because one took the time to do it on one's own. Still, the point is made. Learning takes time, and teachers who allocate enough of it are more effective than those who do not.

Direct Teaching Is Preferred

Direct teaching (or explicit teaching) is a term coined by Rosenshine (1987, 1979) to serve as an umbrella concept to cover six teaching behaviors associated with effective teaching. Essentially, direct teaching is just what the label implies—direct and explicit. It is a method that involves presenting subject matter in small, explicit steps, pausing periodically to check for students' understanding, and encouraging active and successful involvement from as many students as possible. Direct teaching is particularly well-suited for teaching explicit, structured information and skills (e.g., science facts and concepts, mathematical procedures, grammatical rules, vocabulary, and specific reading procedures). The six steps involved in direct teaching include the following:

1. *Begin by reviewing and checking the previous day's work.* Review materials in which errors and misunderstandings are apparent.
2. *Tell students the goals of the day's lesson.* Present new material a little at a time, modeling procedures, giving many examples, and checking often to be sure that students understand.
3. *Provide guided practice.* Allow students to practice using new information with your guidance; ask many questions that give students abundant opportunities to repeat or explain the material just taught. Encourage participation until all students can respond correctly.

4. *During guided practice, give students a great deal of feedback.* Reteach a lesson if necessary. When students answer correctly, explain why the answer is right. It is important that feedback be immediate and thorough.
5. *Allow students time to practice using new information on their own.* Encourage students to help one another, and be available to help out with students' questions.
6. *Provide weekly and monthly reviews.* Go back over material previously learned, test frequently enough to assess learning progress, and reteach material missed on tests.

It should be noted that following these steps is less relevant to teaching in areas that are less structured and less well defined than others, such as composition, analysis of literature or historical trends, writing term papers, or discussion of social issues (Spiro and Meyers, 1984). Although effective teachers might begin their teaching in any of these areas by reviewing what was done on previous days and by stating the goals of the day's lesson, for teaching purposes, they would not necessarily try to break the units into subunits that students had to master one step at a time. Rather, the emphasis would be on exploring a diversity of ways rather than one way, on exploring opinions and attitudes rather than memorizing facts and correct answers.

Essentially, the goal of direct instruction is the mastery of basic skills and knowledge as measured by the tests commonly given in schools. Rosenshine (1979) expressed it this way:

> Direct instruction refers to academically focused, teacher-directed classrooms using sequenced and structured materials. It refers to teaching activities where goals are clear to students, time allocated for instruction is sufficient and continuous, coverage of content is extensive, the performance of students is monitored . . . and feedback to students is immediate and academically oriented. In direct instruction the teacher controls instructional goals, chooses materials appropriate for the student's ability, and paces the instructional episode. Interaction is . . . structured, but not authoritarian. Learning takes place in a convivial academic atmosphere. (p. 38)

The conclusions reached by Rutter, Maugham, Mortimore, Ouston, and Smith, (1979) after studying 1400 students in twelve secondary schools in central London, give added impetus to the direct teaching idea. Basically, their findings showed that students learned and behaved best in schools in which teachers planned their lessons carefully, started teaching promptly when classes began (by not spending large amounts of time distributing books and papers), were less casual about letting classes out early, and put more emphasis on academic achievement. Furthermore, they found that teachers in highly achieving schools gave and checked more homework assignments. Not surprisingly, perhaps, students in these schools made more use of the library.

Successful teachers, far from being harsh, detached, authoritarian martinets, more frequently encouraged their students, put good work on bulletin boards, and made themselves available to students for consultation on problems of a more personal nature. The effective teachers also gave students more responsibility than the less effective ones for taking care of materials, participating in meetings, and holding various posts and offices.

The differences in achievement between students in good schools and bad ones were substantial. The researchers had grade-school records of many of the children and used them to make predictions of how well the children were likely to do in secondary school. Compared with what might have been expected from the student's past achievements, the least able students in the most effective schools scored as well on standardized tests as the most able students in the least effective schools.

It is important to keep in mind that the research related to direct methods of teaching, including Rutter's large study, does not show that teachers using these methods are cold, subject-centered automations insensitive to the human variable of classroom life. For example, because a teacher operates more from the direct influence mode (i.e., lecturing, expressing his or her own ideas, asking rhetorical questions, giving orders, and so forth) does not mean that indirect approaches (i.e., accepting feelings, using students' ideas, praising and encouraging, joking, and the like) are never used by this type of teacher. Research suggests that these two methods of teaching *used in combination* are most likely to result in achievement gains (Flanders, 1960; Rosenshine, 1987). Whereas direct-influence methods have more to do with a teacher's relationship to subject matter in terms of how it is conveyed, indirect-influence methods are more reflective of a teacher's relationship to students in terms of how they are cared about. It is the blend of these two approaches that can make for positive gains in students' cognitive development and personal growth, which brings us to the final, important point in our consideration of who it is that makes an effective or ineffective teacher.

11.10 Something for You to Observe

> You may find it particularly instructive to pay close attention to the instructors you currently have in terms of the directness or indirectness of their instructional styles. How is your learning influenced? How does one style or the other affect your feelings about the class? What can you learn about the kind of teacher that you want to be?

Flexibility—A Key Personal Quality

By far the most repeated adjective used in the research literature to describe good teachers is *flexible*. Both implicitly and explicitly, this characteristic emerges repeatedly when good teaching practices and outcomes are discussed. Flanders (1960), for example, found in his research that superior teachers were inclined to be flexible, in the sense of being able to be more direct or indirect as the occasion demanded, and that *students in all subjects learned more working with flexible teachers.*

Interestingly, those teachers who were not as successful were the ones who were predictably and routinely inclined to use the same instructional procedures and methodology in a rigid fashion. They offered little variation from one classroom situation to the next.

Ongoing studies of teacher effectiveness are continuing to show that there are endless ways for students and teachers to interact with each other (Berliner and Rosenshine, 1987; Davis and Thomas, 1989; Good and Brophy, 1994). It is important to realize that not all students are the same; all will not respond in the same way to any given teaching style. Effective teachers have a readiness to take this fact of classroom life into account. They know that they cannot be just one sort of teacher and use just one type of approach if they intend to meet the multiple needs of their students (Sparks, 1988). They are not overwhelmed by a single point of view to the point of intellectual myopia. Good teachers are, in a sense, "total" teachers. They seem able to move with the shifting tides of classroom life and students' needs, and to do what has to be done to teach a given student in a given subject area under given circumstances.

The success of an effective teacher is not measured in terms of occasional bursts of instructional brilliance and episodic moments of shining student achievement. Rather, it is measured in terms of the cumulative effect of fine instruction done on a continuous basis by teachers who care about their students as human beings, who, along with perhaps occasional flashes of teaching brilliance, offer their students a steady diet of preparedness; enthusiasm; high, but reasonable, expectations; and a willingness to be flexible in the face of changing circumstance.

EPILOGUE

A simple truism about teaching is that "effective" teaching is not done in one, specific way with one, specific type of methodology. Whether we are talking about good teachers or poor teachers, certain observable "patterns," or clusters of behavior, are characteristic of those who fall into one group or the other. Research does not allow us to say that ineffective teachers are always unsuccessful with all students at all times, nor does it allow us to say that effective teachers are always successful with all students at all times. However, current research findings do allow us to say that particular patterns of teacher behaviors are, with greater frequency, more likely to be associated with teachers who are effective or ineffective, as the case might be, than with teachers who fall somewhere in between.

In terms of personality characteristics, intellectual functioning, instructional procedures, and interaction styles, good, or effective, teachers rank high on more of the following behavioral descriptions than poor or ineffective teachers:

1. They are inclined to combine a warm and friendly attitude with firm, but reasonable, expectations.
2. They project an enthusiasm for their work that lends excitement to their teaching.
3. They are by no means perfect, in the sense of doing and saying just the right thing at all times. (This has less to do with something that teachers consciously do, and more to do, perhaps, with the wide latitude of teacher imperfections that students can live with as long as the core person is basically fair and decent.)
4. Intellectually, they are thoroughly grounded in their subject area, which, by virtue of a broad base of interests, they are able to connect to related areas of knowledge.
5. They are ready to assume responsibility for student outcomes, which they reflect in their efforts to make sure that all students have a chance to learn.
6. They make it a point to know their students as individuals and to respond to them as individuals; they go beyond simply seeing them as "students."
7. They provide definite study guidelines; they are as interested in getting their students prepared to know as they are in evaluating what they know.
8. They are able to challenge without being offensive and to encourage without being condescending; more importantly, they challenge when that is appropriate and they encourage when that is needed. Neither behavior is indiscriminately practiced.
9. They give feedback that is personalized, an effect that makes the feedback more believable and powerful.
10. They take time to reflect about their work, their students, and themselves as teachers; they are, in a word, thoughtful.
11. They work on developing a positive rapport that serves as the interpersonal medium within which high, but reasonable, expectations and constructive, critical feedback can be transmitted.
12. They are able to be flexibly adaptive in terms of using direct or indirect methods of teaching to meet various student abilities and needs.

Good teachers are good in many ways, each with his or her own style of relating to students and transmitting knowledge. There is no one, best way for doing this, probably because there is no one type of student. Good teachers are good for many reasons, and one of those reasons might be that they are basically good people to begin with. I have inferred from the research that good teachers like life; are reasonably at peace with themselves; are firm but fair; expect a lot from themselves and their students; have a sense of humor; and generally enjoy their work.

To be a good teacher means that we not only know our subject area and something about our students, but that we know something about ourselves, a topic to which we turn our attention in Chapter 12.

STUDY AND REVIEW QUESTIONS

1. Can you identify the methods and techniques that researchers have used to identify effective teaching?
2. How is good or effective teaching defined?
3. Can you give some examples of ways a teacher's personality can influence students' behavior for better or worse?
4. Why is it that elementary-level students might be more influenced by teacher personality factors than older students?
5. If you were to study teachers' enthusiasm, what particular behaviors would you look for?
6. How would you describe the difference between a proactive and an overreactive teacher?
7. Can you explain why it is that command of one's subject area, although necessary, is not a sufficient condition to be an effective teacher?
8. Why is it that teachers who accept responsibility for students' learning are more likely to have students who, in fact, do learn more than students of teachers who do not accept this responsibility?
9. What is it about the feedback that effective teachers give their students that makes it so effective in the first place?
10. Can you discuss how effective teachers differ from less effective teachers in their use of allocated and engaged time in the classroom?
11. What is "explicit" teaching and when is it best used?
12. Can you explain what the primary differences are between direct and indirect teaching? Is it better to use one method over the other? If so, on what does the choice depend?

REFERENCES

Abrami, P. C., Leventhal, L., and Perry, R. P. "Educational Seduction." *Review of Educational Research*, 1982, *52*, pp. 446–464.

Anderson, L., and Prawat, R. "Responsibility in the Classroom: A Synthesis of Research on Teaching Self-Control." *Educational Leadership*, 1983, *40*, pp. 62–66.

Barr, A. S. *Characteristic Differences in the Teaching Performance of Good and Poor Teachers of Social Studies.* Bloomington, IL: Public School Publishing Co., 1929.

Bereiter, C., Washington, E., Engetmann, S., and Osborn, J. *Research and Development Programs on Preschool Disadvantaged Children.* Final Report, OE Contrast 6-10-235,

Project No. 5-1181. Washington, DC: U. S. Department of Health, Education, and Welfare, Office of Education, Bureau of Research, 1969.

Berliner, D. "But Do They Understand?" In V. Richardson-Koehler (Ed.), *Educator's Handbook: A Research Perspective.* New York: Longman, 1987a.

Berliner, D. "Simple Views of Effective Teaching and a Simple Theory of Classroom Instruction." In D. C. Berliner and B. V. Rosenshine (Eds.), *Talks to Teachers.* New York: Random House, 1987b.

Berliner, D. C., and Rosenshine B. V. (Eds.), *Talks to Teachers.* New York: Random House, 1987.

Bishop, W. E. "Characteristics of Teachers Judged Successful by Intellectually Gifted, High Achieving High School Students." In W. Dennis and M. W. Dennis (Eds.), *The Intellectually Gifted: An Overview.* New York: Grune and Stratton, 1976.

Brattesani, K., Weinstein, R., and Marshall, H. "Student Perceptions of Differential Teacher Treatment as Moderators of Teacher Expectation Effects." *Journal of Educational Psychology,* 1984, *76,* pp. 236–247.

Brophy, J. "Research on the Self-Fulfilling Prophecy and Teacher Expectations." *Journal of Educational Psychology,* 1983, *75,* pp. 631–661.

Brophy, J., and Rohrkemper, M. *The Classroom Strategy Study: Summary of General Findings.* Research Series Report, No. 187. East Lansing: The Institute for Research on Teaching, Michigan State University, 1988.

Centra, J. A. "Student Ratings of Instructors and Their Relationship to Student Learning." *American Educational Research Journal,* 1977, *14,* pp. 17–24.

Collins, M. "Effects of Enthusiasm Training on Preservice Elementary Teachers." *Journal of Teacher Education,* 1978, *24,* pp. 53–57.

Davis, G. A., and Thomas, M. A. *Effective Schools and Effective Teachers.* Boston: Allyn and Bacon, 1989.

Duffy, G., Roehler, L. R., Meloth, M. S., and Vavrus, L. G. "Conceptualizing Instructional Explanation." *Teaching and Teacher Education,* 1986, *2,* pp. 197–214.

Dunkin, M. J., and Biddle, B. J. *The Study of Teaching.* New York: Holt, Rinehart and Winston, 1974.

Ebmeier, H., and Ziomek, R. *Student Academic Achievement Rates.* Final Report of National Institute of Education Grant NIE-G-O-0892. Wheaton, Illinois Public Schools, 1983.

Evertson, C., Anderson, L., and Brophy, J. *Texas Junior High School Study: Final Report of Process-Outcome Relationships, Vol. I.* Report No. 4061, Research and Development Center for Teacher Education, University of Texas, Austin, 1978.

Flanders, N. A. *Teacher Influence, Pupil Attitudes, and Achievement.* U. S. Department of Health, Education, and Welfare, Office of Education, Cooperative Research Project No. 397, Minneapolis, University of Minnesota, 1960.

Gillett, M., and Gall, M. *The Effects of Teacher Enthusiasm on the At-Task Behavior of Students in the Elementary Grades.* Paper presented at the annual meeting of the American Educational Research Association, New York, March, 1982.

Goldsmid, C. A., Gruber, J. E., and Wilson, E. K. "Perceived Attributes of Supervisor Teachers (PAST): An Inquiry into the Giving of Teacher Awards." *American Educational Research Journal,* 1977, *14,* pp. 423–440.

Good, T. L., and Brophy, J. E. *Looking in Classrooms,* 4th ed. New York: Harper and Row, 1987.

Good, T. L., and Brophy, J. E. *Looking in Classrooms,* 6th ed. New York: HarperCollins, 1994.

Good, T. L., and Grouws, D. "Teacher Rapport: Some Stability Data." *Journal of Educational Psychology,* 1975, *67,* pp. 179–182.

Hines, C. V., Cruickshank, D. R., and Kennedy, J. J. "Teacher Clarity and Its Relation to Student Achievement and Satisfaction." *American Educational Research Journal,* 1985, *22,* pp. 87–89.

Jackson, P. *Life in Classrooms.* New York: Holt, Rinehart and Winston, 1968.

Johnson, D. W., Skon, L., and Johnson, R. "Effects of Cooperative, Competitive, and Individualistic Conditions on Children's Problem-Solving Performance." *American Educational Research Journal,* 1980, *17,* pp. 83–93.

Land, M. L. "Vagueness and Clarity." In M. Dunkin, ed., *The International Encyclopedia of Teaching and Teacher Education.* New York: Pergamon, 1987.

Lee, O., and Gallagher, J. J. *Differential Treatment of Individual Students and Whole Classes by Middle School Science Teachers: Causes and Consequences.* Paper presented at the National Association for Research in Science Teaching, San Francisco, March, 1986.

Leinhardt, G. "Expertise in Mathematics Teaching." *Educational Leadership,* 1986, *43,* pp. 28–33.

Leinhardt, G., and Greeno, J. D. "The Cognitive Skill of Teaching." *Journal of Educational Psychology,* 1986, *78,* pp. 75–95.

Leinhardt, G., and Smith, D. "Expertise in Mathematics Instruction: Subject Matter Knowledge." *Journal of Educational Psychology,* 1985, *77,* pp. 241–277.

Mastin, V. E. "Teacher Enthusiasm." *Journal of Educational Research,* 1963, *56,* pp. 385–386.

Mayer, R. E. "Twenty-Five Years of Research on Advance Organizers." *Instructional Science,* 1984, *8,* pp. 133–169.

McDonald, F. *Research on Teaching and Its Implications for Policy Making: Report on Phase II of the Beginning Teacher Evaluation Study.* Princeton, NJ: Educational Testing Service, 1975.

Meyer, W., Bachmann, M., Biermann, U., Hempelmann, M., Ploger, F., and Spiller, H. "The Informational Value of Evaluative Behavior: Influences of Praise and Blame on Perceptions of Ability." *Journal of Educational Psychology,* 1979, *71,* pp. 259–268.

Milgram, R. M. "Perception and Teacher Behavior in Gifted and Nongifted Children." *Journal of Educational Psychology,* 1979, *71,* pp. 125–128.

Monk, M. "Teacher Expectations? Pupil Responses to Teacher Mediated Classroom Climate." *British Educational Research Journal,* 1983, *9,* pp. 153–166.

Morse, W. C., Bloom, R., and Dunn, J. *A Study of Classroom Behavior from Diverse Evaluative Frameworks: Developmental, Mental Health, Substantive Learning, Group Process.* USOE, ESAE-8144, Ann Arbor, University of Michigan, 1961.

Murray, H. G. "Low Inference Classroom Teaching Behavior and Student Ratings of College Teaching Effectiveness." *Journal of Educational Psychology,* 1983, *75,* pp. 138–149.

Page, E. P. "Teacher Comments and Student Performance." *Journal of Educational Psychology,* 1958, *49,* pp. 173–181.

Pedersen, E., Faucher, T., and Eaton, W.W. "A New Perspective on the Effects of First-Grade Teachers on Children's Subsequent Adult Status." *Harvard Educational Review,* 1978, *48,* pp. 1–31.

Porter, A. C., and Brophy, J. E. *Good Teaching: Insights from the Work of the Institute for Research on Teaching* (Occasional Paper No. 114). East Lansing: The Institute for Research on Teaching, College of Education, Michigan State University, 1987.

Purkey, W. W., and Novak, J. M. *Inviting School Success,* 2nd ed. Belmont, CA: Wadsworth, 1984.

Rosenshine, B. "Content, Time, and Direct Instruction." In P. Peterson and H. Walberg (Eds.), *Research on Teaching: Concepts, Findings, and Implications.* Berkeley, CA: McCutchan, 1979.

Rosenshine, B. V. "Explicit Teaching." In D. C. Berliner and B. V. Rosenshine (Eds.), *Talks to Teachers.* New York: Random House, 1987.

Rosenshine, B. V., and Furst, N. "The Use of Direct Observation to Study Teaching." In R. Travers (Ed.), *Second Handbook of Research on Teaching.* Chicago, IL: Rand McNally, 1973.

Rutter, M., Maugham, B., Mortimore, P., Ouston, J., and Smith, A. *Fifteen Thousand Hours: Secondary Schools and Their Effects on Children,* Cambridge, MA: Harvard University Press, 1979.

Schmidt, W., and Buchmann, M. "Six Teachers' Beliefs and Attitudes and Their Curricular Time Allocations." *Elementary School Journal,* 1983, *84,* pp. 162–172.

Sears, P. S. "The Effect of Classroom Conditions on Strength of Achievement Motive and Work Output of Elementary School Children." *Journal of Abnormal Social Psychology,* 1940, *35,* pp. 498–536.

Sherman, B. R., and Blackman, R. T. "Personal Characteristics and Teaching Effectiveness of College Faculty." *Journal of Educational Psychology,* 1975, *67,* pp. 124–131.

Slavin, R. E. *Cooperative Learning: Student Teams,* 2nd ed. Washington, DC: National Education Association, 1987.

Slavin, R. E. *Cooperative Learning: Theory, Research, and Practice.* Englewood Cliffs, NJ: Prentice Hall, 1990.

Soar, R., and Soar, R. *Setting Variables, Classroom Interaction, and Multiple Outcomes.* Final Report for National Institute of Education, Project No. 6–0432. Gainesville, University of Florida, 1978.

Soar, R., and Soar, R. "Emotional Climate and Management." In P. Peterson and H. Walberg (Eds.), *Research on Teaching: Concepts, Findings, and Implications.* Berkeley, CA: McCutchan, 1979.

Sparks, G. M. "Teachers' Attitudes Toward Change and Subsequent Improvements in Classroom Teaching." *Journal of Educational Psychology,* 1988, *80,* pp. 111–117.

Spiro, R. J., and Meyers, A. "Individual Differences and Underlying Cognitive Processes." In P. D. Pearson, R. Barr, M. L. Kamil, and P. Mosenthal (Eds.), *Handbook of Reading Research.* New York: Longman, 1984.

Stallings, J., and Hentzell, S. "Effective Teaching and Learning in Urban Schools." Paper presented at the National Conference on Urban Schools, St. Louis, Missouri, July, 1978.

Tikunoff, W., Berliner, D., and Rist, R. *An Ethnographic Study of the Forty Classrooms of the Beginning Teacher Evaluation Study.* Technical Report No. 75–10–5. Far West Laboratory, San Francisco, 1975.

"Trying the Old-Fashioned Way." *Time,* March 9, 1981.

Wilson, S. M., Shulman, L. S., and Richert, A. R. "150 Different Ways of Knowing: Representations of Knowledge in Teaching." In J. Calderhead (Ed.), *Exploring Teacher Thinking.* London: Cassell, 1987.

Witty, P. "An Analysis of the Personality Traits of the Effective Teacher." *Journal of Educational Research,* 1967, May, pp. 662–671.

Wright, C. J., and Nuthall, G. "Relationships Between Teacher Behaviors and Pupil Achievement in Three Experimental Elementary Science Lessons." *American Educational Research Journal,* 1970, *7,* pp. 477–491.

SELECTED READINGS OF RELATED INTEREST

Arends, R. *Learning to Teach,* 2nd ed. New York: McGraw-Hill, 1991. Organized around the executive, the interactive, and the organizational functions of teaching, this book translates the research based on teaching into workable guidelines for teachers at all grade levels.

Berliner, D. C., and Rosenshine, B. V. (Eds.). *Talks to Teachers.* New York: Random House, 1987. This book is a collection of essays examining motivation, teacher expectations, teacher planning, and a host of other related topics designed to understand more deeply what good teaching is about.

Cohn, M. *To Be a Teacher: Cases, Concepts, Observation Guides.* New York: Random House, 1987. A comprehensive survey and analysis of teaching and schooling at both the elementary and secondary levels featuring five descriptive case studies of highly successful teachers that serve to integrate the concrete realities of teaching with theoretical analysis.

Good, T. L., and Brophy, J. E. *Looking in Classrooms,* 6th ed. New York: Harper and Row, 1994. One of the best available in terms of acquainting people with the nuances and complexities of classroom life, this book is a highly desirable reference book for anyone hoping to be an effective teacher.

Purkey, W. W., and Novak, J. M. *Inviting School Success: A Self-Concept Approach to Teaching and Learning,* 2nd ed. Belmont, CA: Wadsworth, 1984. This small paperback is developed around the idea that "teaching is inviting," and more importantly, everyone and everything in and around school serves as signal systems that invite or disinvite success.

Reynolds, A. "What Is Competent Beginning Teaching?" *Review of Educational Research,* 1992, *62,* pp. 1–35. This article provides a comprehensive review that blends findings from research literature on effective teaching with those of learning to teach in order to answer the question posed in the article's title.

Rubin, L. J. *Artistry in Teaching.* New York: Random House, 1985. This book describes how teacher-induced drama can alleviate habitual classroom tedium through use of the "performance" aspects of teaching, and examines the teacher as an artist and the classroom as a theater; it is a fine source of ideas for teachers at all levels.

12

Understanding Oneself

A Way to Enhance Teaching Effectiveness

CHAPTER OVERVIEW

IMPORTANT CHAPTER IDEAS

1. The kind of teacher you become is influenced by the kind of person you are.
2. Consciously, we teach what we know. Unconsciously, we teach who we are.

3. Teachers' mental health is no better or worse than other professional groups.
4. Expanded self-awareness leads to an expanded range of conscious choices that we can make for our behavior.
5. All defense mechanisms are basically alike in the sense that each serves to protect one against real or imagined personal failures and inadequacies.
6. When used extensively by persons who are unaware of it, defense mechanisms can be easily turned into self-defeating escape routes resorted to (rather than facing problems realistically) as persistent excuses for shortcomings.
7. Engaging in honest, self-disclosing interactions with others enhances the possibility of getting honest feedback, the only type that is useful in making constructive corrections.
8. One way to find out more about one's outer limits is to take on activities that are difficult and challenging periodically.
9. We can learn about ourselves in two ways: (1) observing ourselves in the behavior of others, and (2) paying attention to the outcomes of our own behavior.
10. Personal growth requires both work and courage; work in order to move against the inertia of laziness, and courage to move against the resistance caused by fear of the unknown.
11. Self-understanding can help us to avoid the possible negative outcomes of transference and countertransference interactions.
12. Self-understanding can help us to avoid unnecessarily personalizing particular teacher–student interactions.
13. How people see others and the world is generally related to how they see themselves.
14. Understanding oneself involves accepting one's basic nature and limitations, while simultaneously striving to attain one's full potentialities; it is a continual "tension" between these two polarities.
15. Understanding oneself requires time and effort; there is no shortcut, nor is it a panacea.

PROLOGUE

As teachers, we not only teach a curriculum of study, we also become part of it. The subject matter we teach is mixed with the content of our personalities. When, for example, we think back to our elementary or high school days to a particular grade or subject, it is very difficult to do that without also recalling the teacher associated with that time. The teachers we had (and have) are not lifeless automation's dispensing endless volumes of knowledge in monotonic tones, but living beings, each representing a unique life. We remember our teachers, not so much for what they taught, but for who they were and are. We remember their essence as persons, their style and manner as individuals. We may be attracted to a teacher's mind, but it is that teacher's personhood we remember.

Two types of curriculum infuse the lifeblood of every classroom. One is the curriculum prescribed by teachers. It is reflected in the books students read, the units they study, and the exams they take. It is the central reason students go to school. It shapes what they know. The other type of curriculum is inscribed in teachers. It is reflected in their tone of voice, assorted body language cues, and in their attitudes toward themselves and others, which can have a dramatic impact on the emotional atmosphere of a classroom. This type plays a part in shaping—for better or worse—how students feel about themselves and school.

The more we know about the subject(s) we teach, the better our instructional decisions are likely to be about how to teach what we know. To put it a bit differently, the more we know about our subject matter, the more choices we have for presenting it in a way that makes it learnable.

Somewhat analogously, the more we know about ourselves—the private curriculum within—the better our personal decisions are apt to be about how to pave the way for better teaching. This is not merely wishful, wistful "dreaming" of the way things should be in the best of all worlds. As discussed in Chapter 11, effective teachers tend to be thoughtful about their practice. They take time not only to monitor their instruction, to make sure that worthwhile content is being taught to their students, but also for reflection and self-evaluation.

In all of this, perhaps, there is an implicit bottom line that might be stated in the following way: The kind of teacher we are depends on the kind of person we are. This might seem apparent on the surface, but sometimes in our frantic quest for better teaching methods, more efficient instructional strategies, specifically defined behavioral objectives, and more effective methods of inquiry, we lose sight of the fact that the success of those "better" things we dream up depends very much on the emotional makeup and psychological underpinnings of the teacher who uses them.

We would probably agree that the urgency for understanding oneself is probably not as important for some as it is for others. In the case of, for example, the construction worker, the accountant, the engineer, the chemist, or the plumber, where the relationship is between an individual and buildings, numbers, bridges, test tubes, or pipes, we must admit that knowledge about one's personal dynamics is not as critical. However, where the relationship is between persons, in this case, between teacher and student, then the matter of self-understanding is more critical. Here, processes are more personal, involving, as they do, emotional states, subjective views, and personal preferences.

In Chapter 2, we took the position that an essential function of good education is to help students, at all levels, not only to become knowledgeable, but to develop healthy attitudes of positive self-acceptance. As teachers, we can help in this regard. However, as pointed out by Jersild (1955) in an early study of what happens when teachers face up to themselves:

> Teachers cannot make much headway in understanding others or in helping others understand themselves, unless they are endeavoring to understand themselves. If they are not engaged in this endeavor, they will continue to see those whom they teach through

> the bias and distortions of their own unrecognized needs, fears, desires, anxieties, hostile impulses, and so on. The process of gaining knowledge of self and the struggle for self-fulfillment and self-acceptance is something in which each teacher must be involved. (pp. 13–14)

Being aware of who we are as individuals and how we are perceived by others is an important step in the process of becoming a good teacher. In the absence of functional self-knowledge about our emotional deficits and personal shortcomings, we are in no position either to overhaul or to fine tune those aspects of ourselves that might be blocking our teaching effectiveness. *Consciously, we teach what we know. Unconsciously, we teach who we are.* The "who we are" facet of our teaching personality contributes significantly to the positive or negative tone of our classrooms and, certainly, to the receptivity of our students to learning.

We have all had a teacher whose personality and presentation of self were such that they interfered with our learning in that particular classroom. It does not take much. A personal quirk, an odd mannerism, a communication difficulty, an authoritarian air, a hostile attitude—any one of these can act as a barrier to learning. It does not take an extraordinarily large number of teachers afflicted with psychological problems of one sort or another to touch the lives of a very large number of students. Although Bentz, Hollister, and Edgerton (1971) have shown that maladjustment in its various forms is no greater proportionately for teachers than for other professional groups, Coates and Thoreson's (1976) review of relevant research has shown that the 200,000 teachers who do have emotional difficulties are exposed to some five million students.

That is a very large number of students indeed, which brings us to an important question.

HOW CAN SELF-UNDERSTANDING BE HELPFUL?

If you are like most, there are many facets about yourself and your relationships with others that are difficult to understand. For example, why do you sometimes dislike a person you have just met even when there is no apparent cause for feeling that way? Why do you sometimes lose your temper for no good reason? Why do you sometimes deliberately behave in such a way as to hurt the person you love even though you know you will regret it later?

The fact is, we do not always know the answers to questions such as these because the motives for our behavior reside outside our conscious awareness. Sometimes, for example, we dislike a person we have just met because that person might: (1) unconsciously remind us of something in ourselves we do not like, or (2) trigger the buried memory of some individual in our past experience with whom we had a bad experience. We might lose our temper because we have unconsciously linked tantrumlike behavior to: (1) getting attention, or (2) getting our own way. We might hurt the person we love knowing we will regret it later because of: (1) an unconscious need to be punished, or (2) a fear of intimacy and closeness that triggers a need to do something to create more distance in the relationship. These, of course, are not the only reasons we behave as we do, but they are possibilities. There are many reasons for behavior that, on the surface, seems incomprehensible to us and to others.

Because of the vast complexity of human behavior, it is not likely that any of us will ever totally understand ourselves. However, each of us, if we try, can understand ourselves better. In the struggle to cope with the reality of daily living and to deal firmly with threats, frustrations, and conflicts, we must have a firm grip on our own identity. Indeed, the admonition "know thyself" has been passed through the ages as a major antecedent of wisdom and peace of mind and has been adapted from its religious-philosophical origin as a slogan for better mental health. How can understanding oneself be helpful? Branden (1971) has stated it nicely:

> When we act without knowledge of what we think, feel, need, or want, we do not yet have the option of choosing to act differently. That option comes into existence with self-awareness. This is why self-awareness is the basis of change.
>
> When we become self-aware, we are in a position to acknowledge responsibility for that which we do including that which we do to ourselves, to acknowledge that we are the cause of our actions—and thus to take ownership of our own lives. Self-responsibility grows out of self-awareness.
>
> When we become aware of what we are and take responsibility for what we do, we experience the freedom to express our authentic self. Self-assertiveness becomes possible with the achievement of self-awareness and the acknowledgment of self-responsibility. (p. 171)

Healthy, positive self-understanding is not a mystical psychic station at which one stops during a particular point in life, but is, rather (or at least can be), a dynamic, ongoing process that never ceases.

12.1 Where Was That Knowledge When You Needed It?

Can you think back to a time (or times) in your life when it was precisely because of a lack of self-understanding that you got yourself into trouble? Can you see how you might have done things differently if only you had known what you know now about yourself?

WAYS TO ACQUIRE SELF-UNDERSTANDING

It is sometimes assumed that we get to know ourselves by learning about people in the abstract; that is, people as psychological, social, biological, economic, and religious beings. As a consequence, a person who is "psychologically knowledgeable" knows about a hypothetical being fabricated from theories, and from other persons' experiences, but not very much about him- or herself, the one to whom the personal pronouns *I* or *me* apply. Indeed, it is possible to take a great many courses in psychology and end up knowing a vast amount about psychology, but very little about oneself. Consider, for example, the case of a highly educated woman (she had two degrees and more than 45 credits in psychology) who, although extremely conversant on how children's lives can be affected by their relationships with parents, is unable to see how the unresolved anger she feels toward her father (because of the way he treated her as she grew) is behind her ongoing problems with her husband. Although she knows how defense mechanisms such as denial, repression, displacement, and projection work in the abstract, she is unaware of having used these very mechanisms to bring her unresolved feelings for her father into the marriage and acts as though it is her husband at whom (who is a safer target) she is angry.

A school psychologist of whom I am aware has always had great trouble developing a close relationship with his now teenage son for the very reasons that his own father had such a poor relationship with him as a boy: difficulty being emotionally open and expressing warm feelings. Although this psychologist is able to lecture eloquently to students and parents about the importance of explicit love and open communication between parents and children, he seems to have a blind spot when it comes to applying that knowledge to his own life.

Although both the woman and the man in these examples know a considerable amount about psychology, their knowledge is not wisdom, nor have their intra- and interpersonal lives been particularly enriched because of it.

Clearly, such information is not wisdom nor does it bring peace of mind, nor does positive self-understanding prevail because of it. This type of personal insight is specific knowledge about one's unique individuality. The question is: How can we begin to accumulate such knowledge? Let's turn to some ways for doing this.

Be Aware of How Defense Mechanisms Work

Although we are not always aware of it, each of us uses certain "defense" mechanisms to help us preserve and protect the integrity of our self-systems. Indeed, our ability to mobilize particular defensive processes is to some extent related to how successful we are in handling the daily stresses and strains of living. Regardless of how necessary defense mechanisms might be, they nonetheless can prove to be serious roadblocks to greater self-understanding and self-awareness if one uses them, however consciously, to avoid assuming responsibility, to avoid taking periodic risks, or to manufacture excuses for persisting in behavior that might be immature and self-destructive.

Defense mechanisms can be described both positively and negatively. Positively, they maintain or enhance self-esteem; negatively, they avoid feelings of anxiety and self-doubt. However, all defense mechanisms are fundamentally alike in the sense that each serves as a defense against real or imagined personal failures and inadequacies.

On the whole, defense mechanisms are normal human reactions, unless they are used to such an extreme and with such obliviousness to their presence that they begin to interfere with, rather than to aid, the maintenance of self-esteem. Progress toward greater self-awareness can very easily stagger to a standstill under the weight of extensive practices of self-deception. This is an important point to understand. A defense mechanism is successful only if there is a certain amount of self-deception and reality distortion built into the process. For example, the student who fails an exam and then blames his poor performance on either "an unfair test" or "a lousy teacher" never has to look at his own inadequacies as a possible contributing factor.

Although defense mechanisms are perfectly normal processes designed to protect us from reality onslaughts that might be too harsh for us to handle at a particular moment, they can turn into a self-defeating escape route easily when used as persistent excuses to avoid our shortcomings rather than face them. Recognizing what defense mechanisms are and how they work is the first step to controlling their influence in our lives. Let's turn to a brief consideration of seven frequently used defense mechanisms that figure prominently in everyday life.

Projection (Someone Else's Fault, Not Mine)

By general definition, projection is a means by which people: (1) transfer the blame for their own shortcomings, mistakes, and transgressions to others; and (2) attribute to others their own unacceptable impulses, thoughts, and desires. Projection is a form of blame. It enables us to look outward at others' behaviors rather than inward at our own. For example, who has not taken refuge in the comforting conclusion that it is the other person—certainly not oneself—who is untrustworthy, stupid, phony, unfriendly, or the cause of one's latest problem? Who has not felt at one time or another that life's difficulties would no doubt diminish significantly if we did not have to deal with that other person's manner, temperament, or personality? What person, after having blamed someone else for his or her misfortunes, has not felt some measure of gratifying contempt for the target of that blame, not to mention a particular amount of self-righteousness about his or her own conclusions?

As a verb, *blame* means to find fault with, to hold responsible for. As a noun, *blame* is an expression of disapproval or reproach. In whatever form it is used, blame is always something one puts "out there," something one places on another person or persons.

Projection, then, is an alienated aspect of the self that is aimed at someone else. It helps us maintain the self-image we would like to have by focusing our attention on the world "out there" rather than on the world "in here." When a person's behavior is not allowed into consciousness, there is a tendency to deal with it indirectly by projecting it into the behavior of others.

Projection of alienated feelings has many guises. Some recognizable examples are the following:

Projection	*Alienated Feeling*
"You're angry at me."	"I'm mad at you."
"You're a phony."	"I'm not always sincere."
"Men (or women) can't be trusted."	"I'm not always dependable."
"Welfare cheats should be jailed."	"I'm not always honest."
"You're a hateful person."	"I'm not always very loving."
"You use poor judgment."	"I'm not very smart."
"You put too much emphasis on looks."	"I'm not very attractive."
"All he or she wants is power."	"I'm not a very influential person."

Such projections help maintain our feelings of adequacy and self-esteem when we behave in ways that are inconsistent with how we see ourselves. Placing the blame on others for behavior and/or feelings that originally belonged to us might help us avoid social rejection and disapproval, but over time it is a self-defeating process. If we are so engaged in looking for faults and shortcomings in other people, we might never get around to expanding our awareness of our own. Students who constantly blame teachers, teachers who constantly blame parents, or, for that matter, parents who constantly blame teachers, have a convenient scapegoat for their blame, which is the projection, and a convenient excuse for things not going well, which is the rationalization. You can see that as long as I am able to say it is your fault, there is really nothing in me that I need to change, which, in fact, might be the place that change needs to begin (Hamachek, 1987).

Rationalization (Excuses, Excuses)

Rationalization is probably the most commonly utilized defense mechanism of all. Typically, it involves thinking of logical, socially acceptable reasons for our past, present, or future behavior. Rationalization has two primary objectives: (1) to help us invent excuses for doing what we do not think we should do but want to do anyway, and (2) to aid us in reducing the disappointment connected with not reaching a goal we had set for ourselves.

There are many other examples of rationalization. With not too much effort we can soon think of a reason for not going to class (e.g., "It will probably be a dull lecture anyway"), for goofing off instead of studying (e.g., "There really isn't that much to do; and besides, I can do it tomorrow"), for eating more than we need (e.g., "A little snack won't hurt; and besides, I'll be dieting soon anyway").

Although a certain amount of rationalization is normal in our daily behavior, excessive use of this process can be damaging. How can we be sensitive to its effective use? There are two primary symptoms to which we can be alert: (1) hunting for reasons to justify our behavior and beliefs; and (2) getting emotional (e.g., angry, tense, guarded) when someone questions the reasons we offer. If we find these reactions occurring with any frequency, it usually means that we should stop and examine how factual our reasons really are.

Denial of Reality (Ignoring the Unpleasant)

Denial of reality is a common, everyday mechanism, and one we put into gear every time we turn away from disagreeable realities by ignoring or refusing to acknowledge them. This inclination is reflected in many of our day-to-day behaviors. We turn our attention from unpleasant happenings (e.g., a woman screams for help but six people within hearing distance claim not to have heard her); we refuse to discuss unpleasant topics (e.g., a student receives a low grade on a test but refuses an opportunity to meet with the instructor and a small group of students to find out how to improve); we ignore or disclaim criticism (e.g., "The professor who flunked me doesn't know what he's talking about"); and we sometimes refuse to face our real problems (e.g., "I don't need help. This depression will go away").

The old sayings, "Love is blind" and "None is so blind as he who will not see," are probably fairly accurate illustrations of the inclination to look away from those things that are incompatible with our wishes, desires, and needs. Denial of reality can, indeed, protect us from painful experiences. However, like the proverbial ostrich that buries its head in the sand, denial can also keep us from perceiving things that might otherwise facilitate progress toward greater self-understanding.

12.2 Have You Used These Mechanisms Recently?

Can you think of some recent examples of having used projection, rationalization, or denial as a way of protecting yourself from something (or someone) you did not want to experience or face? What was the outcome? Would you say that your use of any of these defense mechanisms helped or hindered your case? What can you learn from this?

Reaction Formation (Behavior Differs from Feelings)

Reaction formation is a process of doing or thinking the exact opposite of what one really wants to do or think. Why do some persons behave in this contradictory manner? Some persons act this way primarily because they feel their real impulses or desires would get them into trouble if they were actually carried out. For example, a teacher might intensely dislike a particular student in his class, yet go out of his way to be nice to that student for fear of saying something unethical or unprofessional. This might seem desirable on the surface, but, unfortunately, repressed negative feelings usually find expression in more devious and less direct ways, which frequently are more damaging. For example, I recall a fifth-grade teacher who thoroughly disliked a particular boy in her class. She always spoke to him and of him kindly enough—thereby avoiding her real feelings—but not once, during a 6-month period, did she call on him in class, even when he vigorously volunteered. Consciously, she was being "nice" to him. At a less conscious level, when it came to deciding who would be called on in class, her true feelings were expressed.

Reaction-formation behavior is frequently recognizable in extreme and intolerant attitudes, which are usually out of proportion to the importance of the situation. For example, self-appointed guardians of the public's morals, who voluntarily give their time to censoring books and movies, are frequently found to have rather high sexual impulses themselves.

However, the presence of reaction formation in some persons does not mean that motives can never be taken at face value. Not all reformers are moved to action by veiled impulses. Real abuses need to be corrected. If polluted water is spreading disease, rational persons seek to solve the problem. It would be silly exaggeration, for example, to suggest that those looking for a solution are engaged in reaction-formation behavior as a way of managing their own unconscious desires to poison someone.

Reaction-formation behavior can be an effective means of helping us to maintain socially approved behavior and to control unacceptable impulses. However, it can also hinder knowing our true feelings better if we too quickly convert unpleasant impulses to more congenial ones without finding out why the unpleasant ones exist in the first place. For example, it would have been better for both the teacher and the student in the previously mentioned illustration if the teacher had simply admitted her dislike of him to herself and then had made an effort to know more about the boy in order to see him more favorably.

12.3 Is There Any Reaction Formation in Your Life?

Is there anyone in your life you really do not like, but act as if you do? When you think about it, why are you behaving in this manner? If your behavior toward that person were aligned more closely with how you felt, how would that behavior be expressed? What are you protecting yourself from by behaving one way while feeling another way? Could this be an example of reaction formation?

Fantasy (Creating a More Pleasant Reality)

Not only are we inclined to convert an unpleasant feeling into something more palatable, we are also disposed to "embellish" our perceptions so that we see the world more as we would like it to be. Fantasy is nourished by frustrated desires and fed by a need to make existing reality different. In a world of fantasy, it is possible to make one's real or imagined inferiorities vanish in a wink of the mind's eye.

Fantasy can be either productive or nonproductive. It can be used constructively in solving problems, as in creative imagination, or it can be a type of nonproductive wish-fulfilling process aimed at compensating for *lack* of achievement rather than stimulating or promoting achievement. James Thurber's Walter Mitty creation is a classic example of how one can achieve wished-for status by imagining that he or she is rich, powerful, and respected. Einstein, however, used cognitive pictures or "fantasies" in combination with a great deal of factual knowledge to arrive at productive hunches, formulae, and solutions.

As each of us can no doubt testify, the capacity to detach ourselves temporarily from an unfriendly reality and move to a more affable world of fantasy has considerable therapeutic value. Sometimes, for example, a bit of fantasy is just what the doctor ordered to add the dash of excitement and interest we need to spur us to greater efforts toward our goals in real life. However, the individual who *consistently* turns to fantasy as a solution to a troublesome reality is a danger psychologically. No problem ever disappeared by imagining it would.

All in all, there is evidence to suggest that fantasizing and daydreaming are not only normal, but almost universal among persons of both sexes. It is when we use them as a permanent rather than as a temporary escape that we are likely to get ourselves into trouble. It is one thing to build a castle in the sky, it is another to try to live in it.

Displacement (Negative Feelings Given to Someone Else)

Displacement refers to a shift of an impulse, usually hostile and/or aggressive, away from the person or object toward which it was originally intended to a more neutral or less dangerous person or object. If, for example, I am afraid of you (i.e., afraid of the loss of your love, respect, or friendship, or fearful of your retaliation), I might displace or direct to someone else any angry feelings I might have for you. There are many illustrations of how displacement works. A student who suppresses the anger he feels toward his professor might take it out on his unsuspecting (but safe) roommates. A teacher upbraided by her principal for poorly prepared lesson plans might keep her anger at her principal to herself but be grouchy with her students for the remainder of the day.

Displacement is a process whereby one can vent dangerous emotional impulses without loss of love and possible retaliation, and even without the necessity of recognizing the person for whom such feelings were originally intended. By displacing his anger toward the professor, the student maintains an air of cordiality in their relationship. The teacher who was grouchy with her students all day thus avoids showing her hurt and angry feelings to a principal she might fear. Although displacement might serve the needs of the displacer, it obviously places a heavy, not to mention unfair, burden on its misdirected targets.

On the whole, we are psychologically better off when we learn to express and discuss our feelings with the person to whom the feelings are intended in the first place, rather than when we direct them at someone who does not even know what they concern. One very specific advantage to a more direct approach is that it offers the possibility for feedback from the original source of frustrations, which is a much better way to enhance understanding not only of ourselves, but of the other person.

12.4 Why Are Loved Ones Frequent Targets?

Unless we are aware of what we are doing, the persons on whom we displace our negative feelings tend to be those we like or love the most. How would you explain this? Why do you suppose people are inclined to do this?

Compensation (Making Up for Perceived Deficiencies)

The compensation process involves an attempt to disguise the existence of a weak or undesirable characteristic by stressing a more positive one. We can make distinctions among types of compensatory behavior. *Direct* action is one type and occurs when an individual persistently attacks the *source* of an actual shortcoming and attempts to remove it. Participants in the Special Olympics would each be an example of how extraordinary effort can overcome personal handicap. Demosthenes, as the story goes, not only overcame his stammer to become a normal speaker, but a great orator.

We speak of *substitute* compensation when a person cannot overcome or remove the original shortcoming but develops other satisfactions. The unattractive girl might develop a winning personality; the uncoordinated boy might turn from athletics to scholastics; a woman who is deaf and blind might make up for her lack of sight and hearing through extraordinary development of tactile and intellectual ability. In every walk of life, there are personal opportunities that do not involve setting up unreachable goals or the cessation of effort and hope. Legitimate, wholesome compensations can add zest and meaning to anyone's life.

Unfortunately, not all compensatory behaviors are desirable or useful. For example, a girl who feels unloved might become sexually promiscuous; an insecure teacher might turn into an authoritarian despot; a lonely person might eat or drink too much; and a person of low self-worth might boast endlessly about trivial accomplishments.

Watch How Others Behave

Watching how others behave might seem like an odd way to acquire self-understanding, but is it? Perhaps a maxim of Goethe's might help here. "If you want to know yourself, observe what your neighbors are doing," he said. "If you want to understand others, probe within yourself." When you think about it, most of us are inclined to do exactly the opposite. We observe other people in order to understand them, and we probe within ourselves in order to understand ourselves better. This seems an obvious enough route to take, but it does not always work quite that simply. The reason it does not is because we look at other people objectively, but look at ourselves subjectively. We perceive others with the 20–20 vision of sanity and realism: we spot their shortcomings, flaws, self-deceptions, and even recognize their prejudices masquerading as principles.

However, when we look within ourselves, we are not inclined to see the same personal distortions. Indeed, most of us "see" only our good intentions, our purest motives, and our most altruistic inclinations. To the extent that we allow our unremitting calls for love and recognition to distort our self-perceptions, we can never really change anything about ourselves that might, in the interest of more accurate self-understanding, need correcting. There are, however, some specific ways of seeing ourselves more accurately—as Goethe suggests, through "observing what [our] neighbors are doing." Empathy, honesty, and self-disclosure are important parts of this process.

12.5 How Do Your Perceptions Compare with Others?

If you would like to see how your subjective view of yourself compares with someone else's more objective view, try a little experiment. Write down at least three things you think most persons are probably aware of regarding your "physical" self (e.g., appearance, height, weight), and then do the same for your emotional or "feeling" self and your "social" self (i.e., the way you relate to others). Ask a couple of friends who are willing to give you honest feedback to share their perceptions of the physical, emotional, and social aspects of the self you present. How closely do your perceptions match? If your friends' perceptions and yours differ, ask them why they see you the way they do.

Work on Developing Empathy

Empathy, quite simply, is the capacity to put ourselves in another person's shoes in an effort to understand that person's problems and difficulties from his or her point of view. The idea of "social feeling" developed by Alfred Adler provides us with a useful conceptual tool for understanding the empathic process (Crandall, 1980). Essentially, the idea of social feeling refers to a person's ability to empathize with another—to see, hear, and feel with that person. The usefulness of this concept lies in the fact that it combines the idea "social," which is an objective reference to common experiences, with the idea "feelings," which is a subjective reference to private experiences. The synthesis of the objective "social" with the subjective "feeling" is one way, then, of narrowing the gap between "you" and "me."

An empathic response involves a capacity to transcend oneself, to go beyond one's private motives and thoughts in order to better understand and share another person's needs and goals. Social feeling is an attempt to understand one's self through the understanding of others. It is becoming less involved with one's own hopes, fears, shame, and doubt in order to become more in tune with another person's thoughts and feelings. Fromm (1962), for example, has observed: "I discover that I am everybody, and that I discover myself in discovering my fellow man, and vice versa." Self-other understanding through the process of social feeling means to see one's self (i.e., insight) by participating and by sharing concerns with another, or, more succinctly, by being an "I" for a "thou" as Buber (1958) would say. It is a way of doing what Goethe suggested: If you wish to know yourself, watch what others are doing.

We have a great deal in common. When I understand you better this helps me to understand myself better, either because I see myself reflected clearly in the similarities of our behavior, or because your behavior is so different from mine that I am able to see my own more clearly in contrast. Personal insights via this route are a common experience among people in personal-growth-oriented groups, which is an important reason that a positive group experience can facilitate greater self-other understanding. An example from a weekend personal-growth workshop for a group of elementary school and high school teachers might help make this idea clearer:

Our objective in this weekend experience was to focus on personal issues and concerns that the teachers felt were interfering with their effectiveness as teachers and/or their own overall happiness with themselves. During a particular session deep in the weekend, one of the male high school teachers—we'll call him Bob—began to talk about what he saw as his overly developed concern about whether or not students liked him; in his words, "I can get 25 positive student evaluations, but if just one of them is negative, that's the one I worry about. It controls all of my feelings. It's as if I forget that 24 evaluations were positive. It's the same way in class. It can be a good class, things are rolling smoothly, and students seem involved, but if I see just one of them looking disgruntled or bored, I feel myself getting anxious, even angry that student has a negative attitude, which I always feel is toward me."

Mary, a teacher sitting next to him said, "I can't believe how much like me you sound. I hate it when I feel so controlled by my students' opinions of me. And yet I get so anxious when I feel someone doesn't like me." She paused, dropped her eyes, and then hesitantly looked around the circle. In a low voice, she said, "Even now I'm wondering whether any of you may think I'm stupid for how I feel."

Bob reached over and took her hand in his and said gently, "No, I don't think you're stupid, Mary. I just accept how you feel. I've felt that way many times."

Mary looked at him with moist eyes and said nothing for 2 minutes or so. She finally expressed to Bob and to all of us what she was feeling: "You know, I am 26 years old. This is the first time in all those years that I've heard someone say, 'I just accept how you feel.' I cannot tell you the number of times I heard words like, 'Behave yourself—what will people think?' or 'feeling that way is not nice—people won't like you' and on and on. I think I've just realized that I was programmed to believe that everyone—including my students—had to like me or I would not be a good person."

Bob smiled at Mary and said, "You know, I think we had the same programmers. What do you say we write our own?"

Thus, two people were able to recognize a bit of themselves in each other's life. As a result, they each saw more clearly why their feelings about themselves were so controlled by their students' (and others') opinions of them. This new awareness allowed them to begin the process of breaking free from the early conditioning that caused them to think that the only way they could like themselves was to avoid having anyone dislike them. This did not happen overnight, but with an understanding of why they felt the way they did, they were (and are) in a better position to have a healthier perspective—at least a more balanced one—of the feedback they receive from students and others in their lives.

We can learn a great deal about ourselves through being empathic observers of the human scene. When we recognize the common threads that weave us together as a common humanity, some measure of self-understanding is available to us by sharing concerns with another.

12.6 Empathy Has Many Expressions

Does empathy run any deeper? A little girl came home from a neighbor's house where her little friend had died.

"Why did you go?" questioned her father.

"To comfort her mother," said the child.

"What could you do to comfort Jody's mother?"

"I climbed into her lap and cried with her."

Honesty and Self-Disclosure Can Open Doors

We see honesty and self-disclosure in the example above involving Bob and Mary. You can see that practicing these qualities does not mean being brutally and indiscriminately frank, but it does mean showing some of yourself to another person, and exhibiting some of your own deeper feelings and attitudes. This is not an easy thing to do. Self-disclosure and honesty require courage. Not merely the courage to *be,* as the theologian Tillich (1952) eloquently described it, but the courage to *be known,* to be perceived by others as we know ourselves to be. Jourard (1971) whose self-disclosure research opened new doors to the understanding of interpersonal relationships, was among the first to admit that self-disclosure can be a risky business, "You expose yourself not only to a lover's balm, but also to a hater's bombs! When he knows you, he knows just where to plant them for maximum effect."

Honesty sometimes travels along a well-used one-way street rather than a two-lane highway. When a person says to us, "I want to be perfectly honest with you," this often means that he or she wants to be perfectly honest about *us,* rather than about *him- or herself.* Honesty and self-disclosure go hand in hand. You can more easily accept in a nondefensive way my honest feedback—particularly if it is along negatively critical lines—if I am able to be self-disclosing about my own faults and shortcomings. In addition, if I am willing to disclose facets of myself to you, it is very likely that you will feel more open to revealing aspects of yourself to me. It has to do with trust. If you sense that I trust you with my disclosures, you might be more willing to trust me with yours. Research has rather consistently shown the validity of this phenomenon—self-disclosure begets self-disclosure (Miller, Berg, and Archer, 1983; Tolstedt and Stokes, 1984). Timing is an important consideration in whether or not self-disclosure works (Archer and Burkeson, 1980). The person who jumps in with great self-revelations very early in a new relationship is likely to be viewed as immature, insecure, and even somewhat of a phony. If an individual makes a highly personal remark to us early in a conversation, we might conclude that this remark has little to do with his or her feelings toward us and more to do, perhaps, with his or her insecurities or need of attention. For example, a man who, on a first date, launches into deep disclosures about his social and sexual inadequacies is not likely to win the affections of his new lady friend. (Unless, of course, she has a large need to mother someone, in which case he would be a perfect candidate.) However, if someone makes a disclosing comment after knowing us for a while, we are more likely to take the remark personally and infer that it has possible implications for developing a relationship.

A major thesis in Jourard's work was the idea that maladjusted people are individuals who have not made themselves known to other human beings and, as a consequence, do not know themselves. In Jourard's (1963) words:

> When I say that self-disclosure is a means by which one achieves personality health, I mean something like the following: It is not until I am my real self and I act my real self that my real self is in a position to grow . . . People's selves stop growing when they repress them . . . Alienation from one's real self not only arrests one's growth as a person; it tends also to make a farce out of one's relationship with people. (p. 503)

When we repress our inner feelings, we are not only withholding awareness of those feelings from someone else; we are withholding awareness of them from ourselves. *A way to understand ourselves is through the rich diversity of feedback about ourselves from others who see us in a variety of situations.* When the self we present is *consistently* a facade or a mere surface offering of the real person we know ourselves to be, we should not be surprised if we find ourselves wondering, "What do people really think of me?"

Figure 12.1 shows an eight-step continuum of gradations between communications that are least self-disclosing and least difficult to express to those that are more self-disclosing and more difficult to express.

A positive outcome of exposing and sharing feelings is usually greater interpersonal closeness (which might help explain why some people do not easily expose and share themselves at a feeling level—they are fearful of being too close to another person). If I am self-disclosing and honest with you and about myself, this encourages you to be more self-disclosing and honest with me about yourself. If you are honest with me, I am freer to be more honest with you. And so the cycle goes.

Cultivate Friends Who Will Be Honest with You

One of the most consistent findings in interpersonal relations research is that *people tend to relate to other people with whom they agree* (Hamachek, 1982; Jones, 1990; Saks and Krupat, 1988). A fundamental principle of social interaction is the idea that people, when given the choice, will tend to associate with those who think well of them and to avoid those who dislike them, thereby biasing the communications about themselves in a favorable direction.

The outstanding case in point is *friendship,* which is, perhaps, the purest example of selectively choosing one's propaganda. Friends are inclined to say friendly things, which increases the likelihood of hearing more of what we like to hear about ourselves. Indeed, it is possible that we might like someone *because* they like us. Friendship is, at least to some extent, a "mutual admiration unit," whereby each party helps to sustain the desired self-image of the other.

Indeed, one of the most important props of romantic love is the remarkable intensity of mutual admiration. To discover that someone considers us the most wonderful girl in the world, or the most talented boy, is the type of communication we very much like to hear.

Least Self-Disclosing — *Least Difficult to Express*

1. I tell you how Bob feels about Mary, neither person being present.
2. I tell you how Mary feels about Bob, neither person being present.
3. I tell you my past feelings about Bob, who is not present.
4. I tell you my present feelings about Mary, who is not present.
5. I tell you my past feelings about you.
6. I tell you my present feelings about you.
7. I tell you my past feelings about myself.
8. I tell you my present feelings about myself.

Most Self-Disclosing — *Most Difficult to Express*

Figure 12.1. EIGHT-STEP CONTINUUM OF SELF-DISCLOSURE AND EXPRESSION.

What is true for friends and lovers is equally true of groups. The persistent search for social acceptance is a major enterprise of both young and old, and is apparent in our active involvement in groups that accept and approve of us, thereby enhancing our self-esteem.

It is important to note, however, that interpersonal selectivity that is too cautious and defensive can stunt personal growth. For example, both the loner, who has no friends, and the anxious, insecure person, who avoids others because he or she is fearful of negative feedback, limit the possibility of input that might spur them to the type of insights that could help them to be more at peace with themselves. Inasmuch as the self grows best in an interpersonal stream of reflected appraisals, the opportunity for this type of nurturance is severely curtailed when the selectivity is too guarded. *When we interact only with those who agree with us, but who seldom challenge us, we are too infrequently forced into having to reevaluate ourselves and our positions on various issues.* Perhaps the best type of friends are those who can, when it seems appropriate, challenge our most cherished beliefs without being threatened by the possibility of being rejected if they do. A true friend is not necessarily one who believes in us—although we would hope for that—but one who will be honest with us.

12.7 How Would You Handle This Assignment?

Suppose you had to write a short paper for your psychology class on the following topic: "Why Interpersonal Honesty Is So Difficult for People to Practice." What major points would you want to make? Why *is* this kind of honesty so hard? Try to think of why it may be difficult for you.

Allow Your Behavior To Be a Guide to Self-Knowledge

Not long ago, I asked a friend and colleague—a graduate of a nearby university, which happens to be a fierce athletic rival—who he was going to root for at an important upcoming basketball game. Torn as ever between his old ties and his new allegiance, he said, "You know, I just haven't decided yet. I'll have to wait to see which side I yell for." In this candid response lies the central idea behind self-perception theory, which, basically, is a point of view that suggests that we come to know our own attitudes and feelings partly by inferring them from observations of our own behavior (Bem, 1972; Jones, 1990).

One way, for example, that we come to know others is by watching and listening to their nonverbal and verbal behavior, and then making inferences based on those observations. We can use this same technique for knowing ourselves, at least in some instances. The qualifier "in some instances" is added because this process is most likely to work in situations in which our internal feelings are weak, ambiguous, or, as in the case of my friend, in conflict. For example, if we very much like another person and know it, we would not have to infer those positive feelings from the fact that we might look for excuses to be in his or her company. Similarly, we are inclined to use our overt behavior as a guide to our inner feelings only in situations in which this behavior is freely chosen. For example, if you read a book and keep going back to it until you have read it through, you could infer from your behavior that you liked the book because reading it was something you chose to do. If you *have* to read a particular book, you probably could not infer much from your behavior because your reading it was not freely chosen.

There are any number of illustrations of how the idea behind self-perception theory works in our everyday lives without our even knowing it. For example, have you ever found, once you sat down to the table and started eating, that you were hungrier than you thought? Have you ever been in a situation in which, once you started to say good-bye to someone, you found that you were going to miss that person more than you had realized? Have you ever been in an academic situation in which, once an exam was in front of you, you felt more fearful and uncertain than you had imagined? Have you ever been in a situation in which, once you had lost your temper, you discovered that you were much angrier than you believed? Have you ever found yourself, as did my friend, in a situation of conflict, not knowing what your real feelings were until you had to make a choice? (Couples, married and unmarried, frequently discover their *real* feelings for each other—for better or worse—when confronted with the decision of whether to stay together.) My friend, should you be interested, yelled himself hoarse for his alma mater, which told both him and me something about his real feelings on that matter.

Self-perception theory conveys a simple message: Just as we come to know others by watching their behavior, we can learn a great deal about ourselves by observing our own. Thus, we can learn about ourselves in two ways: observing ourselves in the behavior of others, and paying attention to the outcomes of our own behavior.

12.8 What Do You Suppose You Would See?

Try to imagine that, for the past month and unbeknown to you, someone followed you around with a movie camera and made a film of your life. The film is edited into a three-hour version and presented to you for your viewing pleasure. You have a chance, as it were, to watch your behavior. Imagine viewing such a film. How would you describe its central character? What kind of a person is he or she? Would you choose to have a person like that teach your children?

Take Time for Self-Reflection

It is generally true that the better we know ourselves, the more able we will be to forget ourselves—in terms of trying to figure out what certain behaviors mean—for it is usually those things we do *not* know about ourselves, in terms of personal dynamics, that bog us down from time to time. It takes courage to look at oneself (at one's shortcomings and limitations without denying their presence), and to examine one's possibilities and strengths without either fearing their existence or brushing them aside with notions on the order of "Anybody could do it" (or "have it," or "be it," as the case might be). We see this "brushing aside" among persons who are inclined to discount their potential strengths. Consider an example. A teacher says to a student with a low self-concept, "Joe, you have written an exceptional paper and I'm just delighted to have had the opportunity to read it." Joe replies, "Well, gosh, it really isn't that good, and besides, anyone could have done a good job with the topic I chose." Unless we view ourselves as basically worthwhile and capable individuals initially, then it is extremely difficult for us to incorporate the idea of having done worthwhile things, or of having done some things better than someone else. Some individuals feel that if they can do something—which to an outside observer might be perceived as extraordinary, or very well done—this must mean that anyone can do it.

Each of us, no matter who we are or what we do, has strengths and limitations. One outcome typically associated with getting to know oneself better is the discovery of strengths, talents, and healthy personal qualities that frequently have lain dormant in the shadow of overwhelming feelings of worthlessness and inadequacy.

To know our own strengths is a fine thing. Recognizing our own weaknesses is even better. What seems really bad, hurts, and finally defeats us is mistaking a weakness for a strength—misinterpreting and misusing weaknesses. We see examples of this all around us. Stubborn persons might interpret their unbending postures as merely a reflection of their high (and therefore honorable) convictions; cold persons might see themselves as merely detached and "objective" about life; power-driven persons might delude themselves into believing that they are natural leaders; the hard-hearted might call themselves pragmatists; and the smugly intolerant might fancy that they are highly principled.

Ernest Hemingway, for example, swaggered through life behind the front of super-macho manliness, and finally committed suicide when the facade collapsed under the weight of self-deceit. What he wrongly imagined to be a strength turned into megalomania and proved to be his fatal defect.

Take a moment and review the continuum of emotionally healthy and unhealthy behavioral characteristics you see in Table 12.1, which have been culled from a number of sources (Bryant and Veroff, 1982; Corey, 1989; Miller, Yahne, and Rhodes, 1990; Seeman, 1989). How would you rate yourself on each of these categories?

It is not always possible to get a clear picture of our strengths and weaknesses, or of our use of defense mechanisms, through introspection, reading,

Table 12.1. CONTINUUM OF HEALTHY TO LESS HEALTHY BEHAVIORS

A psychologically healthy person might show more of these behaviors:	*A less psychologically healthy person might show more of these behaviors:*
1. Likes self; sees self as essentially OK	Does not like self; sees self as pretty much not OK
2. Able to accept responsibility commensurate with ability and follow-through	Tries to avoid responsibility and has trouble following through
3. Meets daily problems and tensions as they occur; does not run away	Tries to avoid problems and tension; might use denial, fantasy, or chemicals to escape them
4. Able to be a friend and to make friends, enjoys being with others, but can also be alone easily	Does not particularly enjoy people, has few friends, spends much time alone because of general fear of others
5. Has a sense of humor, can take a joke, able to laugh at own self	Tends to be overserious, oversensitive, afraid of being laughed at, resents kidding, does not laugh at own self very often
6. Willing to accept the consequences of behavior, to accept results of errors as well as the fruits of correct decisions	Denies personal liability for wrong decisions, passes the buck, blames others, claims excessive share of credit for successes he or she is part of
7. Does not get defensive when beliefs are challenged or criticized	Tends to get defensive—even angry—when beliefs are challenged or critically evaluated
8. Able to express emotion, but is not controlled by it; does not insist on own way; usually able to control negative emotional expressions and behaviors	Tends to get emotional easily; might cry, pout, holler, or some combination thereof as a matter of course; quite childlike when confronted
9. Usually happy and confident (without being a Pollyanna); relatively free from worry; does not whine for what cannot be achieved	Usually gloomy and fearful; tends to worry needlessly; frequently is fretting or whining about one thing or another
10. Generally in reasonably good health and takes sensible steps to stay that way	Tends to be ill, weak, or physically "down" with some frequency; complains of assorted nonspecific aches and pains; does not follow good health habits

Sources: Bryant and Veroff, 1982; Corey, 1989; Miller, Yahne, and Rhodes, 1990; Seeman, 1989.

or talking to friends. Sometimes, something more is needed to assist the task of self-understanding.

Work and Courage Are Necessary Prerequisites

In M. Scott Peck's (1978) book *The Road Less Traveled,* courage is defined as the ability to move against the resistance engendered by fear. Courage is not the absence of fear; rather, it is taking action in spite of fear, moving against the resistance associated with fear into the unknown and into the future. Work is defined as what it takes on one's part to move against the inertia of laziness. Work requires attention to what needs to be done. Attention is an act of will, of work against the inertia of our own minds.

Courage and work are concepts rich in meaning and implication for personal growth, self-understanding, and self-concept enhancement. After all, what does it take to explore one's outer limits, to build self-confidence, and to find creative means of self-expression if not the courage to override the fear of failure and then willingness to work toward the accomplishment of one's goals? We do not have to go far to find those who have exuded these qualities in their lives. Consider some examples:

1. Failed in business, 1832; defeated for legislature, 1832; again failed in business, 1833; elected to legislature, 1834; sweetheart died, 1835; had nervous breakdown, 1836; defeated for Speaker, 1838; defeated for nomination for Congress, 1843; elected to Congress, 1846: lost renomination, 1848; rejected for land officer, 1849; defeated for Senate, 1854; defeated for nomination for Vice-President, 1856; again defeated for Senate, 1858; but in 1860, Abraham Lincoln was elected President of the United States.

2. After nearly flunking out of military school, he fought with the Spanish in Cuba, then in India and the Sudan. As a high naval officer, his first expedition was a disaster and he was discredited and forced to resign. He was defeated twice at the polls, and remained out of power for a full decade. After his greatest triumph, he was once more defeated at the polls. In 1951, he was again elected prime minister, and in 1953, Winston Churchill was knighted and received the Nobel Prize in Literature for his writing and oratory.

3. Although born black at a time when civil rights barely existed, raised in impoverished conditions, and blind, Ray Charles became a monumental success in the popular music field.

4. Although he was, by his own admission, a hopeless alcoholic, Bill Wilson pulled himself out of the gutter to found Alcoholics Anonymous.

5. Although blind and deaf from the age of 2, she immersed herself in a totally dedicated effort to learn, and in 1904 graduated from Radcliffe College with honors. From that point, Helen Keller devoted her life to writing and lecturing to raise funds for the training of the blind and other social causes.

6. Although addicted to drugs and the victim of a cancer that resulted in radical surgery, Betty Ford (wife of ex-President Ford) found the courage to fight back and "go public" so that others might find the strength to do the same.

There are many other examples of persons who reflect the qualities we are talking about. Which ones come to mind for you?

I suspect that it would be easy enough to conclude that because each of these persons has done exceptional things, they must, therefore, be exceptional people and not comparable to others. Perhaps they are; there is no way of proving that one way or the other. What is subject to proof, however, is the extraordinary courage they exhibited in the face of adversity, and the willingness to work very hard to accomplish what they thought was important.

Success is a relative term. It means accomplishing this, for one person, achieving that, for another. Personally, I have always felt that success is that which enables you to get out of life what you want to get out of life. By whatever criteria success is measured, its psychology remains disarmingly simple: Unless there is the possibility of failure, there can be no success. There are many exceptions to this, of course, not the least of which are the multitude of noncompetitive experiences we have during, say, friendly games or matches in which interactions are more important than outcomes. However, when success makes a difference in our feelings about ourselves, then it seems increasingly important that the success we want is neither guaranteed nor too easily won. For example, in his experimental investigation of the role of choice on feelings of success, Luginbuhl (1972) found that persons who felt the *most* successful on the tasks that they successfully accomplished were those who felt the greatest possibility of failing at those tasks. Persons who felt the *least* successful, even though they successfully completed the tasks before them, were those for whom the sense of possible failure was sharply reduced.

I think that many persons are overwhelmed by the spectacle of superiority, and wrongly imagine that the so-called "best" are endowed with vastly greater capacities than the rest. In sports, for instance, the best batting or passing records are not a great deal higher than the average. In field or track, the differences between winners and losers are measured in fractions of an inch or hundredths of a second. The real difference between those at the top and those at the bottom (in whatever endeavor), might not be so much in raw ability—although, when all other things are equal, that has to be considered—as it is in the willingness to combine the courage to go after a goal and the work necessary to achieve it. The student who studies when others have stopped and the athlete who practices when others have gone are examples of work in action. If the student and that athlete make a decision to try to be the best, or among the best, at what they do, we have examples of courage in action.

I remember a sign that hung in the school counselor's office in my high school. It said: "What you are afraid to do is a clear indication of the next thing you need to do." I always thought there was considerable wisdom in that advice.

12.9 Taking Some Risks May Be Worth It

Is there something in your life that you've wanted to do but have been afraid to go through with it? Sometimes, doing the thing we're afraid to do is where the greatest personal growth potential lies. Why not go ahead and do a thing or two that seem scary to you? What can you learn about yourself in the process?

Counseling Can Help

One does not have to be an emotional wreck to seek the help of a mental health professional. In fact, the majority of a mental health worker's time is spent with "normal" persons, with "normal" problems, who need someone who can be objective and empathic, and thereby help them to sort through confusing life circumstances.

Does counseling help? Evidence suggests that it does. For example, in an investigation involving 302 prospective teachers, Padgett and Gazda (1968) found that group counseling approaches resulted in significant changes for the better in self-concept and professional attitudes.

One advantage of a therapeutic experience, whether in a one-to-one setting or with a group, is that it helps to make unconscious sources of irritation more available to awareness so that they can be dealt with. Sometimes, if we are not careful, trouble spots that remain buried in the unconscious seek other outlets. For example, while discussing one of his teacher self-understanding studies, Jersild (1965) reported that all but one of a representative group of teachers admitted to a variety of personal problems. This lone and sturdy soul replied that he was not a bit anxious. In fact, he was never troubled by his anger or his love life, and his social life and work life were fine. He had no personal problems. He did, however, have ulcers.

A therapy or counseling experience provides no magic cures, and evidence suggests that persons get out of an experience of that sort basically what they expect to get out of it (Senour, 1983). Among other things, a therapeutic experience can lead to greater self-acceptance, a state of mind that has been found to be highly related to a sense of personal well-being, and even to enhanced teacher effectiveness (Foster, 1970; Landman and Dawes, 1982; Smith, Glass, and Miller, 1980).

HOW SELF-UNDERSTANDING CAN HELP US BE BETTER TEACHERS

Whatever else teaching might be, it is an ongoing process of interpersonal dynamics that engages us consciously in interactions with other human beings. Just as knowing about our subject area helps us to present its content in acceptable, appropriate ways (at least that is our goal), so, too, does "knowing" about ourselves as persons help us to present *ourselves* in acceptable, appropriate ways. As teachers, self-understanding can help us to put the interpersonal dynamics of classroom life into their proper perspective. Self-understanding leads to greater self-awareness, which is the type of self-knowledge that helps protect us from unconsciously motivated whims, selfish desires, or unnecessarily defensive behavior. There are at least five ways that self-understanding can help us to be more effective teachers.

Transference Possibilities Are Reduced

Transference is the descriptive label given to the process whereby we unconsciously respond to a person or experience in a way that is similar to the way we felt about, or responded to, some other individual or experience in our lives. For example, sometimes a client in therapy will behave toward the therapist as if that person were a parent figure. A second grader will behave toward his teacher as if she were his mother. In other words, the client and the second grader "transfer" feelings for one person in their lives to another. This can be a conscious process; that is, we can say, "I like this person (or dislike him, as the case might be) because he reminds me of so and so." When the transference phenomenon is conscious, one is more able to control its effect and expression. It is when transference happens without our awareness that we may fail to recognize its possible presence in our students' relationships with us.

Countertransference Behaviors Can Be Controlled

Countertransference has all of the attributes of transference and is the term given to what happens when individual A *responds in kind* to individual B's original transference behavior. If, let us say, a therapist responds to a female client as if she were his daughter, this would be what is called *countertransference.* In varying degrees, both transference and countertransference are processes that occur all of the time with all persons. They surely go on between students and teachers.

There are many examples of how these phenomena work detrimentally in teacher–student interactions. A high school teacher, for instance, finds herself constantly "picking on" girls in her class who are popular and attractive. "My sister was the glamorous one, I wasn't," said in a sneering sort of way, shed some light on her motives when it slipped out one day. In another instance, an elementary teacher, who was the eldest of six children, and who had spent much of her growing years caring for younger siblings, continually complained that, "the children in my class seem like such a burden at times." As she grew to understand herself better, she began to see that she was unconsciously resurrecting old feelings and reliving her youth in her relationships with her students. When she became fully aware of what she had been doing, her attitude changed dramatically. When her attitude changed, so, too, did her perceptions. She no longer saw her students as burdens, as children to be taken care of, but as young persons to be enjoyed and taught. In her words, "I'm their teacher, not their older sister. They have parents who can take care of them." By understanding more about her psychological history, she was able to put the past aside and be more fully in the here and now of her life.

12.10 Could It Be Transference?

Reflect for a moment. Think of someone you simply do not like—whom you have trouble relating to. Who does that person remind you of that you have known before? How are your feelings toward the two people similar or different? To the extent that they are similar, either positively or negatively, this is transference.

Unnecessary Personalization Can Be Reduced

An example of how one very aware and self-understanding teacher behaved in the face of a class's transference behavior is cited by Solomon (1960). Consider the constructive use the teacher in question made of his knowledge of himself and his student's behavior.

> In a [high school] history class . . . the subject of freedom was being discussed. There were muttered swear words, throwing of erasers, sly passing of notes, general disorder. These the teacher recognized, to quote his own words, "not as an affront to me, as I might have formerly thought. But I knew they were mad." And I thought "Better get it out legitimately." So I said, "You seem bothered and mad at me or at somebody in connection with this business of freedom. Suppose you write anything you feel. Anything goes in writing. But no more swearing, etcetera. Here is a way to get out your anger." To give just a sample of the transference evidence, I quote in part from one boy's paper. "There is supposed to be freedom in the U.S. but teachers tell me what to do. The principal tells me what to do. We can't talk. We can't be late. We can't chew gum. We can't do anything but our own school work which is terrible. It's the same at home. The old lady tells me to mow the lawn, sweep the patio, do this, do that. The old man comes home. 'You forgot to do this. You forgot to do that. Leave your car in the garage and walk to school.' And there it starts all over." (p. 88)

This was a wise teacher. He recognized that the students were not angry at him, but at the adults in their lives, whom they saw depriving them of their freedom. A less insightful teacher might have personalized the incident by erroneously concluding that the students were mad at him or the assignment. He could have then gotten angry at them by assuming a defensive and reactive posture (e.g., "How dare you act that way," "I'll teach you for acting up like that"), and the entire happening might have been blown out of proportion.

The transference-countertransference idea comes from sound clinical observations, and is supported by empirical research. For example, research shows that just as students react to the ways in which teachers behave, teachers behave in a manner that is basically consistent with how they perceive their students behaving toward them. A case in point is Klein's (1971) research related to student influence on teacher behavior, her general conclusion being that "when students behaved positively, the teachers were positive, and when the students behaved negatively, the teachers were negative." You can see how teacher behaviors of that type are self-defeating inasmuch as they encourage in students the very behavior that triggers a teacher's reactive behavior in the first place. When teachers are aware of what is happening psychodynamically, they are in a much better position to control their own behavior, or, to put it a bit differently, to be *actors,* not just *reactors.*

Relationships Between Self-Perceptions and Perceptions of Others Are Clearer

Ralph Waldo Emerson insightfully observed that "What we are, that only can we see." As both common sense and research have demonstrated, this simple aphorism stands as the cornerstone on which are built our most important principles of how we see others. Psychoanalyst Fromm (1968) was one of the first to notice the close relationship between persons' feelings toward themselves and their feelings toward others. As Fromm expressed it, "Hatred against oneself is inseparable from hatred against others" (p. 331), an observation that is quite consistent with the research of Kuiper and Rogers (1979), who concluded from their investigation of how persons encode personal information about others that "how we summarize information about other people is bound up with our view of self."

What we are inclined to see "out there" in the behavior of others is quite frequently a projection of our own drives, needs, and fears. Those who tell us that persons are basically untrustworthy and cruel—ignoring the fact that they are also dependable and kind—might be saying more about themselves than about the world. There is solid research evidence to support the idea that when persons think well of themselves, they are more likely to think well of others. Conversely, when persons disapprove of themselves, they are more likely to disapprove of others (Epstein and Feist, 1988; Hamachek, 1992; Markus, Moreland, and Smith, 1985). What we find "out there" is what we put there with our unconscious projections. When we think we are looking out a window, it might be, more often than we realize, that we are really gazing into a looking glass.

Barron (1968) offers some tantalizing evidence to support this looking glass idea. While doing research related to the nature and meaning of psychological health, he and his colleagues first had to develop some operational conceptions about what a healthy person would probably be like. They then studied subjects chosen for their general effectiveness as persons. Following this, each staff member described each subject on a checklist of adjectives. The intention was to derive from these checklists a composite staff description of each subject's so-called "soundness as a person." The results were surprising. Individual staff members used quite different adjectives to describe the same person. The most revealing aspect of this was the great consistency with which staff members described highly effective persons, checking off the same adjectives that in private moments of good will they would use to characterize themselves. Barron (1968) went on to add:

> Moreover, they tended to describe clearly ineffective persons as possessing traits which in themselves they most strongly denied . . . Thus, one staff member noted for his simple and clear thought processes most frequently described an ineffective person as *confused;* another staff member who is exceptionally well-behaved in matters of duty checked adjectives *conscientious* and *responsible* most frequently in describing highly rated subjects . . . another staff member who has subsequently been interested professionally in independence of judgment saw effective subjects as *independent* and *fair-minded. Each of us, in brief, saw his own image in what he judged to be good.* (p. 12)

The inclination to see in others what is in oneself is true as early as adolescence. Rosenberg (1979), for example, found that adolescents who think poorly of themselves tend to think poorly of others, and to feel that others feel poorly of them. Those with high self-regard, however, think well of others, and tend to believe that others think well of them.

Psychiatrist Sullivan (1947) once said: "It is not as ye judge that ye shall be judged, but as you judge yourself so shall you judge others." Clinical and empirical research generally supports Sullivan's observation. We do tend to see others as we see ourselves, *particularly if we are not aware that this is what we are doing.* Seeing others as a projection of our own images might serve several functions: (1) it makes others seem more like us than they really are, and therefore more compatible; and (2) it perpetuates the feeling that the way we are is really the "right" way."

It is generally true that our view of ourselves and our particular life circumstances serve as a filter through which we view the world around us. The angry person sees hurtful motives; the friendly person sees pleasant encounters; the critical person looks around and finds things to correct; the accepting person looks around and finds things to appreciate; the suspicious individual sees ulterior motives; the trusting individual sees honest intentions; and so it goes. The way we interpret the world seems to have a great deal to do with our attempts to make it more that way for ourselves. It might indeed be that our perception of what is reality becomes—for better or worse—a self-fulfilling prophecy. Our perception of reality starts, it seems, with our own self-picture, which is another good reason for expanding our self-understanding—to know what that self-picture is in the first place.

12.11 Are We Reflecting Who We Are?

It has been said that most judgments we make about others are basically autobiographical reflections of ourselves. What do you think of this possibility?

We Can Feel More at Peace with Ourselves

One of the best ways to feel good about ourselves is to know with reasonable certainty what we want, and what it will take to get there. When we know ourselves, we are less likely to delude ourselves into believing that we are happy when we are not. Along with self-understanding comes a degree of self-acceptance. That is, we not only know our strengths, but also are aware of our limitations and are prepared to make the best of them.

Understanding yourself, or "becoming what you are," means two things at once: accepting one's basic nature and limitations while struggling to realize one's full potentialities. A creative and developing life is a continual "tension" between these two factors. In the final analysis, this might be one of those very human characteristics that make good teachers "good": having accepted their own limitations, they are better able to accept their students', and having recognized the unfulfilled potential in themselves, they strive even harder to help their students to do the same.

A TEACHER'S SELF-UNDERSTANDING CAN MAKE A POSITIVE DIFFERENCE

It is important to keep in mind that it is not the teacher's understanding of self, per se, but rather the way it is reflected in behavior toward students, that makes a difference. Thus, teachers who are aware of their personal issues are in a position to be more sympathetic and sensitive to the problems of their students, and more capable of controlling their own behavior. We should also remember that there are many other inputs in the lives of students, and that it is not fair to blame any particular teacher's lack of adjustment for all of the problems of students. Still, the fact is that there are some teachers so busy trying to hold their emotional lives together that they have hardly any energy left over to work effectively in guiding their students' growth.

We might conclude from everything said so far that only "normal," well-adjusted persons should be teachers. To a great extent this is true. The evidence does suggest that healthy, balanced teachers who are warm, flexible, and interested in students, seem better able to affect the attitudes and learning of students positively than do teachers in whom these personal characteristics are less evident. The point can be argued, however, that some teachers are successful precisely because of their neuroticism. For example, the compulsive teacher who places a high premium on order, accuracy, and precision, might teach students the value of order in their lives. We might find another teacher with strong needs for power and domination who vigorously carries students along with his or her own high standards of achievement.

This does not mean, however, that we should recruit more neurotic teachers, or that we should feel more comfortable about our own unresolved personal hang-ups. Absence of self-understanding and flexibility make it difficult for neurotic or emotionally unbalanced teachers to be successful with any group, except that narrow band of students who meet his or her strong, personal needs.

Self-understanding is no panacea, no magic potion that automatically turns a person into a good teacher. It is, however, a door that opens to healthier choices and wiser life decisions.

12.12 What Image Are You Reflecting?

> There is an old adage I've always liked. It says simply, "Life is a mirror; it reflects back whatever image we present to it." What images do you reflect?

EPILOGUE

To achieve the good life, said Socrates, there is one paramount rule: Know thyself. This is not an easy thing to do. Knowing ourselves, deeply and fully, also means facing ourselves, squarely and honestly. This means looking beyond and through the emotional costuming, the sham, and the pretense in order to see ourselves more clearly—as we actually are, and not just the image of what we want to be. It means reconciling, in a realistic way, the discrepancies between our hopes and our accomplishments, and making our peace with the differences that might exist between our ambitions and our talents. It means accepting, in a deep and final way, a simple, psychological truth: The self is not something we find, but something we create. Becoming an emotionally healthy, happy person, or a self-actualized, fully functioning individual—whatever you care to call your version of someone who has it all together—is not something either found by accident or encoded in genes. Rather, it is an emotional position built over time, and constructed by blending reasonable, reachable goals with hard work, some sacrifice, and a willingness to take some risks now and then.

Attaining a healthy self-image—with its concomitant feelings of adequacy, ableness, and personal worth—and self-confidence are not lofty goals beyond mortal reach, standing as a type of poetic ideal. It is an attitude, or cluster of attitudes, that is learned and acquired, which means that sometimes "bad" (i.e., negative, destructive, self-defeating) attitudes must be replaced by healthier attitudes.

Understanding ourselves takes time and effort; it is challenging and exciting, and can open doors to our upper limits and hidden potentials, which might otherwise remain locked away forever. One of the nice things about knowing more about ourselves is that its benefits extend far beyond the classroom to include all arenas of our personal and professional lives.

STUDY AND REVIEW QUESTIONS

1. Consider the following statement: The kind of teacher we are depends largely on the kind of person we are. If someone asked what this means, what would you say?
2. Can you explain why it is possible for a person to know a lot about psychology, but not very much about him- or herself?
3. How could you explain the broad concept "defense mechanism" to someone unfamiliar with its meaning?
4. Can you give an example of each of the following defense mechanisms? (1) projection, (2) rationalization, (3) denial, (4) reaction formation, (5) fantasy, (6) displacement, and (7) compensation.
5. How can watching the behavior of others help us understand ourselves?
6. How does practicing empathy help the process of self-understanding?
7. Can you explain why self-disclosure can facilitate self-understanding?
8. What is the basic idea behind Bem's theory of self-perception?
9. Personal growth and self-understanding requires work and courage. Can you explain what this means?
10. When the point is made that self-understanding can help teachers prevent harmful transference and countertransference interactions, what does that mean?
11. Suppose someone asked you, "What is the relationship between how we see ourselves and how we see others?" How would you respond?
12. How does understanding oneself help a person to be a better teacher?

REFERENCES

Archer, R. L., and Burkeson, J. A. "The Effects of Timing of Self-Disclosure on Attraction and Reciprocity." *Journal of Personality and Social Psychology,* 1980, *38,* pp. 120–130.

Barron, F. *Creativity and Personal Freedom.* New York: Van Nostrand Reinhold, 1968.

Bentz, W. K., Hollister, W. G., and Edgerton, J. W. "An Assessment of the Mental Health of Teachers: A Comparative Analysis." *Psychology in the Schools,* 1971, *8,* pp. 72–76.

Bem, D. J. "Self-Perception Theory." In L. Berkowitz (Ed.), *Advances in Experimental and Social Psychology,* Vol. 6. New York: Academic Press, 1972.

Branden, N. *The Disowned Self.* Los Angeles, CA: Nash, 1971.

Bryant, F. B., and Veroff, J. "The Structure of Psychological Well-Being: A Sociohistorical Analysis." *Journal of Personality and Social Psychology,* 1982, *43,* pp. 653–673.

Buber, M. *I and Thou.* New York: Scribner's, 1958.

Coates, T. S., and Thoreson, C. E. "Teachers Anxiety: A Review with Recommendations." *Review of Educational Research,* 1976, *46,* pp. 159–184.

Corey, S. R. *The 7 Habits of Highly Effective People.* New York: Simon and Schuster, 1989.

Crandall, J. E. "Adler's Concept of Social Interest: Theory, Measurement, and Implications for Adjustment." *Journal of Personality and Social Psychology,* 1980, *39,* pp. 481–485.

Epstein, S., and Feist, G. J. "Relation Between Self- and Other-Acceptance and Its Moderation by Identification." *Journal of Personality and Social Psychology,* 1988, *54,* pp. 309–315.

Foster, S. F. *Self Acceptance and Two Criteria of Elementary Student Teacher Effectiveness.* Paper presented at the American Educational Research Association annual meeting, Minneapolis, MN, March, 1970.

Fromm, E. *Beyond the Chains of Illusion.* New York: Pocket Books, 1962.

Fromm, E. "Selfishness and Self-Love." In C. Gordon and K. J. Gergen (Eds.), *The Self in Social Interaction,* Vol. 1. New York: Wiley, 1968.

Hamachek, D. *Encounters with Others: Interpersonal Relationships and You.* New York: Holt, Rinehart and Winston, 1982.

Hamachek, D. "The Dynamics of Projection: Its Use in Expanding Self-Knowledge." *Journal of Humanistic Education and Development,* 1987, September, pp. 2–11.

Hamachek, D. E. *Encounters with the Self,* 4th ed. Fort Worth: Harcourt Brace Jovanovich, 1992.

Jersild, A. T. *When Teachers Face Themselves.* New York: Bureau of Publications. Teachers College, Columbia University, 1955.

Jersild, A. T. "The Voice of the Self." *NEA Journal,* 1965, *54,* pp. 23–25.

Jones, E. E. *Interpersonal Perception.* New York: W. H. Freeman, 1990.

Jourard, S. M. "Healthy Personality and Self-Disclosure." *Mental Hygiene,* 1963, *43,* pp. 459–507.

Jourard, S. M. *The Transparent Self,* rev. ed. New York: Van Nostrand Reinhold, 1971.

Klein, S. S. "Student Influence on Teacher Behavior." *American Educational Research Journal,* 1971, *8,* pp. 403–421.

Kuiper, N. A., and Rogers, T. B. "Encoding of Personal Information." *Journal of Personality and Social Psychology,* 1979, *37,* pp. 499–514.

Landman, J. T., and Dawes, R. M. "Psychotherapy Outcome." *American Psychologist,* 1982, *37,* pp. 504–516.

Luginbuhl, J. E. R. "Role of Choice and Outcome on Feelings of Success and Estimates of Ability." *Journal of Personality and Social Psychology,* 1972, *22,* pp. 121–127.

Markus, H., Moreland, R. L., and Smith, J. "Role of the Self-Concept in the Perception of Others." *Journal of Personality and Social Psychology.* 1985, *49,* pp. 1494–1512.

Miller, L. C., Berg, J. H., and Archer, R. L. "Openers: Individuals Who Elicit Intimate Self-Disclosure." *Journal of Personality and Social Psychology,* 1983, *44,* pp. 1234–1244.

Miller, W. R., Yahne, C. E., and Rhodes, J. M. *Adjustment: The Psychology of Change.* Englewood Cliffs, NJ: Prentice Hall, 1990.

Padgett, H. G., and Gazda, G. M. "Effects of Group Guidance and Group Counseling on the Self Concept and Professional Attitudes of Prospective Teachers." *SPATE Journal,* 1968, Winter, pp. 42–49.

Peck, M. S. *The Road Less Traveled.* New York: Simon & Schuster, 1978.

Rosenberg, M. *Conceiving the Self.* New York: Basic Books, 1979.

Saks, M. J., and Krupat, E. *Social Psychology and Its Applications.* New York: Harper & Row, 1988.

Seeman, J. "Toward a Model of Positive Health." *American Psychologist,* 1984, *44,* pp. 1099–1109.

Senour, M. N. "How Counselors Influence Clients." *The Personnel & Guidance Journal,* 1983, February, pp. 345–349.

Smith, M. L., Glass, G. V., and Miller, T. I. *The Benefits of Psychotherapy.* Baltimore: Johns Hopkins University Press, 1980.

Solomon, J. C. "Neuroses of School Teachers." *Mental Hygiene,* 1960, *44,* pp. 87–90.

Sullivan, H. S. *Conceptions of Modern Psychiatry.* Washington, DC: William Alanson White Psychiatric Foundations, 1947.

Tillich, P. *The Courage to Be.* New Haven, CT: Yale University Press, 1952.

Tolstedt, B. E., and Stokes, J. P. "Self-Disclosure, Intimacy, and the Depenetration Process." *Journal of Personality and Social Psychology,* 1984, *46,* pp. 84–90.

SELECTED READINGS OF RELATED INTEREST

Brinthaupt, T. M., and Lipka, R. P. (Eds.). *Changing the Self: Philosophies, Techniques, and Experiences.* Albany: State University of New York Press, 1994. This volume examines how the self and self-concept are influenced and changed by personal choices, interpersonal experiences, and life events.

Evans, C. *Understanding Yourself.* New York: New American Library, 1980. This entire book contains a series of self-scoring exercises that explore areas such as extroversion–introversion, popularity, leadership potential, assertiveness, self-concept, physical health, and creativity.

Goleman, D. *Vital Lies, Simple Truths.* New York: Simon and Schuster, 1985. Drawing on a wide variety of evidence from brain function to social dynamics, the author of this book shows how selective perception buries painful memories and insights. Knowledge of its workings allows one to lead a more self-aware life.

Hamachek, D. *Encounters with the Self,* 4th ed. Fort Worth, TX: Harcourt Brace Jovanovich, 1992. This book focuses primarily on self-concept and the countless ways it is shaped and influenced by family and school experiences, physical development, and perceptions. It considers ideas for developing and maintaining a positive self-image.

James, J. J. *Windows.* New York: Newmarket Press, 1987. A series of small, thought-provoking essays, each designed to open a window of insight into one's deeper feelings and sense of being, this book is a delightful reading experience.

Johnson, D. W. *Reaching Out: Interpersonal Effectiveness and Self-Actualization,* 5th ed. Needham Heights, MA: Allyn and Bacon, 1993. This book seeks to provide the theory and experience necessary to develop effective interpersonal skills. It contains a rich array of exercises designed to enhance communication skills and self-knowledge.

Missildine, W. H. *Your Inner Child of the Past.* New York: Pocket Books, 1982. Written by a psychiatrist, this book explores how the child we once were influences the person we currently are. It offers many suggestions for breaking free of the past.

13

Making Teaching Meaningful, Relevant, and Lasting

CHAPTER OVERVIEW

IMPORTANT CHAPTER IDEAS

1. An interesting, competent teacher and relevant school experiences are educational strategies guaranteed to combat student boredom.
2. There are ranges of learning readiness in each grade, which means teachers must be prepared with a variety of teaching approaches to meet the challenge of different learning abilities among students.
3. What is learned in school is likely to transfer to out-of-school areas to the extent that teachers build creative bridges between the academics of school and the realities of everyday living.
4. The "natural" view says that children should not be taught particular subjects until they are maturationally "ready" to learn them. The "guided experience" view says that practically any subject can be taught to any child as long as it is presented at his or her level of development. There is some truth in each view, if it is not carried to extremes.
5. One test of successful teaching is the extent to which what is taught in school is used (i.e., transferred) *outside* of school.
6. Teachers can enhance school's relevancy and meaningfulness by teaching not just *how* things happen, but *why.*
7. School experiences are more meaningful to students when they experience as much early success as possible.
8. Although a particular *type* of teacher question is not clearly related to student achievement, the sheer frequency of teachers' questions is related. Good questions are clear, purposeful, brief, natural, and frequently thought-provoking.
9. Wait time, the period between a teacher asking a question and calling on someone to answer it, is a critical factor for teachers to consider when in a questioning mode.
10. Almost every curricular area has psychological possibilities for being taught in meaningful, relevant ways when viewed in terms of what it might do to

help students find themselves, realize their potential, and use their resources in productive ways.

11. Effective teachers have a knack for "staging," which, basically, is the production of novel approaches or experiences that capture students' attention.
12. Whether a teacher uses the "part" method or the "whole" method as a framework, teaching and learning depend on two factors: (1) characteristics of the students, and (2) nature of the material.
13. Utilizing teaching techniques such as appropriately distributing work and study activities, providing knowledge of results and ample review time, and giving the right "mental set," can dramatically improve learning outcomes.
14. Encouraging overlearning is a good idea when new material is specific and concrete, and when there is a long interval between learning new material and its recall. It is unwise to encourage overlearning abstract principles, or concepts that are not easily understood.
15. Microsociety schools allow students to establish and manage their own miniature society, which encourages them to use their traditional learning in meaningful and relevant ways.
16. When teaching students from varied ethnic and social backgrounds, it is important for teachers to have realistic expectations, and to have an awareness of the ways in which language differences, impoverished living conditions, and uncertain family conditions can affect school performance.
17. When relevance, meaning, purpose, and hope are absent from the curriculum, increased numbers of students lose their motivation to learn.

PROLOGUE

There was a time in the history of education when students' minds were perceived to be the equivalent of blank slates, the teachers' task being that of a person who filled those slates with knowledge. When there were few radios, no television, and not many books, it may well have been that children went to school with relatively "blank slates." Those days are part of a distant past, at least for most young persons.

For increasing numbers of students education begins when they are old enough to look at an attractively presented picturebook or to turn on the television set for a creatively produced children's program. Through the increased efforts of various mass-communication media, students are entering the elementary grades and going into high school better prepared, better read, and more broadly exposed to the language and events of culture than ever before in United States history. Educational systems no longer have exclusive rights to what students learn.

There was a time when students had little with which to compare their schooling. Elementary students could compare this year's teacher to last year's and high school students could compare their English teacher to their science teacher, but these comparisons were usually limited to personal preferences between two personalities, with little thought given to the content or relevancy of one teacher over another. Such is not the case for teachers of today's youth. By and large, young persons might unconsciously expect more of their *formal* education because they have become accustomed to more from their *informal* education. The standards of comparison are not really more available, but higher and more demanding. If students, for example, watch an informative and entertaining science presentation on television, is it any surprise that they might compare their actual schooling with what they see on Channel 18?

Teaching is hard work. Not only are most teachers confronted with a range of individual differences in motivation and intelligence among their students, they are faced with some who are in school only because they have to be. Our objective in this chapter is not to look for ways to make teaching less difficult, but to look for ways to make it more exciting and challenging so that, ultimately, what happens in the classroom is meaningful, relevant, and lasting.

What is a "teachable moment"? How can we help students transfer their learning from one area to another? What does it mean to take advantage of the psychological content of a curriculum? How can we make the results of our teaching more lasting? What factors should we consider when teaching students from varied social and ethnic backgrounds? These and related questions are addressed in this chapter as we continue our exploration of what it takes to become an effective teacher.

PLAN TEACHING WITH AN EYE TO STUDENTS' READINESS TO LEARN

There are wide differences among students when it comes to their intellectual readiness to learn. If we were to pick a class at random, we would soon find that there is no single or standard series of lessons and work materials that are equally effective for all students. This is particularly true during the elementary school years when there can be huge differences among growing youngsters as far as physical, psychological, and cognitive readiness factors are concerned.

Individual differences in reading ability, for example, can be vast. As noted by Zintz (1975): "Teachers may expect to find in classes of unselected children (heterogeneous classes), that the range of reading achievement . . . will be, on the average, three years at the end of grade two; four years at the end of grade three; five years at the end of grade four; six years at the end of grade five; and seven years at the end of grade six" (p. 28). You can quickly see the implications inherent in the readiness idea. If by the end of grade five, there can be up to six years' difference in reading ability among students, that means that a few will be "ready" to read and understand material used at the eleventh-grade level, while a few others will still be struggling along at the first-grade level. Figure 13.1 gives you an overall visual idea of the variations in mental ages in relation to chronological ages, beginning at age 4 and continuing through

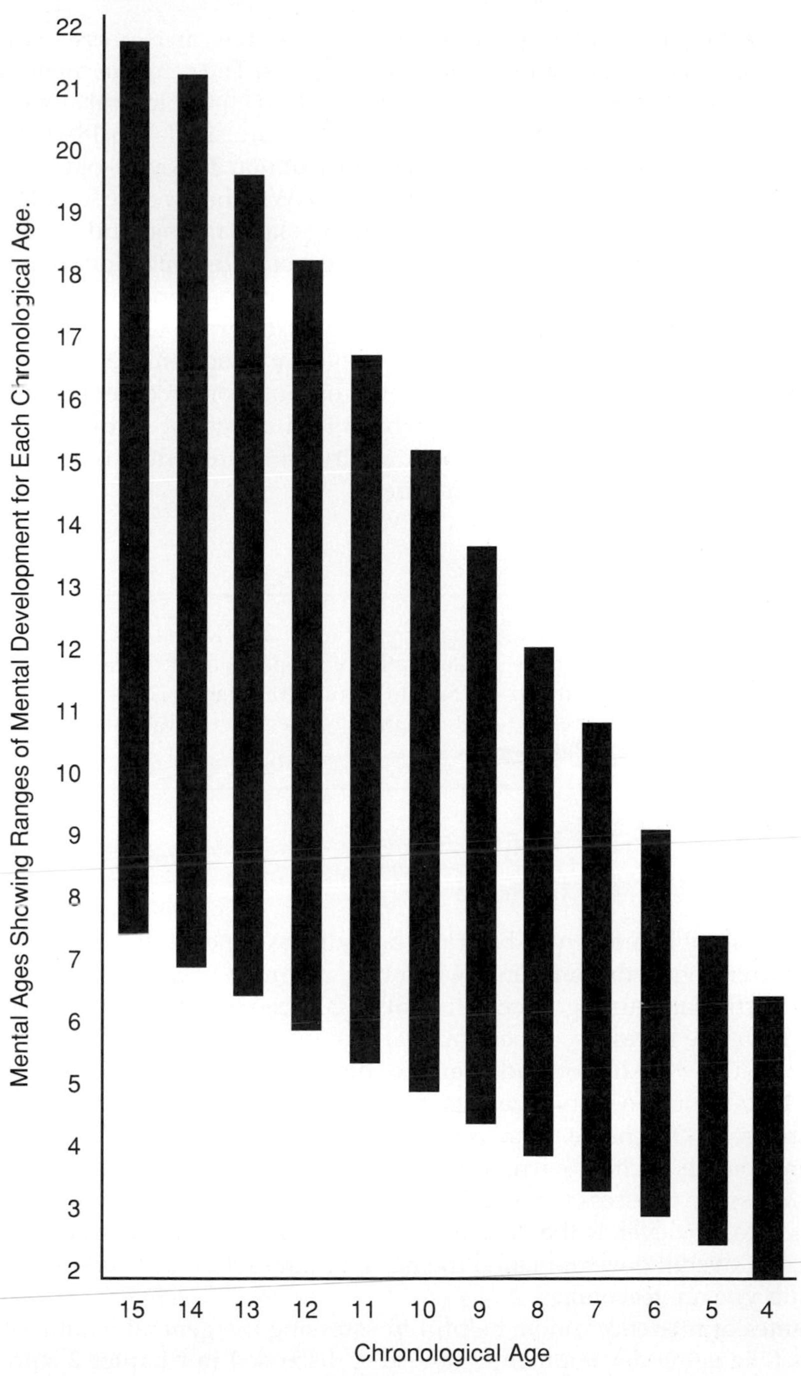

Figure 13.1. RANGES IN MENTAL AGES IN RELATION TO AGES 4 TO 15.

age 15. Note the wide range of differences in mental ages (i.e., an expression of mental ability or capacity) at various chronological ages. The range in mental abilities increases as children grow older. For example, at chronological age 12 there are some children whose overall mental abilities are similar to 18-year-old adolescents, while others have mental abilities similar to 6-year-old first graders. This is a very large spread in mental ability. Whether we are looking at differences in general mental ability or in reading skills among students of similar chronological ages, we come up with the same conclusion: Students are not all ready at the same time to learn, much less comprehend, the same material at the same time. For example, in a typical sixth-grade class, a range of about eight school years will be reflected on tests of reading comprehension, vocabulary, arithmetic reasoning, and arithmetic computation. In other words, in almost any sixth-grade class you are likely to find a student or two with average second-grade reading and arithmetic ability, and a student or two with average tenth-grade abilities in these same areas.

13.1 Mental Age and Chronological Age Differentiated

Mental age (MA) is not the same as chronological age (CA). MA is simply an expression of where a student ranks intellectually in comparison with others his or her age. For example, to say that a 12-year-old has a mental age of 13 years and 7 months means that he has passed the same number of items on an IQ test as the average youngster of 13 years and 7 months.

Have an Idea of When Students Are Most Teachable

The idea of a teachable moment is basically a readiness concept. It refers to a time in a children's growth continuum when they are most "ready" (i.e., able, capable) for particular learning. When students are forced to try to learn a skill before they have the necessary experiential and maturational equipment, the outcomes are usually frustration and a sense of defeat (Corno and Snow, 1986).

What can be done to minimize this possibility? For one thing, we can watch for students' "teachable moments." Because youngsters mature at varied rates, and because school curricula are geared to the average student, it would be impossible to assess the readiness of every student for every subject. What is possible, however, is the development of a sensitivity to, and knowledge about, the overall developmental themes and intellectual possibilities of the age group you are teaching.

Two frames of reference can be helpful in assessing the general readiness of students. One is the developmental task idea discussed in Chapter 2, and the other is Piaget's (1973) stages of intellectual development, which were addressed in Chapter 5.

Assessing General School Readiness with Developmental Tasks Model

Developmental tasks refer to specific behavioral expectations that, according to Havighurst (1980), arise at a particular period in the life of an individual. Successful achievement of each task leads to happiness and success with later tasks, while failure leads to unhappiness, disapproval from others, and difficulty with later tasks.

You might want to quickly review Figure 2.1 in order to reacquaint yourself with the assorted behavioral tasks that can be expected at various age levels. These general guidelines help us to predict what we might reasonably expect, within broad limits, as behavioral tendencies at various stages of growth. Knowing, for example, that developing fundamental skills in reading, writing, and calculating are major tasks normally included in the 6- to 12-year age group enables us to develop instructional objectives and programs that help growing youngsters acquire these skills when they are developmentally ready to do so.

Assessing Intellectual Readiness with Piaget's Model

Because the idea of intellectual readiness is so intimately linked with Piaget's (1973) research on the intellectual development of children, it might be helpful to see an overview of the major periods of intellectual development and the age ranges associated with each. Table 13.1 is a somewhat simplified representation of Piaget's (1973) conception of the stages of intellectual development. It shows the types of mental operations most children are "ready" for at various ages. You can clearly see in Table 13.1 that children progress from a primitive level of sensory learning during their first 2 years of life to a complex level of abstraction in their adolescent years. Remember that there are wide individual differences within each of these age ranges. For example, even though two second graders might be ready to function in the concrete operations stage, does not mean that they will be equally skilled in learning, for example, the basic principles involved in addition and subtraction. Although their *readiness* for learning arithmetic principles might be the same, this does not necessarily mean that they have similar arithmetic *abilities*.

There Are Different Views About Readiness

Although the readiness idea is one that has enjoyed wide acceptance in educational and psychological circles, there is a difference of opinion about how it is expressed and understood. There are, essentially, two ways of looking at the readiness issue.

Table 13.1. BASIC INTELLECTUAL ABILITIES ASSOCIATED WITH EACH OF PIAGET'S STAGES OF INTELLECTUAL DEVELOPMENT

Stage	*Age range*	*Basic characteristics*
1. Sensorimotor period	Birth–2	Infants learn that they are different from other objects and learn primarily through their senses and manipulations. There is a strong desire and need for as much stimulation as possible.
2. Preoperational thought period a. preoperational phase	2–4	An essentially egocentric period insofar as children are unable to see things from others' point of view; they tend to classify in very simple ways—if father is a man, then all men must be fathers.
b. intuitive phase	4–7	Children slowly begin to think in terms of classes, to handle number concepts, and to see simple relationships. Children are "intuitive" (i.e., they are capable of making classifications even though they do not really understand why or how). They develop a gradual awareness of the conservation of mass, weight, and volume (i.e., they can see that the amount may remain the same even if transferred to a different size container).
3. Concrete operations period	7–11	Children grow in ability to consciously use and understand logical operations such as *reversibility* (in arithmetic), classification (i.e., putting objects into hierarchies of classes), and *seriation* (i.e., organizing objects into a specified series, such as increasing size or weight).
4. Formal operations period	11–15	Youngsters further develop the ability to comprehend abstract concepts (e.g., the ability to think about "ideals," to understand cause–effect relationships, to think about the future, and to develop and test hypotheses).

The "Natural" View (Growth Gradually Unfolds)

Those who advocate the "natural" view of development feel that school experiences should be geared to the natural unfolding of each student's developmental pattern. Basically, it is an understanding of growth born of the early work of Gesell (1940), Hilgard (1932), and Olson (1959), whose investigations into developmental processes led them to promote the idea that practically all children will develop the general skills of readiness as they grow. Embedded in their philosophy of natural readiness is the idea that development and behavior at all levels, up to, and including, the teen years, are controlled largely by natural internal forces. Havighurst (1980) and Piaget (1973) fall into this camp. Both of these theorists believed that growth unfolded in a natural and unforced way, a view reflected in Piaget's successive stages of intellectual development and in Havighurst's more general phases of social development.

The "Guided Experience" View (Growth Can Be Helped Along)

The "guided experience" view is favored by those who see little sense in waiting for a child to "naturally unfold," and prefer to speed up this process. We see this point of view favored by those eager to use Vygotsky's (1987) ideas to enhance children's learning. For example, rather than allowing children to make independent discoveries in their own natural time, teachers influenced by a guided experience view promote what is called *assisted discovery.* Within this framework, teachers guide children's learning with explanations, demonstrations, and questions, all in an effort to help each child move into his or her zone of proximal development, an idea discussed more fully in Chapter 5.

In general, readiness is a complex phenomenon influenced by both genetic and social factors. One thing that is more certain today than ever before is that readiness for schooling is being established long before a child enters school. It is certainly true that today's children come to school exposed to a great deal more intellectual and quasi-intellectual stimulation than was true of children a generation ago. Research shows that television, for instance, has had an enormous impact—some of it for the better—on the language readiness of children (Honig, 1983; Williams, Haertel, Haertel, and Walberg, 1982).

13.2 What Do Your Experiences Teach You?

It might be helpful to consider the "natural" and "guided experience" views in light of your own educational experiences. Are there particular skills or abilities that you can see yourself as having had to "grow" into before you were accomplished at them? Are there particular skills and abilities that you have acquired that were, perhaps, developed at a faster rate because of "guided experiences"? What, from your own life experiences, supports, or refutes, either or both of these viewpoints?

TEACHING FOR TRANSFER OF LEARNING

A major challenge facing every teacher is to teach in such a way that what is learned in our classrooms applies (i.e., transfers) to life experiences *outside* of our classrooms. Mathematics teachers want to enable their students to solve everyday math problems; English teachers hope that their courses in composition prepare their students to write coherently; and teachers of American government hope that their students will be prepared to participate as responsible citizens. All of these are worthwhile goals, and at first glance it might seem that their achievement depends primarily on providing sufficient education so that what is learned is remembered, but learning is not as simple as that. Not only must we remember what we learn, we must also be able to select from our experiences those responses that seem most appropriate in a new setting. When learning carries over into new situations, it is known as *transfer* of learning.

Transfer of Knowledge Is Neither General Nor Automatic

It is not uncommon to find that some teachers still believe, in spite of research evidence to the contrary, that rigorous study in particular areas—usually math, science, and English—automatically renders students bright and able in the other things they do in life. In many ways, this is a throwback to early 1900s thinking: that learning mathematics and Latin provided a type of "mental discipline" that taught students how to think and reason. In theory, this mental disciplining could be applied to other subjects in school, and indeed to life itself. Many years ago, Broyler, Thorndike, and Woodyard (1927) put the theory to the test, wanting to see if the study of Latin, Greek, and mathematics really does lead to improved achievement in other subject areas. They found that they do not. What each area of study does, however, is to *transfer to related areas of learning.* For example, learning Latin helps one to learn more Latin, or learning mathematics helps one to improve in subsequent mathematics courses. In other words, transfer from one subject to another occurs only to the extent that two subjects have common elements.

As noted by Travers (1977), early twentieth-century studies in transfer have had a greater, and more lasting, impact on education than any other research completed by psychologists. As a result of widespread publicity given to these research findings, the "mental discipline" idea began to fade as educators recognized that transfer tends to be specific rather than general. So be thankful to educational psychology research that you are not taking four years of Latin and Greek to "discipline" your mind for bigger and better things!

Caution: Transfer Can Be Positive or Negative

Transfer can be either positive or negative. In the case of positive transfer, previous learning is likely to facilitate and enhance subsequent learning. For example:

A student learns	$5 \times 4 = 20$
This should help him or her learn	$4 \times 5 = 20$
And, further	$50 \times 40 = 2{,}000$
And, even further	$400 \times 500 = 200{,}000$

Another illustration of positive transfer is reflected in the considerable success experienced by driver-education students as they make the transition from the driver-education car to the family car. (Well, most of the time.) Other examples of positive transfer include: learning to type on a typewriter and then using those skills on one's personal computer; learning a mathematical concept in second period and then applying it to solve a physics problem in fourth period; learning to do a forward two-and-one-half somersault on the trampoline and then completing it off the one-meter diving board; learning the basic philosophy and framework of various expressions of city government in civics class and then, perhaps ten years later, running as a knowledgeable candidate for a city council slot with a proposal for revamping the system.

Negative transfer occurs when previous learning interferes with learning something new. For example, a T-formation high school quarterback might have trouble adapting to the wishbone formation of his college team; parents who learned to do math the "old" way invariably experience trouble with their children's "new" math; learning the rules of driving on the right-hand side of the road in the United States presents trouble for the sight-seeing American who rents a car in a country where driving occurs on the left-hand side of the road. You might have a better idea of negative transfer by considering a few illustrations derived from the English language. Some words are spelled the same way but are pronounced differently (e.g., read and read); some words sound the same but are spelled differently (e.g., read and red; sight, cite, and site; fair and fare); some words have different sounds for the same initial letter (e.g., city, chime, cook; phone, pet), and some letter combinations seem to follow no consistent sound rules at all (e.g., thought, though, bough).

13.3 When Has Transfer Occurred in Your Life?

What other examples can you think of that illustrate positive and negative transfer? Can you think of instances from your own life experiences in which what you learned in one instance transferred positively or negatively to another situation?

More generally, transfer from one activity to another contains both positive and negative aspects. For example, many of the skills of handball are sufficiently similar to those in paddleball that a person learning to play paddleball might be helped by his previous experience with handball. At the same time, skills are involved in each that are sufficiently incompatible to make it necessary for us to readjust our old skills before we can progress with new ones. A student, a former ballet dancer, talked about her ballet training as both a blessing and a curse when she pursued her interest in modern dance. On one hand, her formal ballet experience helped her with coordination and balance in modern dance; on the other hand, she had to unlearn particular aspects of her disciplined ballet training in order to master the more expansive flow and movement demanded by modern dance.

APPROACHES TO MAXIMIZING POSITIVE TRANSFER

There are at least four interrelated ideas and suggestions for teaching that help to facilitate the possibility of transferring in-school learning to out-of-school experiences.

Relate School Learning to Out-of-School Experiences

This is a principle that coaches are usually skilled in applying. Good coaches, for example, know that the best play diagramming in the world is practically useless information until their players have an opportunity to execute those plays on the court or on the practice field. They know, furthermore, that those plays are more likely to transfer from the board to the actual game as players have an opportunity to execute them in scrimmage under gamelike conditions.

Betty Sumners uses this principle to help her second-grade students apply basic math skills she teaches them in class. Like the good teacher she is, she goes beyond the lesson itself. She appoints four children, different ones each day, to help her manage the lunch program's milk money, for which she is responsible. Thus, in a simple but meaningful way, she is able to create a bridge between the arithmetic they learn in class and its use in real-life situations.

Richard Brooks, a high school math teacher, makes an effort to enhance his students' transfer of learning by involving them in assignments such as computing interest charges; figuring out tax returns; planning family budgets; or estimating the amount, and cost, of paint to cover a house of specified dimensions. These are particularly helpful activities for those several sections of "general" math he teaches, which are designed for non-college–bound students in a more general curriculum. In fact, he had his students help him with a garage he built, not only by pounding nails, but by figuring out the amount of lumber, roofing, and siding he would need to build it, and the gallons of paint it would take to cover it. Six committees of students each worked together to figure out how much of everything it would take to build the garage, and how much it would cost. Then, all six committees got together to compare notes and come up with final estimates. It worked well. The students applied their math, the teacher supplied his guidance (and money), and both teacher and students supplied some elbow grease. Today a garage on Oakland Avenue stands as a tribute to a well-done math lesson. (There is, however, a leak in the roof. None of us is perfect. Besides, it was a class in math, not carpentry.)

Both examples illustrate two basic types of transfer: (1) *lateral*, which is the ability to perform a task similar to, and of about the same level of complexity as, a task previously learned (e.g., Richard Brooks' students used their knowledge of how to multiply to determine how many feet of lumber they would need to build the garage); and (2) *vertical,* which is the ability to learn similar, but more complex, materials (e.g., Betty Sumner's students had to add and subtract in a real money exchange, thereby seeing the relationship between what the school paid for milk and what the school took in from selling it).

Gagné (1977) has shown that both types of transfer are enhanced to the extent to which there is a similarity between what students learn in class and the experiences they have outside of school. If what students learn in school is left in school, we will have greater difficulty helping them to see that their school learning has particular relevance to their lives outside of school.

13.4 How Crucial Is Relevance?

Suppose someone says to you, "Not everything in school needs to be relevant, in the sense of being applicable in everyday life. Knowledge is useful in itself." Does that person have a point? How would you respond?

Help Students Understand the "Whys"

Retention and transfer are more likely to occur if the content students are learning is meaningful to them, or if they can understand the basic principles involved. It is one thing to know that 4 + 4 = 8, it is another to know *why* it does.

As an illustration of this, Brownell and Moser (1949) found, in their classic study, that a group of elementary-age children learned more easily, and remembered longer, the basic principles of subtraction when they were taught in a meaningful (i.e., rational) way than did another group of children who were taught by a mechanical (i.e., rote) method. Students taught in such a way that the material had meaning for them were given a variety of suggestions to help them understand the process of borrowing in subtraction. The second group was taught a mechanical method and then drilled. Although the second group used exercises that required borrowing, no attempt was made to help them understand the meaning of the exercises or the basic principle involved in borrowing. It is interesting to note that although those taught by the rote method made more rapid progress *in the first few days,* at the end of 15 days they began to drop behind those taught by the meaningful method. In addition, when a transfer situation was arranged, those who had been taught *understanding* performed far better than those who had not.

Shuell and Lee's (1976) review of research related to this issue strongly supports the idea that, although teaching for understanding takes more time, the resultant learning lasts longer and can be applied to more situations.

Stress Underlying Principles and Show Applications

An impressive history of research suggests strongly that knowledge of principles and the ability to generalize and to apply learning to as many situations as possible, facilitate transfer (Bigge, 1982; Salomon and Perkins, 1984). There are two basic reasons for this:

1. Thinking in terms of principles allows us to operate deductively (i.e., we can generalize particular principles to a variety of situations). For example, teaching students the meaning of words such as *reaffirm* and *reallocate* is perfectly appropriate, but notice how much more useful it is to learn that the prefix *re* means "again," "anew," "back," or "backward." With this knowledge, student can figure out the meaning of many more words (e.g., *reapply, reinvigorate, repurify*).

2. Whereas teaching students principles helps them to think more broadly along deductive lines, giving them plenty of opportunity to practice what they have learned in a variety of ways is an absolute necessity for transfer of learning. For example, Jill Stockman, a third-grade teacher, has her students set up an in-class grocery store stocked with simple items children bring from home, and gives them play money so that they can practice adding, subtracting, multiplying, and making change in a more real-life way. Charles Handshaw has his entire fifth- grade class contribute to the production of a biweekly newsletter, which includes news about the school in general, and about their room activities in particular. Everyone is at least a reporter, and everyone gets to practice in a very real way the spelling, grammar, and rules of good syntax that are a part of their formal work in English. The children love seeing their names in the paper, and in the fun of putting together *The Room Five Gazette,* rules of good English language usage are being used and absorbed almost unconsciously.

As a teacher, try to figure out as many ways as you can to help your students to use factual information in everyday ways, thus encouraging the generation of general principles that apply to many situations. In order to do this, it is necessary to . . .

Teach Students to Decontextualize

Transfer of learning does not always occur automatically, especially when what is learned is relatively new to us. For example, I remember a fellow student back in my graduate-school days who was an absolute whiz at applying the appropriate principles of positive reinforcement to teaching rats to behave in particular ways. When the rats did what he wanted, he reinforced their behavior and they were eager to oblige him on subsequent occasions with masterful runs through his mazes. However, when his friends or classmates gave him what he might ask for, there was seldom even a word of acknowledgement, much less appreciation. His relationships with his classmates grew increasingly more alienated. He seemed unaware of the possibilities of "transferring" some of the same principles of positive reinforcement he used so well with rats to his relationships with people. He could dispense reinforcing food pellets to rats, but not simple "thank you's" to humans.

As teachers, one of the positive things we can do is remind students to *decontextualize,* or separate, an idea from its original associations so that it can be applied in a new context. Salomon and Globerson (1987) speculate that because transfer across dissimilar contexts requires so much effort and mindfulness, or awareness, it is often avoided. Thus, my psychology classmate was able to positively reinforce rats in a laboratory, but not transfer that knowledge beyond the rodent world. A student might be able to compute the area of a rectangle, and yet be puzzled when figuring out how much carpet it would take to cover a particular floor.

Thus, our job as teachers is to help students see that what they know can be generalized beyond the classroom. When we are more deliberate and more mindful in our attempts to encourage transfer, we can expect to see greater amounts of it among our students.

HONING THE FINE ART OF TEACHER QUESTIONING

Teachers delight in asking questions. It has been estimated that the average high school teacher asks almost 400 questions each day (Gall, 1970). This is a very large number of questions indeed, about sixty-six or so an hour in a typical six-hour teaching day.

Asking questions is a perfectly legitimate way of teaching, but sometimes, in our pursuit of the "right answers," we fall into the trap of asking only one type of question—the memory type. Guilford's (1967) research related to intelligence and creativity has made distinctions among five types of thinking, any one of which could be promoted by its counterpart in question form. One type is *cognition,* which involves immediate discovery, comprehension, or recognition of information in various forms. Another type of thinking is simply *memory,* or a rote recall of fact. A third type is what Guilford calls *convergent,* which demands the sort of mental activity in which data, or "facts," are assembled, shifted, and in some way synthesized in order to arrive at a logical conclusion. A fourth type of thinking is called *divergent,* a process in which one is invited to create something new. A fifth type of thinking is *evaluative,* in which the task is to make a moral or aesthetic judgment about something.

Sadker and Sadker (1987) have suggested seven categories of questions that teachers commonly use to explore cognitively oriented objectives. "You can see illustrations of each of these kinds of question in Table 13.2. Notice that the first three kinds of questions—knowledge, comprehension, and application—are more on the order of the convergent type, and the last three—analysis, synthesis, and evaluation—are more related to divergent questions.

Divergent and Convergent Questions

Convergent questions are those that converge and pull information together so as to ask for one right answer (e.g., When was the first moon landing? What is static electricity? Who invented the telephone? Which principle is demonstrated in the fax machine? Calculate the number of square yards in this room.

Table 13.2. CLASSROOM QUESTIONS FOR OBJECTIVES IN THE COGNITIVE DOMAIN

Category	*Type of thinking expected*	*Examples*
Knowledge (recognition)	Recalling or recognizing information as learned	Define. . . . What is the capital of . . . ? What did the text say about . . . ?
Comprehension	Demonstrating understanding of the material; transforming, reorganizing, or interpreting	Explain in your own words. . . . Compare. . . . What is the main idea of . . . ? Describe what you saw. . . .
Application	Using information to solve a problem with a single correct answer	Which principle is demonstrated in . . . ? Calculate the area of. . . . Apply the rule of . . . to solve. . . .
Analysis	Critical thinking; identifying reasons and motives; making inferences based on specific data; analyzing conclusions to see if supported by evidence	What influenced the writings of . . . ? Why was Washington, D.C. chosen . . . ? Which of the following are facts and which are opinions? Based on your experiment, what is the chemical . . . ?
Synthesis	Divergent, original thinking; original plan, proposal, design, or story	What's a good name for this . . . ? How could we raise money for . . . ? What would the United States be like if the South had won . . . ?
Evaluation	Judging the merits of ideas, offering opinions, applying standards	Which U.S. senator is the most effective? Which painting do you believe to be better? Why? Why would you favor . . . ?

Adapted from Sadker, M., and Sadker, D. "Questioning Skills." In J. Cooper (Ed.), *Classroom Teaching Skills: A Handbook,* 3rd ed. Lexington, MA: D.C. Heath, 1987, pp. 143–160. Used by permission.

How did the United States get involved in the Vietnam Conflict?) Divergent questions, however, invite responses that are original, novel, and creative. To ask a divergent question is to ask not only, "What do you *know* about this?" but also, "What do you *think* of, or how do you *feel* about, this?"

Perhaps a few examples of convergent and divergent questions will help to delineate them clearly. For example, while teaching a social studies unit related to the Vietnam Conflict, a teacher asks, "How many American troops were lost in action in Vietnam, and what percentage of our total budget was allocated for military purposes during the last five years of the conflict?" In this case, only memory, the kind reflected in the knowledge and comprehension categories in Table 13.2, is involved. The student either knows the answer (from reading the assignment, or someone's notes), or he or she does not know it. This is convergent thinking. However, should a teacher ask, "What alternative solutions, short of fighting, do you think the U.S. government should have considered?", the student is invited to think divergently, to think of other ways to handle the problem based on his or her own views, which reflects analysis and synthesis, as in Table 13.2.

Finally, if a teacher asks, "Should the United States have entered the Vietnam Conflict at all?", he or she is attempting to encourage some sort of moral judgment (i.e., an evaluation), which is an open invitation to all sorts of divergent thinking.

Characteristics of Good Questions

Grossier's (1964) investigation of questioning techniques led him to conclude that good questions are: (1) clear, (2) purposeful, (3) brief, (4) natural and adapted to the level of the class, and (5) thought-provoking. A brief elaboration of these characteristics follows:

1. *Clear:* Questions should clearly specify the points to which students are to respond. A clear question might be: "How does stressing the underlying principles of a concept help it to transfer?" A less clear question might be: "What is it about underlying principles that helps transfer one idea to another when they are dissimilar?"

2. *Purposeful:* A purposeful question helps to achieve a teacher's intention in giving a lesson by focusing attention on its major points. A purposeful question might be: "How does transfer of learning enable one to apply knowledge in one area to another?" A less purposeful question might be: "What is it about transfer of learning that helps the learning process?"

3. *Brief:* Brief questions are easier to follow, grasp, and understand than long ones. The benefits of this are obvious. An example of a good brief question might be: "What is a teachable moment?" An example of an overly long

question: "How does the idea of a teachable moment relate to transfer, and how do these moments have positive or negative implications for learning?"

4. *Natural:* Basically, the idea is to phrase questions in natural, simple language (as opposed to highly jargonesque, pedantic language), adapted to the level of a class. A question fitting this criterion might be: "What are five characteristics of good questions?" A less natural question might be: "Given that various possibilities exist for interrogating students' comprehension of substantive knowledge, what five components would one look for in questions designed to probe differential levels of students' knowledge?"

5. *Thought-Provoking:* Not every question, of course, can be (or needs to be) deeply thought-provoking, but when many questions stir a sense of curiosity or ignite a spark of interest, we increase our chances of having a lively, involved group of students. A thought-provoking question might be: "Suppose you have just completed what you feel is one of your best class sessions—your students are lively and interested—but one student says, loud enough for all to hear, that he is bored. What would you say to him? A less thought-provoking question might be: "What can teachers do when students appear to be bored?"

13.5 What's Your Guess?

Research has documented that the average wait time between teachers' asking a question and calling on someone else is about: (1) 2 seconds, (2) 5 seconds, (3) 3 seconds, (4) 7 seconds, or (5) 1 second. Read on for the answer.

The Importance of Wait Time

One important thing a teacher can do after asking a question is simply to wait, something that many teachers have trouble doing. Rowe (1986), for example, reported that the average wait time between teachers' asking a question and calling on someone was *less than one second.* Furthermore, even after calling on a student, the wait time was still only about a second for the student to give an answer before teachers either called on someone else, rephrased the question, or gave the answer themselves.

To see how students' responses would be affected by longer wait-times, Rowe trained a group of teachers to extend their wait times from less than one second to three to five seconds. Surprisingly, some teachers found this difficult, and a few never did manage it. However, in classrooms of teachers who extended their wait-times to *three* to *five* seconds, the following desirable changes were noted:

1. An increase in the average length of students' responses
2. An increase in unsolicited, but appropriate, student responses

3. A decrease in failures to respond
4. An increase in speculative responses
5. An increase in student-to-student comparisons of data
6. An increase in statements that involved drawing inferences from evidence
7. An increase in student-initiated questions
8. A greater variety of oral contributions to lessons by students

Lengthening wait time not only increased the number of students who participated, but also improved the quality of participation. It should be noted that these effects were most pronounced with the less able students in class, something other researchers have also found (Swift and Gooding, 1983; Tobin and Capie, 1982).

Other research has shown a decrease in achievement when wait time is extended for low-level questions, but an increase in achievement when wait time is extended for high- and mixed-cognitive level questions (Anshuntz, 1975; Riley, 1980; Tobin, 1987).

Thus, less wait time, perhaps two to three seconds, works best for lower-level questions covering specific facts, and a longer wait time, somewhere between three and six seconds or even more, is best for questions designed to encourage students to think about the material and to formulate original responses.

Assuming that your question is audible and clearly expressed in the first place, it is not a particularly good idea to repeat it, nor is it a good idea to repeat a student's response.

13.6 A Question About Questions

Why do you suppose that it is not a good idea for teachers to repeat either their own or students' questions?

There are, of course, exceptions to the general no-repeat rule, particularly when working with young children, who have shorter attention spans, and who might need help keeping new information and facts sorted and in order. It might also be necessary to paraphrase answers when information is complex and important. Although this should be done from time to time solely by teachers, it works quite well to have students do this, too. It is a vote of confidence in our students. It is a way of saying, indirectly, "I trust in your ability to understand this material."

Generally, questions that present interesting challenges and stimulate friendly, but spirited, exchanges of views are likely both to maximize motivation and to yield productive answers. Aggressive questions asked in a harsh tone are guaranteed to send students into protective cones of silence. Our effort should be to ask honest questions in order to engage students in the learning of material and to help us assess their understanding of it. Question-and-answer is a form of dialogue that can add zest and color to the life of a classroom.

13.7 Some Things to Look for

You might find it particularly instructive to pay attention to your feelings about, and responses to, the questions raised by your instructors in various classes. What types of questions turn you on? What kinds turn you off? Which arouse your interest? Watch your instructors—how do they keep a dialogue going after it has started? What can you learn from them regarding the use of questions?

USING THE PSYCHOLOGICAL CONTENT OF A CURRICULUM

Nearly everything in a curriculum teems with possibilities for meaningful, relevant learning when viewed in terms of what it might do to help students find themselves, realize their potential, use their personal resources in productive ways, and enter into relationships that have a positive bearing on their ideas about school and their attitudes toward themselves. When we talk about the psychological content of a curriculum, we are referring to those aspects of schooling that offer possibilities for knowing more about oneself, just as one is learning more about English, social studies, physical education, or whatever else one is studying. Let's turn our attention to some ideas for how to do this.

Some Possibilities for Social Studies

In social studies, why not encourage more inquiries into such topics as human values, needs, human aspirations, and competitive tendencies involved in economic affairs? Unfortunately, our social studies offerings frequently do not make much of an impact on the students who take them. For example, a study done at the University of Michigan's Survey Research Center found that social studies courses had little immediate positive effect on more than 1600 seniors in 97 high schools across the United States ("Education Briefs," 1967). Indeed, the study noted that students who had not been exposed to civics courses received almost identical scores on a test of government knowledge as did students who had taken the courses. On other factors, such as interest in politics, keeping up with political news, and developing a sense of political effectiveness, there was even less effect from having taken civics courses. Do the consequences of teaching have to be so dismal? What would happen in a civics class, for instance, if, rather than simply talking about and memorizing forms of city and state government, the class were to actively set them up in the classroom? Students could run for office, conduct campaigns, debate issues—in short, live the government, the election, the victory, and the defeat.

You might get a better idea of what is meant here by taking a look at the following, an example (Rubin, 1985) of what one social studies teacher did to involve students more personally. Notice how the teacher, Mr. Gallardo, lifted the class out of an abstract discussion and deftly placed it in the context of current concerns. He turned boredom into excitement by making the lesson relevant. Here is what happened*:

It was a conventional seventh-grade social studies unit on community government. While the discussion of city administration progressed, a red-headed lad seated near the outside wall gazed absently out the window.

"Larry!"

The boy's gaze turned quickly to the teacher.

"You don't seem very interested in city councils," Mr. Gallardo said pleasantly.

A sheepish look crossed the student's face.

"I don't blame him," a girl across the room muttered. "All this stuff is dumb!"

"Why?" Mr. Gallardo asked.

A silence fell.

"How many of you really think what we've been talking about is dumb?" the teacher asked insistently.

The girl who had complained finally thrust her hand into the air, glancing challengingly at her classmates. Somewhat hesitantly, a few more hands followed. Soon, roughly half the class had raised their hands.

The teacher looked thoughtful. "I'll tell you what: Let's try something different. I want each row to reassemble for group discussion."

Obligingly, the students shifted their chairs and soon were arranged in five circular discussion groups.

"Now," the teacher said, "let's assume each group is a city council. I'll give you a typical problem; you discuss it, agree on a recommendation, then we'll compare the results. O.K.?"

The class nodded.

"Very well," Mr. Gallardo said. "Here's the problem: as you may have read in last week's paper, our county landfill is almost full. We've got to start another one. Where's the best place to put it? Over by the football stadium, near the interstate, next to the old homes on Elm Street, where? Remember now, wherever it's put, some people are going to be very unhappy. There will be a lot of truck noise, trees and other vegetation will have to be removed, there could be some powerful odors, and the value of the houses near the landfill might go down."

He smiled encouragingly at the class. "O.K.," he said, "decide where to put it."

Slowly, at first, and then more animatedly, the discussions began. Soon there was a hum of debate. Twenty minutes later, Mr. Gallardo halted the discussions and asked a representative from each group to summarize the group's conclusions. There was considerable disagreement. As the period came to an end, the teacher said, "Tomorrow we'll compare and analyze each group's suggestions."

The students left the room still talking about a good place for a landfill.

---

*Reprinted from Rubin, L. *Artistry in Teaching*. New York: McGraw-Hill, 1985, pp. 124–125. Used with permission of McGraw-Hill.

Ideas for History and English

Take history as another case in point. What would students learn if history were taught more in terms of people and their experiences than so much in terms of events, institutions, and movements? We all know some significant historical dates, but what do we know about the motivations of the men and women behind them? As another example, is it possible that high school students might get more out of Shakespeare's works by reading them not only as great literary masterpieces, but as unfolding dramas of human greed, love, and hate? How many students actually "see" *Julius Caesar* as an example of what untamed, selfish ambition can do to a person?

13.8 Who Are Some Modern-Day Julius Caesars?

Who are some examples of more contemporary persons who reflect the sort of personal qualities that led to Caesar's downfall? How might these examples be used in a class?

I remember a class of slow-learning ninth-graders who not only read *Romeo and Juliet,* but enjoyed it. Before they even discussed the possibility of reading the Shakespearean classic, Jennifer Holmes, their wise and sensitive teacher, brought her videotape player to class, hooked it up to a television set, and for two hours one Friday morning she and her students enjoyed the movie, *West Side Story.* This was something to which they could relate, and could understand.

True, the characters were Tony and Maria, not Romeo and Juliet, the scene was a fire escape, not a balcony; but they were in love, there were two feuding families, and the movie did end tragically. Thus, through the simple process of exposing students to something they already knew about and liked, the teacher made a study of *Romeo and Juliet* not only possible, but, of all things, fun! What could easily have been a laborious, meaningless English assignment was converted into an exciting adventure as the students puzzled through the similarities and differences between the two stories.

Physical Education Is Rich with Possibilities

Physical education can be more than sweating, running, and push-ups. It can be that part of a curriculum in which students learn to discover and accept their own bodies. They can be introduced to a human laboratory in which they see acts of meanness, aggression, and bad sportsmanship, on the one hand, or behavior that reflects good sportsmanship and dignity in the face of defeat on the other. Moreover, they can learn to recognize the healthy, as well as the unhealthy, features of competition. Some students might discover that winning is more possible than they thought. Others might find that being first is not as important as they had been led to believe. Many could be taught to see that to do anything well, whether in the classroom or in athletic competition, takes persistence, effort, hard work, and discipline. Students could be taught to see that regular exercise can contribute significantly to physical health and a positive self-concept (Hamachek, 1987).

Be Flexible—Take Advantage of Unplanned Moments

Sometimes, in the interpersonal complexity of classroom life, spontaneous interactions occur that are rich with possibilities for a novel experience, a twist in the daily routine, a pleasant excursion away from sameness. Many events will happen in your classroom that you will have no way of anticipating. Some will provide students with real-life object lessons. Other events, when handled properly by teachers, can help students develop a sense of their own power to make constructive things happen. However these unplanned moments turn out, it requires a readiness on our part as teachers to shift gears, to let the unusual happen, flowing with it and making of it what we can.

Two examples may help to clarify what is meant here. Note, in each instance, that the teacher responded to the strong feelings reflected by students. The strength of students' expressed feelings is always one of our best indicators as to how prepared we should be to shift gears. It is usually much more productive to flow *with* a class' mood than to swim against it. A little flexibility and creativity on your part can make a lot happen.

This first example involves a sixth-grade teacher who converted one girl's dismay, another boy's enthusiasm, and the entire class's anxiety into an exciting simulated courtroom trial. This is what happened. As the teacher walked along the side of the room during a class lesson, she accidentally stepped on a cockroach. One of her 11-year-old students, sitting in an aisle seat, saw this and in dismay blurted out, "Ms. Criswell, you meanie, look at what you've done." Another student, also sitting in an aisle seat, immediately responded to the "accuser" by asserting that, "all cockroaches should be killed anyway," and that what Ms. Criswell had done was not only right, but was her "duty." The rest of the class stirred somewhat restlessly, and a few of the youngsters even went so far as to align with one side or the other. Within the span of sixty seconds, or so, several important issues emerged.

One was the "moral" issue of whether the teacher had done something that was good or bad. The other was the "legal" issue of whether the teacher had done something that was right or wrong. The teacher was wise enough to know that a great deal of feeling was being expressed by her students. Therefore, she suggested that this incident be explored from as many points of view as possible and proposed a courtroom trial to settle the issue. The accusing student, naturally, was appointed prosecuting attorney. The youngster who originally defended the teacher was appointed counsel for the defense. Ms.

Criswell's lesson plan was abandoned for the remainder of the afternoon, and each of the "attorneys" talked to witnesses and gathered evidence for their side. (Among the first things that happened, by the way, was the scraping of exhibit A from the bottom of Ms. Criswell's shoe.) A portion of each morning for the next week was set aside for the children to plan the trial, and several students whose fathers were lawyers assumed the responsibility for seeing to it that correct legal procedures were followed. A judge was chosen via a general class election. On the day of the "trial," a jury was picked from another sixth-grade class in the same school, and for the better part of one morning the evidence for and against Ms. Criswell was weighed and debated.

When all was done, the teacher was acquitted. Actually, the outcome was not nearly as important as the process. The children were able to be involved with the concept of "justice" meaningfully, along with some of the social, legal, and moral implications associated with it. Later that term, the students visited a real courtroom and talked to a real judge. By casting the students' experience in the mold of a real courtroom, it was a valuable field trip.

In this next example (Rubin, 1985), notice how the teacher acknowledged and flowed with students' concerns, accomplishing the goal of testing her students—although, with a slightly different twist.*

"Friday's test," the teacher said perfunctorily, "is on the Civil War."

Noting a look of apprehension on several students' faces, she added: "It shouldn't be too bad. You can bone up by reviewing the main ideas in Chapter 11. And you might also find it helpful to go over your notes from Tuesday's discussion. Any questions?"

A long silence filled the room.

"What's wrong?" the teacher asked amiably.

"We have too many tests," a student finally muttered.

"Maybe so," the teacher replied, "but it's the only way to make sure everyone understands the main ideas."

"Tests are really stupid," said another student flatly.

"Why?" the teacher challenged.

A girl raised her hand. Receiving an encouraging nod from the teacher, she said quietly: "We have to spend a lot of time getting ready for the tests. But it's a waste because we forget the stuff as soon as the exam is over. Besides, you grade on percentages so we have to compete. Competition is dumb."

The teacher glanced around the classroom thoughtfully, measuring the reaction of other students. Suddenly, she smiled. "Perhaps you are tired of tests. But I have to be certain you know the material. What would you think of this?" she asked with sudden inspiration. "Instead of taking a test Friday, how about making up a test?"

"What do you mean?" a boy inquired from the back of the room.

"Well, instead of studying for the exam, each of you prepare a test. Just pretend that you are a teacher, and you want to find out whether your students have learned the main ideas."

---

*Reprinted from Rubin, L. *Artistry in Teaching*. New York: McGraw-Hill, 1985, pp. 17–18. Used with permission of McGraw-Hill.

A sudden flash of interest crossed the students faces.
"How will you grade us?" someone asked.
"Well, I'll simply judge the quality of test."
The room grew silent for a moment.
"How do you make out a good test?" a student asked, grinning.
"Ah!" the teacher said. "First of all, a good test is neither so easy that everyone can get all the questions right, nor so hard that everyone will miss every item. Secondly," she continued, "a good test deals with the big ideas, the really significant points, not the minor details. And the test questions must be written clearly enough that their meaning won't be misinterpreted. Finally," the teacher explained, "a good examination is reasonably easy to score. If a teacher has to spend two or three hours grading one student's work, she's probably using the wrong kind of test."
"In other words," a student said, "you'll grade each of us on how good our test is."
"Right."
Once more there was silence.
"Well!" said the teacher.
"Let's try it," exclaimed a boy in the front.
A chorus of agreement followed.

13.9 What Is Your Stand?

Not everyone agrees that teaching and learning might be enhanced—or at least be made more interesting—by teachers taking advantage of the psychological possibilities in a curriculum. Those opposed argue that ideas of this sort are frivolous and unwarranted, that more attention should be given, if anything, to the academic content of a curriculum. Others support the idea that considering the psychological aspects of a curriculum enhances its relevance. If someone asked for your position of this issue, how would you respond?

MAKING THE RESULTS OF TEACHING AND LEARNING MORE LASTING

Exploiting the psychological content of a curriculum, asking divergent questions, and relating subject matter to students' backgrounds, are legitimate methods of helping students learn; what we need now are some strategies to help students *remember* what they learn. We should be clear at the outset that the methods for aiding retention we are about to discuss do not work simply. They are not mere gimmicks pulled randomly from an instructional bag of tricks; they are, rather, research-proven and time-tested strategies that can assist in making the results of teaching more lasting. Each is so basic as to be in the instructional repertoire of every good teacher.

1. Look for novel ways to capture attention.
2. Provide the appropriate mental set.
3. Use elaboration strategies.
4. Utilize the advantages of "part" and "whole" teaching and learning.
5. Distribute work and study activities.

6. Encourage overlearning when appropriate.
7. Provide knowledge, test results, and progress reports.
8. Provide ample review time.

Now let's look at the meaning, implications, and practice of each of the above teaching/learning strategies.

Look for Novel Ways to Capture Attention

Novelty and change of pace are great attention-grabbers. Rubin (1985) suggests that effective teachers have a knack for what he calls "staging," which means that a teacher is at various times playwright, director, and producer. Each role is dedicated to capturing students' attention. Michael Finley, a sixth-grade teacher, reserves a corner of one of his bulletin boards for what he has labeled "Today's Puzzle." One day he had written: "Divide 30 by 1/2. Add 10. What is the answer?" Another day he wrote: "How many animals of each species did Moses take aboard the ark?" On still another day he queried. "I went to bed at eight o'clock in the evening, and set the clock to get up at nine in the morning. How many hours of sleep would this allow me?" His students look forward to these cute brainteasers and are frequently found having animated discussions about possible answers.[†] Michael Finley goes after his students' attention as soon as they arrive in the morning, and manages to keep it at a fairly high level all day long with an array of interesting learning activities.

This next example (Rubin, 1985) is, an illustration of staging at its best.* Do you think this eighth-grade teacher would get your attention?

The teacher entered the eighth-grade science classroom a few moments after the bell had rung. He carried a hammer, a yardstick, and a newspaper. Looking briefly at the class, he said, "Let's begin with a simple experiment today."

Stepping in front of his desk, he carefully centered the yardstick so that half of it was unsupported, extending outward toward the students, with the other half resting on the desk. Then, standing beside the unsupported half of the yardstick, he grasped the hammer, raised it high, and prepared to strike the unsupported end. The hammer began to descend in a furious stoke, but, midway, the teacher abruptly jerked his arm back. Looking intently at the boys in the first row, who, although fascinated, held their arms up protectively in anticipation of a yardstick that would suddenly fly across the room.

"What's going to happen?" the teacher asked. "Why are your hands up?"

"The yardstick could hit us!" a boy exclaimed.

"No way," the teacher responded. "It will break in half."

[†]Answers to Today's Puzzle questions: 70; None; Moses was not involved; 1 hour.

*Reprinted from Rubin, L. *Artistry in Teaching*. New York: McGraw-Hill, 1985, pp. 148–149. Used with permission of McGraw-Hill.

The teacher again raised the hammer high, glanced at the students in the first row, observed that their hands again were guarding their faces, paused reflectively, and abruptly lowered the hammer.

"You might just be right," he said thoughtfully. Gazing about the room for a moment, he asked: "Suppose I really want to hit this yardstick just to see what happens. How can I make sure that no one gets hurt?"

The students were silent at first, and then several absurd suggestions were jokingly offered. Finally, someone said, "You could put a weight over the part of the yardstick on the desk, then it won't fly out when you hit it."

"Not bad," the teacher responded. "Let's try it."

He looked around the room thoughtfully, and finally called on the largest boy in the class. Following the teacher's direction, the heavy lad climbed onto the desk and planted both feet firmly on the yardstick. The teacher again returned to the front of the desk, raised the hammer, looked at the students, and smiled when he saw the first row of students now had their hands down.

The teacher started to bring the hammer down and, midway, again interrupted his swing. Turning to the class, he said: "This really isn't a very nice thing to do; it's kind of mean to make Joey stand on the desk just because he's the largest student in the room. Go back to your seat, Joey."

The teacher then laid the hammer aside and, with a few deliberate movements, covered the entire surface of the desk with a single thickness of newspaper. Picking up the hammer, he returned to the front of the desk, raised it high, and, one more time, looked at the first row. The students' hands were up.

"What's going to happen?" the teacher asked.

"It will break through the paper," a student said quickly. "Put Joey back up there."

"I don't think so," the teacher said, "but let's see."

He brought the hammer high above his head, once more acting as if he intended to strike the yardstick, then, casually glancing at the clock, he exclaimed: "Wow! I've lost track of the time. There are only a few minutes left, and I've got to review Friday's test." Without further ado, the teacher abruptly pushed all of the paraphernalia aside.

"Hit it, hit it!" several students shouted.

Ignoring these entreaties, the teacher calmly opened his text and began reviewing the forthcoming test.

The next day, when class convened, there were immediate questions. Several students, the night before, had taken a yardstick, balanced it on a table top or television set, covered the surface with a newspaper, and struck the yardstick with a hammer. How, they wanted to know, could the newspaper reduce the momentum so much?

The teacher then delivered a technical explanation of area pressure.

Consider the following letter written by Doug Leonard, a junior high school science teacher (*Changing Minds,* 1991, p. 20):

Dear Parents:

I am sorry but due to an unfortunate accident in science class today, I shrunk your kids. They are now invisible to us, but they are okay. I have seen them all by using my classroom microscope. They are living on a glass slide in my supply room.

Sincerely yours,
Mr. Leonard

Although this letter was not actually sent home, it did serve as the starting place for an unusual and novel way of having students discuss their knowledge about the unit on plant cells that they had just completed. It did not take long for Leonard's students to quickly get into the spirit of having been "shrunk." Exploiting this fantasy, Leonard said to them:

> All right kids, let's make the most of this unfortunate accident. I've placed you on a slide along with some very large plant cells. You should be able to survive if you use the knowledge that you have gained in the past couple of weeks about cells. Please write me a letter telling me how you will survive the next few days. Include such things as how you will utilize the plant and its specific parts for: 1) getting food, 2) getting rid of waste, 3) where you will get water and oxygen, 4) what is your source of energy and what will happen if you injure yourself? 5) How will you enter and leave the cell (remember you are about the size of a sugar molecule) . . . ?

A few answers stuck strictly to business, as with the following:

> Dear Mr. Leonard,
>
> It's been hard but I found food from the chloroplasts. I got rid of waste from the vacuole. I get water and oxygen from the cytoplasm. My source of energy comes from the mitochondrion and the ribosomes will fix my injury. I will enter and leave the cell by the cell membrane. I will get information from the nucleus and the endoplasmic reticulum will carry me around.
>
> I'm having fun in the cell parts.
>
> Sincerely,
> Michael

Other students, while answering Leonard's specific questions, livened up their responses with a touch of humor; some examples: "By the way, this pen is very heavy"; "Too bad you didn't shrink a camcorder; we could . . . "; "P.S., shrink a water bed or mattress, this slide is pretty hard"; "We hope mitosis doesn't take place because we might get separated."

Thus, by engaging students in an exercise that was unique, novel, and creatively different, Doug Leonard not only helped his students learn about plant cells, but exercise their imaginations and stretch their thinking in interesting, fun ways. It also shows that when an assessment question generates responses that actually interest students, it can stimulate learning as well as measure it.

Provide the Appropriate Mental Set

When discussing how to provide a proper mental set, we are talking about the importance of being as clear as possible when giving class directions or assignments. Research shows that we tend to remember best those things we *intend to remember* (Hill, 1982). This "lack of intent" phenomenon is demonstrated daily: We forget the name of a person we just met, we forget to do an unpleasant task or assignment, we forget to write a letter we have been meaning to write for weeks, or we take the stairs from the first to the second floor of the Arts and Sciences Building 500 times in a semester and have no idea at all of how many steps there are. It all depends on our intent, or "mental set," to remember.

13.10 A "Mind-Set" Exercise

> Here is a little trick you can try on a friend that demonstrates the effects of mental set. Ask him or her to do it very quickly. You say, "Spell stop." Your friend does. Then quickly add, "What do you do in front of a green light?" Two out of three will say "stop" because of their "mind-set." Try it, and see what happens.

An interesting experiment conducted by Torrance and Harmon (1961) shows the importance of giving students an appropriate mental set. They gave each of three groups of students a distinct set of instructions: (1) to apply *creatively* the content of assigned readings, (2) to *evaluate* the content critically, and (3) to *remember* the content. Then the students were given tests to measure their recall of information, as well as their ability to apply creatively and critically the substance of the content to problems. For each type of test item, the group receiving the related "mental set" scored highest. That is, the group that had been previously instructed to "think creatively" scored highest on the creative items; the group that had been instructed to concentrate on remembering did better on overall recall; and so forth. The investigators also found that the memory set was apparently the easiest of the three to maintain during the three-week period of the experiment. They attribute this effect to the students' extended exposure to this type of mental set, and the one most likely to be induced in many classes and by many teachers.

The evidence suggests that students' mental sets can have a powerful influence on their ability to solve problems and/or to remember newly acquired material for long periods of time. Teachers play a very important role in helping to modify, or to determine, the direction of a student's mental set.

13.11 Directions Make a Difference

> You can verify what you have just read with another experiment. Choose eight words (e.g., adviser, recommend, physiology, ecology, psychology, occasions, dilemma, omission) and tell another person that you are trying to find out how well people can spell. Give the words on the list to that person one at a time. When finished, have that person try to *recall* the words he or she spelled. Most people will have trouble because they were concentrating on spelling, not on remembering. Try the same list with two or three others, but tell them you want to *remember* the words as well as spell them. Compare the results. Do the directions you give make a difference? (You might try a variation of this with words that are easy to spell [e.g., cat, house, boat, and so on).

Use Elaboration Strategies

By definition, to elaborate on something is to expand on it further, to provide more detail, to fill it out more completely. Weinstein, Ridley, Dahl, and Weber (1988/1989) have suggested that elaboration involves putting into use what we already know in order to understand more fully what we are trying to learn. It is a way of building links to existing knowledge, a process that increases the number of memory cues that are helpful when trying to retrieve something from long-term memory. Basically, the idea here is to encourage (and help) students make connections between new material and more familiar material. You may recall from the discussion on information processing in Chapter 6 that the more one item of information is associated with other items, the more mental "routes" there are to get to the original information. Schunk (1991) has pointed out that this gives a person more "handles," or retrieval cues, to "pick up" the information one is seeking. Research has demonstrated repeatedly that well-developed elaborations enhance learning because recall of that learning is more accessible (Stein, Littlefield, Bradsford, and Persampieri, 1984; Weinstein and Mayer, 1986).

One of the ways, for example, I have tried to use the elaboration idea in this text is through the use of the various "boxes" throughout each chapter that invite you to use or think about the content in ways that are more personally relevant and interesting. To the extent that that actually happens you will find yourself "elaborating" your thinking beyond these pages and, in that sense, building links to your existing knowledge and attitudes.

Weinstein et al. (1988/1989) have suggested that teachers can help students to develop their elaborations by asking questions that represent a variety of techniques (e.g., analogies, transformation, comparing and contrasting). Some sample questions include the following:

1. What is the main idea of this story?
2. If this principle were not true, what might happen?
3. How could I represent this in a diagram?
4. How can I put this into my own words?
5. How could I teach this to my dad?
6. How does this apply to my life?
7. How does knowing this make a difference in my life?

13.12 How Could You Prompt Elaboration Thinking?

Now that you have an idea of what elaboration strategies are, can you think of four or five questions that might stimulate elaboration thinking in your students?

Utilize the Advantages of "Part" and "Whole" Approaches

All curriculum areas contain elements of varying size and complexity. In biology, for instance, there are cells, tissues, systems, and members; in addition, there are organisms that are grouped into categories such as species, order, and phyla. In reading, there are letters, groups of letters having particular sounds, words, sentences, paragraphs, chapters, punctuation meanings, and so forth. The question is: In what sequence and in what size units should this material be taught? Should new material or a new skill be approached a step at a time, taking each of its parts in individual order until some level of overall mastery is accomplished? Or would a better approach be to present the "big picture" so that students are not bogged down with too many details? It depends basically on two considerations: (1) the nature of the student (i.e., his or her intelligence, background and readiness for learning, motivation, and need for feedback); and (2) the nature of the material or task (i.e., its length, meaningfulness, complexity, organization, intellectual and/or physical skill demands).

When to Use Each Method

The whole method of teaching is probably better in the following cases:

1. When you want to give a global picture of something without paying particular attention to details (Encouraging students to scan a book, reading only chapter summaries and occasional paragraphs, is an illustration of this process.)
2. When your students have above-average IQs
3. When the material is meaningful, and more concrete than abstract
4. When the material is closely knit, is one theme, and is not too long

The basic idea is to show how smaller units of material fit into larger wholes. Good piano teachers, for example, are not likely to send their budding virtuosos home to practice only finger exercises and the C and F scales. They would make sure that their students had opportunities to use scales by playing simple compositions. The wise piano teacher knows that a piano student takes up the study of music because he or she wants to play real songs, not just practice scales and finger exercises. Unless some whole experiences are introduced into the instructional sequence rather early, students of the piano, or of anything else, are inclined to lose interest. Whether it is learning to play the piano or to paint, or whether it is learning new words or the basic principles of addition and subtraction, it is important that students see that what they are doing fits into a larger context.

The part method of teaching is better in the following cases:

1. When a student is not very capable intellectually (For example, slow learners need to learn new material a step at a time because of the intellec-

tual difficulty they might have in seeing the "whole" picture. Students need the reward and encouragement they can receive more frequently when learning smaller subunits of material. The whole method can be more discouraging because some students have to work too long before they see any return on their efforts.)

2. When the material is long and complicated, and lacks a central theme.

Using a Combination of Both Methods Works Best

As you can see, the *character of the material* has much to do with the relative advantages of these two methods. In terms of motivational and learning results, a combination of the two methods is probably the best idea. For example, whatever you teach, it would be good practice to begin by helping your students to see the "whole" picture. Then divide the whole picture into suitable subsections and approach it by the part method. Finally, review the whole to secure adequate organization of the parts into a total associative train.

Encourage Students to Distribute Work and Study Time

Although teaching and learning can be meaningful and relevant, with the material presented in the form of comprehensive problems or units, there still is the question of spacing and pacing an activity. Teaching and learning new material might be concentrated into relatively long, unbroken periods of work, or spread over several short sessions. Research shows that learning efficiency varies with the length of study or practice periods, with the spacing of such periods, and with the pace at which the material is presented (Hudgins, 1977; Rosenshine, 1989; Underwood, 1961).

Complex and abstract material require more time for assimilation and comprehension than simple material that has immediate meaning. Nothing is more frustrating and defeating than to have new material presented more rapidly than it can be understood. Of course, this varies from student to student and from subject to subject, which means that, as teachers, we have to remain alert to both students and content in order to decide on an appropriate teaching pace. Almost without exception, research concerned with the relative effectiveness of spacing new learning over a period of time, or with cramming it into a shorter time span, indicates that learning should be spaced over longer periods of time in order to facilitate and sustain high motivation and retention (Glaser, 1969; Hill, 1982). For example, a few words of spelling each day for a week will be mastered better than a large number in one lesson.

Four Factors to Consider When Spacing Work and Study

Although the complex interplay of human and subject-matter variables makes it difficult to determine the optimal temporal distribution of practice or study time in a given school subject, nonetheless, some general guidelines can be used to determine the appropriate spacing of work and study activities, including the following:

1. *Complexity of material:* The type of material to be learned is an important consideration. For instance, complex perceptual-motor learning (e.g., learning to write, dive, or drive a car) and difficult memorization require short, frequent (i.e., more than once a week) practice sessions. However, well-integrated and interesting tasks (e.g., learning to play Monopoly or reading an exciting book even though some words are not recognized) might be pursued for longer periods of time without a great loss in motivation.
2. *Similarity of material:* The similarity of material to be learned is another consideration. In order to reduce the possibility that what was previously learned will interfere with what is currently being learned, it is better to have practice or study periods more widely spaced. For example, rather than spending one hour learning fifty new foreign language words, it would be wiser to spend twenty minutes with ten words, and then come back and spend another twenty minutes with ten more words, and then come back and spend another twenty minutes with ten different words, and so on. That is, the more similar the material, the more chance there is of it *interfering* with itself if pursued for long periods of time. Hence, the value of making practice periods short and more widely spaced.
3. *Monotony and fatigue:* Monotony, boredom, and fatigue are most likely to occur when we find ourselves doing the same thing over and over again for long periods of time. The more variety we can introduce into our learning, teaching, and study activities, the less likely it is that this will occur.
4. *Level of motivation:* Because motivation is a key to achievement and learning, encouraging students to map out their own study schedules is an important goal. Predetermined schedules, rigorously imposed on students in an effort to make learning more efficient, might have the reverse effect of stifling interest and initiative. Students who work at meaningful tasks matched with their interests and needs frequently work long and arduously without any apparent detrimental effects.

13.13 How Do You Learn Best?

Do you learn best by first trying to get an idea of the big picture so you can approach a particular topic more holistically, or do you prefer taking a topic a step at a time as in part learning? What type of study works best for you? Do you study over spaced periods, tend to cram, or does what you do depend on the nature of the material? You can learn a lot about learning just by examining your own. Be careful, however, not to overgeneralize your findings. There are many ways to be a good learner.

Promote Overlearning When Appropriate

Forgetting is generally reduced by overlearning; that is, retention of new material can be increased if practice or review continues beyond the point of the first errorless reproduction of the new information. That we can drive a car after years of not driving, type after years of not typing, play the piano after months of not playing, or remember portions of our high school fight song are all example of things we have "overlearned."

Experimental evidence indicates that overlearning results in more accurate retention over longer periods than practice that ceases at the point of original learning (Hulse, Egeth, and Deese, 1980). For instance, the skills of driving a car, swimming, skating, or remembering the multiplication tables are not readily forgotten because we have continued to use these skills on a more or less consistent basis after their original acquisition. However, it is important to keep in mind that gain from overlearning decreases as additional practice continues.

When Overlearning Is Most Desirable

As a technique for increasing motivation and retention, encouraging students to overlearn new material is more advisable when: (1) they are learning specific, concrete material such as grammar rules, multiplication tables, names, dates, the periodic table, or even football plays; or (2) there is a long interval between learning new material and its recall. Overlearning is not achieved through elongated study sessions, but best accomplished through the use of spaced review periods.

As a general rule, overlearning is most efficient when confirmed within one and one-half to twice the number of repetitions required for the original learning. For example, if you were trying to commit a list of names, dates, or formulae to memory and it took ten trials to do so, then you could probably succeed in overlearning this material if you repeated what you had just learned another fifteen or twenty times.

When Not to Encourage Overlearning

Encouraging students to overlearn abstract principles or concepts they do not understand is not wise because it might invite them simply to memorize new material without first understanding it. Furthermore, meaningless repetition might encourage a student to respond mechanically. There is a classic story, illustrating this point, about an elementary school boy who persisted in saying, "I have went." After correcting him dozens of times, his teacher finally could take it no longer and sentenced him to stay after school to write, "I have gone" 100 times on the blackboard. As he wearily reached the ninety-first repetition, the teacher left the room momentarily. When she returned, she discovered that the hapless student had finished his task and departed. On the board were 100 progressively sloppier "I have gone's," and a note:

Dear teacher,
I have wrote "I have gone" 100 times and I have went home.

The moral of this tale, of course, is that repetition does little good unless students *understand what they are doing*. For example, it would be much better for a student who cannot remember how to spell *principal* to write the word five times and utilize a mnemonic aid such as "The principal is a pal," than to write it fifty times and think the teacher is a louse.

Provide Feedback About Progress and Results

Research shows rather clearly that we are more likely to avoid similar mistakes and improve performance if we know what our mistakes are initially (Corno, 1987; Gredler, 1992). Hence, it is important that we indicate to students not only *what* is wrong, but also *why* it is wrong. In addition, the time span should be as short as possible between, for example, handing in a paper or writing an exam and feedback about its results. Nothing stifles motivation and encourages loss of retention more than to have to wait two or three weeks to get back an exam or paper. Even worse is the experience of having to wait two or three weeks and receiving no more feedback than an impersonal grade in the upper-right-hand corner of an exam or paper. You might recall from Chapter 8 that when students get back exams with personalized comments from their teacher, along with a letter grade, they are more likely to improve on subsequent exams than students who receive just grades, but no personalized comments.

Why Feedback Is Important

Knowledge of results leads to improved achievement and greater motivation for at least five reasons:

1. It tends to encourage repetition of those things at which we are successful.
2. It helps us to correct or improve incorrect or unsuccessful responses.
3. It provides an incentive to perform as accurately as possible. Lack of such knowledge reduces this incentive.
4. It helps to capitalize on what has been called the "law of increasing energy," which states that the closer we get to our goals, the greater the effort we put forth. Thus, it is usually easier to write the last two pages of a term paper than the first five.
5. Knowledge of results also has the effect of introducing intermediate, short-term goals in addition to an ultimate goal—thus providing a more frequent resurgence of new energy.

Why Motivation Is Enhanced

Generally, providing knowledge of results can be an excellent way of motivating students to apply themselves to the task at hand. Not only is it a fairly safe method, it is an honest, intrinsic form of motivation. Knowledge of our previous performance tends to make us compete against ourselves, which, for most of us, is a contest in which we can hope for considerable success.

Allow Ample Time for Review

One of the best means of maintaining retention above a given level is through the systematic use of review. Research bears out this supposition. For example, Hudgins (1977) noted in his summary of research related to review that the amount of material remembered is directly related to the amount of time spent on review tests. Immediate review after reading new material is one of the best ways to facilitate retention. For instance, groups that took immediate review tests had more than 60% better retention of material read than those who took their first recall test a week later. Furthermore, a group that took an immediate recall test, and another one the next day, did better on retention tests than a second group that took an immediate recall test, and a second test a week later.

In general, *the more abstract or complicated the new material, the more frequent reviews of it should be.* If one has thoroughly *overlearned* original material, then reviews of it may be less frequent. However, from the standpoint of economy and time, reviews are generally more effective than overlearning. This is especially true inasmuch as effective review is more than just bringing the learning of material up to its original level—it can be an important stepping-stone to more advanced work. Reviews often reveal new meanings, deeper understandings, and relationships that were not apparent the first time.

MICROSOCIETY SCHOOLS: EXPERIMENTS IN EDUCATION RELEVANCY

The following is a description of a different kind of educational experience: Imagine a school where students learn math by holding jobs, paying taxes, and running businesses that sell everything from pencils to pillows; a place where students study logic and law by taking their classmates to court and, when found guilty of their misdeed, fining them in the school's own currency. Imagine a school where students come to understand politics by drawing up their own constitution, drafting laws, and deciding such matters as which days of the week baseball caps may be worn to class. Imagine a school where social studies and civics are not just courses but an ongoing experiment in trying to make school more relevant by making it more real (Fedarko, 1992).

Experiments of this sort are occurring in five American elementary schools, two in Massachusetts and three in New York. Each school represents a "microsociety," a name coined by former fifth-grade teacher, George Richmond (1973), whose book about the possibility of a microsociety school gave birth to the five schools using his model of education. Richmond's first job, at a Brooklyn elementary school in 1967, was a rookie teacher's nightmare. He noted that students frequently skipped class, seldom did their homework, goofed off during lessons, and seemed generally uninterested in learning. Richmond soon became disillusioned with a system in which teachers who pretended to teach and students who pretended to learn did very little of either. From that deep sense of frustration an idea took shape: if discipline, coercion, and the force of reason could not hook students, perhaps freedom and responsibility could.

Richmond viewed grades as representing a basic dilemma. It occurred to him that there was no other place in society where people were expected to work, and rather hard, at that, without some kind of monetary compensation. Thus, Richmond, although he was a Yale graduate with a deep belief in the value of learning for its own sake, began paying his students—in fake money—for completing assignments on time, getting good grades, and not missing class. Students were then free to use their "cash" to play a new game, a sort of life-size version of Monopoly in which they bought, sold, and mortgaged various "properties" around the room.

The first microsociety school opened in 1981 in an empty library in Lowell, Massachusetts. Although a good many doubters dismissed the idea as "futuristic," "dubious," and a "gimmick," by 1987 the school's students were testing two years above the national average in both reading and math. School attendance is consistently around 96% and very few students drop out.

Even more impressive than test scores are changes that are not so easily quantified. For example, in 1981, Lowell's school system was so racially segregated that it took a federal court order to correct the imbalance. When the Lowell microsociety school first opened, the student body was mostly black. Now more than half of the students are from white and Hispanic families *who requested to take part in the program.* Parents frequently comment on their children's positive attitude since attending a microsociety school. Curriculum director Tom Malone believes that, "because students are empowered to create their own society, they see themselves as capable people" (Fedarko, 1992, p. 53).

Under the microsociety model, the school day is split in two. The morning is devoted to traditional classes in math, science, history, and English. In the afternoon, students put their lessons to work. They memorize multiplication tables not just to do well on exams but also so they can keep double-entry books, write checks, bill customers, and complete financial audits. Remember, too, that they set up their own government with its elected officials, rules, regulations, laws, and enforcement agencies. Students experience not only the realities of managing an economic and political system, but they also participate in living experiments in applied moral development. For example, there was an incident at the Lowell school where one boy outbid dozens of his classmates at a Christmas auction and bought a sackful of toys by writing bad checks. His outraged peers took the offender to "court," where the "district attorney" won a guilty verdict. (Unfortunately, none of the items purchased with the bogus checks were able to be recovered. The youthful felon had given everything away to a string of girlfriends.) As punishment, the school court elected to reclaim all of the student's paychecks and ordered him to perform community service for the remainder of the school year.

Concern has been expressed by some skeptics that microsociety's heavy emphasis on grown-up concerns like money, taxes, and employment might force children to grow up too quickly. Supporters of the program have pointed out that the microsociety concept taps into one of childhood's most salient pleasures—the impulse to play—and harnesses it in the service of absorbing knowledge. Fred Hernandez, principal at Yonkers, puts it this way, "Think about what we usually tell kids when they come to school. (We say) 'Sit down. Shut up. Get in line.' That's counterproductive because kids love to play. What Micro does is get them to role-play life" (Fedarko, 1992, p. 53).

The success of microsociety schools can be attributed to at least two factors: (1) they are novel, and (2) they provide a relevant educational experience. Although some of the novelty may wear off with time, so long as what the students learn is associated with meaningful life experiences, the relevancy factor has a chance of remaining a lasting feature. Future research regarding the efficacy of the microsociety concept will provide more definitive answers about its effectiveness.

13.14 Arguments For and Against?

Every idea has two sides to it, and the microsociety concept is no exception. If asked to discuss the possible strengths and weaknesses of such an approach to teaching and learning, how would you respond? Would you choose to have your own children participate in this kind of schooling?

REACHING STUDENTS FROM VARIED ETHNIC AND CULTURAL BACKGROUNDS

America is a pluralistic society unlike every other society in the world. It houses an incredibly large number of different ethnic and cultural groups under its nationalistic roof. In every sense of the word, we are truly a multicultural society and are becoming even more so with the passing of time. Previously, it was thought that new immigrants were expected to be assimilated into a kind of cultural melting pot where, through processes of dilution and diffusion, they would shed the cultural baggage that they had brought with them and become like those who had arrived earlier. American schools were supposed to provide the experiences that enabled children who came for different religious and cultural heritages to become mainstream Americans.

In the 1960s and 1970s, minority-group and poor students who were having trouble in school were referred to as "culturally disadvantaged" or "culturally different." These were labels from the *cultural deficit model,* which was basically a point of view that suggested that the students' home culture was deficient and thus had not prepared them to compete in schools. The cultural deficit model is rejected by most people today. Now, it is rather generally accepted that particular cultures are not necessarily deficient, but that there are basic differences between the students' home culture and the cultural expectations of the school. The challenge is not to invent new labels that unfairly stereotype certain students, but to make the kinds of pedagogical adjustments that make it possible for every student to have a fair chance to find out what his or her strengths are.

The remainder of this chapter examines some strategies teachers can use to make this happen. The following revealing and startling statistics illustrate the importance of this material.

Our Students—Today and in the Future

When thinking about who our students are and who they will be, the following breakdown will give you an idea about the composition of America's multicultural classrooms (Grant and Sleeter, 1989; "You and the System," 1991).

- 1 in 3 children lives with a single parent, usually a working mother.
- 1 in 5 Americans under the age of 18 lives in poverty.
- Nearly 50% of all black children are poor.
- 12% of all students are in bilingual classes.
- 3 in 10 students probably will not finish high school and many of those will be members of minority groups (3 in 10 blacks, 4 in 10 Hispanics, 4 in 10 Native Americans, 1 in 10 whites).
- It is estimated that by the year 2010, 38% of all students will be members of minority groups.

The challenge facing American education is considerable. Multicultural education is not simply a buzz word reflecting a currently popular idea. Banks (1991) has made the point that it is the outgrowth of an expanding awareness and acceptance of the idea that all students—rich, poor, male, female, able, disabled, and regardless of racial or ethnic origin—should have equal access to learning in school and to be respected. It is an idea consistent with the American *ideal* of each person having the right and the opportunity to make as much

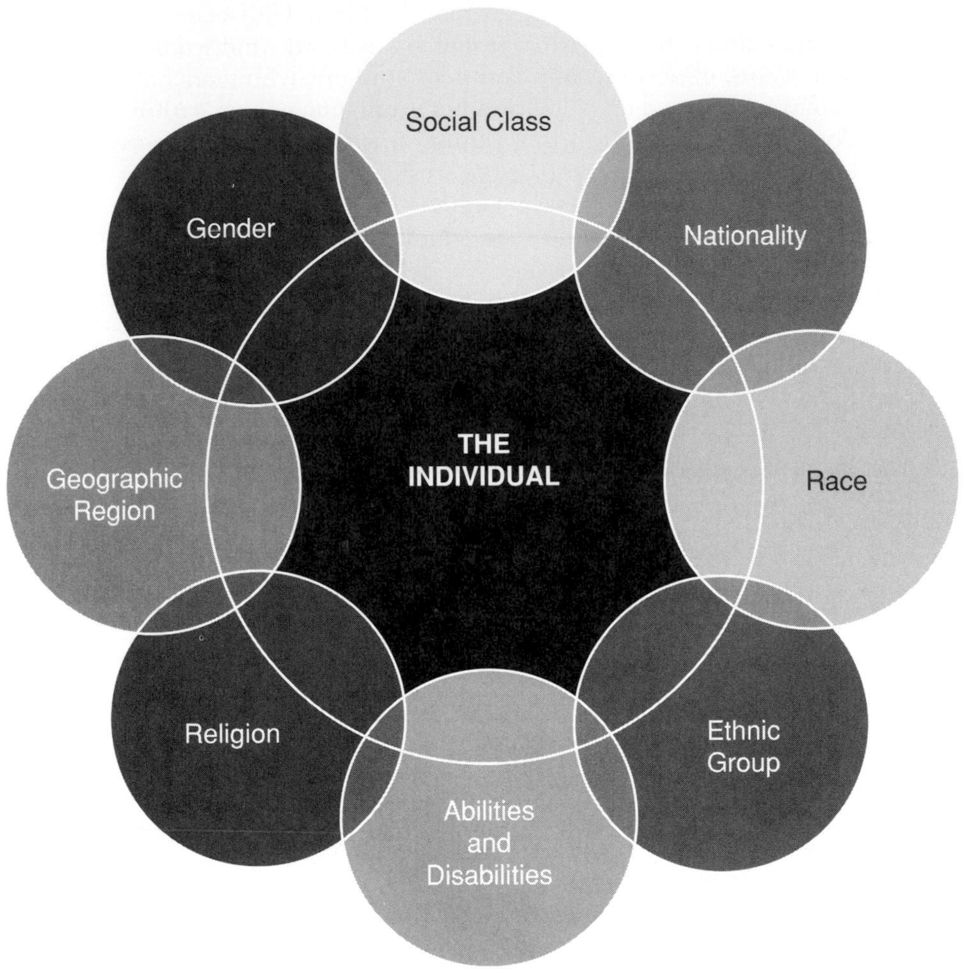

Figure 13.2. EACH INDIVIDUAL BELONGS TO MANY DIFFERENT SOCIAL GROUPS, AND EACH GROUP HAS ITS OWN SET OF INFLUENCES.

(Adapted from James A. Banks, *Multiethnic Education: Theory and Practice 3/e.* Copyright © 1994 by Allyn and Bacon. Adapted by permission.)

of his or her life as possible. This right and opportunity begins in every individual classroom and with the recognition that each student is shaped and influenced by many different groups, as is visually depicted in Figure 13.2. Table 13.3 will give you an idea of how ethnic group diversity has increased since 1980. Some basic principles to remember when teaching students from varied ethnic and cultural backgrounds are reviewed here.

Table 13.3. RESULTS OF 1990 CENSUS FOR SELECTED ETHNIC GROUPS

Group	*Total number*	*Increase since 1980*
African American	30.0 million	13.2%
Asian	7.3 million	107.8%
Native American	2.0 million	37.9%
Hispanic	22.4 million	53.0%
Other	9.8 million	

From U.S. Bureau of the Census, 1990.

When Teaching Students from Different Cultural Backgrounds

If is difficult enough to teach students who come from middle-class backgrounds and environments. Even within this homogeneity there is great diversity. In every classroom, there will be students who are from socioeconomic and ethnic backgrounds that are in the minority, and their needs must be considered, too. Research in recent years has taught us much about what teachers can do to reach these students (Bennett, 1990; Boutte and McCormick, 1992; Brophy, 1982; Fillmore and Valadez, 1986; Slaughter-Defoe, Nakagawki, Takanishi, and Johnson, 1990; Vasquez, 1990). The following are eleven suggestions from research with a multicultural focus that can help you develop the kind of skills that will enable you to be a more effective teacher when dealing with students from differing social and ethnic backgrounds.

13.15 Get to Know Someone Different from Yourself

Make it a point to get to know someone who is, in as many ways possible, different from you. What is that person's views on the value of education, family, individualism, democracy, cooperation versus competition, religion, and so forth? How does that person's cultural and ethnic heritage drive his or her behavior? Try to imagine being a student in his or her country. What do you suppose that would be like?

1. *Recognize that students from diverse social and ethnic backgrounds frequently have learning styles different from middle-class white students.* For example, as a group, African Americans and Native Americans tend to have learning styles that are more visual and global, rather than verbal and analytical, and a preference for reasoning by inference rather than formal logic. Hispanic Americans tend to prefer holistic, concrete, social approaches to learning. Findings like these underscore the importance of incorporating visual aids, hands-on opportunities, small group discussions, and "big picture" plans of

charts, graphs, or diagrams that allow students to see connections and infer relationships.

2. *Have realistic expectations.* Successful teachers do not see "beauty" or "strength" where there is actually poverty and emptiness. They see students from differing social and ethnic backgrounds for what they are—different, yet like all youths, coping in their own way with the trials and frustrations of growing. These teachers also see them, unlike middle-class youths, as struggling to survive in the dog-eat-dog world of their peers, confused by the conflicting pull of the two cultures in which they live—the one of the home, street, and neighborhood and the other of the school and the society that supports their home environment.

3. *Be sensitive to how ethnic group membership influences self-image.* Effective teachers are cognizant of the ethnic group membership of their students and the extent to which such membership shapes persons' images of themselves. In addition, they know something about the history, traditions, and social expectations of various ethnic groups, their status in American society, the obstacles and frustrations they confront, and their perceptions of what life has in store for them.

4. *Allow for language differences.* Good teachers recognize that the language of their pupils is closely tied to the life they lead. Although a particular language may be a distortion of "acceptable English," good teachers will know and accept the idea that it represents the only known and acceptable medium of exchange in the home and neighborhoods from which their students come.

5. *Understand a student's background.* Successful teachers understand the backgrounds from which their students come, the values those backgrounds place on various achievements, and the reasons for students' reluctance to strive toward future goals for which such labor provides limited payoff in the present. For example, it would be helpful to a teacher to realize that, among many Hispanic students, individual accomplishments are not so much prized as is the feeling that one has done something that reflects positively on the family. Thus, a statement to a Hispanic student along the lines of, "Well done, Maria, you should be proud of your work" is likely to be less potent than verbal feedback that says, "Nice job, Maria. Your family will be proud of you." Little nuances like this can make a big motivational difference for certain students.

6. *Realize the effects of intellectual impoverishment.* Good teachers know many of their students bear the scars of the intellectual impoverishment of their early years. Wise teachers realize that such students are rarely helped to name the things they see, feel, and hear, or to recognize similarities and differences, to categorize and classify perceptions, or even to learn the word for an object.

7. *Be aware of the effects of family conditions.* Successful teachers are aware of the array of family structures from which students come: the father-absent, matriarchal family; the home in which both parents are working; the home in which one or both parents are out of work, perhaps on relief; and the home in which the extended family—grandparents, aunts, uncles, and other relatives—lives together. In a word, successful teachers are aware of the physical conditions in which their students live—their lack of privacy, poverty, and absence of basic amenities.

8. *Interpret results of intelligence tests cautiously.* Successful teachers take the results of a student's intelligence test with a grain of salt. They are aware that native potential intelligence is, thus far at least, not measurable, that what tests measure is learned behavior, and that learning results not just from students' native ability, but from their total experience.

Successful teachers are also aware that tests can provide a fairly accurate description of a student's present ability to handle academic material and, unless there are significant changes in his or her life experiences, how a child will function academically in the future. Successful teachers accept test scores as reasonably valid measures of a student's present academic ability, but tend to reject them as measures of active intelligence.

9. *Emphasize teaching for mastery.* Successful teachers spend time actively and aggressively instructing their students in basic skills and monitoring individual students' progress, providing feedback and remedial help. They make a conscientious effort to teach in a hierarchical sequence, recognizing that success at any given level requires mastery of skills taught earlier. They encourage their students to overlearn basic skills (e.g., spelling rules, multiplication tables, grammatical rules) because they realize that this will help their students to: (1) apply their skills appropriately in subsequent situations, and (2) experience positive feelings of success when they do.

10. *Establish firm boundaries that are consistently enforced.* Successful teachers of the disadvantaged are able to meet their students on equal terms—as person to person, individual to individual. Although they accept, they do not condone; that is, they set very clearly defined limits and tolerate few transgressions. They recognize that they cannot control these students through appeals to their sense of shame and/or guilt. Therefore, they set rules and establish boundaries with a minimum of discussion. Here, they are impersonal, undeviating, and strict, but not punitive. Within firmly established boundaries, consistently and fairly enforced, the teacher knows where he or she is going, and students know what to expect. Perhaps most important, teachers are freed from having to spend undue time coping with students who do not know what the rules are. This frees teachers to spend more time relating to students within a clearly defined framework—one that allows teachers to be friendly and outgoing rather than punitive and restrictive.

11. *Use honest praise and avoid harsh criticism.* Successful teachers of culturally abused youths seem to have a deep understanding of the danger of the "self-fulfilling prophecy" of expecting only so much from their students, and, consequently, getting low achievement from them. Rather than expecting less, successful teachers set their standards high, but not so high as to be unattainable. In addition, effective teachers reward each tiny step, are alert to opportunities for honest praise, and, as much as possible, withhold harsh criticism when progress is slow or lacking. Above all, *they are honest.* They do not pretend that a student's work is good when it clearly is not, and they do not condone unacceptable behavior. Pearl (1965), a psychologist who has worked extensively with disadvantaged youth, makes a relevant point:

> Not long ago I heard the dean of a school of education say that the only thing disadvantaged children need is love. If we could only give them enough love, we could solve all our problems, he implied. He became furious with me, however, when I tried to explain to him that love given so promiscuously is known in the streets as prostitution.
>
> By trying to give universal love, the teacher actually punishes the disadvantaged student. In effect, the teacher is asking him to feel guilty for anything he does to displease her because he is hurting or disappointing one who loves him . . . It is not love that disadvantaged children need so much as honest respect. Anything phony will force them to lash out against the teacher and whatever else the school imposes upon them. (p. 21)

Ample research indicates that youths from differing social and ethnic backgrounds do suffer from multiple intellectual handicaps (Banks, 1991). However, research also shows that the academic performance of these students can be improved when, and to the extent that, they feel they are welcome partners in an educational enterprise that is friendly, sympathetic, stimulating, and basically supportive.

EPILOGUE

Students of any age quickly lose their motivation to learn when meaning, purpose, and hope are absent from a curriculum. It is true that children start out with a wonderful, bubbling curiosity about the world in which they live, but that natural zest is soon lost when they find that they have to go to school, have to do homework, have to take tests, have to speak in turn, and so forth. Learning that started out as natural and motivated from within during children's early years becomes, and necessarily so, regimental and imposed during their school years. Children and adolescents, like adults, sometimes lose interest when things they *like* to do become things they *have* to do. School is like that—there are particular subjects to learn at particular times, at a particular pace, and in a particular sequence. The school experience is not an unstructured cafeteria of random learning available on demand. Rather, it is a reasonably structured and changing menu of new skills, experiences, and knowledge served up at specific times in students' development. Students are not all ready for the same learning menu at the same time and, indeed, some students wonder why they are fed when they are not even interested in what is being offered.

It is at this point that the skill and savvy of a good teacher is most important. Just as a fine cook can create a hunger in us that we did not know existed, so, too, it is possible for teachers to create a "hunger" in their students to learn, discover, solve problems, and persist in seeing puzzling, difficult tasks through to completion.

One way to do these things is to help students see that what occurs in school is not unrelated to what occurs outside of school. School and life outside of school do not have to be unconnected experiences left only to the very bright to discern their common components. We can help to make school more meaningful and relevant for more students if we show them how to transfer their learning and provide opportunities for them to do so, if we consider our students' readiness to learn and avoid starting ahead of them, if we relate our teaching to students' backgrounds and experiences, and if we exploit the psychological content available to us in the curriculum.

Microsociety schools represent a fresh and creative approach to making education more meaningful and relevant. By creating, managing, and maintaining a kind of microsociety of their own, students have an opportunity to use, in real-life ways, the knowledge they acquire in their traditional classes. By providing students with opportunities to use their knowledge in practical and meaningful ways, there is evidence to suggest that learning is enhanced and commitment to schooling increases. Which should come as a surprise to no one.

Increasingly, classrooms are becoming more multicultural in their composition. Effective teachers realize that meeting the diverse needs of this kind of student body means that sensitivity to cultural and ethnic differences must be combined with a variety of teaching approaches. Effective teachers appreciate a simple truth: There is no *one* best way to reach all students. There are many *best* ways and what is best depends not only on *what* is taught, but *who* is being taught.

Being an effective teacher—the type who can make teaching meaningful, relevant, and lasting—is hard work, and it requires creative, innovative approaches, *especially* with students who are difficult to reach. I remember an amusing anecdote that illustrates this idea.

An old service navigator was flying with a green and cocksure young pilot for the first time. "Change direction 1 degree to port," advised the navigator.

"Impossible," said the pilot. "No one can fly this old clunker that accurately; give me a decent amount of correction."

The navigator sighed, "Turn starboard 4 degrees."

"Much better," called out the pilot, very pleased with himself.

"Fine," replied the navigator dryly. "Now turn 5 degrees to port."

Teaching can be one of the easiest jobs in the world . . . but not when it is done right.

STUDY AND REVIEW QUESTIONS

1. What is meant by a "teachable moment," and how is this related to learning readiness?
2. Can you explain how Havighurst's developmental-task model and Piaget's intellectual-development model can be used to assess readiness?
3. How does the "natural" view of learning readiness differ from the "guided experience" view? What implications do each of these viewpoints have to teaching practices?
4. How would you explain the difference between positive and negative transfer of learning? Can you give an example of each?
5. What strategies can teachers use to teach for positive transfer?
6. Can you explain what it means to decontextualize an idea from its original associations so that it can be applied in a new context?
7. What is the difference between divergent and convergent questions? Is either any better than the other?
8. If someone asked you to explain the characteristics of a good question, how would you answer?
9. When teachers increase the wait time between asking a question and expecting someone to answer, what outcomes can they expect in their students?
10. What does it mean to consider the "psychological content" of a curriculum?
11. Can you identify five or six ways of making the results of teaching more lasting? That is, what can teachers do to make this more possible?
12. How does "whole" learning differ from "part" learning? When is each advantageous to use?
13. What variables should be considered when thinking about how to distribute time for work and study?
14. How does a microsociety school function?
15. When is it a good idea to promote overlearning? When is it not a good idea?
16. If someone asked you what they could do to make learning more relevant for students from different ethnic and social groups, how would you reply?

REFERENCES

Anshuntz, R. "An Investigation of Wait-time and Questioning Techniques as an Instructional Variable for Science Methods Students Microteaching Elementary School Children." (Doctoral Dissertation, University of Kansas, 1973). *Dissertation Abstracts International, 35,* 1975.

Banks, J. A. *Multiethnic Education,* 3rd ed. Needham Heights, MA: Allyn and Bacon, 1994.

Banks, J. A. *Teaching Strategies for Ethnic Studies.* Boston: Allyn and Bacon, 1991.

Bennett, C. I. *Comprehensive Multicultural Education: Theory and Practice,* 2nd ed. Boston: Allyn and Bacon, 1990.

Bigge, M. L. *Learning Theories for Teachers,* 4th ed. New York: Harper & Row, 1982.

Boutte, G. S., and McCormick, C. B. "Authentic Multicultural Activities." *Childhood Education,* 1992, Spring, pp. 140–144.

Brophy, J. "Successful Teaching Strategies for the Inner-City Child." *Phi Delta Kappan,* 1982, April, pp. 527–530.

Brownell, W. A., and Moser, H. E. "Meaningful Versus Mechanical Learning: A Study in Grade III Subtraction." *Duke University Studies in Education,* No. 8. Durham, NC: Duke University Press, 1949

Broyler, C. R., Thorndike, E. L., and Woodyard, E. R. "A Second Study of Mental Discipline in High School Studies." *Journal of Educational Psychology,* 1927, *18,* pp. 377–404.

Changing Minds, Michigan Educational Extension Service, Michigan State University, East Lansing, Michigan, 1991.

Corno, L. "Teaching and Self-Regulated Learning." In D. C. Berliner and B. V. Rosenshine (Eds.), *Talks to Teachers.* New York: Random House, 1987.

Corno, L., and Snow, R. E. "Adapting Teaching to Individual Differences Among Learners." In M. C. Wittrock (Ed.), *Handbook of Research on Teaching,* 3rd ed. New York: Macmillan, 1986.

"Education Briefs." *Education Digest,* 1967, November, p. 61.

Fedarko, K. "Can I Copy Your Homework—and Represent You in Court?" *Time,* 1992, September *21,* pp. 52–53.

Fillmore, L. W., and Valadez, C. "Teaching Bilingual Learners." In M.C. Wittrock (Ed.), *Handbook of Research on Teaching.* New York: Macmillan, 1986.

Gagne, R. M. *The Conditions of Learning,* 3rd ed. New York: Holt, Rinehart and Winston, 1977.

Gall, M. D. "The Use of Questions in Teaching." *Review of Educational Research,* 1970, *40,* pp. 707–721.

Gesell, A. "The Stability of Mental Growth Careers." *39th Yearbook of the National Society for the Study of Education,* 1940, Part II, pp. 149–159.

Glaser, R. "Learning." In R. L. Ebel and V. H. Noll (Eds.), *Encyclopedia of Educational Research,* 4th ed. London: Collier-Macmillan, 1969.

Good, T. L, and Brophy, J. *Looking in Classrooms,* 5th ed. New York: HarperCollins, 1991.

Grant, C. A., and Sleeter, C. E. "Race, Class, Gender, Exceptionality, and Educational Reform." In J. Banks and C. McGee Banks (Eds.), *Multicultural Education: Issues and Perspectives.* Boston: Allyn and Bacon, 1989.

Gredler, M. E. *Learning and Instruction: Theory into Practice,* 2nd ed. New York: Macmillan, 1992.

Grossier, P. *How to Use the Fine Art of Questioning.* New York: Teachers' Practical Press, 1964.

Guilford, J. P. *The Nature of Human Intelligence.* New York: McGraw-Hill, 1967.

Hamachek, D. "Enhancing the Self's Psychology by Improving Fitness Physiology." *Journal of Human Behavior and Learning,* 1986, *3,* pp. 2–12.

Havighurst, R. S. "More Thoughts on Developmental Tasks." *Personal and Guidance Journal,* 1980, *58,* pp. 330–335.

Hilgard, E. R. "Learning and Maturation in Preschool Children." *Journal of Genetic Psychology,* 1932, *41,* pp. 40–53.

Hill, W. F. *Principles of Learning: A Handbook of Applications.* Palo Alto, CA: Mayfield, 1982.

Honig, A. S. "Television and Young Children." *Young Children,* 1983, *38,* pp. 63–76.

Hudgins, B. R. *Learning and Thinking: A Primer for Teachers.* Itasea, IL: Peacock, 1977.

Hulse, S. H., Egeth, H., and Deese, J. *The Psychology of Learning,* 5th ed. New York: McGraw-Hill, 1980.

Olson, W. C. *Child Development,* 2nd ed. Boston: D. C. Heath, 1959.

Pearl, A. "As a Psychologist Sees Pressures on Disadvantaged Teenagers." *National Education Association Journal,* 1965, *19,* p. 21.

Piaget, J. *The Language and Thought of the Child.* New York: World Publishing, 1973.

Richmond, G. *Microsociety School: Real World in Miniature.* New York: Harper and Row, 1973.

Riley, J. *The Effects of Teachers' Wait-Time and Cognitive Questioning Level on Pupil Science Achievement.* Paper presented at the annual meeting of the National Association for Research in Science Teaching, Boston, 1980.

Rowe, M. "Wait-time: Slowing Down May Be a Way of Speeding Up!" *Journal of Teacher Education,* 1986, *37,* pp. 43–50.

Rosenshine, D. V. "Explicit Teaching." In D. C. Berliner and D. V. Rosenshine (Eds.), *Talks to Teachers.* New York: Random House, 1989.

Rubin, L. J. *Artistry in Teaching.* New York: Random House, 1985.

Sadker, M., and Sadker, D. "Questioning Skills." In J. Cooper (Ed.), *Classroom Teaching Skills: A Handbook,* 3rd ed. Lexington, MA: D.C. Heath, 1987.

Salomon, G., and Globerson, T. *Skill Is Not Enough: The Role of Mindfulness in Learning and Transfer* (Rep. No. 11). Tel Aviv: Tel Aviv University, School of Education, Unit for Communication and Computer Research in Education, 1987.

Salomon, G., and Perkins, D. N. *Rocky Roads to Transfer: Rethinking Mechanisms of a Neglected Phenomenon.* Paper presented at the Harvard University Conference on Thinking, Cambridge, MA, 1984.

Schunk, D. H. *Learning Theories: An Educational Perspective.* New York: Merrill, 1991.

Shuell, T. J., and Lee, C. Z. *Learning and Instruction.* Monterey, CA.: Brooks/Cole, 1976.

Slaughter-Defoe, D. T., Nakagawki, K., Takanishi, R., and Johnson, D. J. "Toward Cultural/Ecological Perspectives on Schooling and Achievement in African- and Asian-American Children." *Child Development,* 1990, *61,* pp. 363–383.

Stein, B. S., Littlefield, J., Bradsford, J. D., and Persampieri, M. "Elaboration and Knowledge Acquisition." *Memory and Cognition,* 1984, *12,* pp. 522–529.

Swift, J., and Gooding, C. "Interaction of Wait-Time Feedback and Questioning Instruction on Middle School Science Teaching." *Journal of Research on Science Teaching,* 1983, *20,* pp. 721–730.

Tobin, K. "The Role of Wait Time in Higher Cognitive Learning." *Review of Educational Research,* 1987, *56,* pp. 69–95.

Tobin, K., and Capie, W. "Relationships Between Classroom Process Variables and Middle School Science Achievement." *Journal of Educational Psychology,* 1982, *74,* pp. 441–454.

Torrance, E. P., and Harmon, J. "Effects of Memory, Evaluative, and Creative Reading Sets on Test Performance." *Journal of Educational Psychology,* 1961, *52,* pp. 207–214.

Travers, R. M. *Essentials of Learning,* 4th ed. New York: Macmillan, 1977.

Underwood, B. J. "Ten Years of Massed Practice on Distributed Practice." *Psychological Review,* 1961, *68,* pp. 229–247.

U. S. Bureau of the Census. *Current Population Reports* (Series P-20.) Washington, DC: U.S. Government Printing Office, 1990.

Vasquez, J. A. "Teaching to the Distinctive Traits of Minority Students." *The Clearing House*, 1990, *63*, pp. 299–304.

Vygotsky, L. S. "Thinking and Speech." In R. W. Rieber, A. S. Carton, and N. Minick (Trans.), *The Collected Works of L. S. Vygotsky: Vol. 1. Problems of General Psychology.* New York: Plenum, 1987. (Original work published 1934).

Weinstein, C. E., and Mayer, R. E. "The Teaching of Learning Strategies." In M.C. Wittrock (Ed.), *Handbook of Research on Teaching.* 3rd ed. New York: Macmillan, 1986.

Weinstein, C. E., Ridley, S., Dahl, T., and Weber, S. "Helping Students Develop Strategies for Effective Learning." *Educational Leadership,* 1988/89, December/January, pp. 17–19.

Williams, P. A., Haertel, E. H., Haertel, G. D., and Walberg, H. J. "The Impact of Leisure-Time Television on School Learning: A Research Synthesis." *American Educational Research Journal,* 1982, *19,* pp. 19–50.

"You and the System: Who You Will Teach." *Teacher Magazine,* 1991, April.

Zintz, M. V. *The Reading Process: The Teacher and the Learner,* 2nd ed. Dubuque, IA: Brown, 1975.

SELECTED READINGS OF RELATED INTEREST

Banks, J. A. *An Introduction to Multicultural Education.* Needham Heights, MA: Allyn and Bacon, 1994. This book discusses multicultural education goals and describes ways that knowledge of multicultural education can help students achieve and develop positive self-attitudes.

Bartz, D. E., and Miller, L. K. *12 Teaching Methods to Enhance Student Learning.* Washington, DC: National Education Association, 1991. This small booklet focuses on 12 specific methods that teachers can use to help students learn more effectively and provides a succinct overview.

Clandinin, D. J., Davies, A., Hogan, P., and Kennard, B. (Eds.). *Learning to Teach, Teaching to Learn.* New York: Teachers College Press, Columbia University, 1993. This book centers on participants in a year-long alternative teacher education program, which included student teachers, cooperating teachers, and university professors exploring new and innovative approaches to teaching.

Davis, G. A., and Thomas, M. A. *Effective Schools and Effective Teachers.* Boston: Allyn and Bacon, 1989. This comprehensive, research-based book provides an excellent overview of the essential ingredients that go into making effective schooling effective.

Mann, P. H., Suiter, P. A., and McClung, R. M. *Handbook in Diagnostic-Prescriptive Teaching,* 3rd ed. Needham Heights, MA: Allyn and Bacon, 1987. This book provides nearly 600 pages of practical tools designed to help teachers in all phases of classroom life and scores of hands-on diagnostic and prescriptive materials for grades K–12.

Nieto, S. *Affirming Diversity: The Sociopolitical Context of Multicultural Education.* New York: Longman, 1992. This book provides a comprehensive framework for analyzing the multiple causes of school failure that occurs for many students representing "multicultures." It aims to help teachers understand what teaching and learning are like from a multicultural perspective.

Reyes, R. *The Ten Commandments for Teaching: A Teacher's View.* Washington, DC: National Education Association, 1991. This book was written by a teacher for teachers; it outlines 10 basic prerequisites to effective teaching.

Wilen, W. W. *Questioning Skills for Teachers.* 3rd ed. Washington, DC: National Education Association, 1991. This small 40 page pamphlet summarizes how teachers can hone questioning skills as a means of enhancing students' learning.

V

TOWARD UNDERSTANDING THE PSYCHOLOGY OF CLASSROOM DYNAMICS AND GROUP BEHAVIOR

Becoming a good teacher or youth worker is a challenging, taxing, and complex activity. It demands a background in psychology in order to understand human behavior, exposure to theories and processes of learning in order to facilitate achievement, understanding of yourself in order to maximize your effectiveness as a person, and exposure to concepts of growth in order to understand the developmental dynamics of the age group with which you are working.

These requirements seem extensive, but one more thing is needed. You must be not only a bit of a behavioral and developmental psychologist, and a learning facilitator, but something of a social psychologist, group worker, and classroom manager as well. Chapters 14 and 15 are intended to give you an understanding of the psychology of group dynamics, and insights into how to promote a positive classroom climate, along with some suggestions that might be helpful to you when it comes to handling management problems in constructive ways.

What does it mean to talk about a classroom as having a unique climate and "personality"? How are these qualities created? How do interpersonal attraction patterns shape the personality of a classroom? Are attractive students given more breaks? What can we do to build constructive group norms? What effect does a teacher's interpersonal-response style have on students' behavior? How serious is the problem of classroom discipline? What strategies can teachers use to cope with classroom discipline? What can teachers do to establish positive classroom discipline? All of these questions, and others, are discussed in Chapters 14 and 15.

14

Psychology and Development of Healthy Classroom Dynamics

CHAPTER OVERVIEW

IMPORTANT CHAPTER IDEAS

1. The "climate" of a classroom refers to the prevailing influence of psychological conditions that characterize the overall interpersonal feeling tones existing within it.
2. A teacher's leadership style has a strong impact on shaping the personality of a classroom.
3. Research indicates that classroom climate affects not only how much is learned, but how long learning lasts and how much future learning there is likely to be.
4. Students are most receptive to, and productive in, classrooms in which they feel they can influence decision making and operating policies.
5. An authoritarian classroom is much more likely to be a positive experience when the emotional tone includes such qualities as acceptance, caring, and mutual respect between teacher and student.
6. Positive-climate teachers tend to be good listeners, good empathizers, high rewarders, and fair evaluators, and are generous with positive feedback to all students.
7. How students and teachers feel about each other, how students handle their peer relations, and who is attracted to whom are important factors in shaping a classroom's teaching/learning environment.
8. Whom a teacher likes or dislikes tends to influence whom other students like or dislike.
9. The development of group norms is important because they serve as behavioral guidelines for the control and regulation of acceptable behavior.
10. When students participate in the development of norms they are more likely to stay within the guidelines of those norms.
11. An informal, supportive leadership style, combined with a group-centered format, enhances the possibility of open communication among group members.
12. Highly cohesive groups usually have a large number of overlapping friendship patterns, and a broad distribution of power.
13. Peer group friendship patterns, which are the basis for cohesive groups, are affected significantly by the instructional behaviors of teachers. Where students' interactions among themselves are minimized by teachers, group cohesiveness is reduced.
14. Teachers who frequently use evaluative and/or interpretive responses tend to make their students feel defensive, and more closed than open.

15. Successful teachers do not get stuck in one type of response mode, but tend to use what is most appropriate at any given time.
16. A climate of open communication is more likely to exist in classrooms where students feel secure enough to take risks and safe enough to make mistakes.

PROLOGUE

It doesn't take long for each classroom to develop its own unique personality, which basically is the collective blend of the individual personalities within it. One classroom, for example, might be somewhat quiet and withdrawn; a second might be outgoing and assertive; a third classroom might be defensive and unresponsive; and a fourth might be open and receptive. The type of personality a class develops is not a chance happening. It is, rather, the outgrowth of student–student and teacher–student interactions that, together, give a classroom's evolving personality both substance and expression.

Specific questions emerge from the study of classroom dynamics. What are the factors and forces that make one classroom quiet and withdrawn, while another, similar classroom seems outgoing and assertive? What part do teachers play in influencing a classroom in one direction or the other? What can teachers do to help students develop positive group norms and a healthy sense of cohesiveness? What steps can be taken to create an open, interactive climate, one that encourages students to stay open to one another, to the teacher, and to new ideas?

It is difficult enough to teach one student at a time in a tutorial format. You can imagine how much more complex it is to teach 20 or more students at a time in a group format. A teacher has to be knowledgeable not only about the psychology of learning and growth, but also about the psychology of groups. Thus, the major purpose of this chapter is to acquaint you with some basic concepts related to group dynamics so that you can begin to think about ways to create a positive group climate—the type that will facilitate both academic learning and personal growth.

PSYCHOLOGY AND DYNAMICS OF CLASSROOM CLIMATE

When we refer to a classroom's emotional "climate," we are talking about the overall psychological tone of a classroom, that amorphous and pervasive feeling that one quickly experiences after being in the room for only a short while. Although it is not easily measured objectively, it is something we can easily sense or subjectively feel. In one classroom, we sense an air of tension. Interactions are cautious and measured. In another classroom, we pick up an air of excitement. Interactions seem spontaneous and free. In a continual cycle of action and reaction, teacher and students simultaneously affect, and are affected by, the emotional climate they create. In this sense, each classroom creates its own ecological system, which is basically an outgrowth of the interrelationships among the persons involved and the social-emotional-intellectual environment spawned from their interactions.

Informally Assessing Classroom Climate: Questions to Ask

Because a classroom's interpersonal climate is constructed largely of feelings, affective tones, and nonverbal messages, it is difficult to know what to look for when trying to assess the emotional frequencies being transmitted. Schmuck and Schmuck (1992) have suggested that a classroom's climate can be diagnosed informally by observing such things as physical movement, gestures, seating arrangements, and patterns of verbal interaction.

There are specific questions to keep in mind that can serve as diagnostic guides when sizing up classroom climate: How do students orient themselves in relation to the teacher; do they stand close or keep a distance? Do students seem physically at ease or are they tight and tense? How often do you see signs of warmth and caring, such as smiles, touching, pats on the back, or verbal praise? Do students walk freely and easily from one spot to another in the room, or do they seem hesitant and cautious? How do students relate to one another; are they somewhat distant and formal, or do they interact freely and laugh spontaneously? Are classrooms neatly organized with everything in place, or are there obvious signs of persons (perhaps even messy ones) living and learning there? What about the seating arrangement; if chairs are movable, are they all facing the front, toward the teacher, or are they arranged in a semicircle or in small, group clusters? Does the seating arrangement shift from time to time, or does it remain the same regardless of the learning activity? Do students look happy and alive, or do they seem sullen, bored, and indifferent?

Pay attention to faces and movement. Happy, excited faces smile a lot. When restless or bored, students tend to slouch, and to drape themselves on their chairs or desks; when excited and involved, their postures are more erect and firm. There are a myriad of cues that can tell us a great deal about the collective feelings of the students we teach, and the emotional climate that those feelings are creating.

14.1 What Has Your Experience Taught You?

From your experience as a student, what four or five considerations come to mind when thinking about factors that most affect whether a classroom has a positive or negative emotional climate? Who contributes the most to that climate—the students, the teacher, or both about equally?

Just as there are particular characteristics of teachers and students that contribute to a classroom's climate, so, too, are there characteristics intrinsic to classrooms that affect climate factors, an idea we turn to next.

Classroom Properties that Affect Climate Factors

Regardless of the manner in which students are organized for learning, or what type of approach to learning is favored by a teacher, classrooms, by virtue of their purpose and function, have distinctive properties affecting each person in them. Doyle (1986) has described six properties in particular that are part of the backdrop affecting the group dynamics of every classroom.

First, classrooms are *multidimensional.* Various activities, involving various groups of students, might be occurring at the same time; meaning that a large number of individuals reflecting individual differences in abilities, goals, and preferences must share available resources, including the teacher, alternately interacting and working quietly, completing assignments, using and reusing materials, and so forth. In addition, there are ongoing actions and reactions. For example, calling on high-ability students might spark their interest, but discourage low-ability students, who might feel "out of it."

Second, there is the related feature of *simultaneity;* that is, many things are happening at the same time. If you are explaining a concept to puzzled students, you must also pay attention to signs of whether or not they understand, decide whether or not Betty's and Joan's whisperings are going too far (and consider how to handle the situation), respond to a call from the principal's office, and decide what to do about Steve, who took Phil's book and refuses to return it. The multidimensionality of a classroom's structure means that many events will be happening simultaneously.

A third characteristic, *immediacy,* has to do with the usually hectic pace of classroom life. Not only is a lot going on, but it is going on quickly. Research (Jackson, 1968) has shown that elementary school teachers can have as many as 1000 interactions in a single day, which is approximately 200 interactions (interruptions, intercessions, and interventions would fit here, too) an hour for the five or so hours that teachers and students are together. Secondary school teachers might have fewer interactions, but they interact with a greater *number* of students—as many as 150—on any given day. Thus, not only are there various types of activities occurring simultaneously, but they are going on at a rather rapid rate.

In this machine-gun-like hum of activity it is not surprising that many classroom happenings are *unpredictable,* which is a fourth characteristic. Even the best laid plans are subject to the unexpected; a film breaks in the middle of an interesting instructional movie, a student gets sick during an exam, two students get into a squabble outside your window while your students are discussing their homework assignment, and so forth.

The manner in which teachers handle these unexpected intrusions is observed and judged by all, because classrooms are *public,* a fifth characteristic of classroom groups. Students—and parents for that matter—are forever evaluating and judging a teacher's behavior. Is the teacher fair? Is there favoritism? Is the teacher too tough or too easy? What happens when discipline is needed?

Finally, classrooms have *histories.* Insofar as a particular classroom group is together for regular periods, it develops a shared sense of itself over time. The meaning of what happens today depends in part on what happened yesterday or last week. If today is the first time the class has had trouble settling down to work, this will no doubt be handled differently than if it were the tenth time in two weeks. In addition, the history of the first few weeks of a new school year or term will have an effect—positive or negative—from that time on.

You can perhaps see why these characteristics of a classroom group are an inherent part of every group, regardless of who the teacher or students might be. Understanding and accepting the reality of these characteristics is the first step toward planning constructive responses to the shifting tides of classroom mood and dynamics.

14.2 How Would You Describe the Differences?

How would you depict the classroom climate in which you feel most comfortable, open, and receptive. What about the climate in which you feel most tentative and guarded? How would you describe the major differences between these classrooms?

A Teacher's Personal Style Affects Group Behavior

The type of emotional climate that evolves in a classroom and the type of "personality" it reflects, depend not only on the students and how well their particular mix of backgrounds and experiences blends together, but very much on the teacher and the type of leadership style he or she projects in everyday behavior (Hamachek, 1978; Joyce and Weil, 1980; Raviv, Raviv, and Reisel, 1990).

For better or worse, the teacher occupies a central position as the leader of the class. How a class behaves as a group, or how it feels about itself, depends on how the teacher handles his or her role. For example, in a detailed series of classroom observations, Anderson and his co-workers (Anderson and Brewer, 1946; Anderson, Brewer, and Reed, 1946) found that emotional chain reactions can be set in motion by particular teacher behaviors. Where a teacher relied heavily on dominating techniques, there were more signs of interpersonal conflict. However, where more cooperation-evoking methods were used, spontaneity and social contributions were more frequent. Moreover, the longer a class was with a teacher, the greater was the effect of that teacher on students. In addition, it was found that when a class changed teachers, the conditions disappeared, only to be replaced by the mood established by the new teacher.

Climate Variables Affect Learning—for Better or Worse

A classroom's emotional climate can make a big difference in how students perform academically, and adjust socially, within a school environment. Research indicates that classroom climate affects not only how much is learned, but also how long learning lasts and how much future learning there is likely to be (Anderson, 1982; Brookover et al., 1978; Ehman, 1980; Fraser and Fisher, 1982). Negative, sullen, or passive emotional climates usually dampen enthusiasm for current learning, and decrease ambition for future learning. Conversely, warm, stimulating, interpersonal classroom relations not only facilitate current learning, but foster positive attitudes toward future learning.

Authoritarian Classrooms Might Produce More, But at a Price

Research shows rather clearly that groups or classrooms that are run in an authoritarian manner produce more products or attain higher achievements than less authoritarian-run groups (Anderson, 1982; Rosenbaum and Rosenbaum, 1971; White and Lippitt, 1968). This fact is sometimes cited by those who favor a more authoritarian approach to teaching. "The way to get results is to get tough," is the way one high school teacher I know expressed it. What this teacher overlooked was another significant finding. Although group/class members from an authoritarian climate might produce more, they are also likely to have negative attitudes about their experiences—an important consideration for any teacher to consider when deciding what type of social-emotional climate to foster. Although participants in more democratic groups tend to be "outproduced," they are usually judged by experimenters and observers to show a much greater degree of creativity in their work and finished products. A tough, autocratic climate might encourage (and even demand) greater productivity in terms of number of tasks completed, but apparently a more democratic we-spirited climate is the most conducive of those feelings of safety and acceptance that allow a student to take the personal risks necessary to do things that are creative and different. Actually, it is not an either/or choice. Sometimes it is necessary to be more authoritarian and directive, particularly when a specific task is to be accomplished or a deadline met. In general, the more specific the assignment (e.g., preparing for an exam, writing a particular type of paper, completing a task in a specific way), the more your students will both want, and expect, direct, focused instructions. However, there are times when it is appropriate and necessary to be more democratic and open-ended. The more unspecific the task (e.g., planning a class party, talking over options for paper assignments, discussing class rules, brainstorming ideas following a lecture or film), the more your students will both appreciate and generally expect more latitude and freedom.

An important implication of research related to authoritarian-democratic methods is that the teacher or leader is a very important variable in determining the social-emotional climate of the group or classroom. We need to be cautious, however, not to overgeneralize the results.

For example, not all authoritarian classroom climates are destructive and harmful. It is possible to lean toward a more authoritarian teaching style in terms of firmness, strict discipline, and careful structure, without necessarily being an angry despot hungry for power. Many fine teachers are authoritarian in their methods, but warm and interpersonally responsive in their styles. A successful class, in terms of attitudes and accomplishments, can exist within an authoritarian framework, but only if the emotional tone of the class includes such qualities as acceptance, caring, and mutual respect between teacher and student.

14.3 What Is Your Experience with Authoritarian Classrooms?

Have you been a student in an authoritarian classroom in which the teacher was tough and autocratic, but lacked the warmth and interpersonal skills necessary to balance that? Have you had experiences with teachers who were authoritarian in their manner, but still managed to be warm and receptive? How do you find yourself affected by teachers in either case?

Performance Improves When Decision Making Is Shared

Students are most receptive to, and productive in, classroom climates in which they can influence decision making and operation policies (Anderson, 1982; Schmuck and Schmuck, 1992). In a democratic society, it is not surprising to find that the satisfaction of group members in organizations such as industry, business, and voluntary enterprises is also related to the degree to which they can influence decision making (Forsyth, 1990; Wofford, 1982). It is not surprising that teachers, too, are found to report their greatest satisfaction and highest morale when they work for principals who are democratic and interpersonally responsive (Blumberg and Greenfield, 1980; Davis and Thomas, 1989).

A major finding that grows from these studies is that a positive working climate is one in which the leadership functions are well distributed and where there are opportunities for all participants to feel some sense of power and self-worth in accomplishing tasks and working together.

14.4 How Do You See Yourself?

Do you see yourself as the type of person who is able to allow others to share in decisions that have to be made, or are you accustomed to making decisions on your own without much consultation? Can you picture yourself talking comfortably and easily with your students about, for example, disciplinary policies, and allowing them to have a voice in the making of these policies, or do you see yourself sitting quietly in the background with students making all of the decisions? What do you feel would be desirable to change in your own behavior that would make you a better teacher when it comes to decision making?

What Good Teachers Do to Create a Positive Classroom Climate

A positive climate is one that involves many opportunities for student participation and involvement. Schmuck (1966), for example, studied twenty-seven classrooms and found that the teachers with the most positive social climates tended to encourage cooperative classroom work more than other teachers. Indeed, positive-climate teachers were more inclined than those with less positive classroom climates to view sound teaching practices as including *both* academic learning and personality development. Consistent with this attitude, teachers with more positive classroom climates mentioned almost twice as many mental health conditions important to their teaching as the other teachers, and, not surprisingly, were more sensitive to conditions that contributed to a positive classroom climate.

It is also worth noting that teachers with more positive climates attended to, and talked with, a larger number of students compared with the other teachers. Teachers with less positive climates tended to call on fewer students for classroom participation and paid little attention to slower, less-involved students. Positive-climate teachers were more likely to reward individual students with such statements as, "John, you've done a very nice job," or "Good work, Jill." They also tended to control class disruptions by making general statements aimed at the total group, such as, "Class, it's really difficult for us to concentrate on what we have to do when there is all this noise." Low-positive-climate teachers, however, tended not only to reward less, but to publicly punish individual students for deviant behavior. (This particular strategy might bring about some peace and quiet, but the cost is usually high in student hostility and alienation toward the teacher.) Generally, positive-climate teachers were good listeners, good empathizers, high rewarders, and were fair with students and generous with positive feedback to all.

INTERPERSONAL ATTRACTION PATTERNS AND THEIR EFFECT ON GROUP CLIMATE

As has been discussed throughout this volume, teaching and learning involve interpersonal processes, sometimes of a very intense nature. When these processes occur, they are affected by the relationships among students, and between students and teachers. How students and teachers feel about each other, how students handle their own peer relations, and who is attracted to whom, are all cogs in the machinery of a dynamic teaching/learning environment.

Interpersonal attraction patterns in classrooms develop in systematic ways, and are influenced by at least four specific factors, which include: (1) intelligence, (2) physical characteristics, (3) mental health characteristics, and (4) teacher behavior. Let's turn our attention to how each of these works.

Intelligence: Attractiveness Reduced When Too Smart or Not Smart Enough

Research shows that one's intelligence, or lack of it, makes a difference as far as acceptance or rejection by peers is concerned. This is particularly true at the extreme ends of the intelligence range. Sadly, mentally retarded students in normal classrooms are usually the ones most severely rejected by their peer group (Johnson and Johnson, 1980a; Johnson and Johnson, 1980b). At the other end of the continuum, Hallahan and Kauffman's (1982) review of research has shown that highly intelligent, conformist students rank high among those who are socially accepted. This is not, however, as likely to be true for intelligent students who are creative but nonconformist. Apparently, considerable social risk is involved in being perceived as either too slow and different, or too smart and different. Nonconformity, especially when it is unexplained and not well understood, is usually an uncomfortable and threatening experience to others. It is worth noting that teachers, too, are among those who rank intelligent, creative students low on the social-acceptance scale.

Research also shows that among students who are socially rejected, there is likely to be a significant discrepancy between intelligence and performance (Berscheid, 1986). What this means is that socially rejected average or above-average students tend to do less well academically than students of comparable intelligence who are socially accepted. Rejection lowers self-esteem, which, in turn, lowers confidence, and this, in turn, can leave students with a feeling of inadequacy and worthlessness that might generalize to their schoolwork. Actually, it is difficult to know which comes first, low performance or low social-acceptance. The most we can say is that an interaction effect results in lowered self-esteem and increased feelings of alienation toward school.

Intelligence, then, is one factor that influences group processes because it affects who likes whom in the classroom. Physical appearance is another.

14.5 What Can You Learn from Your High School Experiences?

When you think back to your high school days, what do you remember about how certain students were treated by their peers and teachers, especially those who got very high grades and those with much lower grades? What does that teach you about the possible connection between intelligence and interpersonal attractiveness?

Physical Characteristics: Attractive Students Have an Edge

We do not have to go any further than our own personal experiences to know that various body types and physical characteristics elicit various feelings, attitudes, and stereotypes in us. Although physical appearance is often considered to be a superficial variable, a great deal of research clearly shows that it is an important factor in forming impressions of others, in making friends, in choosing dating partners, and in selecting marriage partners (Duck, 1977; Hamachek, 1992; Herman, Zanna, and Higgins, 1986).

Responding to others on the basis of appearance is a process that begins early. A case in point is research by Staffieri (1957), who found that boys as young as 6 and as old as 10 years of age are already in close agreement when it comes to assigning specific personality characteristics to particular body types. For instance, there was a remarkably similar tendency for endomorphic types (i.e., heavy for size and frame) to be described as socially offensive and delinquent; mesomorphic types (i.e., muscular, neither too heavy nor too thin) as aggressive, outgoing, active, and having leadership skills; and ectomorphic types (i.e., lean and thin) as retiring, nervous, shy, and introverted. It was also found that ectomorphs were least popular. It is interesting to note that even though this research was done years ago, the stereotypes associated with various body types are as strong now as they were in 1957.

Startling as it might seem, research also suggests that even nursery-school children are responsive to the physical attributes of their peers (Langlois, 1986). The clearest result emerging from this research was that physically unattractive boys were judged to be more aggressive than their more attractive counterparts. In addition, when children were asked to name classmates who "scared them," they tended to nominate unattractive children.

It is not surprising that what is true for younger children and youths is also true for adults. Research shows, for example, that we are more affected by physically attractive persons than by physically unattractive persons, and unless we are specifically abused by them, we tend to like them better (Chaiken, 1986). In addition, this research shows that, as a general rule, attractive persons tend to receive more favorable treatment than less attractive persons. This is an interpersonal process that begins at a very young age. The disquieting aspect of this evidence is that there is a strong possibility that such preferential treatment is the beginning of a cycle of self-fulfilling prophecy. If persons are treated poorly (or well, as the case might be), this treatment affects how they perceive themselves and how they feel about their personal qualities. Thus, unattractive children might come to think of themselves as unlovable, or, at least, as undesirable, if they are continually treated in negative, rejecting ways. Ultimately, they might begin to behave in a style that is consistent with this self-concept, a way that is consistent with how they were treated initially.

As teachers, we need to keep an eye on our own student preferences so that we are not caught in the trap of believing, either consciously or unconsciously, that only that that is beautiful is good.

14.6 Have You Been Swayed by Certain Students?

You might find it instructive to reflect back on experiences you have had with children and/or adolescents and think about how you have responded to those you have perceived as attractive or intelligent, or not so, as the case might be. Remember, we are not always conscious of the biases influencing our responses to particular types of persons. Do you see any signs of your favoring bright or attractive children? How can you use this awareness in your work as a teacher?

Mental Health Attributes: Well-Adjusted Students Tend To Be Favored

Peer-group acceptance is also influenced by the psychological adjustment of individual students. This area has been thoroughly researched, and the results point to rather significant relationships between being rejected by peers on the one hand, and poor interpersonal adjustment on the other hand (Schmuck and Schmuck, 1992). For example, socially rejected youths tend to exhibit more behavioral symptoms typically associated with poor mental health. That is, they are more likely to be overly aggressive and withdrawn, listless and unhealthy, emotionally unstable, or some combination of these characteristics.

Generally, it appears that peer-group acceptance and mental health are highly related; the greater the degree of psychological imbalance, the more likely that such a student will be rejected. Teachers can help reduce the intensity of the rejection process, if not ammeliorate it altogether, by giving public emotional support to those students who need it most. One way of doing this is to make an extra effort to praise uncertain and emotionally wavering students when they do something of note in class, be it no more than a brief comment in a group discussion. Another way is to appoint less-accepted students to groups or committees and see to it that they have specific responsibilities or tasks to conduct. An objective here would be to make it very apparent that the student is *valued*, so that not only he or she knows it, but also that others in the class know it. Students tend to value and appreciate those persons and activities that they perceive the teacher as valuing and appreciating. Teachers can make a big difference in peer-group relationships, an idea we turn to next.

Teacher Preferences: Students Tend To Like Whom Teachers Like

We have suggested that teachers can help reduce the intensity of peer rejections, if not reverse them altogether, by giving public emotional support to those students who need it most. The possibility of this happening has been demonstrated experimentally. For example, Flanders and Havumaki (1960) designed a simple, but clever, experiment in which they instructed teachers to respond positively and consistently to select students and not to others. They had teachers interact with, and praise, only those students in odd-numbered seats; in comparison groups all students were encouraged to speak and the teachers' praise was directed to the entire class. In the first situation, students in the odd-numbered seats, who received most teacher recognition, later received more "liking" votes from their peers than did students in even-numbered seats. This was not true in the comparison groups, in which, teachers made an effort to encourage and praise all students. In these groups, positive peer choices were spread around more evenly, indicating greater general acceptance no matter where one sat.

Schmuck and Schmuck's (1992) review of teacher preference research pointed to the following three consistent findings:

1. When teachers behave in a consistently positive manner toward students who are initially rejected by their peers, within several months these rejected students are more widely accepted by their peer group.

2. Teachers with the most supportive peer groups tend to reward their students with specific comments about their helpful behaviors, and tend to control disruptions with general, group-oriented statements. (It is the difference between saying something such as, "Mitch, Mary, now stop that right now," and saying, "O.K. gang, it's getting a bit noisy—let's settle down." In the first instance, students are picked out and, perhaps later, picked on by their classmates. In the second instance, no one is singled out, but the message is conveyed nonetheless.)

3. Students who are seen as liked by a teacher are more likely to have high status among their peers, and those who are disapproved of by a teacher are more likely to have low status. A word of caution: We should not conclude from this that all it takes for rejection to be reversed for students rejected by their peers is for a teacher to like them. As teachers, we have to translate our positive feelings into actual behaviors. For example, we can speak more positively and affirmatively to particular peer-rejected students, we can give them special responsibilities and publicly praise them for carrying through, and we can make a special effort to recognize their efforts in class. Whom a teacher likes affects whom others like, especially if the teacher is someone the students like and respect. As teachers, we are models in many ways, not the least of which is as a model for who likes whom in our classrooms.

14.7 Can You Think of Some Exceptions?

Human behavior is too complex for there not to be exceptions to any general rule, and what we have just talked about is no exception. Sometimes students who are obviously liked by teachers are *not* liked by their peers. Thinking back on your own experience, when is this likely to happen? What reasons can you think of to explain these times?

CLASSROOM NORMS: THEIR DEVELOPMENT AND EXPRESSION

By definition, group norms are principles of right and wrong, of what is proper and acceptable, that members of a group agree to use as guides to control or regulate behavior. Norms help group members know what is right and wrong. Without such guideposts, group processes can be both confusing and chaotic. When classroom groups behave predictably it is largely because of their adherence to group norms. The existence of norms is important for another reason. When students know what the rules are, they can help monitor one another's behavior. In this way, the group contributes to its own stability.

When talking about a definition of norms, we must also emphasize the idea of sharing. The psychological counterpart of a norm is an attitude, which is a predisposition to think, feel, and act in specific ways in particular circumstances. Thus, norms are individuals' attitudes that are shared in a group.

Norms can be either *static* or *dynamic,* depending on the degree of active interpersonal exchanges, and either *formal* or *informal,* depending on how traditional they are.

Static norms consist of the basic, unconscious culture of groups. These are the norms that people respond to as a matter of course, and take more or less for granted. For example, the shared expectation that all students will have their own tennis shoes for physical education, or their own textbooks for class, is a formal, static norm in most schools. This is not questioned by students, or anyone else, and remains unchanged over time.

Norms of greater interest to the teacher are dynamic and informal. These are norms that can, and indeed do, change; they usually depend for their existence less on tradition and more on the personal style of the teacher and the particular class he or she instructs. In most classrooms, for instance, the existing norm for test taking is each person for him- or herself. Looking at another's paper or talking are definitely not acceptable. If a student tells the teacher that someone is cheating, or if the teacher intercepts a note passed from one student to the next, both informant and teacher are actively supporting the maintenance of a shared norm through their interpersonal influence. In other classrooms, however, talking is not discouraged during examination periods, but encouraged as a valuable learning activity. For instance, during the exam periods of a ninth-grade English teacher I know, students and teacher have agreed that not only is talking all right, but so, too, is looking at notes and books. These exams are like take-home exams except that they are written in class. This procedure would obviously not work if either the teacher or the majority of students were opposed to it.

Norms, then, are group agreements that help direct the course of group processes. They influence how people view things (i.e., their perceptions), how they think about things (i.e., their cognitions), how they feel about things (i.e., their evaluations), and how they act (i.e., their behavior). Each factor plays a part in building the overall norm structure of a classroom. Let's briefly examine how each functions.

Perceptual Norms: Guidelines for What To Believe

Through our perceptual processes we derive meaning from our sensory experiences. Perception research tells us that persons behave in a manner consistent with what they believe to be true, irrespective of what the facts might be (Combs, Richards, and Richards, 1988; Goleman, 1985; Zebrowitz, 1990). It sometimes happens in a group that perception is a straightforward process in which most persons agree with what they see. Many times, however, individual group members differ widely on the meaning they attach to a particular experience. Furthermore, groups, classroom groups in our case, can have a decided effect on the way in which individual students interpret their perceptions.

For instance, if a tenth-grade student who has positive views about a particular teacher hears large numbers of other students describe that teacher negatively, he or she might begin to question his or her initial perceptions. Evidence from group dynamics research indicates that when an individual's personal perceptions deviate from those held by the group as a whole, he or she will tend to change his or her perceptions in the direction of the existing group norms (Forsyth, 1990). Thus, through a process of interpersonal influence, perceptual norms are established, and students are affected psychologically.

The typical classroom, with its vast array of sensory inputs, experiences many ambiguous and unclear events. At the beginning of a school year, particularly, the teacher figures prominently among the many unknowns of the classroom. It is precisely because a teacher has so much power—at least from students' point of view—that he or she is an especially important figure in the development of perceptual norms. What is the teacher like? Will she be tough? Can she be trusted? Will she be consistent? Will she be fair? Beginning with the first day of class, students consciously and unconsciously attach meanings to their perceptions of a teacher's behavior. Not infrequently, students bring from previous experiences negative attitudes toward active participation in class. If a teacher says that he really values participation and hopes that everyone will feel free to speak openly, this is likely to be met with a great deal of initial suspicion. Is he for real? Can I really speak my mind? If the teacher, in fact, does allow different, and even hostile, points of view to be expressed, and behaves in a nondefensive manner toward offerings clearly different from his own leanings, he will go a long way toward encouraging a perceptual norm that says, "He can be trusted; he does mean what he says."

Cognitive Norms: Consensus About What Is Important

The overall academic and intellectual tone of a classroom is determined to a large extent by the types of cognitive norms by which a group abides. It is not coincidence that the intellectual and social development of students occurs more effectively when the expressed educational goals of the school and the basic cognitive norms of the peer group are reasonably consistent. One situation that has always created conflict is when a school places such strong emphasis on academic achievement and the preparation of students for the future that it forgets that students need immediate relevance and satisfaction. During a group discussion related to the "goals of education," a high school student expressed one of the existing conflicts in cognitive norms in the following way:

> Look, I think a basic disagreement my friends and I have with the educational system (specifically, he was referring to his high school) is that it talks about where we're supposed to be before we're even done with understanding what where we are now all means. I mean, we keep talking about all the things we have to know to get along in tomorrow's world. How about today's world? There are a lot of things we don't understand completely about that, you know. Our social studies teacher is a good example. He keeps talking about how important it is to know about our social system so we can survive in it and make a good living. Heck, I'd like to know a little more about the social system of our own city so I can find a job this summer.

This student was saying what many students say: Recognize my needs for what they are and acknowledge their existence. Point me toward the future and encourage my awareness of it, but don't push me out of the relevancy of my own time and needs.

Of course, a conflict in cognitive norms can occur in the other direction, too. For example, a recent article in a major metropolitan newspaper revealed that the principal of a large school system was about to be ousted from his job because he was "too lax in stressing academic goals" as important educational objectives. Even the president of the senior class, acting as a spokesman for his peers, suggested that the principal was "too permissive in his academic philosophy." As with most extreme positions in life, radical stances regarding the importance of this or that educational philosophy run the heavy risk of conflicting with more moderate positions.

One of the most serious conflicts at this time between peer norms and school goals relates to students' role in decision making. More and more, educational technology allows for individualization of instruction. With the assistance of the computer, class schedules can be aligned with individual interests, and curriculum materials can be made more diverse and individualized than ever before. Indeed, schools from the elementary level through high school are finding that students themselves can be used as tutors (Cohen and Kulik, 1982).

However, it is often the case that the cognitive norms are not present to support this type of instructional design in a peer group. All sorts of questions arise. Should students work separately or with adults? To what extent should students and teachers work together in establishing new instructional procedures and curriculum innovations? When new ways evolve, old expectations and rules do not work. Only through ongoing, open discussions, and by arriving at public, group agreements, can such cognitive norms be established.

Evaluative Norms: Criteria for Judgments

Evaluative norms deal with the "goodness" or "badness" of an event or experience. They are norms that members of a group use to judge one another in positive or negative ways. Evaluative norms can vary from one peer group to another. For example, in one peer group, smoking, drinking, and acting out in class might be accepted and even encouraged, while in another group these activities are frowned upon. Whereas cognitive norms are primarily intellectual and static, and involve little intense feeling, evaluative norms are emotionally charged, dynamic, and constantly changing. If, for example, students rush pell mell out of a room at dismissal time and this is taken more or less for granted by the teacher and other students, even though no one likes it, this represents a cognitive norm. There are no active attempts to change that behavior. An evaluative norm is at work when students burst out of their seats and either the teacher or other students advise them to cool it, or in some other way, criticize this behavior. It is judged to be wrong.

As with cognitive norms, it is important that evaluative norms be shared and discussed throughout the school year so that both teachers and students are clear about what constitutes the basic framework for positive self-other feelings and healthy interpersonal relationships. Few things cannot be discussed by a group as far as its evaluations of behavior are concerned. These can range all the way from gum chewing to decisions about whether or not talking during study period is to be allowed, to whether or not it is okay to interrupt when a teacher is talking. When students know what the evaluative norms are, they can be responsible for the consequences of their behavior.

Behavioral Norms: Expectations for Behavior

Behavioral norms serve two functions: (1) they guide a person's actions through a complex psychological network that simultaneously involves perceptual, cognitive, and evaluative norms; and (2) they serve as a barometer indicating the degree of conformity demanded by those in one's immediate social environment.

Interesting work has been done to show how group pressure operates to influence an individual's behavior by making him aware of the group's norms for appropriate or inappropriate behavior. In a famous experiment, Asch (1956) assembled 50 groups, each consisting of eight male college students, and asked them to match the length of a line presented on the board to one of three other lines of varying lengths. Each member was asked to declare his judgment orally for each of 12 different trials. The experimental catch was that all members of each group, except one participant, were instructed to give the wrong answer. Thus, one person in each group was confronted by a situation in which his eyes told him one thing while other group members were telling him another. One-third of the subjects, called, in this instance, *yielders*, conformed to the groups' wrong answers about half of the time. Information from postexperiment interviews suggested that very few of the yielders distorted their perceptions; almost all gave in to avoid standing out and being different. As one yielder expressed it, "I knew I was probably right and the other wrong, but I just didn't want to run the risk of being wrong myself."

14.8 Which Behavior Norms Affect You?

Look about and you will see examples of behavioral norms all over the place. For example, what are the behavioral norms for dress at your school? Is wide diversity of dress style accepted, or is there a more specified mode into which most students fit? How does your own dress style conform to the behavioral norm in this regard? What are the behavioral norms in the various classes you might be taking? Are some classes vocal and interactive? Are others more quiet and passive? How did these norms develop? Do you usually conform to these norms? What would happen if you did not?

Asch's (1956) experiment helps us to understand some of the dynamics of behavioral conformity in schools. As it sometimes happens, students do not completely internalize peer-group norms to the extent that perceptions, cognitions, or feelings are modified. Consequently, they might conform to group standards in order to not appear different or risk being rejected. Even defiant students can conform in ways that do not involve a deep personal commitment. As a ninth-grade boy with something less than a positive attitude toward school expressed it: "The teacher wants me to get my homework in—I will get it in. She wants me to do a paper by Friday—I will do it. But that does not mean I am going to learn anything."

As with other dimensions of the norm structure of a classroom, about the only viable way to arrive at behavioral norms that include the best thinking of both students and teacher is through open, public communication involving the entire class. Under conditions such as this, a teacher can encourage students to discuss circumstances in which superficial allegiance to behavioral pressures keeps them from being effective. As an example of how this works, consider the following excerpt from a paper written by Smith (1991), an eleventh-grade English teacher:

> I had developed the idea that at least one book report per week would be a good idea to help my students develop their writing skills. They all did, although some grumbled a lot. As you might suspect, some reports were better or worse than others, but I guess I expected that. The thing that really got me was when I got wind of what five of my best students were doing. Apparently, each of them took turns being responsible for reading the short story assigned for the week and then wrote a brief outline of it which the other four used as a basis for writing their report. Well, I felt pretty angry at first, but then I got to thinking that maybe my assignment wasn't as interesting as I thought it might be to all students. So, rather than confront the five with what I knew they were doing (and also keeping in mind that there were probably others who were fudging on the assignment while leading me to believe they were digging it), I asked the whole class during one of our open discussion periods to share ideas about projects which could either supplement or replace our weekly book reports.
>
> I never got so many ideas in my life. Some students really enjoyed reading the short stories and writing reports, but others—including the five I originally heard about—had other suggestions that were all the way from writing their own short stories and having others review them, to volunteer oral reports in class (rather than written).
>
> When the discussion was over it was clear that the students would still be reading and writing, which is what I wanted them to do in the first place, but now the standards for what was acceptable were sufficiently broad and encompassing enough to include every student in the class.

This teacher intuitively recognized that what is shared constitutes the essence of its normality, and rather than indignantly confronting the five fudging students, whose behavior was only superficially satisfying the goals of the assignment, she wisely utilized the best of not only her ideas, but of the entire class. The teacher put into practice what group-dynamics research has been saying for a long time: When group members participate in the establishment of group norms and are helped to feel important and valued by the group, they are willing to support both its structure and its goals (Schmuck and Schmuck, 1992). Out of the norm structure of a classroom emerges another dimension—cohesiveness.

14.9 How Will You Develop Norms for Your Classes?

Basically, norms are shared expectations for how participants of a classroom should perceive, think, feel, and behave. They influence the perceptions, cognitions, evaluations, and behaviors of the individual members of the class. What ways can you think of that you and your students could use to develop positive norms in the four areas we've just discussed? Perhaps you can remember teachers you had who were particularly adept at working with students in developing the norms for their classrooms. How did they do it? What part did you play?

COHESIVENESS: A GROUP'S INTERPERSONAL GLUE

Classes can vary enormously with respect to the unity and the amount of togetherness and friendliness exhibited by the students and the teacher. Why, for example, do the members of one sixth-grade class work better together, seem happier, and show more enthusiasm for doing their schoolwork than do the members of a sixth-grade class who come along the following year? What underlying dynamics are responsible for creating enormous group spirit among hundreds of high school youths who, in spite of only casual, sometimes indifferent, and even distant relationships, are nonetheless capable of behaving as a spirited, coordinated unit at a Friday night basketball game?

What It Means To Be a Cohesive Group

Many group-dynamics phenomena are at work in each of the two previously mentioned instances, and one that makes a very large difference in whether or not a classroom group—or any other group for that matter—comes together is its *cohesiveness*. Specifically, cohesiveness has to do with the feelings that class members hold about the classroom group as a whole. It differs from the topic of attraction because of its emphasis on each student's relationship to the group rather than on his or her relationships with specific members, subgroups, or the teacher. Whereas norms refer to shared attitudes about objects and behaviors important to the classroom group, cohesiveness has more to do with relations to group members.

A literal definition of cohesiveness is the tendency to stick together or to be in accord. A cohesive classroom group is characterized by students who are actively involved with one another, who care about one another, and who help one another. Some typical responses of students from a cohesive classroom are: "I really enjoy going to class," "I know my contributions count when I make them," and "The kids in that class are really fun to be with." The question is: What determines the degree of cohesiveness in a classroom group? Let's turn to what research says about this.

14.10 What Does Your Experience Teach You About Group Cohesiveness?

Stop a moment and consider any group of which you are a member that is important to you. What are the forces that keep that group together? What is it that makes it a cohesive group? How are your feelings about being a member of that group influenced by its cohesiveness? What do you do to contribute to its cohesiveness?

Dispersed Friendship and Power Foster Cohesiveness

One basic antecedent to high positive classroom cohesiveness is a relatively wide dispersion of friendship relations among class members. Schmuck (1966), for example, found that classrooms with diffusely structured friendship patterns were more cohesive than classes in which friendship structures were more centralized. The closer and more cohesive classes were those in which most students had at least one or two friends. The less cohesive classes were those in which only a few students were highly liked, in which some were strongly rejected, and in which most were not chosen at all as friends by other students.

For the most part, the more clearly a classroom group labels particular students as popular or unpopular, the less likely it is that the group will function as a unit, work cooperatively under stress (as in preparation for an exam), and behave in friendly ways toward one another. Research into these matters strongly suggests that when there is a wide dispersion of influence, power, and friends, a classroom is likely to be more attractive to students and, as a natural outgrowth, more cohesive (Schmuck and Schmuck, 1992).

As teachers, we can encourage such a dispersion of friendships and power by: (1) paying more obvious attention to students who seem to be lower on the social totem pole (remembering the point made earlier—whom a teacher likes influences whom others like); and (2) giving students with lower social status more status by having them do special things (e.g., appointing them to the patrol force, if in elementary school, giving them special responsibilities as chairperson of a committee, or having them make a special report to the class on a particular subject).

High-Affiliation Teachers Discourage Cohesiveness

A teacher can influence the cohesiveness of a class in still another way. Walberg (1968), for example, found that teachers with a high need for affiliation (i.e., a high need to have friends and to be around persons), tended to have classes with low internal cohesiveness among students. One possible explanation for this is the amount of time a high-need-affiliation teacher spends with students. This is the sort of teacher who might so monopolize the affective behavior of a class that students spend more time relating to the teacher than to one another. If this is true, then students' opportunities for interacting with one another and for developing into a more cohesive, "together" class are minimized.

High-Autonomy Teachers Encourage Cohesiveness

Two other investigations have found that teachers with greater need of autonomy (i.e., the need to be somewhat independent of others, and to feel relatively free to be one's own person without excessive concern about what others are thinking) than need of affiliation, were more likely to have classes that reflected greater intimacy and cohesiveness among students (Anderson, Walberg, and Welch, 1969; Walberg and Welch, 1967). It appears that teachers who are more personally secure and independent are apparently able to allow, and very likely to encourage, more interpersonal interactions among students themselves, a necessary and important condition for the development of classroom cohesiveness. It is perhaps not surprising that if we value autonomy, we will be more comfortable encouraging and allowing students to interact more with one another.

Group-Centered Teachers Foster Involvement

Classroom communication is another antecedent to high group cohesiveness. Frequent interactions among students allow for possibilities of greater cohesiveness to emerge, and minimal interaction generally succeeds in keeping students from getting too highly involved with one another. An interesting early study by Bovard (1956) might help us better understand how various communication patterns influence classroom cohesiveness. In one part of the study, characterized by "group-centered" discussions, students sat in a circle and the teacher participated as a member of the discussion group. In another classroom, called "leadership-centered," the teacher sat in the front of the classroom as the focus of discussion, and most of the interaction consisted of the teacher talking to one student at a time. Interactions in the group-centered discussions were more open and spontaneous, with students more involved and active and the group more cohesive. Communication channels in the leadership-centered group ran primarily through the teacher. What happened was that students seldom talked to one another, were more formal when they did talk, and felt less free to express their ideas and feelings directly. Needless to say, there was little sense of cohesiveness among students in the leadership-centered class.

Group dynamics research has consistently shown that informal, supportive leadership styles, combined with a group-centered format, enhance the possibilities for open communication among group members (Forsyth, 1990; Schmuck and Schmuck, 1992; Shaw, 1981). In this manner, influence is more widely dispersed, a greater number of friendships occur, supportive norms evolve, two-way communication is enhanced, and, from it all, a stronger sense of group unity and cohesiveness emerges as a natural byproduct of a group's having worked together.

There Are Different Kinds of Cohesive Groups

Classroom groups can be described as being cohesive for various reasons. It is possible, for example, for various groups to have various "pulls" on individuals. As an illustration of how this works, Back (1951) arranged to have various pairs of subjects work cooperatively together on a task. The pairs were formed so that they would be either cohesive or noncohesive, with the cohesive pairs arranged in one of three ways: (1) attraction to the group because of a liking for the other member; (2) attraction to the group because of a mutually high interest in the task; and (3) attraction to the group because of its prestige for its members. A major finding was that even though the three types of cohesiveness were distinct, the cohesive groups were more productive, and worked more effectively, than the noncohesive groups.

We can find examples of these three types of cohesiveness in school settings, too. For instance, common interest in an activity or a task is frequently the motivation behind the school's football team or theater group. A liking for other students often serves as the primary cohesion bond for extracurricular clubs, informal get-togethers after school, and, certainly, parties. Prestige is often a powerful motive for the cohesiveness of a basketball squad, a math team, a cheerleader's club, and advanced honors classes. Indeed, it is possible that any group in a school can possess one or more of these motives for cohesiveness, and each gain strength as it incorporates one or more of them. Groups that have fewer bases of cohesiveness work less effectively as a unit.

The sources of attraction for any given group are not necessarily the same for individual students. As an example of this, Schmuck and Schmuck (1992) asked a group of junior high school students, who were very enthusiastic about their local government class, the question, "What do you like most about this government class?" Some of the answers were: "It's interesting to find out how this town operates," "I get to study with my two best friends," "I'm thinking about politics as a career," and "The work is fun to do." Although each response revealed an individual need and several motives for cohesiveness, together they added up to a very cohesive class.

The research findings are clear. Students who are accepted members of a cohesive, reasonably high-morale class with a broadly dispersed friendship structure, have excellent opportunities for working up to their intellectual potential and for enhancing self-esteem.

Implications of Group Cohesiveness for Classroom Life

Based on what group-dynamics research has uncovered about how cohesiveness affects individual behavior and group functioning (Forsyth, 1990; Schmuck and Schmuck, 1992), the following six principles emerge as particularly relevant to our work as classroom teachers:

1. Cohesiveness is an attribute of a group, not of individuals. Feelings of loyalty, membership, closeness, and trust are interactively involved in the development of cohesiveness.
2. Most persons strive to be attractive and likeable to others. Although the degree of affiliation motivation will differ from person to person, most persons look for some degree of friendship in groups of which they are members.

3. Point 2 is important because friendship relationships in classrooms cannot be separated from teaching and learning; they are an intrinsic part of teaching transactions between teachers and students, and among students.
4. Peer-group friendship patterns, which are the basis for cohesive groups, are affected significantly by the instructional behaviors of teachers. For example, teachers who minimize students' interaction among themselves as part of the instructional format have a less cohesive group than teachers who encourage interaction.
5. When students' desires for achievement, power, and affiliation are satisfied through interactions with other group members, their attraction to the classroom group is increased.
6. In classrooms where cohesiveness is high, students' involvement might be high or low depending on the norms of the group. More attention to learning is likely to occur in classes where there is high cohesiveness *and* where norms encourage doing well academically.

CREATING A CLIMATE OF OPEN COMMUNICATION

Some degree of acceptance and warmth in interpersonal relationships is absolutely essential for psychosocial and intellectual growth in a classroom. The need for acceptance is one that begins at birth, and, although it might change in how it expresses itself throughout the maturational process, is a need we have throughout life. When our need for acceptance, which is closely linked to the need to feel adequate or competent, is threatened, our natural tendency is to withdraw, or at least to take some type of defensive measure to parry the threat. In a classroom, this defensive posture is variously reflected in such behaviors as sitting near the back of the room, not participating in class discussions, skipping class, and, as a more extreme reaction, dropping out of school altogether.

As teachers, what can we do to reduce the possibility of these things happening?

14.11 How Do They Do It?

You might find it particularly instructive to watch closely those instructors you have who seem to be good at creating a climate that encourages open communication. What do they do? How do they respond to students? How do they ask questions? How do they involve students? Usually, students feel more free and spontaneous in these classrooms. If you feel this way, *why* do you? What part does the teacher play in your feeling this way? What implications for your own work as a teacher can you derive from your observations?

Make the Emotional Atmosphere a Supportive One

The need for a supportive classroom climate is a critical one if open communication is to exist. The fear of nonsupport and rejection is one of the greatest anxieties typically experiences by class members. Each of us knows from personal experience that some classroom climates make us feel defensive and on guard, while others help us feel safer and more supported. After an intensive study of recordings of discussions occurring in various groups, Gibb (1965) was able to define six pairs of psychological conditions, or categories, that are most frequently associated with defensive or supportive group climates. Behaviors that we perceive as possessing any of the characteristics listed in the left-hand column of Table 14.1 are likely to cause us to feel closed and defensive, whereas behaviors that we perceived as having any of the qualities designated as supportive, help us to be more open and available to another person's ideas and feelings.

As you can see, supportive climates are less judgmental, and more accepting, in nature. Feedback that appears evaluative increases defensiveness. Of course, it does not have to happen that way. If, for example, we perceive the other person as accepting us as an equal, and as simply being helpful and constructive, then the possibility of the message being evaluative might not even occur to us. This same principle is also true of the other five categories of potentially defense-producing climates. The six sets are, in this way, interactive.

How We Respond to Others Makes a Difference

Sometimes, the way we respond to another person turns out to be a real turn-off to him or her, and we might not even be aware of why that individual is suddenly so defensive or is reluctant to say any more to us. Without knowing it, we might have said something quite evaluative or interpretive to that person. As a consequence, our friend feels that we are being judgmental, and the conversation stops.

Table 14.1. CATEGORIES OF BEHAVIOR CHARACTERISTICS OF DEFENSIVE AND SUPPORTIVE CLIMATES

Defensive climates		*Supportive climates*	
1. Evaluation	4. Neutrality	1. Description	4. Empathy
2. Control	5. Superiority	2. Problem orientation	5. Equality
3. Strategy	6. Certainty	3. Spontaneity	6. Provisionalism

Some years ago, Rogers and Roethlisberger (1952) conducted a series of studies on how persons communicate with each other in face-to-face situations. Surprisingly, they found that there were only five basic categories of interpersonal responses, which constituted about 80% of the verbal exchanges between persons. The remaining 20% cut across many individualized responses that were not used frequently enough to be put in a separate category.

From their observations of individuals in a variety of settings—at work, at home, at parties, at conventions, and so forth—five responses kept emerging in the following order of frequency, from most to least used: (1) *advising and evaluating,* (2) *analyzing and interpreting,* (3) *reassuring and supporting,* (4) *questioning and probing,* and (5) *paraphrasing and understanding.* In addition, they found that if a person uses a particular response category as much (or as little) as 40% of the time, then other persons see that persons as *always* responding that way. Actually, the response patterns are, in themselves, neither good nor bad. It is the *overuse* or *underuse* of any particular response pattern that might cause communication handicaps. Each of these response patterns is described below, along with statements illustrating how each might be used in an actual response to another person.

1. *Advising and evaluating:* This response reflects a judgmental, "evaluative" assessment of the relative goodness, appropriateness, effectiveness, or rightness of another person's behavior. One person implies to another how he or she (i.e., the receiver) ought to behave. Examples: "I don't know why you are dating him; he just uses women. And besides, you should be able to do better than that"; "Not only is the format for this paper wrong, it is not even related to our unit of study."

2. *Analyzing and interpreting:* This response reflects an intent to teach, to tell another person what his or her problem "really" means, or to tell him or her how he or she (the other person) "really" feels about the situation. An interpretive response either obviously or subtly tells another person what her behavior means at a deeper level. Examples: "I think the reason you date him is because he is older and this makes you feel more like you're going out with a protecting father"; "You probably wrote this paper the way you did because underneath you feel pretty angry at me and the students in this course."

3. *Reassuring and supporting:* This response reflects an intent to reassure, to pacify, or to reduce another person's intensity of feeling. It helps a person feel more comfortable and less anxious about his or her current circumstances. Examples: "You seem to be concerned about the fact that John is older than you, yet you seem to have a nice time when you're together, don't you?"; "I know that writing papers is difficult for you, but, as you get into it, it may not seem so bad after all."

4. *Questioning and probing:* This response indicates a person's intent to seek further information and to provoke further discussion along a particular line. The speaker implies to the other person that there is something that can be further developed. Examples: "Did you ever think about why it is that the fellows you date always seem so much older than you?"; "Students are motivated for different reasons to choose the topics they do to write about. I wonder what yours was for this paper?"

5. *Paraphrasing and understanding:* The multiple purposes of this response are: (1) to be sure that the listener correctly understands what the sender is saying, (2) to find out how the sender feels about the problem or circumstance, and (3) to find out how the sender sees the problem. Examples: "You feel pretty ambivalent about dating older men, is that it?"; "You've worried about this paper for so long, you're almost afraid to hand it in, right?"

Be Sensitive to the Effects of Different Response Styles

Research tells us that evaluative and interpretive responses are counterproductive in the early phases of a relationship because they leave us with the feeling of being judged and weighed rather than accepted and valued for who we are as individuals (Johnson, 1993).

Conversely, an understanding response is particularly useful in building a positive climate for open communication because it is an open invitation for us to say what we want, and to elaborate and further explore whatever our ideas or feelings are at the moment. An understanding response is also the most helpful for seeing the other person's problem or position from his or her point of view.

Of course, we also have to understand that tone of voice, along with body and facial cues, also communicates acceptance or rejection. Sometimes our voice says one thing, while our nonverbal messages say another. I remember a sixth-grade boy who approached his teacher (a noted grouch, by the way) one day and said, "Mr. Brown, do you like teaching?" Mr. Brown said, sweetly, "Why of course I do," to which the boy replied, "Well, your face does not look like it."

There will be many times when a student tries to discuss something with you that you might not understand. Probing responses might assist you in getting a clear definition of the problem before answering. Supportive responses are useful when another person needs to feel accepted, or when he or she needs support in trying out new behavior that will solve his or her problem. Interpretive responses are sometimes valuable in confronting others with the impact of their behavior on you.

Indeed, both evaluative and interpretive responses, when conveyed within the context of a developed relationship, and when offered with sensitivity, can be powerful stimulants to growth. If done in a friendly manner, both interpretation and evaluation can lead to insight, and insight is the key to deeper understandings and healthier interpersonal relationships.

A key to responding effectively to others, whether it be to our students or other persons in our lives, is to avoid evaluative and interpretive responses, particularly when relationships are new and just developing. This is especially true at the beginning of each school year, term, or semester. As teachers, evaluative and interpretive responses can be used appropriately and constructively under the following conditions: (1) when there is a positive relationship between ourselves and our students (This makes it more possible to see that we are trying to help them clarify their thinking, not trying to attack their personalities); (2) when we need to give students feedback (i.e., evaluation) about how well, or how poorly, they are doing; and (3) when it is necessary to help students understand the possible underlying meanings in their answers or behavior (i.e., interpretive).

14.12 Can You Identify the Responses?

David, a 12-year-old boy, approaches you with a problem. What follows are five possible opening responses to this problem, each of which corresponds to one of the response styles we have just discussed. Can you identify the response category associated with each of the five responses to David's problem?

David: "I'm really worried about that math exam. I almost flunked the last one and my parents will ground me for 2 weeks if I don't get at least a C. They're always comparing me with my stupid brother who always got As in math. I study like crazy, but I just don't seem to get it."

1. "Try not to worry so much, David, it will soon be over and you will wonder why you got so worked up."
2. "I think you should do more studying and less worrying about what your brother did. Why don't you stop trying to be like him?"
3. "You seem really frustrated with so many things to worry about at the same time—the math test, being compared to your brother, and the possibility of being grounded."
4. "I think the reason you are so worried has to do with your competition with your brother."
5. "What have you done so far to prepare for the exam?"*

*Answers to Box 14.12: (1) Evaluating, (2) Supporting, (3) Understanding, (4) Interpreting, (5) Probing.

Reinforce Desired Behaviors: It Facilitates Positive Feelings

Sometimes, a student will make a significant contribution to class discussion and not even receive a nod of approval from the instructor. As you might know from personal experience, nothing is more demoralizing. The principle we are talking about here is a simple one, and is derived from the behavioristic position discussed in Chapter 1: Rewards or reinforcements are most effective when they immediately follow a desired behavior. If, for instance, a student makes an effort to participate in class and is greeted by either no response from the teacher or a negative one (e.g., "That statement doesn't even make sense, John"), it is not likely that he or she will feel greatly moved to participate in the future.

A major value of immediate reinforcement—particularly if it is positive—is that students can feel immediately good about themselves. Success experiences typically lead to feelings of pride and a sense of competence, which, in turn, create new urgency to want to get more of those immediately felt good feelings.

These, then, are some ideas, research findings, and strategies for creating a classroom climate with open communication, which, in the final analysis, is what positive classroom dynamics is all about.

EPILOGUE

There is a large difference between dealing with persons one at a time and working with them in groups of twenty to thirty. One-to-one relationships are not only easier to predict, but also easier to control. This is not so with a class of twenty to thirty first-graders or twelfth-grade high school students. Just as it is important to understand personality dynamics in order to establish healthy interpersonal relationships on a one-to-one basis, so, too, is it important to have a grasp of the basic processes involved in group dynamics in order to facilitate a healthy relationship with an entire class.

There is little question that the social-emotional climate of a classroom influences both individual and group behavior. There is also little question that teachers play a strong part in determining the tone, intensity, and force of a classroom climate. Teachers, by virtue of their behavior, can decidedly affect whether a classroom is warm and supportive, or cold and rejecting. The test is not how they handle the best behavior of the most well-behaved students, but how effectively they deal with the worst behavior of their most troublesome students. Teachers who work at combining fairness and sensitivity with firmness and strength will go a long way toward helping students to trust the teacher's capacity to not only encourage an atmosphere of freedom, but to control a class when control is necessary. Students need to know not only that they are valued by the teacher, but also that the teacher has the personal strength to say, "No" and mean it. For most students, it is scary to be in a classroom in which there is the possibility that the strongest (most vocal, assertive, or aggressive) students might take over and dominate a class if they so choose.

What are healthy group dynamics? Considerations that stand out are such factors as: (1) a wide dispersion of friendship choices, as opposed to small clusters of friends; (2) a dispersion of power so that portions of the authority and responsibility for decision making are shared by as many students as possible; (3) a psychological atmosphere that is more supportive and democratic than rejecting and authoritarian; (4) a norm structure that the entire class has participated in developing; (5) response styles by both teacher and students that are geared more toward probing and understanding than toward evaluating and interpreting; and (6) a general spirit of unification and "we-ness"—a spirit that is usually the natural outgrowth of the first five factors.

STUDY AND REVIEW QUESTIONS

1. What does it mean when we say "each classroom develops its own personality?" How does this happen? Why is it important to be aware of this phenomenon?
2. What factors go into creating a classroom's "climate?" How can one informally diagnose this climate?
3. Can you identify the six major properties of classrooms that affect their group dynamics?
4. If you were asked how a teacher's personal "style" influences a classroom's climate, how would you respond?
5. The observation was made that students in authoritarian classrooms produce more, but at a price. What does this statement mean?
6. Can you explain how interpersonal attraction patterns affect group climate?
7. Why is it that whom a teacher likes affects whom others like?
8. How would you define the idea of "group norms" to someone who did not know what these were for or about?
9. What is the difference between *static* and *dynamic* norms, and between *formal* and *informal* norms?
10. What are the advantages of encouraging students to help to develop group norms?
11. There are basically four types of norms that fit under the umbrella of static or dynamic norms and formal or informal norms: (1) perceptual norms, (2) cognitive norms, (3) evaluative norms, and (4) behavioral norms. Explain how each functions in a classroom setting?
12. Why is it that classrooms with widely diffuse friendship patterns are more cohesive than those with less diffuse friendship patterns?
13. What behavioral characteristics are most frequently associated with teachers who are good at creating high group cohesiveness?

14. As a teacher, what can you do to create a more supportive, as opposed to a more defensive, classroom climate?
15. If someone asked you what types of responses to persons are most destructive to healthy, open relationships, how would you reply?
16. What advice would you give teachers for using response styles appropriately and constructively?

REFERENCES

Anderson, C. S. "The Search for School Climate: A Review of the Research." *Review of Educational Research,* 1982, *52,* pp. 368–420.

Anderson, G. J., Walberg, H. J., and Welch, W. W. "Curriculum Effects of the Social Climate of Learning: A New Representation of Discriminant Functions." *American Educational Research Journal,* 1969, *6,* pp. 315–328.

Anderson, H. H., and Brewer, J. E. "Studies of Teachers' Classroom Personalities, II." *Applied Psychology Monographs,* 1946, No. 8.

Anderson, H. H., Brewer, J. E., and Reed, M. F. "Studies of Teachers' Classroom Personalities, II." *Applied Psychology Monographs,* 1946, No. 46.

Asch, S. E. "Studies of Independence and Conformity: I. A Minority of One Against an Unanimous Majority." *Psychological Monographs,* 1956, *70,* 9 (Whole No. 416).

Back, K. "Influence Through Social Communication." *Journal of Abnormal and Normal Psychology,* 1951, *46,* pp. 9–23.

Berscheid, E. "The Question of the Importance of Physical Attractiveness." In C. P. Herman, M. P. Zanna, and E. T. Higgins (Eds.), *Physical Appearance, Stigma, and Social Behavior: The Ontario Symposium,* Vol. 3. Hillsdale, NJ: Lawrence Erlbaum, 1986.

Blumberg, A., and Greenfield, W. *The Effective Principal.* Needham Heights, MA: Allyn and Bacon, 1980.

Brookover, W. B., Schweitzer, J. H., Schneider, J. M., Beady, C. H., Flood, P. K., and Wisenbaker, J. M. "Elementary School Social Climate and School Achievement." *American Educational Research Journal.* 1978, *15,* pp. 301–318.

Bovard, E. "Interaction and Attraction to the Group." *Human Relations,* 1956, *9,* pp. 481–489.

Chaiken, S. "Physical Appearance and Social Influence." In C. P. Herman, M. P. Zanna, and E. T. Higgins (Eds.), *Physical Appearance, Stigma, and Social Behavior: The Ontario Symposium,* Vol. 3. Hillsdale, NJ: Lawrence Erlbaum, 1986.

Cohen, P., and Kulik, C. "Educational Outcomes of Tutoring: A Meta-Analysis of Findings." *American Educational Research Journal,* 1982, *19,* pp. 237–248.

Combs, A. W., Richards, A. C., and Richards, F. *Perceptual Psychology.* Lanham, MD: University Press of America, 1988.

Davis, G. A., and Thomas, M. A. *Effective Schools and Effective Teachers.* Needham Heights, MA: Allyn and Bacon, 1989.

Doyle, W. "Classroom Organization and Management." In M. Wittrock (Ed.), *Handbook of Research of Teaching,* 3rd ed. New York: Macmillan, 1986.

Duck, S. (Ed.). *Theory and Practice in Interpersonal Attraction.* New York: Academic Press, 1977.

Ehman, L. H. "Change in High School Students' Political Attitudes as a Function of Social Studies Classroom Climate." *American Educational Research Journal*, 1980, *17*, pp. 253–265.

Flanders, N. A., and Havumaki, S. "The Effect of Teacher–Pupil Contacts Involving Praise on the Sociometric Choices of Students." *Journal of Educational Psychology*, 1960, *51*, pp. 65–68.

Forsyth, D. R. *Group Dynamics*, 2nd ed. Pacific Grove, CA: Brooks/Cole, 1990.

Fraser, B. J., and Fisher, D. L. "Predicting Students' Outcomes from Their Perceptions of Classroom Psychosocial Environment." *American Educational Research Journal*, 1982, *19*, pp. 498–518.

Gibb, J. R. "Defensive Communication." *ETC: A Review of General Semantics*, 1965, *22*, pp. 14–24.

Goleman, D. *Vital Lies, Simple Truths*. New York: Simon and Schuster, 1985.

Hallahan, D. P., and Kauffman, J. M. *Exceptional Children*, 2nd ed. Englewood Cliffs, NJ: Prentice Hall, 1982.

Hamachek, D. "Dynamics of Self-Other Perceptions and Their Relationship to Leadership Style." *Humanities: Journal of the Institute of Man*, 1978, *14*, pp. 355–366.

Hamachek, D. *Encounters with the Self*, 4th ed. Fort Worth, TX: Harcourt Brace Jovanovich, 1992.

Herman, C. P., Zanna, M. P., and Higgins, E. T. *Physical Appearance, Stigma, and Social Behavior: The Ontario Symposium*, Vol. 3. Hillsdale, NJ: Lawrence Erlbaum, 1986.

Jackson, P. *Life in Classrooms*. New York: Holt, Rinehart and Winston, 1968.

Johnson, D. W. *Reading Out: Interpersonal Effectiveness and Self-Actualization*, 5th ed. Needham Heights, MA: Allyn and Bacon, 1993.

Johnson, D. W., and Johnson, R. T. "Integrating Handicapped Students into the Mainstream." *Exceptional Children*, 1980a, October, pp. 90–98.

Johnson, R. T., and Johnson, D. W. "The Social Integration of Handicapped Students into the Mainstream." In L. M. Reynolds (Ed.), *Social Acceptance and Peer Relationships of the Exceptional Child in the Regular Classroom*. Reston, VA: The Council for Exceptional Children, 1980b.

Joyce, B., and Weil, M. *Models of Teaching*, 2nd ed. Englewood Cliffs, NJ: Prentice Hall, 1980.

Langlois, J. H. "From the Eye of the Beholder to Behavioral Reality: Development of Social Behaviors and Social Relations as a Function of Physical Attractiveness." In C. P. Herman, M. P. Zanna, and E. T. Higgins (Eds.), *Physical Appearance, Stigma, and Social Behavior: The Ontario Symposium*, Vol. 3. Hillsdale, NJ: Lawrence Erlbaum, 1986.

Raviv, A., Raviv, A., and Reisel, E. "Teachers and Students: Two Different Perspectives? Measuring Social Climate in the Classroom." *American Educational Research Journal*, 1990, *27*, pp. 141–157.

Rogers, C. R., and Roethlisberger, F. J. "Barriers and Gateways to Communication." *Harvard Business Review*, 1952, July–August, pp. 28–35.

Rosenbaum, L. L., and Rosenbaum, W. B. "Morale and Productivity Consequences of Group Leadership Style, Stress, and Type of Stress." *Journal of Applied Psychology*, 1971, *55*, pp. 343–348.

Schmuck, R. A. "Some Aspects of Classroom Social Climate." *Psychology in the Schools*, 1966, *3*, pp. 59–65.

Schmuck, R. A., and Schmuck, P. A. *Group Processes in the Classroom,* 6th ed. Dubuque, IA: Wm. C. Brown, 1992.

Shaw, M. E. *Group Dynamics: The Psychology of Small Group Behavior,* 3rd ed. New York, McGraw-Hill, 1981.

Smith, J. *Group Dynamics at Work.* Term paper excerpt, Michigan State University, April, 1991.

Staffieri, J. "A Study of Social Stereotype of Body Image in Children." *Journal of Personality and Social Psychology,* 1957, *7,* pp. 101–104.

Walberg, H. J. "Teacher Personality and Classroom Climate." *Psychology in the Schools,* 1968, *5,* pp. 163–169.

Walberg, H. J., and Welch, W. W. "Personality Characteristics of Innovative Physics Teachers." *Journal of Creative Behavior,* 1967, *1,* pp. 163–171.

White, R., and Lippitt, R. "Leader Behavior and Member Reaction in Three Social Climates." In Cartwright, D., and Zander, A. (eds.), Group Dynamics, 3rd ed. New York: Harper & Row, 1968.

Wofford, J. C. *Organization Behavior: Foundation for Organizational Effectiveness.* Boston: Kent, 1982.

Zebrowitz, L. A. *Social Perception.* Pacific Grove, CA: Brooks/Cole, 1990.

SELECTED READINGS OF RELATED INTEREST

Corey, M. S., and Corey, G. *Groups: Process and Practice,* 4th ed. Monterey, CA: Brooks/Cole, 1992. This is an excellent volume for anyone wanting to know more about the skills that are necessary for keeping groups running smoothly and effectively, whether inside or outside of a classroom setting.

Forsyth, D. R. *Group Dynamics,* 2nd ed. Pacific Grove, CA: Brooks/Cole, 1990. This solid basic text on group dynamics has particularly good chapters on the qualities of effective group leaders and group decision making.

Johnson, D. W. *Reaching Out: Interpersonal Effectiveness and Self-Actualization,* 5th ed. Needham Heights, MA: Allyn and Bacon, 1993. This is an excellent book for helping one develop the kind of skills necessary to work effectively with groups.

McGrath, J. E. ed. *Groups: Interaction and Performance.* Englewood Cliffs, NJ: Prentice Hall, 1984. This book contains a broad array of topics related to how groups affect behavior and performance; there is an excellent section on the effects of interaction on group members.

Schmuck, R. A., and Schmuck, P. A. *Group Processes in the Classroom,* 5th ed. Dubuque, IA: Wm. C. Brown, 1992. This is probably one of the very best books you will find that deals exclusively with group dynamics in classroom settings. I highly recommend it for your professional library.

15

Strategies for Achieving Positive Classroom Management

CHAPTER OVERVIEW

IMPORTANT CHAPTER IDEAS

1. Surveys show that approximately 90% of all teachers view disruptive student behavior as one of their major problems.
2. Although today's generation of young persons is no better nor worse behaved than their predecessors, adults who raise them and teach them usually manage to feel that "this generation is the worst one yet."
3. A key to effective classroom management is the existence of clear rules and procedures, which are established early in the school year.
4. Effective classroom managers are particularly aware of what is going on throughout the classroom, attend to more than one thing at a time, keep the class moving along at a steady pace, and do a lot of advance preparation.
5. Teachers who are effective classroom managers realize that the manner in which they begin with a new class, in terms of being firm, fair, and enforcing the rules consistently, has a dramatic effect on how the class functions from that point.
6. Another key to successful classroom management is in what teachers do to create a positive learning environment, which is the best type of preventative medicine a teacher can practice.
7. Stressing positive, desirable behavior in firm "I-statements" is much more effective than negative emphases that underscore the "do nots" and "should nots."
8. Assertive discipline is an approach to classroom management that says, in effect, that teachers will have fewer problems when they tell students in an assertive way (not in a passive or hostile manner) exactly what is expected of them and then give them choices, which, theoretically at least, help them learn more responsible behavior.
9. Critics of the assertive discipline model maintain that it teaches children too much in the way of obedience and too little about responsibility.
10. Praise, when used appropriately, can have a positive effect on the attitudes of students and on the morale of a class.
11. When students have a chance to participate in making rules, they are less likely to break them.

12. Diagnostic thinking is an approach to classroom management and dealing with disciplinary problems that prepares one for sizing up a situation, getting the facts, and then experimenting with various measure to cope with it.
13. Disciplinary measures are necessary when there are real dangers, when there is too much excitement and loss of control is imminent, when learning is disrupted, or when a teacher's mental health needs protecting.
14. Although punishment might control misbehavior, it will not, by itself, teach desirable behavior. It is best used as a last resort and should be a natural consequence of the offense.
15. Teachers who work on developing a warm, positive relationship with their students, while, at the same time being firm and consistent, will go a very long way in keeping problem behavior at a minimum.

PROLOGUE

In every classroom, in every school, and in every grade from kindergarten through high school, there will always be moments when certain students will bend the rules, stretch the limits, and test the patience of even the most forbearing teacher. Managing a roomful of students so that learning can proceed as smoothly as possible is one of the great challenges of teaching. It is also done in a variety of ways. For example, I remember an elementary school teacher I had who ritualistically dealt with problem students by having them sit in the hallway to "think about what they had done." On any number of occasions, particular students would cause a problem *just so* they would be put in the hallway, not to sit in sober reflection about their shenanigans, but to get into further mischief with unsuspecting passersby. I recall another teacher—of fifth grade—who always sent troublemakers to the principal's office and left the problem for someone else to handle. Not many students liked this teacher. Some of us felt the principal took more time to know us than our teacher did. Still another teacher spelled out the rules at the beginning, asked for our input, and we all agreed on the consequences associated with particular misdeeds. True to her word, she followed through by doing exactly as she said she would when someone broke a rule. We did not always like what she did (she was not always thrilled with what we did either), but we knew where she stood and where we stood. She was consistent, and there were no surprises.

It might be helpful at the outset to be aware of an important distinction between classroom management and discipline. Put simply, *classroom management* refers to the overall coordination of a classroom's activities in order to facilitate teaching and learning. *Discipline* has reference to teacher actions prompted by students whose behaviors disrupt classroom activity. Because discipline tends to be equated with punishment, it is preferable to use the term *classroom management* when thinking about ways to facilitate a positive teaching/learning environment. Not only does this help to avoid the negative connotations associated with punishment, but it encourages one to think more creatively about how to prevent problems *before* they occur rather than to focus solely on how to punish them *after* they happen.

Actually, much of what has been discussed in this volume fits under the heading of classroom management. For example, motivating a class, using a variety of teaching strategies, evaluating learning, and developing group dynamics are all classroom management techniques in a more general sense of the word. What we really have not looked at is how the management concept is related to problems of classroom discipline, and at approaches to handling these problems when they occur.

There are many ways for dealing with disciplinary problems and classroom management issues. To be sure, there are good ways and bad ways. Our purpose in this chapter is to identify some of the "good" ways and to discuss how these ways can be implemented as part of the ongoing life of a classroom.

HOW SERIOUS IS THE PROBLEM OF SCHOOL DISCIPLINE?

Every year since 1968, the Gallup poll includes the following question in its survey of the nation's attitude toward public schools: "What do you think are the biggest problems with which the *public* schools in the community must deal?" Until 1986, respondents to that survey ranked school discipline first on the list, and every year since that time it has ranked it second only to drugs as the biggest educational headache. In a national survey of 22,000 teachers, 89% of them pointed to disruptive student behavior as one of their major problems (Carnegie Foundation, 1988). In an earlier nationwide teacher opinion poll conducted by the National Education Association, 90% of teachers said that student misbehavior interferes with teaching, and 25% said it interferes greatly. In addition, it was found that 110,000 teachers were subjected to physical attacks by students during the previous twelve months, most of which occurred in the classroom ("Opinion Poll," 1981).

Although physical encounters between teachers and students are always serious, it should be noted that none of the 110,000 reported attacks resulted in serious physical injury. Only a very small percentage of teachers ever experience anything of a serious nature. Research in hundreds of classrooms indicates that even serious oral confrontations occur rarely (Charles, 1992). Actually, the vast majority of disciplinary problems consist overwhelmingly of what are, by comparison, rather innocuous behaviors such as not listening, talking without permission, goofing off and disturbing others in the process, and in other nonviolent ways disrupting the flow of classroom activity. These types of behaviors constitute approximately 99% of disciplinary problems typically encountered by teachers (Jones, 1979). Although these problems are not major, they are persistent, which is why discipline problems are one of the major reasons for teacher failure and stress (Blase and Pajak, 1985).

Are Today's Youths Different from Previous Generations?

The late Earl Kelley (1962), a sensitive, wise psychologist and educator, once observed that the complaint about the deterioration of today's youths is a wail recorded in the literature almost as far as the beginning of written language. He went on to note:

> In Boston in 1850, it took 65 beatings a day to keep a school of four hundred going. About 1875, an uncle of mine decided on teaching as a career and started with a country one-room school. His professional career ended when the pupils tipped the outhouse over, door down, with him in it. I never heard how he got out, but by the time I knew he was an aging farmer. (p. 5)

Consider another observation that has been made about young people: "Children now love luxury. They have bad manners and contempt for authority. They show disrespect for elders and love chatter in the place of exercise. Children are now tyrants, not the servants of their households." That was Socrates, 2500 years ago, describing the youths of his time. Does it sound familiar?

Each new generation of adults looks at its young people and sees problems and misdeeds that they are certain never existed previously. Somehow, the youths of this generation are always a bit worse than those of any other era, or so it seems. The fact is children and adolescents have always been a bit wild and untamed, some more so than others. Growing up means assimilating the rules of the game, learning to control impulses, and socializing childhood's need for fun and immediate gratification into a more balanced and responsible outlook. As adults, we know that school is important, a fact that many youngsters do not fully appreciate. We want them to learn and be serious at the very time in life that they want to play and have fun.

Kids will be kids. Some will be handfuls for teachers because to cut up occasionally is a natural outgrowth of their youthful exuberance. Others, sadly, will be handfuls because their life circumstances are leading them to feel frustrated and angry, emotional states that get acted out in the classroom.

The recognition that kids are no different than they have ever been does not mean that we should throw up our hands in helpless desperation. Rather, it can help sensitize us to the idea that today's youths are probably no better or no worse than at any other time in recorded history, a reality that may encourage us to be somewhat more understanding of the young people in our charge.

MANAGING A CLASSROOM: WHAT EFFECTIVE TEACHERS DO

One of the best ways of figuring out how to manage a classroom so that it runs smoothly and efficiently is to watch how effective teachers make this happen.

Which is exactly what a group of researchers did with a group of high school teachers (Emmer, Evertson, Sanford, Clements, and Worsham, 1989) and a group of elementary school teachers (Evertson, Emmer, Clements, Sanford, and Worsham, 1989). The way they conducted their research was to observe teachers in a large number of classrooms as they went about their daily teaching activities. After months of observations, the researchers noted that there were striking differences among the classes. Some had few disciplinary problems; others had many. The most and least effective teachers were identified on the basis of how their students behaved and how smoothly their classrooms operated.

The next thing the researchers did was to study their observation records to see how effective teachers got started during the initial weeks of a new school year. These observations were compared with those made of teachers who were confronted with disciplinary problems constantly. Principles of classroom management were developed on the basis of these comparisons. The researchers then taught these management principles to other groups of elementary and secondary school teachers. Generally, the results were quite positive. Teachers exposed to the management principles, as opposed to those who weren't, had few discipline problems; their students spent more time working on their assignments and less time disrupting the class, and achievement (the bottom line) was higher.

Prerequisites for Effective Management: Procedures and Rules

A characteristic of teachers who are effective classroom managers is that they establish clear procedures and rules early in the school year (Emmer et. al., 1989; Evertson et. al., 1989). By definition, procedures refer to established ways for doing things. Effective teachers recognize that clear-cut procedures are useful in giving students a sense of direction and clarity about when and how certain things are to be done. Weinstein and Mignano (1993) suggest that classroom procedures are particularly important in relation to the following activities:

1. Administrative routines (e.g., taking attendance)
2. Student movement (e.g., entering and leaving the room, getting a drink, going to someone else's desk)
3. Housekeeping (e.g., storing personal items, watering plants, hanging up jackets or sweaters)
4. Routines for accomplishing lessons (e.g., how to collect or hand in homework assignments or return completed homework)
5. Teacher–student interactions (e.g., how to get the teacher's attention when help is needed)
6. Interaction among students (e.g., helping each other with schoolwork or socializing)

Another characteristic of effective classroom managers is that they establish clear rules, frequently with input from the students. Rules reflect the do's and don'ts of a classroom. They provide guidelines that students can use to monitor their own behavior. Weinstein and Mignano (1993) have pointed to the importance of being sure that the rules are consistent with what is known about principles of learning. For example, small-group learning research shows that students benefit when they work and study together. Thus, a rule that prevents students from helping each other is inconsistent with known principles of learning. Or a rule that says, "Erasing is not allowed when writing" may promote unnecessary anxiety about making mistakes, and thus interfere with cognitive processing and clear communication.

It is better to have a few general rules that cover a broad array of specific possibilities than a lengthy listing of all of the do's and don'ts.

General Rules for Elementary School Students

Evertson et al. (1989) found in their research that the behavior of elementary school students was enhanced when they were aware of the following five general rules (or similar versions):

1. Be polite and helpful to classmates and teachers: Examples of the expectations here include things like saying "please" and "thank you," not fighting or calling names, and waiting for your turn. It is practicing the rules of common courtesy.

2. Respect other people's property: This includes such things as not writing on walls, desks, or buses; getting permission to borrow other people's belongings; and returning library books and anything else borrowed.

3. Listen quietly while others are speaking: This means being attentive while anyone else is speaking during class discussions and applies equally to students and the teacher. It is a basic act of respect for others.

4. No hitting, shoving, or hurting others: Students have a right and a need to feel safe at their school and in their classrooms. Teachers are advised to remind their students that "hurting others" involves not only hurt bodies, but also hurt feelings, which can happen with name-calling.

5. Obey all school rules: When stated in this manner, it reminds students that all school rules also apply to the classroom. If, for example, not chewing gum is a school rule, they are aware that that is a regulation for their classroom decorum, as well. (Gentle reminders about these school rules always helps.)

Note that, with the exception of number 4, each of these rules is stated in terms of what students *should* do rather than in terms of what they *should not* do, wording which helps to underscore the desirable behavior. Remember that elementary-level students, in particular, have a short attention span, are restless, and tend to "forget" easily. To minimize "forgetting," it is important that they have a voice in making the rules and that the rules are posted where they can be easily seen. Research is clear in pointing out that rules are more likely to be followed (but never *always*) when they are stated clearly, positively, given rationales, kept short, and when they incorporate student input (Evertson, 1987).

15.1 Do Some Teachers Stand Out for You?

When you think back over your elementary school years, what comes to mind when you consider the differences between what you consider to be the effective and ineffective teachers you had when it came to classroom management? What did the effective ones do? Can you think of a particular teacher or two that you'd like to emulate?

General Rules for Secondary School Students

From their observations of secondary school teachers, Emmer et al. (1989) noted that the ones who were among the more effective classroom managers had at least six somewhat similar basic rules for their students, which were as follows:

1. Bring all of the necessary materials you need to class. It is helpful for the teacher to specify what this includes (e.g., paper, notebook, texts, pen, pencil).
2. Be in your seat and ready to work when the bell rings. Many teachers combine this with a particular routine they go through for starting class, which may include a warm-up exercise associated with the lesson, or a request that they have their workbooks open and ready to go.
3. Respect and be polite to everyone. Effective teachers make it clear that they value courteous behavior, and that they do not like to hear verbal abuse or to see fighting.
4. Listen and stay seated when someone else is speaking. The teacher makes it clear that this applies when the teacher or other students are talking.
5. Respect other people's property. This applies to property belonging to the school, the teacher, or to other students.
6. Obey all school rules. This is similar to the elementary class rules in that it covers many behaviors and situations, so that a teacher does not have to repeat every school rule for the class.

The advantage of having basic rules of this sort is that they describe, simply and clearly, expectations that are seen by most students as fair and reasonable. They are rules designed to protect both a student's physical and psychological safety, a feeling they need to have in order to open themselves to new learning.

15.2 Was School Always a Safe Place for You?

When you think back over your own school experiences, can you recall times when you feared for your own physical or psychological safety? How did this affect your performance as a student? Did it affect your enthusiasm for school? Perhaps you can see from your own experience why being fearful and learning are incompatible.

Starting on the Right Foot: Practices that Work

One of the things I did while still in college was to serve as the waterfront director for several summers at a camp for emotionally disturbed boys. I quickly learned that the way I ran the waterfront during the first week, in particular, had a great deal to do with whether things went well or badly in the following weeks. A tone was set. I soon learned that if my initial interactions with the boys were essentially positive but firm and if the rules were fair and enforced consistently that the waterfront activities were likely to run more smoothly for the remainder of the session.

Research has shown repeatedly that the same thing is true for classroom teachers. The way they begin with new classes very much sets the tone for how students behave from that point (Davis and Thomas, 1989; Emmer, Evertson, and Anderson, 1980; Evertson, 1987; Weinstein and Mignano, 1993).

Evertson (1987), for example, noted that effective teachers pay particular attention to three important components of the physical environment, which include *visibility, accessibility,* and *distractibility.*

Visibility: Effective teachers arrange their rooms so that its important features can be easily seen (e.g., the chalkboard, overhead projector screen, bulletin board announcements). They make it a point to write with large letters on the blackboard so those in the back can see without straining.

Accessibility: Effective teachers make sure that there is easy access to high traffic areas (e.g., the bookcase, the pencil sharpener, the classroom door). There is room for both the teacher and the students to move about without people running into each other or inanimate objects.

Distractibility: Effective teachers arrange their rooms to minimize distractions. For example, they tend to arrange chairs so they face away from windows.

They do not put eye-catching, attention-grabbing pictures by the blackboard where lessons are written. Effective teachers realize that it is always a good idea to have students seated in such a manner that they face the teacher, especially when their attention is expected.

Although these may seem self-evident principles, beginning teachers, in particular, have a tendency to overlook their importance. Veteran teachers are more likely to recognize that each of these represents nuances in preparation that help make classroom management a little easier.

In addition to arranging the physical properties of classrooms in certain ways and establishing procedures and rules, there are certain other practices that effective classroom managers are likely to conduct during the first couple of weeks of new classes; some examples include the following:

1. They plan their class time carefully to avoid last-minute details that take them away from their students; for example, they may have name tags prepared and something interesting for students to do.

2. They help students deal with immediate concerns first (e.g., where to put their things, where to sit, how to get the teacher's attention, when they can talk and when to pay attention).

3. Effective teachers have some simple, easily understood rules and teach these to their students right away. In fact, they teach these rules like they would any other subject, which means a lot of explanation, examples of how they work, and practice in carrying them out. A third-grade teacher I know has taught her students to stop what they are doing and return to their seats when they hear her ring a small bell she has on her desk. During the first week of school, she made a fun contest out of it by having them see who could return to their seat the quickest and give their attention. The kids loved it and now do it automatically, having learned in a painless way that a bell means play is over and work begins.

4. When students misbehave, they are stopped quickly and firmly, but not punitively. In one case, I recall watching a teacher step between two sixth-grade boys, who were about to erupt at each other, and say, "Now come on, fellas—you know the rule about fighting and bad-mouthing. It makes my ears hurt, you know." Her accompanying smile and light-hearted attitude defused the tension, and the boys quickly dropped their hostilities. I witnessed a seventh-grade teacher grab two boys who were in each other's faces and, squeezing their arms, remind them in a loud, stern voice that he "did not want to see anymore of this nonsense" and "to knock it off." The boys did knock it off, but later that morning ended up in the principal's office for fighting in gym class. A fire is not stopped by fanning the flames.

5. Effective classroom managers recognize the importance of establishing some kind of rapport with their students, and they realize that this will probably happen—for better or worse—during the first days or weeks of a new class. Effective teachers realize that they are not likely to have the kind of positive relationship with students that will facilitate either learning or a smooth-running classroom if on the first day of a new class they jump to page 1 and expect students to pay attention automatically and learn. Much of what happens in a classroom that is pedagogically sound and psychologically healthy occurs within the medium of mutual respect and liking between the teacher and the students. Research shows that even in tough inner-city schools, teachers who are successful classroom managers are likely to be those who take time to know their students and allow their students to know them (Moskowitz and Hayman, 1976).

It should come as no surprise that teachers who are less successful classroom managers tend to be less organized, less attentive to the immediate concerns of students, and inconsistent about setting and enforcing the rules. In addition, disciplinary measures are frequently inconsistent and unfairly practiced, behavior that usually fuels students' resentments. Less effective classroom managers seem not as appreciative of the idea that quality of teacher–student relationships have a lot to do with the intellectual and psychological climate of a classroom (Brophy, 1982, 1983; Davis and Thomas, 1989; Doyle, 1990; Evertson, 1987).

15.3 An Argument You Will Hear

The argument is sometimes advanced that learning suffers when teachers take time to "establish relationships" with their students and that these kinds of teachers get taken advantage of. How would you respond to this position? What has your own experience as a student taught you?

PREVENTION: THE BEST MANAGEMENT STRATEGY OF ALL

Research done originally by Kounin (1970), and verified by other investigators, has found that good classroom managers do not react to student misbehavior much differently than poor managers (Doyle, 1990; Good and Brophy, 1994). The skill with which good managers do things to *prevent* misbehavior distinguishes them from poor managers. The key to successful classroom management is in what teachers do to create a positive learning environment, which is the best type of preventative medicine a teacher can practice.

Using interviews and on-the-spot note taking, Kounin (1970) used the strategy of simply observing teachers in their classrooms as a way of understanding more about the relationship between teacher and student behavior. Successful classroom managers, he found, were particularly adept at minimizing potentially disruptive student behavior in two ways: (1) they maximized the time students spent involved in academic activities, and (2) they resolved incidents of minor inattention before they escalated into major disruptions. Successful managers were more skilled than less successful managers in the following behaviors: (1) with-it-ness, (2) overlapping, (3) movement management, (4) group focusing and (5) avoiding satiation.

Let's briefly consider each of these behaviors.

With-it-ness (Being Aware of What Is Happening)

To say that someone is "with it" is to suggest that the person is tuned in to what is happening, which is one of the characteristics of teachers who are effective classroom managers. They have, it seems, a sense of the total classroom, almost as if they had eyes in the backs of their heads. I still remember my sixth-grade teacher's adeptness at this. She might be talking to a group of students in one corner of the room and, without even turning her head, say to Michael, who was fooling around behind her in another corner of the room, "Michael . . . study time please." I can tell you that instances of this sort were impressive displays of seemingly magical powers to those of us who witnessed it. We didn't fool around much in Ms. Eliot's room.

There are three components of with-it-ness that contribute to its effectiveness. One is the ability to select the right student for a desist. Suppose, for example, that while the teacher is working with a reading group, Bobby and Jimmy, sitting in the far corner of the room, keep hitting Debbie's hand while she is trying to write. Finally, in exasperation, she says, "You boys stop that!" Although the teacher did not actually see the incident, she turns around and, in a firm voice, tells Bobby and Jimmy to move to another table. When students see enough examples of this type of teacher behavior, they soon get the idea that the teacher is not easy to fool.

A second component of with-it-ness is the ability to attend to a more serious problem when two or more are going on simultaneously. For example: Jackie and Barbara are giggling and passing notes during a study period, while in the back of the room John and David are snapping paper wads at each other at close range. The teacher looks up and says, "John, David, please bring those rubber bands up to my desk; and John, I'd like you to sit up here in the front for a while." Students soon learn that the teacher is aware of what is serious and what is not. As a result, the teacher's credibility increases and students think twice about misbehaving, knowing that they might get caught.

Timing is the third component of with-it-ness. A major mistake in timing is to wait until the misbehavior has gone on too long before intervening. For example, if the teacher had not put an immediate stop to John and David snapping paper wads, this could have easily gotten out of control and involved many other students. Good timing is nipping a problem in the bud. It is a powerful preventative tactic.

Overlapping (Attending to Two Events Simultaneously)

Overlapping is the ability to give attention to simultaneous events. Not surprisingly, Kounin (1970) found that teachers who were skilled at overlapping also had a high level of with-it-ness. For example: A teacher is helping several students with a math problem and notices William hitting the boy in front of him in the head with his pencil. Stopping mid-sentence, the teacher says, simply, "William, your math problems please." The teacher looks at William for two or three seconds and says nothing more. He gets the message, the teacher gets compliance, and the other students continue getting help with the math problem.

Teachers are endlessly interrupted in the course of a normal teaching day; those skilled at overlapping are more able to encourage a smooth flow of activities. While checking a student's paper to see if a problem was done correctly, a teacher might glance periodically at a small group she is helping and give them encouraging comments such as, "You are on the right track" or "You're doing well. You've almost got it." In ways such as this, two issues are attended to simultaneously.

Movement Management (Keeping the Ball Rolling Smoothly)

Basically, movement management refers to a teacher's skill in dealing with pace, momentum, transition when it comes to lesson presentations, and changes from one activity to another. Teachers' ability to move smoothly from one activity to the next, and to maintain the momentum within an activity, have a great deal to do with their effectiveness in controlling classroom behavior. Busy, involved students simply do not have as much time to cause trouble.

Effective movement managers tend to have a plan of action; they know where they want to go and how to get there. They ignore minor, fleeting inattentiveness but deal quickly with behaviors that promise to escalate into trouble. They do this by using eye contact, by giving a short oral reminder ("Billy, not now"), or by moving closer to a brewing trouble spot. Teachers who are good classroom managers recognize, among other things, that students are more likely to be attentive when there is something to which to attend. Hence, their efforts to keep lessons moving at a brisk, but achievable, pace are rewarded.

15.4 Did Your Teachers Have These Skills?

Can you think of some teachers you have had who had some of the qualities just discussed—with-it-ness, overlapping, and movement management skills? What was it like being in their classrooms? What particular behaviors conveyed to you the idea that they were in control?

Group Focusing (Working with Groups, not just with Individuals)

Essential to the creation of a productive, efficient classroom is a teacher's ability to maintain a concerted group focus. This is done by having the entire class work as a large group whenever feasible and whenever consistent with achieving the objectives of the lesson at hand. A large group format is a means of encouraging broader participation because the teacher can call on many students, instead of just a few.

Group focusing is enhanced when teachers show that they are aware of how each student is progressing. This can be done in any number of ways, including these two examples: (1) The teacher attracts the group's attention by looking around in a suspenseful manner, or saying, "Let's see now—who can respond to this question?"; (2) Nonreciters are alerted that they might be called on in connection with a reciter's response (e.g., "Listen carefully to David, and let's see who can figure out who took the cookie jar").

Kounin (1970) found that practices such as these draw a group's attention to the lesson because every member of the group is alerted. Diane and Dave are less likely to fool around if they realize that they might be called on. A teacher can discourage group attention by focusing on one student at a time, thereby excluding others from the lesson, or by choosing a reciter before asking the question, which conveys the idea to others that perhaps they can listen less carefully because they know they won't have to respond.

Avoiding Satiation (Being Cautious About Too Much Repetition)

Satiation means getting filled up with something, getting enough of it, or getting bored. Simple, repetitive behaviors or exercises make it easy to get careless because what we are doing becomes mechanical and boring. When students are satiated with an activity, they not only become less involved, but surprisingly inventive in finding creative ways to enliven things. Hence, the task of the teacher is to involve students in tasks that are familiar, and that are easy enough for them to accomplish successfully, but that also offer enough variety and challenge to help them maintain interest and motivation.

Kounin (1970) found that one element effective in slowing the rate of satiation is the feeling of progress. Students who believed they were making definite headway took longer to become satiated. Those who repeated the same task over and over and believed they were getting nowhere, became satiated quickly.

It was also found that teachers who found ways to challenge students throughout a lesson had a few bored students, and therefore fewer troublesome students. They might challenge their students with comments such as the following: "I have a special, magical math formula. Watch what you can do with it."; "Listen carefully. This is a tricky question. See if you can think it through."; and "I have a question I think you're really going to enjoy." Notice the positive, upbeat tone of these questions.

Preparing in Advance (Spelling out Expectations Early)

Teachers who are successful in preventing, or at least reducing, disciplinary problems get an early jump on things. As you saw earlier in this chapter, teachers with fewer disciplinary problems implement their methods at the beginning of the school year (Evertson and Harris, 1992; Weinstein and Mignano, 1993). The seemingly automatic, smoothly functioning classrooms of successful managers are not chance happenings, but a direct outgrowth of thorough preparation and organization at the beginning of the year. Such things as room arrangement, materials storage, and other physical factors are prepared in advance, and good managers take considerable time in early weeks to spell out their rules and expectations. Beginning on the first day, and continuing throughout the first week, students are gradually introduced to the routines of classroom life—review of the daily schedule, times and procedures for lunch and recess, use of the bathroom, where to put personal materials, information about teacher and students, and so forth.

Successful managers not only told their students what they expected, but also took time to answer questions and model correct procedures. In short, good managers formally taught key procedures to their students in much the same way they would teach academic content.

This is not as easy as it might sound. Considerable time was invested in repeating expectations, discussing rules, getting feedback from students, and dealing with students who were testing to see if their teachers really meant what they said.

Effective managers gradually reduce the time they have spent on procedural instruction and practice in the first two weeks of school, but they do give reminders whenever needed, and they practice cardinal principles of classroom management: fairness and consistency.

TEACHER BEHAVIORS THAT HELP SET A POSITIVE, COOPERATIVE TONE

When students like their teacher and feel liked in return and when they feel both valued as individuals and are treated fairly, chances are good that more of their energy will go into getting on with learning rather than getting into trouble. There are at least five things that teachers can do to encourage this outcome: (1) recognize and reinforce desired behavior, (2) stress desirable behavior in positive language, (3) use praise frequently, but appropriately, (4) use "I-messages," and (5) practice active listening. Let's briefly examine each of these methods.

Recognize and Reinforce Desired Behavior

The basic principle here is simply stated: Behavior that is reinforced is likely to be repeated, and behavior that is not reinforced is likely to be extinguished. When we translate this into practical classroom applications, it means we should reinforce behaviors we would like to see more on a daily basis.

It is possible to carry this idea to extremes. Some psychologists and educators (Martin and Pear, 1992; Walker and Shea, 1988), for example, promote the ideas of setting up schedules of reinforcement, developing reinforcement preference scales and reinforcement preference lists, and encouraging the development of a "token economy." This is a system whereby students earn "tokens" for good behavior and turn them in for their choice of reward (e.g., ten minutes of free time, a library pass, a school-shown movie, listening to records, being first in the lunch line).

Approaches to behavior management that use reinforcement principles in this way have about as many opposed to this idea as there are those in favor. The major argument against it is that the emphasis is too little on students' own inner control and too much on the reward, which, it is feared, increases dependence on external controls rather than encouraging students to develop greater self-control (Gallagher, 1980; Good and Brophy, 1994).

Generally speaking, students who are prone to cause trouble are frequently those who have not had a lot of positive reinforcement in their lives. Being disruptive is frequently a way of getting what they lack—attention. Even negative attention is better than no attention at all. Most of our students need much more reinforcement than the type that occurs naturally as a result of their efforts to do well. Other students hunger for the positive validations that might be missing from their lives, and it is they who profit most from extra efforts on our part to recognize and reinforce even the small things they do well.

Teacher reinforcements come in a variety of expressions. Many are in the form of simple verbal rewards (e.g., "Great job, Jimmy."; "Fine effort, Joni."; "Fantastic, Ginny, just fantastic."). Others take the form of tokens or passes as mentioned above, or perhaps stars after one's name on the bulletin board for work well done. (College football players frequently have stars—reinforcements—plastered all over their helmets. Coaches are particularly smart about using this system.)

Usually, when students feel good about themselves, they behave better. Teachers, by virtue of their use of appropriate and wise use of reinforcements, can have a great impact on how students feel about themselves.

15.5 An Example of Positive Reinforcement

A seventh-grade teacher I know approached a student who had been particularly troublesome in class the day before and, focusing on the one thing that the student did that was positive, said, "I really liked the idea you expressed in class yesterday when we were talking about how culture influences values. I'm looking forward to hearing more from you." The student beamed, mumbled "thanks," and smiled all the way to his seat. During class there were no more monkeyshines as there had been the day before and he contributed, it seemed, twice as often. Has anything like this ever happened to you?

Use Positive Language to Stress Desirable Behavior

Among the many choices we have in life, there is the choice to be positive or negative. A glass is either half full or half empty, depending on your point of view. It is a particularly important choice for teachers because a negative emphasis is more likely to trigger a negative reaction, not just from one person, but from many. Ordinarily, persons do not like being told what not to do. It typically causes them to feel defensive and reactive. In fact, so universal is this response to autocratic behavior, that an entire theory, known as *psychological reactance,* has been developed to explain why most healthy persons object to being told what they cannot do (Brehm, 1972).

Thus, a long string of "don'ts," with an emphasis on what students should *not* be doing, runs a high risk of generating considerable resistance to, and resentment toward, teachers who come across as negative and domineering. Consider the following examples, by Good and Brophy (1994), of differences between positive and negative language. Try to hear the teacher's tone and inflection in each case.

Positive Language	*Negative Language*
Close the door quietly.	Don't slam the door.
Try to work these out on your own without help.	Don't cheat by copying from your neighbor.
Quiet down—you're getting too loud.	Don't make so much noise.
Sharpen your pencils like this (demonstration).	That's not how you use the pencil sharpener.
Carry your chair like this (demonstration).	Don't make so much noise with your chair.
Sit up straight.	Don't slouch in your chair.
Raise your hand if you think you know the answer.	Don't yell out the answer.

Positive Language	*Negative Language*
When you finish, put the scissors in the box and the bits of paper in the wastebasket.	Don't leave a mess.
These crayons are for you to share—use one color at a time and then put it back so that others can use it too.	Stop fighting over those crayons.
Use your own ideas. When you do borrow ideas from another author, be sure to acknowledge them. Even here, try to put them in your own words.	Don't plagiarize.
Speak naturally, as you would when talking to a friend.	Don't just read your report to us.
Note the caution statements in the instructions. Be sure to check things mentioned there before proceeding to the next step.	Take your time when doing this experiment or you'll mess it up.
Be ready to explain your answer—why you think it is correct.	Don't just guess.

Sometimes, it is necessary to say something sharp, pointed, and essentially negative, as when a fight needs to be stopped immediately. However, even in these cases a teacher can model the value of positive thinking by following up with what he or she would like to see in their behavior as more constructive.

15.6 How Do You Usually Respond?

What is *your* usual reaction when someone such as a friend, loved one, parent, or instructor tells you what you *cannot* do? Are you open, receptive, and eager to please? Do you feel warm and friendly toward that person? What happens inside? How is your behavior affected?

Use Praise, But Do So Appropriately

Praise is tricky. Although it is usually described as a form of reinforcement, it does not always have this effect. For example, suppose a teacher tried to influence the entire class by saying something such as, "I really like the way Jeannie is continuing to do her assignment, even though the lunch bell will ring soon." Jeannie is not likely to experience this as "praise," especially if her classmates make fun of her after class. Assume, a teacher says to John, whom he doesn't particularly like, "Well, you were quiet all morning—that's good." The words might be okay, but if you can hear this said in somewhat of a monotone, and without much feeling, you have a sense of why this might trigger a sneer on John's face rather than a smile.

Good and Brophy (1994) suggest the following seven guidelines for using praise appropriately and effectively:

1. Praise should be given in a natural voice without gushing or going overboard. Keep it simple. That way it will be more easily heard and longer remembered.
2. Praise should be given in straightforward, declarative sentences (e.g., "An interesting idea, Joe. I like that."), rather than syrupy exclamations (e.g., "Oh wow, that's a wonderful idea!"). The more straightforward the praise, the more believable it will be.
3. Point to the particulars being praised and recognize any noteworthy effort or special outcome (e.g., "I like the way you used the formula to figure that out. I know you worked hard.")
4. Stay away from stock phrases, which is anything said repeatedly (e.g., "Nice job"; "Well done"; "Excellent work"). After a while these statements sound insincere (usually because they are).
5. Accompany verbal praise with nonverbals that fit—a smile, energy in the voice, a warm tone, or a touch on the shoulder or arm.
6. Avoid general statements such as, "This was a good morning for you." This could easily be interpreted as praise for compliance rather than learning. Rather, be more specific (e.g., "You really came through with a fine solution for that problem set. I like the way you stayed with it. Keep up the good work.").
7. Use public praise sparingly; it embarrasses some students and might cause peer group problems with others. It is difficult to praise students publicly because it might seem as though you are holding them up as examples for the rest of the class. This sometimes causes negative feelings toward the person being praised. Private praise is more likely to be considered genuine. (This should not be interpreted as an absolute rule. Some students need to be praised publicly so that their peers can see they have credibility with the teacher, something that is important for students who are struggling.)

When used appropriately—delivered with genuine feeling about real accomplishments—teacher praise is a powerful way of letting students know their efforts and progress are valued and appreciated. When students feel they are liked and part of the life of a classroom, they are far less likely to disrupt or upset a system that brings them good things.

Use "I-Messages"

Consider the following two statements made to a student by two hypothetical teachers:

Teacher A: "You are constantly talking out of turn and being disruptive. All you do is cause trouble."

Teacher B: "I feel very frustrated with the constant interruptions. The rule is that we do not talk when others are talking. I find it very difficult to concentrate on board work with that buzzing in the background."

Which of these two teachers is probably going to have less trouble in this situation? All things being equal, chances are fairly good that teacher B will ride this out with fewer problems and repercussions than teacher A. According to T. Gordon (1974), long an advocate of using the proper communication skills, whether in parenting or teaching, teacher B is more likely to get positive results because she is using strong *"I-messages."* A good "I-message" contains three basic components: (1) it addresses the behavior in question rather than the student's character or personality; (2) it describes the problem in terms of its effect on the teacher; and (3) it describes the feelings stirred within the teacher because of the problem.

Teacher B does all of these things. By reminding the student of the rule, she focuses on the behavior and avoids attacking the student's personality (and thus, minimizes the possibility of a defensive response). By framing the problem in terms of its effects on her (it interferes with her concentration), she takes a step in the direction of helping the student see the link between his action and her reaction (thus, allowing the student to see clearly and forcefully that how he behaves has definite effects on others, the teacher in this instance). By describing the feelings that his behavior generates in her (she feels very frustrated), teacher B is, in a little different way, helping the student to understand the effects of his actions on others, which may be a small step toward helping him toward more responsible behavior.

Using "I-statements" when dealing with disciplinary problems is also useful in helping one to avoid labeling, judging, and evaluating students in critical and usually negative ways. Suppose that I am your student and you say to me, "Don, you are a very inconsiderate boy. You are constantly causing trouble and being insensitive of others." My response to that will probably be to feel put down and to behave defensively. My reply could easily be, "I am not" and thus to feel neither responsibility nor remorse. But suppose you had said to me, "Don, I feel troubled when you behave like that in class. When you take things that don't belong to you, it is very frustrating to me. Class is disrupted when things like this occur." You have accused me of nothing, nor have you called me a name or judged me right or wrong. You have, however, pointed out what I did and its effects. I cannot say to you (and have it make sense) that you are not troubled, or frustrated, or that the class is not disrupted. By reporting to me the *effects* of my behavior, I am less apt to get defensive because I am less likely to feel attacked. Basically, you have given me no reason to be angry. Thus, my behavior is more likely to be reflective and thoughtful than reactive and revengeful.

15.7 How Would You Respond?

Consider the following scenarios:

1. Two students are constantly whispering and passing notes during class.
2. For the third time in a week, John claims to have forgotten to bring his homework assignment.
3. You hear a group of students call another student derogatory names.

What are some appropriate "I-messages" you might use in these instances?

Practice Active Listening

Active listening is an important part of good communication between teachers and students (Gordon, 1974; Sokolove, Garrett, Sadker, and Sadker, 1986). Notice that the emphasis is on "active," which suggests that the teacher is an involved participant and not merely a passive recipient. Consider an example of active listening between a ninth-grade English teacher and one of his students:

Student: "Mr. Johnson, I feel I should've gotten more than a C on my essay answer."

Teacher: "You don't think the grade was fair?"

Student: "Well, no . . ." (shifts uncomfortably in his chair) "I felt my answer was as good as Joe's. We both said about the same thing and he got a B."

Teacher: "I think I can understand why you might feel disappointed, Bill, especially when you saw the similarities. Did you notice anything that was different?"

Student: "Well, what we wrote about was pretty similar, but he didn't have as many of your corrections as I did."

Teacher: "I think that's the key, Chuck. Although your and Bob's answers were somewhat similar, a major difference was in punctuation and grammar usage. You will recall that that was to be considered in the overall evaluation."

Student: "Yeah, I know. But still, my answer was pretty good."

Teacher: "I agree, it was, and if I were you I'd probably feel as frustrated as you do. I'm confident you can do better on next week's test, and I'd like to suggest that you really study the handout material related to punctuation and grammar usage. With your motivation, you've got an excellent chance of bringing up that grade."

Notice that Mr. Johnson responded to both the intellectual and emotional content of the student's message. He understands Bill's disappointment (i.e., the emotional content), and he could see why Bill might have questions about the grade, given the similarity Bill saw between himself and the student who received a higher grade (i.e., the intellectual content). Notice, too, that the teacher did not cave in to the student's suggestion of unfairness. Rather, Mr. Johnson listened to Bill nonjudgmentally, made an effort to understand his feelings, did not get defensive, pointed to specific reasons the grade wasn't any higher, and explained what Bill could do to improve on the next test. The essential ingredients of active listening involve: (1) listening nondefensively, (2) paying attention to the intellectual *and* emotional content, (3) rephrasing what is heard to be sure that you've understood it (and to let the other person know you're really listening), (4) avoiding judgmental and evaluative feedback, and (5) exploring for positive solutions that all parties can accept. The willingness simply to listen and to do so nonjudgmentally and without criticism will short-circuit many small problems before they get larger.

ASSERTIVE DISCIPLINE: THE CANTER MODEL OF CLASSROOM MANAGEMENT

It has been estimated that more than 750,000 teachers have been trained to apply the principles of Assertive Discipline in their classrooms (Hill, 1990). The basis for this program is explained in Canter's (1976) book, *Assertive Discipline: A Take-Charge Approach to Today's Educator,* which is now in its 26th printing. The main focus of Canter's model is on teachers assertively insisting that students follow the rules and behave properly, and on providing teachers with step-by-step procedures for following through when students misbehave.

Canter has identified three common response styles that teachers frequently use, which he labels *passive, hostile,* and *assertive.* Consider how each might be expressed in relation to the following classroom incident:

As different students get up to read various passages during English class, Brian and Kevin, sitting next to each other near the back of the room, keep whispering back and forth and being generally disruptive. Some possible teacher reactions:

A passive response: "Boys, please. Class will soon be over and then you can talk all you want."

A hostile response: "If I hear one more peep out of you two, you're gone. Now knock it off!"

An assertive response: "Brian, Kevin, please stop whispering when others are reading. It is very disruptive."

Note that the *passive response* has a certain solicitous, pleading quality about it, a response that lacks the kind of muscle that might otherwise get attention. The *hostile response* is just that—hostile. Although it probably gets immediate results, it also generates resentment in the students that will be expressed at a later time. The *assertive response* is neither passive nor hostile, but one that communicates clearly what the teacher wants to happen and why. It is the kind of response that can be expressed in a firm and controlled voice. The idea about being firm and assertive is a stance found in a number of approaches to classroom management, including Kounin's (1970) teacher-awareness system, Glasser's (1990) reality-based approach, Jones' (1987) positive-discipline system, and Dreikurs, Grunwald, and Pepper's (1982) democratically oriented system. By assertiveness, we are not referring to teacher responses that are critical, harsh, and authoritarian. Rather, we are referring to teacher responses that are stated clearly, firmly, authoritatively, and, when possible, in "I-statements." The fact that it is advocated by so many different management systems reflects its potency.

The way Assertive Discipline works is for teachers to establish a systematic discipline plan that explains exactly what will happen when students choose to misbehave. Canter maintains that the key to this program is consistency, which means that the rules and consequences for breaking them are applied fairly to all students.

It is suggested that the plan include a maximum of five consequences for misbehavior. For example, the first time a rule is broken, the student is warned. The second infraction carries with it a 10-minute time out (i.e., isolation) and the third infraction, a 15-minute time out. If there's a fourth infraction, the teacher calls the parents, and if there's a fifth time, the student goes to the principal.

A basic outcome of Assertive Discipline, according to Canter, is teaching children responsibility, something he feels is best done by telling them exactly what is expected and then giving them a choice. For example, a teacher might say to a student, "Sarah, you have a choice. If you choose to continue knocking your book on the floor when someone else is talking, you will get a 10-minute time out. If, however, you choose to behave, I will greatly appreciate that."

One of the ways that Canter suggests that teachers recognize positive behaviors (e.g., obeying the rules, doing as they are requested, making positive choices) is to drop marbles into a jar every time a student behaves in a nondisruptive manner. When the jar is full, the entire class is rewarded by, for example, 10 minutes of free time or, at times, with material objects such as cookies, ice cream, or a special party.

A basic tenet of Assertive Discipline is that students are given opportunities to learn self-discipline and responsible behavior by being given clear, consistent choices. In this way, they learn that their actions have an impact and that they themselves control the consequences.

Not everyone, however, agrees.

Criticisms of the Canter Model

One of the criticisms of Assertive Discipline is that, while it may stop misbehavior in the short term, the long-term effects may be damaging. Curwin and

Mendler (1988) note, for example, that the main objective of Assertive Discipline is to teach children to be obedient rather than to be responsible. Students do as they are told because they are told to, which leads to the kind of obedience that brings short-term obedience, offers teachers temporary relief, and gives them a sense of control and power.

A second criticism is heard from those who believe that there is too little research support for the idea of Assertive Discipline. For example, Render, Padilla, and Krank (1989) were able to find only 16 systematic studies of Assertive Discipline and concluded that the claims made by Canter "are simply not supported by the existing and available literature" (p. 72).

Support for the Canter Model

Although researchers are somewhat skeptical of Canter's system, practitioners who use it are far more enthusiastic. For example, McCormack (1989) found that 78% to 99% of 8700 teachers from four school districts and a confederation of schools in Oregon reported that they saw improvements in student behavior when they applied the principles of Assertive Discipline. Charles Warner, principal of a New Haven, Connecticut, middle school has nothing but praise for the system, noting that there's been a "drastic decrease" in discipline problems since the plan was implemented. He believes that assertive discipline provides teachers with the kind of consistency that students need (Hill, 1990). Canter (1989), who has more than a passing interest in this debate, notes that several studies have pointed to improvements in both teachers' and students' self-concepts when Assertive Discipline principles are followed.

15.8 How Do Your Feelings Line Up?

Canter's system of Assertive Discipline appears to be a no-nonsense approach to classroom management with clear-cut rules and consequences, which are supposed to help students control their behavior and make responsible choices. Critics say that it undermines students' self-worth and sense of responsibility by making it appear that students have choices when they really do not. Would you be comfortable using this system? How would you feel about your children being exposed to teachers who used Assertive Discipline?

DIAGNOSTIC THINKING: A PSYCHODYNAMIC APPROACH TO CLASSROOM MANAGEMENT

Diagnostic thinking is not merely another way for handling classroom problems, but, in a more general sense, it provides a cognitive framework for thinking about constructive ways to handle various disciplinary incidents. It is a time-tested method, one that Redl (1966) and Redl and Wattenberg (1959) referred to as a *psychodynamic* approach because of the emphasis on staying alert to the interacting components of classroom life. It is an approach that stresses the idea of *diagnostic thinking,* which, basically, refers to a general problem-solving attitude that prepares one for sizing up a situation, getting the facts, and experimenting with various measures to cope with it.

A Classroom Incident: Diagnostic Thinking in Action

In order to understand better the process involved in the diagnostic-thinking approach, consider the following incident that occurs in an ordinary classroom setting and how the teacher handles it:

> As her fourth-grade class worked in their spelling workbooks, Ms. Rinehart noticed that Billy was looking very anxious and making no effort at all to get into his workbook. He was a quiet, frail boy, but well liked by the others. Her first thought was that he couldn't do the assignment. She asked him if that was the case, but he said that it wasn't. She then wondered if he was feeling sick. He answered that he was feeling fine and sounded as though he really meant it. During this exchange, Ms. Rinehart noted that Billy kept glancing at Sam, who had been watching this exchange with a scowl on his face.
>
> When Ms. Rinehart looked around the class, Sam began working in his spelling book with what seemed to be uncommon vigor and enthusiasm. Her hunch was that there had been something going on between the two boys, but, recognizing the juvenile code against tattling, she kept the hunch to herself. However, she did want more information, so she pressed Billy to tell her what was wrong. As she did so, she sensed that the rest of the class was more quiet that it usually was. She suspected that the rest of the students knew something. Billy finally relented and allowed that he had lost his arithmetic homework assignment, which was due during the period after lunch. Ms. Rinehart was sure that Sam had something to do with the assignment being lost, but she could not be certain.

Ms. Rinehart's conclusions felt right to her, but the question was: What should she do? Tell Billy to forget about it? That would not do because the very fact that he was so upset suggested that he could not forget it easily. Give him time to do the assignment again? It did not seem fair that he should have to do it over again. Besides, the issue seemed more deeply related to how it was lost, as opposed to it being a simple matter of accidentally losing something. Should she force him to tell the whole story? That would not be a good idea because she felt it would turn the class against Billy and give Sam social reinforcement outside of school. Should she brow-beat Sam or some other youngster into telling the truth? They might still blame Billy. She decided she had to show that Billy was not a tattletale and yet let Sam discover that the actions she suspected had social consequences. Ms. Rinehart recognized that Sam was larger than average for the class and was using his greater size to feel powerful by bullying other students, but that was a problem that could be handled later. A vivid lesson now might make him more ready to accept her intervention later, especially if she did not confront him directly.

Before reading any further, what would *you* do if you were Ms. Rinehart?

All of these possibilities for action flashed through Ms. Rinehart's mind as she was talking to Billy. She decided to take a chance on one of the possibilities that occurred to her. What she did was to tell the class that Billy had lost his completed arithmetic assignment, and then she good-naturedly admonished him to be more careful in the future. She then said she had to go to the principal's office, and asked the class to see if they could help Billy find his missing homework while she was gone. To make the request a bit more striking, she dwelt a little on how frustrating it feels to complete a homework assignment only to lose it before it is handed in.

As she hoped, no sooner was the door closed behind her than there was a noisy chattering. Although she could not be sure, she thought she heard several loud voices saying, "Come on, Sam, give it back to him." At any rate, when she returned, after 10 minutes or so, the class was quiet. Billy had "found" his completed arithmetic assignment, and Sam was working busily in his spelling book. All she said was, "You found your paper, Billy? That's good. I'm sure you must be pleased."

Five Steps Involved in Diagnostic Thinking

In this simple classroom incident, Ms. Rinehart illustrated five steps usually involved in diagnostic thinking. Essentially, it is the same type of thinking a lawyer, physician, auto mechanic, or plumber might use to define and locate a problem, and then to work out an appropriate plan of action for taking care of it. Redl and Wattenberg (1959) have identified five basic components of diagnostic thinking, which, in somewhat modified form, include: (1) listening to the first hunch, (2) looking for hidden factors, (3) using behavior as a guide to action, (4) reality-testing hunches by action, and (5) trying new approaches when original ones fail. Let's briefly examine each of these.

Listening to Your First Hunch

In the face of any new problem, we almost invariably form a hunch as to what it means and what we should do to solve it. These are not carefully developed and reasoned hunches, but more on the order of unconscious reflexes based on our past experiences. Ms. Rinehart, for example, had no doubt seen many students look anxious and worried when they could not do an assignment, and thus her first hunch was that Billy could not handle the class work.

It makes no difference whether a first hunch is correct or not. What is important is that it is an essential first step toward working out a solution. It helps to focus observation and reduce aimless thinking. First hunches can be used to act out an empathic response to a troublesome situation. When Ms. Rinehart, for instance, asked Billy if he was having trouble with the assignment or feeling sick, it was as much a response to how he was feeling as it was a search for a solution. Note, too, that Ms. Rinehart had to drop her first two guesses before she hit on a promising lead. A hunch is a point of departure, not a final destination.

Looking for Hidden Factors

Looking for hidden factors involves using information concerning psychological dynamics by combining the facts we already know with those we can gather by observation. One of the hidden factors Ms. Rinehart paid attention to was the natural aversion most children have to tattling. Other hidden factors she took into account included the idea that Billy was liked by most of the class members (which meant she could probably count on them not to be destructive if she left the problem, as she did, for the group to solve), and the fact that Sam was giving Billy dirty looks.

Using Behavior As a Guide to Action

Even when we cannot see the cause of behavior, we can still see some meaning in it. Consider a few illustrations. During the course of discussion in an eighth-grade social studies class about the importance of the family unit and various styles of parent–child relationships, a girl in the back of the room began crying softly to herself. We cannot know on the basis of so few facts the cause of the crying, but we can see a clear meaning—the girl was upset or sad. Whatever caused the girl to cry might not be known for a time. To see that the girl was softly crying, and therefore that she was upset or sad, would be important readings of first clues. The nature of a problem can be read directly from the "language of behavior" and the events that led up to the behavior.

Although our understanding of causation is incomplete, it is possible to take a first step on the basis of our interpretation of conduct. In the incident just described, the teacher simply reflected to each of the students involved what she thought the behavior meant. Rather than saying to the girl, "You shouldn't feel this way" or "You must learn to control yourself," the teacher simply said, "Sally, you looked very unhappy in class today." Sally admitted that she did and was able to relate some of the sad feelings she was experiencing as the class was talking about family togetherness. The tears, as the teacher soon discovered, were very real, reflecting as they did Sally's hurt about her parents' ensuing divorce.

By responding to the behavior and what it might have meant, the teacher avoided making an emotional situation more difficult, while at the same time allowing a hurt student to vent her feelings.

Reality-Testing Your Hunches with Action

As soon as we feel reasonably confident in our hunches, we should test them. This is a way of assessing the accuracy of our hunches rather than a course of behavior to which we are irrevocably committed.

Indeed, when a hypothesis is actually tested, it is sometimes found to be wrong or incomplete. For instance, Richard, a boy with a very fine high school record, began not only misbehaving and acting up in his chemistry class, but also was late handing in his assignments and slow in finishing his lab work. The teacher first suspected that Richard's behavior was related to not understanding some basic concepts very well. Because the teacher's first hunch about lack of knowledge did not fit, he reasoned that something of a more emotional nature might have been amiss. With this hunch in mind, he asked Richard to stay after class one day. The teacher approached the problem directly, and simply asked Richard why his chemistry work seemed so inconsistent with his high achievement in all other classes. As they talked, it became apparent that there was, indeed, an emotional base to the problem—one that was directly linked to the boy's father wanting Richard to be a doctor. Richard was resisting this idea (He wanted to be a lawyer.), and one expression of this resistance was poor work in chemistry, which he knew was an important course to do well in to be accepted into a pre-med program. Richard talked his problem through with one of the high school counselors and in the process discovered that there were more constructive ways of resisting his father than flunking chemistry.

Being Flexible—Trying Alternative Approaches

Richard's chemistry teacher is a good example of the basic principle in being flexible. In the process of action-testing his hunch, the teacher found that he had to give up his initial hypothesis about Richard not understanding the material and develop a new one related to the possibility of an emotional problem. An essential characteristic of diagnostic thinking is that it is flexible. Our hunches are revised not only in terms of what happens as a result of action, but by new developments in the individual or the group.

For instance, in a tenth-grade class we might have a boy who seems to enjoy disrupting the class by constantly getting into arguments about the most trivial issues with the teacher or other class members. A friendship sociogram (i.e., a measure of liking patterns) may show that the boy is an isolate. We might also know that his father is an overbearing businessman in town who has a reputation for bulldozing his employees and making a lot of enemies. One diagnosis, based on these facts, might be that the boy identifies with his father and is also being excluded and rejected by his classmates, and that his troublesome argumentativeness is both a cause and effect of the situation. We would, therefore, do what we could to help him to be more accepted by his peers. One approach, for example, might be to put him in charge of a special planning group so that he could experience power in natural ways, without having to fight for it. We might also confront him with the consequences of his actions so that he could develop a greater awareness of the links between his behavior and others' feelings toward him.

We would do well to remember that an individual or group, if given the opportunity, will often work out problems without interference. For many persons, trouble, like pain, is a signal that something is wrong, and that it is time for them to bring their own resources into play. The wise teacher does not rush in when trouble occurs, but takes time to size up the situation, and then intervene only if necessary. Ms. Rinehart, for example, wisely recognized that she could count on the class—or at least she had enough faith to be able to *take the risk* of counting on the class—to settle the immediate problem of getting Sam to return the arithmetic assignment, which brings us to an important question.

WHEN ARE DISCIPLINARY MEASURES NECESSARY?

No matter how skilled a teacher is in relating to students and conducting a class, and no matter how "normal" a class might be, there will always be those moments when either an individual student or the entire class needs to be taken in tow. Before examining some practical intervention strategies, the question of *when* a teacher should intervene must be considered. This is an important question because school psychologists have observed that many teachers fail to set limits or to intervene until they are so frustrated, angry, and choked with counteraggressive feelings that they cannot discipline in a constructive way. Long and Newman (1980) have discussed seven criteria which, in somewhat modified form, we will examine here as guidelines to help determine when some form of disciplinary intervention is necessary. They are as follows:

1. When there are real dangers: (e.g., Steve is hit on the head by another student, Joe tries to set fire to the trash basket) Obvious, real threats must be curbed at once.

2. When someone needs psychological protection: Just as we want to protect students from physical hurt, so, too, do we want to protect them from psychological injury. A student being scapegoated or called racial names is as much in need of protection as the one who gets hit in the mouth by the class bully.

3. When there is too much excitement: Sometimes a teacher has to intervene in order to avoid the development of too much excitement, anxiety, and guilt in students, particularly younger ones. For example, if a game is getting out of

hand and goes on for another 5 minutes, all of the children might begin to lose control, run wild, and maybe even hurt someone. It is the teacher's responsibility to stop this before it happens.

4. When an ongoing program is threatened: When a class is involved in a particular task and the students have an investment in its outcome, it is not fair to have it ruined by one or two students, who, for any number of reasons, want to act up. In this instance, the teacher intervenes and asks the student, or students, involved to change seats or whatever seems appropriate to ensure program continuity.

5. When there is the possibility of negative contagion: This is related to point 4, and refers to the disruptive behavior of one student spreading to the rest of the class. For example, when a teacher is aware that tension is mounting in the classroom, and a child with high social power begins to lightly kick the legs of his desk, the teacher might ask him to stop in order to prevent this behavior from spreading to other students (called the "ripple effect") and disrupting the entire class.

6. When there is the possibility of conflict with the outside world: The outside world can mean the classroom next door, or the public. It is certainly justifiable, indeed necessary, to expect that students have more control over themselves while at an assembly or on a tour of an art museum than when they are in their own classrooms.

7. When a teacher's mental health needs protection: This point is not made often, but teachers, after all, are only human. Although it is true that they must have a fairly high frustration level if they want to be successful teachers, it is also true that all people have their limits. Sometimes teachers have to say "stop that" because their own upper limits have been reached.

There are at least three counterindications *against* taking disciplinary steps:

1. It might seem to the teacher that the fuss created by an intervention is not worth the trouble or the time at the moment. For example, the teacher might decide that it is better to let Sue pass notes and whisper to Sean than to disrupt an otherwise smooth lesson. Of course, if the teacher sensed that Sue's and Sean's behavior would ripple across the room with negative consequences, intervening would be a good idea.
2. A second counterindication might be that the teacher believes that it would be wiser to wait until a misbehavior deviates to the point that it is obvious not only to the student, but to the entire group. This is one way of neutralizing the usual defenses, such as projection (i.e., "You're always picking on me") or denial (i.e., "I didn't do it").

3. A third counterindication might be that the teacher is in too good a mood to work up enough concern to impress the student and/or the group with the seriousness of the student's behavior.

SOME CAUTIONS ABOUT THE USE OF PUNISHMENT

The effects of punishment are limited and specific. A large body of research shows clearly that although punishment might control misbehavior, by itself, it will not teach desirable behavior or even reduce the desire to misbehave (Martin and Pear, 1992; Wielkiewicz, 1986). Punishment, by definition, is an essentially negative consequence, usually physical or emotional, or both, administered because of wrong or bad behavior. If it is used, it should be used only as a last resort for students who persist in *repeated* behavior.

Punishment is seldom appropriate for coping with isolated incidents, no matter how severe, particularly if there is reason to believe that the student will not repeat the action in the future. Even with repeated misbehavior, punishment should be avoided if there are signs that students are trying to improve. For example, if Joseph, who has been working all week at controlling his easily triggered aggression, gives a swinging hip bump to one of his classmates while coming into the room, it might be better to say, "Careful there, Joe, that aggression of yours is showing" than to make him sit outside the room for half an hour.

As a general rule, we are better off in the long run giving students the benefit of the doubt by assuming that they are acting with good will and by expressing confidence in their ability to improve. If I am one of your students and I sense that you *expect* me to misbehave, chances are very good that I will not disappoint you. When children know they are not trusted, they tend to live up to that expectation. Fortunately, it works the other way, too.

15.10 A Question of Trust

Perhaps you can relate to the trust issue more personally. Have you ever felt distrusted by someone reasonably close to you (parents, girlfriend or boyfriend, a teacher)? When you have not felt trusted, how has this affected your inclination to behave in a trustworthy manner? Conversely, when you feel you *are* trusted, how does this affect your behavior? What implications can you see here for your work as a teacher?

Any punishment that is arbitrary, cruel, or prolonged is both unnecessary and unhealthy. It typically generates hostility, and frequently leaves a lingering aroma of bad air that permeates relationships for days or even weeks. Standing a child in a corner, making the offender go for an hour with chewing gum stuck to his or her nose, or subjecting students to shame and ridicule are all punishments guaranteed to make things worse. Not only do punishments such as these serve no corrective function, they confirm students' suspicions that the teacher administering them cannot be trusted.

Ways to Use Punishment Effectively

It should be clear to students that punishment will be used as a last resort, and not because the teacher enjoys punishing or wants to get even. If students get the idea that the teacher likes to punish, it is easy for them to conclude that the punishments are the result of a mean streak in the teacher rather than the consequence of misbehavior on their part.

To be effective, a punishment should be a natural consequence of the offense. If students misuse classroom materials, for example, a fitting punishment might be to restrict their use of the materials for a time. If they are always fighting in the lunchroom, they might be made to eat in a room by themselves for a while. If they are constantly disruptive, they might have to sit outside of the room for specified periods, or be sent to the principal's office, if the offense warrants it.

Punishment that is related to the offense is more easily seen as fair, even though it might not be liked. Students can only blame themselves if a privilege is lost because they have abused it, but they can easily feel picked on if the punishment is unrelated to the crime. For example, an inexperienced high school math teacher soon learned that lowering students' grades on math quizzes when they misbehaved not only failed to solve the problem, but discouraged particular students from trying as hard in math. Except for instances in which children might be given failing grades for cheating on a test, it is *never* a good idea to lower grades as a form of punishment. A lowered grade is there forever. Effective punishment should have a terminal point; when it is over with, a fresh start begins.

When punishment is used effectively, students know what they are being punished for, and they know what they must do to restore their good standing in the classroom. This involves making a clear distinction between their unacceptable behavior and their overall acceptance as persons. For example, if I am a misbehaving student in your class and you are finally fed up with my behavior, you might say to me, "You are a thoughtless, disruptive person and I do not like people who behave like that." This is a sweeping condemnation, one that indicts my entire character. No distinction is made between who I am as a person and what I have done. Still, you *are* angry, and I *have* been disruptive. The key is to focus on the specific misbehavior rather than on the entire person. It would be better, for example, to say to me, "Don, when you behave like this it is very disruptive to those trying to study. I do not like it when you seem so unconcerned about others." Here, the focus is on my behavior and its effects on others, rather than on my personality and its implied hopelessness. It is a strong "I-statement."

In summary, to be effective, a punishment should be a natural consequence of the offense. It should be prompt. It should be simple and short. It should be applied consistently. As soon as the penalty is paid, it is a fine idea to do two things: (1) let bygones be bygones, and (2) take an early opportunity to let the student know that the slate is clean and that you know he or she will try hard in the future. (Saying something like this will make not a whit of difference unless it can be said sincerely and genuinely.)

GUIDELINES FOR DEVELOPING POSITIVE CLASSROOM DISCIPLINE

1. An ounce of prevention is worth tons of punishment. Be sure you are using methods that will minimize occasions for disorder. If one strategy does not work, try another.
2. Be yourself—your best self. This does not mean that we should go around self-actualizing at the expense of our students, but it does mean that we should keep in mind that students—no matter what grade they are in—respond as much to who we are as what we say.
3. Keep an eye on physical conditions—light, ventilation, temperature, and seating. Any one of these conditions can influence individual and group behavior for better or worse.
4. Be firm, fair, and friendly.
5. Avoid punishing an entire class for the misbehavior of one or two students. Very seldom, if ever, is every pupil involved.
6. Avoid threatening or ridiculing.
7. Be consistent.
8. Be prompt. Make an effort to discipline as soon after the misdeed as possible.
9. Avoid all unusual, long, and cruel punishments; rather, keep the penalty to the minimum that you judge to be effective.
10. Let the punishment fit the crime. Deprivation of a possession or privilege that has been abused, and rectification or reparation, are the two types of action that most frequently fulfill this condition.
11. Be sure the student understands his or her case. Give students an opportunity to state their case.
12. Let bygones be bygones.
13. Always search for the causes of misbehavior. If misbehavior is general, the cause might be in bad conditions or a poor curriculum. It might be in attitude or teaching methods. The most frequent problem, however, is that of chronic offenders driven by circumstances beyond their control. Reform here depends not on punishment of the behavior, but on a cure for the cause.
14. Remember that the goal of all discipline is self-discipline.
15. Do not lose your sense of humor. It will help lighten many otherwise heavy moments.

EPILOGUE

Teaching is a demanding activity. The business of running a classroom or a gym class or a shop/laboratory is a complicated technology that requires initiating and maintaining classroom activity with smoothness and momentum, observing and giving feedback, and coping with events simultaneously. When combined with the knowledge that students learn at various rates and that some students not only do not want to learn but also interfere with the learning of others, teaching and managing a classroom can be even more demanding.

Teachers who are good at preventing disciplinary problems are identified by particular behaviors. Among other things, they quickly establish general rules on which everyone in the class agrees (*Following* the rules is another story, of course.); they are aware of what is happening around them; they have the ability to keep things running smoothly without long interruptions between lessons; they are able to work with groups of students, not just individuals; they avoid excessive repetition, which can be boring; and they prepare thoroughly for their classes.

Effective teachers recognize that creating a positive, cooperative tone in the classroom involves reinforcing the behavior they would like to encourage; using "I-statements" that address the behavior and describe the problem rather than attack the person; and practicing active listening, a skill that enables teachers to be active participants, not merely passive recipients, in communications with students.

Assertive Discipline is an approach to classroom management that advocates a model whereby teachers are taught to insist assertively that students follow the rules and behave properly. Teachers are provided with step-by-step procedures for following through when students misbehave. Thousands of teachers swear by it, although opponents of the system argue that it teaches students to be obedient rather than responsible for their own behavior. Its effectiveness may have as much to do with the teachers who use it as it does with the system itself.

The ability to think diagnostically—in terms of using students' behavior as a guide to action, looking for hidden factors, reality-testing hunches, and being willing to try various remedial approaches when initial efforts fail—is an overall approach to classroom management that is easily coupled with other techniques because of its generic qualities.

The use of punishment is risky. Because it can so easily trigger negative feelings, create lingering resentment, and contaminate the mutual trust so necessary for positive teacher–student relationships, it should be used only as a last resort. When used by involved, caring teachers, punishment might be just the thing that gets particular students to face the consequences of their behavior and mend their troublesome ways. When used by teachers who come across as cold and distant, punishment is not likely to do much more than confirm what the student might have thought in the first place—namely, that the teacher doesn't like him or her and is just an old "so and so."

Classroom discipline is a complex task. What contributes to its complexity is the lack of a universally agreed upon criterion for what constitutes a disciplinary problem. For the most part, it depends on the teachers who judge the problem. It also depends on the teacher's tolerance for unplanned, unanticipated behavior. Some teachers actually look forward to the unexpected with a sense of excitement because they view it as a challenge. Other teachers have little tolerance for even the smallest infraction and, as a consequence, find themselves in a state of emotional distress most of the time. It is probably safe to say that if you value a quiet and, more or less predictable, orderly lifestyle, then you might want to think twice about whether teaching is really for you.

STUDY AND REVIEW QUESTIONS

1. If you were asked whether the youths of today were any better or worse than they have ever been, how would you respond?
2. Why do explicit rules and procedures set out at the beginning of class help reduce discipline problems?
3. What general rules for behavior have been found effective in helping elementary-level students control their behavior? How about rules for secondary students? What components do these two sets of rules have in common. Can you explain *why* those common components have been found to be effective?
4. Can you explain why and how timing is such an important part of successful classroom management?
5. What are the advantages of discussing and spelling out your rules and expectations early in the school year rather than bringing them up later?
6. What is the basic idea behind "recognizing and reinforcing desired behavior" as a way of working toward positive classroom management?
7. You want your students to behave in particular ways. Can you explain why it is better to use positive language to communicate your desires than negative language? Can you give some examples of each?
8. How does appropriate praise differ from inappropriate (and therefore, less effective) praise?
9. What are the basic principles associated with the Assertive Discipline model of classroom management?
10. Can you spell out the arguments for and against Assertive Discipline?
11. What basic steps are involved in diagnostic thinking?
12. What types of classroom situations usually require immediate disciplinary action on the teacher's part?
13. Techniques a teacher can use to maintain control involve such measures as signal intervention, proximity control, nonpunitive exile, and hurdle assistance. What is involved in each instance?

14. Can you explain why punishment is not usually effective as a primary mode of discipline?
15. A teacher asks you, "If I do have to use punishment, how can I use it effectively?" How would you respond?

REFERENCES

Blase, J. J., and Pajak, E. F. "How Discipline Creates Stress for Teachers." *Canadian School Executive*, 1985, *4*, pp. 8–11.

Brehm, J. W. *Responses to Loss of Freedom: A Theory of Psychological Resistance.* Morristown, NJ. General Learning Press, 1972.

Brophy, J. E. "How Teachers Influence What Is Taught in the Classroom." *Elementary School Journal*, 1982, *83*, pp. 1–13.

Brophy, J. E. "Classroom Organization and Management." *Elementary School Journal*, 1983, *83*, pp. 265–286.

Canter, L. *Assertive Discipline: A Take-Charge Approach for Today's Educator.* Seal Beach, CA: Canter and Associates, 1976.

Canter, L. *Assertive Discipline for Secondary Educators.* Santa Monica, CA: Canter and Associates, 1989.

Carnegie Foundation. *The Conditions of Teaching: A State by State Analysis.* Lawrenceville, NJ: Princeton University Press, 1988.

Charles, C. M. *Building Positive Classroom Discipline*, 4th ed. New York: Longman, 1992.

Curwin, R. L., and Mendler, A. N. "Packaged Discipline Programs: Let the Buyer Beware." *Educational Leadership*, 1988, *46*, pp. 68–71.

Davis, G. A., and Thomas, M. A. *Effective Schools and Effective Teachers.* Needham Heights, MA: Allyn and Bacon, 1980.

Doyle, W. "Classroom Management Techniques." In O. C. Moles (Ed.), *Student Discipline Strategies: Research and Practice.* Albany: State University of New York Press, 1990.

Dreikurs, R., Grunwald, B., and Pepper, F. *Maintaining Sanity in the Classroom.* New York: Harper and Row, 1982.

Emmer, E. T., Evertson, C. M., and Anderson, L. M. "Effective Classroom Management at the Beginning of the School Year." *Elementary School Journal*, 1980, *80*, spp. 219–231.

Emmer, E. T., Evertson, C. M., Sanford, J. P., Clements, B., and Worsham, M. *Classroom Management for Secondary Teachers*, 2nd ed. Englewood Cliffs, NJ: Prentice Hall, 1989.

Evertson, C. M. "Managing Classrooms: A Framework for Teachers." In D. Berliner and B. Rosenshine (Eds.), *Talks to Teachers.* New York: Random House, 1987.

Evertson, C. M., Emmer, E. T., Clements, B. S., Sanford, J. P., and Worsham, M. E. *Classroom Management for Elementary Teachers*, 2nd ed. Englewood Cliffs, NJ: Prentice Hall, 1989.

Evertson, C. M., and Harris, A. H. "What We Know About Managing Classrooms." *Educational Leadership*, 1992, April, pp. 74–78.

Gallagher, P. A. "Behavior Modification? Caution!" In N. J. Long, W. C. Morse, and R. G. Newman, (Eds.), *Conflict in the Classroom*, 4th ed. Belmont, CA: Wadsworth, 1980.

Glasser, W. *The Quality School: Managing Students Without Coercion.* New York: Harper and Row, 1990.

Good, T. L., and Brophy, J. E. *Looking in Classrooms,* 6th ed. New York: HarperCollins, 1994.

Gordon, T. *Teacher Effectiveness Training.* New York: Wyden, 1974.

Hill, D. "Order in the Classroom." *Teacher Magazine,* 1990, April, pp. 70–73, 75–77.

Jones, F. "The Gentle Art of Classroom Discipline." *National Elementary Principal,* 1979, *58,* pp. 26–32.

Kelley, E. C. *In Defense of Youth.* Englewood Cliffs, NJ: Prentice Hall, 1962.

Kounin, J. *Discipline and Group Management in Classrooms.* New York: Holt, Rinehart and Winston, 1970.

Long, N. J., and Newman, R. G. "Managing Surface Behavior of Children in School." In N. J. Long, W. C. Morse, and R. G. Newman (Eds.), *Conflict in the Classroom,* 4th ed. Belmont, CA: Wadsworth, 1980.

Martin, G., and Pear, J. *Behavior Modification: What It Is and How To Do It,* 4th ed. Englewood Cliffs, NJ: Prentice Hall, 1992.

McCormack, S. "Response to Render, Padilla, and Krank: But Practitioners Say It Works!" *Educational Leadership,* 1989, *46,* pp. 77–79.

Moskowitz, G., and Hayman, M. L. "Successful Strategies of Inner-City Teachers." *Journal of Educational Research,* 1976, *69,* pp. 283–289.

"Opinion Poll: Disruptive Behavior." *Today's Education,* 1981, November–December, p. 10.

Redl, F. *When We Deal with Children.* New York: Free Press, 1966.

Redl, F., and Wattenberg, W. *Mental Hygiene in Teaching.* New York: Harcourt Brace Jovanovich, 1959.

Render, G. F., Padilla, J. N. M., and Krank, H. M. "What Research Really Shows About Assertive Discipline." *Educational Leadership,* 1989, *46,* pp. 72–75.

Sokolove, S., Garrett, S., Sadker, M., and Sadker, D. "Interpersonal Communication Skills." In J. Cooper (Ed.), *Classroom Teaching Skills.* Lexington, MA: D.C. Heath, 1986.

Walker, J. E., and Shea, T. M. *Behavior Management: A Practical Approach for Educators,* 4th ed. Columbus, OH: Merrill, 1988.

Weinstein, C. S., and Mignano, A. *Organizing the Elementary School Classroom: Lessons from Research and Practice.* New York: McGraw-Hill, 1993.

Wielkiewicz, R. M. *Behavior Management in the Schools: Principles and Procedures.* New York: Pergamon Press, 1986.

SELECTED READINGS OF RELATED INTEREST

Charles, C. M. *Building Classroom Discipline,* 4th ed. New York: Longman, 1992. This book discusses seven models of discipline, including Kounin, Ginott, Glasser, Dreikurs, Jones, Canter, and behavior modification and contains a fine discussion on building one's personal system of discipline.

Doyle, W. "Classroom Organization and Management." In M. Wittrock (ed.), *Handbook of Research on Teaching,* 3rd ed. New York: Macmillan, 1986. This is a comprehensive overview of the research on classroom discipline and its implications for classroom management.

Emmer, E., Evertson, C., Sanford, J., Clements, B., and Worsham, M. *Classroom Management for Secondary Teachers,* 2nd ed. Englewood Cliffs, NJ: Prentice Hall, 1989. Based on research done with secondary teachers, this volume is a source of excellent ideas and practical suggestions for secondary-level teachers.

Evertson, C., Emmer, E., Clements, B., Sanford, J., and Worsham, M. *Classroom Management for Elementary Teachers,* 2nd ed. Englewood Cliffs, NJ: Prentice Hall, 1989. Based on the practice of effective elementary school teachers, this book is a rich source of ideas and practical suggestions for how to manage elementary-level classrooms successfully.

Gordon, T. *Teacher Effectiveness Training.* New York: Peter H. Wyden, 1974. This continues to be a very popular and helpful book; it promotes the idea of active listening and negotiation as a way toward a "no lose" solution in which each party wins.

Kauffman, J. M., Hallahan, D. P., Mostert, M. P., Trent, S. C., and Nuttycombe, D. G. *Managing Classroom Behavior: A Reflective Case Approach.* Needham Heights, MA: Allyn and Bacon, 1993. This book provides an overview of basic concepts related to classroom management followed by extensive case-study presentations of how those concepts are applied.

Levin, J., and Nolan, J. F. *Principles of Classroom Management: A Hierarchical Approach.* Englewood Cliffs, NJ: Prentice Hall, 1991. This is an excellent source of practical approaches to common classroom problems and steps teachers can take to cope effectively. It contains an excellent section on prevention.

Wood, M. M., and Long, N. J. *Life Space Intervention: Talking with Children and Youth in Crisis.* Austin, TX: PRO-ED, 1991. The title captures the essence of this book, which is to promote a particular way to talk to children when there are problems to resolve. Life space intervention is a technique that has been around a long time, and this volume is the best you will find on the topic.

Name Index

Subject Index